MANHATTAN LSAT

15 Real, Recent LSATs

LSAT Practice Book II

This Practice Book contains 15 recent official LSATs, PrepTests 51–65 from December 2006 through December 2011, including experimental sections and essay topics.

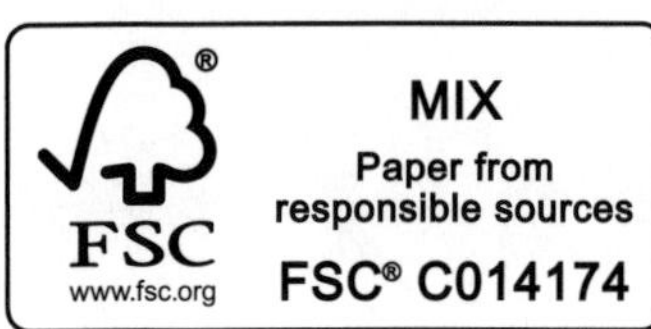

15 Real, Recent LSATs: Manhattan LSAT Practice Book, 2013 Edition

10-digit International Standard Book Number: 1-937707-12-1
13-digit International Standard Book Number: 978-1-937707-12-5

Layout Design: Dan McNaney and Cathy Huang
Cover Design: Evyn Williams and Dan McNaney

INSTRUCTIONAL GUIDE SERIES

Logic Games
(ISBN: 978-1-935707-13-4)

Logical Reasoning
(ISBN: 978-1-935707-11-0)

Reading Comprehension
(ISBN: 978-1-935707-12-7)

PRACTICE BOOKS

10 Real LSATs Grouped by Question Type
Practice Book I
(ISBN: 978-1-937707-11-8)

15 Real, Recent LSATs
Practice Book II
(ISBN: 978-1-937707-12-5)

HOW TO ACCESS YOUR ONLINE STUDY CENTER

If you...

are a registered Manhattan LSAT student

and have received this book as part of your course materials, you have AUTOMATIC access to ALL of our online resources. To access these resources, follow the instructions in the Welcome Guide provided to you at the start of your program.

Do NOT follow the instructions below.

purchased this book from the Manhattan LSAT Online store or at one of our Centers

1. Go to: http://www.manhattanlsat.com/studentcenter.cfm.

2. Log in using the username and password used when your account was set up.
Your one year of online access begins on the day that you purchase the book from the Manhattan LSAT online store or at one of our centers.

purchased this book at a retail location

1. Create an account with Manhattan LSAT at the website https://www.manhattanlsat.com/createaccount.cfm.

2. Go to: http://www.manhattanlsat.com/access.cfm.

3. Follow the instructions on the screen.

Your one year of online access begins on the day that you register your book at the above URL.

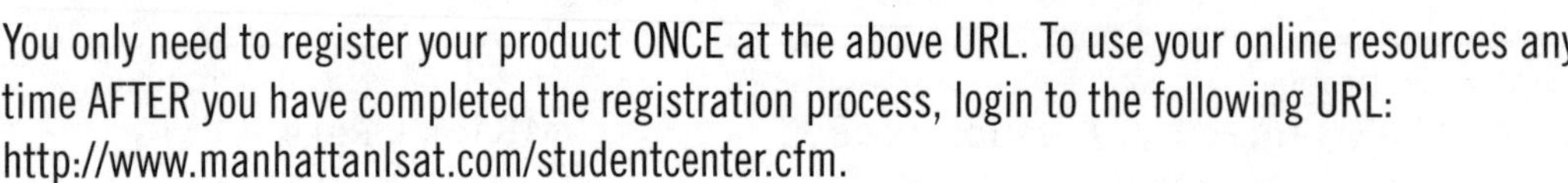

You only need to register your product ONCE at the above URL. To use your online resources any time AFTER you have completed the registration process, login to the following URL: http://www.manhattanlsat.com/studentcenter.cfm.

Please note that online access is non-transferable. This means that only NEW and UNREGISTERED copies of the book will grant you online access. Previously used books will not provide any online resources.

purchased an eBook version of this book

1. Create an account with Manhattan LSAT at the website https://www.manhattanlsat.com/createaccount.cfm.

2. Email a copy of your purchase receipt to books@manhattanlsat.com to activate your resources. Please be sure to use the same email address to create an account that you used to purchase the eBook.

For any technical issues, email books@manhattanlsat.com or call 800-576-4628.

June 5th, 2012

Dear Student,

You're holding one of the keys to LSAT success: practice! While our other Practice Book, *10 Real LSATs Grouped by Question Type*, breaks up LSATs by question type, this book is 15 pure, un-cut LSATs. However, since endurance matters, we've added an extra section to each test to simulate the un-scored experimental section that you'll face on test day. We've taken those experimental from earlier LSATs. Take a look at the note on the next page for a bit more information about the experimental sections.

The basic structure of our program is that you first learn a strategy through one of our classes, self-study programs, or strategy guides. You then hone that strategy on concentrated practice sets, and then you fold it into the full LSATs you'll find in this book. Be sure to take your tests timed, 35 minutes per section, with a 15-minute break between sections three and four. If you'd like a proctor to keep time for you, you're welcome to use our online proctor, which you'll find at www.manhattanlsat.com/LSAT-proctor.cfm. While you're there, we also give you some tips about how to review your work after the test.

If what you want is to learn some strategies, you should look at our three Strategy Guides—*Logic Games*, *Logical Reasoning*, and *Reading Comprehension*. If you'd like to read explanations for any of the questions, check out our online explanation forums at www.manhattanlsat.com/forums. Feel free to read the explanations, join the conversation, and, if a question hasn't been explained yet, tell us how you approached it and any questions you have about it. One of our instructors is sure to reply to your question!

While we can't take credit for the questions in this book—LSAC wrote each and every one—we are proud of our curriculum and the way we approach the questions. If you'd like to get a taste of what we do, look at the free samples of our guides online, or attend a trial class or one of our free introductory workshops online.

If you notice any problems with this book, or have some suggestions for us, please email me at noah@manhattanlsat.com.

Sincerely,

Noah Teitelbaum
Executive Director of Academics
Manhattan LSAT

www.manhattanlsat.com 138 West 25th St., 7th Floor, NY, NY 10001 Tel: 646-254-6480

Some Notes About Using this Book

If you are a few sessions into a Manhattan LSAT Class or Self-Study Program, you might want to skip PrepTests 51 and 52 since we borrow some questions, games, and passages from those for our classes. It won't hurt to do those tests—especially if you plan to do each and every LSAT in this book—but they won't necessarily be the most authentic as you may have been exposed to a small portion of those tests.

Talking about authentic, each of the LSATs in this book includes an **experimental section**. We grabbed those from earlier LSATs. We do this because the real LSAT will have *five* sections, one of which will be used to test new questions on you. Thus, in terms of the number of sections, these tests are realistic. However, the experimental sections we have included are from older LSATs, specifically from PrepTests 25–28, some of which include question types that are no longer in use. In this sense, these tests are not realistic. Furthermore, in order to make it easy for you to look up explanations on our forums, we've labeled the top of the experimental section differently—**"E"**—and we have retained the "official" numbering of the other sections. On test day, you will not know which section is the experimental one (historically, the experimental has always been one of the first three sections, though there was a recent exam in which it appears that many test-takers had an experimental fourth section). If you'd like to make the experimental section "anonymous," take a thick black magic marker and draw over the section numbers at the top of the pages well before you take the tests.

Remember that the official timing for LSAT is 35 minutes per section, with a 10 minute break between sections three and four. (Consider using our online proctor at www.manhattanlsat.com/LSAT-proctor.cfm.)

On your mark, get set...

TABLE *of* CONTENTS

PrepTest 51
December 2006

SECTION I

Time—35 minutes

25 Questions

Directions: The questions in this section are based on the reasoning contained in brief statements or passages. For some questions, more than one of the choices could conceivably answer the question. However, you are to choose the best answer; that is, the response that most accurately and completely answers the question. You should not make assumptions that are by commonsense standards implausible, superfluous, or incompatible with the passage. After you have chosen the best answer, blacken the corresponding space on your answer sheet.

1. Editorial: Almost every year the Smithfield River floods the coastal fishing community of Redhook, which annually spends $3 million on the cleanup. Some residents have proposed damming the river, which would cost $5 million but would prevent the flooding. However, their position is misguided. A dam would prevent nutrients in the river from flowing into the ocean. Fish that now feed on those nutrients would start feeding elsewhere. The loss of these fish would cost Redhook $10 million annually.

Which one of the following most accurately expresses the main conclusion of the editorial's argument?

(A) The Smithfield River should be dammed to prevent flooding.
(B) Nutrients from the Smithfield River are essential to the local fish population.
(C) Damming the Smithfield River is not worth the high construction costs for such a project.
(D) For Redhook to build a dam on the Smithfield River would be a mistake.
(E) The Smithfield River floods cost Redhook $3 million every year.

2. We already knew from thorough investigation that immediately prior to the accident, either the driver of the first vehicle changed lanes without signaling or the driver of the second vehicle was driving with excessive speed. Either of these actions would make a driver liable for the resulting accident. But further evidence has proved that the first vehicle's turn signal was not on, though the driver of that vehicle admits to having changed lanes. So the driver of the second vehicle is not liable for the accident.

Which one of the following would be most important to know in evaluating the conclusion drawn above?

(A) whether the second vehicle was being driven at excessive speed
(B) whether the driver of the first vehicle knew that the turn signal was not on
(C) whether any other vehicles were involved in the accident
(D) whether the driver of the first vehicle was a reliable witness
(E) whether the driver of the second vehicle would have seen the turn signal flashing had it been on

3. In some places, iceberg lilies are the mainstay of grizzly bears' summer diets. The bears forage meadows for the lilies, uprooting them and eating their bulbs. Although the bears annually destroy a large percentage of the lilies, scientists have determined that the bears' feeding habits actually promote the survival of iceberg lilies.

Which one of the following, if true, most helps to resolve the apparent discrepancy in the statements above?

(A) When grizzly bears forage for iceberg lilies, they generally kill many more lilies than they eat.
(B) Iceberg lilies produce so many offspring that, when undisturbed, they quickly deplete the resources necessary for their own survival.
(C) A significantly smaller number of iceberg lily flowers are produced in fields where grizzly bears forage than in fields of undisturbed iceberg lilies.
(D) The geographic regions in which iceberg lilies are most prevalent are those regions populated by grizzly bears.
(E) Iceberg lilies contain plentiful amounts of some nutrients that are necessary for grizzly bears' survival.

GO ON TO THE NEXT PAGE.

4. Advertisement: Seventy-five percent of dermatologists surveyed prefer Dermactin to all other brands of skin cream. Why? We consulted dermatologists during the development of Dermactin to ensure that you have the best skin cream on the market. So if you need a skin cream, use Dermactin.

The reasoning in the advertisement is questionable because the advertisement

(A) overlooks the possibility that other types of doctors have cause to use Dermactin, which would render the sample unrepresentative
(B) fails to state the number of dermatologists surveyed, which leaves open the possibility that the sample of doctors is too small to be reliable
(C) presumes, without providing justification, that some dermatologists are less qualified than others to evaluate skin cream
(D) relies on an inappropriate appeal to the opinions of consumers with no special knowledge of skin care
(E) overlooks the possibility that for a few people, using no skin cream is preferable to using even the best skin cream

5. Landscape architect: If the screen between these two areas is to be a hedge, that hedge must be of either hemlocks or Leyland cypress trees. However, Leyland cypress trees cannot be grown this far north. So if the screen is to be a hedge, it will be a hemlock hedge.

In which one of the following is the pattern of reasoning most similar to that in the landscape architect's argument?

(A) If there is to be an entrance on the north side of the building, it will have to be approached by a ramp. However, a ramp would become impossibly slippery in winter, so there will be no entrance on the north side.
(B) If visitors are to travel to this part of the site by automobile, there will be a need for parking spaces. However, no parking spaces are allowed for in the design. So if visitors are likely to come by automobile, the design will be changed.
(C) The subsoil in these five acres either consists entirely of clay or consists entirely of shale. Therefore, if one test hole in the area reveals shale, it will be clear that the entire five acres has a shale subsoil.
(D) Any path along this embankment must be either concrete or stone. But a concrete path cannot be built in this location. So if there is to be a path on the embankment, it will be a stone path.
(E) A space the size of this meadow would be suitable for a playground or a picnic area. However, a playground would be noisy and a picnic area would create litter. So it will be best for the area to remain a meadow.

6. Deirdre: Many philosophers have argued that the goal of every individual is to achieve happiness—that is, the satisfaction derived from fully living up to one's potential. They have also claimed that happiness is elusive and can be achieved only after years of sustained effort. But these philosophers have been unduly pessimistic, since they have clearly exaggerated the difficulty of being happy. Simply walking along the seashore on a sunny afternoon causes many people to experience feelings of happiness.

Which one of the following most accurately describes a reasoning flaw in Deirdre's argument?

(A) It dismisses a claim because of its source rather than because of its content.
(B) It fails to take into account that what brings someone happiness at one moment may not bring that person happiness at another time.
(C) It allows the key term "happiness" to shift in meaning illicitly in the course of the argument.
(D) It presumes, without providing justification, that happiness is, in fact, the goal of life.
(E) It makes a generalization based on the testimony of a group whose views have not been shown to be representative.

7. Global ecological problems reduce to the problem of balancing supply and demand. Supply is strictly confined by the earth's limitations. Demand, however, is essentially unlimited, as there are no limits on the potential demands made by humans. The natural tendency for there to be an imbalance between demand and sustainable supply is the source of these global problems. Therefore, any solutions require reducing current human demand.

Which one of the following is an assumption on which the argument depends?

(A) Supply and demand tend to balance themselves in the long run.
(B) It is possible to determine the limitations of the earth's sustainable supply.
(C) Actual human demand exceeds the earth's sustainable supply.
(D) It is never possible to achieve a balance between the environmental supply and human demand.
(E) Human consumption does not decrease the environmental supply.

GO ON TO THE NEXT PAGE.

8. We can now dismiss the widely held suspicion that sugar consumption often exacerbates hyperactivity in children with attention deficit disorder. A scientific study of the effects of three common sugars—sucrose, fructose, and glucose—on children who have attention deficit disorder, with experimental groups each receiving a type of sugar in their diets and a control group receiving a sugar substitute instead of sugar, showed no statistically significant difference between the groups in thinking or behavior.

Which one of the following, if true, would most weaken the argument above?

(A) Only one of the three types of sugar used in the study was ever widely suspected of exacerbating hyperactivity.
(B) The consumption of sugar actually has a calming effect on some children.
(C) The consumption of some sugar substitutes exacerbates the symptoms of hyperactivity.
(D) The study included some observations of each group in contexts that generally tend to make children excited and active.
(E) Some children believe that they can tell the difference between the taste of sugar and that of sugar substitutes.

9. Philosopher: An action is morally good if it both achieves the agent's intended goal and benefits someone other than the agent.

Which one of the following judgments most closely conforms to the principle cited by the philosopher?

(A) Colin chose to lie to the authorities questioning him, in an attempt to protect his friends. The authorities discovered his deception and punished Colin and his friends severely. But because he acted out of love for his friends, Colin's action was morally good.
(B) Derek prepared a steak dinner to welcome his new neighbors to the neighborhood. When they arrived for dinner, Derek found out that the newcomers were strict vegetarians. Though the new neighbors were still grateful for Derek's efforts to welcome them, Derek's action was not morally good.
(C) Ellen worked overtime hoping to get a promotion. The extra money she earned allowed her family to take a longer vacation that year, but she failed to get the promotion. Nevertheless, Ellen's action was morally good.
(D) Louisa tried to get Henry into serious trouble by making it appear that he stole some expensive clothes from a store. But the store's detective realized what Louisa did, and so Louisa was punished rather than Henry. Since she intended to harm Henry, Louisa's action was not morally good.
(E) Yolanda took her children to visit their grandfather because she wanted her children to enjoy their vacation and she knew they adored their grandfather. The grandfather and the children all enjoyed the visit. Though Yolanda greatly enjoyed the visit, her action was morally good.

GO ON TO THE NEXT PAGE.

10. Columnist: A recent research report suggests that by exercising vigorously, one significantly lowers one's chances of developing certain cardio-respiratory illnesses. But exercise has this effect, the report concludes, only if the exercise is vigorous. Thus, one should not heed older studies purporting to show that nonstrenuous walking yields the same benefits.

The reasoning in the columnist's argument is most vulnerable to criticism on the grounds that this argument

(A) fails to consider the possibility that the risk of developing certain cardio-respiratory illnesses can be reduced by means other than exercise
(B) fails to consider that those who exercise vigorously are at increased risk of physical injury caused by exercise
(C) overlooks the possibility that vigorous exercise may prevent life-endangering diseases that have little to do with the cardio-respiratory system
(D) fails to consider the possibility that those who engage in vigorous physical exercise are more likely than others to perceive themselves as healthy
(E) fails to show that a certain conclusion of the recent report is better justified than an opposing conclusion reached in older studies

11. Some statisticians believe that the method called extreme value theory (EVT) is a powerful analytical tool. The curves generated by traditional statistical methods to analyze empirical data on human longevity predict that some humans would live beyond 130 years. According to the curves EVT generates, however, the limit on human life spans is probably between 113 and 124 years. To date, no one has lived beyond the upper limits indicated by EVT analysis.

Which one of the following can be properly inferred from the statements above?

(A) EVT is, in general, a more reliable method for projecting future trends based on past observations than are traditional statistical methods.
(B) EVT fits the data about the highest observed human life spans more closely than do traditional statistical methods.
(C) According to the findings derived through the use of EVT, it is physically impossible for any human being to live longer than 124 years.
(D) Given the results generated by EVT, there is no point in conducting research aimed at greatly extending the upper limit on human life spans.
(E) Traditional statistical methods of empirical data analysis should eventually be replaced by some version of EVT.

12. The number of different synthetic chemical compounds that are known to be carcinogenic but are nonetheless used as pesticides, preservatives, or food additives is tiny compared to the number of nonsynthetic carcinogenic compounds widely found in plants and animals. It is therefore absurd to suppose that the rise in the cancer rate in recent decades is due to synthetic carcinogens.

The reasoning above is most vulnerable to criticism on the grounds that it overlooks the possibility that

(A) the rise in the cancer rate in recent decades is due to increased exposure to nonsynthetic pollutants
(B) the rise in the cancer rate in recent decades is due to something other than increased exposure to carcinogens
(C) some synthetic chemical compounds that are not known to be carcinogenic are in other respects toxic
(D) people undergo significantly less exposure to carcinogens that are not synthetic than to those that are synthetic
(E) people can vary greatly in their susceptibility to cancers caused by nonsynthetic carcinogens

13. It is a mistake to think, as ecologists once did, that natural selection will eventually result in organisms that will be perfectly adapted to their environments. After all, perfect adaptation of an individual to its environment is impossible, for an individual's environment can vary tremendously; no single set of attributes could possibly prepare an organism to cope with all the conditions that it could face.

Which one of the following most accurately expresses the main conclusion of the argument?

(A) It is not possible for an individual to be perfectly adapted to its environment.
(B) Natural selection will never result in individuals that will be perfectly adapted to their environments.
(C) No single set of attributes could enable an individual organism to cope with all of the conditions that it might face.
(D) Because an individual's environment can vary tremendously, no individual can be perfectly adapted to its environment.
(E) Ecologists once believed that natural selection would eventually result in individuals that will be perfectly adapted to their environments.

14. It would not be surprising to discover that the trade routes between China and the West were opened many centuries, even millennia, earlier than 200 B.C., contrary to what is currently believed. After all, what made the Great Silk Road so attractive as a trade route linking China and the West—level terrain, easily traversable mountain passes, and desert oases—would also have made it an attractive route for the original emigrants to China from Africa and the Middle East, and this early migration began at least one million years ago.

That a migration from Africa and the Middle East to China occurred at least one million years ago figures in the above reasoning in which one of the following ways?

(A) It is cited as conclusive evidence for the claim that trade links between China and the Middle East were established long before 200 B.C.
(B) It is an intermediate conclusion made plausible by the description of the terrain along which the migration supposedly took place.
(C) It is offered as evidence in support of the claim that trade routes between China and the West could easily have been established much earlier than is currently believed.
(D) It is offered as evidence against the claim that trade routes between China and Africa preceded those eventually established between China and the Middle East.
(E) It is the main conclusion that the argument attempts to establish about intercourse between China and the West.

15. The typological theory of species classification, which has few adherents today, distinguishes species solely on the basis of observable physical characteristics, such as plumage color, adult size, or dental structure. However, there are many so-called "sibling species," which are indistinguishable on the basis of their appearance but cannot interbreed and thus, according to the mainstream biological theory of species classification, are separate species. Since the typological theory does not count sibling species as separate species, it is unacceptable.

The reasoning in the argument is most vulnerable to criticism on the grounds that

(A) the argument does not evaluate all aspects of the typological theory
(B) the argument confuses a necessary condition for species distinction with a sufficient condition for species distinction
(C) the argument, in its attempt to refute one theory of species classification, presupposes the truth of an opposing theory
(D) the argument takes a single fact that is incompatible with a theory as enough to show that theory to be false
(E) the argument does not explain why sibling species cannot interbreed

16. Chiu: The belief that a person is always morally blameworthy for feeling certain emotions, such as unjustifiable anger, jealousy, or resentment, is misguided. Individuals are responsible for only what is under their control, and whether one feels such an emotion is not always under one's control.

Chiu's conclusion follows logically if which one of the following is assumed?

(A) Individuals do not have control over their actions when they feel certain emotions.
(B) If a person is morally blameworthy for something, then that person is responsible for it.
(C) Although a person may sometimes be unjustifiably angry, jealous, or resentful, there are occasions when these emotions are appropriate.
(D) If an emotion is under a person's control, then that person cannot hold others responsible for it.
(E) The emotions for which a person is most commonly blamed are those that are under that person's control.

GO ON TO THE NEXT PAGE.

17. Industrial adviser: If two new processes under consideration are not substantially different in cost, then the less environmentally damaging process should be chosen. If, however, a company already employs an environmentally damaging process and retooling for a less damaging process would involve substantial cost, then that company should retool only if retooling is either legally required or likely to bring long-term savings substantially greater than the cost.

Which one of the following judgments conforms most closely to the principles described by the industrial adviser?

(A) A new law offering companies tax credits for reducing pollution would enable a company to realize a slight long-term savings by changing to a more environmentally sound process for manufacturing dye, despite the substantial cost of retooling. In light of the new law, the company should change its process.
(B) In manufacturing pincushions, a company uses a process that, though legal, has come under heavy public criticism for the environmental damage it causes. The company should change its process to preserve its public image, despite some expected long-term losses from doing so.
(C) A company is considering two new processes for the manufacture of staples. Process A is more expensive than process B but not substantially so. However, process A is substantially less environmentally damaging than process B. The company should implement process A.
(D) Two new processes are being considered for the manufacture of ball bearings. The processes are similar, except that the chemicals used in process A will pollute a nearby river slightly more than will the chemicals for process B. Process A is also slightly cheaper than process B. The company should use process A.
(E) A company is considering changing its process for manufacturing shoelaces. The new process is cheaper and less environmentally damaging than the old. Both are legal. Changing processes would be costly, but the cost would be almost entirely recovered in long-term savings. The company should switch processes.

18. In a poll of a representative sample of a province's residents, the provincial capital was the city most often selected as the best place to live in that province. Since the capital is also the largest of that province's many cities, the poll shows that most residents of that province generally prefer life in large cities to life in small cities.

The argument is most vulnerable to the criticism that it

(A) overlooks the possibility that what is true of the residents of the province may not be true of other people
(B) does not indicate whether most residents of other provinces also prefer life in large cities to life in small cities
(C) takes for granted that when people are polled for their preferences among cities, they tend to vote for the city that they think is the best place to live
(D) overlooks the possibility that the people who preferred small cities over the provincial capital did so not because of their general feelings about the sizes of cities, but because of their general feelings about capital cities
(E) overlooks the possibility that most people may have voted for small cities even though a large city received more votes than any other single city

19. Geneticist: Genes, like viruses, have a strong tendency to self-replicate; this has led some biologists to call genes "selfish." This term is, in this instance, intended to be defined behaviorally: it describes what genes do without ascribing intentions to them. But even given that genes are ascribed no intentions, the label "selfish" as applied to genes is a misnomer. Selfishness only concerns bringing about the best conditions for oneself; creating replicas of oneself is not selfish.

Which one of the following, if assumed, allows the geneticist's conclusion to be properly drawn?

(A) Bringing about the best conditions for oneself is less important than doing this for others.
(B) Creating replicas of oneself does not help bring about the best conditions for oneself.
(C) The behavioral definition of "selfish" is incompatible with its everyday definition.
(D) To ignore the fact that self-replication is not limited to genes is to misunderstand genetic behavior.
(E) Biologists have insufficient evidence about genetic behavior to determine whether it is best described as selfish.

GO ON TO THE NEXT PAGE.

20. Only experienced salespeople will be able to meet the company's selling quota. Thus, I must not count as an experienced salesperson, since I will be able to sell only half the quota.

The pattern of flawed reasoning exhibited by the argument above is most similar to that exhibited by which one of the following?

(A) Only on Fridays are employees allowed to dress casually. Today is Friday but Hector is dressed formally. So he must not be going to work.
(B) Only music lovers take this class. Thus, since Hillary is not taking this class, she apparently does not love music.
(C) Only oceanographers enjoy the Atlantic in midwinter. Thus, we may expect that Gerald does not enjoy the Atlantic in midwinter, since he is not an oceanographer.
(D) As this tree before us is a giant redwood, it follows that we must be in a northern latitude, since it is only in northern latitudes that one finds giant redwoods.
(E) Only accomplished mountain climbers can scale El Capitan. Thus, Michelle must be able to scale El Capitan, since she is an accomplished mountain climber.

21. Designer: Any garden and adjoining living room that are separated from one another by sliding glass doors can visually merge into a single space. If the sliding doors are open, as may happen in summer, this effect will be created if it does not already exist and intensified if it does. The effect remains quite strong during colder months if the garden is well coordinated with the room and contributes strong visual interest of its own.

The designer's statements, if true, most strongly support which one of the following?

(A) A garden separated from an adjoining living room by closed sliding glass doors cannot be well coordinated with the room unless the garden contributes strong visual interest.
(B) In cold weather, a garden and an adjoining living room separated from one another by sliding glass doors will not visually merge into a single space unless the garden is well coordinated with the room.
(C) A garden and an adjoining living room separated by sliding glass doors cannot visually merge in summer unless the doors are open.
(D) A garden can visually merge with an adjoining living room into a single space even if the garden does not contribute strong visual interest of its own.
(E) Except in summer, opening the sliding glass doors that separate a garden from an adjoining living room does not intensify the effect of the garden and room visually merging into a single space.

22. Last summer, after a number of people got sick from eating locally caught anchovies, the coastal city of San Martin advised against eating such anchovies. The anchovies were apparently tainted with domoic acid, a harmful neurotoxin. However, a dramatic drop in the population of *P. australis* plankton to numbers more normal for local coastal waters indicates that it is once again safe to eat locally caught anchovies.

Which one of the following, if true, would most help to explain why it is now safe to lift the advisory?

(A) *P. australis* is one of several varieties of plankton common to the region that, when ingested by anchovies, cause the latter to secrete small amounts of domoic acid.
(B) *P. australis* naturally produces domoic acid, though anchovies consume enough to become toxic only when the population of *P. australis* is extraordinarily large.
(C) Scientists have used *P. australis* plankton to obtain domoic acid in the laboratory.
(D) A sharp decline in the population of *P. australis* is typically mirrored by a corresponding drop in the local anchovy population.
(E) *P. australis* cannot survive in large numbers in seawater that does not contain significant quantities of domoic acid along with numerous other compounds.

23. Constance: The traditional definition of full employment as a 5 percent unemployment rate is correct, because at levels below 5 percent, inflation rises.

Brigita: That traditional definition of full employment was developed before the rise of temporary and part-time work and the fall in benefit levels. When people are juggling several part-time jobs with no benefits, or working in a series of temporary assignments, as is now the case, 5 percent unemployment is not full employment.

The dialogue most strongly supports the claim that Constance and Brigita disagree with each other about which one of the following?

(A) what definition of full employment is applicable under contemporary economic conditions
(B) whether it is a good idea, all things considered, to allow the unemployment level to drop below 5 percent
(C) whether a person with a part-time job should count as fully employed
(D) whether the number of part-time and temporary workers has increased since the traditional definition of full employment was developed
(E) whether unemployment levels above 5 percent can cause inflation levels to rise

GO ON TO THE NEXT PAGE.

24. The supernova event of 1987 is interesting in that there is still no evidence of the neutron star that current theory says should have remained after a supernova of that size. This is in spite of the fact that many of the most sensitive instruments ever developed have searched for the tell-tale pulse of radiation that neutron stars emit. Thus, current theory is wrong in claiming that supernovas of a certain size always produce neutron stars.

Which one of the following, if true, most strengthens the argument?

(A) Most supernova remnants that astronomers have detected have a neutron star nearby.
(B) Sensitive astronomical instruments have detected neutron stars much farther away than the location of the 1987 supernova.
(C) The supernova of 1987 was the first that scientists were able to observe in progress.
(D) Several important features of the 1987 supernova are correctly predicted by the current theory.
(E) Some neutron stars are known to have come into existence by a cause other than a supernova explosion.

25. On average, corporations that encourage frequent social events in the workplace show higher profits than those that rarely do. This suggests that the EZ Corporation could boost its profits by having more staff parties during business hours.

Which one of the following, if true, most weakens the argument above?

(A) The great majority of corporations that encourage frequent social events in the workplace do so at least in part because they are already earning above-average profits.
(B) Corporations that have frequent staff parties after business hours sometimes have higher profits than do corporations that have frequent staff parties during business hours.
(C) The EZ Corporation already earns above-average profits, and it almost never brings play into the workplace.
(D) Frequent social events in a corporate workplace leave employees with less time to perform their assigned duties than they would otherwise have.
(E) At one time the EZ Corporation encouraged social events in the workplace more frequently than it currently does, but it has not always been one of the most profitable corporations of its size.

S T O P

IF YOU FINISH BEFORE TIME IS CALLED, YOU MAY CHECK YOUR WORK ON THIS SECTION ONLY. DO NOT WORK ON ANY OTHER SECTION IN THE TEST.

Time–35 minutes

23 Questions

Directions: Each group of questions in this section is based on a set of conditions. In answering some of the questions, it may be useful to draw a rough diagram. Choose the response that most accurately and completely answers each question and blacken the corresponding space on your answer sheet.

Questions 1-5

Six racehorses—K, L, M, N, O, and P—will be assigned to six positions arranged in a straight line and numbered consecutively 1 through 6. The horses are assigned to the positions, one horse per position, according to the following conditions:

K and L must be assigned to positions that are separated from each other by exactly one position.
K and N cannot be assigned to positions that are next to each other.
N must be assigned to a higher-numbered position than M.
P must be assigned to position 3.

1. Which one of the following lists an acceptable assignment of horses to positions 1 though 6, respectively?

(A) K, L, P, M, N, O
(B) M. K, P, L, N, O
(C) M, N, K, P, L, O
(D) N, O, P, K, M, L
(E) O, M, P, L, N, K

2. Which one of the following is a complete and accurate list of the positions any one of which can be the position to which K is assigned?

(A) 1, 2
(B) 2, 3
(C) 2, 4
(D) 2, 4, 5
(E) 2, 4, 6

3. Which one of the following CANNOT be true?

(A) K is assigned to position 2.
(B) L is assigned to position 2.
(C) M is assigned to position 1.
(D) M is assigned to position 5.
(E) O is assigned to position 2.

4. Which one of the following must be true?

(A) Either K or else L is assigned to position 2.
(B) Either K or else L is assigned to position 4.
(C) Either M or else N is assigned to position 2.
(D) Either M or else N is assigned to position 5.
(E) Either M or else O is assigned to position 6.

5. Which one of the following CANNOT be true?

(A) L and N are assigned to positions that are next to each other.
(B) M and K are assigned to positions that are next to each other.
(C) M and O are assigned to positions that are next to each other.
(D) L and N are assigned to positions that are separated from each other by exactly one position.
(E) M and P are assigned to positions that are separated from each other by exactly one position.

GO ON TO THE NEXT PAGE.

Questions 6-12

To prepare for fieldwork, exactly four different researchers—a geologist, a historian, a linguist, and a paleontologist—will learn at least one and at most three of four languages—Rundi, Swahili, Tigrinya, and Yoruba. They must learn the languages according to the following specifications:

Exactly one researcher learns Rundi.
Exactly two researchers learn Swahili.
Exactly two researchers learn Tigrinya.
Exactly three researchers learn Yoruba.
Any language learned by the linguist or paleontologist is not learned by the geologist.
Any language learned by the geologist is learned by the historian.

6. Which one of the following could be true?
   (A) The linguist learns three languages—Rundi, Swahili, and Tigrinya.
   (B) The linguist learns three languages—Swahili, Tigrinya, and Yoruba.
   (C) The historian learns three languages—Rundi, Swahili, and Tigrinya.
   (D) The historian learns three languages—Swahili, Tigrinya, and Yoruba.
   (E) The paleontologist learns three languages—Rundi, Swahili, and Tigrinya.

7. If the linguist learns three of the languages, then which one of the following must be true?
   (A) The linguist learns Tigrinya.
   (B) The linguist learns Rundi.
   (C) The linguist learns Swahili.
   (D) The paleontologist learns Rundi.
   (E) The paleontologist learns Swahili.

8. Each of the following could be true of the researcher who learns Rundi EXCEPT:
   (A) The researcher also learns Tigrinya but not Swahili.
   (B) The researcher learns neither Tigrinya nor Swahili.
   (C) The researcher also learns Tigrinya but not Yoruba.
   (D) The researcher also learns both Tigrinya and Yoruba.
   (E) The researcher also learns Yoruba but not Tigrinya.

9. Each of the following could be a complete and accurate list of the researchers who learn both Swahili and Yoruba EXCEPT:
   (A) the historian
   (B) the paleontologist
   (C) the historian, the linguist
   (D) the historian, the paleontologist
   (E) the linguist, the paleontologist

10. If the geologist learns exactly two of the languages, then which one of the following could be true?
   (A) The paleontologist learns Rundi.
   (B) The paleontologist learns Swahili.
   (C) The historian learns Rundi.
   (D) The paleontologist learns exactly three of the languages.
   (E) The historian learns exactly two of the languages.

11. Which one of the following must be true?
   (A) Fewer of the languages are learned by the historian than are learned by the paleontologist.
   (B) Fewer of the languages are learned by the geologist than are learned by the historian.
   (C) Fewer of the languages are learned by the geologist than are learned by the linguist.
   (D) Fewer of the languages are learned by the paleontologist than are learned by the linguist.
   (E) Fewer of the languages are learned by the paleontologist than are learned by the historian.

12. If exactly two of the languages are learned by the historian, then which one of the following must be true?
   (A) The paleontologist does not learn Rundi.
   (B) The geologist does not learn Swahili.
   (C) The linguist does not learn Rundi.
   (D) The historian does not learn Rundi.
   (E) The paleontologist does not learn Swahili.

GO ON TO THE NEXT PAGE.

Questions 13-18

During three days—Monday through Wednesday—a health officer will inspect exactly six buildings—three hotels: Grace, Jacaranda, and Lido; and three restaurants: Seville, Vesuvio, and Zeno. Each day, exactly two buildings are inspected: one in the morning and one in the afternoon. Inspections must occur according to the following conditions:

Hotels are not inspected on Wednesday.
Grace is inspected at some time before Jacaranda.
Grace is not inspected on the same day as Seville.
If Zeno is inspected in the morning, Lido is also inspected in the morning.

13. Which one of the following could be the order in which the buildings are inspected, listed in order from Monday morning through Wednesday afternoon?

(A) Grace, Seville, Jacaranda, Lido, Vesuvio, Zeno
(B) Grace, Vesuvio, Zeno, Jacaranda, Lido, Seville
(C) Lido, Jacaranda, Grace, Vesuvio, Zeno, Seville
(D) Lido, Seville, Grace, Jacaranda, Zeno, Vesuvio
(E) Zeno, Grace, Jacarnada, Lido, Seville, Vesuvio

14. Which one of the following could be the buildings inspected in the mornings, listed in order from Monday through Wednesday?

(A) Grace, Jacaranda, Zeno
(B) Jacaranda, Vesuvio, Seville
(C) Lido, Jacaranda, Vesuvio
(D) Seville, Jacaranda, Vesuvio
(E) Seville, Lido, Zeno

15. Which one of the following is a pair of buildings that, if inspected on the same day as each other, must be inspected on Monday?

(A) Grace and Jacaranda
(B) Grace and Vesuvio
(C) Jacaranda and Lido
(D) Lido and Seville
(E) Lido and Vesuvio

16. If Grace is inspected on Tuesday, which one of the following could be the buildings inspected in the afternoons, listed in order from Monday through Wednesday?

(A) Lido, Jacaranda, Vesuvio
(A) Lido, Jacranda, Zeno
(A) Lido, Vesuvio, Zeno
(A) Seville, Grace, Vesuvio
(A) Seville, Jacaranda, Lido

17. If Seville is inspected on Monday morning, which one of the following must be true?

(A) Grace is inspected on Tuesday afternoon.
(A) Jacaranda is inspected on Monday afternoon.
(A) Lido is inspected on Tuesday morning.
(A) Vesuvio is inspected on Wednesday morning.
(A) Zeno is inspected on Wednesday morning.

18. If Grace is inspected on Monday morning and Zeno is inspected on Wednesday morning, which one of the following must be true?

(A) Jacaranda is inspected before Lido is inspected.
(A) Jacaranda is inspected after Lido is inspected.
(A) Jacaranda is inspected after Seville is inspected.
(A) Lido is inspected before Seville is inspected.
(A) Lido is inspected before Vesuvio is inspected.

GO ON TO THE NEXT PAGE.

Questions 19-23

Morrisville's town council has exactly three members: Fu, Gianola, and Herstein. During one week, the council members vote on exactly three bills: a recreation bill, a school bill, and a tax bill. Each council member votes either for or against each bill. The following is known:

Each member of the council votes for at least one of the bills and against at least one of the bills.
Exactly two members of the council vote for the recreation bill.
Exactly one member of the council votes for the school bill.
Exactly one member of the council votes for the tax bill.
Fu votes for the recreation bill and against the school bill.
Gianola votes against the recreation bill.
Herstein votes against the tax bill.

19. Which one of the following statements could be true?

(A) Fu and Gianola vote the same way on the tax bill.
(B) Gianola and Herstein vote the same way on the recreation bill.
(C) Gianola and Herstein vote the same way on the school bill.
(D) Fu votes for one of the bills and Gianola votes for two of the bills.
(E) Fu votes for two of the bills and Gianola votes for two of the bills.

20. If the set of members of the council who vote against the school bill is the same set of members who vote against the tax bill, then which one of the following statements must be true?

(A) Fu votes for the tax bill.
(B) Gianola votes for the recreation bill.
(C) Gianola votes against the school bill.
(D) Herstein votes against the recreation bill.
(E) Herstein votes against the school bill.

21. If Gianola votes for the tax bill, then which one of the following statements could be true?

(A) Fu and Gianola each vote for exactly one bill.
(B) Gianola and Herstein each vote for exactly one bill.
(C) Fu votes for exactly two bills.
(D) Gianola votes for the recreation bill.
(E) Herstein votes against the recreation bill.

22. If Gianola votes for exactly two of the three bills, which one of the following statements must be true?

(A) Fu votes for the tax bill.
(B) Gianola votes for the recreation bill.
(C) Gianola votes for the school bill.
(D) Gianola votes against the tax bill.
(E) Herstein votes for the school bill.

23. If one of the members of the council votes against exactly the same bills as does another member of the council, then which one of the following statements must be true?

(A) Fu votes for the tax bill.
(B) Gianola votes for the recreation bill.
(C) Gianola votes against the school bill.
(D) Gianola votes for exactly one bill
(E) Herstein votes for exactly one bill.

S T O P

IF YOU FINISH BEFORE TIME IS CALLED, YOU MAY CHECK YOUR WORK ON THIS SECTION ONLY. DO NOT WORK ON ANY OTHER SECTION IN THE TEST.

SECTION II

Time—35 minutes

28 Questions

Directions: Each passage in this section is followed by a group of questions to be answered on the basis of what is stated or implied in the passage. For some of the questions, more than one of the choices could conceivably answer the question. However, you are to choose the best answer; that is, the response that most accurately and completely answers the question, and blacken the corresponding space on your answer sheet.

The work of South African writer Ezekiel Mphahlele has confounded literary critics, especially those who feel compelled to draw a sharp distinction between autobiography and fiction. These critics point to Mphahlele's best-known works—his 1959 autobiography *Down Second Avenue* and his 1971 novel *The Wanderers*—to illustrate the problem of categorizing his work. While his autobiography traces his life from age five until the beginning of his self-imposed 20-year exile at age thirty-eight, *The Wanderers* appears to pick up at the beginning of his exile and go on from there. Critics have variously decried the former as too fictionalized and the latter as too autobiographical, but those who focus on traditional labels inevitably miss the fact that Mphahlele manipulates different prose forms purely in the service of the social message he advances.

Even where critics give him a favorable reading, all too often their reviews carry a negative subtext. For example, one critic said of *The Wanderers* that if anger, firsthand experiences, compassion, and topicality were the sole requirements for great literature, the novel might well be one of the masterpieces of this declining part of the twentieth century. And although this critic may not have meant to question the literary contribution of the novel, there are those who are outright dismissive of *The Wanderers* because it contains an autobiographical framework and is populated with real-world characters. Mphahlele briefly defends against such charges by pointing out the importance of the fictional father-son relationship that opens and closes the novel. But his greater concern is the social vision that pervades his work, though it too is prone to misunderstandings and underappreciation. Mphahlele is a humanist and an integrationist, and his writings wonderfully articulate his vision of the future; but critics often balk at this vision because Mphahlele provides no road maps for bringing such a future about.

Mphahlele himself shows little interest in establishing guidelines to distinguish autobiography from fiction. Though he does refer to *Down Second Avenue* as an autobiography and *The Wanderers* as a novel, he asserts that no novelist can write complete fiction or absolute fact. It is the nature of writing, at least the writing he cares about, that the details must be drawn from the writer's experiences, and thus are in some sense fact, but conveyed in such a way as to maximize the effectiveness of the social message contained in the work, and thus inevitably fiction. As he claims, the whole point of the exercise of writing has nothing to do with classification; in all forms writing is the transmission of ideas, and important ideas at that: "Whenever you write prose or poetry or drama you are writing a social criticism of one kind or another. If you don't, you are completely irrelevant—you don't count."

1. Based on the passage, with which one of the following statements would Mphahlele be most likely to agree?

(A) All works of literature should articulate a vision of the future.
(B) It is not necessary for a writer to write works to fit predetermined categories.
(C) Literary categories are worth addressing only when literary works are being unjustifiably dismissed.
(D) Most works of literature that resemble novels could accurately be classified as autobiographies.
(E) The most useful categories in literature are those that distinguish prose from poetry and poetry from drama.

2. The passage states that Mphahlele believes which one of the following?

(A) Writing should provide a guide for achieving social change.
(B) Writing should have as its goal the transmission of ideas.
(C) Writing is most effective when it minimizes the use of real people and events to embellish a story.
(D) Good writing is generally more autobiographical than fictional.
(E) Fiction and autobiography are clearly identifiable literary forms if the work is composed properly.

GO ON TO THE NEXT PAGE.

3. In lines 18–25, the author uses the phrase "negative subtext" in reference to the critic's comment to claim that

   (A) the critic believes that Mphahlele himself shows little interest in establishing guidelines that distinguish fact from fiction in literature
   (B) the comment is unfairly one-sided and gives no voice to perspectives that Mphahlele might embrace
   (C) the requirement of firsthand experiences mentioned in the comment is in direct contradiction to the requirements of fiction
   (D) the requirements for great literature mentioned in the comment are ill conceived, thus the requirements have little bearing on what great literature really is
   (E) the requirements for great literature mentioned in the comment are not the sole requirements, thus Mphahlele's work is implied by the critic not to be great literature

4. According to the passage, critics offer which one of the following reasons for their dismissal of *The Wanderers*?

   (A) It should not have been populated with real-world characters.
   (B) It should have been presented as an autobiography.
   (C) It does not clearly display Mphahlele's vision.
   (D) It intends to deliver controversial social criticisms.
   (E) It places too much emphasis on relationships.

5. The author quotes Mphahlele (lines 55–58) primarily in order to

   (A) demonstrate Mphahlele's eloquence as a writer
   (B) provide a common goal of writing among novelists
   (C) further elaborate the kind of writing Mphahlele values
   (D) introduce the three literary forms Mphahlele uses to write social criticism
   (E) show that Mphahlele makes no distinction among prose, poetry, and drama

6. Which one of the following aspects of Mphahlele's work does the author of the passage appear to value most highly?

   (A) his commitment to communicating social messages
   (B) his blending of the categories of fiction and autobiography
   (C) his ability to redefine established literary categories
   (D) his emphasis on the importance of details
   (E) his plan for bringing about the future he envisions

7. Which one of the following is most strongly suggested by the information in the passage?

   (A) Mphahlele's stance as a humanist and an integrationist derives from an outlook on writing that recognizes a sharp distinction between fiction and autobiography.
   (B) The social vision contained in a work is irrelevant to critics who feel compelled to find distinct categories in which to place literary works.
   (C) Critics are concerned with categorizing the works they read not as a means to judge the quality of the works but as a way of discovering tendencies within literary traditions.
   (D) If Mphahlele were to provide direction as to how his vision of the future might be realized, more critics might find this vision acceptable.
   (E) For a work to be classified as a novel, it must not contain any autobiographical elements.

GO ON TO THE NEXT PAGE.

A vigorous debate in astronomy centers on an epoch in planetary history that was first identified by analysis of rock samples obtained in lunar missions. Scientists discovered that the major craters on the Moon were created by a vigorous bombardment of debris approximately four billion years ago—the so-called late heavy bombardment (LHB). Projectiles from this bombardment that affected the Moon should also have struck Earth, a likelihood with profound consequences for the history of Earth since, until the LHB ended, life could not have survived here.

Various theoretical approaches have been developed to account for both the evidence gleaned from samples of Moon rock collected during lunar explorations and the size and distribution of craters on the Moon. Since the sizes of LHB craters suggest they were formed by large bodies, some astronomers believe that the LHB was linked to the disintegration of an asteroid or comet orbiting the Sun. In this view, a large body broke apart and peppered the inner solar system with debris. Other scientists disagree and believe that the label "LHB" is in itself a misnomer. These researchers claim that a cataclysm is not necessary to explain the LHB evidence. They claim that the Moon's evidence merely provides a view of the period concluding billions of years of a continuous, declining heavy bombardment throughout the inner solar system. According to them, the impacts from the latter part of the bombardment were so intense that they obliterated evidence of earlier impacts. A third group contends that the Moon's evidence supports the view that the LHB was a sharply defined cataclysmic cratering period, but these scientists believe that because of its relatively brief duration, this cataclysm did not extend throughout the inner solar system. They hold that the LHB involved only the disintegration of a body within the Earth-Moon system, because the debris from such an event would have been swept up relatively quickly.

New support for the hypothesis that a late bombardment extended throughout the inner solar system has been found in evidence from the textural features and chemical makeup of a meteorite that has been found on Earth. It seems to be a rare example of a Mars rock that made its way to Earth after being knocked from the surface of Mars. The rock has recently been experimentally dated at about four billion years old, which means that, if the rock is indeed from Mars, it was knocked from the planet at about the same time that the Moon was experiencing the LHB. This tiny piece of evidence suggests that at least two planetary systems in the inner solar system experienced bombardment at the same time. However, to determine the pervasiveness of the LHB, scientists will need to locate many more such rocks and perhaps obtain surface samples from other planets in the inner solar system.

8. Which one of the following most accurately expresses the main point of the passage?
   (A) The LHB is an intense meteorite bombardment that occurred about four billion years ago and is responsible for the cratering on the Moon and perhaps on other members of the inner solar system as well.
   (B) Astronomers now believe that they may never collect enough evidence to determine the true nature of the LHB.
   (C) If scientists continue to collect new clues at their current rate, the various LHB hypotheses can soon be evaluated and a clear picture will emerge.
   (D) The Moon's evidence shows that the LHB was linked to a small body that disintegrated while in solar orbit and sprayed the inner solar system with debris.
   (E) New evidence has been found that favors the view that the LHB was widespread, but before competing theories of the LHB can be excluded, more evidence needs to be gathered.

9. The author's attitude toward arguments that might be based on the evidence of the rock mentioned in the passage as being from Mars (lines 44–46) can most accurately be described as
   (A) ambivalence because the theory of the rock's migration to Earth is at once both appealing and difficult to believe
   (B) caution because even if the claims concerning the rock's origins can be proven, it is unwise to draw general conclusions without copious evidence
   (C) skepticism because it seems unlikely that a rock could somehow make its way from Mars to Earth after being dislodged
   (D) curiosity because many details of the rock's interplanetary travel, its chemical analysis, and its dating analysis have not yet been published
   (E) outright acceptance because the origins of the rock have been sufficiently corroborated

10. The author mentions that the LHB "should also have struck Earth" (lines 8–9) primarily to
   (A) support a particular theory of the extent of the LHB
   (B) question the lack of LHB evidence found on Earth
   (C) advocate certain scientific models for the origins of life on Earth
   (D) provide a reason why scientists are interested in studying the LHB
   (E) introduce additional support for the dating of the LHB

GO ON TO THE NEXT PAGE.

11. The author implies that all theoretical approaches to the LHB would agree on which one of the following?

(A) the approximate duration of the LHB
(B) the origin of the debris involved in the LHB
(C) the idea that cratering decreased significantly after the LHB
(D) the idea that the LHB destroyed the life that existed on Earth four billion years ago
(E) the approximate amount of debris involved in the LHB

12. According to the passage, the third group of scientists (line 31) believes that the LHB

(A) affected only the Moon
(B) was so brief that its extent had to be fairly localized
(C) consisted of so little debris that it was absorbed quickly by the planets in the inner solar system
(D) occurred more recently than four billion years ago
(E) may have lasted a long time, but all its debris remained within the Earth-Moon system

13. Which one of the following, if true, would lend the most support to the view that the LHB was limited to Earth and the Moon?

(A) An extensive survey of craters on Mars shows very little evidence for an increase in the intensity of projectiles striking Mars during the period from three billion to five billion years ago.
(B) Scientists discover another meteorite on Earth that they conclude had been knocked from the surface of the Moon during the LHB.
(C) A re-analysis of Moon rocks reveals that several originated on Earth during the LHB.
(D) Based on further testing, scientists conclude that the rock believed to have originated on Mars actually originated on the Moon.
(E) Excavations on both Earth and the Moon yield evidence that the LHB concluded billions of years of heavy bombardment.

GO ON TO THE NEXT PAGE.

Specialists in international communications almost unanimously assert that the broadcasting in developing nations of television programs produced by industrialized countries amounts to cultural imperialism: the phenomenon of one culture's productions overwhelming another's, to the detriment of the flourishing of the latter. This assertion assumes the automatic dominance of the imported productions and their negative effect on the domestic culture. But the assertion is polemical and abstract, based on little or no research into the place held by imported programs in the economies of importing countries or in the lives of viewers. This is not to deny that dominance is sometimes a risk in relationships between cultures, but rather to say that the assertion lacks empirical foundation and in some cases goes against fact. For one example, imported programs rarely threaten the economic viability of the importing country's own television industry. For another, imported programs do not uniformly attract larger audiences than domestically produced programs; viewers are not part of a passive, undifferentiated mass but are individuals with personal tastes, and most of them tend to prefer domestically produced television over imported television.

The role of television in developing nations is far removed from what the specialists assert. An anthropological study of one community that deals in part with residents' viewing habits where imported programs are available cites the popularity of domestically produced serial dramas and points out that, because viewers enjoy following the dramas from day to day, television in the community can serve an analogous function to that of oral poetry, which the residents often use at public gatherings as a daily journal of events of interest.

An empirical approach not unlike that of anthropologists is needed if communications specialists are to understand the impact of external cultural influences on the lives of people in a society. The first question they must investigate is: Given the evidence suggesting that the primary relationship of imported cultural productions to domestic ones is not dominance, then what model best represents the true relationship? One possibility is that, rather than one culture's productions dominating another's, the domestic culture absorbs the imported productions and becomes enriched. Another is that the imported productions fuse with domestic culture only where the two share common aspects, such as the use of themes, situations, or character types that are relevant and interesting to both cultures.

Communications researchers will also need to consider how to assess the position of the individual viewer in their model of cultural relationships. This model must emphasize the diversity of human responses, and will require engaging with the actual experiences of viewers, taking into account the variable contexts in which productions are experienced, and the complex manner in which individuals ascribe meanings to those productions.

14. The primary purpose of the passage is to

(A) determine which of two hypotheses considered by a certain discipline is correct
(B) discredit the evidence offered for a claim made by a particular discipline
(C) argue that a certain discipline should adopt a particular methodology
(D) examine similar methodological weaknesses in two different disciplines
(E) compare the views of two different disciplines on an issue

15. Which one of the following most accurately describes the organization of the passage?

(A) The author takes issue with an assertion, suggests reasons why the assertion is supported by its proponents, introduces a new view that runs counter to the assertion, and presents examples to support the new view.
(B) The author takes issue with an assertion, presents examples that run counter to the assertion, suggests that a particular approach be taken by the proponents of the assertion, and discusses two questions that should be addressed in the new approach.
(C) The author takes issue with an assertion, introduces a new view that runs counter to the assertion, presents examples that support the new view, and gives reasons why proponents of the assertion should abandon it and adopt the new view.
(D) The author takes issue with an assertion, presents examples that run counter to the assertion, suggests a change in the approach taken by the proponents of the assertion, and discusses two ways in which the new approach will benefit the proponents.
(E) The author takes issue with an assertion, presents examples that run counter to the assertion, introduces a new view that runs counter to the assertion, and suggests ways in which a compromise may be found between the view and the assertion.

GO ON TO THE NEXT PAGE.

16. Which one of the following is the most logical continuation of the last paragraph of the passage?

(A) Lacking such an emphasis, we cannot judge conclusively the degree to which cultural relationships can be described by an abstract model.
(B) Without such an emphasis, we can be confident that the dominance view asserted by communications specialists will survive the criticisms leveled against it.
(C) Unless they do so, we cannot know for certain whether the model developed describes accurately the impact of external cultural influences on the lives of people.
(D) Until they agree to do so, we can remain secure in the knowledge that communications specialists will never fully gain the scientific credibility they so passionately crave.
(E) But even with such an emphasis, it will be the extent to which the model accurately describes the economic relationship between cultures that determines its usefulness.

17. The author most likely discusses an anthropological study in the second paragraph primarily in order to

(A) provide to international communications specialists a model of cultural relationships
(B) describe to international communications specialists new ways of conducting their research
(C) highlight the flaws in a similar study conducted by international communications specialists
(D) cite evidence that contradicts claims made by international communications specialists
(E) support the claim that international communications specialists need to take the diversity of individual viewing habits into account

18. Which one of the following can most reasonably be concluded about the television viewers who were the subject of the study discussed in the second paragraph?

(A) They will gradually come to prefer imported television programs over domestic ones.
(B) They are likely someday to give up oral poetry in favor of watching television exclusively.
(C) They would likely watch more television if they did not have oral poetry.
(D) They enjoy domestic television programs mainly because they have little access to imported ones.
(E) They watch television for some of the same reasons that they enjoy oral poetry.

19. According to the author, an empirical study of the effect of external cultural influences on the lives of people in a society must begin by identifying

(A) the viewing habits and tastes of the people in the society
(B) an accurate model of how imported cultural productions influence domestic ones
(C) the role of the external cultural influences in the daily life of the people in the society
(D) shared aspects of domestic and imported productions popular with mass audiences
(E) social factors that affect how external cultural productions are given meaning by viewers

20. Suppose a study is conducted that measures the amount of airtime allotted to imported television programming in the daily broadcasting schedules of several developing nations. Given the information in the passage, the results of that study would be most directly relevant to answering which one of the following questions?

(A) How does the access to imported cultural productions differ among these nations?
(B) What are the individual viewing habits of citizens in these nations?
(C) How influential are the domestic television industries in these nations?
(D) Do imported programs attract larger audiences than domestic ones in these nations?
(E) What model best describes the relationship between imported cultural influences and domestic culture in these nations?

GO ON TO THE NEXT PAGE.

Computers have long been utilized in the sphere of law in the form of word processors, spreadsheets, legal research systems, and practice management systems. Most exciting, however, has been the prospect of using artificial intelligence techniques to create so-called legal reasoning systems—computer programs that can help to resolve legal disputes by reasoning from and applying the law. But the practical benefits of such automated reasoning systems have fallen short of optimistic early predictions and have not resulted in computer systems that can independently provide expert advice about substantive law. This is not surprising in light of the difficulty in resolving problems involving the meaning and applicability of rules set out in a legal text.

Early attempts at automated legal reasoning focused on the doctrinal nature of law. They viewed law as a set of rules, and the resulting computer systems were engineered to make legal decisions by determining the consequences that followed when its stored set of legal rules was applied to a collection of evidentiary data. Such systems underestimated the problems of interpretation that can arise at every stage of a legal argument. Examples abound of situations that are open to differing interpretations: whether a mobile home in a trailer park is a house or a motor vehicle, whether a couple can be regarded as married in the absence of a formal legal ceremony, and so on. Indeed, many notions invoked in the text of a statute may be deliberately left undefined so as to allow the law to be adapted to unforeseen circumstances. But in order to be able to apply legal rules to novel situations, systems have to be equipped with a kind of comprehensive knowledge of the world that is far beyond their capabilities at present or in the foreseeable future.

Proponents of legal reasoning systems now argue that accommodating reference to, and reasoning from, cases improves the chances of producing a successful system. By focusing on the practice of reasoning from precedents, researchers have designed systems called case-based reasoners, which store individual example cases in their knowledge bases. In contrast to a system that models legal knowledge based on a set of rules, a case-based reasoner, when given a concrete problem, manipulates the cases in its knowledge base to reach a conclusion based on a similar case. Unfortunately, in the case-based systems currently in development, the criteria for similarity among cases are system dependent and fixed by the designer, so that similarity is found only by testing for the presence or absence of predefined factors. This simply postpones the apparently intractable problem of developing a system that can discover for itself the factors that make cases similar in relevant ways.

21. Which one of the following most accurately expresses the main point of the passage?

(A) Attempts to model legal reasoning through computer programs have not been successful because of problems of interpreting legal discourse and identifying appropriate precedents.
(B) Despite signs of early promise, it is now apparent that computer programs have little value for legal professionals in their work.
(C) Case-based computer systems are vastly superior to those computer systems based upon the doctrinal nature of the law.
(D) Computers applying artificial intelligence techniques show promise for revolutionizing the process of legal interpretation in the relatively near future.
(E) Using computers can expedite legal research, facilitate the matching of a particular case to a specific legal principle, and even provide insights into possible flaws involving legal reasoning.

22. The logical relationship of lines 8–13 of the passage to lines 23–25 and 49–53 of the passage is most accurately described as

(A) a general assertion supported by two specific observations
(B) a general assertion followed by two arguments, one of which supports and one of which refutes the general assertion
(C) a general assertion that entails two more specific assertions
(D) a theoretical assumption refuted by two specific observations
(E) a specific observation that suggests two incompatible generalizations

23. In the passage as a whole, the author is primarily concerned with

(A) arguing that computers can fundamentally change how the processes of legal interpretation and reasoning are conducted in the future
(B) indicating that the law has subtle nuances that are not readily dealt with by computerized legal reasoning programs
(C) demonstrating that computers are approaching the point where they can apply legal precedents to current cases
(D) suggesting that, because the law is made by humans, computer programmers must also apply their human intuition when designing legal reasoning systems
(E) defending the use of computers as essential and indispensable components of the modern legal profession

GO ON TO THE NEXT PAGE.

24. The passage suggests that the author would be most likely to agree with which one of the following statements about computerized automated legal reasoning systems?

(A) These systems have met the original expectations of computer specialists but have fallen short of the needs of legal practitioners.
(B) Progress in research on these systems has been hindered, more because not enough legal documents are accessible by computer than because theoretical problems remain unsolved.
(C) These systems will most likely be used as legal research tools rather than as aids in legal analysis.
(D) Rule systems will likely replace case-based systems over time.
(E) Developing adequate legal reasoning systems would require research breakthroughs by computer specialists.

25. It can be most reasonably inferred from the passage's discussion of requirements for developing effective automated legal reasoning systems that the author would agree with which one of the following statements?

(A) Focusing on the doctrinal nature of law is the fundamental error made by developers of automated legal systems.
(B) Contemporary computers do not have the required memory capability to store enough data to be effective legal reasoning systems.
(C) Questions of interpretation in rule-based legal reasoning systems must be settled by programming more legal rules into the systems.
(D) Legal statutes and reasoning may involve innovative applications that cannot be modeled by a fixed set of rules, cases, or criteria.
(E) As professionals continue to use computers in the sphere of law they will develop the competence to use legal reasoning systems effectively.

26. Based on the passage, which one of the following can be most reasonably inferred concerning case-based reasoners?

(A) The major problem in the development of these systems is how to store enough cases in their knowledge bases.
(B) These systems are more useful than rule systems because case-based reasoners are based on a simpler view of legal reasoning.
(C) Adding specific criteria for similarity among cases to existing systems would not overcome an important shortcoming of these systems.
(D) These systems can independently provide expert advice about legal rights and duties in a wide range of cases.
(E) These systems are being designed to attain a much more ambitious goal than had been set for rule systems.

27. Which one of the following is mentioned in the passage as an important characteristic of many statutes that frustrates the application of computerized legal reasoning systems?

(A) complexity of syntax
(B) unavailability of relevant precedents
(C) intentional vagueness and adaptability
(D) overly narrow intent
(E) incompatibility with previous statutes

28. The examples of situations that are open to differing interpretations (lines 25–30) function in the passage to

(A) substantiate the usefulness of computers in the sphere of law
(B) illustrate a vulnerability of rule systems in computerized legal reasoning
(C) isolate issues that computer systems are in principle incapable of handling
(D) explain how legal rules have been adapted to novel situations
(E) question the value of reasoning from precedents in interpreting legal rules

S T O P

IF YOU FINISH BEFORE TIME IS CALLED, YOU MAY CHECK YOUR WORK ON THIS SECTION ONLY. DO NOT WORK ON ANY OTHER SECTION IN THE TEST.

SECTION III

Time—35 minutes

25 Questions

Directions: The questions in this section are based on the reasoning contained in brief statements or passages. For some questions, more than one of the choices could conceivably answer the question. However, you are to choose the best answer; that is, the response that most accurately and completely answers the question. You should not make assumptions that are by commonsense standards implausible, superfluous, or incompatible with the passage. After you have chosen the best answer, blacken the corresponding space on your answer sheet.

1. Studies have shown that treating certain illnesses with treatment X produces the same beneficial changes in patients' conditions as treating the same illnesses with treatment Y. Furthermore, treatment X is quicker and less expensive than treatment Y. Thus, in treating these illnesses, treatment X should be preferred to treatment Y.

Which one of the following, if true, would most weaken the argument above?

(A) Unlike treatment Y, treatment X has produced harmful side effects in laboratory animals.
(B) There are other illnesses for which treatment Y is more effective than treatment X.
(C) Until recently, treatment X was more expensive than treatment Y.
(D) Treatment Y is prescribed more often by physicians than treatment X.
(E) A third treatment, treatment Z, is even quicker and less expensive than treatment X.

2. Some political thinkers hope to devise a form of government in which every citizen's rights are respected. But such a form of government is impossible. For any government must be defined and controlled by laws that determine its powers and limits; and it is inevitable that some individuals will learn how to interpret these laws to gain a greater share of political power than others have.

Which one of the following is an assumption required by the argument?

(A) In any form of government that leads to unequal distribution of political power, the rights of the majority of people will be violated.
(B) A government can ensure that every citizen's rights are respected by keeping the citizens ignorant of the laws.
(C) Not all the laws that define a government's power and limits can be misinterpreted.
(D) In any form of government, if anybody gains a greater share of political power than others have, then somebody's rights will be violated.
(E) People who have more political power than others have tend to use it to acquire an even greater share of political power.

3. Safety considerations aside, nuclear power plants are not economically feasible. While the cost of fuel for nuclear plants is significantly lower than the cost of conventional fuels, such as coal and oil, nuclear plants are far more expensive to build than are conventional power plants.

Which one of the following, if true, most strengthens the argument?

(A) Safety regulations can increase the costs of running both conventional and nuclear power plants.
(B) Conventional power plants spend more time out of service than do nuclear power plants.
(C) The average life expectancy of a nuclear power plant is shorter than that of a conventional one.
(D) Nuclear power plants cost less to build today than they cost to build when their technology was newly developed.
(E) As conventional fuels become scarcer their cost will increase dramatically, which will increase the cost of running a conventional power plant.

4. Pundit: The average salary for teachers in our society is lower than the average salary for athletes. Obviously, our society values sports more than it values education.

The reasoning in the pundit's argument is questionable because the argument

(A) presumes, without providing justification, that sports have some educational value
(B) fails to consider that the total amount of money spent on education may be much greater than the total spent on sports
(C) fails to consider both that most teachers are not in the classroom during the summer and that most professional athletes do not play all year
(D) compares teachers' salaries only to those of professional athletes rather than also to the salaries of other professionals
(E) fails to compare salaries for teachers in the pundit's society to salaries for teachers in other societies

GO ON TO THE NEXT PAGE.

5. The area of mathematics called "gauge field theory," though investigated in the nineteenth century, has only relatively recently been applied to problems in contemporary quantum mechanics. Differential geometry, another area of mathematics, was investigated by Gauss in the early nineteenth century, long before Einstein determined that one of its offspring, tensor analysis, was the appropriate mathematics for exploring general relativity.

   Which one of the following is best illustrated by the examples presented above?

   (A) Applications of some new theories or techniques in mathematics are unrecognized until long after the discovery of those theories or techniques.
   (B) Mathematicians are sometimes able to anticipate which branches of their subject will prove useful to future scientists.
   (C) The discoveries of modern physics would not have been possible without major mathematical advances made in the nineteenth century.
   (D) The nineteenth century stands out among other times as a period of great mathematical achievement.
   (E) Mathematics tends to advance more quickly than any of the physical sciences.

6. Recently discovered bird fossils are about 20 million years older than the fossils of the birdlike dinosaurs from which the birds are generally claimed to have descended. So these newly discovered fossils show, contrary to the account espoused by most paleontologists, that no bird descended from any dinosaur.

   The reasoning in the argument is flawed in that the argument

   (A) draws a generalization that is broader than is warranted by the findings cited
   (B) rejects the consensus view of experts in the field without providing any counterevidence
   (C) attacks the adherents of the opposing view personally instead of addressing any reason for their view
   (D) fails to consider the possibility that dinosaurs descended from birds
   (E) ignores the possibility that dinosaurs and birds descended from a common ancestor

7. Whether one is buying men's or women's clothing, it pays to consider fashion trends. A classic suit may stay in style for as long as five years, so it is worthwhile to pay more to get a well-constructed one. A trendy hat that will go out of style in a year or two should be purchased as cheaply as possible.

   Which one of the following most accurately expresses the principle underlying the reasoning above?

   (A) Formal attire tends to be designed and constructed to last longer than casual attire.
   (B) The amount of money one spends on a garment should be roughly proportionate to the length of time one plans to keep wearing it.
   (C) One should not buy a cheaply made garment when a well-constructed garment is available.
   (D) The amount of money one spends on clothing should be roughly the same whether one is purchasing men's or women's attire.
   (E) It is more appropriate to spend money on office attire than on casual attire.

8. Engineers are investigating the suitability of Wantastiquet Pass as the site of a new bridge. Because one concern is whether erosion could eventually weaken the bridge's foundations, they contracted for two reports on erosion in the region. Although both reports are accurate, one claims that the region suffers relatively little erosion, while the other claims that regional erosion is heavy and a cause for concern.

   Which one of the following, if true, most helps to explain how both reports could be accurate?

   (A) Neither report presents an extensive chemical analysis of the soil in the region.
   (B) Both reports include computer-enhanced satellite photographs.
   (C) One report was prepared by scientists from a university, while the other report was prepared by scientists from a private consulting firm.
   (D) One report focuses on regional topsoil erosion, while the other report focuses on riverbank erosion resulting from seasonal floods.
   (E) One report cost nearly twice as much to prepare as did the other report.

GO ON TO THE NEXT PAGE.

9. Letter to the editor: I have never seen such flawed reasoning and distorted evidence as that which you tried to pass off as a balanced study in the article "Speed Limits, Fatalities, and Public Policy." The article states that areas with lower speed limits had lower vehicle-related fatality rates than other areas. However, that will not be true for long, since vehicle-related fatality rates are rising in the areas with lower speed limits. So the evidence actually supports the view that speed limits should be increased.

The reasoning in the letter writer's argument is flawed because the argument

(A) bases its conclusion on findings from the same article that it is criticizing
(B) fails to consider the possibility that automobile accidents that occur at high speeds often result in fatalities
(C) fails to consider the possibility that not everyone wants to drive faster
(D) fails to consider the possibility that the vehicle-related fatality rates in other areas are also rising
(E) does not present any claims as evidence against the opposing viewpoint

10. Human settlement of previously uninhabited areas tends to endanger species of wildlife. However, the Mississippi kite, a bird found on the prairies of North America, flourishes in areas that people have settled. In fact, during the five years since 1985 its population has risen far more rapidly in towns than in rural areas.

Which one of the following, if true, most helps to explain why the Mississippi kite population does not follow the usual pattern?

(A) Residents of prairie towns have been setting off loud firecrackers near kites' roosting spots because of the birds' habit of diving at people and frightening them.
(B) Towns on the prairies tend to be small, with a low density of human population and large numbers of wild birds and animals.
(C) Since the international migratory bird protection treaty of 1972, it has been illegal to shoot kites, and the treaty has been effectively enforced.
(D) Wildlife such as pigeons and raccoons had already adapted successfully to towns and cities long before there were towns on the North American prairies.
(E) Trees are denser in towns than elsewhere on the prairie, and these denser trees provide greater protection from hail and windstorms for kites' nests and eggs.

11. When a major record label signs a contract with a band, the label assumes considerable financial risk. It pays for videos, album art, management, and promotions. Hence, the band does not need to assume nearly as much risk as it would if it produced its own records independently. For this reason, it is only fair for a major label to take a large portion of the profits from the record sales of any band signed with it.

Which one of the following most accurately describes the role played in the argument by the claim that a band signed with a major label does not need to assume nearly as much risk as it would if it produced its own records independently?

(A) It is the only conclusion that the argument attempts to establish.
(B) It is one of two unrelated conclusions, each of which the same premises are used to support.
(C) It is a general principle from which the argument's conclusion follows as a specific instance.
(D) It describes a phenomenon for which the rest of the argument offers an explanation.
(E) Premises are used to support it, and it is used to support the main conclusion.

12. Commentator: Recently, articles criticizing the environmental movement have been appearing regularly in newspapers. According to Winslow, this is due not so much to an antienvironmental bias among the media as to a preference on the part of newspaper editors for articles that seem "daring" in that they seem to challenge prevailing political positions. It is true that editors like to run antienvironmental pieces mainly because they seem to challenge the political orthodoxy. But serious environmentalism is by no means politically orthodox, and antienvironmentalists can hardly claim to be dissidents, however much they may have succeeded in selling themselves as renegades.

The commentator's statements, if true, most strongly support which one of the following?

(A) Winslow is correct about the preference of newspaper editors for controversial articles.
(B) Critics of environmentalism have not successfully promoted themselves as renegades.
(C) Winslow's explanation is not consonant with the frequency with which critiques of environmentalism are published.
(D) The position attacked by critics of environmentalism is actually the prevailing political position.
(E) Serious environmentalism will eventually become a prevailing political position.

GO ON TO THE NEXT PAGE.

13. Philosopher: Some of the most ardent philosophical opponents of democracy have rightly noted that both the inherently best and the inherently worst possible forms of government are those that concentrate political power in the hands of a few. Thus, since democracy is a consistently mediocre form of government, it is a better choice than rule by the few.

Which one of the following principles, if valid, most helps to justify the philosopher's argument?

(A) A society should adopt a democratic form of government if and only if most members of the society prefer a democratic form of government.
(B) In choosing a form of government, it is better for a society to avoid the inherently worst than to seek to attain the best.
(C) The best form of government is the one that is most likely to produce an outcome that is on the whole good.
(D) Democratic governments are not truly equitable unless they are designed to prevent interest groups from exerting undue influence on the political process.
(E) It is better to choose a form of government on the basis of sound philosophical reasons than on the basis of popular preference.

14. Expert: What criteria distinguish addictive substances from nonaddictive ones? Some have suggested that any substance that at least some habitual users can cease to use is nonaddictive. However, if this is taken to be the sole criterion of nonaddictiveness, some substances that most medical experts classify as prime examples of addictive substances would be properly deemed nonaddictive. Any adequate set of criteria for determining a substance's addictiveness must embody the view, held by these medical experts, that a substance is addictive only if withdrawal from its habitual use causes most users extreme psychological and physiological difficulty.

Which one of the following can be properly inferred from the expert's statements?

(A) If a person experiences extreme psychological and physiological difficulty in ceasing to use a substance habitually, that substance is addictive.
(B) Fewer substances would be deemed addictive than are deemed so at present if an adequate definition of "addictive" were employed.
(C) A substance that some habitual users can cease to use with little or no psychological or physiological difficulty is addictive only if that is not true for most habitual users.
(D) A chemical substance habitually used by a person throughout life without significant psychological or physiological difficulty is nonaddictive.
(E) "Addiction" is a term that is impossible to define with precision.

GO ON TO THE NEXT PAGE.

15. Sociologist: A contention of many of my colleagues—that the large difference between the wages of the highest- and lowest-paid workers will inevitably become a source of social friction—is unfounded. Indeed, the high differential should have an opposite effect, for it means that companies will be able to hire freely in response to changing conditions. Social friction arises not from large wage differences, but from wage levels that are static or slow changing.

Which one of the following is an assumption required by the sociologist's argument?

(A) When companies can hire freely in response to changing conditions, wage levels do not tend to be static or slow changing.
(B) People who expect their wages to rise react differently than do others to obvious disparities in income.
(C) A lack of financial caution causes companies to expand their operations.
(D) A company's ability to respond swiftly to changing conditions always benefits its workers.
(E) Even relatively well-paid workers may become dissatisfied with their jobs if their wages never change.

16. Publisher: The new year is approaching, and with it the seasonal demand for books on exercise and fitness. We must do whatever it takes to ship books in that category on time; our competitors have demonstrated a high level of organization, and we cannot afford to be outsold.

Which one of the following most accurately expresses the main conclusion drawn in the publisher's argument?

(A) The company should make shipping books its highest priority.
(B) By increasing its efficiency, the company can maintain its competitive edge.
(C) The company will be outsold if it does not maintain its competitors' high level of organization.
(D) It is imperative that the company ship fitness and exercise books on time.
(E) The company should do whatever is required in order to adopt its competitors' shipping practices.

17. Advertiser: There's nothing wrong with a tool that has ten functions until you need a tool that can perform an eleventh function! The VersaTool can perform more functions than any other tool. If you use the VersaTool, therefore, you will need additional tools less often than you would using any other multiple-function tool.

The reasoning in the advertiser's argument is most vulnerable to criticism on the grounds that the VersaTool might

(A) include some functions that are infrequently or never needed
(B) include a number of functions that are difficult to perform with any tool
(C) cost more than the combined cost of two other multiple-function tools that together perform more functions than the VersaTool
(D) be able to perform fewer often-needed functions than some other multiple-function tool
(E) not be able to perform individual functions as well as single-function tools

18. The flagellum, which bacteria use to swim, requires many parts before it can propel a bacterium at all. Therefore, an evolutionary ancestor of bacteria that had only a few of these parts would gain no survival advantage from them.

Which one of the following is an assumption on which the argument depends?

(A) Any of bacteria's evolutionary ancestors that had only a few of the parts of the flagellum would be at a disadvantage relative to similar organisms that had none of these parts.
(B) For parts now incorporated into the flagellum to have aided an organism's survival, they would have had to help it swim.
(C) All parts of the flagellum are vital to each of its functions.
(D) No evolutionary ancestor of bacteria had only a few of the parts of the flagellum.
(E) Any of bacteria's evolutionary ancestors that lacked a flagellum also lacked the capacity to swim.

GO ON TO THE NEXT PAGE.

19. Style manual: Archaic spellings and styles of punctuation in direct quotations from older works are to be preserved if they occur infrequently and do not interfere with a reader's comprehension. However, if they occur frequently, the editor may modernize them, inserting a note with an explanation to this effect in the text, or if similar modernizing has been done in more than one quotation, inserting a general statement in the preface. On the other hand, obvious typographical errors in quotations from modern works may be corrected without explanation.

Which one of the following follows logically from the statements above?

(A) If an editor corrects the spelling of a quoted word and the word occurs only once in the text, then an explanation should appear in a note or in the text.
(B) An editor may modernize an archaic spelling of a word found in a modern work without providing an explanation.
(C) An editor should modernize an archaic spelling of a word that is quoted from an older work if the spelling interferes with reader comprehension.
(D) An editor may modernize punctuation directly quoted from an older work if that punctuation occurs frequently and interferes with reader comprehension.
(E) If an editor modernizes only one of several similar instances of quoted archaic punctuation, an explanation should appear in the preface of the work.

20. Whoever murdered Jansen was undoubtedly in Jansen's office on the day of the murder, and both Samantha and Herbert were in Jansen's office on that day. If Herbert had committed the murder, the police would have found either his fingerprints or his footprints at the scene of the crime. But if Samantha was the murderer, she would have avoided leaving behind footprints or fingerprints. The police found fingerprints but no footprints at the scene of the crime. Since the fingerprints were not Herbert's, he is not the murderer. Thus Samantha must be the killer.

Which one of the following, if assumed, allows the conclusion that Samantha was the killer to be properly inferred?

(A) If there had been footprints at the scene of the crime, the police would have found them.
(B) Jansen's office was the scene of the crime.
(C) No one but Herbert and Samantha was in Jansen's office on the day of the murder.
(D) The fingerprints found at the scene of the crime were not Jansen's.
(E) The fingerprints found at the scene of the crime were not Samantha's.

21. Most opera singers who add demanding roles to their repertoires at a young age lose their voices early. It has been said that this is because their voices have not yet matured and hence lack the power for such roles. But young singers with great vocal power are the most likely to ruin their voices. The real problem is that most young singers lack the technical training necessary to avoid straining their vocal cords—especially when using their full vocal strength. Such misuse of the cords inevitably leads to a truncated singing career.

Which one of the following does the information above most strongly support?

(A) Young opera singers without great vocal power are unlikely to ruin their voices by singing demanding roles.
(B) Some young opera singers ruin their voices while singing demanding roles because their vocal cords have not yet matured.
(C) Only opera singers with many years of technical training should try to sing demanding roles.
(D) Only mature opera singers can sing demanding roles without undue strain on their vocal cords.
(E) Most young opera singers who sing demanding roles strain their vocal cords.

GO ON TO THE NEXT PAGE.

22. Food that is very high in fat tends to be unhealthy. These brownies are fat-free, while those cookies contain a high percentage of fat. Therefore, these fat-free brownies are healthier than those cookies are.

Which one of the following exhibits flawed reasoning most similar to the flawed reasoning exhibited by the argument above?

(A) Canned foods always contain more salt than frozen foods do. Therefore, these canned peas contain more salt than those frozen peas do.
(B) Vegetables that are overcooked generally have few vitamins. Therefore, these carrots, which are overcooked, contain fewer vitamins than those peas, which are uncooked.
(C) The human body needs certain amounts of many minerals to remain healthy. Therefore, this distilled water, which has no minerals, is unhealthy.
(D) Some types of nuts make Roy's throat itch. These cookies contain a greater percentage of nuts than that pie contains. Therefore, these cookies are more likely to make Roy's throat itch.
(E) Eating at a restaurant costs more than eating food prepared at home. Therefore, this home-cooked meal is less expensive than a restaurant meal of the same dishes would be.

23. Ethicist: It would be a mistake to say that just because someone is not inclined to do otherwise, she or he does not deserve to be praised for doing what is right, for although we do consider people especially virtuous if they successfully resist a desire to do what is wrong, they are certainly no less virtuous if they have succeeded in extinguishing all such desires.

The assertion that people are considered especially virtuous if they successfully resist a desire to do what is wrong plays which one of the following roles in the ethicist's argument?

(A) It is a claim for which the argument attempts to provide justification.
(B) It makes an observation that, according to the argument, is insufficient to justify the claim that the argument concludes is false.
(C) It is a claim, acceptance of which, the argument contends, is a primary obstacle to some people's having an adequate conception of virtue.
(D) It is, according to the argument, a commonly held opinion that is nevertheless false.
(E) It reports an observation that, according to the argument, serves as evidence for the truth of its conclusion.

GO ON TO THE NEXT PAGE.

24. Ecologists predict that the incidence of malaria will increase if global warming continues or if the use of pesticides is not expanded. But the use of pesticides is known to contribute to global warming, so it is inevitable that we will see an increase in malaria in the years to come.

    The pattern of reasoning in which one of the following is most similar to that in the argument above?

    (A) The crime rate will increase if the economy does not improve or if we do not increase the number of police officers. But we will be able to hire more police officers if the economy does improve. Therefore, the crime rate will not increase.
    (B) If educational funds remain at their current level or if we fail to recruit qualified teachers, student performance will worsen. But we will fail to recruit qualified teachers. Therefore, student performance will worsen.
    (C) If interest rates increase or demand for consumer goods does not decline, inflation will rise. But if there is a decline in the demand for consumer goods, that will lead to higher interest rates. Therefore, inflation will rise.
    (D) If global warming continues or if the rate of ozone depletion is not reduced, there will be an increase in the incidence of skin cancer. But reduced use of aerosols ensures both that global warming will not continue and that ozone depletion will be reduced. Thus, the incidence of skin cancer will not increase.
    (E) If deforestation continues at the current rate and the use of chemicals is not curtailed, wildlife species will continue to become extinct. But because of increasing population worldwide, it is inevitable that the current rate of deforestation will continue and that the use of chemicals will not be curtailed. Thus, wildlife species will continue to become extinct.

25. In ancient Greece, court witnesses were not cross-examined and the jury, selected from the citizenry, received no guidance on points of law; thus, it was extremely important for litigants to make a good impression on the jurors. For this reason, courtroom oratory by litigants is a good source of data on the common conceptions of morality held by the citizens of ancient Greece.

    Which one of the following, if true, would most strengthen the argument?

    (A) Litigants believed jurors were more likely to be impressed by litigants whose personality they preferred.
    (B) Litigants believed jurors were more likely to subject the litigants' personal moral codes to close critical scrutiny than were people who did not sit on juries.
    (C) Litigants believed jurors were likely to be impressed by litigants whose professed moral code most resembled their own.
    (D) Litigants believed jurors to be more impressed by litigants who were of the same economic class as the jurors.
    (E) Litigants believed jurors were likely to render their decisions based on a good understanding of the law.

S T O P

IF YOU FINISH BEFORE TIME IS CALLED, YOU MAY CHECK YOUR WORK ON THIS SECTION ONLY.
DO NOT WORK ON ANY OTHER SECTION IN THE TEST.

SECTION IV

Time—35 minutes

22 Questions

Directions: Each group of questions in this section is based on a set of conditions. In answering some of the questions, it may be useful to draw a rough diagram. Choose the response that most accurately and completely answers each question and blacken the corresponding space on your answer sheet.

Questions 1–5

A clown will select a costume consisting of two pieces and no others: a jacket and overalls. One piece of the costume will be entirely one color, and the other piece will be plaid. Selection is subject to the following restrictions:

If the jacket is plaid, then there must be exactly three colors in it.
If the overalls are plaid, then there must be exactly two colors in them.
The jacket and overalls must have exactly one color in common.
Green, red, and violet are the only colors that can be in the jacket.
Red, violet, and yellow are the only colors that can be in the overalls.

1. Which one of the following could be a complete and accurate list of the colors in the costume?

	Jacket	Overalls
(A)	red	red
(B)	red	violet, yellow
(C)	violet	green, violet
(D)	violet	red, violet
(E)	violet	red, violet, yellow

2. If there are exactly two colors in the costume, then which one of the following must be false?

(A) At least part of the jacket is green.
(B) At least part of the jacket is red.
(C) The overalls are red and violet.
(D) The overalls are red and yellow.
(E) The overalls are violet and yellow.

3. If at least part of the jacket is green, then which one of the following could be true?

(A) The overalls are plaid.
(B) No part of the jacket is red.
(C) No part of the jacket is violet.
(D) At least part of the overalls are yellow.
(E) At least part of the overalls are violet.

4. Which one of the following must be false?

(A) Both green and red are colors used in the costume.
(B) Both green and violet are colors used in the costume.
(C) Both green and yellow are colors used in the costume.
(D) Both red and violet are colors used in the costume.
(E) Both violet and yellow are colors used in the costume.

5. If there are exactly three colors in the costume, the overalls must be

(A) entirely red or else red and violet plaid
(B) entirely yellow or else violet and yellow plaid
(C) entirely violet or else red and violet plaid
(D) entirely red or else entirely yellow
(E) entirely red or else entirely violet

GO ON TO THE NEXT PAGE.

Questions 6–10

Six hotel suites—F, G, H, J, K, L—are ranked from most expensive (first) to least expensive (sixth). There are no ties. The ranking must be consistent with the following conditions:

H is more expensive than L.
If G is more expensive than H, then neither K nor L is more expensive than J.
If H is more expensive than G, then neither J nor L is more expensive than K.
F is more expensive than G, or else F is more expensive than H, but not both.

6. Which one of the following could be the ranking of the suites, from most expensive to least expensive?

(A) G, F, H, L, J, K
(B) H, K, F, J, G, L
(C) J, H, F, K, G, L
(D) J, K, G, H, L, F
(E) K, J, L, H, F, G

7. If G is the second most expensive suite, then which one of the following could be true?

(A) H is more expensive than F.
(B) H is more expensive than G.
(C) K is more expensive than F.
(D) K is more expensive than J.
(E) L is more expensive than F.

8. Which one of the following CANNOT be the most expensive suite?

(A) F
(B) G
(C) H
(D) J
(E) K

9. If L is more expensive than F, then which one of the following could be true?

(A) F is more expensive than H.
(B) F is more expensive than K.
(C) G is more expensive than H.
(D) G is more expensive than J.
(E) G is more expensive than L.

10. If H is more expensive than J and less expensive than K, then which one of the following could be true?

(A) F is more expensive than H.
(B) G is more expensive than F.
(C) G is more expensive than H.
(D) J is more expensive than L.
(E) L is more expensive than K.

GO ON TO THE NEXT PAGE.

Questions 11–15

A locally known guitarist's demo CD contains exactly seven different songs—S, T, V, W, X, Y, and Z. Each song occupies exactly one of the CD's seven tracks. Some of the songs are rock classics; the others are new compositions. The following conditions must hold:

S occupies the fourth track of the CD.
Both W and Y precede S on the CD.
T precedes W on the CD.
A rock classic occupies the sixth track of the CD.
Each rock classic is immediately preceded on the CD by a new composition.
Z is a rock classic.

11. Which one of the following could be the order of the songs on the CD, from the first track through the seventh?

(A) T, W, V, S, Y, X, Z
(B) V, Y, T, S, W, Z, X
(C) X, Y, W, S, T, Z, S
(D) Y, T, W, S, X, Z, V
(E) Z, T, X, W, V, Y, S

12. Which one of the following is a pair of songs that must occupy consecutive tracks on the CD?

(A) S and V
(B) S and W
(C) T and Z
(D) T and Y
(E) V and Z

13. Which one of the following songs must be a new composition?

(A) S
(B) T
(C) W
(D) X
(E) Y

14. If W precedes Y on the CD, then which one of the following must be true?

(A) S is a rock classic.
(B) V is a rock classic.
(C) Y is a rock classic.
(D) T is a new composition.
(E) W is a new composition.

15. If there are exactly two songs on the CD that both precede V and are preceded by Y, then which one of the following could be true?

(A) V occupies the seventh track of the CD.
(B) X occupies the fifth track of the CD.
(C) Y occupies the third track of the CD.
(D) T is a rock classic.
(E) W is a rock classic.

GO ON TO THE NEXT PAGE.

Questions 16–22

A courier delivers exactly eight parcels—G, H, J, K, L, M, N, and O. No two parcels are delivered at the same time, nor is any parcel delivered more than once. The following conditions must apply:

L is delivered later than H.
K is delivered earlier than O.
H is delivered earlier than M.
O is delivered later than G.
M is delivered earlier than G.
Both N and J are delivered earlier than M.

16. Which one of the following could be the order of deliveries from first to last?

(A) N, H, K, M, J, G, O, L
(B) H, N, J, K, G, O, L, M
(C) J, H, N, M, K, O, G, L
(D) N, J, H, L, M, K, G, O
(E) K, N, J, M, G, H, O, L

17. Which one of the following must be true?

(A) At least one parcel is delivered earlier than K is delivered.
(B) At least two parcels are delivered later than G is delivered.
(C) At least four parcels are delivered later than H is delivered.
(D) At least four parcels are delivered later than J is delivered.
(E) At least four parcels are delivered earlier than M is delivered.

18. If M is the fourth parcel delivered, then which one of the following must be true?

(A) G is the fifth parcel delivered.
(B) O is the seventh parcel delivered.
(C) J is delivered later than H.
(D) K is delivered later than N.
(E) G is delivered later than L.

19. If H is the fourth parcel delivered, then each of the following could be true EXCEPT:

(A) K is the fifth parcel delivered.
(B) L is the sixth parcel delivered.
(C) M is the sixth parcel delivered.
(D) G is the seventh parcel delivered.
(E) O is the seventh parcel delivered.

20. Each of the following could be true EXCEPT:

(A) H is delivered later than K.
(B) J is delivered later than G.
(C) L is delivered later than O.
(D) M is delivered later than L.
(E) N is delivered later than H.

21. If K is the seventh parcel delivered, then each of the following could be true EXCEPT:

(A) G is the fifth parcel delivered.
(B) M is the fifth parcel delivered.
(C) H is the fourth parcel delivered.
(D) L is the fourth parcel delivered.
(E) J is the third parcel delivered.

22. If L is delivered earlier than K, then which one of the following must be false?

(A) N is the second parcel delivered.
(B) L is the third parcel delivered.
(C) H is the fourth parcel delivered.
(D) K is the fifth parcel delivered.
(E) M is the sixth parcel delivered.

S T O P

IF YOU FINISH BEFORE TIME IS CALLED, YOU MAY CHECK YOUR WORK ON THIS SECTION ONLY. DO NOT WORK ON ANY OTHER SECTION IN THE TEST.

Acknowledgment is made to the following sources from which material has been adapted for use in this test booklet:

Clark R. Chapman, "Bombarding Mars Lately." ©1996 by Nature Publishing Group.

James P. Draper, ed., *Black Literature Criticism.* ©1992 by Gale Research Inc.

Garrett Hardin, *Living Within Limits: Ecology, Economics, and Population Taboos.* ©1993 by Oxford University Press.

Michael Tracey, "The Poisoned Chalice? International Television and the Idea of Dominance." ©1985 by the American Academy of Arts and Sciences.

LSAT WRITING SAMPLE TOPICS

Directions: The scenario presented below describes two choices, either one of which can be supported on the basis of the information given. Your essay should consider both choices and argue for one and against the other, based on the two specified criteria and the facts provided. There is no "right" or "wrong" choice: a reasonable argument can be made for either.

The charitable grants manager of Highland Electricity has received funding requests for two worthy programs—*Market Your Art*, a business program for artists, and *Get Certified*, a technical skills program for adults seeking to change careers—but can grant only one. Write an essay in which you argue for one program over the other, keeping in mind the following two criteria:

- Highland wants to help as many people as possible through its charitable giving.
- Grants should enhance the company's corporate stature within its service area.

The first funding request is to provide a grant to an arts center that serves several communities in the utility's defined service territory. The grant money would be used to establish a year-long entrepreneurship program called *Market Your Art*, designed for artists who are new to the business of selling their art. Participants will learn about pricing their work, running a small business, working with art galleries, soliciting corporate work, and bidding for public contracts. Business professionals will work closely with individual artists, and enrollment is limited to around a dozen or so participants. Highland is well known for its financial support of local community projects, yet the utility has in the past turned down numerous funding requests from arts and cultural organizations because the proposed programs did not directly further its economic development objectives.

The second request is for a grant to a nonprofit jobs training program called *Get Certified*. Participants are generally those looking for a career change, and the focus is on needed technical skills. *Get Certified* is now in the final phase of a one-time multi-year grant and is in need of new funding. Although several hundred participants have successfully completed the program, it is not heavily represented inside the utility's service area. Nonetheless, *Get Certified* is well established, increasingly in demand, and may eventually expand to locations in Highland's service area. The utility's involvement at this early stage may provide opportunities for building additional relationships and good will.

Scratch Paper

Do not write your essay in this space.

DIRECTIONS:

1. Use the Answer Key on the next page to check your answers.

2. Use the Scoring Worksheet below to compute your raw score.

3. Use the Score Conversion Chart to convert your raw score into the 120–180 scale.

SCORING WORKSHEET

1. Enter the number of questions you answered correctly in each section

	NUMBER CORRECT
SECTION I.	______
SECTION II	______
SECTION III	______
SECTION IV	______

2. Enter the sum here: ______ THIS IS YOUR RAW SCORE.

CONVERSION CHART

For converting Raw Score to the 120–180 LSAT Scaled Score LSAT Prep Test 51

REPORTED SCORE	LOWEST RAW SCORE	HIGHEST RAW SCORE
180	98	100
179	97	97
178	96	96
177	95	95
176	94	94
175	__*	__*
174	93	93
173	92	92
172	91	91
171	90	90
170	89	89
169	87	88
168	86	86
167	85	85
166	83	84
165	82	82
164	80	81
163	79	79
162	77	78
161	75	76
160	74	74
159	72	73
158	70	71
157	68	69
156	67	67
155	65	66
154	63	64
153	61	62
152	60	60
151	58	59
150	56	57
149	54	55
148	53	53
147	51	52
146	49	50
145	47	48
144	46	46
143	44	45
142	42	43
141	41	41
140	39	40
139	38	38
138	36	37
137	35	35
136	33	34
135	32	32
134	30	31
133	29	29
132	28	28
131	26	27
130	25	25
129	24	24
128	22	23
127	21	21
126	20	20
125	19	19
124	18	18
123	16	17
122	15	15
121	14	14
120	0	13

*There is no raw score that will produce this scaled score for this form.

SECTION I

1.	D	8.	C	15.	C	22.	B
2.	A	9.	E	16.	B	23.	A
3.	B	10.	E	17.	C	24.	B
4.	B	11.	B	18.	E	25.	A
5.	D	12.	D	19.	B		
6.	C	13.	B	20.	B		
7.	C	14.	C	21.	D		

SECTION II

1.	B	8.	E	15.	B	22.	A
2.	B	9.	B	16.	C	23.	B
3.	E	10.	D	17.	D	24.	E
4.	A	11.	C	18.	E	25.	D
5.	C	12.	B	19.	B	26.	C
6.	A	13.	A	20.	A	27.	C
7.	D	14.	C	21.	A	28.	B

SECTION III

1.	A	8.	D	15.	A	22.	B
2.	D	9.	D	16.	D	23.	B
3.	C	10.	E	17.	D	24.	C
4.	B	11.	E	18.	B	25.	C
5.	A	12.	A	19.	D		
6.	A	13.	B	20.	C		
7.	B	14.	C	21.	E		

SECTION IV

1.	D	8.	A	15.	E	22.	C
2.	A	9.	D	16.	D		
3.	E	10.	D	17.	C		
4.	C	11.	D	18.	D		
5.	E	12.	E	19.	A		
6.	B	13.	D	20.	B		
7.	C	14.	D	21.	C		

Experimental Section Answer Key
June 1999, PrepTest 28, Section 2

1.	B	8.	C	15.	B	22.	C
2.	E	9.	B	16.	B	23.	E
3.	E	10.	A	17.	D		
4.	B	11.	B	18.	D		
5.	C	12.	D	19.	D		
6.	D	13.	D	20.	E		
7.	B	14.	C	21.	A		

PrepTest 52
September 2007

SECTION I

Time—35 minutes

25 Questions

Directions: The questions in this section are based on the reasoning contained in brief statements or passages. For some questions, more than one of the choices could conceivably answer the question. However, you are to choose the best answer; that is, the response that most accurately and completely answers the question. You should not make assumptions that are by commonsense standards implausible, superfluous, or incompatible with the passage. After you have chosen the best answer, blacken the corresponding space on your answer sheet.

1. Certain companies require their managers to rank workers in the groups they supervise from best to worst, giving each worker a unique ranking based on job performance. The top 10 percent of the workers in each group are rewarded and the bottom 10 percent are penalized or fired. But this system is unfair to workers. Good workers could receive low rankings merely because they belong to groups of exceptionally good workers. Furthermore, managers often give the highest rankings to workers who share the manager's interests outside of work.

   Which one of the following most accurately expresses the conclusion drawn in the argument?

   (A) Some companies require their managers to give unique rankings to the workers they supervise.
   (B) Under the ranking system, the top 10 percent of the workers in each group are rewarded and the bottom 10 percent are penalized or fired.
   (C) The ranking system is not a fair way to determine penalties or rewards for workers.
   (D) Workers in exceptionally strong work groups are unfairly penalized under the ranking system.
   (E) Managers often give the highest rankings to workers who share the manager's outside interests.

2. Psychologist: A study of 436 university students found that those who took short naps throughout the day suffered from insomnia more frequently than those who did not. Moreover, people who work on commercial fishing vessels often have irregular sleep patterns that include frequent napping, and they also suffer from insomnia. So it is very likely that napping tends to cause insomnia.

   The reasoning in the psychologist's argument is most vulnerable to criticism on the grounds that the argument

   (A) presumes, without providing justification, that university students suffer from insomnia more frequently than do members of the general population
   (B) presumes that all instances of insomnia have the same cause
   (C) fails to provide a scientifically respectable definition for the term "napping"
   (D) fails to consider the possibility that frequent daytime napping is an effect rather than a cause of insomnia
   (E) presumes, without providing justification, that there is such a thing as a regular sleep pattern for someone working on a commercial fishing vessel

GO ON TO THE NEXT PAGE.

3. Whenever Joe's car is vacuumed, the employees of K & L Auto vacuum it; they are the only people who ever vacuum Joe's car. If the employees of K & L Auto vacuumed Joe's car, then Joe took his car to K & L Auto to be fixed. Joe's car was recently vacuumed. Therefore, Joe took his car to K & L Auto to be fixed.

The pattern of reasoning exhibited by the argument above is most similar to that exhibited by which one of the following?

(A) Emily's water glass is wet and it would be wet only if she drank water from it this morning. Since the only time she drinks water in the morning is when she takes her medication, Emily took her medication this morning.
(B) Lisa went to the hair salon today since either she went to the hair salon today or she went to the bank this morning, but Lisa did not go to the bank this morning.
(C) There are no bills on John's kitchen table. Since John gets at least one bill per day and he always puts his bills on his kitchen table, someone else must have checked John's mail today.
(D) Linda is grumpy only if she does not have her coffee in the morning, and Linda does not have her coffee in the morning only if she runs out of coffee. Therefore, Linda runs out of coffee only on days that she is grumpy.
(E) Jeff had to choose either a grapefruit or cereal for breakfast this morning. Given that Jeff is allergic to grapefruit, Jeff must have had cereal for breakfast this morning.

4. Editorialist: In a large corporation, one of the functions of the corporation's president is to promote the key interests of the shareholders. Therefore, the president has a duty to keep the corporation's profits high.

Which one of the following, if true, would most strengthen the editorialist's argument?

(A) Shareholders sometimes will be satisfied even if dividends paid to them from company profits are not high.
(B) The president and the board of directors of a corporation are jointly responsible for advancing the key interests of the shareholders.
(C) Keeping a corporation's profits high is likely to advance the important interests of the corporation's shareholders.
(D) In considering where to invest, most potential shareholders are interested in more than just the profitability of a corporation.
(E) The president of a corporation has many functions besides advancing the important interests of the corporation's shareholders.

5. Everyone in Biba's neighborhood is permitted to swim at Barton Pool at some time during each day that it is open. No children under the age of 6 are permitted to swim at Barton Pool between noon and 5 P.M. From 5 P.M. until closing, Barton Pool is reserved for adults only.

If all the sentences above are true, then which one of the following must be true?

(A) Few children under the age of 6 live in Biba's neighborhood.
(B) If Biba's next-door neighbor has a child under the age of 6, then Barton Pool is open before noon.
(C) If most children who swim in Barton Pool swim in the afternoon, then the pool is generally less crowded after 5 P.M.
(D) On days when Barton Pool is open, at least some children swim there in the afternoon.
(E) Any child swimming in Barton Pool before 5 P.M. must be breaking Barton Pool rules.

6. Beck: Our computer program estimates municipal automotive use based on weekly data. Some staff question the accuracy of the program's estimates. But because the figures it provides are remarkably consistent from week to week, we can be confident of its accuracy.

The reasoning in Beck's argument is flawed in that it

(A) fails to establish that consistency is a more important consideration than accuracy
(B) fails to consider the program's accuracy in other tasks that it may perform
(C) takes for granted that the program's output would be consistent even if its estimates were inaccurate
(D) regards accuracy as the sole criterion for judging the program's value
(E) fails to consider that the program could produce consistent but inaccurate output

GO ON TO THE NEXT PAGE.

7. Inertia affects the flow of water pumped through a closed system of pipes. When the pump is first switched on, the water, which has mass, takes time to reach full speed. When the pump is switched off, inertia causes the decrease in the water flow to be gradual. The effects of inductance in electrical circuits are similar to the effects of inertia in water pipes.

The information above provides the most support for which one of the following?

(A) The rate at which electrical current flows is affected by inductance.
(B) The flow of electrical current in a circuit requires inertia.
(C) Inertia in the flow of water pumped by an electrically powered pump is caused by inductance in the pump's circuits.
(D) Electrical engineers try to minimize the effects of inductance in electrical circuits.
(E) When a water pump is switched off it continues to pump water for a second or two.

8. Journalist: To reconcile the need for profits sufficient to support new drug research with the moral imperative to provide medicines to those who most need them but cannot afford them, some pharmaceutical companies feel justified in selling a drug in rich nations at one price and in poor nations at a much lower price. But this practice is unjustified. A nation with a low average income may still have a substantial middle class better able to pay for new drugs than are many of the poorer citizens of an overall wealthier nation.

Which one of the following principles, if valid, most helps to justify the journalist's reasoning?

(A) People who are ill deserve more consideration than do healthy people, regardless of their relative socioeconomic positions.
(B) Wealthy institutions have an obligation to expend at least some of their resources to assist those incapable of assisting themselves.
(C) Whether one deserves special consideration depends on one's needs rather than on characteristics of the society to which one belongs.
(D) The people in wealthy nations should not have better access to health care than do the people in poorer nations.
(E) Unequal access to health care is more unfair than an unequal distribution of wealth.

9. Robert: The school board is considering adopting a year-round academic schedule that eliminates the traditional three-month summer vacation. This schedule should be adopted, since teachers need to cover more new material during the school year than they do now.

Samantha: The proposed schedule will not permit teachers to cover more new material. Even though the schedule eliminates summer vacation, it adds six new two-week breaks, so the total number of school days will be about the same as before.

Which one of the following, if true, is a response Robert could make that would counter Samantha's argument?

(A) Teachers would be willing to accept elimination of the traditional three-month summer vacation as long as the total vacation time they are entitled to each year is not reduced.
(B) Most parents who work outside the home find it difficult to arrange adequate supervision for their school-age children over the traditional three-month summer vacation.
(C) In school districts that have adopted a year-round schedule that increases the number of school days per year, students show a deeper understanding and better retention of new material.
(D) Teachers spend no more than a day of class time reviewing old material when students have been away from school for only a few weeks, but have to spend up to a month of class time reviewing after a three-month summer vacation.
(E) Students prefer taking a long vacation from school during the summer to taking more frequent but shorter vacations spread throughout the year.

GO ON TO THE NEXT PAGE.

10. In order to reduce traffic congestion and raise revenue for the city, the mayor plans to implement a charge of $10 per day for driving in the downtown area. Payment of this charge will be enforced using a highly sophisticated system that employs digital cameras and computerized automobile registration. This system will not be ready until the end of next year. Without this system, however, mass evasion of the charge will result. Therefore, when the mayor's plan is first implemented, payment of the charge will not be effectively enforced.

Which one of the following is an assumption on which the argument depends for its conclusion to be properly drawn?

(A) The mayor's plan to charge for driving downtown will be implemented before the end of next year.
(B) The city will incur a budget deficit if it does not receive the revenue it expects to raise from the charge for driving downtown.
(C) The plan to charge for driving downtown should be implemented as soon as payment of the charge can be effectively enforced.
(D) Raising revenue is a more important consideration for the city than is reducing traffic congestion.
(E) A daily charge for driving downtown is the most effective way to reduce traffic congestion.

11. A recent study revealed that the percentage of people treated at large, urban hospitals who recover from their illnesses is lower than the percentage for people treated at smaller, rural hospitals.

Each of the following, if true, contributes to an explanation of the difference in recovery rates EXCEPT:

(A) Because there are fewer patients to feed, nutritionists at small hospitals are better able to tailor meals to the dietary needs of each patient.
(B) The less friendly, more impersonal atmosphere of large hospitals can be a source of stress for patients at those hospitals.
(C) Although large hospitals tend to draw doctors trained at the more prestigious schools, no correlation has been found between the prestige of a doctor's school and patients' recovery rate.
(D) Because space is relatively scarce in large hospitals, doctors are encouraged to minimize the length of time that patients are held for observation following a medical procedure.
(E) Doctors at large hospitals tend to have a greater number of patients and consequently less time to explain to staff and to patients how medications are to be administered.

12. Perry: Worker-owned businesses require workers to spend time on management decision-making and investment strategy, tasks that are not directly productive. Also, such businesses have less extensive divisions of labor than do investor-owned businesses. Such inefficiencies can lead to low profitability, and thus increase the risk for lenders. Therefore, lenders seeking to reduce their risk should not make loans to worker-owned businesses.

Which one of the following, if true, most seriously weakens Perry's argument?

(A) Businesses with the most extensive divisions of labor sometimes fail to make the fullest use of their most versatile employees' potential.
(B) Lenders who specialize in high-risk loans are the largest source of loans for worker-owned businesses.
(C) Investor-owned businesses are more likely than worker-owned businesses are to receive start-up loans.
(D) Worker-owned businesses have traditionally obtained loans from cooperative lending institutions established by coalitions of worker-owned businesses.
(E) In most worker-owned businesses, workers compensate for inefficiencies by working longer hours than do workers in investor-owned businesses.

13. Some paleontologists believe that certain species of dinosaurs guarded their young in protective nests long after the young hatched. As evidence, they cite the discovery of fossilized hadrosaur babies and adolescents in carefully designed nests. But similar nests for hatchlings and adolescents are constructed by modern crocodiles, even though crocodiles guard their young only for a very brief time after they hatch. Hence, ______.

Which one of the following most logically completes the argument?

(A) paleontologists who believe that hadrosaurs guarded their young long after the young hatched have no evidence to support this belief
(B) we will never be able to know the extent to which hadrosaurs guarded their young
(C) hadrosaurs guarded their young for at most very brief periods after hatching
(D) it is unclear whether what we learn about hadrosaurs from their fossilized remains tells us anything about other dinosaurs
(E) the construction of nests for hatchlings and adolescents is not strong evidence for the paleontologists' belief

14. For one academic year all the students at a high school were observed. The aim was to test the hypothesis that studying more increased a student's chances of earning a higher grade. It turned out that the students who spent the most time studying did not earn grades as high as did many students who studied less. Nonetheless, the researchers concluded that the results of the observation supported the initial hypothesis.

Which one of the following, if true, most helps to explain why the researchers drew the conclusion described above?

(A) The students who spent the most time studying earned higher grades than did some students who studied for less time than the average.
(B) The students tended to get slightly lower grades as the academic year progressed.
(C) In each course, the more a student studied, the better his or her grade was in that course.
(D) The students who spent the least time studying tended to be students with no more than average involvement in extracurricular activities.
(E) Students who spent more time studying understood the course material better than other students did.

15. Researchers had three groups of professional cyclists cycle for one hour at different levels of intensity. Members of groups A, B, and C cycled at rates that sustained, for an hour, pulses of about 60 percent, 70 percent, and 85 percent, respectively, of the recommended maximum pulse rate for recreational cyclists. Most members of Group A reported being less depressed and angry afterward. Most members of Group B did not report these benefits. Most members of Group C reported feeling worse in these respects than before the exercise.

Which one of the following is most strongly supported by the information above?

(A) The higher the pulse rate attained in sustained exercise, the less psychological benefit the exercise tends to produce.
(B) The effect that a period of cycling has on the mood of professional cyclists tends to depend at least in part on how intense the cycling is.
(C) For professional cyclists, the best exercise from the point of view of improving mood is cycling that pushes the pulse no higher than 60 percent of the maximum pulse rate.
(D) Physical factors, including pulse rate, contribute as much to depression as do psychological factors.
(E) Moderate cycling tends to benefit professional cyclists physically as much or more than intense cycling.

16. Anyone who believes in extraterrestrials believes in UFOs. But the existence of UFOs has been conclusively refuted. Therefore a belief in extraterrestrials is false as well.

Which one of the following arguments contains flawed reasoning most similar to that in the argument above?

(A) Anyone who believes in unicorns believes in centaurs. But it has been demonstrated that there are no centaurs, so there are no unicorns either.
(B) Anyone who believes in unicorns believes in centaurs. But you do not believe in centaurs, so you do not believe in unicorns either.
(C) Anyone who believes in unicorns believes in centaurs. But you do not believe in unicorns, so you do not believe in centaurs either.
(D) Anyone who believes in unicorns believes in centaurs. But there is no good reason to believe in centaurs, so a belief in unicorns is unjustified as well.
(E) Anyone who believes in unicorns believes in centaurs. But it has been conclusively proven that there is no such thing as a unicorn, so a belief in centaurs is mistaken as well.

17. People want to be instantly and intuitively liked. Those persons who are perceived as forming opinions of others only after cautiously gathering and weighing the evidence are generally resented. Thus, it is imprudent to appear prudent.

Which one of the following, if assumed, enables the argument's conclusion to be properly drawn?

(A) People who act spontaneously are well liked.
(B) Imprudent people act instantly and intuitively.
(C) People resent those less prudent than themselves.
(D) People who are intuitive know instantly when they like someone.
(E) It is imprudent to cause people to resent you.

GO ON TO THE NEXT PAGE.

18. Journalist: Recent studies have demonstrated that a regular smoker who has just smoked a cigarette will typically display significantly better short-term memory skills than a nonsmoker, whether or not the nonsmoker has also just smoked a cigarette for the purposes of the study. Moreover, the majority of those smokers who exhibit this superiority in short-term memory skills will do so for at least eight hours after having last smoked.

If the journalist's statements are true, then each of the following could be true EXCEPT:

(A) The short-term memory skills exhibited by a nonsmoker who has just smoked a cigarette are usually substantially worse than the short-term memory skills exhibited by a nonsmoker who has not recently smoked a cigarette.
(B) The short-term memory skills exhibited by a nonsmoker who has just smoked a cigarette are typically superior to those exhibited by a regular smoker who has just smoked a cigarette.
(C) The short-term memory skills exhibited by a nonsmoker who has just smoked a cigarette are typically superior to those exhibited by a regular smoker who has not smoked for more than eight hours.
(D) A regular smoker who, immediately after smoking a cigarette, exhibits short-term memory skills no better than those typically exhibited by a nonsmoker is nevertheless likely to exhibit superior short-term memory skills in the hours following a period of heavy smoking.
(E) The short-term memory skills exhibited by a regular smoker who last smoked a cigarette five hours ago are typically superior to those exhibited by a regular smoker who has just smoked a cigarette.

19. Educator: It has been argued that our professional organization should make decisions about important issues—such as raising dues and taking political stands—by a direct vote of all members rather than by having members vote for officers who in turn make the decisions. This would not, however, be the right way to decide these matters, for the vote of any given individual is much more likely to determine organizational policy by influencing the election of an officer than by influencing the result of a direct vote on a single issue.

Which one of the following principles would, if valid, most help to justify the educator's reasoning?

(A) No procedure for making organizational decisions should allow one individual's vote to weigh more than that of another.
(B) Outcomes of organizational elections should be evaluated according to their benefit to the organization as a whole, not according to the fairness of the methods by which they are produced.
(C) Important issues facing organizations should be decided by people who can devote their full time to mastering the information relevant to the issues.
(D) An officer of an organization should not make a particular decision on an issue unless a majority of the organization's members would approve of that decision.
(E) An organization's procedures for making organizational decisions should maximize the power of each member of the organization to influence the decisions made.

GO ON TO THE NEXT PAGE.

20. Neural connections carrying signals from the cortex (the brain region responsible for thought) down to the amygdala (a brain region crucial for emotions) are less well developed than connections carrying signals from the amygdala up to the cortex. Thus, the amygdala exerts a greater influence on the cortex than vice versa.

The argument's conclusion follows logically if which one of the following is assumed?

(A) The influence that the amygdala exerts on the rest of the brain is dependent on the influence that the cortex exerts on the rest of the brain.
(B) No other brain region exerts more influence on the cortex than does the amygdala.
(C) The region of the brain that has the most influence on the cortex is the one that has the most highly developed neural connections to the cortex.
(D) The amygdala is not itself controlled by one or more other regions of the brain.
(E) The degree of development of a set of neural connections is directly proportional to the influence transmitted across those connections.

21. The *Iliad* and the *Odyssey* were both attributed to Homer in ancient times. But these two poems differ greatly in tone and vocabulary and in certain details of the fictional world they depict. So they are almost certainly not the work of the same poet.

Which one of the following statements, if true, most weakens the reasoning above?

(A) Several hymns that were also attributed to Homer in ancient times differ more from the *Iliad* in the respects mentioned than does the *Odyssey*.
(B) Both the *Iliad* and the *Odyssey* have come down to us in manuscripts that have suffered from minor copying errors and other textual corruptions.
(C) Works known to have been written by the same modern writer are as different from each other in the respects mentioned as are the *Iliad* and the *Odyssey*.
(D) Neither the *Iliad* nor the *Odyssey* taken by itself is completely consistent in all of the respects mentioned.
(E) Both the *Iliad* and the *Odyssey* were the result of an extended process of oral composition in which many poets were involved.

22. Moralist: A statement is wholly truthful only if it is true and made without intended deception. A statement is a lie if it is intended to deceive or if its speaker, upon learning that the statement was misinterpreted, refrains from clarifying it.

Which one of the following judgments most closely conforms to the principles stated by the moralist?

(A) Ted's statement to the investigator that he had been abducted by extraterrestrial beings was wholly truthful even though no one has ever been abducted by extraterrestrial beings. After all, Ted was not trying to deceive the investigator.
(B) Tony was not lying when he told his granddaughter that he did not wear dentures, for even though Tony meant to deceive his granddaughter, she made it clear to Tony that she did not believe him.
(C) Siobhan did not tell a lie when she told her supervisor that she was ill and hence would not be able to come to work for an important presentation. However, even though her statement was true, it was not wholly truthful.
(D) Walter's claim to a potential employer that he had done volunteer work was a lie. Even though Walter had worked without pay in his father's factory, he used the phrase "volunteer work" in an attempt to deceive the interviewer into thinking he had worked for a socially beneficial cause.
(E) The tour guide intended to deceive the tourists when he told them that the cabin they were looking at was centuries old. Still, his statement about the cabin's age was not a lie, for if he thought that this statement had been misinterpreted, he would have tried to clarify it.

GO ON TO THE NEXT PAGE.

23. Principle: It is healthy for children to engage in an activity that promotes their intellectual development only if engaging in that activity does not detract from their social development.

Application: Although Megan's frequent reading stimulates her intellectually, it reduces the amount of time she spends interacting with other people. Therefore, it is not healthy for her to read as much as she does.

The application of the principle is most vulnerable to criticism on which one of the following grounds?

(A) It misinterprets the principle as a universal claim intended to hold in all cases without exception, rather than as a mere generalization.
(B) It overlooks the possibility that the benefits of a given activity may sometimes be important enough to outweigh the adverse health effects.
(C) It misinterprets the principle to be, at least in part, a claim about what is unhealthy, rather than solely a claim about what is healthy.
(D) It takes for granted that any decrease in the amount of time a child spends interacting with others detracts from that child's social development.
(E) It takes a necessary condition for an activity's being healthy as a sufficient condition for its being so.

24. In response to several bacterial infections traced to its apple juice, McElligott now flash pasteurizes its apple juice by quickly heating and immediately rechilling it. Intensive pasteurization, in which juice is heated for an hour, eliminates bacteria more effectively than does any other method, but is likely to destroy the original flavor. However, because McElligott's citrus juices have not been linked to any bacterial infections, they remain unpasteurized.

The statements above, if true, provide the most support for which one of the following claims?

(A) McElligott's citrus juices contain fewer infectious bacteria than do citrus juices produced by other companies.
(B) McElligott's apple juice is less likely to contain infectious bacteria than are McElligott's citrus juices.
(C) McElligott's citrus juices retain more of the juices' original flavor than do any pasteurized citrus juices.
(D) The most effective method for eliminating bacteria from juice is also the method most likely to destroy flavor.
(E) Apple juice that undergoes intensive pasteurization is less likely than McElligott's apple juice is to contain bacteria.

25. Sociologist: Widespread acceptance of the idea that individuals are incapable of looking after their own welfare is injurious to a democracy. So legislators who value democracy should not propose any law prohibiting behavior that is not harmful to anyone besides the person engaging in it. After all, the assumptions that appear to guide legislators will often become widely accepted.

The sociologist's argument requires the assumption that

(A) democratically elected legislators invariably have favorable attitudes toward the preservation of democracy
(B) people tend to believe what is believed by those who are prominent and powerful
(C) legislators often seem to be guided by the assumption that individuals are incapable of looking after their own welfare, even though these legislators also seem to value democracy
(D) in most cases, behavior that is harmful to the person who engages in it is harmful to no one else
(E) a legislator proposing a law prohibiting an act that can harm only the person performing the act will seem to be assuming that individuals are incapable of looking after their own welfare

S T O P

IF YOU FINISH BEFORE TIME IS CALLED, YOU MAY CHECK YOUR WORK ON THIS SECTION ONLY.
DO NOT WORK ON ANY OTHER SECTION IN THE TEST.

Time–35 minutes

26 Questions

Directions: Each passage in this section is followed by a group of questions to be answered on the basis of what is stated or implied in the passage. For some of the questions, more than one of the choices could conceivably answer the question. However, you are to choose the best answer; that is, the response that most accurately and completely answers the question, and blacken the corresponding space on your answer sheet.

Some Native American tribes have had difficulty establishing their land claims because the United States government did not recognize their status as tribes; therefore during the 1970's some Native Americans attempted to obtain such recognition through the medium of U.S. courts. In presenting these suits, Native Americans had to operate within a particular sphere of U.S. government procedure, that of its legal system, and their arguments were necessarily interpreted by the courts in terms the law could understand: e.g., through application of precedent or review of evidence. This process brought to light some of the differing perceptions and definitions that can exist between cultures whose systems of discourse are sometimes at variance.

In one instance, the entire legal dispute turned on whether the suing community—a group of Mashpee Wampanoag in the town of Mashpee, Massachusetts—constituted a tribe. The area had long been occupied by the Mashpee, who continued to have control over land use after the town's incorporation. But in the 1960's after an influx of non-Mashpee people shifted the balance of political power in the town, the new residents were able to buy Mashpee-controlled land from the town and develop it for commercial or private use. The Mashpee's 1976 suit claimed that these lands were taken in violation of a statute prohibiting transfers of land from any tribe of Native Americans without federal approval. The town argued that the Mashpee were not a tribe in the sense intended by the statute and so were outside its protection. As a result, the Mashpee were required to demonstrate their status as a tribe according to a definition contained in an earlier ruling: a body of Native Americans "governing themselves under one leadership and inhabiting a particular territory."

The town claimed that the Mashpee were not self-governing and that they had no defined territory: the Mashpee could legally be self-governing, the town argued, only if they could show written documentation of such a system, and could legally inhabit territory only if they had precisely delineated its boundaries and possessed a deed to it. The Mashpee marshaled oral testimony against these claims, arguing that what the town perceived as a lack of evidence was simply information that an oral culture such as the Mashpee's would not have recorded in writing. In this instance, the disjunction between U.S. legal discourse and Mashpee culture—exemplified in the court's inability to "understand" the Mashpee's oral testimony as documentary evidence—rendered the suit unsuccessful. Similar claims have recently met with greater success, however, as U.S. courts have begun to acknowledge that the failure to accommodate differences in discourse between cultures can sometimes stand in the way of guaranteeing the fairness of legal decisions.

1. Which one of the following most completely and accurately expresses the main point of the passage?

(A) Land claim suits such as the Mashpee's establish that such suits must be bolstered by written documentation if they are to succeed in U.S. courts.

(B) Land claim suits such as the Mashpee's underscore the need for U.S. courts to modify their definition of "tribe."

(C) Land claim suits such as the Mashpee's illustrate the complications that can result when cultures with different systems of discourse attempt to resolve disputes.

(D) Land claim suits such the Mashpee's point out discrepancies between what U.S. courts claim they will recognize as evidence and what forms of evidence they actually accept.

(E) Land claim suits such as the Mashpee's bring to light the problems faced by Native American tribes attempting to establish their claims within a legal system governed by the application of precedent.

GO ON TO THE NEXT PAGE.

2. According to the passage, the Mashpee's lawsuit was based on their objection to
   (A) the increase in the non-Mashpee population of the town during the 1960s
   (B) the repeal of a statute forbidding land transfers without U.S. government approval
   (C) the loss of Mashpee control over land use immediately after the town's incorporation
   (D) the town's refusal to recognize the Mashpee's deed to the land in dispute
   (E) the sale of Mashpee-controlled land to non-Mashpee residents without U.S. government approval

3. The author's attitude toward the court's decision in the Mashpee's lawsuit is most clearly revealed by the author's use of which one of the following phrases?
   (A) "operate within a particular sphere" (lines 7-8)
   (B) "continued to have control" (line 20)
   (C) "required to demonstrate" (line 32)
   (D) "precisely delineated its boundaries" (line 42)
   (E) "failure to accommodate" (line 54)

4. Based on the passage, which one of the following can most reasonably be said to have occurred in the years since the Mashpee's lawsuit?
   (A) The Mashpee have now regained control over the land they inhabit.
   (B) Native American tribes have won all of their land claim suits in U.S. courts.
   (C) U.S. courts no longer abide by the statute requiring federal approval of certain land transfers.
   (D) U.S. courts have become more likely to accept oral testimony as evidence in land claim suits.
   (E) U.S. courts have changed their definition of what legally constitutes a tribe.

5. The passage is primarily concerned with
   (A) evaluating various approaches to solving a problem
   (B) illuminating a general problem by discussing a specific example
   (C) reconciling the differences in how two opposing sides approach a problem
   (D) critiquing an earlier solution to a problem in light of new information
   (E) reinterpreting an earlier analysis and proposing a new solution to the problem.

GO ON TO THE NEXT PAGE.

Long after the lava has cooled, the effects of a major volcanic eruption may linger on. In the atmosphere a veil of fine dust and sulfuric acid droplets can spread around the globe and persist for years. Researchers have generally thought that this veil can block enough sunlight to have a chilling influence on Earth's climate. Many blame the cataclysmic eruption of the Indonesian volcano Tambora in 1815 for the ensuing "year without a summer" of 1816—when parts of the northeastern United States and southeastern Canada were hit by snowstorms in June and frosts in August.

The volcano-climate connection seems plausible, but, say scientists Clifford Mass and Davit Portman, it is not as strong as previously believed. Mass and Portman analyzed global temperature data for the years before and after nine volcanic eruptions, from Krakatau in 1883 to El Chichón in 1982. In the process they tried to filter out temperature changes caused by the cyclic weather phenomenon known as the El Niño-Southern Oscillation, which warms the sea surface in the equatorial Pacific and thereby warms the atmosphere. Such warming can mask the cooling brought about by an eruption, but it can also mimic volcanic cooling if the volcano happens to erupt just as an El Niño-induced warm period is beginning to fade.

Once El Niño effects had been subtracted from the data, the actual effects of the eruptions came through more clearly. Contrary to what earlier studies had suggested, Mass and Portman found that minor eruptions have no discernible effect on temperature. And major, dust-spitting explosions, such as Krakatau or El Chichón, cause a smaller drop than expected in the average temperature in the hemisphere (Northern or Southern) of the eruption—only half a degree centigrade or less—a correspondingly smaller drop in the opposite hemisphere.

Other researchers, however, have argued that even a small temperature drop could result in a significant regional fluctuation in climate if its effects were amplified by climatic feedback loops. For example, a small temperature drop in the northeastern U.S. and southeastern Canada in early spring might delay the melting of snow, and the unmelted snow would continue to reflect sunlight away from the surface, amplifying the cooling. The cool air over the region could, in turn, affect the jet stream. The jet stream tends to flow at the boundary between cool northern air and warm southern air, drawing its power from the sharp temperature contrast and the consequent difference in pressure. An unusual cooling in the region could cause the stream to wander farther south than normal, allowing more polar air to come in behind it and deepen the region's cold snap. Through such a series of feedbacks a small temperature drop could be blown up into a year without a summer.

6. Which one of the following most accurately expresses the main idea of the passage?
   - (A) The effect of volcanic eruptions on regional temperature is greater than it was once thought to be.
   - (B) The effect of volcanic eruptions on regional temperature is smaller than the effect of volcanic eruptions on global temperature.
   - (C) The effect of volcanic eruptions on global temperature appears to be greater than was previously supposed.
   - (D) Volcanic eruptions appear not to have the significant effect on global temperature they were once thought to have but might have a significant effect on regional temperature.
   - (E) Researchers tended to overestimate the influence of volcanic eruptions on global temperature because they exaggerated the effect of cyclical weather phenomena in making their calculations.

7. Not taking the effects of El Niño into account when figuring the effect of volcanic eruptions on Earth's climate is most closely analogous to not taking into account the
   - (A) weight of a package as a whole when determining the weight of its contents apart from the packing material
   - (B) monetary value of the coins in a pile when counting the number of coins in the pile
   - (C) magnification of a lens when determining the shape of an object seen through the lens
   - (D) number of false crime reports in a city when figuring the average annual number of crimes committed in that city
   - (E) ages of new immigrants to a country before attributing a change in the average of the country's population to a change in the number of births

8. The passage indicates that each of the following can be an effect of the El Niño phenomenon EXCEPT:
   - (A) making the cooling effect of a volcanic eruption appear to be more pronounced than it actually is
   - (B) making the cooling effect of a volcanic eruption appear to be less pronounced than it actually is
   - (C) increasing atmospheric temperature through cyclic warming of equatorial waters
   - (D) initiating a feedback loop that masks cooling brought about by an eruption
   - (E) confounding the evidence for a volcano-climate connection

GO ON TO THE NEXT PAGE.

9. Which one of the following most accurately characterizes what the author of the passage means by a "minor" volcanic eruption (line 30)?

(A) an eruption that produces less lava than either Krakatau or El Chichón did
(B) an eruption that has less of an effect on global temperature than either Krakatau or El Chichón did
(C) an eruption whose effect on regional temperature can be masked by conditions in the hemisphere of the eruption
(D) an eruption that introduces a relatively small amount of debris into the atmosphere
(E) an eruption that causes average temperature in the hemisphere of the eruption to drop by less than half a degree centigrade

10. To which one of the following situations would the concept of a feedback loop, as it is employed in the passage, be most accurately applied?

(A) An increase in the amount of decaying matter in the soil increases the amount of nutrients in the soil, which increases the number of plants, which further increases the amount of decaying matter in the soil.
(B) An increase in the number of wolves in an area decreases the number of deer, which decreases the grazing of shrubs, which increases the amount of food available for other animals, which increases the number of other animals in the area.
(C) An increase in the amount of rain in an area increases the deterioration of the forest floor, which makes it harder for wolves to prey on deer, which increases the number of deer, which gives wolves more opportunities to prey upon deer.
(D) An increase in the amount of sunlight on the ocean increases the ocean temperature, which increases the number of phytoplankton in the ocean, which decreases the ocean temperature by blocking sunlight.
(E) As increase in the number of outdoor electric lights in an area increases the number of insects in the area, which increases the number of bats in the area, which decreases the number of insects in the area, which decreases the number of bats in the area.

11. The author of the passage would be most likely to agree with which one of the following hypotheses?

(A) Major volcanic eruptions sometimes cause average temperature in the hemisphere of the eruption to drop by more than a degree centigrade.
(B) Major volcanic eruptions can induce the El Niño phenomenon when it otherwise might not occur.
(C) Major volcanic eruptions do not directly cause unusually cold summers.
(D) The climatic effects of minor volcanic eruptions differ from those of major eruptions only in degree.
(E) El Niño has no discernible effect on average hemispheric temperature.

12. The information in the passage provides the LEAST support for which one of the following claims?

(A) Major volcanic eruptions have a discernible effect on global temperature.
(B) The effect of major volcanic eruptions on global temperature is smaller than was previously thought.
(C) Major volcanic eruptions have no discernible effect on regional temperature.
(D) Minor volcanic eruptions have no discernible effect on temperature in the hemisphere in which they occur.
(E) Minor volcanic eruptions have no discernible effect on temperature in the hemisphere opposite the hemisphere of the eruption.

13. The primary purpose of the last paragraph of the passage is to

(A) describe how the "year without a summer" differs from other examples of climatic feedback loops
(B) account for the relatively slight hemispheric cooling effect of a major volcanic eruption
(C) explain how regional climatic conditions can be significantly affected by a small drop in temperature
(D) indicate how researchers are sometimes led to overlook the effects of El Niño on regional temperature
(E) suggest a modification to the current model of how feedback loops produce changes in regional temperature

GO ON TO THE NEXT PAGE.

Recently, a new school of economics called steady-state economics has seriously challenged neoclassical economics, the reigning school in Western economic decision making. According to the neoclassical model, an economy is a closed system involving only the circular flow of exchange value between producers and consumers. Therefore, no noneconomic constraints impinge upon the economy and growth has no limits. Indeed, some neoclassical economists argue that growth itself is crucial, because, they claim, the solutions to problems often associated with growth (income inequities, for example) can be found only in the capital that further growth creates.

Steady-state economists believe the neoclassical model to be unrealistic and hold that the economy is dependent on nature. Resources, they argue, enter the economy as raw material and exit as consumed products or waste; the greater the resources, the greater the size of the economy. According to these economists, nature's limited capacity to regenerate raw material and absorb waste suggests that there is an optimal size for the economy, and that growth beyond this ideal point would increase the cost to the environment at a faster rate than the benefit to producers and consumers, generating cycles that impoverish rather than enrich. Steady-state economists thus believe that the concept of an ever growing economy is dangerous, and that the only alternative is to maintain a state in which the economy remains in equilibrium with nature. Neoclassical economists, on the other hand, consider nature to be just one element of the economy rather than an outside constraint, believing that natural resources, if depleted, can be replaced with other elements—i.e., human-made resources—that will allow the economy to continue with its process of unlimited growth.

Some steady-state economists, pointing to the widening disparity between indices of actual growth (which simply count the total monetary value of goods and services) and the index of environmentally sustainable growth (which is based on personal consumption, factoring in depletion of raw materials and production costs), believe that Western economies have already exceeded their optimal size. In response to the warnings from neoclassical economists that checking economic growth only leads to economic stagnation, they argue that there are alternatives to growth that still accomplish what is required of any economy: the satisfaction of human wants. One of the alternatives is conservation. Conservation—for example, increasing the efficiency of resource use through means such as recycling—differs from growth in that it is qualitative, not quantitative, requiring improvement in resource management rather than an increase in the amount of resources. One measure of the success of a steady-state economy would be the degree to which it could implement alternatives to growth, such as conservation, without sacrificing the ability to satisfy the wants of producers and consumers.

14. Which one of the following most completely and accurately expresses the main point of the passage?

(A) Neoclassical economists, who, unlike steady-state economists, hold that economic growth is not subject to outside constraints, believe that nature is just one element of the economy and that if natural resources in Western economies are depleted they can be replaced with human-made resources.

(B) Some neoclassical economists, who, unlike steady-state economists, hold that growth is crucial to the health of economies, believe that the solutions to certain problems in Western economies can thus be found in the additional capital generated by unlimited growth.

(C) Some steady-state economists, who, unlike neoclassical economists, hold that unlimited growth is neither possible nor desirable, believe that Western economies should limit economic growth by adopting conservation strategies, even if such strategies lead temporarily to economic stagnation.

(D) Some steady-state economists, who, unlike neoclassical economists, hold that the optimal sizes of economies are limited by the availability of natural resources, believe that Western economies should limit economic growth and that, with alternatives like conservation, satisfaction of human wants need not be sacrificed.

(E) Steady-state and neoclassical economists, who both hold that economies involve the circular flow of exchange value between producers and consumers, nevertheless differ over the most effective way of guaranteeing that a steady increase in this exchange value continues unimpeded in Western economies.

15. Based on the passage, neoclassical economists would likely hold that steady-state economists are wrong to believe each of the following EXCEPT:

(A) The environment's ability to yield raw material is limited.

(B) Natural resources are an external constraint on economies.

(C) The concept of unlimited economic growth is dangerous.

(D) Western economies have exceeded their optimal size.

(E) Economies have certain optimal sizes.

GO ON TO THE NEXT PAGE.

16. According to the passage, steady-state economists believe that unlimited economic growth is dangerous because it

(A) may deplete natural resources faster than other natural resources are discovered to replace them
(B) may convert natural resources into products faster than more efficient resource use can compensate for
(C) may proliferate goods and services faster than it generates new markets for them
(D) may create income inequities faster than it creates the capital needed to redress them
(E) may increase the cost to the environment faster than it increases benefits to producers and consumers

17. A steady-state economist would be LEAST likely to endorse which one of the following as a means of helping a steady-state economy reduce growth without compromising its ability to satisfy human wants?

(A) a manufacturer's commitment to recycle its product packaging
(B) a manufacturer's decision to use a less expensive fuel in its production process
(C) a manufacturer's implementation of a quality-control process to reduce the output of defective products
(D) a manufacturer's conversion from one type of production process to another with greater fuel efficiency
(E) a manufacturer's reduction of output in order to eliminate an overproduction problem

18. Based on the passage, a steady-state economist is most likely to claim that a successful economy is one that satisfies which one of the following principles?

(A) A successful economy uses human-made resources in addition to natural resources.
(B) A successful economy satisfies human wants faster than it creates new ones.
(C) A successful economy maintains an equilibrium with nature while still satisfying human wants.
(D) A successful economy implements every possible means to prevent growth.
(E) A successful economy satisfies the wants of producers and consumers by using resources to spur growth.

19. In the view of steady-state economists, which one of the following is a noneconomic constraint as referred to in line 7?

(A) the total amount of human wants
(B) the index of environmentally sustainable growth
(C) the capacity of nature to absorb waste
(D) the problems associated with economic growth
(E) the possibility of economic stagnation

20. Which one of the following most accurately describes what the last paragraph does in the passage?

(A) It contradicts the ways in which the two economic schools interpret certain data and gives a criterion for judging between them based on the basic goals of an economy.
(B) It gives an example that illustrates the weakness of the new economic school and recommends an economic policy based on the basic goals of the prevailing economic school.
(C) It introduces an objection to the new economic school and argues that the policies of the new economic school would be less successful than growth-oriented economic policies at achieving the basic goal an economy must meet.
(D) It notes an objection to implementing the policies of the new economic school and identifies an additional policy that can help avoid that objection and still meet the goal an economy must meet.
(E) It contrasts the policy of the prevailing economic school with the recommendation mentioned earlier of the new economic school and shows that they are based on differing views on the basic goal an economy must meet.

21. The passage suggests which one of the following about neoclassical economists?

(A) They assume that natural resources are infinitely available.
(B) They assume that human-made resources are infinitely available.
(C) They assume that availability of resources places an upper limit on growth.
(D) They assume that efficient management of resources is necessary to growth.
(E) They assume that human-made resources are preferable to natural resources.

GO ON TO THE NEXT PAGE.

As one of the most pervasive and influential popular arts, the movies feed into and off of the rest of the culture in various ways. In the United States, the star system of the mid-1920s—in which actors were placed under exclusive contract to particular Hollywood film studios—was a consequence of studios' discovery that the public was interested in actor's private lives, and that information about actors could be used to promote their films. Public relations agents fed the information to gossip columnists, whetting the public's appetite for the films—which, audiences usually discovered, had the additional virtue of being created by talented writers, directors, and producers devoted to the art of storytelling. The important feature of this relationship was not the benefit to Hollywood, but rather to the press; in what amounted to a form of cultural cross-fertilization, the press saw that they could profit from studios' promotion of new films.

Today this arrangement has mushroomed into an intricately interdependent mass-media entertainment industry. The faith by which this industry sustains itself is the belief that there is always something worth promoting. A vast portion of the mass media—television and radio interviews, magazine articles, even product advertisements—now does most of the work for Hollywood studios attempting to promote their movies. It does so not out of altruism but because it makes for good business: If you produce a talk show or edit a newspaper, and other media are generating public curiosity about a studio's forthcoming film, it would be unwise for you not to broadcast or publish something about the film, too, because the audience for your story is already guaranteed.

The problem with this industry is that it has begun to affect the creation of films as well as their promotion. Choices of subject matter and actors are made more and more frequently by studio executives rather than by producers, writers, or directors. This problem is often referred to simply as an obsession with turning a profit, but Hollywood movies have almost always been produced to appeal to the largest possible audience. The new danger is that, increasingly, profit comes only from exciting an audience's curiosity about a movie instead of satisfying its desire to have an engaging experience watching the film. When movies can pull people into theaters instantly on the strength of media publicity rather than relying on the more gradual process of word of mouth among satisfied moviegoers, then the intimate relationship with the audience—on which the vitality of all popular art depends—is lost. But studios are making more money than ever by using this formula, and for this reason it appears that films whose appeal is due not merely to their publicity value but to their ability to affect audiences emotionally will become increasingly rare in the U.S. film industry.

22. The passage suggests that the author would be most likely to agree with which one of the following statements?

(A) The Hollywood films of the mid-1920s were in general more engaging to watch than are Hollywood films produced today.
(B) The writers, producers, and directors in Hollywood in the mid-1920s were more talented than are their counterparts today.
(C) The Hollywood film studios of the mid-1920s had a greater level of dependence on the mass-media industry than do Hollywood studios today.
(D) The publicity generated for Hollywood films in the mid-1920s was more interesting than is the publicity generated for these films today.
(E) The star system of the mid-1920s accounts for most of the difference in quality between the Hollywood films of that period and Hollywood films today.

23. According to the author, the danger of mass-media promotion of films is that it

(A) discourages the work of filmmakers who attempt to draw the largest possible audiences to their films
(B) discourages the critical review of the content of films that have been heavily promoted
(C) encourages the production of films that excite an audience's curiosity but that do not provide satisfying experiences
(D) encourages decisions to make the content of films parallel the private lives of the actors that appear in them
(E) encourages cynicism among potential audience members about the merits of the films publicized

24. The phrase "cultural cross-fertilization" (line 17) is used in the passage to refer to which one of the following?

(A) competition among different segments of the U.S. mass media
(B) the interrelationship of Hollywood movies with other types of popular art
(C) Hollywood film studios' discovery that the press could be used to communicate with the public
(D) the press's mutually beneficial relationship with Hollywood film studios
(E) interactions between public relations agents and the press

GO ON TO THE NEXT PAGE.

25. Which one of the following most accurately describes the organization of the passage?

(A) description of the origins of a particular aspect of a popular art; discussion of the present state of this aspect; analysis of a problem associated with this aspect; introduction of a possible solution to the problem
(B) description of the origins of a particular aspect of a popular art; discussion of the present state of this aspect; analysis of a problem associated with this aspect; suggestion of a likely consequence of the problem
(C) description of the origins of a particular aspect of a popular art; analysis of a problem associated with this aspect; introduction of a possible solution to the problem; suggestion of a likely consequence of the solution
(D) summary of the history of a particular aspect of a popular art; discussion of a problem that accompanied the growth of this aspect; suggestion of a likely consequence of the problem; appraisal of the importance of avoiding this consequence
(E) summary of the history of a particular aspect of a popular art; analysis of factors that contributed to the growth of this aspect; discussion of a problem that accompanied the growth of this aspect; appeal for assistance in solving the problem

26. The author's position in lines 35-47 would be most weakened if which one of the following were true?

(A) Many Hollywood studio executives do consider a film's ability to satisfy moviegoers emotionally.
(B) Many Hollywood studio executives achieved their positions as a result of demonstrating talent at writing, producing, or directing films that satisfy audiences emotionally.
(C) Most writers, producers, and directors in Hollywood continue to have a say in decisions about the casting and content of films despite the influence of studio executives.
(D) The decisions made by most Hollywood studio executives to improve a film's chances of earning a profit also add to its ability to satisfy moviegoers emotionally.
(E) Often the U.S. mass media play an indirect role in influencing the content of the films that Hollywood studios make by whetting the public's appetite for certain performers or subjects.

S T O P

IF YOU FINISH BEFORE TIME IS CALLED, YOU MAY CHECK YOUR WORK ON THIS SECTION ONLY.
DO NOT WORK ON ANY OTHER SECTION IN THE TEST.

SECTION II

Time—35 minutes

23 Questions

Directions: Each group of questions in this section is based on a set of conditions. In answering some of the questions, it may be useful to draw a rough diagram. Choose the response that most accurately and completely answers each question and blacken the corresponding space on your answer sheet.

Questions 1–7

Workers at a water treatment plant open eight valves—G, H, I, K, L, N, O, and P—to flush out a system of pipes that needs emergency repairs. To maximize safety and efficiency, each valve is opened exactly once, and no two valves are opened at the same time. The valves are opened in accordance with the following conditions:

Both K and P are opened before H.
O is opened before L but after H.
L is opened after G.
N is opened before H.
I is opened after K.

1. Which one of the following could be the order, from first to last, in which the valves are opened?

(A) P, I, K, G, N, H, O, L
(B) P, G, K, N, L, H, O, I
(C) G, K, I, P, H, O, N, L
(D) N, K, P, H, O, I, L, G
(E) K, I, N, G, P, H, O, L

2. Each of the following could be the fifth valve opened EXCEPT:

(A) H
(B) I
(C) K
(D) N
(E) O

3. If I is the second valve opened, then each of the following could be true EXCEPT:

(A) G is the third valve opened.
(B) H is the fourth valve opened.
(C) P is the fifth valve opened.
(D) O is the sixth valve opened.
(E) G is the seventh valve opened.

4. If L is the seventh valve opened, then each of the following could be the second valve opened EXCEPT:

(A) G
(B) I
(C) K
(D) N
(E) P

5. Which one of the following must be true?

(A) At least one valve is opened before P is opened.
(B) At least two valves are opened before G is opened.
(C) No more than two valves are opened after O is opened.
(D) No more than three valves are opened after H is opened.
(E) No more than four valves are opened before N is opened.

6. If K is the fourth valve opened, then which one of the following could be true?

(A) I is the second valve opened.
(B) N is the third valve opened.
(C) G is the fifth valve opened.
(D) O is the fifth valve opened.
(E) P is the sixth valve opened.

7. If G is the first valve opened and I is the third valve opened, then each of the following must be true EXCEPT:

(A) K is the second valve opened.
(B) N is the fourth valve opened.
(C) H is the sixth valve opened.
(D) O is the seventh valve opened.
(E) L is the eighth valve opened.

Questions 8–12

On a field trip to the Museum of Natural History, each of six children—Juana, Kyle, Lucita, Salim, Thanh, and Veronica—is accompanied by one of three adults—Ms. Margoles, Mr. O'Connell, and Ms. Podorski. Each adult accompanies exactly two of the children, consistent with the following conditions:

If Ms. Margoles accompanies Juana, then Ms. Podorski accompanies Lucita.
If Kyle is not accompanied by Ms. Margoles, then Veronica is accompanied by Mr. O'Connell.
Either Ms. Margoles or Mr. O'Connell accompanies Thanh.
Juana is not accompanied by the same adult as Kyle; nor is Lucita accompanied by the same adult as Salim; nor is Thanh accompanied by the same adult as Veronica.

8. Which one of the following could be an accurate matching of the adults to the children they accompany?
   (A) Ms. Margoles: Juana, Thanh; Mr. O'Connell: Lucita, Veronica; Ms. Podorski: Kyle, Salim
   (B) Ms. Margoles: Kyle, Thanh; Mr. O'Connell: Juana, Salim; Ms. Podorski: Lucita, Veronica
   (C) Ms. Margoles: Lucita, Thanh; Mr. O'Connell: Juana, Salim; Ms. Podorski: Kyle, Veronica
   (D) Ms. Margoles: Kyle, Veronica; Mr. O'Connell: Juana, Thanh; Ms. Podorski: Lucita, Salim
   (E) Ms. Margoles: Salim, Veronica; Mr. O'Connell: Kyle, Lucita; Ms. Podorski: Juana, Thanh

9. If Ms. Margoles accompanies Lucita and Thanh, then which one of the following must be true?
   (A) Juana is accompanied by the same adult as Veronica.
   (B) Kyle is accompanied by the same adult as Salim.
   (C) Juana is accompanied by Mr. O'Connell.
   (D) Kyle is accompanied by Ms. Podorski.
   (E) Salim is accompanied by Ms. Podorski.

10. If Ms. Podorski accompanies Juana and Veronica, then Ms. Margoles could accompany which one of the following pairs of children?
   (A) Kyle and Salim
   (B) Kyle and Thanh
   (C) Lucita and Salim
   (D) Lucita and Thanh
   (E) Salim and Thanh

11. Ms. Podorski CANNOT accompany which one of the following pairs of children?
   (A) Juana and Lucita
   (B) Juana and Salim
   (C) Kyle and Salim
   (D) Salim and Thanh
   (E) Salim and Veronica

12. Mr. O'Connell CANNOT accompany which one of the following pairs of children?
   (A) Juana and Lucita
   (B) Juana and Veronica
   (C) Kyle and Thanh
   (D) Lucita and Thanh
   (E) Salim and Veronica

Questions 13–17

Three short seminars—Goals, Objections, and Persuasion—and three long seminars—Humor, Negotiating, and Telemarketing—will be scheduled for a three-day sales training conference. On each day, two of the seminars will be given consecutively. Each seminar will be given exactly once. The schedule must conform to the following conditions:

Exactly one short seminar and exactly one long seminar will be given each day.
Telemarketing will not be given until both Goals and Objections have been given.
Negotiating will not be given until Persuasion has been given.

13. Which one of the following could be an accurate schedule for the sales training conference?

(A) first day: Persuasion followed by Negotiating
second day: Objections followed by Telemarketing
third day: Goals followed by Humor
(B) first day: Objections followed by Humor
second day: Goals followed by Telemarketing
third day: Persuasion followed by Negotiating
(C) first day: Objections followed by Negotiating
second day: Persuasion followed by Humor
third day: Goals followed by Telemarketing
(D) first day: Objections followed by Goals
second day: Telemarketing followed by Persuasion
third day: Negotiating followed by Humor
(E) first day: Goals followed by Humor
second day: Persuasion followed by Telemarketing
third day: Objections followed by Negotiating

14. If Goals is given on the first day of the sales training conference, then which one of the following could be true?

(A) Negotiating is given on the first day.
(B) Objections is given on the first day.
(C) Persuasion is given on the first day.
(D) Humor is given on the second day.
(E) Telemarketing is given on the second day.

15. If Negotiating is given at some time before Objections, then which one of the following must be true?

(A) Negotiating is given at some time before Goals.
(B) Persuasion is given at some time before Goals.
(C) Persuasion is given at some time before Objections.
(D) Humor is given at some time before Objections.
(E) Negotiating is given at some time before Humor.

16. Which one of the following CANNOT be the second seminar given on the second day of the sales training conference?

(A) Humor
(B) Persuasion
(C) Objections
(D) Negotiating
(E) Goals

17. If Humor is given on the second day of the sales training conference, then which one of the following could be true?

(A) Telemarketing is given on the first day.
(B) Negotiating is given on the second day.
(C) Telemarketing is given on the second day.
(D) Objections is given on the third day.
(E) Persuasion is given on the third day.

GO ON TO THE NEXT PAGE.

Questions 18–23

A bread truck makes exactly one bread delivery to each of six restaurants in succession—Figueroa's, Ginsberg's, Harris's, Kanzaki's, Leacock's, and Malpighi's—though not necessarily in that order. The following conditions must apply:

Ginsberg's delivery is earlier than Kanzaki's but later than Figueroa's.
Harris's delivery is earlier than Ginsberg's.
If Figueroa's delivery is earlier than Malpighi's, then Leacock's delivery is earlier than Harris's.
Either Malpighi's delivery is earlier than Harris's or it is later than Kanzaki's, but not both.

18. Which one of the following accurately represents an order in which the deliveries could occur, from first to last?

(A) Harris's, Figueroa's, Leacock's, Ginsberg's, Kanzaki's, Malpighi's
(B) Leacock's, Harris's, Figueroa's, Ginsberg's, Malpighi's, Kanzaki's
(C) Malpighi's, Figueroa's, Harris's, Ginsberg's, Leacock's, Kanzaki's
(D) Malpighi's, Figueroa's, Kanzaki's, Harris's, Ginsberg's, Leacock's
(E) Malpighi's, Figueroa's, Ginsberg's, Kanzaki's, Harris's, Leacock's

19. If Figueroa's delivery is fourth, then which one of the following must be true?

(A) Ginsberg's delivery is fifth.
(B) Harris's delivery is second.
(C) Harris's delivery is third.
(D) Leacock's delivery is second.
(E) Malpighi's delivery is first.

20. If Malpighi's delivery is first and Leacock's delivery is third, then which one of the following must be true?

(A) Figueroa's delivery is second.
(B) Harris's delivery is second.
(C) Harris's delivery is fourth.
(D) Kanzaki's delivery is fifth.
(E) Kanzaki's delivery is last.

21. Which one of the following must be true?

(A) Figueroa's delivery is earlier than Leacock's.
(B) Ginsberg's delivery is earlier than Leacock's.
(C) Harris's delivery is earlier than Kanzaki's.
(D) Leacock's delivery is earlier than Ginsberg's.
(E) Malpighi's delivery is earlier than Harris's.

22. If Kanzaki's delivery is earlier than Leacock's, then which one of the following could be true?

(A) Figueroa's delivery is first.
(B) Ginsberg's delivery is third.
(C) Harris's delivery is third.
(D) Leacock's delivery is fifth.
(E) Malpighi's delivery is second.

23. Which one of the following must be false?

(A) Figueroa's delivery is first.
(B) Ginsberg's delivery is fifth.
(C) Harris's delivery is third.
(D) Leacock's delivery is second.
(E) Malpighi's delivery is fourth.

S T O P

IF YOU FINISH BEFORE TIME IS CALLED, YOU MAY CHECK YOUR WORK ON THIS SECTION ONLY.
DO NOT WORK ON ANY OTHER SECTION IN THE TEST.

SECTION III
Time—35 minutes
25 Questions

Directions: The questions in this section are based on the reasoning contained in brief statements or passages. For some questions, more than one of the choices could conceivably answer the question. However, you are to choose the best answer; that is, the response that most accurately and completely answers the question. You should not make assumptions that are by commonsense standards implausible, superfluous, or incompatible with the passage. After you have chosen the best answer, blacken the corresponding space on your answer sheet.

1. Any museum that owns the rare stamp that features an airplane printed upside down should not display it. Ultraviolet light causes red ink to fade, and a substantial portion of the stamp is red. If the stamp is displayed, it will be damaged. It should be kept safely locked away, even though this will deny the public the chance to see it.

   The reasoning above most closely conforms to which one of the following principles?

   (A) The public should judge the quality of a museum by the rarity of the objects in its collection.
   (B) Museum display cases should protect their contents from damage caused by ultraviolet light.
   (C) Red ink should not be used on items that will not be exposed to ultraviolet light.
   (D) A museum piece that would be damaged by display should not be displayed.
   (E) The primary purpose of a museum is to educate the public.

2. Dietitian: Many diet-conscious consumers are excited about new "fake fat" products designed to give food the flavor and consistency of fatty foods, yet without fat's harmful effects. Consumers who expect the new fat substitute to help them lose weight arc likely to be disappointed, however. Research has shown that when people knowingly or unknowingly eat foods containing "fake fat," they tend to take in at least as many additional calories as are saved by eating "fake fat."

   Which one of the following most accurately expresses the conclusion of the dietitian's argument?

   (A) People tend to take in a certain number of daily calories, no matter what types of food they eat
   (B) Most consumers who think that foods with "fake fat" are more nutritious than fatty foods are destined to be disappointed.
   (C) "Fake fat" products are likely to contribute to obesity more than do other foods.
   (D) "Fake fat" in foods is probably not going to help consumers meet weight loss goals.
   (E) "Fake fat" in foods is indistinguishable from genuine fat by most consumers on the basis of taste alone.

3. Banking analyst: Banks often offer various services to new customers at no charge. But this is not an ideal business practice, since regular, long-term customers, who make up the bulk of the business for most banks, are excluded from these special offers.

   Which one of the following, if true, most strengthens the banking analyst's argument'?

   (A) Most banks have similar charges for most services and pay similar interest rates on deposits.
   (B) Banks do best when offering special privileges only to their most loyal customers.
   (C) Offering services at no charge to all of its current customers would be prohibitively expensive for a bank.
   (D) Once they have chosen a bank, people tend to remain loyal to that bank.
   (E) Some banks that offer services at no charge to new customers are very successful.

GO ON TO THE NEXT PAGE.

4. Panelist: Medical research articles cited in popular newspapers or magazines are more likely than other medical research articles to be cited in subsequent medical research. Thus, it appears that medical researchers' judgments of the importance of prior research are strongly influenced by the publicity received by that research and do not strongly correspond to the research's true importance.

The panelist's argument is most vulnerable to criticism on the grounds that it

(A) presents counterarguments to a view that is not actually held by any medical researcher
(B) fails to consider the possibility that popular newspapers and magazines do a good job of identifying the most important medical research articles
(C) takes for granted that coverage of medical research in the popular press is more concerned with the eminence of the scientists involved than with the content of their research
(D) fails to consider the possibility that popular newspapers and magazines are able to review only a minuscule percentage of medical research articles
(E) draws a conclusion that is logically equivalent to its premise

5. Lahar: We must now settle on a procedure for deciding on meeting agendas. Our club's constitution allows three options: unanimous consent, majority vote, or assigning the task to a committee. Unanimous consent is unlikely. Forming a committee has usually led to factionalism and secret deals. Clearly, we should subject meeting agendas to majority vote.

Lahar's argument does which one of the following?

(A) rejects suggested procedures on constitutional grounds
(B) claims that one procedure is the appropriate method for reaching every decision in the club
(C) suggests a change to a constitution on the basis of practical considerations
(D) recommends a choice based on the elimination of alternative options
(E) supports one preference by arguing against those who have advocated alternatives

6. Mayor: Local antitobacco activists are calling for expanded antismoking education programs paid for by revenue from heavily increased taxes on cigarettes sold in the city. Although the effectiveness of such education programs is debatable, there is strong evidence that the taxes themselves would produce the sought-after reduction in smoking. Surveys show that cigarette sales drop substantially in cities that impose stiff tax increases on cigarettes.

Which one of the following, if true, most undermines the reasoning in the argument above?

(A) A city-imposed tax on cigarettes will substantially reduce the amount of smoking in the city if the tax is burdensome to the average cigarette consumer.
(B) Consumers are more likely to continue buying a product if its price increases due to higher taxes than if its price increases for some other reason.
(C) Usually, cigarette sales will increase substantially in the areas surrounding a city after that city imposes stiff taxes on cigarettes.
(D) People who are well informed about the effects of long-term tobacco use are significantly less likely to smoke than are people who are not informed.
(E) Antismoking education programs that are funded by taxes on cigarettes will tend to lose their funding if they are successful.

GO ON TO THE NEXT PAGE.

7. Gotera: Infants lack the motor ability required to voluntarily produce particular sounds, but produce various babbling sounds randomly. Most children are several years old before they can voluntarily produce most of the vowel and consonant sounds of their language. We can conclude that speech acquisition is entirely a motor control process rather than a process that is abstract or mental.

   Which one of the following is an assumption required by Gotera's argument?

   (A) Speech acquisition is a function only of one's ability to produce the sounds of spoken language.
   (B) During the entire initial babbling stage, infants cannot intentionally move their tongues while they are babbling.
   (C) The initial babbling stage is completed during infancy.
   (D) The initial babbling stage is the first stage of the speech acquisition process.
   (E) Control of tongue and mouth movements requires a sophisticated level of mental development.

8. Caldwell: The government recently demolished a former naval base. Among the complex's facilities were a gymnasium, a swimming pool, office buildings, gardens, and housing for hundreds of people. Of course the government was legally permitted to use these facilities as it wished. But clearly, using them for the good of the community would have benefited everyone, and thus the government's actions were not only inefficient but immoral.

   Caldwell's argument is most vulnerable to criticism on the grounds that it

   (A) fails to consider that an action may be morally permissible even if an alternative course of action is to everyone's advantage
   (B) presumes, without providing justification, that the actual consequences of an action are irrelevant to the action's moral permissibility
   (C) presumes, without providing justification, that the government never acts in the most efficient manner
   (D) presumes, without providing justification, that any action that is efficient is also moral
   (E) inappropriately treats two possible courses of action as if they were the only options

9. Reducing stress lessens a person's sensitivity to pain. This is the conclusion reached by researchers who played extended audiotapes to patients before they underwent surgery and afterward while they were recovering. One tape consisted of conversation; the other consisted of music. Those who listened only to the latter tape required less anesthesia during surgery and fewer painkillers afterward than those who listened only to the former tape.

   Which one of the following is an assumption on which the researchers' reasoning depends?

   (A) All of the patients in the study listened to the same tape before surgery as they listened to after surgery.
   (B) Anticipating surgery is no less stressful than recovering from surgery.
   (C) Listening to music reduces stress.
   (D) The psychological effects of music are not changed by anesthesia or painkillers.
   (E) Both anesthesia and painkillers tend to reduce stress.

10. Samuel: Because communication via computer is usually conducted privately and anonymously between people who would otherwise interact in person, it contributes to the dissolution, not the creation, of lasting communal bonds.

    Tova: You assume that communication via computer replaces more intimate forms of communication and interaction, when more often it replaces asocial or even antisocial behavior.

    On the basis of their statements, Samuel and Tova are committed to disagreeing about which one of the following?

    (A) A general trend of modern life is to dissolve the social bonds that formerly connected people.
    (B) All purely private behavior contributes to the dissolution of social bonds.
    (C) Face-to-face communication is more likely to contribute to the creation of social bonds than is anonymous communication.
    (D) It is desirable that new social bonds be created to replace the ones that have dissolved.
    (E) If people were not communicating via computer, they would most likely be engaged in activities that create stronger social bonds.

GO ON TO THE NEXT PAGE.

11. Spreading iron particles over the surface of the earth's oceans would lead to an increase in phytoplankton, decreasing the amount of carbon dioxide in the atmosphere and thereby counteracting the greenhouse effect. But while counteracting the greenhouse effect is important, the side effects of an iron-seeding strategy have yet to be studied. Since the oceans represent such an important resource, this response to the greenhouse effect should not be implemented immediately.

The reasoning above most closely conforms to which one of the following principles?

(A) A problem-solving strategy should be implemented if the side effects of the strategy are known.
(B) Implementing a problem-solving strategy that alters an important resource is impermissible if the consequences are not adequately understood.
(C) We should not implement a problem-solving strategy if the consequences of doing so are more serious than the problem itself.
(D) We should not implement a problem-solving strategy if that strategy requires altering an important resource.
(E) As long as there is a possibility that a strategy for solving a problem may instead exacerbate that problem, such a solution should not be adopted.

12. No matter how conscientious they are, historians always have biases that affect their work. Hence, rather than trying to interpret historical events, historians should instead interpret what the people who participated in historical events thought about those events.

The reasoning in the argument is most vulnerable to criticism on the grounds that the argument fails to consider the possibility that

(A) historians who have different biases often agree about many aspects of some historical events
(B) scholars in disciplines other than history also risk having their biases affect their work
(C) many of the ways in which historians' biases affect their work have been identified
(D) not all historians are aware of the effect that their particular biases have on their work
(E) the proposed shift in focus is unlikely to eliminate the effect that historians' biases have on their work

13. Humanitarian considerations aside, sheer economics dictates that country X should institute, as country Y has done, a nationwide system of air and ground transportation for conveying seriously injured persons to specialized trauma centers. Timely access to the kind of medical care that only specialized centers can provide could save the lives of many people. The earnings of these people would result in a substantial increase in country X's gross national product, and the taxes paid on those earnings would substantially augment government revenues.

The argument depends on the assumption that

(A) lifetime per-capita income is roughly the same in country X as it is in country Y
(B) there are no specialized trauma centers in country X at present
(C) the treatment of seriously injured persons in trauma centers is not more costly than treatment elsewhere
(D) there would be a net increase in employment in country X if more persons survived serious injury
(E) most people seriously injured in automobile accidents in country X do not now receive treatment in specialized trauma centers

14. Early urban societies could not have been maintained without large-scale farming nearby. This is because other methods of food acquisition, such as foraging, cannot support populations as dense as urban ones. Large-scale farming requires irrigation, which remained unfeasible in areas far from rivers or lakes until more recent times.

Which one of the following is most strongly supported by the information above?

(A) Most peoples who lived in early times lived in areas near rivers or lakes.
(B) Only if farming is possible in the absence of irrigation can societies be maintained in areas far from rivers or lakes.
(C) In early times it was not possible to maintain urban societies in areas far from rivers or lakes.
(D) Urban societies with farms near rivers or lakes do not have to rely upon irrigation to meet their farming needs.
(E) Early rural societies relied more on foraging than on agriculture for food.

GO ON TO THE NEXT PAGE.

15. Economist: A country's rapid emergence from an economic recession requires substantial new investment in that country's economy. Since people's confidence in the economic policies of their country is a precondition for any new investment, countries that put collective goals before individuals' goals cannot emerge quickly from an economic recession.

Which one of the following, if assumed, enables the economist's conclusion to be properly drawn?

(A) No new investment occurs in any country that does not emerge quickly from an economic recession.
(B) Recessions in countries that put collective goals before individuals' goals tend not to affect the country's people's support for their government's policies.
(C) If the people in a country that puts individuals' goals first are willing to make new investments in their country's economy, their country will emerge quickly from an economic recession.
(D) People in countries that put collective goals before individuals' goals lack confidence in the economic policies of their countries.
(E) A country's economic policies are the most significant factor determining whether that country's economy will experience a recession.

16. The average length of stay for patients at Edgewater Hospital is four days, compared to six days at University Hospital. Since studies show that recovery rates at the two hospitals are similar for patients with similar illnesses, University Hospital could decrease its average length of stay without affecting quality of care.

The reasoning in the argument is most vulnerable to criticism on the grounds that the argument

(A) equates the quality of care at a hospital with patients' average length of stay
(B) treats a condition that will ensure the preservation of quality of care as a condition that is required to preserve quality of care
(C) fails to take into account the possibility that patients at Edgewater Hospital tend to be treated for different illnesses than patients at University Hospital
(D) presumes, without providing justification, that the length of time patients stay in the hospital is never relevant to the recovery rates of these patients
(E) fails to take into account the possibility that patients at University Hospital generally prefer longer hospital stays

17. Philosopher: Graham argues that since a person is truly happy only when doing something, the best life is a life that is full of activity. But we should not be persuaded by Graham's argument. People sleep, and at least sometimes when sleeping, they are truly happy, even though they are not doing anything.

Which one of the following most accurately describes the role played in the philosopher's argument by the claim that at least sometimes when sleeping, people are truly happy, even though they are not doing anything?

(A) It is a premise of Graham's argument.
(B) It is an example intended to show that a premise of Graham's argument is false.
(C) It is an analogy appealed to by Graham but that the philosopher rejects.
(D) It is an example intended to disprove the conclusion of Graham's argument.
(E) It is the main conclusion of the philosopher's argument.

GO ON TO THE NEXT PAGE.

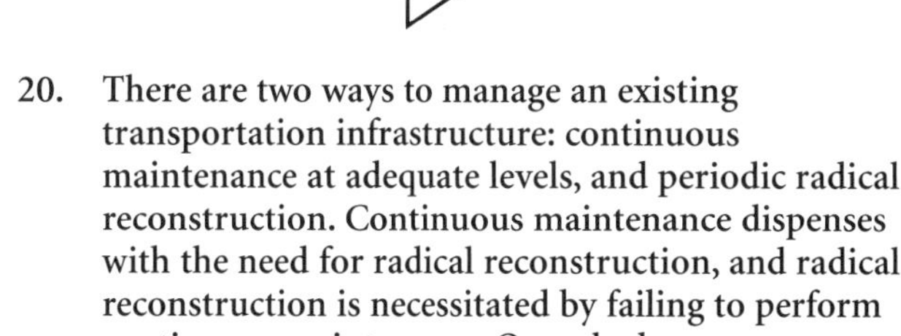

18. Historian: In rebuttal of my claim that West influenced Stuart, some people point out that West's work is mentioned only once in Stuart's diaries. But Stuart's diaries mention several meetings with West, and Stuart's close friend, Abella, studied under West. Furthermore, Stuart's work often uses West's terminology which, though now commonplace, none of Stuart's contemporaries used.

Which one of the following propositions is most supported by the historian's statements, if those statements are true?

(A) Stuart's discussions with Abella were one of the means by which West influenced Stuart.
(B) It is more likely that Stuart influenced West than that West influenced Stuart.
(C) Stuart's contemporaries were not influenced by West.
(D) Stuart's work was not entirely free from West's influence
(E) Because of Stuart's influence on other people, West's terminology is now commonplace.

19. One theory to explain the sudden extinction of all dinosaurs points to "drug overdoses" as the cause. Angiosperms, a certain class of plants, first appeared at the time that dinosaurs became extinct. These plants produce amino-acid-based alkaloids that are psychoactive agents. Most plant-eating mammals avoid these potentially lethal poisons because they taste bitter. Moreover, mammals have livers that help detoxify such drugs. However, dinosaurs could neither taste the bitterness nor detoxify the substance once it was ingested. This theory receives its strongest support from the fact that it helps explain why so many dinosaur fossils are found in unusual and contorted positions.

Which one of the following, if true, would most undermine the theory presented above?

(A) Many fossils of large mammals are found in contorted positions.
(B) Angiosperms provide a great deal of nutrition.
(C) Carnivorous dinosaurs mostly ate other, vegetarian, dinosaurs that fed on angiosperms.
(D) Some poisonous plants do not produce amino-acid-based alkaloids.
(E) Mammals sometimes die of drug overdoses from eating angiosperms.

20. There are two ways to manage an existing transportation infrastructure: continuous maintenance at adequate levels, and periodic radical reconstruction. Continuous maintenance dispenses with the need for radical reconstruction, and radical reconstruction is necessitated by failing to perform continuous maintenance. Over the long run, continuous maintenance is far less expensive; nevertheless, it almost never happens.

Which one of the following, if true, most contributes to an explanation of why the first alternative mentioned is almost never adopted?

(A) Since different parts of the transportation infrastructure are the responsibility of different levels of government, radical reconstruction projects are very difficult to coordinate efficiently.
(B) When funds for transportation infrastructure maintenance are scarce, they are typically distributed in proportion to the amount of traffic that is borne by different elements of the infrastructure.
(C) If continuous maintenance is performed at less-than-adequate levels, the need for radical reconstruction will often arise later than if maintenance had been restricted to responding to emergencies.
(D) Radical reconstruction projects are, in general, too costly to be paid for from current revenue.
(E) For long periods, the task of regular maintenance lacks urgency, since the consequences of neglecting it are very slow to manifest themselves.

GO ON TO THE NEXT PAGE.

21. A good way to get over one's fear of an activity one finds terrifying is to do it repeatedly. For instance, over half of people who have parachuted only once report being extremely frightened by the experience, while less than 1 percent of those who have parachuted ten times or more report being frightened by it.

The reasoning in the argument is most vulnerable to criticism on the grounds that the argument

(A) takes for granted that the greater the number of dangerous activities one engages in the less one is frightened by any one of them
(B) neglects to consider those people who have parachuted more than once but fewer than ten times
(C) takes for granted that people do not know how frightening something is unless they have tried it
(D) fails to take into account the possibility that people would be better off if they did not do things that terrify them
(E) overlooks the possibility that most people who have parachuted many times did not find it frightening initially

22. Most economists believe that reducing the price of any product generally stimulates demand for it. However, most wine merchants have found that reducing the price of domestic wines to make them more competitive with imported wines with which they were previously comparably priced is frequently followed by an increase in sales of those imported wines.

Which one of the following, if true, most helps to reconcile the belief of most economists with the consequences observed by most wine merchants?

(A) Economists' studies of the prices of grocery items and their rates of sales rarely cover alcoholic beverages.
(B) Few merchants of any kind have detailed knowledge of economic theories about the relationship between item prices and sales rates.
(C) Consumers are generally willing to forgo purchasing other items they desire in order to purchase a superior wine.
(D) Imported wines in all price ranges are comparable in quality to domestic wines that cost less.
(E) An increase in the demand for a consumer product is compatible with an increase in demand for a competing product.

23. Certain bacteria that produce hydrogen sulfide as a waste product would die if directly exposed to oxygen. The hydrogen sulfide reacts with oxygen, removing it and so preventing it from harming the bacteria. Furthermore, the hydrogen sulfide tends to kill other organisms in the area, thereby providing the bacteria with a source of food. As a result, a dense colony of these bacteria produces for itself an environment in which it can continue to thrive indefinitely.

Which one of the following is most strongly supported by the information above?

(A) A dense colony of the bacteria can indefinitely continue to produce enough hydrogen sulfide to kill other organisms in the area and to prevent oxygen from harming the bacteria.
(B) The hydrogen sulfide produced by the bacteria kills other organisms in the area by reacting with and removing oxygen.
(C) Most organisms, if killed by the hydrogen sulfide produced by the bacteria, can provide a source of food for the bacteria.
(D) The bacteria can continue to thrive indefinitely only in an environment in which the hydrogen sulfide they produce has removed all oxygen and killed other organisms in the area.
(E) If any colony of bacteria produces hydrogen sulfide as a waste product, it thereby ensures that it is both provided with a source of food and protected from harm by oxygen.

GO ON TO THE NEXT PAGE.

24. Books that present a utopian future in which the inequities and sufferings of the present are replaced by more harmonious and rational social arrangements will always find enthusiastic buyers. Since gloomy books predicting that even more terrifying times await us are clearly not of this genre, they are unlikely to be very popular.

The questionable pattern of reasoning in which one of the following arguments is most similar to that in the argument above?

(A) Art that portrays people as happy and contented has a tranquilizing effect on the viewer, an effect that is appealing to those who are tense or anxious. Thus, people who dislike such art are neither tense nor anxious.
(B) People who enjoy participating in activities such as fishing or hiking may nevertheless enjoy watching such spectator sports as boxing or football. Thus, one cannot infer from someone's participating in vigorous contact sports that he or she is not also fond of less violent forms of recreation.
(C) Action movies that involve complicated and dangerous special-effects scenes are enormously expensive to produce. Hence, since traditional dramatic or comedic films contain no such scenes, it is probable that they are relatively inexpensive to produce.
(D) Adults usually feel a pleasant nostalgia when hearing the music they listened to as adolescents, but since adolescents often like music specifically because they think it annoys their parents, adults rarely appreciate the music that their children will later listen to with nostalgia.
(E) All self-employed businesspeople have salaries that fluctuate with the fortunes of the general economy, but government bureaucrats are not self-employed. Therefore, not everyone with an income that fluctuates with the fortunes of the general economy is a government bureaucrat.

25. Some people mistakenly believe that since we do not have direct access to the distant past we cannot learn much about it. Contemporary historians and archaeologists find current geography, geology, and climate to be rich in clues about a given region's distant history. However, the more distant the period we are studying is, the less useful the study of the present becomes.

Of the following, which one most closely conforms to the principle that the passage illustrates?

(A) Astronomers often draw inferences about the earlier years of our solar system on the basis of recently collected data. Unfortunately, they have been able to infer comparatively little about the origin of our solar system.
(B) Much can be learned about the perpetrator of a crime by applying scientific methods of investigation to the crime scene. But the more the crime scene has been studied the less likely anything will be learned from further study.
(C) To understand a literary text one needs to understand the author's world view. However, the farther that world view gets from one's own the less one will be able to appreciate the text.
(D) We often extrapolate from ordinary sensory experience to things beyond such experience and form a rash judgment, such as the claim that the earth is the center of the universe because it appears that way to us.
(E) One crucial clue to the extent of the ancient Egyptians' mathematical knowledge came from studying the pyramids. The more we studied such structures, the more impressed we were by how much the Egyptians knew.

S T O P

IF YOU FINISH BEFORE TIME IS CALLED, YOU MAY CHECK YOUR WORK ON THIS SECTION ONLY.
DO NOT WORK ON ANY OTHER SECTION IN THE TEST.

SECTION IV

Time—35 minutes

27 Questions

Directions: Each set of questions in this section is based on a single passage or a pair of passages. The questions are to be answered on the basis of what is stated or implied in the passage or pair of passages. For some of the questions, more than one of the choices could conceivably answer the question. However, you are to choose the best answer; that is, the response that must accurately and completely answers the question, and blacken the corresponding space on your answer sheet.

Many critics agree that the primary characteristic of Senegalese filmmaker Ousmane Sembène's work is its sociopolitical commitment. Sembène was trained in Moscow in the cinematic methods of socialist realism, and he asserts that his films are not meant to entertain his compatriots, but rather to raise their awareness of the past and present realities of their society. But his originality as a filmmaker lies most strikingly in his having successfully adapted film, originally a Western cultural medium, to the needs, pace, and structures of West African culture. In particular, Sembène has found within African oral culture techniques and strategies that enable him to express his views and to reach both literate and nonliterate Senegalese viewers.

A number of Sembène's characters and motifs can be traced to those found in traditional West African storytelling. The tree, for instance, which in countless West African tales symbolizes knowledge, life, death, and rebirth, is a salient motif in *Emitaï*. The trickster, usually a dishonest individual who personifies antisocial traits, appears in *Borom Sarret*, *Mandabi*, and *Xala* as a thief, a corrupted civil servant, and a member of the elite, respectively. In fact, most of Sembène's characters, like those of many oral West African narratives, are types embodying collective ideas or attitudes. And in the oral tradition, these types face archetypal predicaments, as is true, for example, of the protagonist of *Borom Sarret*, who has no name and is recognizable instead by his trade—he is a street merchant—and by the difficulties he encounters but is unable to overcome.

Moreover, many of Sembène's films derive their structure from West African dilemma tales, the outcomes of which are debated and decided by their audiences. The open-endedness of most of his plots reveals that Sembène similarly leaves it to his viewers to complete his narratives: in such films as *Borom Sarret*, *Mandabi*, and *Ceddo*, for example, he provides his spectators with several alternatives as the films end. The openness of his narratives is also evidenced by his frequent use of freeze-frames, which carry the suggestion of continued action.

Finally, like many West African oral tales, Sembène's narratives take the form of initiatory journeys that bring about a basic change in the worldview of the protagonist and ultimately, Sembène hopes, in that of the viewer. His films denounce social and political injustice. and his protagonists' social consciousness emerges from an acute self-consciousness brought about by the juxtaposition of opposites within the films' social context: good versus evil, powerlessness versus power, or poverty versus wealth. Such binary oppositions are used analogously in West African tales, and it seems likely that these dialectical elements are related to African oral storytelling more than, as many critics have supposed, to the Marxist components of his ideology.

1. Which one of the following most accurately states the main point of the passage?
   (A) Sembène's originality as a filmmaker lies in his adaptation of traditional archetypal predicaments and open-ended plots, both of which are derived from West African oral tales.
   (B) Many of the characters in Sembène's films are variations on character types common to traditional West African storytelling.
   (C) Sembène's films derive their distinctive characteristics from oral narrative traditions that had not previously been considered suitable subject matter for films.
   (D) Sembène's films give vivid expression to the social and political beliefs held by most of the Senegalese people.
   (E) Sembène's films are notable in that they use elements derived from traditional West African storytelling to comment critically on contemporary social and political issues.

GO ON TO THE NEXT PAGE.

2. The author says that Sembène does which one of the following in at least some of his films?

(A) uses animals as symbols
(B) uses slow motion for artistic effect
(C) provides oral narration of the film's story
(D) juxtaposes West African images and Marxist symbols
(E) leaves part of the story to be filled in by audiences

3. Which one of the following would, if true, most strengthen the claim made by the author in the last sentence of the passage (lines 54–58)?

(A) Several African novelists who draw upon the oral traditions of West Africa use binary oppositions as fundamental structures in their narratives, even though they have not read Marxist theory.
(B) Folklorists who have analyzed oral storytelling traditions from across the world have found that the use of binary oppositions to structure narratives is common to many of these traditions.
(C) When he trained in Moscow, Sembène read extensively in Marxist political theory and worked to devise ways of synthesizing Marxist theory and the collective ideas expressed in West African storytelling.
(D) Very few filmmakers in Europe or North America make use of binary oppositions to structure their narratives.
(E) Binary oppositions do not play an essential structuring role in the narratives of some films produced by other filmmakers who subscribe to Marxist principles.

4. Which one of the following inferences about Sembène is most strongly supported by the passage?

(A) His films have become popular both in parts of Africa and elsewhere.
(B) He has not received support from government agencies for his film production.
(C) His films are widely misunderstood by critics in Senegal.
(D) His characters are drawn from a broad range of social strata.
(E) His work has been subjected to government censorship.

5. Which one of the following most closely expresses the author's intended meaning in using the word "initiatory" (line 45)?

(A) beginning a series
(B) experimental
(C) transformative
(D) unprecedented
(E) prefatory

6. The passage does NOT provide evidence that Sembène exhibits which one of the following attitudes in one or more of his films?

(A) disenchantment with attempts to reform Senegalese government
(B) confidence in the aptness of using traditional motifs to comment on contemporary issues
(C) concern with social justice
(D) interest in the vicissitudes of ordinary people's lives
(E) desire to educate his audience

GO ON TO THE NEXT PAGE.

Passage A

Readers, like writers, need to search for answers. Part of the joy of reading is in being surprised, but academic historians leave little to the imagination. The perniciousness of the historiographic approach became fully evident to me when I started teaching. Historians require undergraduates to read scholarly monographs that sap the vitality of history; they visit on students what was visited on them in graduate school. They assign books with formulaic arguments that transform history into an abstract debate that would have been unfathomable to those who lived in the past. Aimed so squarely at the head, such books cannot stimulate students who yearn to connect to history emotionally as well as intellectually.

In an effort to address this problem, some historians have begun to rediscover stories. It has even become something of a fad within the profession. This year, the American Historical Association chose as the theme for its annual conference some putative connection to storytelling: "Practices of Historical Narrative." Predictably, historians responded by adding the word "narrative" to their titles and presenting papers at sessions on "Oral History and the Narrative of Class Identity," and "Meaning and Time: The Problem of Historical Narrative." But it was still historiography. intended only for other academics. At meetings of historians, we still encounter very few historians telling stories or moving audiences to smiles, chills, or tears.

Passage B

Writing is at the heart of the lawyer's craft, and so, like it or not, we who teach the law inevitably teach aspiring lawyers how lawyers write. We do this in a few stand-alone courses and, to a greater extent, through the constraints that we impose on their writing throughout the curriculum. Legal writing, because of the purposes it serves, is necessarily ruled by linear logic, creating a path without diversions, surprises, or reversals. Conformity is a virtue, creativity suspect, humor forbidden, and voice mute.

Lawyers write as they see other lawyers write, and, influenced by education, profession, economic constraints, and perceived self-interest, they too often write badly. Perhaps the currently fashionable call for attention to narrative in legal education could have an effect on this. It is not yet exactly clear what role narrative should play in the law, but it is nonetheless true that every case has at its heart a story—of real events and people, of concerns, misfortunes, conflicts, feelings. But because legal analysis strips the human narrative content from the abstract, canonical legal form of the case, law students learn to act as if there is no such story.

It may well turn out that some of the terminology and public rhetoric of this potentially subversive movement toward attention to narrative will find its way into the law curriculum, but without producing corresponding changes in how legal writing is actually taught or in how our future colleagues will write. Still, even mere awareness of the value of narrative could perhaps serve as an important corrective.

7. Which one of the following does each of the passages display?

(A) a concern with the question of what teaching methods are most effective in developing writing skills
(B) a concern with how a particular discipline tends to represent points of view it does not typically deal with
(C) a conviction that writing in specialized professional disciplines cannot be creatively crafted
(D) a belief that the writing in a particular profession could benefit from more attention to storytelling
(E) a desire to see writing in a particular field purged of elements from other disciplines

8. The passages most strongly support which one of the following inferences regarding the authors' relationships to the professions they discuss?

(A) Neither author is an active member of the profession that he or she discusses.
(B) Each author is an active member of the profession he or she discusses.
(C) The author of passage A is a member of the profession discussed in that passage, but the author of passage B is not a member of either of the professions discussed in the passages.
(D) Both authors are active members of the profession discussed in passage B.
(E) The author of passage B, but not the author of passage A, is an active member of both of the professions discussed in the passages.

GO ON TO THE NEXT PAGE.

9. Which one of the following does each passage indicate is typical of writing in the respective professions discussed in the passages?

(A) abstraction
(B) hyperbole
(C) subversion
(D) narrative
(E) imagination

10. In which one of the following ways are the passages NOT parallel?

(A) Passage A presents and rejects arguments for an opposing position, whereas passage B does not.
(B) Passage A makes evaluative claims, whereas passage B does not.
(C) Passage A describes specific examples of a phenomenon it criticizes, whereas passage B does not.
(D) Passage B offers criticism, whereas passage A does not.
(E) Passage B outlines a theory, whereas passage A does not.

11. The phrase "scholarly monographs that sap the vitality of history" in passage A (lines 6–7) plays a role in that passage's overall argument that is most analogous to the role played in passage B by which one of the following phrases?

(A) "Writing is at the heart of the lawyer's craft" (line 29)
(B) "Conformity is a virtue, creativity suspect, humor forbidden, and voice mute" (lines 37–38)
(C) "Lawyers write as they see other lawyers write" (line 39)
(D) "every case has at its heart a story" (line 46)
(E) "Still, even mere awareness of the value of narrative could perhaps serve as an important corrective" (lines 57–59)

12. Suppose that a lawyer is writing a legal document describing the facts that are at issue in a case. The author of passage B would be most likely to expect which one of the following to be true of the document?

(A) It will be poorly written because the lawyer who is writing it was not given explicit advice by law professors on how lawyers should write.
(B) It will be crafted to function like a piece of fiction in its description of the characters and motivations of the people involved in the case.
(C) It will be a concise, well-crafted piece of writing that summarizes most, if not all, of the facts that are important in the case.
(D) It will not genuinely convey the human dimension of the case, regardless of how accurate the document may be in its details.
(E) It will neglect to make appropriate connections between the details of the case and relevant legal doctrines.

GO ON TO THE NEXT PAGE.

Traditional theories of animal behavior assert that animal conflict within a species is highly ritualized and does not vary from contest to contest. This species-specific model assumes that repetitive use of the same visual and vocal displays and an absence of escalated fighting evolved to prevent injury. The contestant that exhibits the "best" display wins the contested resource. Galápagos tortoises, for instance, settle contests on the basis of height: the ritualized display consists of two tortoises facing one another and stretching their necks skyward; the tortoise perceived as being "taller" wins.

In populations of the spider *Agelenopsis aperta*, however, fighting behavior varies greatly from contest to contest. In addition, fighting is not limited to displays: biting and shoving are common. Susan Riechert argues that a recently developed model, evolutionary game theory, provides a closer fit to *A. aperta* territorial disputes than does the species-specific model, because it explains variations in conflict behavior that may result from varying conditions, such as differences in size, age, and experience of combatants. Evolutionary game theory was adapted from the classical game theory that was developed by von Neumann and Morganstern to explain human behavior in conflict situations. In both classical and evolutionary game theory, strategies are weighed in terms of maximizing the average payoff against contestants employing both the same and different strategies. For example, a spider may engage in escalated fighting during a dispute only if the disputed resource is valuable enough to warrant the risk of physical injury. There are, however, two major differences between the classical and evolutionary theories. First, whereas in classical game theory it is assumed that rational thought is used to determine which action to take, evolutionary game theory assumes that instinct and long-term species advantage ultimately determine the strategies that are exhibited. The other difference is in the payoffs: in classical game theory, the payoffs are determined by an individual's personal judgment of what constitutes winning; in evolutionary game theory, the payoffs are defined in terms of reproductive success.

In studying populations of *A. aperta* in a grassland habitat and a riparian habitat, Riechert predicts that such factors as the size of the opponents, the potential rate of predation in a habitat, and the probability of winning a subsequent site if the dispute is lost will all affect the behavior of spiders in territorial disputes. In addition, she predicts that the markedly different levels of competition for web sites in the two habitats will affect the spiders' willingness to engage in escalated fighting. In the grassland, where 12 percent of the habitat is available for occupation by *A. aperta*, Riechert predicts that spiders will be more willing to engage in escalated fighting than in the riparian habitat, where 90 percent of the habitat is suitable for occupation.

13. Which one of the following best states the main idea of the passage?

(A) Evolutionary game theory and classical game theory can be used to analyze the process of decision-making used by humans and animals in settling disputes.
(B) *A. aperta* in grassland habitats and riparian habitats exhibit an unusually wide variety of fighting behaviors in territorial disputes.
(C) Evolutionary game theory may be useful in explaining the behavior of certain spiders during territorial disputes.
(D) The traditional theory of animal behavior in conflict situations cannot be used to explain the fighting behavior of most species.
(E) Evolutionary game theory, adapted from classical game theory, is currently used by scientists to predict the behavior of spiders in site selection.

14. The author of the passage mentions Galápagos tortoises in the first paragraph most likely in order to

(A) describe a kind of fighting behavior that is used by only a few species
(B) suggest that repetitive use of the same visual and vocal displays is a kind of fighting behavior used by some but not all species
(C) provide evidence to support the claim that fighting behavior does not vary greatly from contest to contest for most species
(D) provide an example of a fighting behavior that is unique to a particular species
(E) provide an example of a ritualized fighting behavior of the kind that traditional theorists assume is the norm for most species

GO ON TO THE NEXT PAGE.

15. Item Removed From Scoring.

16. Which one of the following, if true, is LEAST consistent with Riechert's theory about fighting behavior in spiders?

(A) Spiders in the grassland habitat engage in escalated fighting when a disputed site is highly desirable.
(B) Spiders in the riparian habitat are not willing to engage in escalated fighting for less-than-suitable sites.
(C) Spiders in the riparian habitat confine their fighting to displays more regularly than do spiders in the grassland habitat.
(D) Spiders in the riparian habitat are as willing to engage in escalated fighting as are spiders in the grassland habitat.
(E) Spiders in the riparian habitat are more likely to withdraw when faced with a larger opponent in territorial disputes than are spiders in the grassland habitat.

17. Which one of the following best states the function of the third paragraph of the passage?

(A) It develops a comparison of the two theories that were introduced in the preceding paragraph.
(B) It continues a discussion of a controversial theory described in the first two paragraphs of the passage.
(C) It describes an experiment that provides support for the theory described in the preceding paragraph.
(D) It describes a rare phenomenon that cannot be accounted for by the theory described in the first paragraph.
(E) It describes predictions that can be used to test the validity of a theory described in a preceding paragraph.

18. The passage suggests which one of the following about the behavior of *A. aperta* in conflict situations?

(A) They exhibit variations in fighting behavior from contest to contest primarily because of the different levels of competition for suitable sites in different habitats.
(B) They may confine their fighting behavior to displays if the value of a disputed resource is too low and the risk of physical injury is too great.
(C) They exhibit variations in fighting behavior that are similar to those exhibited by members of most other species of animals.
(D) They are more likely to engage in escalated fighting during disputes than to limit their fighting behavior to visual and vocal displays.
(E) They are more willing to engage in escalated fighting during conflict situations than are members of most other species of animals.

19. The primary purpose of the passage is to

(A) present an alternative to a traditional approach
(B) describe a phenomenon and provide specific examples
(C) evaluate evidence used to support an argument
(D) present data that refutes a controversial theory
(E) suggest that a new theory may be based on inadequate research

GO ON TO THE NEXT PAGE.

Most people acknowledge that not all governments have a moral right to govern and that there are sometimes morally legitimate reasons for disobeying the law, as when a particular law prescribes behavior that is clearly immoral. It is also commonly supposed that such cases are special exceptions and that, in general, the fact that something is against the law counts as a moral, as well as legal, ground for not doing it; i.e., we generally have a moral duty to obey a law simply because it is the law. But the theory known as philosophical anarchism denies this view, arguing instead that people who live under the jurisdiction of governments have no moral duty to those governments to obey their laws. Some commentators have rejected this position because of what they take to be its highly counterintuitive implications: (1) that no existing government is morally better than any other (since all are, in a sense, equally illegitimate), and (2) that, lacking any moral obligation to obey any laws, people may do as they please without scruple. In fact, however, philosophical anarchism does not entail these claims.

First, the conclusion that no government is morally better than any other does not follow from the claim that nobody owes moral obedience to any government. Even if one denies that there is a moral obligation to follow the laws of any government, one can still evaluate the morality of the policies and actions of various governments. Some governments do more good than harm, and others more harm than good, to their subjects. Some violate the moral rights of individuals more regularly, systematically, and seriously than others. In short, it is perfectly consistent with philosophical anarchism to hold that governments vary widely in their moral stature.

Second, philosophical anarchists maintain that all individuals have basic, nonlegal moral duties to one another—duties not to harm others in their lives, liberty, health, or goods. Even if governmental laws have no moral force, individuals still have duties to refrain from those actions that constitute crimes in the majority of legal systems (such as murder, assault, theft, and fraud). Moreover, philosophical anarchists hold that people have a positive moral obligation to care for one another, a moral obligation that they might even choose to discharge by supporting cooperative efforts by governments to help those in need. And where others are abiding by established laws, even those laws derived from mere conventions, individuals are morally bound not to violate those laws when doing so would endanger others. Thus, if others obey the law and drive their vehicles on the right, one must not endanger them by driving on the left, for, even though driving on the left is not inherently immoral, it is morally wrong to deliberately harm the innocent.

20. Which one of the following most accurately expresses the main point of the passage?

(A) Some views that certain commentators consider to be implications of philosophical anarchism are highly counterintuitive.
(B) Contrary to what philosophical anarchists claim, some governments are morally superior to others, and citizens under legitimate governments have moral obligations to one another.
(C) It does not follow logically from philosophical anarchism that no government is morally better than any other or that people have no moral duties toward one another.
(D) Even if, as certain philosophical anarchists claim, governmental laws lack moral force, people still have a moral obligation to refrain from harming one another.
(E) Contrary to what some of its opponents have claimed, philosophical anarchism does not conflict with the ordinary view that one should obey the law because it is the law.

21. The author identifies which one of the following as a commonly held belief?

(A) In most cases we are morally obligated to obey the law simply because it is the law.
(B) All governments are in essence morally equal.
(C) We are morally bound to obey only those laws we participate in establishing.
(D) Most crimes are morally neutral, even though they are illegal.
(E) The majority of existing laws are intended to protect others from harm.

22. The author's stance regarding the theory of philosophical anarchism can most accurately be described as one of

(A) ardent approval of most aspects of the theory
(B) apparent acceptance of some of the basic positions of the theory
(C) concerned pessimism about the theory's ability to avoid certain extreme views
(D) hesitant rejection of some of the central features of the theory
(E) resolute antipathy toward both the theory and certain of its logical consequences

GO ON TO THE NEXT PAGE.

23. By attributing to commentators the view that philosophical anarchism has implications that are "counterintuitive" (line 17), the author most likely means that the commentators believe that

(A) the implications conflict with some commonly held beliefs
(B) there is little empirical evidence that the implications are actually true
(C) common sense indicates that philosophical anarchism does not have such implications
(D) the implications appear to be incompatible with each other
(E) each of the implications contains an internal logical inconsistency

24. Which one of the following scenarios most completely conforms to the views attributed to philosophical anarchists in lines 37–44?

(A) A member of a political party that is illegal in a particular country divulges the names of other members because he fears legal penalties.
(B) A corporate executive chooses to discontinue her company's practice of dumping chemicals illegally when she learns that the chemicals are contaminating the water supply.
(C) A person who knows that a coworker has stolen funds from their employer decides to do nothing because the coworker is widely admired.
(D) A person neglects to pay her taxes, even though it is likely that she will suffer severe legal penalties as a consequence, because she wants to use the money to finance a new business.
(E) A driver determines that it is safe to exceed the posted speed limit, in spite of poor visibility, because there are apparently no other vehicles on the road.

25. It can be inferred that the author would be most likely to agree that

(A) people are subject to more moral obligations than is generally held to be the case
(B) governments that are morally superior recognize that their citizens are not morally bound to obey their laws
(C) one may have good reason to support the efforts of one's government even if one has no moral duty to obey its laws
(D) there are some sound arguments for claiming that most governments have a moral right to require obedience to their laws
(E) the theory of philosophical anarchism entails certain fundamental principles regarding how laws should be enacted and enforced

26. The author's discussion of people's positive moral duty to care for one another (lines 44–49) functions primarily to

(A) demonstrate that governmental efforts to help those in need are superfluous
(B) suggest that philosophical anarchists maintain that laws that foster the common good are extremely rare
(C) imply that the theoretical underpinnings of philosophical anarchism are inconsistent with certain widely held moral truths
(D) indicate that philosophical anarchists recognize that people are subject to substantial moral obligations
(E) illustrate that people are morally obligated to refrain from those actions that arc crimes in most legal systems

27. In the passage, the author seeks primarily to

(A) describe the development and theoretical underpinnings of a particular theory
(B) establish that a particular theory conforms to the dictates of common sense
(C) argue that two necessary implications of a particular theory are morally acceptable
(D) defend a particular theory against its critics by showing that their arguments are mistaken
(E) demonstrate that proponents of a particular theory are aware of the theory's defects

S T O P

IF YOU FINISH BEFORE TIME IS CALLED, YOU MAY CHECK YOUR WORK ON THIS SECTION ONLY.
DO NOT WORK ON ANY OTHER SECTION IN THE TEST.

Acknowledgment is made to the following sources from which material has been adapted for use in this test booklet:

Dinha Kaplan, “When Less Is More.” ©1997 by Sussex Publishers, Inc.

Françoise Pfaff, “The Uniqueness of Ousmane Sembène’s Cinema.” ©1993 by Five Colleges, Inc.

A. John Simmons, *On the Edge of Anarchy: Locke, Consent, and the Limits of Society.* ©1993 by Princeton University Press.

LSAT WRITING SAMPLE TOPIC

Directions: The scenario presented below describes two choices, either one of which can be supported on the basis of the information given. Your essay should consider both choices and argue for one over the other, based on the two specified criteria and the facts provided. There is no "right" or "wrong" choice: a reasonable argument can be made for either.

A neighborhood association is planning to sponsor a public event on the first day of summer—either a walking tour or a 5 kilometer run. Using the facts below, write an essay in which you argue for one event over the other based on the following two criteria:

- The association wants to encourage more neighborhood residents to become association members.
- In order to conduct other activities during the year, the association wants to minimize the time and resources required by the event.

The first event is a free, self-guided walking tour of some of the neighborhood's private homes and historic buildings. The tour would feature the association's promotional table and exhibits of crafts, music, and cooking. Many neighborhood residents have expressed interest in such a tour. Some of the responsibility for organizing the event would be borne by those who own the homes and buildings; the association would be responsible for the remaining details. The costs of this event would consume most of the association's annual budget. Other neighborhood associations that have conducted similar tours report robust neighborhood participation and accompanying increases in membership.

The second event is a 5 kilometer run through the neighborhood. The association has sponsored this yearly event for almost a decade. In recent years, the association has hired a third-party company to manage the race and would do so again. Registration fees collected from race participants would cover administrative costs. In the past the event has led to modest increases in membership for the association. At its peak, almost 1,000 people participated in the race, most of them from out of town. This year more people are expected to participate, because the course has been professionally certified and the race would serve as a qualifying race for a national championship.

Scratch Paper

Do not write your essay in this space.

DIRECTIONS:

1. Use the Answer Key on the next page to check your answers.

2. Use the Scoring Worksheet below to compute your raw score.

3. Use the Score Conversion Chart to convert your raw score into the 120–180 scale.

SCORING WORKSHEET

1. Enter the number of questions you answered correctly in each section

	NUMBER CORRECT
SECTION I	______
SECTION II	______
SECTION III	______
SECTION IV	______

2. Enter the sum here: ______ THIS IS YOUR RAW SCORE.

CONVERSION CHART

For converting Raw Score to the 120–180 LSAT Scaled Score
LSAT Prep Test 52

REPORTED SCORE	LOWEST RAW SCORE	HIGHEST RAW SCORE
180	97	99
179	_*	_*
178	96	96
177	95	95
176	94	94
175	_*	_*
174	93	93
173	92	92
172	91	91
171	90	90
170	89	89
169	88	88
168	87	87
167	86	86
166	84	85
165	83	83
164	82	82
163	80	81
162	78	79
161	77	77
160	75	76
159	73	74
158	72	72
157	70	71
156	68	69
155	66	67
154	64	65
153	62	63
152	61	61
151	59	60
150	57	58
149	55	56
148	53	54
147	51	52
146	50	50
145	48	49
144	46	47
143	45	45
142	43	44
141	41	42
140	40	40
139	38	39
138	36	37
137	35	35
136	33	34
135	32	32
134	31	31
133	29	30
132	28	28
131	27	27
130	25	26
129	24	24
128	23	23
127	22	22
126	21	21
125	20	20
124	19	19
123	18	18
122	16	17
121	_*	_*
120	0	15

*There is no raw score that will produce this scaled score for this form.

SECTION I

1.	C	8.	C	15.	B	22.	D
2.	D	9.	D	16.	A	23.	D
3.	A	10.	A	17.	E	24.	E
4.	C	11.	C	18.	B	25.	E
5.	B	12.	E	19.	E		
6.	E	13.	E	20.	E		
7.	A	14.	C	21.	C		

SECTION II

1.	E	8.	B	15.	C	22.	C
2.	C	9.	E	16.	B	23.	E
3.	B	10.	A	17.	D		
4.	B	11.	D	18.	C		
5.	E	12.	C	19.	A		
6.	B	13.	B	20.	E		
7.	B	14.	E	21.	C		

SECTION III

1.	D	8.	A	15.	D	22.	E
2.	D	9.	C	16.	C	23.	A
3.	B	10.	E	17.	B	24.	C
4.	B	11.	B	18.	D	25.	A
5.	D	12.	E	19.	A		
6.	C	13.	D	20.	E		
7.	A	14.	C	21.	E		

SECTION IV

1.	E	8.	B	15.	*	22.	B
2.	E	9.	A	16.	D	23.	A
3.	A	10.	C	17.	E	24.	B
4.	D	11.	B	18.	B	25.	C
5.	C	12.	D	19.	A	26.	D
6.	A	13.	C	20.	C	27.	D
7.	D	14.	E	21.	A		

*Item removed from scoring.

Experimental Section Answer Key
June 1999, PrepTest 28, Section 4

1.	C	8.	D	15.	A	22.	A
2.	E	9.	D	16.	E	23.	C
3.	E	10.	A	17.	B	24.	D
4.	D	11.	C	18.	C	25.	B
5.	B	12.	C	19.	C	26.	D
6.	D	13.	C	20.	D		
7.	E	14.	D	21.	B		

PrepTest 53
December 2007

Time—35 minutes

26 Questions

Directions: The questions in this section are based on the reasoning contained in brief statements or passages. For some questions, more than one of the choices could conceivably answer the question. However, you are to choose the best answer; that is, the response that most accurately and completely answers the question. You should not make assumptions that are by commonsense standards implausible, superfluous, or incompatible with the passage. After you have chosen the best answer, blacken the corresponding space on your answer sheet.

1. A student has taken twelve courses and received a B in a majority of them. The student is now taking another course and will probably, given her record, receive a B in it.

Each of the following, if true, strengthens the argument EXCEPT:

(A) The student previously studied alone but is receiving help from several outstanding students during the present course.
(B) The twelve courses together covered a broad range of subject matter.
(C) The student previously studied in the library and continues to do so.
(D) The student received a B in all but one of the twelve courses.
(E) The current course is a continuation of one of the twelve courses in which the student received a B.

2. If the government increases its funding for civilian scientific research, private patrons and industries will believe that such research has become primarily the government's responsibility. When they believe that research is no longer primarily their responsibility, private patrons and industries will decrease their contributions toward research. Therefore, in order to keep from depressing the overall level of funding for civilian scientific research, the government should not increase its own funding.

Which one of the following is an assumption on which the argument relies?

(A) Governments should bear the majority of the financial burden of funding for civilian scientific research.
(B) Any increase in government funding would displace more private funding for funding for civilian scientific research than it would provide.
(C) Private donations toward research are no longer welcomed by researchers whose work receives government funding.
(D) Civilian scientific research cannot be conducted efficiently with more than one source of funding.
(E) Funding for civilian scientific research is currently at the highest possible level.

3. For any given ticket in a 1000-ticket lottery, it is reasonable to believe that that ticket will lose. Hence, it is reasonable to believe that no ticket will win.

Which one of the following exhibits flawed reasoning most similar to the flawed reasoning in the argument above?

(A) It is reasonable to believe for any randomly drawn playing card that it will not be an ace, so it is reasonable to believe that an ace will never be drawn.
(B) When the chances of a certain horse winning the race are 999 out of 1000, it is reasonable to believe that that horse will win. So it is reasonable to believe that no one other than that horse can win.
(C) It is unreasonable to believe that 1000 consecutive coin flips will turn up heads, so it is reasonable to believe that this never happens.
(D) It is reasonable to believe that if the most recent flip of a given coin was tails, the next flip will be heads. So if a coin has turned up tails the last 1000 times it was flipped, it is reasonable to believe that it will turn up heads the next time it is flipped.
(E) For any given group of five-year-old children, the average height is one meter, so it is reasonable to believe that if Pat is five years old, she is exactly one meter tall.

GO ON TO THE NEXT PAGE.

4. Dental researcher: Filling a cavity in a tooth is not a harmless procedure: it inevitably damages some of the healthy parts of the tooth. Cavities are harmful only if the decay reaches the nerves inside the tooth, and many cavities, if left untreated, never progress to that point. Therefore, dentists should not fill a cavity unless the nerves inside the tooth are in imminent danger from that cavity.

Which one of the following principles, if valid, most strongly supports the researcher's reasoning?

(A) Dentists should perform any procedure that it likely to be beneficial in the long term, but only if the procedure does not cause immediate damage.
(B) Dentists should help their patients to prevent cavities rather than waiting until cavities are present to begin treatment.
(C) A condition that is only potentially harmful should not be treated using a method that is definitely harmful.
(D) A condition that is typically progressive should not be treated using methods that provide only temporary relief.
(E) A condition that is potentially harmful should not be left untreated unless it can be kept under constant surveillance.

5. The number of codfish in the North Atlantic has declined substantially as the population of harp seals has increased from two million to more than three million. Some blame the seal for the shrinking cod population, but cod plays a negligible role in the seal's diet. It is therefore unlikely that the increase in the seal population has contributed significantly to the decline in the cod population.

Which one of the following, if true, most seriously weakens the argument?

(A) People who fish for cod commercially are inconvenienced by the presence of large numbers of seals near traditional fishing grounds.
(B) Water pollution poses a more serious threat to cod than to the harp seal.
(C) The harp seal thrives in water that is too cold to support a dense population of cod.
(D) Cod feed almost exclusively on capelin, a fish that is a staple of the harp seal's diet.
(E) The cod population in the North Atlantic began to decline before the harp-seal population began to increase.

Questions 6-7

Hospital auditor: The Rodríguez family stipulated that the funds they donated to the neurological clinic all be used to minimize patients' suffering. The clinic administration is clearly violating those terms, since it has allocated nearly one fifth of those funds for research into new diagnostic technologies, instead of letting that money flow directly to its patients.

Clinic administrator: But the successful development of new technologies will allow early diagnosis of many neurological disorders. In most cases, patients who are treated in the early stages of neurological disorders suffer far less than do patients who are not treated until their neurological disorders reach advanced stages.

6. Which one of the following is the main point at issue between the hospital auditor and the clinic administrator?

(A) whether early treatment of many neurological disorders lessens the suffering associated with those disorders rather than completely eliminating such suffering
(B) whether the patients being treated at the neurological clinic are currently receiving adequate treatment for the neurological disorders from which they suffer
(C) whether the Rodríguez family clearly stipulated that the funds they donated to the neurological clinic be used to minimize patients' suffering
(D) whether the neurological clinic is adhering strictly to the conditions the Rodríguez family placed on the allocation of the funds they donated to the clinic
(E) whether the Rodríguez family anticipated that some of the funds they donated to the neurological clinic would be used to pay for research into new diagnostic technologies

7. The clinic administrator responds to the hospital auditor by doing which one of the following?

(A) demonstrating that the hospital auditor's conclusion, though broadly correct, stands in need of a minor qualification
(B) showing that the hospital auditor's argument fails to separate what is the case from what ought to be the case
(C) reminding the hospital auditor that, in the case at issue, being told what to do is tantamount to being told how to do it
(D) arguing that, in assessing the severity of a violation, the reasoning motivating the violation needs to be considered
(E) reinterpreting a key phrase in the hospital auditor's argument so as to undermine an assumption underlying that argument

GO ON TO THE NEXT PAGE.

8. Generally speaking, if the same crop is sown in a field for several successive years, growth in the later years is poorer than growth in the earlier years, since nitrogen in the soil becomes depleted. Even though alfalfa is a nitrogen-fixing plant and thus increases the amount of nitrogen in the soil, surprisingly, it too, if planted in the same field year after year, grows less well in the later years than it does in the earlier years.

Which one of the following, if true, most helps to explain the similarity described above between alfalfa and non-nitrogen-fixing plants?

(A) Some kinds of plants grow more rapidly and are more productive when they are grown among other kinds of plants rather than being grown only among plants of their own kind.
(B) Alfalfa increases the amount of nitrogen in the soil by taking nitrogen from the air and releasing it in a form that is usable by most kinds of plants.
(C) Certain types of plants, including alfalfa, produce substances that accumulate in the soil and that are toxic to the plants that produce those substances.
(D) Alfalfa increases nitrogen in the soil in which it grows only if a certain type of soil bacteria is present in the soil.
(E) Alfalfa is very sensitive to juglone, a compound that is exuded from the leaves of black walnut trees.

9. Political commentators see recent policies of the government toward Country X as appeasement, pure and simple. This view is fundamentally mistaken, for polls show that most people disagree with the political commentators' assessment of government policies toward Country X.

The reasoning in the argument is questionable because

(A) the term "policies" is used ambiguously in the argument
(B) the political commentators discussed in the passage are not identified
(C) a claim is inferred to be false merely because a majority of people believe it to be false
(D) the claim that the political commentators are mistaken is both a premise and a conclusion in the argument
(E) it is assumed that what is true of persons individually is true of a country as a whole

10. It is a principle of economics that a nation can experience economic growth only when consumer confidence is balanced with a small amount of consumer skepticism.

Which one of the following is an application of the economic principle above?

(A) Any nation in which consumer confidence is balanced with a small amount of consumer skepticism will experience economic growth.
(B) Any nation in which the prevailing attitude of consumers is not skepticism will experience economic growth.
(C) Any nation in which the prevailing attitude of consumers is either exclusively confidence or exclusively skepticism will experience economic growth.
(D) Any nation in which the prevailing attitude of consumers is exclusively confidence will not experience economic growth.
(E) Any nation in which consumer skepticism is balanced with a small amount of consumer confidence will experience economic growth.

11. Sharks have a higher ratio of cartilage mass to body mass than any other organism. They also have a greater resistance to cancer than any other organism. Shark cartilage contains a substance that inhibits tumor growth by stopping the development of a new blood network. In the past 20 years, none of the responses among terminal cancer patients to various therapeutic measures has been more positive than the response among those who consumed shark cartilage.

If the claims made above are true, then each of the following could be true EXCEPT:

(A) No organism resists cancer better than sharks do, but some resist cancer as well as sharks.
(B) The organism most susceptible to cancer has a higher percentage of cartilage than some organisms that are less susceptible to cancer.
(C) The substance in shark cartilage that inhibits tumor growth is found in most organisms.
(D) In the past 20 years many terminal cancer patients have improved dramatically following many sorts of therapy.
(E) Some organisms have immune systems more efficient than a shark's immune system.

GO ON TO THE NEXT PAGE.

Questions 12-13

People who say that Dooney County is flat are clearly wrong. On flat land, soil erosion by water is not a problem. Consequently, farmers whose land is flat do not build terraces to prevent erosion. Yet I hear that the farms in Dooney County are dotted with terraces.

12. The author's conclusion in the passage depends on the assumption that

(A) the only cause of soil erosion is water
(B) there are terraces on farmland in Dooney County which were built to prevent soil erosion
(C) terraces of the kind found on farmland in Dooney County have been shown to prevent soil erosion
(D) on flat land there is no soil erosion
(E) the only terraces in Dooney County are on farmland

13. The reasoning in the passage is most similar to that in which one of the following?

(A) If we paint the room white, it will get smudged, and we will have to paint it again soon. Therefore, we should paint it dark blue.
(B) People with children need more space than those without children. Yet people with no children can usually afford bigger houses.
(C) People who get a lot of exercise have no trouble falling asleep; hence, people who get a lot of exercise do not use medication to help them fall asleep. Jack is taking many kinds of medication, so he must not be getting a lot of exercise.
(D) If I go grocery shopping when I am hungry, I buy snack foods and cannot resist eating them. Therefore, I cannot lose weight.
(D) People who have many friends tend to go out often, so they need cars. Therefore, if Joe wants to have many friends, he must buy a car.

14. The axis of Earth's daily rotation is tilted with respect to the plane of its orbit at an angle of roughly 23 degrees. That angle can be kept fairly stable only by the gravitational influence of Earth's large, nearby Moon. Without such a stable and moderate axis tilt, a planet's climate is too extreme and unstable to support life. Mars, for example, has only very small moons, tilts at wildly fluctuating angles, and cannot support life.

If the statements above are true, which one of the following must also be true on the basis of them?

(A) If Mars had a sufficiently large nearby moon, Mars would be able to support life.
(B) If Earth's Moon were to leave Earth's orbit, Earth's climate would be unable to support life.
(C) Any planet with a stable, moderate axis tilt can support life.
(D) Gravitational influences other than moons have little or no effect on the magnitude of the tilt angle of either Earth's or Mars's axis.
(E) No planet that has more than one moon can support life.

GO ON TO THE NEXT PAGE.

15. The town of Springhill frequently must declare a water emergency, making it temporarily unlawful to use water for such nonessential purposes as car washing. These emergencies could be avoided if Springhill would introduce permanent economic incentives for water conservation. Actually, Springhill discourages conservation because each household pays a modest monthly flat fee for any amount of water below a certain usage threshold, and a substantial per-liter rate only after the threshold is reached.

    Which one the following, if true, most strengthens the argument?

    (A) The Springhill authorities do a poor job of enforcing its water emergency laws and many people break the laws without incurring a penalty.
    (B) The town council of Springhill recently refused to raise the threshold.
    (C) The threshold is kept at a high enough level to exceed the water requirements of most households in Springhill.
    (D) The threshold is not as high in Springhill as it is in neighboring towns.
    (E) The threshold remains at the predetermined level specified by law until a change is approved by the Springhill town council.

16. Poppy petals function to attract pollinating insects. The pollination of a poppy flower triggers the release into that flower of a substance that causes its petals to wilt within one or two days. If the flower is not pollinated, the substance will not be released and the petals will remain fresh for a week or longer, as long as the plant can nourish them. Cutting an unpollinated poppy flower from the plant triggers the release into the flower of the same substance whose release is triggered by pollination.

    The statement above, if true, most strongly support which one of the following?

    (A) Pollinating insects are not attracted to wilted poppy flowers.
    (B) Even if cut poppies are given all necessary nutrients, their petals will tend to wilt within a few days.
    (C) Flowers of all plants release the substance that causes wilting when they are cut, although the amount released may vary.
    (D) The pollen on pollinated poppy flowers prevents their petals from absorbing the nutrients carried to them by their stems.
    (E) Poppy plants are unable to draw nutrients from soil or water after the substance that causes wilting has been released.

17. When a community opens a large shopping mall, it often expects a boost to the local economy, and in fact a large amount of economic activity goes on in these malls. Yet the increase in the local economy is typically much smaller than the total amount of economic activity that goes on in the mall.

    Which one of the following, if true, most helps to explain the discrepancy described above?

    (A) When large shopping malls are new they attract a lot of shoppers but once the novelty has worn off they usually attract fewer shoppers than does the traditional downtown shopping district.
    (B) Most of the money spent in a large shopping mall is spent by tourists who are drawn specifically by the mall and who would not have visited the community had that mall not been built.
    (C) Most of the jobs created by large shopping malls are filled by people who recently moved to the community and who would not have moved had there been no job offer in the community.
    (D) Most of the money spent in a large shopping mall is money that would have been spent elsewhere in the same community had that mall not been built.
    (E) Most of the jobs created by the construction of a large shopping mall are temporary, and most of the permanent jobs created are low paying.

GO ON TO THE NEXT PAGE.

18. Essayist: The way science is conducted and regulated can be changed. But we need to determine whether the changes are warranted, taking into account their price. The use of animals in research could end immediately, but only at the cost of abandoning many kinds of research and making others very expensive. The use of recombinant DNA could be drastically curtailed. Many other restrictions could be imposed, complete with a system of fraud police. But such massive interventions would be costly and would change the character of science.

Which one of the following most accurately expresses the main conclusion of the essayist's argument?

(A) We should not make changes that will alter the character of science.
(B) If we regulate science more closely, we will change the character of science.
(C) The regulation of science and the conducting of science can be changed.
(D) The imposition of restrictions on the conduct of science would be very costly.
(E) We need to be aware of the impact of change in science before changes are made.

19. The postmodern view involves the rejection of modern assumptions about order and the universality of truth. The grand theories of the modern era are now seen as limited by the social and historical contexts in which they were elaborated. Also, the belief in order has given way to a belief in the importance of irregularity and chaos. It follows that we inhabit a world full of irregular events, and in which there are no universal truths.

The argument's reasoning is questionable because the argument

(A) infers that something is the case because it is believed to be the case
(B) uses the term "universal" ambiguously
(C) relies on the use of emotional terms to bolster its conclusion
(D) uses the term "order" ambiguously
(E) fails to cite examples of modern theories that purport to embody universal truths

20. If the economy is weak, then prices remain constant although unemployment rises. But unemployment rises only if investment decreases. Fortunately, investment is not decreasing.

If the statements above are true, then which one of the following must be false?

(A) Either the economy is weak or investment is decreasing.
(B) If unemployment rises, the prices remain constant.
(C) The economy is weak only if investment decreases.
(D) Either the economy is weak or prices are remaining constant.
(E) Either unemployment is rising or the economy is not weak.

21. Psychologist: Some astrologers claim that our horoscopes completely determine our personalities, but this claim is false. I concede that identical twins—who are, of course, born at practically the same time—often do have similar personalities. However, birth records were examined to find two individuals who were born 40 years ago on the same day and at exactly the same time—one in a hospital in Toronto and one in a hospital in New York. Personality tests revealed that the personalities of these two individuals are in fact different.

Which one of the following is an assumption on which the psychologist's argument depends?

(A) Astrologers have not subjected their claims to rigorous experimentation.
(B) The personality differences between the two individuals cannot be explained by the cultural differences between Toronto and New York.
(C) The geographical difference between Toronto and New York did not result in the two individuals having different horoscopes.
(D) Complete birth records for the past 40 years were kept at both hospitals.
(E) Identical twins have identical genetic structures and usually have similar home environments.

GO ON TO THE NEXT PAGE.

22. Under the influence of today's computer-oriented culture, publishing for children has taken on a flashy new look that emphasizes illustrations and graphic design; the resulting lack of substance leads to books that are short-lived items covering mainly trendy subjects. The changes also include more humorous content, simplification of difficult material, and a narrower focus on specific topics.

Which one of the following is most strongly supported by the information above?

(A) The inclusion of humorous material and a narrower focus detract from the substance of a children's book.
(B) The substance of a children's book is important to its longevity.
(C) Children of the computer generation cannot concentrate on long, unbroken sections of prose.
(D) Children judge books primarily on the basis of graphic design.
(E) The lack of substance of a children's book is unlikely to be important to its popularity.

23. Further evidence of a connection between brain physiology and psychological states has recently been uncovered in the form of a correlation between electroencephalograph patterns and characteristic moods. A study showed that participants who suffered form clinical depression exhibited less left frontal lobe activity than right, while, conversely, characteristically good-natured participants exhibited greater left lobe activity. Thus one's general disposition is a result of the activity of one's frontal lobe.

Each of the following, if true, weakens the argument EXCEPT:

(A) Many drugs prescribed to combat clinical depression act by causing increased left lobe activity.
(B) Excessive sleep, a typical consequence of clinical depression, is known to suppress left lobe activity.
(C) Frontal lobe activity is not subject to variation the way general disposition is.
(D) Earlier studies indicated that frontal lobe activity and emotive states are both caused by activity in the brain's limbic system.
(E) Social interaction of the kind not engaged in by most clinically depressed people is known to stimulate left lobe activity.

24. We ought to pay attention only to the intrinsic properties of a work of art. Its other, extrinsic properties are irrelevant to our aesthetic interactions with it. For example, when we look at a painting we should consider only what is directly presented in our experience of it. What is really aesthetically relevant, therefore, is not what a painting symbolizes, but what it directly presents to experience.

The conclusion follows logically if which one of the following is added to the premises?

(A) What an artwork symbolizes involves only extrinsic properties of that work.
(B) There are certain properties of our experiences of artworks that can be distinguished as symbolic properties.
(C) Only an artwork's intrinsic properties are relevant to our aesthetic interactions with it.
(D) It is possible in theory for an artwork to symbolize nothing.
(E) An intrinsic property of an artwork is one that relates the work to itself.

GO ON TO THE NEXT PAGE.

25. McKinley: A double-blind study, in which neither the patient nor the primary researcher knows whether the patient is being given the drug being tested or a placebo, is the most effective procedure for testing the efficacy of a drug. But we will not be able to perform such a study on this new drug, since the drug will have various effects on the patients' bodies, which will make us aware of whether the patients are getting the drug or a placebo.

Engle: You cannot draw that conclusion at this point, for you are assuming you know what the outcome of the study will be.

Engle's statement indicates that he is most likely interpreting McKinley's remarks to be

(A) presuming that a double-blind study is the only effective way to test new drugs
(B) denying that the drug will be effective
(C) presuming that the placebo will produce no effects whatever on the patients' bodies
(D) referring to the drug's therapeutic effects rather than to any known side effects
(E) based on a confusion about when a drug is efficacious

26. Modern navigation systems, which are found in most of today's commercial aircraft, are made with low-power circuitry, which is more susceptible to interference than the vacuum-tube circuitry found in older planes. During landing, navigation systems receive radio signals from the airport to guide the plane to the runway. Recently, one plane with low-power circuitry veered off course during landing, its dials dimming, when a passenger turned on a laptop computer. Clearly, modern aircraft navigation systems are being put at risk by the electronic devices that passengers carry on board, such as cassette players and laptop computers.

Which one of the following, if true, LEAST strengthens the argument above?

(A) After the laptop computer was turned off, the plane regained course and its navigation instruments and dials returned to normal.
(B) When in use all electronic devices emit electromagnetic radiation, which is known to interfere with circuitry.
(C) No problems with navigational equipment or instrument dials have been reported on flights with no passenger-owned electronic devices on board.
(D) Significant electromagnetic radiation from portable electronic devices can travel up to eight meters, and some passenger seats on modern aircraft are located within four meters of the navigation systems.
(E) Planes were first equipped with low-power circuitry at about the same time portable electronic devices became popular.

S T O P

IF YOU FINISH BEFORE TIME IS CALLED, YOU MAY CHECK YOUR WORK ON THIS SECTION ONLY.
DO NOT WORK ON ANY OTHER SECTION IN THE TEST.

SECTION I

Time—35 minutes

25 Questions

Directions: The questions in this section are based on the reasoning contained in brief statements or passages. For some questions, more than one of the choices could conceivably answer the question. However, you are to choose the best answer; that is, the response that most accurately and completely answers the question. You should not make assumptions that are by commonsense standards implausible, superfluous, or incompatible with the passage. After you have chosen the best answer, blacken the corresponding space on your answer sheet.

1. Consumer advocate: Businesses are typically motivated primarily by the desire to make as great a profit as possible, and advertising helps businesses to achieve this goal. But it is clear that the motive of maximizing profits does not impel businesses to present accurate information in their advertisements. It follows that consumers should be skeptical of the claims made in advertisements.

   Each of the following, if true, would strengthen the consumer advocate's argument EXCEPT:

   (A) Businesses know that they can usually maximize their profits by using inaccurate information in their advertisements.
   (B) Businesses have often included inaccurate information in their advertisements.
   (C) Many consumers have a cynical attitude toward advertising.
   (D) Those who create advertisements are less concerned with the accuracy than with the creativity of advertisements.
   (E) The laws regulating truth in advertising are not applicable to many of the most common forms of inaccurate advertising.

2. Elaine: The purpose of art museums is to preserve artworks and make them available to the public. Museums, therefore, should seek to acquire and display the best examples of artworks from each artistic period and genre, even if some of these works are not recognized by experts as masterpieces.

   Frederick: Art museums ought to devote their limited resources to acquiring the works of recognized masters in order to ensure the preservation of the greatest artworks.

   Elaine's and Frederick's statements provide the most support for the claim that they would disagree about whether

   (A) many artistic masterpieces are not recognized as such by art experts
   (B) museums should seek to represent all genres of art in their collections
   (C) art museums should seek to preserve works of art
   (D) an art museum ought to acquire an unusual example of a period or genre if more characteristic examples are prohibitively expensive
   (E) all of the artworks that experts identify as masterpieces are actually masterpieces

3. Science columnist: It is clear why humans have so many diseases in common with cats. Many human diseases are genetically based, and cats are genetically closer to humans than are any other mammals except nonhuman primates. Each of the genes identified so far in cats has an exact counterpart in humans.

   Which one of the following, if true, most weakens the science columnist's explanation for the claim that humans have so many diseases in common with cats?

   (A) Cats have built up resistance to many of the diseases they have in common with humans.
   (B) Most diseases that humans have in common with cats have no genetic basis.
   (C) Cats have more diseases in common with nonhuman primates than with humans.
   (D) Many of the diseases humans have in common with cats are mild and are rarely diagnosed.
   (E) Humans have more genes in common with nonhuman primates than with cats.

4. This region must find new ways to help business grow. After all, shoe manufacturing used to be a major local industry, but recently has experienced severe setbacks due to overseas competition, so there is a need for expansion into new manufacturing areas. Moreover, our outdated public policy generally inhibits business growth.

   Which one of the following most accurately expresses the main conclusion drawn in the argument?

   (A) The region needs to find new ways to enhance business growth.
   (B) Shoe manufacturing is no longer a major source of income in the region.
   (C) Shoe manufacturing in the region has dramatically declined due to overseas competition.
   (D) Business in the region must expand into new areas of manufacturing.
   (E) Outdated public policy inhibits business growth in the region.

GO ON TO THE NEXT PAGE.

5. As a result of modern medicine, more people have been able to enjoy long and pain-free lives. But the resulting increase in life expectancy has contributed to a steady increase in the proportion of the population that is of advanced age. This population shift is creating potentially devastating financial problems for some social welfare programs.

Which one of the following propositions is most precisely exemplified by the situation presented above?

(A) Technical or scientific innovation cannot be the solution to all problems.
(B) Implementing technological innovations should be delayed until the resulting social changes can be managed.
(C) Every enhancement of the quality of life has unavoidable negative consequences.
(D) All social institutions are affected by a preoccupation with prolonging life.
(E) Solving one set of problems can create a different set of problems.

6. Since Jackie is such a big fan of Moral Vacuum's music, she will probably like The Cruel Herd's new album. Like Moral Vacuum, The Cruel Herd on this album plays complex rock music that employs the acoustic instrumentation and harmonic sophistication of early sixties jazz. The Cruel Herd also has very witty lyrics, full of puns and sardonic humor, like some of Moral Vacuum's best lyrics.

Which one of the following, if true, most strengthens the argument?

(A) Jackie has not previously cared for The Cruel Herd, but on the new album The Cruel Herd's previous musical arranger has been replaced by Moral Vacuum's musical arranger.
(B) Though The Cruel Herd's previous albums' production quality was not great, the new album is produced by one of the most widely employed producers in the music industry.
(C) Like Moral Vacuum, The Cruel Herd regularly performs in clubs popular with many students at the university that Jackie attends.
(D) All of the music that Jackie prefers to listen to on a regular basis is rock music.
(E) Jackie's favorite Moral Vacuum songs have lyrics that are somber and marked by a strong political awareness.

7. Superconductors are substances that conduct electricity without resistance at low temperatures. Their use, however, will never be economically feasible, unless there is a substance that superconducts at a temperature above minus 148 degrees Celsius. If there is such a substance, that substance must be an alloy of niobium and germanium. Unfortunately, such alloys superconduct at temperatures no higher than minus 160 degrees Celsius.

If the statements above are true, which one of the following must also be true?

(A) The use of superconductors will never be economically feasible.
(B) If the alloys of niobium and germanium do not superconduct at temperatures above minus 148 degrees Celsius, then there are other substances that will do so.
(C) The use of superconductors could be economically feasible if there is a substance that superconducts at temperatures below minus 148 degrees Celsius.
(D) Alloys of niobium and germanium do not superconduct at temperatures below minus 160 degrees Celsius.
(E) No use of alloys of niobium and germanium will ever be economically feasible.

8. Doctor: In three separate studies, researchers compared children who had slept with night-lights in their rooms as infants to children who had not. In the first study, the children who had slept with night-lights proved more likely to be nearsighted, but the later studies found no correlation between night-lights and nearsightedness. However, the children in the first study were younger than those in the later studies. This suggests that if night-lights cause nearsightedness, the effect disappears with age.

Which one of the following, if true, would most weaken the doctor's argument?

(A) A fourth study comparing infants who were currently sleeping with night-lights to infants who were not did not find any correlation between night-lights and nearsightedness.
(B) On average, young children who are already very nearsighted are no more likely to sleep with night-lights than young children who are not already nearsighted.
(C) In a study involving children who had not slept with night-lights as infants but had slept with night-lights when they were older, most of the children studied were not nearsighted.
(D) The two studies in which no correlation was found did not examine enough children to provide significant support for any conclusion regarding a causal relationship between night-lights and nearsightedness.
(E) In a fourth study involving 100 children who were older than those in any of the first three studies, several of the children who had slept with night-lights as infants were nearsighted.

GO ON TO THE NEXT PAGE.

9. Global surveys estimate the earth's population of nesting female leatherback turtles has fallen by more than two-thirds in the past 15 years. Any species whose population declines by more than two-thirds in 15 years is in grave danger of extinction, so the leatherback turtle is clearly in danger of extinction.

Which one of the following is an assumption that the argument requires?

(A) The decline in the population of nesting female leatherback turtles is proportional to the decline in the leatherback turtle population as a whole.
(B) If the global population of leatherback turtles falls by more than two-thirds over the next 15 years, the species will eventually become extinct.
(C) The global population of leatherback turtles consists in roughly equal numbers of females and males.
(D) Very few leatherback turtles exist in captivity.
(E) The only way to ensure the continued survival of leatherback turtles in the wild is to breed them in captivity.

10. Public health experts have waged a long-standing educational campaign to get people to eat more vegetables, which are known to help prevent cancer. Unfortunately, the campaign has had little impact on people's diets. The reason is probably that many people simply dislike the taste of most vegetables. Thus, the campaign would probably be more effective if it included information on ways to make vegetables more appetizing.

Which one of the following, if true, most strengthens the argument?

(A) The campaign to get people to eat more vegetables has had little impact on the diets of most people who love the taste of vegetables.
(B) Some ways of making vegetables more appetizing diminish vegetables' ability to help prevent cancer.
(C) People who find a few vegetables appetizing typically do not eat substantially more vegetables than do people who dislike the taste of most vegetables.
(D) People who dislike the taste of most vegetables would eat many more vegetables if they knew how to make them more appetizing.
(E) The only way to make the campaign to get people to eat more vegetables more effective would be to ensure that anyone who at present dislikes the taste of certain vegetables learns to find those vegetables appetizing.

11. Pure science—research with no immediate commercial or technological application—is a public good. Such research requires a great amount of financial support and does not yield profits in the short term. Since private corporations will not undertake to support activities that do not yield short-term profits, a society that wants to reap the benefits of pure science ought to use public funds to support such research.

The claim about private corporations serves which one of the following functions in the argument?

(A) It expresses the conclusion of the argument.
(B) It explains what is meant by the expression "pure research" in the context of the argument.
(C) It distracts attention from the point at issue by introducing a different but related goal.
(D) It supports the conclusion by ruling out an alternative way of achieving the benefits mentioned.
(E) It illustrates a case where unfortunate consequences result from a failure to accept the recommendation offered.

12. Melinda: Hazard insurance decreases an individual's risk by judiciously spreading the risk among many policyholders.

Jack: I disagree. It makes sense for me to buy fire insurance for my house, but I don't see how doing so lessens the chances that my house will burn down.

Jack's response most clearly trades on an ambiguity in which one of the following expressions used by Melinda?

(A) judiciously spreading
(B) many policyholders
(C) risk
(D) decreases
(E) hazard insurance

GO ON TO THE NEXT PAGE.

13. Some doctors believe that a certain drug reduces the duration of episodes of vertigo, claiming that the average duration of vertigo for people who suffer from it has decreased since the drug was introduced. However, during a recent three-month shortage of the drug, there was no significant change in the average duration of vertigo. Thus, we can conclude that the drug has no effect on the duration of vertigo.

Which one of the following is an assumption required by the argument?

(A) If a drug made a difference in the duration of vertigo, a three-month shortage of that drug would have caused a significant change in the average duration of vertigo.
(B) If there were any change in the average duration of vertigo since the introduction of the drug, it would have demonstrated that the drug has an effect on the duration of vertigo.
(C) A period of time greater than three months would not have been better to use in judging whether the drug has an effect on the duration of vertigo.
(D) Changes in diet and smoking habits are not responsible for any change in the average duration of vertigo since the introduction of the drug.
(E) There are various significant factors other than drugs that decrease the duration of vertigo for many people who suffer from it.

14. It has been suggested that a television set should be thought of as nothing more than "a toaster with pictures" and that since we let market forces determine the design of kitchen appliances we can let them determine what is seen on television. But that approach is too simple. Some governmental control is needed, since television is so important politically and culturally. It is a major source of commercial entertainment. It plays an important political role because it is the primary medium through which many voters obtain information about current affairs. It is a significant cultural force in that in the average home it is on for more than five hours a day.

Which one of the following most accurately expresses the role played in the argument by the claim that television is so important politically and culturally?

(A) It states a view that the argument as a whole is designed to discredit.
(B) It is an intermediate conclusion that is offered in support of the claim that a television set should be thought of as nothing more than "a toaster with pictures" and for which the claim that we can let market forces determine what is seen on television is offered as support.
(C) It is a premise that is offered in support of the claim that we let market forces determine the design of kitchen appliances.
(D) It is an intermediate conclusion that is offered in support of the claim that some governmental control of television is needed and for which the claim that the television is on for more than five hours a day in the average home is offered as partial support.
(E) It is a premise that is offered in support of the claim that television is the primary medium through which many voters obtain information about current affairs.

GO ON TO THE NEXT PAGE.

15. Earthworms, vital to the health of soil, prefer soil that is approximately neutral on the acid-to-alkaline scale. Since decomposition of dead plants makes the top layer of soil highly acidic, application of crushed limestone, which is highly alkaline, to the soil's surface should make the soil more attractive to earthworms.

Which one of the following is an assumption on which the argument depends?

(A) As far as soil health is concerned, aiding the decomposition of dead plants is the most important function performed by earthworms.
(B) After its application to the soil's surface, crushed limestone stays in the soil's top layer long enough to neutralize some of the top layer's acidity.
(C) Crushed limestone contains available calcium and magnesium, both of which are just as vital as earthworms to healthy soil.
(D) By itself, acidity of soil does nothing to hasten decomposition of dead plants.
(E) Alkaline soil is significantly more likely to benefit from an increased earthworm population than is highly acidic soil.

16. Jurist: A nation's laws must be viewed as expressions of a moral code that transcends those laws and serves as a measure of their adequacy. Otherwise, a society can have no sound basis for preferring any given set of laws to all others. Thus, any moral prohibition against the violation of statutes must leave room for exceptions.

Which one of the following can be properly inferred from the jurist's statements?

(A) Those who formulate statutes are not primarily concerned with morality when they do so.
(B) Sometimes criteria other than the criteria derived from a moral code should be used in choosing one set of laws over another.
(C) Unless it is legally forbidden ever to violate some moral rules, moral behavior and compliance with laws are indistinguishable.
(D) There is no statute that a nation's citizens have a moral obligation to obey.
(E) A nation's laws can sometimes come into conflict with the moral code they express.

17. An association between two types of conditions does not establish that conditions of one type cause conditions of the other type. Even persistent and inviolable association is inconclusive; such association is often due to conditions of both types being effects of the same kind of cause.

Which one of the following judgments most closely conforms to the principle stated above?

(A) Some people claim that rapid growth of the money supply is what causes inflation. But this is a naive view. What these people do not realize is that growth in the money supply and inflation are actually one and the same phenomenon.
(B) People who have high blood pressure tend to be overweight. But before we draw any inferences, we should consider that an unhealthy lifestyle can cause high blood pressure, and weight gain can result from living unhealthily.
(C) In some areas, there is a high correlation between ice cream consumption and the crime rate. Some researchers have proposed related third factors, but we cannot rule out that the correlation is purely coincidental.
(D) People's moods seem to vary with the color of the clothes they wear. Dark colors are associated with gloomy moods, and bright colors are associated with cheerful moods. This correlation resolves nothing, however. We cannot say whether it is the colors that cause the moods or the converse.
(E) Linguists propose that the similarities between Greek and Latin are due to their common descent from an earlier language. But how are we to know that the similarities are not actually due to the two languages having borrowed structures from one another, as with the languages Marathi and Telegu?

GO ON TO THE NEXT PAGE.

18. Salesperson: When a salesperson is successful, it is certain that that person has been in sales for at least three years. This is because to succeed as a salesperson, one must first establish a strong client base, and studies have shown that anyone who spends at least three years developing a client base can eventually make a comfortable living in sales.

The reasoning in the salesperson's argument is vulnerable to criticism on the grounds that it fails to consider the possibility that

(A) salespeople who have spent three years developing a client base might not yet be successful in sales
(B) some salespeople require fewer than three years in which to develop a strong client base
(C) a salesperson who has not spent three years developing a client base may not succeed in sales
(D) it takes longer than three years for a salesperson to develop a strong client base
(E) few salespeople can afford to spend three years building a client base

19. People who have habitually slept less than six hours a night and then begin sleeping eight or more hours a night typically begin to feel much less anxious. Therefore, most people who sleep less than six hours a night can probably cause their anxiety levels to fall by beginning to sleep at least eight hours a night.

The reasoning in which one of the following arguments is most similar to that in the argument above?

(A) When a small company first begins to advertise on the Internet, its financial situation generally improves. This shows that most small companies that have never advertised on the Internet can probably improve their financial situation by doing so.
(B) Certain small companies that had never previously advertised on the Internet have found that their financial situations began to improve after they started to do so. So most small companies can probably improve their financial situations by starting to advertise on the Internet.
(C) It must be true that any small company that increases its Internet advertising will improve its financial situation, since most small companies that advertise on the Internet improved their financial situations soon after they first began to do so.
(D) Usually, the financial situation of a small company that has never advertised on the Internet will improve only if that company starts to advertise on the Internet. Therefore, a typical small company that has never advertised on the Internet can probably improve its financial situation by doing so.
(E) A small company's financial situation usually improves soon after that company first begins to advertise on the Internet. Thus, most small companies that have never advertised on the Internet could probably become financially strong.

GO ON TO THE NEXT PAGE.

20. Biologist: Lions and tigers are so similar to each other anatomically that their skeletons are virtually indistinguishable. But their behaviors are known to be quite different: tigers hunt only as solitary individuals, whereas lions hunt in packs. Thus, paleontologists cannot reasonably infer solely on the basis of skeletal anatomy that extinct predatory animals, such as certain dinosaurs, hunted in packs.

The conclusion is properly drawn if which one of the following is assumed?

(A) The skeletons of lions and tigers are at least somewhat similar in structure in certain key respects to the skeletons of at least some extinct predatory animals.
(B) There have existed at least two species of extinct predatory dinosaurs that were so similar to each other that their skeletal anatomy is virtually indistinguishable.
(C) If skeletal anatomy alone is ever an inadequate basis for inferring a particular species' hunting behavior, then it is never reasonable to infer, based on skeletal anatomy alone, that a species of animals hunted in packs.
(D) If any two animal species with virtually indistinguishable skeletal anatomy exhibit quite different hunting behaviors, then it is never reasonable to infer, based solely on the hunting behavior of those species, that the two species have the same skeletal anatomy.
(E) If it is unreasonable to infer, solely on the basis of differences in skeletal anatomy, that extinct animals of two distinct species differed in their hunting behavior, then the skeletal remains of those two species are virtually indistinguishable.

21. The trees always blossom in May if April rainfall exceeds 5 centimeters. If April rainfall exceeds 5 centimeters, then the reservoirs are always full on May 1. The reservoirs were not full this May 1 and thus the trees will not blossom this May.

Which one of the following exhibits a flawed pattern of reasoning most similar to the flawed pattern of reasoning in the argument above?

(A) If the garlic is in the pantry, then it is still fresh. And the potatoes are on the basement stairs if the garlic is in the pantry. The potatoes are not on the basement stairs, so the garlic is not still fresh.
(B) The jar reaches optimal temperature if it is held over the burner for 2 minutes. The contents of the jar liquefy immediately if the jar is at optimal temperature. The jar was held over the burner for 2 minutes, so the contents of the jar must have liquefied immediately.
(C) A book is classified "special" if it is more than 200 years old. If a book was set with wooden type, then it is more than 200 years old. This book is not classified "special," so it is not printed with wooden type.
(D) The mower will operate only if the engine is not flooded. The engine is flooded if the foot pedal is depressed. The foot pedal is not depressed, so the mower will operate.
(E) If the kiln is too hot, then the plates will crack. If the plates crack, then the artisan must redo the order. The artisan need not redo the order. Thus, the kiln was not too hot.

22. Doctor: Being overweight has long been linked with a variety of health problems, such as high blood pressure and heart disease. But recent research conclusively shows that people who are slightly overweight are healthier than those who are considerably underweight. Therefore, to be healthy, it suffices to be slightly overweight.

The argument's reasoning is flawed because the argument

(A) ignores medical opinions that tend to lead to a conclusion contrary to the one drawn
(B) never adequately defines what is meant by "healthy"
(C) does not take into account the fact that appropriate weight varies greatly from person to person
(D) holds that if a person lacks a property that would suffice to make the person unhealthy, then that person must be healthy
(E) mistakes a merely relative property for one that is absolute

GO ON TO THE NEXT PAGE.

23. Robust crops not only withstand insect attacks more successfully than other crops, they are also less likely to be attacked in the first place, since insects tend to feed on weaker plants. Killing insects with pesticides does not address the underlying problem of inherent vulnerability to damage caused by insect attacks. Thus, a better way to reduce the vulnerability of agricultural crops to insect pest damage is to grow those crops in good soil—soil with adequate nutrients, organic matter, and microbial activity.

Which one of the following is an assumption on which the argument depends?

(A) The application of nutrients and organic matter to farmland improves the soil's microbial activity.
(B) Insects never attack crops grown in soil containing adequate nutrients, organic matter, and microbial activity.
(C) The application of pesticides to weak crops fails to reduce the extent to which they are damaged by insect pests.
(D) Crops that are grown in good soil tend to be more robust than other crops.
(E) Growing crops without the use of pesticides generally produces less robust plants than when pesticides are used.

24. People perceive color by means of certain photopigments in the retina that are sensitive to certain wavelengths of light. People who are color-blind are unable to distinguish between red and green, for example, due to an absence of certain photopigments. What is difficult to explain, however, is that in a study of people who easily distinguish red from green, 10 to 20 percent failed to report distinctions between many shades of red that the majority of the subjects were able to distinguish.

Each of the following, if true, helps to explain the result of the study cited above EXCEPT:

(A) People with abnormally low concentrations of the photopigments for perceiving red can perceive fewer shades of red than people with normal concentrations.
(B) Questions that ask subjects to distinguish between different shades of the same color are difficult to phrase with complete clarity.
(C) Some people are uninterested in fine gradations of color and fail to notice or report differences they do not care about.
(D) Some people are unable to distinguish red from green due to an absence in the retina of the photopigment sensitive to green.
(E) Some people fail to report distinctions between certain shades of red because they lack the names for those shades.

25. Occultist: The issue of whether astrology is a science is easily settled: it is both an art and a science. The scientific components are the complicated mathematics and the astronomical knowledge needed to create an astrological chart. The art is in the synthesis of a multitude of factors and symbols into a coherent statement of their relevance to an individual.

The reasoning in the occultist's argument is most vulnerable to criticism on the grounds that the argument

(A) presumes, without providing justification, that any science must involve complicated mathematics
(B) incorrectly infers that a practice is a science merely from the fact that the practice has some scientific components
(C) denies the possibility that astrology involves components that are neither artistic nor scientific
(D) incorrectly infers that astronomical knowledge is scientific merely from the fact that such knowledge is needed to create an astrological chart
(E) presumes, without providing justification, that any art must involve the synthesis of a multitude of factors and symbols

S T O P

IF YOU FINISH BEFORE TIME IS CALLED, YOU MAY CHECK YOUR WORK ON THIS SECTION ONLY.
DO NOT WORK ON ANY OTHER SECTION IN THE TEST.

SECTION II

Time—35 minutes

23 Questions

Directions: Each group of questions in this section is based on a set of conditions. In answering some of the questions, it may be useful to draw a rough diagram. Choose the response that most accurately and completely answers each question and blacken the corresponding space on your answer sheet.

Questions 1–5

Five performers—Traugott, West, Xavier, Young, and Zinser—are recruited by three talent agencies—Fame Agency, Premier Agency, and Star Agency. Each performer signs with exactly one of the agencies and each agency signs at least one of the performers. The performers' signing with the agencies is in accord with the following:

Xavier signs with Fame Agency.
Xavier and Young do not sign with the same agency as each other.
Zinser signs with the same agency as Young.
If Traugott signs with Star Agency, West also signs with Star Agency.

1. Which one of the following could be a complete and accurate list of the performers who sign with each agency?

(A) Fame Agency: Xavier
Premier Agency: West
Star Agency: Traugott, Young, Zinser
(B) Fame Agency: Xavier
Premier Agency: Traugott, West
Star Agency: Young, Zinser
(C) Fame Agency: Xavier
Premier Agency: Traugott, Young
Star Agency: West, Zinser
(D) Fame Agency: Young, Zinser
Premier Agency: Xavier
Star Agency: Traugott, West
(E) Fame Agency: Xavier, Young, Zinser
Premier Agency: Traugott
Star Agency: West

2. Which one of the following could be true?

(A) West is the only performer who signs with Star Agency.
(B) West, Young, and Zinser all sign with Premier Agency.
(C) Xavier signs with the same agency as Zinser.
(D) Zinser is the only performer who signs with Star Agency.
(E) Three of the performers sign with Fame Agency.

3. Which one of the following must be true?

(A) West and Zinser do not sign with the same agency as each other.
(B) Fame Agency signs at most two of the performers.
(C) Fame Agency signs the same number of the performers as Star Agency.
(D) Traugott signs with the same agency as West.
(E) West does not sign with Fame Agency.

4. The agency with which each of the performers signs is completely determined if which one of the following is true?

(A) Traugott signs with Fame Agency.
(B) Traugott signs with Star Agency.
(C) West signs with Premier Agency.
(D) Xavier signs with Fame Agency.
(E) Zinser signs with Premier Agency.

5. If Zinser signs with Star Agency, which one of the following must be false?

(A) Premier Agency signs exactly one performer.
(B) Star Agency signs exactly three of the performers.
(C) Traugott signs with Star Agency.
(D) West signs with Star Agency.
(E) None of the other performers signs with the same agency as Xavier.

GO ON TO THE NEXT PAGE.

Questions 6–11

A competition is being held to select a design for Yancy College's new student union building. Each of six architects— Green, Jackson, Liu, Mertz, Peete, and Valdez—has submitted exactly one design. There are exactly six designs, and they are presented one at a time to the panel of judges, each design being presented exactly once, consistent with the following conditions:

Mertz's design is presented at some time before Liu's and after Peete's.
Green's design is presented either at some time before Jackson's or at some time after Liu's, but not both.
Valdez's design is presented either at some time before Green's or at some time after Peete's, but not both.

6. Which one of the following could be the order in which the designs are presented, from first to last?

(A) Jackson's, Peete's, Mertz's, Green's, Valdez's, Liu's
(B) Peete's, Jackson's, Liu's, Mertz's, Green's, Valdez's
(C) Peete's, Mertz's, Jackson's, Liu's, Green's, Valdez's
(D) Peete's, Mertz's, Valdez's, Green's, Liu's, Jackson's
(E) Valdez's, Liu's, Jackson's, Peete's, Mertz's, Green's

7. Mertz's design CANNOT be presented

(A) sixth
(B) fifth
(C) fourth
(D) third
(E) second

8. If Liu's design is presented sixth, then which one of the following must be true?

(A) Green's design is presented at some time before Jackson's.
(B) Jackson's design is presented at some time before Mertz's.
(C) Peete's design is presented at some time before Green's.
(D) Peete's design is presented at some time before Valdez's.
(E) Valdez's design is presented at some time before Green's.

9. If Jackson's design is presented at some time before Mertz's, then each of the following could be true EXCEPT:

(A) Jackson's design is presented second.
(B) Peete's design is presented third.
(C) Peete's design is presented fourth.
(D) Jackson's design is presented fifth.
(E) Liu's design is presented fifth.

10. Which one of the following designs CANNOT be the design presented first?

(A) Green's
(B) Jackson's
(C) Liu's
(D) Peete's
(E) Valdez's

11. Which one of the following could be an accurate partial list of the architects, each matched with his or her design's place in the order in which the designs are presented?

(A) first: Mertz; fourth: Liu; fifth: Green
(B) second: Green; third: Peete; fourth: Jackson
(C) second: Mertz; fifth: Green; sixth: Jackson
(D) fourth: Peete; fifth: Liu; sixth: Jackson
(E) fourth:Valdez; fifth: Green; sixth: Liu

GO ON TO THE NEXT PAGE.

Questions 12–17

Detectives investigating a citywide increase in burglaries questioned exactly seven suspects—S, T, V, W, X, Y, and Z—each on a different one of seven consecutive days. Each suspect was questioned exactly once. Any suspect who confessed did so while being questioned. The investigation conformed to the following:

T was questioned on day three.
The suspect questioned on day four did not confess.
S was questioned after W was questioned.
Both X and V were questioned after Z was questioned.
No suspects confessed after W was questioned.
Exactly two suspects confessed after T was questioned.

12. Which one of the following could be true?

(A) X was questioned on day one.
(B) V was questioned on day two.
(C) Z was questioned on day four.
(D) W was questioned on day five.
(E) S was questioned on day six.

13. If Z was the second suspect to confess, then each of the following statements could be true EXCEPT:

(A) T confessed.
(B) T did not confess.
(C) V did not confess.
(D) X confessed.
(E) Y did not confess.

14. If Y was questioned after V but before X, then which one of the following could be true?

(A) V did not confess.
(B) Y confessed.
(C) X did not confess.
(D) X was questioned on day four.
(E) Z was questioned on day two.

15. Which one of the following suspects must have been questioned before T was questioned?

(A) V
(B) W
(C) X
(D) Y
(E) Z

16. If X and Y both confessed, then each of the following could be true EXCEPT:

(A) V confessed.
(B) X was questioned on day five.
(C) Y was questioned on day one.
(D) Z was questioned on day one.
(E) Z did not confess.

17. If neither X nor V confessed, then which one of the following must be true?

(A) T confessed.
(B) V was questioned on day two.
(C) X was questioned on day four.
(D) Y confessed.
(E) Z did not confess.

GO ON TO THE NEXT PAGE.

Questions 18–23

The three highest-placing teams in a high school debate tournament are the teams from Fairview, Gillom, and Hilltop high schools. Each team has exactly two members. The individuals on these three teams are Mei, Navarro, O'Rourke, Pavlovich, Sethna, and Tsudama. The following is the case:

Sethna is on the team from Gillom High.
Tsudama is on the second-place team.
Mei and Pavlovich are not on the same team.
Pavlovich's team places higher than Navarro's team.
The team from Gillom High places higher than the team from Hilltop High.

18. Which one of the following could be an accurate list of the members of each of the three highest-placing teams?

(A) first place: Mei and O'Rourke
second place: Pavlovich and Sethna
third place: Navarro and Tsudama
(B) first place: Mei and Pavlovich
second place: Sethna and Tsudama
third place: Navarro and O'Rourke
(C) first place: Navarro and Sethna
second place: Pavlovich and Tsudama
third place: Mei and O'Rourke
(D) first place: O'Rourke and Pavlovich
second place: Navarro and Tsudama
third place: Mei and Sethna
(E) first place: Pavlovich and Sethna
second place: O'Rourke and Tsudama
third place: Mei and Navarro

19. If Pavlovich is on the team from Hilltop High, then which one of the following could be true?

(A) O'Rourke is on the first-place team.
(B) Pavlovich is on the first-place team.
(C) Mei is on the second-place team.
(D) Navarro is on the second-place team.
(E) Sethna is on the second-place team.

20. If O'Rourke is on the second-place team, then which one of the following could be true?

(A) Mei is on the team from Gillom High.
(B) Navarro is on the team from Fairview High.
(C) O'Rourke is on the team from Gillom High.
(D) Pavlovich is on the team from Hilltop High.
(E) Tsudama is on the team from Gillom High.

21. If Pavlovich and Tsudama are teammates, then for how many of the individuals can it be exactly determined where his or her team places?

(A) two
(B) three
(C) four
(D) five
(E) six

22. If Mei is on a team that places higher than the Hilltop team, then which one of the following could be true?

(A) The Fairview team places first.
(B) The Gillom team places second.
(C) Navarro is on the second-place team.
(D) O'Rourke is on the first-place team.
(E) Pavlovich is on the first-place team.

23. Sethna's teammate could be any one of the following EXCEPT:

(A) Mei
(B) Navarro
(C) O'Rourke
(D) Pavlovich
(E) Tsudama

S T O P

IF YOU FINISH BEFORE TIME IS CALLED, YOU MAY CHECK YOUR WORK ON THIS SECTION ONLY.
DO NOT WORK ON ANY OTHER SECTION IN THE TEST.

SECTION III

Time—35 minutes

25 Questions

Directions: The questions in this section are based on the reasoning contained in brief statements or passages. For some questions, more than one of the choices could conceivably answer the question. However, you are to choose the best answer; that is, the response that most accurately and completely answers the question. You should not make assumptions that are by commonsense standards implausible, superfluous, or incompatible with the passage. After you have chosen the best answer, blacken the corresponding space on your answer sheet.

1. At many electronics retail stores, the consumer has the option of purchasing product warranties that extend beyond the manufacturer's warranty. However, consumers are generally better off not buying extended warranties. Most problems with electronic goods occur within the period covered by the manufacturer's warranty.

   Which one of the following, if true, most strengthens the argument?

   (A) Problems with electronic goods that occur after the manufacturer's warranty expires are generally inexpensive to fix in comparison with the cost of an extended warranty.
   (B) Because problems are so infrequent after the manufacturer's warranty expires, extended warranties on electronic goods are generally inexpensive.
   (C) Most of those who buy extended warranties on electronic goods do so because special circumstances make their item more likely to break than is usually the case.
   (D) Some extended warranties on electronic goods cover the product for the period covered by the manufacturer's warranty as well as subsequent years.
   (E) Retail stores sell extended warranties in part because consumers who purchase them are likely to purchase other products from the same store.

2. Since the 1970s, environmentalists have largely succeeded in convincing legislators to enact extensive environmental regulations. Yet, as environmentalists themselves not only admit but insist, the condition of the environment is worsening, not improving. Clearly, more environmental regulations are not the solution to the environment's problems.

   The argument's reasoning is flawed because the argument

   (A) attacks the environmentalists themselves instead of their positions
   (B) presumes, without providing warrant, that only an absence of environmental regulations could prevent environmental degradation
   (C) fails to consider the possibility that the condition of the environment would have worsened even more without environmental regulations
   (D) fails to justify its presumption that reducing excessive regulations is more important than preserving the environment
   (E) fails to consider the views of the environmentalists' opponents

GO ON TO THE NEXT PAGE.

3. Although it is unwise to take a developmental view of an art like music—as if Beethoven were an advance over Josquin, or Miles Davis an advance over Louis Armstrong—there are ways in which it makes sense to talk about musical knowledge growing over time. We certainly know more about certain sounds than was known five centuries ago; that is, we understand how sounds that earlier composers avoided can be used effectively in musical compositions. For example, we now know how the interval of the third, which is considered dissonant, can be used in compositions to create consonant musical phrases.

Which one of the following most accurately expresses the main conclusion of the argument?

(A) Sounds that were never used in past musical compositions are used today.
(B) Sounds that were once considered dissonant are more pleasing to modern listeners.
(C) It is inappropriate to take a developmental view of music.
(D) It is unwise to say that one composer is better than another.
(E) Our understanding of music can improve over the course of time.

4. A recent test of an electric insect control device discovered that, of the more than 300 insects killed during one 24-hour period, only 12 were mosquitoes. Thus this type of device may kill many insects, but will not significantly aid in controlling the potentially dangerous mosquito population.

Which one of the following, if true, most seriously weakens the argument?

(A) A careful search discovered no live mosquitoes in the vicinity of the device after the test.
(B) A very large proportion of the insects that were attracted to the device were not mosquitoes.
(C) The device is more likely to kill beneficial insects than it is to kill harmful insects.
(D) Many of the insects that were killed by the device are mosquito-eating insects.
(E) The device does not succeed in killing all of the insects that it attracts.

5. Brain-scanning technology provides information about processes occurring in the brain. For this information to help researchers understand how the brain enables us to think, however, researchers must be able to rely on the accuracy of the verbal reports given by subjects while their brains are being scanned. Otherwise brain-scan data gathered at a given moment might not contain information about what the subject reports thinking about at that moment, but instead about some different set of thoughts.

Which one of the following most accurately expresses the main conclusion of the argument?

(A) It is unlikely that brain-scanning technology will ever enable researchers to understand how the brain enables us to think.
(B) There is no way that researchers can know for certain that subjects whose brains are being scanned are accurately reporting what they are thinking.
(C) Because subjects whose brains are being scanned may not accurately report what they are thinking, the results of brain-scanning research should be regarded with great skepticism.
(D) Brain scans can provide information about the accuracy of the verbal reports of subjects whose brains are being scanned.
(E) Information from brain scans can help researchers understand how the brain enables us to think only if the verbal reports of those whose brains are being scanned are accurate.

GO ON TO THE NEXT PAGE.

6. Ornithologist: This bird species is widely thought to subsist primarily on vegetation, but my research shows that this belief is erroneous. While concealed in a well-camouflaged blind, I have observed hundreds of these birds every morning over a period of months, and I estimate that over half of what they ate consisted of insects and other animal food sources.

The reasoning in the ornithologist's argument is most vulnerable to criticism on the grounds that the argument

(A) assumes, without providing justification, that the feeding behavior of the birds observed was not affected by the ornithologist's act of observation
(B) fails to specify the nature of the animal food sources, other than insects, that were consumed by the birds
(C) adopts a widespread belief about the birds' feeding habits without considering the evidence that led to the belief
(D) neglects the possibility that the birds have different patterns of food consumption during different parts of the day and night
(E) fails to consider the possibility that the birds' diet has changed since the earlier belief about their diet was formed

7. Educator: Only those students who are genuinely curious about a topic can successfully learn about that topic. They find the satisfaction of their curiosity intrinsically gratifying, and appreciate the inherent rewards of the learning process itself. However, almost no child enters the classroom with sufficient curiosity to learn successfully all that the teacher must instill. A teacher's job, therefore, _______.

Which one of the following most logically completes the educator's argument?

(A) requires for the fulfillment of its goals the stimulation as well as the satisfaction of curiosity
(B) necessitates the creative use of rewards that are not inherent in the learning process itself
(C) is to focus primarily on those topics that do not initially interest the students
(D) is facilitated by students' taking responsibility for their own learning
(E) becomes easier if students realize that some learning is not necessarily enjoyable

8. Environmentalist: When bacteria degrade household cleaning products, vapors that are toxic to humans are produced. Unfortunately, household cleaning products are often found in landfills. Thus, the common practice of converting landfills into public parks is damaging human health.

Which one of the following is an assumption the environmentalist's argument requires?

(A) In at least some landfills that have been converted into public parks there are bacteria that degrade household cleaning products.
(B) Converting a landfill into a public park will cause no damage to human health unless toxic vapors are produced in that landfill and humans are exposed to them.
(C) If a practice involves the exposure of humans to vapors from household cleaning products, then it causes at least some damage to human health.
(D) When landfills are converted to public parks, measures could be taken that would prevent people using the parks from being exposed to toxic vapors.
(E) If vapors toxic to humans are produced by the degradation of household cleaning products by bacteria in any landfill, then the health of at least some humans will suffer.

9. Tea made from camellia leaves is a popular beverage. However, studies show that regular drinkers of camellia tea usually suffer withdrawal symptoms if they discontinue drinking the tea. Furthermore, regular drinkers of camellia tea are more likely than people in general to develop kidney damage. Regular consumption of this tea, therefore, can result in a heightened risk of kidney damage.

Which one of the following, if true, most seriously weakens the argument?

(A) Several other popular beverages contain the same addictive chemical that is found in camellia tea.
(B) Addictive chemicals are unlikely to cause kidney damage solely by virtue of their addictive qualities.
(C) Some people claim that regular consumption of camellia tea helps alleviate their stress.
(D) Most people who regularly drink camellia tea do not develop kidney damage.
(E) Many people who regularly consume camellia tea also regularly consume other beverages suspected of causing kidney damage.

GO ON TO THE NEXT PAGE.

10. Artist: Avant-garde artists intend their work to challenge a society's mainstream beliefs and initiate change. And some art collectors claim that an avant-garde work that becomes popular in its own time is successful. However, a society's mainstream beliefs do not generally show any significant changes over a short period of time. Therefore, when an avant-garde work becomes popular it is a sign that the work is not successful, since it does not fulfil the intentions of its creator.

The reference to the claim of certain art collectors plays which one of the following roles in the artist's argument?

(A) It serves to bolster the argument's main conclusion.
(B) It identifies a view that is ultimately disputed by the argument.
(C) It identifies a position supported by the initial premise in the argument.
(D) It provides support for the initial premise in the argument.
(E) It provides support for a counterargument to the initial premise.

11. A recent epidemiological study found that businesspeople who travel internationally on business are much more likely to suffer from chronic insomnia than are businesspeople who do not travel on business. International travelers experience the stresses of dramatic changes in climate, frequent disruption of daily routines, and immersion in cultures other than their own, stresses not commonly felt by those who do not travel. Thus, it is likely that these stresses cause the insomnia.

Which one of the following would, if true, most strengthen the reasoning above?

(A) Most international travel for the sake of business occurs between countries with contiguous borders.
(B) Some businesspeople who travel internationally greatly enjoy the changes in climate and immersion in another culture.
(C) Businesspeople who already suffer from chronic insomnia are no more likely than businesspeople who do not to accept assignments from their employers that require international travel.
(D) Experiencing dramatic changes in climate and disruption of daily routines through international travel can be beneficial to some people who suffer from chronic insomnia.
(E) Some businesspeople who once traveled internationally but no longer do so complain of various sleep-related ailments.

12. Many mountain climbers regard climbing Mount Everest as the ultimate achievement. But climbers should not attempt this climb since the risk of death or serious injury in an Everest expedition is very high. Moreover, the romantic notion of gaining "spiritual discovery" atop Everest is dispelled by climbers' reports that the only profound experiences they had at the top were of exhaustion and fear.

Which one of the following principles, if valid, most helps to justify the reasoning above?

(A) Projects undertaken primarily for spiritual reasons ought to be abandoned if the risks are great.
(B) Dangerous activities that are unlikely to result in significant spiritual benefits for those undertaking them should be avoided.
(C) Activities that are extremely dangerous ought to be legally prohibited unless they are necessary to produce spiritual enlightenment.
(D) Profound spiritual experiences can be achieved without undergoing the serious danger involved in mountain climbing.
(E) Mountain climbers and other athletes should carefully examine the underlying reasons they have for participating in their sports.

13. Each of the smallest particles in the universe has an elegantly simple structure. Since these particles compose the universe, we can conclude that the universe itself has an elegantly simple structure.

Each of the following arguments exhibits flawed reasoning similar to that in the argument above EXCEPT:

(A) Each part of this car is nearly perfectly engineered. Therefore this car is nearly perfect, from an engineering point of view.
(B) Each part of this desk is made of metal. Therefore this desk is made of metal.
(C) Each brick in this wall is rectangular. Therefore this wall is rectangular.
(D) Each piece of wood in this chair is sturdy. Therefore this chair is sturdy.
(E) Each sentence in this novel is well constructed. Therefore this is a well-constructed novel.

GO ON TO THE NEXT PAGE.

14. Criminologist: A judicial system that tries and punishes criminals without delay is an effective deterrent to violent crime. Long, drawn-out trials and successful legal maneuvering may add to criminals' feelings of invulnerability. But if potential violent criminals know that being caught means prompt punishment, they will hesitate to break the law.

Which one of the following, if true, would most seriously weaken the criminologist's argument?

(A) It is in the nature of violent crime that it is not premeditated.
(B) About one-fourth of all suspects first arrested for a crime are actually innocent.
(C) Many violent crimes are committed by first-time offenders.
(D) Everyone accused of a crime has the right to a trial.
(E) Countries that promptly punish suspected lawbreakers have lower crime rates than countries that allow long trials.

15. Journalist: Many people object to mandatory retirement at age 65 as being arbitrary, arguing that people over 65 make useful contributions. However, if those who reach 65 are permitted to continue working indefinitely, we will face unacceptable outcomes. First, young people entering the job market will not be able to obtain decent jobs in the professions for which they were trained, resulting in widespread dissatisfaction among the young. Second, it is not fair for those who have worked 40 or more years to deprive others of opportunities. Therefore, mandatory retirement should be retained.

The journalist's argument depends on assuming which one of the following?

(A) Anyone who has worked 40 years is at least 65 years old.
(B) All young people entering the job market are highly trained professionals.
(C) It is unfair for a person not to get a job in the profession for which that person was trained.
(D) If people are forced to retire at age 65, there will be much dissatisfaction among at least some older people.
(E) If retirement ceases to be mandatory at age 65, at least some people will choose to work past age 65.

16. Editorial: Contrary to popular belief, teaching preschoolers is not especially difficult, for they develop strict systems (e.g., for sorting toys by shape), which help them to learn, and they are always intensely curious about something new in their world.

Which one of the following, if true, most seriously weakens the editorial's argument?

(A) Preschoolers have a tendency to imitate adults, and most adults follow strict routines.
(B) Children intensely curious about new things have very short attention spans.
(C) Some older children also develop strict systems that help them learn.
(D) Preschoolers ask as many creative questions as do older children.
(E) Preschool teachers generally report lower levels of stress than do other teachers.

17. Lawyer: A body of circumstantial evidence is like a rope, and each item of evidence is like a strand of that rope. Just as additional pieces of circumstantial evidence strengthen the body of evidence, adding strands to the rope strengthens the rope. And if one strand breaks, the rope is not broken nor is its strength much diminished. Thus, even if a few items of a body of circumstantial evidence are discredited, the overall body of evidence retains its basic strength.

The reasoning in the lawyer's argument is most vulnerable to criticism on the grounds that the argument

(A) takes for granted that no items in a body of circumstantial evidence are significantly more critical to the strength of the evidence than other items in that body
(B) presumes, without providing justification, that the strength of a body of evidence is less than the sum of the strengths of the parts of that body
(C) fails to consider the possibility that if many items in a body of circumstantial evidence were discredited, the overall body of evidence would be discredited
(D) offers an analogy in support of a conclusion without indicating whether the two types of things compared share any similarities
(E) draws a conclusion that simply restates a claim presented in support of that conclusion

GO ON TO THE NEXT PAGE.

18. Ethicist: Many environmentalists hold that the natural environment is morally valuable for its own sake, regardless of any benefits it provides us. However, even if nature has no moral value, nature can be regarded as worth preserving simply on the grounds that people find it beautiful. Moreover, because it is philosophically disputable whether nature is morally valuable but undeniable that it is beautiful, an argument for preserving nature that emphasizes nature's beauty will be less vulnerable to logical objections than one that emphasizes its moral value.

The ethicist's reasoning most closely conforms to which one of the following principles?

(A) An argument in favor of preserving nature will be less open to logical objections if it avoids the issue of what makes nature worth preserving.
(B) If an argument for preserving nature emphasizes a specific characteristic of nature and is vulnerable to logical objections, then that characteristic does not provide a sufficient reason for preserving nature.
(C) If it is philosophically disputable whether nature has a certain characteristic, then nature would be more clearly worth preserving if it did not have that characteristic.
(D) Anything that has moral value is worth preserving regardless of whether people consider it to be beautiful.
(E) An argument for preserving nature will be less open to logical objections if it appeals to a characteristic that can be regarded as a basis for preserving nature and that philosophically indisputably belongs to nature.

19. An editor is compiling a textbook containing essays by several different authors. The book will contain essays by Lind, Knight, or Jones, but it will not contain essays by all three. If the textbook contains an essay by Knight, then it will also contain an essay by Jones.

If the statements above are true, which one of the following must be true?

(A) If the textbook contains an essay by Lind, then it will not contain an essay by Knight.
(B) The textbook will contain an essay by only one of Lind, Knight, and Jones.
(C) The textbook will not contain an essay by Knight.
(D) If the textbook contains an essay by Lind, then it will also contain an essay by Jones.
(E) The textbook will contain an essay by Lind.

20. The ability of mammals to control their internal body temperatures is a factor in the development of their brains and intelligence. This can be seen from the following facts: the brain is a chemical machine, all chemical reactions are temperature dependent, and any organism that can control its body temperature can assure that these reactions occur at the proper temperatures.

Which one of the following is an assumption on which the argument depends?

(A) Organisms unable to control their body temperatures do not have the capacity to generate internal body heat without relying on external factors.
(B) Mammals are the only animals that have the ability to control their internal body temperatures.
(C) The brain cannot support intelligence if the chemical reactions within it are subject to uncontrolled temperatures.
(D) The development of intelligence in mammals is not independent of the chemical reactions in their brains taking place at the proper temperatures.
(E) Organisms incapable of controlling their internal body temperatures are subject to unpredictable chemical processes.

21. People who object to the proposed hazardous waste storage site by appealing to extremely implausible scenarios in which the site fails to contain the waste safely are overlooking the significant risks associated with delays in moving the waste from its present unsafe location. If we wait to remove the waste until we find a site certain to contain it safely, the waste will remain in its current location for many years, since it is currently impossible to guarantee that any site can meet that criterion. Yet keeping the waste at the current location for that long clearly poses unacceptable risks.

The statements above, if true, most strongly support which one of the following?

(A) The waste should never have been stored in its current location.
(B) The waste should be placed in the most secure location that can ever be found.
(C) Moving the waste to the proposed site would reduce the threat posed by the waste.
(D) Whenever waste must be moved, one should limit the amount of time allotted to locating alternative waste storage sites.
(E) Any site to which the waste could be moved will be safer than its present site.

22. A recent survey indicates that the average number of books read annually per capita has declined in each of the last three years. However, it also found that most bookstores reported increased profits during the same period.

    Each of the following, if true, helps to resolve the survey's apparently paradoxical results EXCEPT:

    (A) Recent cutbacks in government spending have forced public libraries to purchase fewer popular contemporary novels.
    (B) Due to the installation of sophisticated new antitheft equipment, the recent increase in shoplifting that has hit most retail businesses has left bookstores largely unaffected.
    (C) Over the past few years many bookstores have capitalized on the lucrative coffee industry by installing coffee bars.
    (D) Bookstore owners reported a general shift away from the sale of inexpensive paperback novels and toward the sale of lucrative hardback books.
    (E) Citing a lack of free time, many survey respondents indicated that they had canceled magazine subscriptions in favor of purchasing individual issues at bookstores when time permits.

23. Naturalist: A species can survive a change in environment, as long as the change is not too rapid. Therefore, the threats we are creating to woodland species arise not from the fact that we are cutting down trees, but rather from the rate at which we are doing so.

    The reasoning in which one of the following is most similar to that in the naturalist's argument?

    (A) The problem with burning fossil fuels is that the supply is limited; so, the faster we expend these resources, the sooner we will be left without an energy source.
    (B) Many people gain more satisfaction from performing a job well—regardless of whether they like the job—than from doing merely adequately a job they like; thus, people who want to be happy should choose jobs they can do well.
    (C) Some students who study thoroughly do well in school. Thus, what is most important for success in school is not how much time a student puts into studying, but rather how thoroughly the student studies.
    (D) People do not fear change if they know what the change will bring; so, our employees' fear stems not from our company's undergoing change, but from our failing to inform them of what the changes entail.
    (E) Until ten years ago, we had good soil and our agriculture flourished. Therefore, the recent decline of our agriculture is a result of our soil rapidly eroding and there being nothing that can replace the good soil we lost.

GO ON TO THE NEXT PAGE.

24. Professor: A person who can select a beverage from among 50 varieties of cola is less free than one who has only these 5 choices: wine, coffee, apple juice, milk, and water. It is clear, then, that meaningful freedom cannot be measured simply by the number of alternatives available; the extent of the differences among the alternatives is also a relevant factor.

The professor's argument proceeds by

(A) supporting a general principle by means of an example
(B) drawing a conclusion about a particular case on the basis of a general principle
(C) supporting its conclusion by means of an analogy
(D) claiming that whatever holds for each member of a group must hold for the whole group
(E) inferring one general principle from another, more general, principle

25. Principle: Meetings should be kept short, addressing only those issues relevant to a majority of those attending. A person should not be required to attend a meeting if none of the issues to be addressed at the meeting are relevant to that person.

Application: Terry should not be required to attend today's two o'clock meeting.

Which one of the following, if true, most justifies the stated application of the principle?

(A) The only issues on which Terry could make a presentation at the meeting are issues irrelevant to at least a majority of those who could attend.
(B) If Terry makes a presentation at the meeting, the meeting will not be kept short.
(C) No issue relevant to Terry could be relevant to a majority of those attending the meeting.
(D) If Terry attends the meeting a different set of issues will be relevant to a majority of those attending than if Terry does not attend.
(E) The majority of the issues to be addressed at the meeting are not relevant to Terry.

S T O P

IF YOU FINISH BEFORE TIME IS CALLED, YOU MAY CHECK YOUR WORK ON THIS SECTION ONLY.
DO NOT WORK ON ANY OTHER SECTION IN THE TEST.

SECTION IV

Time—35 minutes

27 Questions

Directions: Each set of questions in this section is based on a single passage or a pair of passages. The questions are to be answered on the basis of what is stated or implied in the passage or pair of passages. For some of the questions, more than one of the choices could conceivably answer the question. However, you are to choose the best answer; that is, the response that most accurately and completely answers the question, and blacken the corresponding space on your answer sheet.

Asian American poetry from Hawaii, the Pacific island state of the United States, is generally characterizable in one of two ways: either as portraying a model multicultural paradise, or as exemplifying familiar Asian American literary themes such as generational conflict. In this light, the recent work of Wing Tek Lum in *Expounding the Doubtful Points* is striking for its demand to be understood on its own terms. Lum offers no romanticized notions of multicultural life in Hawaii, and while he does explore themes of family, identity, history, and literary tradition, he does not do so at the expense of attempting to discover and retain a local sensibility. For Lum such a sensibility is informed by the fact that Hawaii's population, unlike that of the continental U.S., has historically consisted predominantly of people of Asian and Pacific island descent, making the experience of its Asian Americans somewhat different than that of mainland Asian Americans.

In one poem, Lum meditates on the ways in which a traditional Chinese lunar celebration he is attending at a local beach both connects him to and separates him from the past. In the company of new Chinese immigrants, the speaker realizes that while ties to the homeland are comforting and necessary, it is equally important to have "a sense of new family" in this new land of Hawaii, and hence a new identity—one that is sensitive to its new environment. The role of immigrants in this poem is significant in that, through their presence, Lum is able to refer both to the traditional culture of his ancestral homeland as well as to the flux within Hawaiian society that has been integral to its heterogeneity. Even in a laudatory poem to famous Chinese poet Li Po (701–762 A.D.), which partly serves to place Lum's work within a distinguished literary tradition, Lum refuses to offer a stereotypical nostalgia for the past, instead pointing out the often elitist tendencies inherent in the work of some traditionally acclaimed Chinese poets.

Lum closes his volume with a poem that further points to the complex relationships between heritage and local culture in determining one's identity. Pulling together images and figures as vastly disparate as a famous Chinese American literary character and an old woman selling bread, Lum avoids an excessively romantic vision of U.S. culture, while simultaneously acknowledging the dream of this culture held by many newly arrived immigrants. The central image of a communal pot where each person chooses what she or he wishes to eat but shares with others the "sweet soup / spooned out at the end of the meal" is a hopeful one; however, it also appears to caution that the strong cultural emphasis in the U.S. on individual drive and success that makes retaining a sense of homeland tradition difficult should be identified and responded to in ways that allow for a healthy new sense of identity to be formed.

1. Which one of the following most accurately expresses the main point of the passage?

(A) The poetry of Lum departs from other Asian American poetry from Hawaii in that it acknowledges its author's heritage but also expresses the poet's search for a new local identity.

(B) Lum's poetry is in part an expression of the conflict between a desire to participate in a community with shared traditions and values and a desire for individual success.

(C) Lum writes poetry that not only rejects features of the older literary tradition in which he participates but also rejects the popular literary traditions of Hawaiian writers.

(D) The poetry of Lum illustrates the extent to which Asian American writers living in Hawaii have a different cultural perspective than those living in the continental U.S.

(E) Lum's poetry is an unsuccessful attempt to manage the psychological burdens of reconciling a sense of tradition with a healthy sense of individual identity.

GO ON TO THE NEXT PAGE.

2. Given the information in the passage, which one of the following is Lum most likely to believe?
   (A) Images in a poem should be explained in that poem so that their meaning will be widely understood.
   (B) The experience of living away from one's homeland is necessary for developing a healthy perspective on one's cultural traditions.
   (C) It is important to reconcile the values of individual achievement and enterprise with the desire to retain one's cultural traditions.
   (D) One's identity is continually in transition and poetry is a way of developing a static identity.
   (E) One cannot both seek a new identity and remain connected to one's cultural traditions.

3. The author of the passage uses the phrase "the flux within Hawaiian society" (line 33) primarily in order to
   (A) describe the social tension created by the mix of attitudes exhibited by citizens of Hawaii
   (B) deny that Hawaiian society is culturally distinct from that of the continental U.S.
   (C) identify the process by which immigrants learn to adapt to their new communities
   (D) refer to the constant change to which the culture in Hawaii is subject due to its diverse population
   (E) emphasize the changing attitudes of many immigrants to Hawaii toward their traditional cultural norms

4. According to the passage, some Asian American literature from Hawaii has been characterized as which one of the following?
   (A) inimical to the process of developing a local sensibility
   (B) centered on the individual's drive to succeed
   (C) concerned with conflicts between different age groups
   (D) focused primarily on retaining ties to one's homeland
   (E) tied to a search for a new sense of family in a new land

5. The author of the passage describes *Expounding the Doubtful Points* as "striking" (lines 7–8) primarily in order to
   (A) underscore the forceful and contentious tone of the work
   (B) indicate that the work has not been properly analyzed by literary critics
   (C) stress the radical difference between this work and Lum's earlier work
   (D) emphasize the differences between this work and that of other Asian American poets from Hawaii
   (E) highlight the innovative nature of Lum's experiments with poetic form

6. With which one of the following statements regarding Lum's poetry would the author of the passage be most likely to agree?
   (A) It cannot be used to support any specific political ideology.
   (B) It is an elegant demonstration of the poet's appreciation of the stylistic contributions of his literary forebears.
   (C) It is most fruitfully understood as a meditation on the choice between new and old that confronts any human being in any culture.
   (D) It conveys thoughtful assessments of both his ancestral homeland tradition and the culture in which he is attempting to build a new identity.
   (E) It conveys Lum's antipathy toward tradition by juxtaposing traditional and nontraditional images.

GO ON TO THE NEXT PAGE.

In England the burden of history weighs heavily on common law, that unwritten code of time-honored laws derived largely from English judicial custom and precedent. Students of contemporary British law are frequently required to study medieval cases, to interpret archaic Latin maxims, or to confront doctrinal principles whose validity is based solely on their being part of the "timeless reason" of the English legal tradition. Centuries-old custom serves as the basis both for the divisions of law school subject matter and for much of the terminology of legal redress. Connected not only with legal history but also with the cultural history of the English people, common law cannot properly be understood without taking a long historical view.

Yet the academic study of jurisprudence has seldom treated common law as a constantly evolving phenomenon rooted in history; those interpretive theories that do acknowledge the antiquity of common law ignore the practical contemporary significance of its historical forms. The reasons for this omission are partly theoretical and partly political. In theoretical terms, modern jurisprudence has consistently treated law as a unified system of rules that can be studied at any given moment in time as a logical whole. The notion of jurisprudence as a system of norms or principles deemphasizes history in favor of the coherence of a system. In this view, the past of the system is conceived as no more than the continuous succession of its states of presence. In political terms, believing in the logic of law is a necessary part of believing in its fairness; even if history shows the legal tradition to be far from unitary and seldom logical, the prestige of the legal institution requires that jurisprudence treat the tradition as if it were, in essence, the application of known rules to objectively determined facts. To suggest otherwise would be dispiriting for the student and demoralizing for the public.

Legal historian Peter Goodrich has argued, however, that common law is most fruitfully studied as a continually developing tradition rather than as a set of rules. Taking his cue from the study of literature, Goodrich sees common law as a sort of literary text, with history and tradition serving as the text's narrative development. To study the common law historically, says Goodrich, is to study a text in which fiction is as influential as analysis, perception as significant as rule, and the play of memory as strong as the logic of argument. The concept of tradition, for Goodrich, implies not only the preservation and transmission of existing forms, but also the continuous rewriting of those forms to adapt them to contemporary legal circumstances.

7. Which one of the following statements best expresses the main idea of the passage?

(A) The residual influences of common law explain not only the divisions of subject matter but also the terminology associated with many legal procedures.
(B) In the academic study of jurisprudence, theoretical interpretations of common law have traditionally been at odds with political interpretations of common law.
(C) Common law, while often treated as an oral history of the English people, would, according to one scholar, be more fruitfully studied as a universally adaptable and constantly changing system of rules.
(D) Although obviously steeped in history and tradition, common law has seldom been studied in relation to its development, as one theorist proposes that it be understood.
(E) Although usually studied as a unitary and logical system of rules and norms, the history of common law shows that body of law to be anything but consistent and fair.

8. It can be inferred that the author of the passage believes which one of the following about the history of law in relation to modern jurisprudence?

(A) Modern jurisprudence misinterprets the nature of the legal tradition.
(B) The history of law proves the original forms of common law to be antiquated and irrelevant to modern jurisprudence.
(C) The history of law, if it is to be made applicable to modern jurisprudence, is best studied as a system of rules rather than as a literary text.
(D) Mainstream theories of modern jurisprudence overlook the order and coherence inherent in legal history.
(E) Mainstream theories of modern jurisprudence, by and large devoid of a sense of legal history, are unnecessarily dispiriting to students and the public alike.

GO ON TO THE NEXT PAGE.

9. Which one of the following would best exemplify the kind of interpretive theory referred to in the first sentence of the second paragraph of the passage?

(A) a theory that traced modern customs involving property ownership to their origins in medieval practice
(B) a theory that relied on a comparison between modern courtroom procedures and medieval theatrical conventions
(C) a theory that analyzed medieval marriage laws without examining their relationship to modern laws
(D) a theory that compared the development of English common law in the twentieth century with simultaneous developments in German common law without examining the social repercussions of either legal system
(E) a theory that compared rules of evidence in civil courts with those in criminal courts

10. It can be inferred from the passage that Peter Goodrich would be most likely to agree with which one of the following statements concerning common law?

(A) Common law is more fruitfully studied as a relic of the history of the English people than as a legal code.
(B) The "text" of common law has degenerated from an early stage of clarity to a current state of incoherence.
(C) Without the public's belief in the justness of common law, the legal system cannot be perpetuated.
(D) While rich in literary significance, the "text" of common law has only a very limited applicability to modern life.
(E) The common law "text" inherited by future generations will differ from the one currently in use.

11. Which one of the following best defines the word "political" as it is used in the second paragraph of the passage?

(A) concerned with the ways by which people seek to advance themselves in a profession
(B) concerned with the covert and possibly unethical methods by which governments achieve their goals
(C) having to do with the maintenance of ethical standards between professions and the citizenry
(D) having to do with the maintenance of an institution's effectiveness
(E) having to do with the manner in which institutions are perceived by radical theorists

12. The passage states that students of British law are frequently required to study

(A) histories of English politics
(B) episodes of litigation from the Middle Ages
(C) treatises on political philosophy
(D) histories of ancient Roman jurisprudence
(E) essays on narrative development

13. Which one of the following best describes the author's opinion of most modern academic theories of common law?

(A) They are overly detailed and thus stultifying to both the student and the public.
(B) They lack an essential dimension that would increase their accuracy.
(C) They overemphasize the practical aspects of the common law at the expense of the theoretical.
(D) They excuse students of the law from the study of important legal disputes of the past.
(E) They routinely treat the study of the law as an art rather than as a science.

14. The primary purpose of the passage is to

(A) explain a paradoxical situation and discuss a new view of the situation
(B) supply a chronological summary of the history of an idea
(C) trace the ideas of an influential theorist and evaluate the theorist's ongoing work
(D) contrast the legal theories of past eras with those of today and suggest how these theories should be studied
(E) advocate a traditional school of thought while criticizing a new trend

GO ON TO THE NEXT PAGE.

The passages discuss relationships between business interests and university research.

Passage A

As university researchers working in a "gift economy" dedicated to collegial sharing of ideas, we have long been insulated from market pressures. The recent tendency to treat research findings as commodities, tradable for cash, threatens this tradition and the role of research as a public good.

The nurseries for new ideas are traditionally universities, which provide an environment uniquely suited to the painstaking testing and revision of theories. Unfortunately, the market process and values governing commodity exchange are ill suited to the cultivation and management of new ideas. With their shareholders impatient for quick returns, businesses are averse to wide-ranging experimentation. And, what is even more important, few commercial enterprises contain the range of expertise needed to handle the replacement of shattered theoretical frameworks.

Further, since entrepreneurs usually have little affinity for adventure of the intellectual sort, they can buy research and bury its products, hiding knowledge useful to society or to their competitors. The growth of industrial biotechnology, for example, has been accompanied by a reduction in the free sharing of research methods and results—a high price to pay for the undoubted benefits of new drugs and therapies.

Important new experimental results once led university scientists to rush down the hall and share their excitement with colleagues. When instead the rush is to patent lawyers and venture capitalists, I worry about the long-term future of scientific discovery.

Passage B

The fruits of pure science were once considered primarily a public good, available for society as a whole. The argument for this view was that most of these benefits were produced through government support of universities, and thus no individual was entitled to restrict access to them.

Today, however, the critical role of science in the modern "information economy" means that what was previously seen as a public good is being transformed into a market commodity. For example, by exploiting the information that basic research has accumulated about the detailed structures of cells and genes, the biotechnology industry can derive profitable pharmaceuticals or medical screening technologies. In this context, assertion of legal claims to "intellectual property"—not just in commercial products but in the underlying scientific knowledge—becomes crucial.

Previously, the distinction between a scientific "discovery" (which could not be patented) and a technical "invention" (which could) defined the limits of industry's ability to patent something. Today, however, the speed with which scientific discoveries can be turned into products and the large profits resulting from this transformation have led to a blurring of both the legal distinction between discovery and invention and the moral distinction between what should and should not be patented.

Industry argues that if it has supported—either in its own laboratories or in a university—the makers of a scientific discovery, then it is entitled to seek a return on its investment, either by charging others for using the discovery or by keeping it for its own exclusive use.

15. Which one of the following is discussed in passage B but not in passage A?

(A) the blurring of the legal distinction between discovery and invention
(B) the general effects of the market on the exchange of scientific knowledge
(C) the role of scientific research in supplying public goods
(D) new pharmaceuticals that result from industrial research
(E) industry's practice of restricting access to research findings

16. Both passages place in opposition the members of which one of the following pairs?

(A) commercially successful research and commercially unsuccessful research
(B) research methods and research results
(C) a marketable commodity and a public good
(D) a discovery and an invention
(E) scientific research and other types of inquiry

GO ON TO THE NEXT PAGE.

17. Both passages refer to which one of the following?

(A) theoretical frameworks
(B) venture capitalists
(C) physics and chemistry
(D) industrial biotechnology
(E) shareholders

18. It can be inferred from the passages that the authors believe that the increased constraint on access to scientific information and ideas arises from

(A) the enormous increase in the volume of scientific knowledge that is being generated
(B) the desire of individual researchers to receive credit for their discoveries
(C) the striving of commercial enterprises to gain a competitive advantage in the market
(D) moral reservations about the social impact of some scientific research
(E) a drastic reduction in government funding for university research

19. Which one of the following statements is most strongly supported by both passages?

(A) Many scientific researchers who previously worked in universities have begun to work in the biotechnology industry.
(B) Private biotechnology companies have invalidly patented the basic research findings of university researchers.
(C) Because of the nature of current scientific research, patent authorities no longer consider the distinction between discoveries and inventions to be clear-cut.
(D) In the past, scientists working in industry had free access to the results of basic research conducted in universities.
(E) Government-funded research in universities has traditionally been motivated by the goals of private industry.

GO ON TO THE NEXT PAGE.

Sometimes there is no more effective means of controlling an agricultural pest than giving free rein to its natural predators. A case in point is the cyclamen mite, a pest whose population can be effectively controlled by a predatory mite of the genus *Typhlodromus*. Cyclamen mites infest strawberry plants; they typically establish themselves in a strawberry field shortly after planting, but their populations do not reach significantly damaging levels until the plants' second year. *Typhlodromus* mites usually invade the strawberry fields during the second year, rapidly subdue the cyclamen mite populations, and keep them from reaching significantly damaging levels.

Typhlodromus owes its effectiveness as a predator to several factors in addition to its voracious appetite. Its population can increase as rapidly as that of its prey. Both species reproduce by parthenogenesis—a mode of reproduction in which unfertilized eggs develop into fertile females. Cyclamen mites lay three eggs per day over the four or five days of their reproductive life span; *Typhlodromus* lay two or three eggs per day for eight to ten days. Seasonal synchrony of *Typhlodromus* reproduction with the growth of prey populations and ability to survive at low prey densities also contribute to the predatory efficiency of *Typhlodromus*. During winter, when cyclamen mite populations dwindle to a few individuals hidden in the crevices and folds of leaves in the crowns of the strawberry plants, the predatory mites subsist on the honeydew produced by aphids and white flies. They do not reproduce except when they are feeding on the cyclamen mites. These features, which make *Typhlodromus* well-suited for exploiting the seasonal rises and falls of its prey, are common among predators that control prey populations.

Greenhouse experiments have verified the importance of *Typhlodromus* predation for keeping cyclamen mites in check. One group of strawberry plants was stocked with both predator and prey mites; a second group was kept predator-free by regular application of parathion, an insecticide that kills the predatory species but does not affect the cyclamen mite. Throughout the study, populations of cyclamen mites remained low in plots shared with *Typhlodromus*, but their infestation attained significantly damaging proportions on predator-free plants.

Applying parathion in this instance is a clear case in which using a pesticide would do far more harm than good to an agricultural enterprise. The results were similar in field plantings of strawberries, where cyclamen mites also reached damaging levels when predators were eliminated by parathion, but they did not attain such levels in untreated plots. When cyclamen mite populations began to increase in an untreated planting, the predator populations quickly responded to reduce the outbreak. On average, cyclamen mites were about 25 times more abundant in the absence of predators than in their presence.

20. Which one of the following most accurately expresses the main point of the passage?

(A) Control of agricultural pests is most effectively and safely accomplished without the use of pesticides, because these pesticides can kill predators that also control the pests.
(B) Experimental verification is essential in demonstrating the effectiveness of natural controls of agricultural pests.
(C) The relationship between *Typhlodromus* and cyclamen mites demonstrates how natural predation can keep a population of agricultural pests in check.
(D) Predation by *Typhlodromus* is essential for the control of cyclamen mite populations in strawberry fields.
(E) Similarity in mode and timing of reproduction is what enables *Typhlodromus* effectively to control populations of cyclamen mites in fields of strawberry plants.

21. Based on the passage, the author would probably hold that which one of the following principles is fundamental to long-term predatory control of agricultural pests?

(A) The reproduction of the predator population should be synchronized with that of the prey population, so that the number of predators surges just prior to a surge in prey numbers.
(B) The effectiveness of the predatory relationship should be experimentally demonstrable in greenhouse as well as field applications.
(C) The prey population should be able to survive in times of low crop productivity, so that the predator population will not decrease to very low levels.
(D) The predator population's level of consumption of the prey species should be responsive to variations in the size of the prey population.
(E) The predator population should be vulnerable only to pesticides to which the prey population is also vulnerable.

22. Which one of the following is mentioned in the passage as a factor contributing to the effectiveness of *Typhlodromus* as a predator?

(A) its ability to withstand most insecticides except parathion
(B) its lack of natural predators in strawberry fields
(C) its ability to live in different climates in different geographic regions
(D) its constant food supply in cyclamen mite populations
(E) its ability to survive when few prey are available

GO ON TO THE NEXT PAGE.

23. Suppose that pesticide X drastically slows the reproductive rate of cyclamen mites and has no other direct effect on cyclamen mites or *Typhlodromus*. Based on the information in the passage, which one of the following would most likely have occurred if, in the experiments mentioned in the passage, pesticide X had been used instead of parathion, with all other conditions affecting the experiments remaining the same?

(A) In both treated and untreated plots inhabited by both *Typhlodromus* and cyclamen mites, the latter would have been effectively controlled.
(B) Cyclamen mite populations in all treated plots from which *Typhlodromus* was absent would have been substantially lower than in untreated plots inhabited by both kinds of mites.
(C) In the treated plots, slowed reproduction in cyclamen mites would have led to a loss of reproductive synchrony between *Typhlodromus* and cyclamen mites.
(D) In the treated plots, *Typhlodromus* populations would have decreased temporarily and would have eventually increased.
(E) In the treated plots, cyclamen mite populations would have reached significantly damaging levels more slowly, but would have remained at those levels longer, than in untreated plots.

24. It can be inferred from the passage that the author would be most likely to agree with which one of the following statements about the use of predators to control pest populations?

(A) If the use of predators to control cyclamen mite populations fails, then parathion should be used to control these populations.
(B) Until the effects of the predators on beneficial insects that live in strawberry fields are assessed, such predators should be used with caution to control cyclamen mite populations.
(C) Insecticides should be used to control certain pest populations in fields of crops only if the use of natural predators has proven inadequate.
(D) If an insecticide can effectively control pest populations as well as predator populations, then it should be used instead of predators to control pest populations.
(E) Predators generally control pest populations more effectively than pesticides because they do not harm the crops that their prey feed on.

25. The author mentions the egg-laying ability of each kind of mite (lines 20–23) primarily in order to support which one of the following claims?

(A) Mites that reproduce by parthenogenesis do so at approximately equal rates.
(B) Predatory mites typically have a longer reproductive life span than do cyclamen mites.
(C) *Typhlodromus* can lay their eggs in synchrony with cyclamen mites.
(D) *Typhlodromus* can reproduce at least as quickly as cyclamen mites.
(E) The egg-laying rate of *Typhlodromus* is slower in the presence of cyclamen mites than it is in their absence.

26. Which one of the following would, if true, most strengthen the author's position regarding the practical applicability of the information about predatory mites presented in the passage?

(A) The individual *Typhlodromus* mites that have the longest reproductive life spans typically also lay the greatest number of eggs per day.
(B) The insecticides that are typically used for mite control on strawberry plants kill both predatory and nonpredatory species of mites.
(C) In areas in which strawberry plants become infested by cyclamen mites, winters tend to be short and relatively mild.
(D) *Typhlodromus* are sometimes preyed upon by another species of mites that is highly susceptible to parathion.
(E) *Typhlodromus* easily tolerate the same range of climatic conditions that strawberry plants do.

27. Information in the passage most strongly supports which one of the following statements?

(A) Strawberry crops can support populations of both cyclamen mites and *Typhlodromus* mites without significant damage to those crops.
(B) For control of cyclamen mites by another mite species to be effective, it is crucial that the two species have the same mode of reproduction.
(C) Factors that make *Typhlodromus* effective against cyclamen mites also make it effective against certain other pests of strawberry plants.
(D) When *Typhlodromus* is relied on to control cyclamen mites in strawberry crops, pesticides may be necessary to prevent significant damage during the first year.
(E) Strawberry growers have unintentionally caused cyclamen mites to become a serious crop pest by the indiscriminate use of parathion.

S T O P

IF YOU FINISH BEFORE TIME IS CALLED, YOU MAY CHECK YOUR WORK ON THIS SECTION ONLY.
DO NOT WORK ON ANY OTHER SECTION IN THE TEST.

Acknowledgment is made to the following sources from which material has been adapted for use in this test booklet:

Brenda Kwon, review of *Expanding the Doubtful Points* by Wing Tek Lum. ©1995 by the Regents of the University of California.

Robert E. Ricklefs and Gary L. Miller, *Ecology*, Third Edition. ©1990 by W.H. Freeman and Company.

Edward Rothstein, *Emblems of Mind*. ©1995 by Edward Rothstein.

LSAT WRITING SAMPLE TOPIC

Directions: The scenario presented below describes two choices, either one of which can be supported on the basis of the information given. Your essay should consider both choices and argue for one over the other, based on the two specified criteria and the facts provided. There is no "right" or "wrong" choice: a reasonable argument can be made for either.

Dennis, a photographer and local historian, has been commissioned to write a book about the preservation of photographs. He has worked out two different approaches to completing the book, which must be finished in two years. Using the facts below, write an essay in which you argue for one approach over the other based on the following two criteria:

- Dennis would like to improve his knowledge of photographic preservation through practical, hands-on experience.
- Dennis wants to produce a draft of the book as soon as possible.

One approach is for Dennis to take a two-year, part-time position at the photographic archives of a prestigious portrait gallery. He would help people locate visual images for publication, exhibition, research, or personal use from the archives. He would also perform various administrative tasks. Over the two-year period, Dennis would learn a great deal about the methodologies and techniques relating to photographic preservation through routine contact with professional archivists and visiting researchers. He would also enjoy extensive access to the portrait gallery's resources during that time.

Alternatively, Dennis can take a one-year, full-time position with the local public archives, which has a vast collection of photographs from the surrounding region dating back to 1865. Dennis would be helping to complete the cataloging and scanning of those photographs for inclusion in an online system. His extensive responsibilities would include entering historic photographs into a web-based database, determining the street address or location of scenes depicted in the photographs, transferring historic photographic negatives to acid-free storage, and retouching scanned images. He would work alongside skilled archivists and would gain a working knowledge of photographic conservation-preservation procedures.

Scratch Paper

Do not write your essay in this space.

DIRECTIONS:

1. Use the Answer Key on the next page to check your answers.

2. Use the Scoring Worksheet below to compute your raw score.

3. Use the Score Conversion Chart to convert your raw score into the 120–180 scale.

SCORING WORKSHEET

1. Enter the number of questions you answered correctly in each section

	NUMBER CORRECT
SECTION I..........	______
SECTION II..........	______
SECTION III	______
SECTION IV	______

2. Enter the sum here: ______ THIS IS YOUR RAW SCORE.

CONVERSION CHART

For converting Raw Score to the 120–180 LSAT Scaled Score LSAT Prep Test 53

REPORTED SCORE	LOWEST RAW SCORE	HIGHEST RAW SCORE
180	98	100
179	97	97
178	96	96
177	—*	—*
176	95	95
175	94	94
174	93	93
173	92	92
172	91	91
171	90	90
170	89	89
169	88	88
168	87	87
167	86	86
166	84	85
165	83	83
164	81	82
163	80	80
162	78	79
161	77	77
160	75	76
159	73	74
158	71	72
157	70	70
156	68	69
155	66	67
154	64	65
153	62	63
152	61	61
151	59	60
150	57	58
149	55	56
148	53	54
147	52	52
146	50	51
145	48	49
144	46	47
143	45	45
142	43	44
141	41	42
140	40	40
139	38	39
138	36	37
137	35	35
136	33	34
135	32	32
134	30	31
133	29	29
132	28	28
131	26	27
130	25	25
129	24	24
128	22	23
127	21	21
126	20	20
125	19	19
124	18	18
123	17	17
122	16	16
121	15	15
120	0	14

*There is no raw score that will produce this scaled score for this form.

SECTION I

1.	C	8.	D	15.	B	22.	E
2.	B	9.	A	16.	E	23.	D
3.	B	10.	D	17.	B	24.	D
4.	A	11.	D	18.	B	25.	B
5.	E	12.	C	19.	A		
6.	A	13.	A	20.	C		
7.	A	14.	D	21.	A		

SECTION II

1.	B	8.	A	15.	E	22.	E
2.	A	9.	D	16.	A	23.	B
3.	B	10.	C	17.	D		
4.	B	11.	B	18.	E		
5.	C	12.	B	19.	A		
6.	C	13.	E	20.	B		
7.	A	14.	A	21.	C		

SECTION III

1.	A	8.	A	15.	E	22.	B
2.	C	9.	E	16.	B	23.	D
3.	E	10.	B	17.	A	24.	A
4.	A	11.	C	18.	E	25.	C
5.	E	12.	B	19.	A		
6.	D	13.	B	20.	D		
7.	A	14.	A	21.	C		

SECTION IV

1.	A	8.	A	15.	A	22.	E
2.	C	9.	C	16.	C	23.	A
3.	D	10.	E	17.	D	24.	C
4.	C	11.	D	18.	C	25.	D
5.	D	12.	B	19.	D	26.	E
6.	D	13.	B	20.	C	27.	A
7.	D	14.	A	21.	D		

Experimental Section Answer Key
June 1999, PrepTest 28, Section 1

1.	A	8.	C	15.	C	22.	B
2.	B	9.	C	16.	B	23.	A
3.	A	10.	D	17.	D	24.	A
4.	C	11.	A	18.	E	25.	D
5.	D	12.	B	19.	A	26.	E
6.	D	13.	C	20.	A		
7.	E	14.	B	21.	C		

PrepTest 54
June 2008

Time–35 minutes

26 Questions

Directions: The questions in this section are based on the reasoning contained in brief statements or passages. For some questions, more than one of the choices could conceivably answer the question. However, you are to choose the best answer; that is, the response that most accurately and completely answers the question. You should not make assumptions that are by commonsense standards implausible, superfluous, or incompatible with the passage. After you have chosen the best answer, blacken the corresponding space on your answer sheet.

1. Flavonoids are a common component of almost all plants, but a specific variety of flavonoid in apples has been found to be an antioxidant. Antioxidants are known to be a factor in the prevention of heart disease.

   Which one of the following can be properly inferred from the passage?

   (A) A diet composed largely of fruits and vegetables will help to prevent heart disease.
   (B) Flavonoids are essential to preventing heart disease.
   (C) Eating at least one apple each day will prevent heart disease.
   (D) At least one type of flavonoid helps to prevent heart disease.
   (E) A diet deficient in antioxidants is a common cause of heart disease.

2. A number of Grandville's wealthiest citizens have been criminals. So, since it is of utmost importance that the Grandville Planning Committee be composed solely of individuals whose personal standards of ethics are beyond reproach, no wealthy person should be appointed to that committee.

   The argument is most vulnerable to the criticism that it

   (A) confuses a result with something that is sufficient for bringing about that result
   (B) mistakes a temporal relationship for a causal relationship
   (C) assumes that because a certain action has a certain result the person taking that action intended that result
   (D) judges only by subjective standards something that can be readily evaluated according to objective standards
   (E) generalizes on the basis of what could be exceptional cases

3. Birds startled by potential predators generally try to take cover in nearby vegetation. Yet many birds that feed at bird feeders placed in suburban gardens are killed when, thus startled, they fly away from the vegetation in the gardens and into the windowpanes of nearby houses.

   Which one of the following, if true, most helps to explain the anomalous behavior of the birds that fly into windowpanes?

   (A) Predator attacks are as likely to occur at bird feeders surrounded by dense vegetation as they are at feeders surrounded by little or no vegetation.
   (B) The bird feeders in some suburban gardens are placed at a considerable distance from the houses.
   (C) Large birds are as likely s small birds to fly into windowpanes.
   (D) Most of the birds startled while feeding at bird feeders placed in suburban gardens are startled by loud noises rather than by predators.
   (E) The windowpanes of many houses clearly reflect surrounding vegetation.

4. Raising the humidity of a room protects furniture, draperies, and computers from damage caused by excessively dry air. Further, it can make people feel warmer, helps the body's defenses against viruses, and alleviates some skin rashes.

   Each of the following is supported by the information above EXCEPT:

   (A) Humidity can be bad for computers.
   (B) A room can be too dry for the optimal maintenance of its furnishings.
   (C) Dry air can feel cooler than humid air of the same temperature.
   (D) Increased humidity can be beneficial to the skin.
   (E) The human immune system can benefit from humidity.

GO ON TO THE NEXT PAGE.

Questions 5-6

Jane: Television programs and movies that depict violence among teenagers are extremely popular. Given how influential these media are, we have good reason to believe that these depictions cause young people to engage in violent behavior. Hence, depictions of violence among teenagers should be prohibited from movies and television programs, if only in those programs and movies promoted to young audiences.

Maurice: But you are recommending nothing short of censorship! Besides which, your claim that television and movie depictions of violence cause violence is mistaken: violence among young people predates movies and television by centuries.

5. Maurice's attempted refutation of Jane's argument is vulnerable to criticism on which one of the following grounds?

(A) It presupposes that an unpopular policy cannot possibly achieve its intended purpose.
(B) It confuses a subjective judgment of private moral permissibility with an objective description of social fact.
(C) It rules out something as a cause of a current phenomenon solely on the ground that the phenomenon used to occur without that thing.
(D) It cites purported historical facts that cannot possibly be verified.
(E) It relies on an ambiguity in the term "violence" to justify a claim.

6. Which one of the following, if true, most strengthens Jane's argument?

(A) The most violent characters depicted in movies and on television programs are adult characters who are portrayed by adult actors.
(B) The movies that have been shown to have the most influence on young people's behavior are those that are promoted to young audiences.
(C) The people who make the most profits in the movie and television industry are those who can successfully promote their work to both young and old audiences.
(D) Many adolescents who engage in violent behavior had already displayed such behavior before they were exposed to violence in movies.
(E) Among the producers who make both movies and television programs, many voluntarily restrict the subject matter of films directed toward young audiences.

7. Sam: In a recent survey, over 95 percent of people who purchased a Starlight automobile last year said they were highly satisfied with their purchase. Since people who have purchased a new car in the last year are not highly satisfied if that car has a manufacturing defect, Starlight automobiles are remarkably free from such defects.

Tiya: But some manufacturing defects in automobiles become apparent only after several years of use.

Which one of the following most accurately describes how Tiya's response is related to Sam's argument?

(A) It argues that Sam's conclusion is correct, though not for the reasons Sam gives.
(B) It provides evidence indicating that the survey results Sam relies on in his argument do not accurately characterize the attitudes of those surveyed.
(C) It offers a consideration that undermines the support Sam offers for his conclusion.
(D) It points out that Sam's argument presupposes the truth of the conclusion Sam is defending.
(E) It presents new information that implies that Sam's conclusion is false.

8. Some environmentalists question the prudence of exploiting features of the environment, arguing that there are no economic benefits to be gained from forests, mountains, or wetlands that no longer exist. Many environmentalists claim that because nature has intrinsic value it would be wrong to destroy such features of the environment, even if the economic costs of doing so were outweighed by the economic costs of not doing so.

Which one of the following can be logically inferred from the passage?

(A) It is economically imprudent to exploit features of the environment.
(B) Some environmentalists appeal to a noneconomic justification in questioning the defensibility of exploiting features of the environment.
(C) Most environmentalists appeal to economic reasons in questioning the defensibility of exploiting features of the environment.
(D) Many environmentalists provide only a noneconomic justification in questioning the defensibility of exploiting features of the environment.
(E) Even if there is no economic reason for protecting the environment, there is a sound noneconomic justification for doing so.

9. Market research traditionally entails surveying consumers about why they buy and use particular products and brands. Observational research—actually watching consumers shopping and interacting with products—is now increasingly used by market researchers to supplement surveys. Market researchers claim that observational research yields information about consumer behavior that surveys alone cannot provide.

Which one of the following, if true, provides the strongest support for the market researchers' claim?

(A) Even consumers who are unable to explain their preference for or rejection of particular brands reveal which brands they are considering by picking up and putting down products while they are shopping.
(B) Market researchers find that consumers are almost always willing to participate in observational research for which the consumer is paid by the hour.
(C) Consumers are becoming increasingly self-conscience about their buying habits, and some consumers have stopped buying some items that they normally used to buy.
(D) Market researchers say they find data collection more enjoyable in observational research than in survey research, because observational research requires more creative judgment on their part.
(E) Consumers are more likely to respond to oral surveys than they are to respond to written questionnaires.

10. Laura: Harold is obviously lonely. He should sell his cabin in the woods and move into town. In town he will be near other people all the time, so he will not be lonely anymore.

Ralph: Many very lonely people live in towns. What is needed to avoid loneliness is not only the proximity of other people but also genuine interaction with them.

Ralph responds to Laura by pointing out that

(A) something needed for a certain result does not necessarily guarantee that result
(B) what is appropriate in one case is not necessarily appropriate in all cases
(C) what is logically certain is not always intuitively obvious
(D) various alternative solutions are possible for a single problem
(E) a proposed solution for a problem could actually worsen that problem

11. A rise in the percentage of all 18-year-olds who were recruited by the armed services of a small republic between 1980 and 1986 correlates with a rise in the percentage of young people who dropped out of high school in that republic. Since 18-year-olds in the republic are generally either high school graduates or high school dropouts, the correlation leads to the conclusion that the republic's recruitment rates for 18-year-olds depend substantially on recruitment rates for high school dropouts.

Which one of the following statements, if true, most weakens the argument?

(A) A larger number of 18-year-old high school graduates were recruited for the republic's armed services in 1986 than in 1980.
(B) Many of the high-technology systems used by the republic's armed services can be operated only by individuals who have completed a high school education.
(C) Between 1980 and 1986 the percentage of high school graduates among 18-year-olds recruited in the republic rose sharply.
(D) Personnel of the republic's armed services are strongly encouraged to finish their high school education.
(E) The proportion of recruits who had completed at least two years of college education was greater in 1986 than in 1980.

12. Letter to the Editor: Your article on effective cockroach control states that vexone is effective against only one of the more than 4,000 cockroach species that infest North America: the German cockroach. In actuality, vexone has been utilized effectively for almost a decade against all of the species that infest North America. In testing our product, Roach Ender, which contains vexone, we have conducted many well-documented studies that prove this fact.

Each of the following statements conflicts with the letter writer's view EXCEPT:

(A) Vexone is effective against only two species of cockroach that infest North America.
(B) Not all of the major species of cockroach that infest North America can be controlled by Roach Ender.
(C) Every species of cockroach that infests North America can be controlled by vexone.
(D) The cockroach infestations that have been combated with vexone have not included all of the cockroach species that infest North America.
(E) Roach Ender was tested against exactly 4,000 cockroach species that infest North America.

13. A recent study concludes that prehistoric birds, unlike modern birds, were cold-blooded. This challenges a widely held view that modern birds descended from warm-blooded birds. The conclusion is based on the existence of growth rings in prehistoric birds' bodily structures, which are thought to be found only in cold-blooded animals. Another study, however, disputes this view. It concludes that prehistoric birds had dense blood vessels in their bones, which suggests that they were active creatures and therefore had to be warm-blooded.

    Which one of the following, if true, would most help to resolve the dispute described above in favor of one party to it?

    (A) Some modern warm-blooded species other than birds have been shown to have descended from cold-blooded species.
    (B) Having growth rings is not the only physical trait of cold-blooded species.
    (C) Modern birds did not evolve from prehistoric species of birds.
    (D) Dense blood vessels are not found in all warm-blooded species.
    (E) In some cold-blooded species the gene that is responsible for growth rings is also responsible for dense blood vessels.

14. If citizens do not exercise their right to vote, then democratic institutions will crumble and, as a consequence, much valuable social cohesion will be lost. Of course, one person's vote can only make an imperceptible difference to the result of an election, but one must consider the likely effects of large numbers of people failing to vote. An act or omission by one person is not right if such an act or omission done by large numbers of people would be socially damaging. Organized society would be impossible if theft were common, though a single dishonest act on the part of a single person is likely to have an insignificant effect upon society.

    Which one of the following most accurately expresses the main conclusion of the argument?

    (A) People in a democracy should not neglect to vote.
    (B) Dishonest acts and failure to vote are equally damaging.
    (C) There is a risk that individual antisocial acts will be imitated by others.
    (D) A single person's vote or wrongful act can in fact make a great deal of difference.
    (E) Large-scale dishonesty and neglect of public duty will be destructive of democratic and other societies.

15. Human beings have cognitive faculties that are superior to those of other animals, and once humans become aware of these, they cannot be made happy by anything that does not involve gratification of these faculties.

    Which one of the following statements, if true, most calls into question the view above?

    (A) Certain animals—dolphins and chimpanzees, for example—appear to be capable of rational communication.
    (B) Many people familiar both with intellectual stimulation and with physical pleasures enjoy the latter more.
    (C) Someone who never experienced classical music as a child will usually prefer popular music as an adult.
    (D) Many people who are serious athletes consider themselves to be happy.
    (E) Many people who are serious athletes love gourmet food.

16. Historian: We can learn about the medical history of individuals through chemical analysis of their hair. It is likely, for example, that Isaac Newton's psychological problems were due to mercury poisoning; traces of mercury were found in his hair. Analysis is now being done on a lock of Beethoven's hair. Although no convincing argument has shown that Beethoven ever had a venereal disease, some people hypothesize that venereal disease caused his deafness. Since mercury was commonly ingested in Beethoven's time to treat venereal disease, if researchers find a trace of mercury in his hair, we can conclude that this hypothesis is correct.

    Which one of the following is an assumption on which the historian's argument depends?

    (A) None of the mercury introduced into the body can be eliminated.
    (B) Some people in Beethoven's time did not ingest mercury.
    (C) Mercury is an effective treatment for venereal disease.
    (D) Mercury poisoning can cause deafness in people with venereal disease.
    (E) Beethoven suffered from psychological problems of the same severity as Newton's.

GO ON TO THE NEXT PAGE.

17. In 1992, a major newspaper circulated throughout North America paid its reporters an average salary that was much lower than the average salary paid by its principal competitors to their reporters. An executive of the newspaper argued that this practice was justified, since any shortfall that might exist in the reporters' salaries is fully compensated by the valuable training they receive through their assignments.

Which one of the following, if true about the newspaper in 1992, most seriously undermines the justification offered by the executive?

(A) Senior reporters at the newspaper earned as much as reporters of similar stature who worked for the newspaper's principal competitors.
(B) Most of the newspaper's reporters had worked there for more than ten years.
(C) The circulation of the newspaper had recently reached a plateau, after it had increased steadily throughout the 1980s.
(D) The union that represented reporters at the newspaper was different from the union that represented reporters at the newspaper's competitors.
(E) The newspaper was widely read throughout continental Europe and Great Britain as well as North America.

18. The human brain and its associated mental capacities evolved to assist self-preservation. Thus, the capacity of make aesthetic judgments is an adaptation to past environments in which humans lived. So an individual's aesthetic judgments must be evaluated in terms of the extent to which they promote the survival of that individual.

Which one of the following is a principle that would, if valid, provide the strongest justification for the reasoning above?

(A) All human adaptations to past environments were based on the human brain and its associated mental capacities.
(B) Human capacities that do not contribute to the biological success of the human species cannot be evaluated.
(C) If something develops to serve a given function, the standard by which it must be judged is how well it serves that function.
(D) Judgments that depend on individual preference or taste cannot be evaluated as true or false.
(E) Anything that enhances the proliferation of a species is to be valued highly.

19. On a certain day, nine scheduled flights on Swift Airlines were canceled. Ordinarily, a cancellation is due to mechanical problems with the airplane scheduled for a certain flight. However, since it is unlikely that Swift would have mechanical problems with more than one or two airplanes on a single day, some of the nine cancellations were probably due to something else.

The argument depends on which one of the following assumptions?

(A) More than one or two airplanes were scheduled for the nine canceled flights.
(B) Swift Airlines has fewer mechanical problems than do other airlines of the same size.
(C) Each of the canceled flights would have been longer than the average flight on Swift Airlines.
(D) Swift Airlines had never before canceled more than one or two scheduled flights on a single day.
(E) All of the airplanes scheduled for the canceled flights are based at the same airport.

GO ON TO THE NEXT PAGE.

20. Game show host: Humans are no better than apes at investing, that is, they do not attain a better return on their investments than apes do. We gave five stock analysts and one chimpanzee $1,350 each to invest. After one month, the chimp won, having increased its net worth by $210. The net worth of the analyst who came in second increased by only $140.

Each of the following describes a flaw in the game show host's reasoning EXCEPT:

(A) A conclusion is drawn about apes in general on the basis of an experiment involving one chimpanzee.
(B) No evidence is offered that chimpanzees are capable of understanding stock reports and making reasoned investment decisions.
(C) A broad conclusion is drawn about the investment skills of humans on the basis of what is known about five humans.
(D) Too general a conclusion is made about investing on the basis of a single experiment involving short-term investing but not long-term investing.
(E) No evidence is considered about the long-term performance of the chimpanzee's portfolio versus that of the analysts' portfolios.

21. If the law punishes littering, then the city has an obligation to provide trash cans. But the law does not punish littering, so the city has no such obligation.

Which one of the following exhibits a flawed pattern of reasoning most similar to that in the argument above?

(A) If today is a holiday, then the bakery will not be open. The bakery is not open for business. Thus today is a holiday.
(B) Jenny will have lots of balloons at her birthday party. There are no balloons around yet, so today is not her birthday.
(C) The new regulations will be successful only if most of the students adhere to them. Since most of the students will adhere to those regulations, the new regulations will be successful.
(D) In the event that my flight had been late, I would have missed the committee meeting. Fortunately, my flight is on time. Therefore, I will make it to the meeting.
(E) When the law is enforced, some people are jailed. But no one is in jail, so clearly the law is not enforced.

22. Researcher: The role of chemicals called pheromones in determining the sexual behavior of some animals is well documented. But, even though humans also produce these chemicals, it is clear that psychological factors have taken over this role in us. Whereas for animals these behaviors are involuntary, which is a clear sign of chemical control, humans, by virtue of their free will, choose how they behave, and thus psychological factors take over. So pheromones are merely a vestige of our evolutionary past.

The researcher's argument requires the assumption that

(A) whatever does not have a chemical explanation must have a purely psychological one
(B) voluntary action cannot have a chemical explanation
(C) free will can be found only in humans
(D) voluntary action cannot have an evolutionary explanation
(E) there is a psychological explanation for the continuing presence of pheromones in humans

GO ON TO THE NEXT PAGE.

23. Ethicist: It is widely believed that it is always wrong to tell lies, but this is a rule almost no one fully complies with. In fact, lying is often the morally appropriate thing to do. It is morally correct to lie when telling the truth carries the reasonable expectation of producing considerable physical or psychological harm to others.

Which one of the following most closely conforms to the principle the ethicist endorses?

(A) When Juan asked Judy if the movie they were going to was *North by Northwest*, Judy said yes, though she knew that *Persona* was playing instead. This was the only way Juan would see the film and avoid losing an opportunity for an aesthetically pleasing experience.
(B) A daughter asked her father which candidate he supported, McBride or Chang. Though in fact he preferred Chang, the father responded by saying he preferred McBride, in order to avoid discussion.
(C) A husband told his wife he felt ready to go on a canoe trip, though he had recently had severe chest pains; his wife had determined a year ago that they would go on this trip, so to ask to cancel now would be inconvenient.
(D) A young boy asked his mother if she loved his older sister more than she loved him. The mother said she loved them both to the same degree, even though it was not true.
(E) A friend invited Jamal to a party, but Jamal was afraid that he might see his ex-wife and her new husband there. To spare himself emotional pain, as well as the embarrassment of telling his friend why he did not want to go, Jamal falsely claimed he had to work.

24. Surviving seventeenth-century Dutch landscapes attributed to major artists now equal in number those attributed to minor ones. But since in the seventeenth century many prolific minor artists made a living supplying the voracious market for Dutch landscapes, while only a handful of major artists painted in the genre, many attributions of seventeenth-century Dutch landscape paintings to major artists are undoubtedly erroneous.

Which one of the following, if true, most strengthens the argument?

(A) Technically gifted seventeenth-century Dutch landscape artists developed recognizable styles that were difficult to imitate.
(B) In the workshops of major seventeenth-century artists, assistants were employed to prepare the paints, brushes, and other materials that the major artists then used.
(C) In the eighteenth century, landscapes by minor seventeenth-century artists were often simply thrown away or else destroyed through improper storage.
(D) Seventeenth-century art dealers paid minor artists extra money to leave their landscapes unsigned so that the dealers could add phony signatures and pass such works off as valuable paintings.
(E) More seventeenth-century Dutch landscapes were painted than have actually survived, and that is true of those executed by minor artists as well as of those executed by major artists.

GO ON TO THE NEXT PAGE.

25. The interstitial nucleus, a subregion of the brain's hypothalamus, is typically smaller for male cats than for female cats. A neurobiologist performed autopsies on male cats who died from disease X, a disease affecting no more than .05 percent of male cats, and found that these male cats had interstitial nuclei that were as large as those generally found in female cats. Thus, the size of the interstitial nucleus determines whether or not male cats can contract disease X.

Which of the following statements, if true, most seriously weakens the argument?

(A) No female cats have been known to contract disease X, which is a subtype of disease Y.
(B) Many male cats who contract disease X also contract disease Z, the cause of which is unknown.
(C) The interstitial nuclei of female cats who contract disease X are larger than those of female cats who do not contract disease X.
(D) Of 1,000 autopsies on male cats who did not contract disease X, 5 revealed interstitial nuclei larger than those of the average male cat.
(E) The hypothalamus is known not to be causally linked to disease Y, and disease X is a subtype of disease Y.

26. It is common to respond to a person who is exhorting us to change our behavior by drawing attention to that person's own behavior. This response, however, is irrational. Whether or not someone in fact heeds his or her own advice is irrelevant to whether that person's advice should be heeded.

Which one of the following arguments is most similar in its reasoning to the argument above?

(A) Other countries argue that if we are serious about disarming we should go ahead and disarm to show our good intentions, but this is irrational, for we could make the same argument about them.
(B) My neighbor urges me to exercise, but I see no good reason to do so; despite his strenuous exercise, he has failed to exhibit any real benefits from it.
(C) When one country accuses another country of violating human rights standards, the accused country can reduce the damage to its reputation by drawing attention to the human rights record of its accuser because this tactic distracts critical attention.
(D) One should not dismiss the philosopher's argument that matter does not exist by pointing out that the philosopher acts as though matter exists. People's actions have no effect on the strength of their arguments.
(E) We should not be too severe in our condemnation of the salesperson; we have all lied at one point or another. It is irrational to condemn a person for wrongs committed by everybody.

S T O P

IF YOU FINISH BEFORE TIME IS CALLED, YOU MAY CHECK YOUR WORK ON THIS SECTION ONLY.
DO NOT WORK ON ANY OTHER SECTION IN THE TEST.

SECTION I

Time—35 minutes

27 Questions

Directions: Each set of questions in this section is based on a single passage or a pair of passages. The questions are to be answered on the basis of what is stated or implied in the passage or pair of passages. For some of the questions, more than one of the choices could conceivably answer the question. However, you are to choose the best answer; that is, the response that most accurately and completely answers the question, and blacken the corresponding space on your answer sheet.

This passage was adapted from an article published in 1996.

The Internet is a system of computer networks that allows individuals and organizations to communicate freely with other Internet users throughout the world. As a result, an astonishing variety of information is able to flow unimpeded across national and other political borders, presenting serious difficulties for traditional approaches to legislation and law enforcement, to which such borders are crucial.

Control over physical space and the objects located in it is a defining attribute of sovereignty. Lawmaking presupposes some mechanism for enforcement, i.e., the ability to control violations. But jurisdictions cannot control the information and transactions flowing across their borders via the Internet. For example, a government might seek to intercept transmissions that propagate the kinds of consumer fraud that it regulates within its jurisdiction. But the volume of electronic communications crossing its territorial boundaries is too great to allow for effective control over individual transmissions. In order to deny its citizens access to specific materials, a government would thus have to prevent them from using the Internet altogether. Such a draconian measure would almost certainly be extremely unpopular, since most affected citizens would probably feel that the benefits of using the Internet decidedly outweigh the risks.

One legal domain that is especially sensitive to geographical considerations is that governing trademarks. There is no global registration of trademarks; international protection requires registration in each country. Moreover, within a country, the same name can sometimes be used proprietarily by businesses of different kinds in the same locality, or by businesses of the same kind in different localities, on the grounds that use of the trademark by one such business does not affect the others. But with the advent of the Internet, a business name can be displayed in such a way as to be accessible from any computer connected to the Internet anywhere in the world. Should such a display advertising a restaurant in Norway be deemed to infringe a trademark in Brazil just because it can be accessed freely from Brazil? It is not clear that any particular country's trademark authorities possess, or should possess, jurisdiction over such displays. Otherwise, any use of a trademark on the Internet could be subject to the jurisdiction of every country simultaneously.

The Internet also gives rise to situations in which regulation is needed but cannot be provided within the existing framework. For example, electronic communications, which may pass through many different territorial jurisdictions, pose perplexing new questions about the nature and adequacy of privacy protections. Should French officials have lawful access to messages traveling via the Internet from Canada to Japan? This is just one among many questions that collectively challenge the notion that the Internet can be effectively controlled by the existing system of territorial jurisdictions.

1. Which one of the following most accurately expresses the main point of the passage?
   (A) The high-volume, global nature of activity on the Internet undermines the feasibility of controlling it through legal frameworks that presuppose geographic boundaries.
   (B) The system of Internet communications simultaneously promotes and weakens the power of national governments to control their citizens' speech and financial transactions.
   (C) People value the benefits of their participation on the Internet so highly that they would strongly oppose any government efforts to regulate their Internet activity.
   (D) Internet communications are responsible for a substantial increase in the volume and severity of global crime.
   (E) Current Internet usage and its future expansion pose a clear threat to the internal political stability of many nations.

GO ON TO THE NEXT PAGE.

2. The author mentions French officials in connection with messages traveling between Canada and Japan (lines 57–59) primarily to

(A) emphasize that the Internet allows data to be made available to users worldwide
(B) illustrate the range of languages that might be used on the Internet
(C) provide an example of a regulatory problem arising when an electronic communication intended for a particular destination passes through intermediate jurisdictions
(D) show why any use of a trademark on the Internet could be subject to the jurisdiction of every country simultaneously
(E) highlight the kind of international cooperation that made the Internet possible

3. According to the passage, which one of the following is an essential property of political sovereignty?

(A) control over business enterprises operating across territorial boundaries
(B) authority over communicative exchanges occurring within a specified jurisdiction
(C) power to regulate trademarks throughout a circumscribed geographic region
(D) control over the entities included within a designated physical space
(E) authority over all commercial transactions involving any of its citizens

4. Which one of the following words employed by the author in the second paragraph is most indicative of the author's attitude toward any hypothetical measure a government might enact to deny its citizens access to the Internet?

(A) benefits
(B) decidedly
(C) unpopular
(D) draconian
(E) risks

5. What is the main purpose of the fourth paragraph?

(A) to call into question the relevance of the argument provided in the second paragraph
(B) to provide a practical illustration that questions the general claim made in the first paragraph
(C) to summarize the arguments provided in the second and third paragraphs
(D) to continue the argument that begins in the third paragraph
(E) to provide an additional argument in support of the general claim made in the first paragraph

GO ON TO THE NEXT PAGE.

Passage A

Drilling fluids, including the various mixtures known as drilling muds, play essential roles in oil-well drilling. As they are circulated down through the drill pipe and back up the well itself, they lubricate the drill bit, bearings, and drill pipe; clean and cool the drill bit as it cuts into the rock; lift rock chips (cuttings) to the surface; provide information about what is happening downhole, allowing the drillers to monitor the behavior, flow rate, pressure, and composition of the drilling fluid; and maintain well pressure to control cave-ins.

Drilling muds are made of bentonite and other clays and polymers, mixed with a fluid to the desired viscosity. By far the largest ingredient of drilling muds, by weight, is barite, a very heavy mineral of density 4.3 to 4.6. It is also used as an inert filler in some foods and is more familiar in its medical use as the "barium meal" administered before X-raying the digestive tract.

Over the years individual drilling companies and their expert drillers have devised proprietary formulations, or mud "recipes," to deal with specific types of drilling jobs. One problem in studying the effects of drilling waste discharges is that the drilling fluids are made from a range of over 1,000, sometimes toxic, ingredients—many of them known, confusingly, by different trade names, generic descriptions, chemical formulae, and regional or industry slang words, and many of them kept secret by companies or individual formulators.

Passage B

Drilling mud, cuttings, and associated chemicals are normally released only during the drilling phase of a well's existence. These discharges are the main environmental concern in offshore oil production, and their use is tightly regulated. The discharges are closely monitored by the offshore operator, and releases are controlled as a condition of the operating permit.

One type of mud—water-based mud (WBM)—is a mixture of water, bentonite clay, and chemical additives, and is used to drill shallow parts of wells. It is not particularly toxic to marine organisms and disperses readily. Under current regulations, it can be dumped directly overboard. Companies typically recycle WBMs until their properties are no longer suitable and then, over a period of hours, dump the entire batch into the sea.

For drilling deeper wells, oil-based mud (OBM) is normally used. The typical difference from WBM is the high content of mineral oil (typically 30 percent). OBMs also contain greater concentrations of barite, a powdered heavy mineral, and a number of additives. OBMs have a greater potential for negative environmental impact, partly because they do not disperse as readily. Barite may impact some organisms, particularly scallops, and the mineral oil may have toxic effects. Currently only the residues of OBMs adhering to cuttings that remain after the cuttings are sieved from the drilling fluids may be discharged overboard, and then only mixtures up to a specified maximum oil content.

6. A primary purpose of each of the passages is to
   - (A) provide causal explanations for a type of environmental pollution
   - (B) describe the general composition and properties of drilling muds
   - (C) point out possible environmental impacts associated with oil drilling
   - (D) explain why oil-well drilling requires the use of drilling muds
   - (E) identify difficulties inherent in the regulation of oil-well drilling operations

7. Which one of the following is a characteristic of barite that is mentioned in both of the passages?
   - (A) It does not disperse readily in seawater.
   - (B) It is not found in drilling muds containing bentonite.
   - (C) Its use in drilling muds is tightly regulated.
   - (D) It is the most commonly used ingredient in drilling muds.
   - (E) It is a heavy mineral.

8. Each of the following is supported by one or both of the passages EXCEPT:
   - (A) Clay is an important constituent of many, if not all, drilling muds.
   - (B) At least one type of drilling mud is not significantly toxic to marine life.
   - (C) There has been some study of the environmental effects of drilling-mud discharges.
   - (D) Government regulations allow drilling muds to contain 30 percent mineral oil.
   - (E) During the drilling of an oil well, drilling mud is continuously discharged into the sea.

GO ON TO THE NEXT PAGE.

9. Which one of the following can be most reasonably inferred from the two passages taken together, but not from either one individually?

(A) Barite is the largest ingredient of drilling muds, by weight, and also the most environmentally damaging.
(B) Although barite can be harmful to marine organisms, it can be consumed safely by humans.
(C) Offshore drilling is more damaging to the environment than is land-based drilling.
(D) The use of drilling muds needs to be more tightly controlled by government.
(E) If offshore drilling did not generate cuttings, it would be less harmful to the environment.

10. Each of the following is supported by one or both of the passages EXCEPT:

(A) Drillers monitor the suitability of the mud they are using.
(B) The government requires drilling companies to disclose all ingredients used in their drilling muds.
(C) In certain quantities, barite is not toxic to humans.
(D) Oil reserves can be found within or beneath layers of rock.
(E) Drilling deep oil wells requires the use of different mud recipes than does drilling shallow oil wells.

11. Based on information in the passages, which one of the following, if true, provides the strongest support for a prediction that the proportion of oil-well drilling using OBMs will increase in the future?

(A) The cost of certain ingredients in WBMs is expected to increase steadily over the next several decades.
(B) The deeper an offshore oil well, the greater the concentration of barite that must be used in the drilling mud.
(C) Oil reserves at shallow depths have mostly been tapped, leaving primarily much deeper reserves for future drilling.
(D) It is unlikely that oil drillers will develop more efficient ways of removing OBM residues from cuttings that remain after being sieved from drilling fluids.
(E) Barite is a common mineral, the availability of which is virtually limitless.

12. According to passage B, one reason OBMs are potentially more environmentally damaging than WBMs is that OBMs

(A) are slower to disperse
(B) contain greater concentrations of bentonite
(C) contain a greater number of additives
(D) are used for drilling deeper wells
(E) cannot be recycled

GO ON TO THE NEXT PAGE.

Aida Overton Walker (1880–1914), one of the most widely acclaimed African American performers of the early twentieth century, was known largely for popularizing a dance form known as the cakewalk through her choreographing, performance, and teaching of the dance. The cakewalk was originally developed prior to the United States Civil War by African Americans, for whom dance was a means of maintaining cultural links within a slave society. It was based on traditional West African ceremonial dances, and like many other African American dances, it retained features characteristic of African dance forms, such as gliding steps and an emphasis on improvisation.

To this African-derived foundation, the cakewalk added certain elements from European dances: where African dances feature flexible body postures, large groups and separate-sex dancing, the cakewalk developed into a high-kicking walk performed by a procession of couples. Ironically, while these modifications later enabled the cakewalk to appeal to European Americans and become one of the first cultural forms to cross the racial divide in North America, they were originally introduced with satiric intent. Slaves performed the grandiloquent walks in order to parody the processional dances performed at slave owners' balls and, in general, the self-important manners of slave owners. To add a further irony, by the end of the nineteenth century, the cakewalk was itself being parodied by European American stage performers, and these parodies in turn helped shape subsequent versions of the cakewalk.

While this complex evolution meant that the cakewalk was not a simple cultural phenomenon—one scholar has characterized this layering of parody upon parody with the phrase "mimetic vertigo"—it is in fact what enabled the dance to attract its wide audience. In the cultural and socioeconomic flux of the turn-of-the-century United States, where industrialization, urbanization, mass immigration, and rapid social mobility all reshaped the cultural landscape, an art form had to be capable of being many things to many people in order to appeal to a large audience.

Walker's remarkable success at popularizing the cakewalk across otherwise relatively rigid racial boundaries rested on her ability to address within her interpretation of it the varying and sometimes conflicting demands placed on the dance. Middle-class African Americans, for example, often denounced the cakewalk as disreputable, a complaint reinforced by the parodies circulating at the time. Walker won over this audience by refining the cakewalk and emphasizing its fundamental grace. Meanwhile, because middle- and upper-class European Americans often felt threatened by the tremendous cultural flux around them, they prized what they regarded as authentic art forms as bastions of stability; much of Walker's success with this audience derived from her distillation of what was widely acclaimed as the most authentic cakewalk. Finally, Walker was able to gain the admiration of many newly rich industrialists and financiers, who found in the grand flourishes of her version of the cakewalk a fitting vehicle for celebrating their newfound social rank.

13. Which one of the following most accurately expresses the main point of the passage?

(A) Walker, who was especially well known for her success in choreographing, performing, and teaching the cakewalk, was one of the most widely recognized African American performers of the early twentieth century.

(B) In spite of the disparate influences that shaped the cakewalk, Walker was able to give the dance broad appeal because she distilled what was regarded as the most authentic version in an era that valued authenticity highly.

(C) Walker popularized the cakewalk by capitalizing on the complex cultural mix that had developed from the dance's original blend of satire and cultural preservation, together with the effects of later parodies.

(D) Whereas other versions of the cakewalk circulating at the beginning of the twentieth century were primarily parodic in nature, the version popularized by Walker combined both satire and cultural preservation.

(E) Because Walker was able to recognize and preserve the characteristics of the cakewalk as African Americans originally performed it, it became the first popular art form to cross the racial divide in the United States.

14. The author describes the socioeconomic flux of the turn-of-the-century United States in the third paragraph primarily in order to

(A) argue that the cakewalk could have become popular only in such complex social circumstances

(B) detail the social context that prompted performers of the cakewalk to fuse African and European dance forms

(C) identify the target of the overlapping parodic layers that characterized the cakewalk

(D) indicate why a particular cultural environment was especially favorable for the success of the cakewalk

(E) explain why European American parodies of the cakewalk were able to reach wide audiences

GO ON TO THE NEXT PAGE.

15. Which one of the following is most analogous to the author's account in the second paragraph of how the cakewalk came to appeal to European Americans?

(A) Satirical versions of popular music songs are frequently more popular than the songs they parody.
(B) A style of popular music grows in popularity among young listeners because it parodies the musical styles admired by older listeners.
(C) A style of music becomes admired among popular music's audience in part because of elements that were introduced in order to parody popular music.
(D) A once popular style of music wins back its audience by incorporating elements of the style of music that is currently most popular.
(E) After popular music begins to appropriate elements of a traditional style of music, interest in that traditional music increases.

16. The passage asserts which one of the following about the cakewalk?

(A) It was largely unknown outside African American culture until Walker popularized it.
(B) It was mainly a folk dance, and Walker became one of only a handful of people to perform it professionally.
(C) Its performance as parody became uncommon as a result of Walker's popularization of its authentic form.
(D) Its West African origins became commonly known as a result of Walker's work.
(E) It was one of the first cultural forms to cross racial lines in the United States.

17. It can be inferred from the passage that the author would be most likely to agree with which one of the following statements?

(A) Because of the broad appeal of humor, satiric art forms are often among the first to cross racial or cultural divisions.
(B) The interactions between African American and European American cultural forms often result in what is appropriately characterized as "mimetic vertigo."
(C) Middle-class European Americans who valued the cakewalk's authenticity subsequently came to admire other African American dances for the same reason.
(D) Because of the influence of African dance forms, some popular dances that later emerged in the United States featured separate-sex dancing.
(E) Some of Walker's admirers were attracted to her version of the cakewalk as a means for bolstering their social identities.

18. The passage most strongly suggests that the author would be likely to agree with which one of the following statements about Walker's significance in the history of the cakewalk?

(A) Walker broadened the cakewalk's appeal by highlighting elements that were already present in the dance.
(B) Walker's version of the cakewalk appealed to larger audiences than previous versions did because she accentuated its satiric dimension.
(C) Walker popularized the cakewalk by choreographing various alternative interpretations of it, each tailored to the interests of a different cultural group.
(D) Walker added a "mimetic vertigo" to the cakewalk by inserting imitations of other performers' cakewalking into her dance routines.
(E) Walker revitalized the cakewalk by disentangling its complex admixture of African and European elements.

19. The passage provides sufficient information to answer which one of the following questions?

(A) What were some of the attributes of African dance forms that were preserved in the cakewalk?
(B) Who was the first performer to dance the cakewalk professionally?
(C) What is an aspect of the cakewalk that was preserved in other North American dance forms?
(D) What features were added to the original cakewalk by the stage parodies circulating at the end of the nineteenth century?
(E) For about how many years into the twentieth century did the cakewalk remain widely popular?

GO ON TO THE NEXT PAGE.

In principle, a cohesive group—one whose members generally agree with one another and support one another's judgments—can do a much better job at decision making than it could if it were noncohesive. When cohesiveness is low or lacking entirely, compliance out of fear of recrimination is likely to be strongest. To overcome this fear, participants in the group's deliberations need to be confident that they are members in good standing and that the others will continue to value their role in the group, whether or not they agree about a particular issue under discussion. As members of a group feel more accepted by the others, they acquire greater freedom to say what they really think, becoming less likely to use deceitful arguments or to play it safe by dancing around the issues with vapid or conventional comments. Typically, then, the more cohesive a group becomes, the less its members will deliberately censor what they say out of fear of being punished socially for antagonizing their fellow members.

But group cohesiveness can have pitfalls as well: while the members of a highly cohesive group can feel much freer to deviate from the majority, their desire for genuine concurrence on every important issue often inclines them not to use this freedom. In a highly cohesive group of decision makers, the danger is not that individuals will conceal objections they harbor regarding a proposal favored by the majority, but that they will think the proposal is a good one without attempting to carry out a critical scrutiny that could reveal grounds for strong objections. Members may then decide that any misgivings they feel are not worth pursuing—that the benefit of any doubt should be given to the group consensus. In this way, they may fall victim to a syndrome known as "groupthink," which one psychologist concerned with collective decision making has defined as "a deterioration of mental efficiency, reality testing, and moral judgment that results from in-group pressures."

Based on analyses of major fiascoes of international diplomacy and military decision making, researchers have identified groupthink behavior as a recurring pattern that involves several factors: overestimation of the group's power and morality, manifested, for example, in an illusion of invulnerability, which creates excessive optimism; closed-mindedness to warnings of problems and to alternative viewpoints; and unwarranted pressures toward uniformity, including self-censorship with respect to doubts about the group's reasoning and a concomitant shared illusion of unanimity concerning group decisions. Cohesiveness of the decision-making group is an essential antecedent condition for this syndrome but not a sufficient one, so it is important to work toward identifying the additional factors that determine whether group cohesiveness will deteriorate into groupthink or allow for effective decision making.

20. Which one of the following most accurately expresses the main point of the passage?

(A) Despite its value in encouraging frank discussion, high cohesion can lead to a debilitating type of group decision making called groupthink.
(B) Group members can guard against groupthink if they have a good understanding of the critical role played by cohesion.
(C) Groupthink is a dysfunctional collective decision-making pattern that can occur in diplomacy and military affairs.
(D) Low cohesion in groups is sometimes desirable when higher cohesion involves a risk of groupthink behavior.
(E) Future efforts to guard against groupthink will depend on the results of ongoing research into the psychology of collective decision making.

21. A group of closely associated colleagues has made a disastrous diplomatic decision after a series of meetings marked by disagreement over conflicting alternatives. It can be inferred from the passage that the author would be most likely to say that this scenario

(A) provides evidence of chronic indecision, thus indicating a weak level of cohesion in general
(B) indicates that the group's cohesiveness was coupled with some other factor to produce a groupthink fiasco
(C) provides no evidence that groupthink played a role in the group's decision
(D) provides evidence that groupthink can develop even in some groups that do not demonstrate an "illusion of unanimity"
(E) indicates that the group probably could have made its decision-making procedure more efficient by studying the information more thoroughly

GO ON TO THE NEXT PAGE.

22. Which one of the following, if true, would most support the author's contentions concerning the conditions under which groupthink takes place?

(A) A study of several groups, each made up of members of various professions, found that most fell victim to groupthink.
(B) There is strong evidence that respectful dissent is more likely to occur in cohesive groups than in groups in which there is little internal support.
(C) Extensive analyses of decisions made by a large number of groups found no cases of groupthink in groups whose members generally distrust one another's judgments.
(D) There is substantial evidence that groupthink is especially likely to take place when members of a group develop factions whose intransigence prolongs the group's deliberations.
(E) Ample research demonstrates that voluntary deference to group opinion is not a necessary factor for the formation of groupthink behavior.

23. The passage mentions which one of the following as a component of groupthink?

(A) unjustified suspicions among group members regarding an adversary's intentions
(B) strong belief that the group's decisions are right
(C) group members working under unusually high stress, leading to illusions of invulnerability
(D) the deliberate use of vapid, clichéd arguments
(E) careful consideration of objections to majority positions

24. It can be inferred from the passage that both the author of the passage and the researchers mentioned in the passage would be most likely to agree with which one of the following statements about groupthink?

(A) Groupthink occurs in all strongly cohesive groups, but its contribution to collective decision making is not fully understood.
(B) The causal factors that transform group cohesion into groupthink are unique to each case.
(C) The continued study of cohesiveness of groups is probably fruitless for determining what factors elicit groupthink.
(D) Outside information cannot influence group decisions once they have become determined by groupthink.
(E) On balance, groupthink cannot be expected to have a beneficial effect in a group's decision making.

25. In the passage, the author says which one of the following about conformity in decision-making groups?

(A) Enforced conformity may be appropriate in some group decision situations.
(B) A high degree of conformity is often expected of military decision-making group members.
(C) Inappropriate group conformity can result from inadequate information.
(D) Voluntary conformity occurs much less frequently than enforced conformity.
(E) Members of noncohesive groups may experience psychological pressure to conform.

26. In line 5, the author mentions low group cohesiveness primarily in order to

(A) contribute to a claim that cohesiveness can be conducive to a freer exchange of views in groups
(B) establish a comparison between groupthink symptoms and the attributes of low-cohesion groups
(C) suggest that there may be ways to make both cohesive and noncohesive groups more open to dissent
(D) indicate that both cohesive and noncohesive groups may be susceptible to groupthink dynamics
(E) lay the groundwork for a subsequent proposal for overcoming the debilitating effects of low cohesion

27. Based on the passage, it can be inferred that the author would be most likely to agree with which one of the following?

(A) Highly cohesive groups are more likely to engage in confrontational negotiating styles with adversaries than are those with low cohesion.
(B) It is difficult for a group to examine all relevant options critically in reaching decisions unless it has a fairly high degree of cohesiveness.
(C) A group with varied viewpoints on a given issue is less likely to reach a sound decision regarding that issue than is a group whose members are unified in their outlook.
(D) Intense stress and high expectations are the key factors in the formation of groupthink.
(E) Noncohesive groups can, under certain circumstances, develop all of the symptoms of groupthink.

S T O P

IF YOU FINISH BEFORE TIME IS CALLED, YOU MAY CHECK YOUR WORK ON THIS SECTION ONLY.
DO NOT WORK ON ANY OTHER SECTION IN THE TEST.

SECTION II

Time—35 minutes

26 Questions

Directions: The questions in this section are based on the reasoning contained in brief statements or passages. For some questions, more than one of the choices could conceivably answer the question. However, you are to choose the best answer; that is, the response that most accurately and completely answers the question. You should not make assumptions that are by commonsense standards implausible, superfluous, or incompatible with the passage. After you have chosen the best answer, blacken the corresponding space on your answer sheet.

1. Executive: Our company is proud of its long history of good relations with its employees. In fact, a recent survey of our retirees proves that we treat our employees fairly, since 95 percent of the respondents reported that they had always been treated fairly during the course of their careers with us.

   The executive's argument is flawed in that it

   (A) presents as its sole premise a claim that one would accept as true only if one already accepted the truth of the conclusion
   (B) relies on evidence that cannot be verified
   (C) equivocates on the word "fairly"
   (D) bases a generalization on a sample that may not be representative
   (E) presumes, without providing justification, that older methods of managing employees are superior to newer ones

2. Many of those who are most opposed to cruelty to animals in the laboratory, in the slaughterhouse, or on the farm are people who truly love animals and who keep pets. The vast majority of domestic pets, however, are dogs and cats, and both of these species are usually fed meat. Therefore, many of those who are most opposed to cruelty to animals do, in fact, contribute to such cruelty.

   Which one of the following is an assumption made by the argument?

   (A) Loving pets requires loving all forms of animal life.
   (B) Many of those who are opposed to keeping dogs and cats as pets are also opposed to cruelty to animals.
   (C) Some people who work in laboratories, in slaughterhouses, or on farms are opposed to cruelty to animals.
   (D) Many popular pets are not usually fed meat.
   (E) Feeding meat to pets contributes to cruelty to animals.

3. Statistics from the National Booksellers Association indicate that during the last five years most bookstores have started to experience declining revenues from the sale of fiction, despite national campaigns to encourage people to read more fiction. Therefore, these reading campaigns have been largely unsuccessful.

   Which one of the following statements, if true, most seriously weakens the argument?

   (A) Mail order book clubs have enjoyed substantial growth in fiction sales throughout the last five years.
   (B) During the last five years the most profitable items in bookstores have been newspapers and periodicals rather than novels.
   (C) Fierce competition has forced booksellers to make drastic markdowns on the cover price of best-selling biographies.
   (D) Due to the poor economic conditions that have prevailed during the last five years, most libraries report substantial increases in the number of patrons seeking books on changing careers and starting new businesses.
   (E) The National Booksellers Association statistics do not include profits from selling novels by mail to overseas customers.

4. People who consume a lot of honey tend to have fewer cavities than others have. Yet, honey is high in sugar, and sugar is one of the leading causes of tooth decay.

   Which one of the following, if true, most helps to resolve the apparent paradox described above?

   (A) People who eat a lot of honey tend to consume very little sugar from other sources.
   (B) Many people who consume a lot of honey consume much of it dissolved in drinks.
   (C) People's dental hygiene habits vary greatly.
   (D) Refined sugars have been linked to more health problems than have unrefined sugars.
   (E) Honey contains bacteria that inhibit the growth of the bacteria that cause tooth decay.

5. Byrne: One of our club's bylaws specifies that any officer who fails to appear on time for any one of the quarterly board meetings, or who misses two of our monthly general meetings, must be suspended. Thibodeaux, an officer, was recently suspended. But Thibodeaux has never missed a monthly general meeting. Therefore, Thibodeaux must have failed to appear on time for a quarterly board meeting.

The reasoning in Byrne's argument is flawed in that the argument

(A) fails to consider the possibility that Thibodeaux has arrived late for two or more monthly general meetings
(B) presumes, without providing justification, that if certain events each produce a particular result, then no other event is sufficient to produce that result
(C) takes for granted that an assumption required to establish the argument's conclusion is sufficient to establish that conclusion
(D) fails to specify at what point someone arriving at a club meeting is officially deemed late
(E) does not specify how long Thibodeaux has been an officer

6. Manufacturers of writing paper need to add mineral "filler" to paper pulp if the paper made from the pulp is to look white. Without such filler, paper products look grayish. To make writing paper that looks white from recycled paper requires more filler than is required to make such paper from other sources. Therefore, barring the more efficient use of fillers in paper manufacturing or the development of paper-whitening technologies that do not require mineral fillers, if writing paper made from recycled paper comes to replace other types of writing paper, paper manufacturers will have to use more filler than they now use.

Which one of the following is an assumption on which the argument depends?

(A) Certain kinds of paper cannot be manufactured from recycled paper.
(B) The fillers that are used to make paper white are harmful to the environment.
(C) Grayish writing paper will not be a universally acceptable alternative to white writing paper.
(D) Beyond a certain limit, increasing the amount of filler added to paper pulp does not increase the whiteness of the paper made from the pulp.
(E) The total amount of writing paper manufactured worldwide will increase significantly in the future.

7. Environmentalist: The excessive atmospheric buildup of carbon dioxide, which threatens the welfare of everyone in the world, can be stopped only by reducing the burning of fossil fuels. Any country imposing the strict emission standards on the industrial burning of such fuels that this reduction requires, however, would thereby reduce its gross national product. No nation will be willing to bear singlehandedly the costs of an action that will benefit everyone. It is obvious, then, that the catastrophic consequences of excessive atmospheric carbon dioxide are unavoidable unless _______.

Which one of the following most logically completes the argument?

(A) all nations become less concerned with pollution than with the economic burdens of preventing it
(B) multinational corporations agree to voluntary strict emission standards
(C) international agreements produce industrial emission standards
(D) distrust among nations is eliminated
(E) a world government is established

8. A clear advantage of digital technology over traditional printing is that digital documents, being patterns of electronic signals rather than patterns of ink on paper, do not generate waste in the course of their production and use. However, because patterns of electronic signals are necessarily ephemeral, a digital document can easily be destroyed and lost forever.

The statements above best illustrate which one of the following generalizations?

(A) A property of a technology may constitute an advantage in one set of circumstances and a disadvantage in others.
(B) What at first appears to be an advantage of a technology may create more problems than it solves.
(C) It is more important to be able to preserve information than it is for information to be easily accessible.
(D) Innovations in document storage technologies sometimes decrease, but never eliminate, the risk of destroying documents.
(E) Advances in technology can lead to increases in both convenience and environmental soundness.

9. Museum visitor: The national government has mandated a 5 percent increase in the minimum wage paid to all workers. This mandate will adversely affect the museum-going public. The museum's revenue does not currently exceed its expenses, and since the mandate will significantly increase the museum's operating expenses, the museum will be forced either to raise admission fees or to decrease services.

Which one of the following is an assumption required by the museum visitor's argument?

(A) Some of the museum's employees are not paid significantly more than the minimum wage.
(B) The museum's revenue from admission fees has remained constant over the past five years.
(C) Some of the museum's employees are paid more than the current minimum wage.
(D) The annual number of visitors to the museum has increased steadily.
(E) Not all visitors to the museum are required to pay an admission fee.

10. Helen: Reading a book is the intellectual equivalent of investing money: you're investing time, thereby foregoing other ways of spending that time, in the hope that what you learn will later afford you more opportunities than you'd get by spending the time doing something other than reading that book.

Randi: But that applies only to vocational books. Reading fiction is like watching a sitcom: it's just wasted time.

Which one of the following most accurately describes the technique Randi uses in responding to Helen's claims?

(A) questioning how the evidence Helen uses for a claim was gathered
(B) disputing the scope of Helen's analogy by presenting another analogy
(C) arguing that Helen's reasoning ultimately leads to an absurd conclusion
(D) drawing an analogy to an example presented by Helen
(E) denying the relevance of an example presented by Helen

11. Contrary to recent speculations, no hardware store will be opening in the shopping plaza. If somebody were going to open a store there, they would already have started publicizing it. But there has been no such publicity.

Which one of the following most accurately expresses the conclusion drawn in the argument?

(A) Some people have surmised that a hardware store will be opening in the shopping plaza.
(B) A hardware store will not be opening in the shopping plaza.
(C) If somebody were going to open a hardware store in the shopping plaza, that person would already have started publicizing it.
(D) It would be unwise to open a hardware store in the shopping plaza.
(E) There has been no publicity concerning the opening of a hardware store in the shopping plaza.

12. Ethicist: Although science is frequently said to be morally neutral, it has a traditional value system of its own. For example, scientists sometimes foresee that a line of theoretical research they are pursuing will yield applications that could seriously harm people, animals, or the environment. Yet, according to science's traditional value system, such consequences do not have to be considered in deciding whether to pursue that research. Ordinary morality, in contrast, requires that we take the foreseeable consequences of our actions into account whenever we are deciding what to do.

The ethicist's statements, if true, most strongly support which one of the following?

(A) Scientists should not be held responsible for the consequences of their research.
(B) According to the dictates of ordinary morality, scientists doing research that ultimately turns out to yield harmful applications are acting immorally.
(C) Science is morally neutral because it assigns no value to the consequences of theoretical research.
(D) It is possible for scientists to both adhere to the traditional values of their field and violate a principle of ordinary morality.
(E) The uses and effects of scientifically acquired knowledge can never be adequately foreseen.

GO ON TO THE NEXT PAGE.

13. Consumers seek to purchase the highest quality at the lowest prices. Companies that do not offer products that attract consumers eventually go bankrupt. Therefore, companies that offer neither the best quality nor the lowest price will eventually go bankrupt.

The conclusion above follows logically if which one of the following is assumed?

(A) No company succeeds in producing a product that is both highest in quality and lowest in price.
(B) Products that are neither highest in quality nor lowest in price do not attract consumers.
(C) Any company that offers either the highest quality or the lowest price will avoid bankruptcy.
(D) Some consumers will not continue to patronize a company purely out of brand loyalty.
(E) No company is driven from the market for reasons other than failing to meet consumer demands.

14. The number of serious traffic accidents (accidents resulting in hospitalization or death) that occurred on Park Road from 1986 to 1990 was 35 percent lower than the number of serious accidents from 1981 to 1985. The speed limit on Park Road was lowered in 1986. Hence, the reduction of the speed limit led to the decrease in serious accidents.

Which one of the following statements, if true, most weakens the argument?

(A) The number of speeding tickets issued annually on Park Road remained roughly constant from 1981 to 1990.
(B) Beginning in 1986, police patrolled Park Road much less frequently than in 1985 and previous years.
(C) The annual number of vehicles using Park Road decreased significantly and steadily from 1981 to 1990.
(D) The annual number of accidents on Park Road that did not result in hospitalization remained roughly constant from 1981 to 1990.
(E) Until 1986 accidents were classified as "serious" only if they resulted in an extended hospital stay.

15. Humans are supposedly rational: in other words, they have a capacity for well-considered thinking and behavior. This is supposedly the difference that makes them superior to other animals. But humans knowingly pollute the world's precious air and water and, through bad farming practices, deplete the soil that feeds them. Thus, humans are not rational after all, so it is absurd to regard them as superior to other animals.

The reasoning above is flawed in that it

(A) relies crucially on an internally contradictory definition of rationality
(B) takes for granted that humans are aware that their acts are irrational
(C) neglects to show that the irrational acts perpetrated by humans are not also perpetrated by other animals
(D) presumes, without offering justification, that humans are no worse than other animals
(E) fails to recognize that humans may possess a capacity without displaying it in a given activity

16. "Good hunter" and "bad hunter" are standard terms in the study of cats. Good hunters can kill prey that weigh up to half their body weight. All good hunters have a high muscle-to-fat ratio. Most wild cats are good hunters, but some domestic cats are good hunters as well.

If the statements above are true, which one of the following must also be true?

(A) Some cats that have a high muscle-to-fat ratio are not good hunters.
(B) A smaller number of domestic cats than wild cats have a high muscle-to-fat ratio.
(C) All cats that are bad hunters have a low muscle-to-fat ratio.
(D) Some cats that have a high muscle-to-fat ratio are domestic.
(E) All cats that have a high muscle-to-fat ratio can kill prey that weigh up to half their body weight.

GO ON TO THE NEXT PAGE.

17. Ethicist: The penalties for drunk driving are far more severe when the drunk driver accidentally injures people than when no one is injured. Moral responsibility for an action depends solely on the intentions underlying the action and not on the action's results. Therefore, legal responsibility, depending as it does in at least some cases on factors other than the agent's intentions, is different than moral responsibility.

The claim that the penalties for drunk driving are far more severe when the drunk driver accidentally injures people than when no one is injured plays which one of the following roles in the ethicist's argument?

(A) It is a premise offered in support of the claim that legal responsibility for an action is based solely upon features of the action that are generally unintended by the agent.
(B) It is offered as an illustration of the claim that the criteria of legal responsibility for an action include but are not the same as those for moral responsibility.
(C) It is offered as an illustration of the claim that people may be held morally responsible for an action for which they are not legally responsible.
(D) It is a premise offered in support of the claim that legal responsibility depends in at least some cases on factors other than the agent's intentions.
(E) It is a premise offered in support of the claim that moral responsibility depends solely on the intentions underlying the action and not on the action's result.

18. Columnist: Taking a strong position on an issue makes one likely to misinterpret or ignore additional evidence that conflicts with one's stand. But in order to understand an issue fully, it is essential to consider such evidence impartially. Thus, it is best not to take a strong position on an issue unless one has already considered all important evidence conflicting with that position.

The columnist's reasoning most closely conforms to which one of the following principles?

(A) It is reasonable to take a strong position on an issue if one fully understands the issue and has considered the evidence regarding that issue impartially.
(B) To ensure that one has impartially considered the evidence regarding an issue on which one has taken a strong position, one should avoid misinterpreting or ignoring evidence regarding that issue.
(C) Anyone who does not understand an issue fully should avoid taking a strong position on it.
(D) One should try to understand an issue fully if doing so will help one to avoid misinterpreting or ignoring evidence regarding that issue.
(E) It is reasonable to take a strong position on an issue only if there is important evidence conflicting with that position.

GO ON TO THE NEXT PAGE.

19. The coach of the Eagles used a computer analysis to determine the best combinations of players for games. The analysis revealed that the team has lost only when Jennifer was not playing. Although no computer was needed to discover this information, this sort of information is valuable, and in this case it confirms that Jennifer's presence in the game will ensure that the Eagles will win.

The argument above is most vulnerable to criticism on the grounds that it

(A) infers from the fact that a certain factor is sufficient for a result that the absence of that factor is necessary for the opposite result
(B) presumes, without providing justification, that a player's contribution to a team's win or loss can be reliably quantified and analyzed by computer
(C) draws conclusions about applications of computer analyses to sports from the evidence of a single case
(D) presumes, without providing justification, that occurrences that have coincided in the past must continue to coincide
(E) draws a conclusion about the value of computer analyses from a case in which computer analysis provided no facts beyond what was already known

20. Of the various food containers made of recycled Styrofoam, egg cartons are among the easiest to make. Because egg shells keep the actual food to be consumed from touching the Styrofoam, used Styrofoam need not be as thoroughly cleaned when made into egg cartons as when made into other food containers.

Which one of the following is most strongly supported by the information above?

(A) No food containers other than egg cartons can safely be made of recycled Styrofoam that has not been thoroughly cleaned.
(B) There are some foods that cannot be packaged in recycled Styrofoam no matter how the Styrofoam is recycled.
(C) The main reason Styrofoam must be thoroughly cleaned when recycled is to remove any residual food that has come into contact with the Styrofoam.
(D) Because they are among the easiest food containers to make from recycled Styrofoam, most egg cartons are made from recycled Styrofoam.
(E) Not every type of food container made of recycled Styrofoam is effectively prevented from coming into contact with the food it contains.

GO ON TO THE NEXT PAGE.

21. Most people who become migraine sufferers as adults were prone to bouts of depression as children. Hence it stands to reason that a child who is prone to bouts of depression is likely to suffer migraines during adulthood.

The flawed pattern of reasoning in the argument above is most parallel to that in which one of the following?

(A) Most good-tempered dogs were vaccinated against rabies as puppies. Therefore, a puppy that is vaccinated against rabies is likely to become a good-tempered dog.
(B) Most vicious dogs were ill-treated when young. Hence it can be concluded that a pet owner whose dog is vicious is likely to have treated the dog badly when it was young.
(C) Most well-behaved dogs have undergone obedience training. Thus, if a dog has not undergone obedience training, it will not be well behaved.
(D) Most of the pets taken to veterinarians are dogs. Therefore, it stands to reason that dogs are more prone to illness or accident than are other pets.
(E) Most puppies are taken from their mothers at the age of eight weeks. Thus, a puppy that is older than eight weeks is likely to have been taken from its mother.

22. Student: The publications of Professor Vallejo on the origins of glassblowing have reopened the debate among historians over whether glassblowing originated in Egypt or elsewhere. If Professor Vallejo is correct, there is insufficient evidence for claiming, as most historians have done for many years, that glassblowing began in Egypt. So, despite the fact that the traditional view is still maintained by the majority of historians, if Professor Vallejo is correct, we must conclude that glassblowing originated elsewhere.

Which one of the following is an error in the student's reasoning?

(A) It draws a conclusion that conflicts with the majority opinion of experts.
(B) It presupposes the truth of Professor Vallejo's claims.
(C) It fails to provide criteria for determining adequate historical evidence.
(D) It mistakes the majority view for the traditional view.
(E) It confuses inadequate evidence for truth with evidence for falsity.

23. At Southgate Mall, mattresses are sold only at Mattress Madness. Every mattress at Mattress Madness is on sale at a 20 percent discount. So every mattress for sale at Southgate Mall is on sale at a 20 percent discount.

Which one of the following arguments is most similar in its reasoning to the argument above?

(A) The only food in Diane's apartment is in her refrigerator. All the food she purchased within the past week is in her refrigerator. Therefore, she purchased all the food in her apartment within the past week.
(B) Diane's refrigerator, and all the food in it, is in her apartment. Diane purchased all the food in her refrigerator within the past week. Therefore, she purchased all the food in her apartment within the past week.
(C) All the food in Diane's apartment is in her refrigerator. Diane purchased all the food in her refrigerator within the past week. Therefore, she purchased all the food in her apartment within the past week.
(D) The only food in Diane's apartment is in her refrigerator. Diane purchased all the food in her refrigerator within the past week. Therefore, all the food she purchased within the past week is in her apartment.
(E) The only food that Diane has purchased within the past week is in her refrigerator. All the food that she has purchased within the past week is in her apartment. Therefore, all the food in her apartment is in her refrigerator.

GO ON TO THE NEXT PAGE.

24. There are 1.3 billion cows worldwide, and this population is growing to keep pace with the demand for meat and milk. These cows produce trillions of liters of methane gas yearly, and this methane contributes to global warming. The majority of the world's cows are given relatively low-quality diets even though cows produce less methane when they receive better-quality diets. Therefore, methane production from cows could be kept in check if cows were given better-quality diets.

Which one of the following, if true, adds the most support for the conclusion of the argument?

(A) Cows given good-quality diets produce much more meat and milk than they would produce otherwise.
(B) Carbon and hydrogen, the elements that make up methane, are found in abundance in the components of all types of cow feed.
(C) Most farmers would be willing to give their cows high-quality feed if the cost of that feed were lower.
(D) Worldwide, more methane is produced by cows raised for meat production than by those raised for milk production.
(E) Per liter, methane contributes more to global warming than does carbon dioxide, a gas that is thought to be the most significant contributor to global warming.

25. To face danger solely because doing so affords one a certain pleasure does not constitute courage. Real courage is manifested only when a person, in acting to attain a goal, perseveres in the face of fear prompted by one or more dangers involved.

Which one of the following statements can be properly inferred from the statements above?

(A) A person who must face danger in order to avoid future pain cannot properly be called courageous for doing so.
(B) A person who experiences fear of some aspects of a dangerous situation cannot be said to act courageously in that situation.
(C) A person who happens to derive pleasure from some dangerous activities is not a courageous person.
(D) A person who faces danger in order to benefit others is acting courageously only if the person is afraid of the danger.
(E) A person who has no fear of the situations that everyone else would fear cannot be said to be courageous in any situation.

26. The government will purchase and install new severe weather sirens for this area next year if replacement parts for the old sirens are difficult to obtain. The newspaper claims that public safety in the event of severe weather would be enhanced if new sirens were to be installed. The local company from which replacement parts were purchased last year has since gone out of business. So, if the newspaper is correct, the public will be safer during severe weather in the future.

The argument's conclusion follows logically from its premises if which one of the following is assumed?

(A) If public safety in the event of severe weather is enhanced next year, it will be because new sirens have been purchased.
(B) The newspaper was correct in claiming that public safety in the event of severe weather would be enhanced if new sirens were purchased.
(C) The local company from which replacement parts for the old sirens were purchased last year was the only company in the area that sold them.
(D) Replacement parts for the old sirens will be difficult to obtain if the government cannot obtain them from the company it purchased them from last year.
(E) Because the local company from which replacement parts had been purchased went out of business, the only available parts are of such inferior quality that use of them would make the sirens less reliable.

S T O P

IF YOU FINISH BEFORE TIME IS CALLED, YOU MAY CHECK YOUR WORK ON THIS SECTION ONLY.
DO NOT WORK ON ANY OTHER SECTION IN THE TEST.

SECTION III

Time—35 minutes

23 Questions

Directions: Each group of questions in this section is based on a set of conditions. In answering some of the questions, it may be useful to draw a rough diagram. Choose the response that most accurately and completely answers each question and blacken the corresponding space on your answer sheet.

Questions 1–5

A dance is being choreographed for six dancers: three men—Felipe, Grant, and Hassan—and three women—Jaclyn, Keiko, and Lorena. At no time during the dance will anyone other than the dancers be on stage. Who is on stage and who is off stage at any particular time in the dance is determined by the following constraints:

If Jaclyn is on stage, Lorena is off stage.
If Lorena is off stage, Jaclyn is on stage.
If Felipe is off stage, Jaclyn is also off stage.
If any of the women are on stage, Grant is also on stage.

1. Which one of the following is a list of all of the dancers who could be on stage at a particular time?

(A) Grant
(B) Keiko, Lorena
(C) Grant, Hassan, Lorena
(D) Grant, Hassan, Jaclyn
(E) Felipe, Grant, Jaclyn, Lorena

2. Which one of the following CANNOT be true at any time during the dance?

(A) Felipe and Grant are the only men on stage.
(B) Grant and Hassan are the only men on stage.
(C) Jaclyn is the only woman on stage.
(D) Keiko is the only woman on stage.
(E) Jaclyn and Keiko are the only women on stage.

3. Which one of the following is a complete and accurate list of the dancers any one of whom could be off stage when Jaclyn is on stage?

(A) Lorena
(B) Felipe, Lorena
(C) Hassan, Lorena
(D) Hassan, Keiko
(E) Hassan, Keiko, Lorena

4. If there are more women than men on stage, then exactly how many dancers must be on stage?

(A) five
(B) four
(C) three
(D) two
(E) one

5. What is the minimum number of dancers that must be on stage at any given time?

(A) zero
(B) one
(C) two
(D) three
(E) four

GO ON TO THE NEXT PAGE.

Questions 6–12

A critic has prepared a review of exactly six music CDs—*Headstrong*, *In Flight*, *Nice*, *Quasi*, *Reunion*, and *Sounds Good*. Each CD received a rating of either one, two, three, or four stars, with each CD receiving exactly one rating. Although the ratings were meant to be kept secret until the review was published, the following facts have been leaked to the public:

For each of the ratings, at least one but no more than two of the CDs received that rating.
Headstrong received exactly one more star than *Nice* did.
Either *Headstrong* or *Reunion* received the same number of stars as *In Flight* did.
At most one CD received more stars than *Quasi* did.

6. Which one of the following could be an accurate matching of ratings to the CDs that received those ratings?
   (A) one star: *In Flight*, *Reunion*; two stars: *Nice*; three stars: *Headstrong*; four stars: *Quasi*, *Sounds Good*
   (B) one star: *In Flight*, *Reunion*; two stars: *Quasi*, *Sounds Good*; three stars: *Nice*; four stars: *Headstrong*
   (C) one star: *Nice*; two stars: *Headstrong*; three stars: *In Flight*, *Sounds Good*; four stars: *Quasi*, *Reunion*
   (D) one star: *Nice*, *Sounds Good*; two stars: *In Flight*, *Reunion*; three stars: *Quasi*; four stars: *Headstrong*
   (E) one star: *Sounds Good*; two stars: *Reunion*; three stars: *Nice*, *Quasi*; four stars: *Headstrong*, *In Flight*

7. If *Headstrong* is the only CD that received a rating of two stars, then which one of the following must be true?
   (A) *In Flight* received a rating of three stars.
   (B) *Nice* received a rating of three stars.
   (C) *Quasi* received a rating of three stars.
   (D) *Reunion* received a rating of one star.
   (E) *Sounds Good* received a rating of one star.

8. If *Reunion* received the same rating as *Sounds Good*, then which one of the following must be true?
   (A) *Headstrong* received a rating of two stars.
   (B) *In Flight* received a rating of three stars.
   (C) *Nice* received a rating of two stars.
   (D) *Quasi* received a rating of four stars.
   (E) *Sounds Good* received a rating of one star.

9. If *Nice* and *Reunion* each received a rating of one star, then which one of the following could be true?
   (A) *Headstrong* received a rating of three stars.
   (B) *Headstrong* received a rating of four stars.
   (C) *In Flight* received a rating of three stars.
   (D) *Sounds Good* received a rating of two stars.
   (E) *Sounds Good* received a rating of three stars.

10. Which one of the following CANNOT be true?
    (A) *Quasi* is the only CD that received a rating of three stars.
    (B) *Quasi* is the only CD that received a rating of four stars.
    (C) *Reunion* is the only CD that received a rating of one star.
    (D) *Reunion* is the only CD that received a rating of two stars.
    (E) *Reunion* is the only CD that received a rating of three stars.

11. If *Reunion* is the only CD that received a rating of one star, then which one of the following could be true?
    (A) *Headstrong* received a rating of four stars.
    (B) *In Flight* received a rating of two stars.
    (C) *Nice* received a rating of three stars.
    (D) *Quasi* received a rating of three stars.
    (E) *Sounds Good* received a rating of two stars.

12. Which one of the following CANNOT have received a rating of four stars?
    (A) *Headstrong*
    (B) *In Flight*
    (C) *Quasi*
    (D) *Reunion*
    (E) *Sounds Good*

GO ON TO THE NEXT PAGE.

Questions 13–17

A cake has exactly six layers—lemon, marzipan, orange, raspberry, strawberry, and vanilla. There is exactly one bottom layer (the first layer), and each succeeding layer (from second through sixth) completely covers the layer beneath it. The following conditions must apply:

The raspberry layer is neither immediately above nor immediately below the strawberry layer.
The marzipan layer is immediately above the lemon layer.
The orange layer is above the marzipan layer but below the strawberry layer.

13. Which one of the following could be an accurate list of the layers of the cake, from bottom to top?

(A) lemon, marzipan, orange, strawberry, vanilla, raspberry
(B) lemon, marzipan, orange, strawberry, raspberry, vanilla
(C) marzipan, lemon, raspberry, vanilla, orange, strawberry
(D) raspberry, lemon, marzipan, vanilla, strawberry, orange
(E) raspberry, orange, lemon, marzipan, strawberry, vanilla

14. If the strawberry layer is not immediately above the orange layer, then which one of the following could be true?

(A) The raspberry layer is immediately above the vanilla layer.
(B) The raspberry layer is immediately above the orange layer.
(C) The raspberry layer is immediately below the marzipan layer.
(D) The raspberry layer is the second layer.
(E) The raspberry layer is the top layer.

15. If the strawberry layer is not the top layer, then which one of the following is a complete and accurate list of the layers that could be the vanilla layer?

(A) the first, the second, the third, the fourth, the fifth, the sixth
(B) the second, the third, the fourth, the fifth, the sixth
(C) the third, the fourth, the fifth, the sixth
(D) the fourth, the fifth, the sixth
(E) the fifth, the sixth

16. If the lemon layer is third, then which one of the following could be true?

(A) The vanilla layer is fifth.
(B) The vanilla layer is immediately above the raspberry layer.
(C) The orange layer is not immediately above the marzipan layer.
(D) The raspberry layer is above the marzipan layer.
(E) The strawberry layer is not the top layer.

17. Which one of the following could be an accurate list of the two lowest layers of the cake, listed in order from the bottom up?

(A) lemon, raspberry
(B) vanilla, raspberry
(C) marzipan, raspberry
(D) raspberry, marzipan
(E) raspberry, strawberry

GO ON TO THE NEXT PAGE.

Questions 18–23

A panel reviews six contract bids—H, J, K, R, S, and T. No two bids have the same cost. Exactly one of the bids is accepted. The following conditions must hold:

The accepted bid is either K or R and is either the second or the third lowest in cost.
H is lower in cost than each of J and K.
If J is the fourth lowest in cost, then J is lower in cost than each of S and T.
If J is not the fourth lowest in cost, then J is higher in cost than each of S and T.
Either R or S is the fifth lowest in cost.

18. Which one of the following could be an accurate list of the bids in order from lowest to highest in cost?

(A) T, K, H, S, J, R
(B) H, T, K, S, R, J
(C) H, S, T, K, R, J
(D) H, K, S, J, R, T
(E) H, J, K, R, S, T

19. Which one of the following bids CANNOT be the fourth lowest in cost?

(A) H
(B) J
(C) K
(D) R
(E) T

20. Which one of the following bids CANNOT be the second lowest in cost?

(A) H
(B) J
(C) K
(D) R
(E) T

21. If R is the accepted bid, then which one of the following must be true?

(A) T is the lowest in cost.
(B) K is the second lowest in cost.
(C) R is the third lowest in cost.
(D) S is the fifth lowest in cost.
(E) J is the highest in cost.

22. Which one of the following must be true?

(A) H is lower in cost than S.
(B) H is lower in cost than T.
(C) K is lower in cost than J.
(D) S is lower in cost than J.
(E) S is lower in cost than K.

23. If R is the lowest in cost, then which one of the following could be false?

(A) J is the highest in cost.
(B) S is the fifth lowest in cost.
(C) K is the third lowest in cost.
(D) H is the second lowest in cost.
(E) K is the accepted bid.

S T O P

IF YOU FINISH BEFORE TIME IS CALLED, YOU MAY CHECK YOUR WORK ON THIS SECTION ONLY.
DO NOT WORK ON ANY OTHER SECTION IN THE TEST.

SECTION IV

Time—35 minutes

25 Questions

Directions: The questions in this section are based on the reasoning contained in brief statements or passages. For some questions, more than one of the choices could conceivably answer the question. However, you are to choose the best answer; that is, the response that most accurately and completely answers the question. You should not make assumptions that are by commonsense standards implausible, superfluous, or incompatible with the passage. After you have chosen the best answer, blacken the corresponding space on your answer sheet.

1. Editorialist: Advertisers devote millions of dollars to the attempt to instill attitudes and desires that lead people to purchase particular products, and advertisers' techniques have been adopted by political strategists in democratic countries, who are paid to manipulate public opinion in every political campaign. Thus, the results of elections in democratic countries cannot be viewed as representing the unadulterated preferences of the people.

   Which one of the following, if true, most strengthens the editorialist's argument?

   (A) Public opinion can be manipulated more easily by officials of nondemocratic governments than by those of democratic governments.
   (B) Advertisers' techniques are often apparent to the people to whom the advertisements are directed.
   (C) Many democratic countries have laws limiting the amount that may be spent on political advertisements in any given election.
   (D) People who neither watch television nor read any print media are more likely to vote than people who do one or both of these activities.
   (E) Unlike advertisements for consumer products, most of which only reinforce existing beliefs, political advertisements often change voters' beliefs.

2. Kris: Years ago, the chemical industry claimed that technological progress cannot occur without pollution. Today, in the name of technological progress, the cellular phone industry manufactures and promotes a product that causes environmental pollution in the form of ringing phones and loud conversations in public places. Clearly, the cellular industry must be regulated, just as the chemical industry is now regulated.

   Terry: That's absurd. Chemical pollution can cause physical harm, but the worst harm that cellular phones can cause is annoyance.

   Terry responds to Kris's argument by doing which one of the following?

   (A) questioning the reliability of the source of crucial information in Kris's argument
   (B) attacking the accuracy of the evidence about the chemical industry that Kris puts forward
   (C) arguing that an alleged cause of a problem is actually an effect of that problem
   (D) questioning the strength of the analogy on which Kris's argument is based
   (E) rejecting Kris's interpretation of the term "technological progress"

GO ON TO THE NEXT PAGE.

3. Researcher: Any country can determine which type of public school system will work best for it by investigating the public school systems of other countries. Nationwide tests could be given in each country and other countries could adopt the system of the country that has the best scores on these tests.

Which one of the following is an assumption required by the researcher's argument?

(A) A type of school system that works well in one country will work well in any other country.
(B) A number of children in each country in the research sample are educated in private schools.
(C) If two countries performed differently on these nationwide tests, further testing could determine what features of the school systems account for the differences.
(D) Most countries in the research sample already administer nationwide tests to their public school students.
(E) The nationwide testing in the research sample will target as closely as possible grade levels that are comparable in the different countries in the research sample.

4. Ray: Cynthia claims that her car's trunk popped open because the car hit a pothole. Yet, she also acknowledged that the trunk in that car had popped open on several other occasions, and that on none of those other occasions had the car hit a pothole. Therefore, Cynthia mistakenly attributed the trunk's popping open to the car's having hit a pothole.

The reasoning in Ray's argument is most vulnerable to criticism in that the argument

(A) fails to consider the possibility that the trunks of other cars may pop open when those cars hit potholes
(B) fails to consider the possibility that potholes can have negative effects on a car's engine
(C) presumes, without providing justification, that if one event causes another, it cannot also cause a third event
(D) fails to consider the possibility that one type of event can be caused in many different ways
(E) presumes the truth of the claim that it is trying to establish

5. Journalists agree universally that lying is absolutely taboo. Yet, while many reporters claim that spoken words ought to be quoted verbatim, many others believe that tightening a quote from a person who is interviewed is legitimate on grounds that the speaker's remarks would have been more concise if the speaker had written them instead. Also, many reporters believe that, to expose wrongdoing, failing to identify oneself as a reporter is permissible, while others condemn such behavior as a type of lying.

Which one of the following is most supported by the information above?

(A) Reporters make little effort to behave ethically.
(B) There is no correct answer to the question of whether lying in a given situation is right or wrong.
(C) Omission of the truth is the same thing as lying.
(D) Since lying is permissible in some situations, reporters are mistaken to think that it is absolutely taboo.
(E) Reporters disagree on what sort of behavior qualifies as lying.

6. Wood-frame houses withstand earthquakes far better than masonry houses do, because wooden frames have some flexibility; their walls can better handle lateral forces. In a recent earthquake, however, a wood-frame house was destroyed, while the masonry house next door was undamaged.

Which one of the following, if true, most helps to explain the results of the earthquake described above?

(A) In earthquake-prone areas, there are many more wood-frame houses than masonry houses.
(B) In earthquake-prone areas, there are many more masonry houses than wood-frame houses.
(C) The walls of the wood-frame house had once been damaged in a flood.
(D) The masonry house was far more expensive than the wood-frame house.
(E) No structure is completely impervious to the destructive lateral forces exerted by earthquakes.

GO ON TO THE NEXT PAGE.

7. In an experiment, biologists repeatedly shone a bright light into a tank containing a sea snail and simultaneously shook the tank. The snail invariably responded by tensing its muscular "foot," a typical reaction in sea snails to ocean turbulence. After several repetitions of this procedure, the snail tensed its "foot" whenever the biologists shone the light into its tank, even when the tank was not simultaneously shaken. Therefore, the snail must have learned to associate the shining of the bright light with the shaking of the tank.

Which one of the following is an assumption required by the argument?

(A) All sea snails react to ocean turbulence in the same way as the sea snail in the experiment did.
(B) Sea snails are not ordinarily exposed to bright lights such as the one used in the biologists' experiment.
(C) The sea snail used in the experiment did not differ significantly from other members of its species in its reaction to external stimuli.
(D) The appearance of a bright light alone would ordinarily not result in the sea snail's tensing its "foot."
(E) Tensing of the muscular "foot" in sea snails is an instinctual rather than a learned response to ocean turbulence.

8. The university's purchasing department is highly efficient overall. We must conclude that each of its twelve staff members is highly efficient.

Which one of the following arguments exhibits flawed reasoning most similar to that exhibited by the argument above?

(A) The employees at this fast-food restaurant are the youngest and most inexperienced of any fast-food workers in the city. Given this, it seems obvious that customers will have to wait longer for their food at this restaurant than at others.
(B) The outside audit of our public relations department has exposed serious deficiencies in the competence of each member of that department. We must conclude that the department is inadequate for our needs.
(C) This supercomputer is the most sophisticated—and the most expensive—ever built. It must be that each of its components is the most sophisticated and expensive available.
(D) Literature critics have lavished praise on every chapter of this book. In light of their reviews, one must conclude that the book is excellent.
(E) Passing a driving test is a condition of employment at the city's transportation department. It follows that each of the department's employees has passed the test.

9. The Jacksons regularly receive wrong-number calls for Sara, whose phone number was misprinted in a directory. Sara contacted the Jacksons, informing them of the misprint and her correct number. The Jacksons did not lead Sara to believe that they would pass along the correct number, but it would be helpful to Sara and of no difficulty for them to do so. Thus, although it would not be wrong for the Jacksons to tell callers trying to reach Sara merely that they have dialed the wrong number, it would be laudable if the Jacksons passed along Sara's correct number.

Which one of the following principles, if valid, most helps to justify the reasoning in the argument?

(A) It is always laudable to do something helpful to someone, but not doing so would be wrong only if one has led that person to believe one would do it.
(B) Being helpful to someone is laudable whenever it is not wrong to do so.
(C) If one can do something that would be helpful to someone else and it would be easy to do, then it is laudable and not wrong to do so.
(D) Doing something for someone is laudable only if it is difficult for one to do so and it is wrong for one not to do so.
(E) The only actions that are laudable are those that it would not be wrong to refrain from doing, whether or not it is difficult to do so.

GO ON TO THE NEXT PAGE.

10. Albert: The government has proposed new automobile emissions regulations designed to decrease the amount of polycyclic aromatic hydrocarbons (PAHs) released into the atmosphere by automobile exhaust. I don't see the need for such regulations; although PAHs are suspected of causing cancer, a causal link has never been proven.

Erin: Scientists also blame PAHs for 10,000 premature deaths in this country each year from lung and heart disease. So the proposed regulations would save thousands of lives.

Which one of the following, if true, is the logically strongest counter that Albert can make to Erin's argument?

(A) Most automobile manufacturers are strongly opposed to additional automobile emissions regulations.
(B) It is not known whether PAHs are a causal factor in any diseases other than heart and lung disease and cancer.
(C) Even if no new automobile emissions regulations are enacted, the amount of PAHs released into the atmosphere will decrease if automobile usage declines.
(D) Most of the PAHs released into the atmosphere are the result of wear and tear on automobile tires.
(E) PAHs are one of several components of automobile exhaust that scientists suspect of causing cancer.

11. Australia has considerably fewer species of carnivorous mammals than any other continent does but about as many carnivorous reptile species as other continents do. This is probably a consequence of the unusual sparseness of Australia's ecosystems. To survive, carnivorous mammals must eat much more than carnivorous reptiles need to; thus carnivorous mammals are at a disadvantage in ecosystems in which there is relatively little food.

Which one of the following most accurately expresses the main conclusion of the argument?

(A) Australia has considerably fewer species of carnivorous mammals than any other continent does but about as many carnivorous reptile species as other continents do.
(B) In ecosystems in which there is relatively little food carnivorous mammals are at a disadvantage relative to carnivorous reptiles.
(C) The unusual sparseness of Australia's ecosystems is probably the reason Australia has considerably fewer carnivorous mammal species than other continents do but about as many carnivorous reptile species.
(D) The reason that carnivorous mammals are at a disadvantage in ecosystems in which there is relatively little food is that they must eat much more in order to survive than carnivorous reptiles need to.
(E) Because Australia's ecosystems are unusually sparse, carnivorous mammals there are at a disadvantage relative to carnivorous reptiles.

12. Linguist: The Sapir-Whorf hypothesis states that a society's world view is influenced by the language or languages its members speak. But this hypothesis does not have the verifiability of hypotheses of physical science, since it is not clear that the hypothesis could be tested.

If the linguist's statements are accurate, which one of the following is most supported by them?

(A) The Sapir-Whorf hypothesis is probably false.
(B) Only the hypotheses of physical science are verifiable.
(C) Only verifiable hypotheses should be seriously considered.
(D) We do not know whether the Sapir-Whorf hypothesis is true or false.
(E) Only the hypotheses of physical science should be taken seriously.

GO ON TO THE NEXT PAGE.

13. The highest mountain ranges are formed by geological forces that raise the earth's crust: two continent-bearing tectonic plates of comparable density collide and crumple upward, causing a thickening of the crust. The erosive forces of wind and precipitation inexorably wear these mountains down. Yet the highest mountain ranges tend to be found in places where these erosive forces are most prevalent.

Which one of the following, if true, most helps to reconcile the apparent conflict described above?

(A) Patterns of extreme wind and precipitation often result from the dramatic differences in elevation commonly found in the highest mountain ranges.
(B) The highest mountain ranges have less erosion-reducing vegetation near their peaks than do other mountain ranges.
(C) Some lower mountain ranges are formed by a different collision process, whereby one tectonic plate simply slides beneath another of lesser density.
(D) The amount of precipitation that a given region of the earth receives may vary considerably over the lifetime of an average mountain range.
(E) The thickening of the earth's crust associated with the formation of the highest mountain ranges tends to cause the thickened portion of the crust to sink over time.

14. Expert: A group of researchers claims to have shown that for an antenna to work equally well at all frequencies, it must be symmetrical in shape and have what is known as a fractal structure. Yet the new antenna developed by these researchers, which satisfies both of these criteria, in fact works better at frequencies below 250 megahertz than at frequencies above 250 megahertz. Hence, their claim is incorrect.

The reasoning in the expert's argument is flawed because the argument

(A) fails to provide a definition of the technical term "fractal"
(B) contradicts itself by denying in its conclusion the claim of scientific authorities that it relies on in its premises
(C) concludes that a claim is false merely on the grounds that there is insufficient evidence that it is true
(D) interprets an assertion that certain conditions are necessary as asserting that those conditions are sufficient
(E) takes for granted that there are only two possible alternatives, either below or above 250 megahertz

15. Singletary: We of Citizens for Cycling Freedom object to the city's new ordinance requiring bicyclists to wear helmets. If the city wanted to become a safer place for cyclists, it would not require helmets. Instead, it would construct more bicycle lanes and educate drivers about bicycle safety. Thus, passage of the ordinance reveals that the city is more concerned with the appearance of safety than with bicyclists' actual safety.

Which one of the following most accurately describes the role played in Singletary's argument by the statement that mentions driver education?

(A) It is cited as evidence for the claim that the city misunderstands the steps necessary for ensuring bicyclists' safety.
(B) It is used as partial support for a claim about the motivation of the city.
(C) It is offered as evidence of the total ineffectiveness of the helmet ordinance.
(D) It is offered as an example of further measures the city will take to ensure bicyclists' safety.
(E) It is presented as an illustration of the city's overriding interest in its public image.

16. Max: Although doing so would be very costly, humans already possess the technology to build colonies on the Moon. As the human population increases and the amount of unoccupied space available for constructing housing on Earth diminishes, there will be a growing economic incentive to construct such colonies to house some of the population. Thus, such colonies will almost certainly be built and severe overcrowding on Earth relieved.

Max's argument is most vulnerable to criticism on which one of the following grounds?

(A) It takes for granted that the economic incentive to construct colonies on the Moon will grow sufficiently to cause such a costly project to be undertaken.
(B) It takes for granted that the only way of relieving severe overcrowding on Earth is the construction of colonies on the Moon.
(C) It overlooks the possibility that colonies will be built on the Moon regardless of any economic incentive to construct such colonies to house some of the population.
(D) It overlooks the possibility that colonies on the Moon might themselves quickly become overcrowded.
(E) It takes for granted that none of the human population would prefer to live on the Moon unless Earth were seriously overcrowded.

GO ON TO THE NEXT PAGE.

17. Ethicist: An action is wrong if it violates a rule of the society in which the action is performed and that rule promotes the general welfare of people in the society. An action is right if it is required by a rule of the society in which the action is performed and the rule promotes the general welfare of the people in that society.

Which one of the following judgments most closely conforms to the principle cited by the ethicist?

(A) Amelia's society has a rule against lying. However, she lies anyway in order to protect an innocent person from being harmed. While the rule against lying promotes the general welfare of people in the society, Amelia's lie is not wrong because she is preventing harm.
(B) Jordan lives in a society that requires its members to eat certain ceremonial foods during festivals. Jordan disobeys this rule. Because the rule is not detrimental to the general welfare of people in her society, Jordan's disobedience is wrong.
(C) Elgin obeys a certain rule of his society. Because Elgin knows that this particular rule is detrimental to the general welfare of the people in his society, his obedience is wrong.
(D) Dahlia always has a cup of coffee before getting dressed in the morning. Dahlia's action is right because it does not violate any rule of the society in which she lives.
(E) Edward's society requires children to take care of their aged parents. Edward's taking care of his aged parents is the right thing for him to do because the rule requiring this action promotes the general welfare of people in the society.

18. Teresa: If their goal is to maximize profits, film studios should concentrate on producing big-budget films rather than small-budget ones. For, unlike big-budget films, small-budget films never attract mass audiences. While small-budget films are less expensive to produce and, hence, involve less risk of unprofitability than big-budget films, low production costs do not guarantee the highest possible profits.

Which one of the following is an assumption required by Teresa's argument?

(A) Each big-budget film is guaranteed to attract a mass audience.
(B) A film studio cannot make both big-budget films and small-budget films.
(C) A film studio will not maximize its profits unless at least some of its films attract mass audiences.
(D) It is impossible to produce a big-budget film in a financially efficient manner.
(E) A film studio's primary goal should be to maximize profits.

19. Cyclists in the Tour de France are extremely physically fit: all of the winners of this race have had abnormal physiological constitutions. Typical of the abnormal physiology of these athletes are exceptional lung capacity and exceptionally powerful hearts. Tests conducted on last year's winner did not reveal an exceptionally powerful heart. That cyclist must, therefore, have exceptional lung capacity.

The reasoning in the argument is most vulnerable to criticism on the grounds that it overlooks the possibility that

(A) having exceptional lung capacity and an exceptionally powerful heart is an advantage in cycling
(B) some winners of the Tour de France have neither exceptional lung capacity nor exceptionally powerful hearts
(C) cyclists with normal lung capacity rarely have exceptionally powerful hearts
(D) the exceptional lung capacity and exceptionally powerful hearts of Tour de France winners are due to training
(E) the notions of exceptional lung capacity and exceptional heart function are relative to the physiology of most cyclists

20. TV meteorologist: Our station's weather forecasts are more useful and reliable than those of the most popular news station in the area. After all, the most important question for viewers in this area is whether it will rain, and on most of the occasions when we have forecast rain for the next day, we have been right. The same cannot be said for either of our competitors.

Which one of the following, if true, most strengthens the meteorologist's argument?

(A) The meteorologist's station forecast rain more often than did the most popular news station in the area.
(B) The less popular of the competing stations does not employ any full-time meteorologists.
(C) The most popular news station in the area is popular because of its investigative news reports.
(D) The meteorologist's station has a policy of not making weather forecasts more than three days in advance.
(E) On most of the occasions when the meteorologist's station forecast that it would not rain, at least one of its competitors also forecast that it would not rain.

GO ON TO THE NEXT PAGE.

21. In an experiment, volunteers witnessed a simulated crime. After they witnessed the simulation the volunteers were first questioned by a lawyer whose goal was to get them to testify inaccurately about the event. They were then cross-examined by another lawyer whose goal was to cause them to correct the inaccuracies in their testimony. The witnesses who gave testimony containing fewer inaccurate details than most of the other witnesses during the first lawyer's questioning also gave testimony containing a greater number of inaccurate details than most of the other witnesses during cross-examination.

Which one of the following, if true, most helps to resolve the apparent conflict in the results concerning the witnesses who gave testimony containing fewer inaccurate details during the first lawyer's questioning?

(A) These witnesses were more observant about details than were most of the other witnesses.
(B) These witnesses had better memories than did most of the other witnesses.
(C) These witnesses were less inclined than most of the other witnesses to be influenced in their testimony by the nature of the questioning.
(D) These witnesses were unclear about the details at first but then began to remember more accurately as they answered questions.
(E) These witnesses tended to give testimony containing more details than most of the other witnesses.

22. The short-term and long-term interests of a business often conflict; when they do, the morally preferable act is usually the one that serves the long-term interest. Because of this, businesses often have compelling reasons to execute the morally preferable act.

Which one of the following, if assumed, enables the conclusion of the argument to be properly drawn?

(A) A business's moral interests do not always provide compelling reasons for executing an act.
(B) A business's long-term interests often provide compelling reasons for executing an act.
(C) The morally preferable act for a business to execute and the long-term interests of the business seldom conflict.
(D) The morally preferable act for a business to execute and the short-term interests of the business usually conflict.
(E) When a business's short-term and long-term interests conflict, morality alone is rarely the overriding consideration.

23. Politician: The current crisis in mathematics education must be overcome if we are to remain competitive in the global economy. Alleviating this crisis requires the employment of successful teaching methods. No method of teaching a subject can succeed that does not get students to spend a significant amount of time outside of class studying that subject.

Which one of the following statements follows logically from the statements above?

(A) If students spend a significant amount of time outside of class studying mathematics, the current crisis in mathematics education will be overcome.
(B) The current crisis in mathematics education will not be overcome unless students spend a significant amount of time outside of class studying mathematics.
(C) Few subjects are as important as mathematics to the effort to remain competitive in the global economy.
(D) Only if we succeed in remaining competitive in the global economy will students spend a significant amount of time outside of class studying mathematics.
(E) Students' spending a significant amount of time outside of class studying mathematics would help us to remain competitive in the global economy.

GO ON TO THE NEXT PAGE.

24. Downtown Petropolis boasted over 100 large buildings 5 years ago. Since then, 60 of those buildings have been demolished. Since the number of large buildings in a downtown is an indicator of the economic health of that downtown, it is clear that downtown Petropolis is in a serious state of economic decline.

Which one of the following is an assumption required by the argument?

(A) The demolitions that have taken place during the past 5 years have been evenly spread over that period.
(B) There have never been significantly more than 100 large buildings in downtown Petropolis.
(C) Most of the buildings demolished during the past 5 years were torn down because they were structurally unsound.
(D) The large buildings demolished over the past 5 years have been replaced with small buildings built on the same sites.
(E) Significantly fewer than 60 new large buildings have been built in downtown Petropolis during the past 5 years.

25. To get the free dessert, one must order an entree and a salad. But anyone who orders either an entree or a salad can receive a free soft drink. Thus, anyone who is not eligible for a free soft drink is not eligible for a free dessert.

The reasoning in the argument above is most similar to the reasoning in which one of the following arguments?

(A) To get an executive position at Teltech, one needs a university diploma and sales experience. But anyone who has worked at Teltech for more than six months who does not have sales experience has a university diploma. Thus, one cannot get an executive position at Teltech unless one has worked there for six months.
(B) To be elected class president, one must be well liked and well known. Anyone who is well liked or well known has something better to do than run for class president. Therefore, no one who has something better to do will be elected class president.
(C) To grow good azaleas, one needs soil that is both rich in humus and low in acidity. Anyone who has soil that is rich in humus or low in acidity can grow blueberries. So, anyone who cannot grow blueberries cannot grow good azaleas.
(D) To drive to Weller, one must take the highway or take Old Mill Road. Anyone who drives to Weller on the highway will miss the beautiful scenery. Thus, one cannot see the beautiful scenery without taking Old Mill Road to Weller.
(E) To get a discount on ice cream, one must buy frozen raspberries and ice cream together. Anyone who buys ice cream or raspberries will get a coupon for a later purchase. So, anyone who does not get the discount on ice cream will not get a coupon for a later purchase.

S T O P

IF YOU FINISH BEFORE TIME IS CALLED, YOU MAY CHECK YOUR WORK ON THIS SECTION ONLY. DO NOT WORK ON ANY OTHER SECTION IN THE TEST.

Acknowledgment is made to the following sources from which material has been adapted for use in this test booklet:

Irving L. Janis, *Groupthink: Psychological Studies of Policy Decisions and Fiascoes.* ©1982 by Houghton Mifflin Co.

David R. Johnson and David Post, "Law and Borders—The Rise of Law in Cyberspace." ©1996 by the Board of Trustees of the Leland Stanford Jr. University.

David Krasner, "Rewriting the Body: Aida Overton Walker and the Social Formation of Cakewalking." ©1996 by the American Society for Theatre Research.

LSAT WRITING SAMPLE TOPIC

Directions: The scenario presented below describes two choices, either one of which can be supported on the basis of the information given. Your essay should consider both choices and argue for one over the other, based on the two specified criteria and the facts provided. There is no "right" or "wrong" choice: a reasonable argument can be made for either.

Carol Hudson, the concert coordinator for Jordan Arena, a very large entertainment venue, must schedule one of two musical groups to perform on an open date in the arena's schedule. Using the facts below, write an essay in which you argue for one group over the other based on the following two criteria:

- Carol wants to continue Jordan Arena's long-standing record of sold-out concerts.
- Carol wants to attract an audience at least a third of whom are aged 14 to 24.

The first group, The Mustangs, plays cutting-edge music of a sort popular with the 14- to 24-year-old demographic. The Mustangs, gradually growing in popularity, have filled steadily larger venues. The group recently sold out in record time its largest venue ever, the Midvale Arena, located in a large metropolitan area. Jorden Arena, which is located in a different large metropolitan area, has twice the seating capacity of Midvale Arena. The Mustangs' video of the cover song for their debut album is scheduled for release a few weeks before the Jordan Arena concert date. If the music video is a success, as many expect, The Mustangs' popularity will rapidly soar.

The second group, Radar Love, is an aging but well-established hard rock band, which has consistently appealed to a wide-ranging audience. It has sold out all appearances for the past 20 years, including venues considerably larger than Jordan Arena. A song on the group's latest album quickly became a runaway hit among the 14- to 24-year-old demographic, the first time the group has appealed to this extent to this audience. Twenty percent of the audience at the group's most recent concert, which featured songs from the group's latest album, constituted 14- to 24-year-olds, a significant increase from prior concerts.

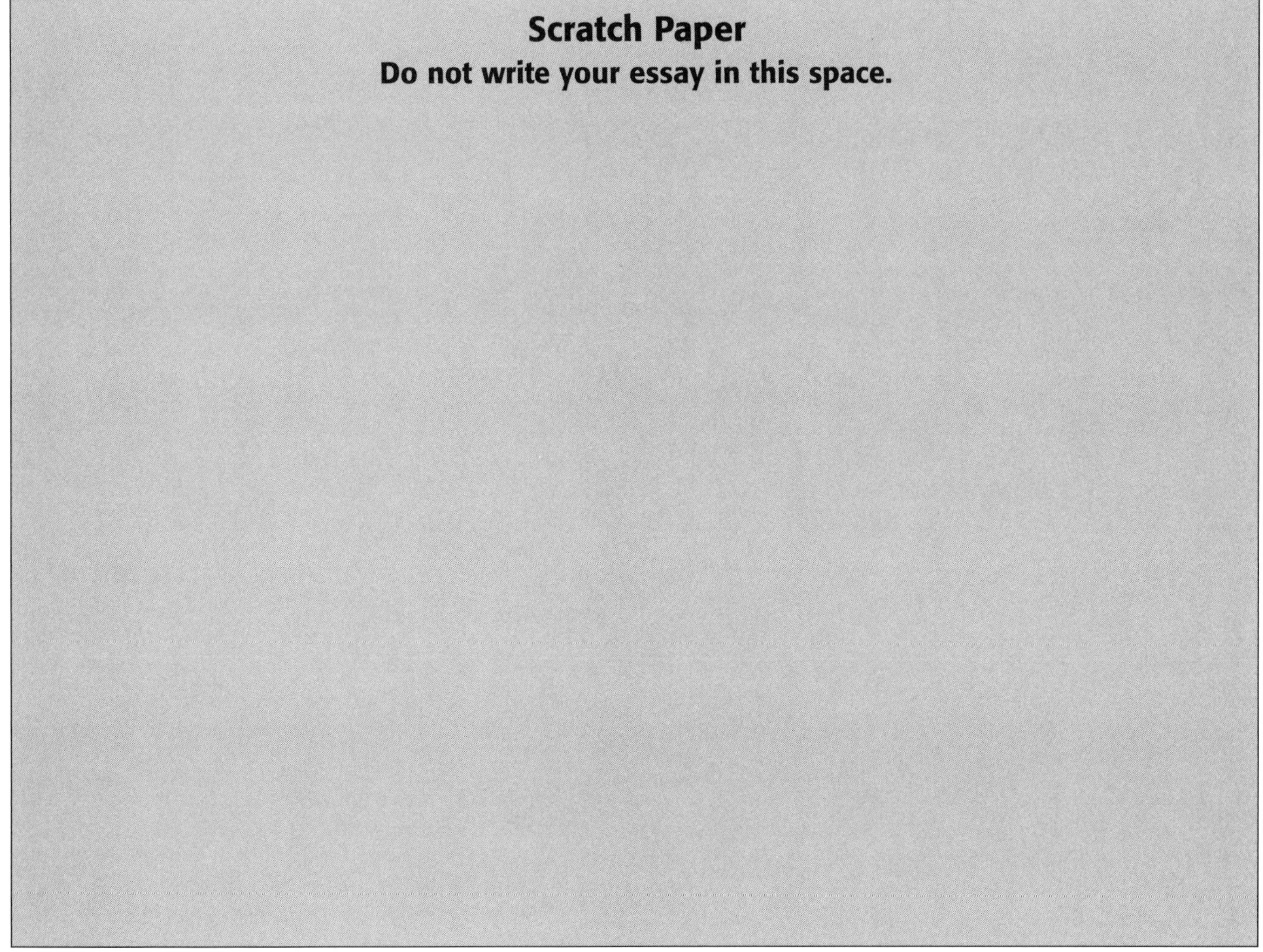
Scratch Paper
Do not write your essay in this space.

Directions:

1. Use the Answer Key on the next page to check your answers.

2. Use the Scoring Worksheet below to compute your raw score.

3. Use the Score Conversion Chart to convert your raw score into the 120–180 scale.

Scoring Worksheet

1. Enter the number of questions you answered correctly in each section

	Number Correct
SECTION I.	______
SECTION II	______
SECTION III	______
SECTION IV	______

2. Enter the sum here: ______ **This is your Raw Score.**

Conversion Chart

For Converting Raw Score to the 120–180 LSAT Scaled Score
LSAT PrepTest 54

Reported Score	Lowest Raw Score	Highest Raw Score
180	99	101
179	98	98
178	—*	—*
177	97	97
176	96	96
175	95	95
174	—*	—*
173	94	94
172	93	93
171	92	92
170	91	91
169	90	90
168	89	89
167	88	88
166	87	87
165	85	86
164	84	84
163	83	83
162	81	82
161	80	80
160	78	79
159	76	77
158	75	75
157	73	74
156	71	72
155	69	70
154	67	68
153	66	66
152	64	65
151	62	63
150	60	61
149	58	59
148	56	57
147	54	55
146	52	53
145	50	51
144	49	49
143	47	48
142	45	46
141	43	44
140	42	42
139	40	41
138	38	39
137	37	37
136	35	36
135	33	34
134	32	32
133	30	31
132	29	29
131	28	28
130	26	27
129	25	25
128	24	24
127	23	23
126	21	22
125	20	20
124	19	19
123	18	18
122	16	17
121	—*	—*
120	0	15

*There is no raw score that will produce this scaled score for this PrepTest.

SECTION I

1.	A	8.	E	15.	C	22.	C
2.	C	9.	B	16.	E	23.	B
3.	D	10.	B	17.	E	24.	E
4.	D	11.	C	18.	A	25.	E
5.	E	12.	A	19.	A	26.	A
6.	B	13.	C	20.	A	27.	B
7.	E	14.	D	21.	C		

SECTION II

1.	D	8.	A	15.	E	22.	E
2.	E	9.	A	16.	D	23.	C
3.	A	10.	B	17.	D	24.	A
4.	E	11.	B	18.	C	25.	D
5.	B	12.	D	19.	D	26.	D
6.	C	13.	B	20.	E		
7.	C	14.	C	21.	A		

SECTION III

1.	C	8.	D	15.	E	22.	C
2.	D	9.	E	16.	B	23.	A
3.	E	10.	D	17.	B		
4.	C	11.	E	18.	B		
5.	C	12.	B	19.	A		
6.	A	13.	A	20.	B		
7.	A	14.	B	21.	D		

SECTION IV

1.	E	8.	C	15.	B	22.	B
2.	D	9.	A	16.	A	23.	B
3.	A	10.	D	17.	E	24.	E
4.	D	11.	C	18.	C	25.	C
5.	E	12.	D	19.	B		
6.	C	13.	A	20.	A		
7.	D	14.	D	21.	C		

Experimental Section Answer Key
June 1999, PrepTest 28, Section 3

1.	D	8.	B	15.	B	22.	B
2.	E	9.	A	16.	B	23.	D
3.	E	10.	A	17.	B	24.	D
4.	A	11.	C	18.	C	25.	E
5.	C	12.	C	19.	A	26.	D
6.	B	13.	E	20.	B		
7.	C	14.	A	21.	D		

PrepTest 55
October 2008

SECTION I

Time—35 minutes

25 Questions

Directions: The questions in this section are based on the reasoning contained in brief statements or passages. For some questions, more than one of the choices could conceivably answer the question. However, you are to choose the best answer; that is, the response that most accurately and completely answers the question. You should not make assumptions that are by commonsense standards implausible, superfluous, or incompatible with the passage. After you have chosen the best answer, blacken the corresponding space on your answer sheet.

1. The editor of a magazine has pointed out several errors of spelling and grammar committed on a recent TV program. But she can hardly be trusted to pass judgment on such matters: similar errors have been found in her own magazine.

   The flawed reasoning in the argument above is most similar to that in which one of the following?

   (A) Your newspaper cannot be trusted with the prerogative to criticize the ethics of our company: you misspelled our president's name.
   (B) Your news program cannot be trusted to judge our hiring practices as unfair: you yourselves unfairly discriminate in hiring and promotion decisions.
   (C) Your regulatory agency cannot condemn our product as unsafe: selling it is allowed under an existing-product clause.
   (D) Your coach cannot be trusted to judge our swimming practices: he accepted a lucrative promotional deal from a soft-drink company.
   (E) Your teen magazine should not run this feature on problems afflicting modern high schools: your revenue depends on not alienating the high school audience.

2. Soaking dried beans overnight before cooking them reduces cooking time. However, cooking without presoaking yields plumper beans. Therefore, when a bean dish's quality is more important than the need to cook that dish quickly, beans should not be presoaked.

   Which one of the following is an assumption required by the argument?

   (A) Plumper beans enhance the quality of a dish.
   (B) There are no dishes whose quality improves with faster cooking.
   (C) A dish's appearance is as important as its taste.
   (D) None of the other ingredients in the dish need to be presoaked.
   (E) The plumper the bean, the better it tastes.

3. Durth: Increasingly, businesses use direct mail advertising instead of paying for advertising space in newspapers, in magazines, or on billboards. This practice is annoying and also immoral. Most direct mail advertisements are thrown out without ever being read, and the paper on which they are printed is wasted. If anyone else wasted this much paper, it would be considered unconscionable.

   Which one of the following most accurately describes Durth's method of reasoning?

   (A) presenting a specific counterexample to the contention that direct mail advertising is not immoral
   (B) asserting that there would be very undesirable consequences if direct mail advertising became a more widespread practice than it is now
   (C) claiming that direct mail advertising is immoral because one of its results would be deemed immoral in other contexts
   (D) basing a conclusion on the claim that direct mail advertising is annoying to those who receive it
   (E) asserting that other advertising methods do not have the negative effects of direct mail advertising

GO ON TO THE NEXT PAGE.

4. Among the various models of Delta vacuum cleaners, one cannot accurately predict how effectively a particular model cleans simply by determining how powerful its motor is. The efficiency of dust filtration systems varies significantly, even between models of Delta vacuum cleaners equipped with identically powerful motors.

The argument's conclusion is properly drawn if which one of the following is assumed?

(A) For each Delta vacuum cleaner, the efficiency of its dust filtration system has a significant impact on how effectively it cleans.
(B) One can accurately infer how powerful a Delta vacuum cleaner's motor is from the efficiency of the vacuum cleaner's dust filtration system.
(C) All Delta vacuum cleaners that clean equally effectively have identically powerful motors.
(D) For any two Delta vacuum cleaners with equally efficient dust filtration systems, the one with the more powerful motor cleans more effectively.
(E) One cannot accurately assess how effectively any Delta vacuum cleaner cleans without knowing how powerful that vacuum cleaner's motor is.

5. Many scientists believe that bipedal locomotion (walking on two feet) evolved in early hominids in response to the move from life in dense forests to life in open grasslands. Bipedalism would have allowed early hominids to see over tall grasses, helping them to locate food and to detect and avoid predators. However, because bipedalism also would have conferred substantial advantages upon early hominids who never left the forest—in gathering food found within standing reach of the forest floor, for example—debate continues concerning its origins. It may even have evolved, like the upright threat displays of many large apes, because it bettered an individual's odds of finding a mate.

Which one of the following statements is most supported by the information above?

(A) For early hominids, forest environments were generally more hospitable than grassland environments.
(B) Bipedal locomotion would have helped early hominids gather food.
(C) Bipedal locomotion actually would not be advantageous to hominids living in open grassland environments.
(D) Bipedal locomotion probably evolved among early hominids who exclusively inhabited forest environments.
(E) For early hominids, gathering food was more relevant to survival than was detecting and avoiding predators.

6. Mathematics teacher: Teaching students calculus before they attend university may significantly benefit them. Yet if students are taught calculus before they are ready for the level of abstraction involved, they may abandon the study of mathematics altogether. So if we are going to teach pre-university students calculus, we must make sure they can handle the level of abstraction involved.

Which one of the following principles most helps to justify the mathematics teacher's argument?

(A) Only those who, without losing motivation, can meet the cognitive challenges that new intellectual work involves should be introduced to it.
(B) Only those parts of university-level mathematics that are the most concrete should be taught to pre-university students.
(C) Cognitive tasks that require exceptional effort tend to undermine the motivation of those who attempt them.
(D) Teachers who teach university-level mathematics to pre-university students should be aware that students are likely to learn effectively only when the application of mathematics to concrete problems is shown.
(E) The level of abstraction involved in a topic should not be considered in determining whether that topic is appropriate for pre-university students.

GO ON TO THE NEXT PAGE.

7. In 1955, legislation in a certain country gave the government increased control over industrial workplace safety conditions. Among the high-risk industries in that country, the likelihood that a worker will suffer a serious injury has decreased since 1955. The legislation, therefore, has increased overall worker safety within high-risk industries.

Which one of the following, if true, most weakens the argument above?

(A) Because of technological innovation, most workplaces in the high-risk industries do not require as much unprotected interaction between workers and heavy machinery as they did in 1955.
(B) Most of the work-related injuries that occurred before 1955 were the result of worker carelessness.
(C) The annual number of work-related injuries has increased since the legislation took effect.
(D) The number of work-related injuries occurring within industries not considered high-risk has increased annually since 1955.
(E) Workplace safety conditions in all industries have improved steadily since 1955.

8. Economist: Historically, sunflower seed was one of the largest production crops in Kalotopia, and it continues to be a major source of income for several countries. The renewed growing of sunflowers would provide relief to Kalotopia's farming industry, which is quite unstable. Further, sunflower oil can provide a variety of products, both industrial and consumer, at little cost to Kalotopia's already fragile environment.

The economist's statements, if true, most strongly support which one of the following?

(A) Kalotopia's farming industry will deteriorate if sunflowers are not grown there.
(B) Stabilizing Kalotopia's farming industry would improve the economy without damaging the environment.
(C) Kalotopia's farming industry would be better off now if it had never ceased to grow any of the crops that historically were large production crops.
(D) A crop that was once a large production crop in Kalotopia would, if it were grown there again, benefit that country's farmers and general economy.
(E) Sunflower seed is a better crop for Kalotopia from both the environmental and the economic viewpoints than are most crops that could be grown there.

9. Several major earthquakes have occurred in a certain region over the last ten years. But a new earthquake prediction method promises to aid local civil defense officials in deciding exactly when to evacuate various towns. Detected before each of these major quakes were certain changes in the electric current in the earth's crust.

Which one of the following, if true, most weakens the argument?

(A) Scientists do not fully understand what brought about the changes in the electric current in the earth's crust that preceded each of the major quakes in the region over the last ten years.
(B) Most other earthquake prediction methods have been based on a weaker correlation than that found between the changes in the electric current in the earth's crust and the subsequent earthquakes.
(C) The frequency of major earthquakes in the region has increased over the last ten years.
(D) There is considerable variation in the length of time between the changes in the electric current and the subsequent earthquakes.
(E) There is presently only one station in the region that is capable of detecting the electric current in the earth's crust.

10. Unlike many machines that are perfectly useful in isolation from others, fax machines must work with other fax machines. Thus, in the fax industry, the proliferation of incompatible formats, which resulted from the large number of competing manufacturers, severely limited the usefulness—and hence the commercial viability—of fax technology until the manufacturers agreed to adopt a common format for their machines.

The information above provides the most support for which one of the following propositions?

(A) Whenever machines are dependent on other machines of the same type, competition among manufacturers is damaging to the industry.
(B) In some industries it is in the interest of competitors to cooperate to some extent with one another.
(C) The more competitors there are in a high-tech industry, the more they will have to cooperate in determining the basic design of their product.
(D) Some cooperation among manufacturers in the same industry is more beneficial than is pure competition.
(E) Cooperation is beneficial only in industries whose products depend on other products of the same type.

11. In comparing different methods by which a teacher's performance can be evaluated and educational outcomes improved, researchers found that a critique of teacher performance leads to enhanced educational outcomes if the critique is accompanied by the information that teacher performance is merely one of several factors that, in concert with other factors, determines the educational outcomes.

Which one of the following best illustrates the principle illustrated by the finding of the researchers?

(A) Children can usually be taught to master subject matter in which they have no interest if they believe that successfully mastering it will earn the respect of their peers.
(B) People are generally more willing to accept a negative characterization of a small group of people if they do not see themselves as members of the group being so characterized.
(C) An actor can more effectively evaluate the merits of her own performance if she can successfully convince herself that she is really evaluating the performance of another actor.
(D) The opinions reached by a social scientist in the study of a society can be considered as more reliable and objective if that social scientist is not a member of that society.
(E) It is easier to correct the mistakes of an athlete if it is made clear to him that the criticism is part of an overarching effort to rectify the shortcomings of the entire team on which he plays.

12. Critic: A novel cannot be of the highest quality unless most readers become emotionally engaged with the imaginary world it describes. Thus shifts of narrative point of view within a novel, either between first and third person or of some other sort, detract from the merit of the work, since such shifts tend to make most readers focus on the author.

Which one of the following is an assumption necessary for the critic's conclusion to be properly drawn?

(A) Most readers become emotionally engaged with the imaginary world described by a novel only if the novel is of the highest quality.
(B) A novel is generally not considered to be of high quality unless it successfully engages the imagination of most readers.
(C) Most readers cannot become emotionally involved with a novel's imaginary world if they focus on the author.
(D) Most readers regard a novel's narrative point of view as representing the perspective of the novel's author.
(E) Shifts in narrative point of view serve no literary purpose.

13. People aged 46 to 55 spend more money per capita than people of any other age group. So it is puzzling that when companies advertise consumer products on television, they focus almost exclusively on people aged 25 and under. Indeed, those who make decisions about television advertising think that the value of a television advertising slot depends entirely on the number of people aged 25 and under who can be expected to be watching at that time.

Which one of the following, if true, most helps to explain the puzzling facts stated above?

(A) The expense of television advertising slots makes it crucial for companies to target people who are most likely to purchase their products.
(B) Advertising slots during news programs almost always cost far less than advertising slots during popular sitcoms whose leading characters are young adults.
(C) When television executives decide which shows to renew, they do so primarily in terms of the shows' ratings among people aged 25 and under.
(D) Those who make decisions about television advertising believe that people older than 25 almost never change their buying habits.
(E) When companies advertise consumer products in print media, they focus primarily on people aged 26 and over.

14. Eighteenth-century moralist: You should never make an effort to acquire expensive new tastes, since they are a drain on your purse and in the course of acquiring them you may expose yourself to sensations that are obnoxious to you. Furthermore, the very effort that must be expended in their acquisition attests their superfluity.

The moralist's reasoning is most vulnerable to criticism on the grounds that the moralist

(A) draws a conclusion that simply restates a claim presented in support of that conclusion
(B) takes for granted that the acquisition of expensive tastes will lead to financial irresponsibility
(C) uses the inherently vague term "sensations" without providing a definition of that term
(D) mistakes a cause of acquisition of expensive tastes for an effect of acquisition of such tastes
(E) rejects trying to achieve a goal because of the cost of achieving it, without considering the benefits of achieving it

GO ON TO THE NEXT PAGE.

15. Zack's Coffeehouse schedules free poetry readings almost every Wednesday. Zack's offers half-priced coffee all day on every day that a poetry reading is scheduled.

Which one of the following can be properly inferred from the information above?

(A) Wednesday is the most common day on which Zack's offers half-priced coffee all day.
(B) Most free poetry readings given at Zack's are scheduled for Wednesdays.
(C) Free poetry readings are scheduled on almost every day that Zack's offers half-priced coffee all day.
(D) Zack's offers half-priced coffee all day on most if not all Wednesdays.
(E) On some Wednesdays Zack's does not offer half-priced coffee all day.

16. Philosopher: An event is intentional if it is a human action performed on the basis of a specific motivation. An event is random if it is not performed on the basis of a specific motivation and it is not explainable by normal physical processes.

Which one of the following inferences conforms most closely to the philosopher's position?

(A) Tarik left the keys untouched on the kitchen counter, but he did not do so on the basis of a specific motivation. Therefore, the keys' remaining on the kitchen counter was a random event.
(B) Ellis tore the envelope open in order to read its contents, but the envelope was empty. Nevertheless, because Ellis acted on the basis of a specific motivation, tearing the envelope open was an intentional event.
(C) Judith's hailing a cab distracted a driver in the left lane. She performed the action of hailing the cab on the basis of a specific motivation, so the driver's becoming distracted was an intentional event.
(D) Yasuko continued to breathe regularly throughout the time that she was asleep. This was a human action, but it was not performed on the basis of a specific motivation. Therefore, her breathing was a random event.
(E) Henry lost his hold on the wrench and dropped it because the handle was slippery. This was a human action and is explainable by normal physical processes, so it was an intentional event.

17. It is a mistake to conclude, as some have, that ancient people did not know what moral rights were simply because no known ancient language has an expression correctly translatable as "a moral right." This would be like saying that a person who discovers a wild fruit tree and returns repeatedly to harvest from it and study it has no idea what the fruit is until naming it or learning its name.

Which one of the following is an assumption required by the argument?

(A) To know the name of something is to know what that thing is.
(B) People who first discover what something is know it better than do people who merely know the name of the thing.
(C) The name or expression that is used to identify something cannot provide any information about the nature of the thing that is identified.
(D) A person who repeatedly harvests from a wild fruit tree and studies it has some idea of what the fruit is even before knowing a name for the fruit.
(E) One need not know what something is before one can name it.

18. There is little plausibility to the claim that it is absurd to criticize anyone for being critical. Obviously, people must assess one another and not all assessments will be positive. However, there is wisdom behind the injunction against being judgmental. To be judgmental is not merely to assess someone negatively, but to do so prior to a serious effort at understanding.

Which one of the following most accurately expresses the main conclusion drawn in the argument?

(A) To be judgmental is to assess someone negatively prior to making a serious effort at understanding.
(B) It is absurd to criticize anyone for being critical.
(C) There is some plausibility to the claim that it is absurd to criticize anyone for being critical.
(D) Not all assessments people make of one another will be positive.
(E) There is wisdom behind the injunction against being judgmental.

GO ON TO THE NEXT PAGE.

19. Even those who believe that the art of each age and culture has its own standards of beauty must admit that some painters are simply superior to others in the execution of their artistic visions. But this superiority must be measured in light of the artist's purposes, since the high merits, for example, of Jose Rey Toledo's work and his extraordinary artistic skills are not in doubt, despite the fact that his paintings do not literally resemble what they represent.

The claim that some painters are superior to others in the execution of their artistic visions plays which one of the following roles in the argument?

(A) It is a hypothesis that the argument attempts to refute.
(B) It is a generalization, one sort of objection to which the argument illustrates by giving an example.
(C) It is a claim that, according to the argument, is to be understood in a manner specified by the conclusion.
(D) It is a claim that the argument derives from another claim and that it uses to support its conclusion.
(E) It is a generalization that the argument uses to justify the relevance of the specific example it cites.

20. A study of rabbits in the 1940s convinced many biologists that parthenogenesis—reproduction without fertilization of an egg—sometimes occurs in mammals. However, the study's methods have since been shown to be flawed, and no other studies have succeeded in demonstrating mammalian parthenogenesis. Thus, since parthenogenesis is known to occur in a wide variety of nonmammalian vertebrates, there must be something about mammalian chromosomes that precludes the possibility of parthenogenesis.

A flaw in the reasoning of the argument is that the argument

(A) takes for granted that something that has not been proven to be true is for that reason shown to be false
(B) infers that a characteristic is shared by all nonmammalian vertebrate species merely because it is shared by some nonmammalian vertebrate species
(C) rules out an explanation of a phenomenon merely on the grounds that there is another explanation that can account for the phenomenon
(D) confuses a necessary condition for parthenogenesis with a sufficient condition for it
(E) assumes that the methods used in a study of one mammalian species were flawed merely because the study's findings cannot be generalized to all other mammalian species

21. Advertiser: Most TV shows depend on funding from advertisers and would be canceled without such funding. However, advertisers will not pay to have their commercials aired during a TV show unless many people watching the show buy the advertised products as a result. So if people generally fail to buy the products advertised during their favorite shows, these shows will soon be canceled. Thus, anyone who feels that a TV show is worth preserving ought to buy the products advertised during that show.

The advertiser's reasoning most closely conforms to which one of the following principles?

(A) If a TV show that one feels to be worth preserving would be canceled unless one took certain actions, then one ought to take those actions.
(B) If a TV show would be canceled unless many people took certain actions, then everyone who feels that the show is worth preserving ought to take those actions.
(C) If a TV show is worth preserving, then everyone should take whatever actions are necessary to prevent that show from being canceled.
(D) If one feels that a TV show is worth preserving, then one should take at least some actions to reduce the likelihood that the show will be canceled.
(E) If a TV show would be canceled unless many people took certain actions, then those who feel most strongly that it is worth preserving should take those actions.

GO ON TO THE NEXT PAGE.

22. Psychologist: It is well known that becoming angry often induces temporary incidents of high blood pressure. A recent study further showed, however, that people who are easily angered are significantly more likely to have permanently high blood pressure than are people who have more tranquil personalities. Coupled with the long-established fact that those with permanently high blood pressure are especially likely to have heart disease, the recent findings indicate that heart disease can result from psychological factors.

Which one of the following would, if true, most weaken the psychologist's argument?

(A) Those who are easily angered are less likely to recover fully from episodes of heart disease than are other people.
(B) Medication designed to control high blood pressure can greatly affect the moods of those who use it.
(C) People with permanently high blood pressure who have tranquil personalities virtually never develop heart disease.
(D) Those who discover that they have heart disease tend to become more easily frustrated by small difficulties.
(E) The physiological factors that cause permanently high blood pressure generally make people quick to anger.

23. A professor of business placed a case-study assignment for her class on her university's computer network. She later found out that instead of reading the assignment on the computer screen, 50 out of the 70 students printed it out on paper. Thus, it is not the case that books delivered via computer will make printed books obsolete.

Which one of the following, if true, most strengthens the argument?

(A) Several colleagues of the professor have found that, in their non-business courses, several of their students behave similarly in relation to assignments placed on the computer network.
(B) Studies consistently show that most computer users will print reading material that is more than a few pages in length rather than read it on the computer screen.
(C) Some people get impaired vision from long periods of reading printed matter on computer screens, even if they use high quality computer screens.
(D) Scanning technology is very poor, causing books delivered via computer to be full of errors unless editors carefully read the scanned versions.
(E) Books on cassette tape have only a small fraction of the sales of printed versions of the same books, though sales of videos of books that have been turned into movies remain strong.

GO ON TO THE NEXT PAGE.

24. Advertisement: Researchers studied a group of people trying to lose weight and discovered that those in the group who lost the most weight got more calories from protein than from carbohydrates and ate their biggest meal early in the day. So anyone who follows our diet, which provides more calories from protein than from anything else and which requires that breakfast be the biggest meal of the day, is sure to lose weight.

The reasoning in the advertisement is most vulnerable to criticism on the grounds that the advertisement overlooks the possibility that

(A) eating foods that derive a majority of their calories from carbohydrates tends to make one feel fuller than does eating foods that derive a majority of their calories from protein
(B) a few of the people in the group studied who lost significant amounts of weight got nearly all of their calories from carbohydrates and ate their biggest meal at night
(C) the people in the group studied who increased their activity levels lost more weight, on average, than those who did not, regardless of whether they got more calories from protein or from carbohydrates
(D) some people in the group studied lost no weight yet got more calories from protein than from carbohydrates and ate their biggest meal early in the day
(E) people who eat their biggest meal at night tend to snack more during the day and so tend to take in more total calories than do people who eat their biggest meal earlier in the day

25. Some twentieth-century art is great art. All great art involves original ideas, and any art that is not influential cannot be great art.

Each of the following statements follows logically from the set of statements above EXCEPT:

(A) Some influential art involves original ideas.
(B) Some twentieth-century art involves original ideas.
(C) Only art that involves original ideas is influential.
(D) Only art that is influential and involves original ideas is great art.
(E) Some twentieth-century art is influential and involves original ideas.

S T O P

IF YOU FINISH BEFORE TIME IS CALLED, YOU MAY CHECK YOUR WORK ON THIS SECTION ONLY.
DO NOT WORK ON ANY OTHER SECTION IN THE TEST.

SECTION II

Time—35 minutes

27 Questions

Directions: Each set of questions in this section is based on a single passage or a pair of passages. The questions are to be answered on the basis of what is stated or implied in the passage or pair of passages. For some of the questions, more than one of the choices could conceivably answer the question. However, you are to choose the best answer; that is, the response that most accurately and completely answers the question, and blacken the corresponding space on your answer sheet.

Often when a highly skilled and experienced employee leaves one company to work for another, there is the potential for a transfer of sensitive information between competitors. Two basic principles in such cases appear irreconcilable: the right of the company to its intellectual property—its proprietary data and trade secrets—and the right of individuals to seek gainful employment and to make free use of their abilities. Nevertheless, the courts have often tried to preserve both parties' legal rights by refusing to prohibit the employee from working for the competitor, but at the same time providing an injunction against disclosure of any of the former employer's secrets. It has been argued that because such measures help generate suspicions and similar psychological barriers to full and free utilization of abilities in the employee's new situation, they are hardly effective in upholding the individual's rights to free employment decisions. But it is also doubtful that they are effective in preserving trade secrets.

It is obviously impossible to divest oneself of that part of one's expertise that one has acquired from former employers and coworkers. Nor, in general, can one selectively refrain from its use, given that it has become an integral part of one's total intellectual capacity. Nevertheless, almost any such information that is not public knowledge may legitimately be claimed as corporate property: normal employment agreements provide for corporate ownership of all relevant data, including inventions, generated by the employee in connection with the company's business.

Once an employee takes a position with a competitor, the trade secrets that have been acquired by that employee may manifest themselves clearly and consciously. This is what court injunctions seek to prohibit. But they are far more likely to manifest themselves subconsciously and inconspicuously—for example, in one's daily decisions at the new post, or in the many small contributions one might make to a large team effort—often in the form of an intuitive sense of what to do or to avoid. Theoretically, an injunction also prohibits such inadvertent "leakage." However, the former employer faces the practical problem of securing evidence of such leakage, for little will usually be apparent from the public activities of the new employer. And even if the new employee's activities appear suspicious, there is the further problem of distinguishing trade secrets from what may be legitimately asserted as technological skills developed independently by the employee or already possessed by the new employer. This is a major stumbling block in the attempt to protect trade secrets, since the proprietor has no recourse against others who independently generate the same information. It is therefore unlikely that an injunction against disclosure of trade secrets to future employers actually prevents any transfer of information except for the passage of documents and other concrete embodiments of the secrets.

1. Which one of the following most accurately expresses the main point of the passage?

(A) There are more effective ways than court injunctions to preserve both a company's right to protect its intellectual property and individuals' rights to make free use of their abilities.

(B) Court injunctions must be strengthened if they are to remain a relevant means of protecting corporations' trade secrets.

(C) Enforcement of court injunctions designed to protect proprietary information is impossible when employees reveal such information to new employers.

(D) Court injunctions prohibiting employees from disclosing former employers' trade secrets to new employers probably do not achieve all of their intended objectives.

(E) The rights of employees to make full use of their talents and previous training are being seriously eroded by the prohibitions placed on them by court injunctions designed to prevent the transfer of trade secrets.

GO ON TO THE NEXT PAGE.

2. Given the passage's content and tone, which one of the following statements would most likely be found elsewhere in a work from which this passage is an excerpt?

(A) Given the law as it stands, corporations concerned about preserving trade secrets might be best served by giving their employees strong incentives to stay in their current jobs.
(B) While difficult to enforce and interpret, injunctions are probably the most effective means of halting the inadvertent transfer of trade secrets while simultaneously protecting the rights of employees.
(C) Means of redress must be made available to companies that suspect, but cannot prove, that former employees are revealing protected information to competitors.
(D) Even concrete materials such as computer disks are so easy to copy and conceal that it will be a waste of time for courts to try to prevent the spread of information through physical theft.
(E) The psychological barriers that an injunction can place on an employee in a new workplace are inevitably so subtle that they have no effect on the employee.

3. The author's primary purpose in the passage is to

(A) suggest that injunctions against the disclosure of trade secrets not only create problems for employees in the workplace, but also are unable to halt the illicit spread of proprietary information
(B) suggest that the information contained in "documents and other concrete embodiments" is usually so trivial that injunctions do little good in protecting intellectual property
(C) argue that new methods must be found to address the delicate balance between corporate and individual rights
(D) support the position that the concept of protecting trade secrets is no longer viable in an age of increasing access to information
(E) argue that injunctions are not necessary for the protection of trade secrets

4. The passage provides the most support for which one of the following assertions?

(A) Injunctions should be imposed by the courts only when there is strong reason to believe that an employee will reveal proprietary information.
(B) There is apparently no reliable way to protect both the rights of companies to protect trade secrets and the rights of employees to seek new employment.
(C) Employees should not be allowed to take jobs with their former employers' competitors when their new job could compromise trade secrets of their former employers.
(D) The multiplicity of means for transferring information in the workplace only increases the need for injunctions.
(E) Some companies seek injunctions as a means of punishing employees who take jobs with their competitors.

5. With which one of the following statements regarding documents and other concrete embodiments mentioned in line 58 would the author be most likely to agree?

(A) While the transfer of such materials would be damaging, even the seemingly innocuous contributions of an employee to a competitor can do more harm in the long run.
(B) Such materials are usually less informative than what the employee may recollect about a previous job.
(C) Injunctions against the disclosure of trade secrets should carefully specify which materials are included in order to focus on the most damaging ones.
(D) Large-scale transfer of documents and other materials cannot be controlled by injunctions.
(E) Such concrete materials lend themselves to control and identification more readily than do subtler means of transferring information.

6. In the passage, the author makes which one of the following claims?

(A) Injunctions against the disclosure of trade secrets limit an employee's chances of being hired by a competitor.
(B) Measures against the disclosure of trade secrets are unnecessary except in the case of documents and other concrete embodiments of the secrets.
(C) Employees who switch jobs to work for a competitor usually unintentionally violate the law by doing so.
(D) Employers are not restricted in the tactics they can use when seeking to secure protected information from new employees.
(E) What may seem like intellectual theft may in fact be an example of independent innovation.

GO ON TO THE NEXT PAGE.

The following passages concern a plant called purple loosestrife. Passage A is excerpted from a report issued by a prairie research council; passage B from a journal of sociology.

Passage A

Purple loosestrife (*Lythrum salicaria*), an aggressive and invasive perennial of Eurasian origin, arrived with settlers in eastern North America in the early 1800s and has spread across the continent's midlatitude wetlands. The impact of purple loosestrife on native vegetation has been disastrous, with more than 50 percent of the biomass of some wetland communities displaced. Monospecific blocks of this weed have maintained themselves for at least 20 years. Impacts on wildlife have not been well studied, but serious reductions in waterfowl and aquatic furbearer productivity have been observed. In addition, several endangered species of vertebrates are threatened with further degradation of their breeding habitats. Although purple loosestrife can invade relatively undisturbed habitats, the spread and dominance of this weed have been greatly accelerated in disturbed habitats. While digging out the plants can temporarily halt their spread, there has been little research on long-term purple loosestrife control. Glyphosate has been used successfully, but no measure of the impact of this herbicide on native plant communities has been made.

With the spread of purple loosestrife growing exponentially, some form of integrated control is needed. At present, coping with purple loosestrife hinges on early detection of the weed's arrival in areas, which allows local eradication to be carried out with minimum damage to the native plant community.

Passage B

The war on purple loosestrife is apparently conducted on behalf of nature, an attempt to liberate the biotic community from the tyrannical influence of a life-destroying invasive weed. Indeed, purple loosestrife control is portrayed by its practitioners as an environmental initiative intended to save nature rather than control it. Accordingly, the purple loosestrife literature, scientific and otherwise, dutifully discusses the impacts of the weed on endangered species—and on threatened biodiversity more generally. Purple loosestrife is a pollution, according to the scientific community, and all of nature suffers under its pervasive influence.

Regardless of the perceived and actual ecological effects of the purple invader, it is apparent that popular pollution ideologies have been extended into the wetlands of North America. Consequently, the scientific effort to liberate nature from purple loosestrife has failed to decouple itself from its philosophical origin as an instrument to control nature to the satisfaction of human desires. Birds, particularly game birds and waterfowl, provide the bulk of the justification for loosestrife management. However, no bird species other than the canvasback has been identified in the literature as endangered by purple loosestrife. The impact of purple loosestrife on furbearing mammals is discussed at great length, though none of the species highlighted (muskrat, mink) can be considered threatened in North America. What is threatened by purple loosestrife is the economics of exploiting such preferred species and the millions of dollars that will be lost to the economies of the United States and Canada from reduced hunting, trapping, and recreation revenues due to a decline in the production of the wetland resource.

7. Both passages explicitly mention which one of the following?

    (A) furbearing animals
    (B) glyphosate
    (C) the threat purple loosestrife poses to economies
    (D) popular pollution ideologies
    (E) literature on purple loosestrife control

8. Each of the passages contains information sufficient to answer which one of the following questions?

    (A) Approximately how long ago did purple loosestrife arrive in North America?
    (B) Is there much literature discussing the potential benefit that hunters might derive from purple loosestrife management?
    (C) What is an issue regarding purple loosestrife management on which both hunters and farmers agree?
    (D) Is the canvasback threatened with extinction due to the spread of purple loosestrife?
    (E) What is a type of terrain that is affected in at least some parts of North America by the presence of purple loosestrife?

9. It can be inferred that the authors would be most likely to disagree about which one of the following?

    (A) Purple loosestrife spreads more quickly in disturbed habitats than in undisturbed habitats.
    (B) The threat posed by purple loosestrife to local aquatic furbearer populations is serious.
    (C) Most people who advocate that eradication measures be taken to control purple loosestrife are not genuine in their concern for the environment.
    (D) The size of the biomass that has been displaced by purple loosestrife is larger than is generally thought.
    (E) Measures should be taken to prevent other non-native plant species from invading North America.

GO ON TO THE NEXT PAGE.

10. Which one of the following most accurately describes the attitude expressed by the author of passage B toward the overall argument represented by passage A?

    (A) enthusiastic agreement
    (B) cautious agreement
    (C) pure neutrality
    (D) general ambivalence
    (E) pointed skepticism

11. It can be inferred that both authors would be most likely to agree with which one of the following statements regarding purple loosestrife?

    (A) As it increases in North America, some wildlife populations tend to decrease.
    (B) Its establishment in North America has had a disastrous effect on native North American wetland vegetation in certain regions.
    (C) It is very difficult to control effectively with herbicides.
    (D) Its introduction into North America was a great ecological blunder.
    (E) When it is eliminated from a given area, it tends to return to that area fairly quickly.

12. Which one of the following is true about the relationship between the two passages?

    (A) Passage A presents evidence that directly counters claims made in passage B.
    (B) Passage B assumes what passage A explicitly argues for.
    (C) Passage B displays an awareness of the arguments touched on in passage A, but not vice versa.
    (D) Passage B advocates a policy that passage A rejects.
    (E) Passage A downplays the seriousness of claims made in passage B.

13. Which one of the following, if true, would cast doubt on the argument in passage B but bolster the argument in passage A?

    (A) Localized population reduction is often a precursor to widespread endangerment of a species.
    (B) Purple loosestrife was barely noticed in North America before the advent of suburban sprawl in the 1950s.
    (C) The amount by which overall hunting, trapping, and recreation revenues would be reduced as a result of the extinction of one or more species threatened by purple loosestrife represents a significant portion of those revenues.
    (D) Some environmentalists who advocate taking measures to eradicate purple loosestrife view such measures as a means of controlling nature.
    (E) Purple loosestrife has never become a problem in its native habitat, even though no effort has been made to eradicate it there.

GO ON TO THE NEXT PAGE.

With their recognition of Maxine Hong Kingston as a major literary figure, some critics have suggested that her works have been produced almost *ex nihilo*, saying that they lack a large traceable body of direct literary antecedents especially within the Chinese American heritage in which her work is embedded. But these critics, who have examined only the development of written texts, the most visible signs of a culture's narrative production, have overlooked Kingston's connection to the long Chinese tradition of a highly developed genre of song and spoken narrative known as "talk-story" (*gong gu tsai*).

Traditionally performed in the dialects of various ethnic enclaves, talk-story has been maintained within the confines of the family and has rarely surfaced into print. The tradition dates back to Sung dynasty (A.D. 970–1279) storytellers in China, and in the United States it is continually revitalized by an overlapping sequence of immigration from China. Thus, Chinese immigrants to the U.S. had a fully established, sophisticated oral culture, already ancient and capable of producing masterpieces, by the time they began arriving in the early nineteenth century. This transplanted oral heritage simply embraced new subject matter or new forms of Western discourse, as in the case of Kingston's adaptations written in English.

Kingston herself believes that as a literary artist she is one in a long line of performers shaping a recalcitrant history into talk-story form. She distinguishes her "thematic" storytelling memory processes, which sift and reconstruct the essential elements of personally remembered stories, from the memory processes of a print-oriented culture that emphasizes the retention of precise sequences of words. Nor does the entry of print into the storytelling process substantially change her notion of the character of oral tradition. For Kingston, "writer" is synonymous with "singer" or "performer" in the ancient sense of privileged keeper, transmitter, and creator of stories whose current stage of development can be frozen in print, but which continue to grow both around and from that frozen text.

Kingston's participation in the tradition of talk-story is evidenced in her book *China Men*, which utilizes forms typical of that genre and common to most oral cultures including: a fixed "grammar" of repetitive themes; a spectrum of stock characters; symmetrical structures, including balanced oppositions (verbal or physical contests, antithetical characters, dialectical discourse such as question-answer forms and riddles); and repetition. In *China Men*, Kingston also succeeds in investing idiomatic English with the allusive texture and oral-aural qualities of the Chinese language, a language rich in aural and visual puns, making her work a written form of talk-story.

14. Which one of the following most accurately states the main point of the passage?
    (A) Despite some critics' comments, Kingston's writings have significant Chinese American antecedents, which can be found in the traditional oral narrative form known as talk-story.
    (B) Analysis of Kingston's writings, especially *China Men*, supports her belief that literary artists can be performers who continue to reconstruct their stories even after they have been frozen in print.
    (C) An understanding of Kingston's work and of Chinese American writers in general reveals that critics of ethnic literatures in the United States have been mistaken in examining only written texts.
    (D) Throughout her writings Kingston uses techniques typical of the talk-story genre, especially the retention of certain aspects of Chinese speech in the written English text.
    (E) The writings of Kingston have rekindled an interest in talk-story, which dates back to the Sung dynasty, and was extended to the United States with the arrival of Chinese immigrants in the nineteenth century.

15. Which one of the following can be most reasonably inferred from the passage?
    (A) In the last few years, written forms of talk-story have appeared in Chinese as often as they have in English.
    (B) Until very recently, scholars have held that oral storytelling in Chinese ethnic enclaves was a unique oral tradition.
    (C) Talk-story has developed in the United States through a process of combining Chinese, Chinese American, and other oral storytelling forms.
    (D) Chinese American talk-story relies upon memory processes that do not emphasize the retention of precise sequences of words.
    (E) The connection between certain aspects of Kingston's work and talk-story is argued by some critics to be rather tenuous and questionable.

GO ON TO THE NEXT PAGE.

16. It can be inferred from the passage that the author uses the phrase "personally remembered stories" (line 32) primarily to refer to

    (A) a literary genre of first-person storytelling
    (B) a thematically organized personal narrative of one's own past
    (C) partially idiosyncratic memories of narratives
    (D) the retention in memory of precise sequences of words
    (E) easily identifiable thematic issues in literature

17. In which one of the following is the use of cotton fibers or cotton cloth most analogous to Kingston's use of the English language as described in lines 51–55?

    (A) Scraps of plain cotton cloth are used to create a multicolored quilt.
    (B) The surface texture of woolen cloth is simulated in a piece of cotton cloth by a special process of weaving.
    (C) Because of its texture, cotton cloth is used for a certain type of clothes for which linen is inappropriate.
    (D) In making a piece of cloth, cotton fiber is substituted for linen because of the roughly similar texture of the two materials.
    (E) Because of their somewhat similar textures, cotton and linen fibers are woven together in a piece of cloth to achieve a savings in price over a pure linen cloth.

18. The passage most clearly suggests that Kingston believes which one of the following about at least some of the stories contained in her writings?

    (A) Since they are intimately tied to the nature of the Chinese language, they can be approximated, but not adequately expressed, in English.
    (B) They should be thought of primarily as ethnic literature and evaluated accordingly by critics.
    (C) They will likely be retold and altered to some extent in the process.
    (D) Chinese American history is best chronicled by traditional talk-story.
    (E) Their significance and beauty cannot be captured at all in written texts.

19. The author's argument in the passage would be most weakened if which one of the following were true?

    (A) Numerous writers in the United States have been influenced by oral traditions.
    (B) Most Chinese American writers' work is very different from Kingston's.
    (C) Native American storytellers use narrative devices similar to those used in talk-story.
    (D) *China Men* is for the most part atypical of Kingston's literary works.
    (E) Literary critics generally appreciate the authenticity of Kingston's work.

20. The author's specific purpose in detailing typical talk-story forms (lines 43–51) is to

    (A) show why Kingston's book *China Men* establishes her as a major literary figure
    (B) support the claim that Kingston's use of typically oral techniques makes her work a part of the talk-story tradition
    (C) dispute the critics' view that Chinese American literature lacks literary antecedents
    (D) argue for Kingston's view that the literary artist is at best a "privileged keeper" of stories
    (E) provide an alternative to certain critics' view that Kingston's work should be judged primarily as literature

21. Which one of the following most accurately identifies the attitude shown by the author in the passage toward talk-story?

    (A) scholarly appreciation for its longstanding artistic sophistication
    (B) mild disappointment that it has not distinguished itself from other oral traditions
    (C) tentative approval of its resistance to critical evaluations
    (D) clear respect for the diversity of its ancient sources and cultural derivations
    (E) open admiration for the way it uses song to express narrative

GO ON TO THE NEXT PAGE.

In economics, the term "speculative bubble" refers to a large upward move in an asset's price driven not by the asset's fundamentals—that is, by the earnings derivable from the asset—but rather by mere speculation that someone else will be willing to pay a higher price for it. The price increase is then followed by a dramatic decline in price, due to a loss in confidence that the price will continue to rise, and the "bubble" is said to have burst. According to Charles Mackay's classic nineteenth-century account, the seventeenth-century Dutch tulip market provides an example of a speculative bubble. But the economist Peter Garber challenges Mackay's view, arguing that there is no evidence that the Dutch tulip market really involved a speculative bubble.

By the seventeenth century, the Netherlands had become a center of cultivation and development of new tulip varieties, and a market had developed in which rare varieties of bulbs sold at high prices. For example, a Semper Augustus bulb sold in 1625 for an amount of gold worth about U.S.$11,000 in 1999. Common bulb varieties, on the other hand, sold for very low prices. According to Mackay, by 1636 rapid price rises attracted speculators, and prices of many varieties surged upward from November 1636 through January 1637. Mackay further states that in February 1637 prices suddenly collapsed; bulbs could not be sold at 10 percent of their peak values. By 1739, the prices of all the most prized kinds of bulbs had fallen to no more than one two-hundredth of 1 percent of Semper Augustus's peak price.

Garber acknowledges that bulb prices increased dramatically from 1636 to 1637 and eventually reached very low levels. But he argues that this episode should not be described as a speculative bubble, for the increase and eventual decline in bulb prices can be explained in terms of the fundamentals. Garber argues that a standard pricing pattern occurs for new varieties of flowers. When a particularly prized variety is developed, its original bulb sells for a high price. Thus, the dramatic rise in the price of some original tulip bulbs could have resulted as tulips in general, and certain varieties in particular, became fashionable. However, as the prized bulbs become more readily available through reproduction from the original bulb, their price falls rapidly; after less than 30 years, bulbs sell at reproduction cost. But this does not mean that the high prices of original bulbs are irrational, for earnings derivable from the millions of bulbs descendent from the original bulbs can be very high, even if each individual descendent bulb commands a very low price. Given that an original bulb can generate a reasonable return on investment even if the price of descendent bulbs decreases dramatically, a rapid rise and eventual fall of tulip bulb prices need not indicate a speculative bubble.

22. Which one of the following most accurately expresses the main point of the passage?

(A) The seventeenth-century Dutch tulip market is widely but mistakenly believed by economists to provide an example of a speculative bubble.
(B) Mackay did not accurately assess the earnings that could be derived from rare and expensive seventeenth-century Dutch tulip bulbs.
(C) A speculative bubble occurs whenever the price of an asset increases substantially followed by a rapid and dramatic decline.
(D) Garber argues that Mackay's classic account of the seventeenth-century Dutch tulip market as a speculative bubble is not supported by the evidence.
(E) A tulip bulb can generate a reasonable return on investment even if the price starts very high and decreases dramatically.

23. Given Garber's account of the seventeenth-century Dutch tulip market, which one of the following is most analogous to someone who bought a tulip bulb of a certain variety in that market at a very high price, only to sell a bulb of that variety at a much lower price?

(A) someone who, after learning that many others had withdrawn their applications for a particular job, applied for the job in the belief that there would be less competition for it
(B) an art dealer who, after paying a very high price for a new painting, sells it at a very low price because it is now considered to be an inferior work
(C) someone who, after buying a box of rare motorcycle parts at a very high price, is forced to sell them at a much lower price because of the sudden availability of cheap substitute parts
(D) a publisher who pays an extremely high price for a new novel only to sell copies at a price affordable to nearly everyone
(E) an airline that, after selling most of the tickets for seats on a plane at a very high price, must sell the remaining tickets at a very low price

GO ON TO THE NEXT PAGE.

24. The passage most strongly supports the inference that Garber would agree with which one of the following statements?

(A) If speculative bubbles occur at all, they occur very rarely.
(B) Many of the owners of high-priced original tulip bulbs could have expected to at least recoup their original investments from sales of the many bulbs propagated from the original bulbs.
(C) If there is not a speculative bubble in a market, then the level of prices in that market is not irrational.
(D) Most people who invested in Dutch tulip bulbs in the seventeenth century were generally rational in all their investments.
(E) Mackay mistakenly infers from the fact that tulip prices dropped rapidly that the very low prices that the bulbs eventually sold for were irrational.

25. The passage states that Mackay claimed which one of the following?

(A) The rapid rise in price of Dutch tulip bulbs was not due to the fashionability of the flowers they produced.
(B) The prices of certain varieties of Dutch tulip bulbs during the seventeenth century were, at least for a time, determined by speculation.
(C) The Netherlands was the only center of cultivation and development of new tulip varieties in the seventeenth century.
(D) The very high prices of bulbs in the seventeenth-century Dutch tulip market were not irrational.
(E) Buyers of rare and very expensive Dutch tulip bulbs were ultimately able to derive earnings from bulbs descendent from the original bulbs.

26. The main purpose of the second paragraph is to

(A) present the facts that are accepted by all experts in the field
(B) identify the mistake that one scholar alleges another scholar made
(C) explain the basis on which one scholar makes an inference with which another scholar disagrees
(D) undermine the case that one scholar makes for the claim with which another scholar disagrees
(E) outline the factual errors that led one scholar to draw the inference that he drew

27. The phrase "standard pricing pattern" as used in line 38 most nearly means a pricing pattern

(A) against which other pricing patterns are to be measured
(B) that conforms to a commonly agreed-upon criterion
(C) that is merely acceptable
(D) that regularly recurs in certain types of cases
(E) that serves as an exemplar

S T O P

IF YOU FINISH BEFORE TIME IS CALLED, YOU MAY CHECK YOUR WORK ON THIS SECTION ONLY. DO NOT WORK ON ANY OTHER SECTION IN THE TEST.

Time—35 minutes

24 Questions

Directions: Each group of questions in this section is based on a set of conditions. In answering some of the questions, it may be useful to draw a rough diagram. Choose the response that most accurately and completely answers each question and blacken the corresponding space on your answer sheet.

Questions 1–6

During a period of seven consecutive days—from day 1 through day 7—seven investors—Fennelly, Gupta, Hall, Jones, Knight, López, and Moss—will each view a building site exactly once. Each day exactly one investor will view the site. The investors must view the site in accordance with the following conditions:

Fennelly views the site on day 3 or else day 5.
López views the site on neither day 4 nor day 6.
If Jones views the site on day 1, Hall views the site on day 2.
If Knight views the site on day 4, López views the site on day 5.
Gupta views the site on the day after the day on which Hall views the site.

1. Which one of the following could be the order in which the investors view the site, from day 1 through day 7?

(A) Hall, Gupta, Fennelly, Moss, Knight, López, Jones
(B) Hall, Gupta, López, Fennelly, Moss, Knight, Jones
(C) López, Gupta, Hall, Moss, Fennelly, Jones, Knight
(D) López, Jones, Fennelly, Knight, Hall Gupta, Moss
(E) López, Jones, Knight, Moss, Fennelly, Hall, Gupta

2. If Jones views the site on day 1, which one of the following investors must view the site on day 4?

(A) Fennelly
(B) Gupta
(C) Knight
(D) López
(E) Moss

3. If Knight views the site on day 4 and Moss views the site on some day after the day on which Jones views the site, which one of the following must be true?

(A) Jones views the site on day 1.
(B) Jones views the site on day 2.
(C) Jones views the site on day 6.
(D) Moss views the site on day 2.
(E) Moss views the site on day 6.

4. If Hall views the site on day 2, which one of the following is a complete and accurate list of investors any one of whom could be the investor who views the site on day 4?

(A) Knight
(B) Moss
(C) Jones, Moss
(D) Knight, Moss
(E) Jones, Knight, Moss

5. If Hall views the site on the day after the day Knight views the site and if Fennelly views the site on the day after the day López views the site, then Jones must view the site on day

(A) 1
(B) 2
(C) 3
(D) 4
(E) 5

6. If the day on which Gupta views the site and the day on which López views the site both come at some time before the day on which Fennelly views the site, which one of the following is an investor who could view the site on day 3?

(A) Fennelly
(B) Gupta
(C) Jones
(D) Knight
(E) Moss

GO ON TO THE NEXT PAGE.

Questions 7–12

A zoo's reptile house has a straight row of exactly five consecutive habitats—numbered 1 through 5 from left to right—for housing exactly seven reptiles—four snakes and three lizards. Five of the reptiles are female and two are male. The reptiles must be housed as follows:

No habitat houses more than two reptiles.
No habitat houses both a snake and a lizard.
No female snake is housed in a habitat that is immediately next to a habitat housing a male lizard.

7. Which one of the following could be a complete and accurate matching of habitats to reptiles?

(A) 1: two female snakes; 2: one male snake; 3: one female lizard; 4: one male snake, one female lizard; 5: one female lizard
(B) 1: empty; 2: two female snakes; 3: two female lizards; 4: two male snakes; 5: one female lizard
(C) 1: one female snake, one male snake; 2: two female snakes; 3: one male lizard; 4: one female lizard; 5: one female lizard
(D) 1: two male snakes; 2: empty; 3: one female lizard; 4: one female lizard; 5: two female snakes, one female lizard
(E) 1: one female snake, one male snake; 2: one female snake, one male snake; 3: one male lizard; 4: one female lizard; 5: one female lizard

8. If habitat 2 contains at least one female snake and habitat 4 contains two male lizards, then which one of the following could be true?

(A) Habitat 3 contains two reptiles.
(B) Habitat 5 contains two reptiles.
(C) Habitat 1 contains a female lizard.
(D) Habitat 2 contains a female lizard.
(E) Habitat 5 contains a female lizard.

9. Which one of the following must be true?

(A) At least one female reptile is alone in a habitat.
(B) At least one male reptile is alone in a habitat.
(C) At least one lizard is alone in a habitat.
(D) At least one lizard is male.
(E) At least one snake is male.

10. Which one of the following CANNOT be the complete housing arrangement for habitats 1 and 2?

(A) 1: one female snake, one male snake; 2: one male snake
(B) 1: one male lizard; 2: one male snake
(C) 1: two female lizards; 2: one female snake
(D) 1: one male snake; 2: empty
(E) 1: empty; 2: one female lizard

11. If habitat 3 is empty, and no snake is housed in a habitat that is immediately next to a habitat containing a snake, then which one of the following could be false?

(A) All snakes are housed in even-numbered habitats.
(B) None of the lizards is male.
(C) No snake is alone in a habitat.
(D) No lizard is housed in a habitat that is immediately next to a habitat containing a lizard.
(E) Exactly one habitat contains exactly one reptile.

12. If all snakes are female and each of the lizards has a habitat to itself, then which one of the following habitats CANNOT contain any snakes?

(A) habitat 1
(B) habitat 2
(C) habitat 3
(D) habitat 4
(E) habitat 5

GO ON TO THE NEXT PAGE.

Questions 13–19

Exactly seven film buffs—Ginnie, Ian, Lianna, Marcos, Reveka, Viktor, and Yow—attend a showing of classic films. Three films are shown, one directed by Fellini, one by Hitchcock, and one by Kurosawa. Each of the film buffs sees exactly one of the three films. The films are shown only once, one film at a time. The following restrictions must apply:

Exactly twice as many of the film buffs see the Hitchcock film as see the Fellini film.
Ginnie and Reveka do not see the same film as each other.
Ian and Marcos do not see the same film as each other.
Viktor and Yow see the same film as each other.
Lianna sees the Hitchcock film.
Ginnie sees either the Fellini film or the Kurosawa film.

13. Which one of the following could be an accurate matching of film buffs to films?

(A) Ginnie: the Hitchcock film; Ian: the Kurosawa film; Marcos: the Hitchcock film
(B) Ginnie: the Kurosawa film; Ian: the Fellini film; Viktor: the Fellini film
(C) Ian: the Hitchcock film; Reveka: the Kurosawa film; Viktor: the Fellini film
(D) Marcos: the Kurosawa film; Reveka: the Kurosawa film; Viktor: the Kurosawa film
(E) Marcos: the Hitchcock film; Reveka: the Hitchcock film; Yow: the Hitchcock film

14. Each of the following must be false EXCEPT:

(A) Reveka is the only film buff to see the Fellini film.
(B) Reveka is the only film buff to see the Hitchcock film.
(C) Yow is the only film buff to see the Kurosawa film.
(D) Exactly two film buffs see the Kurosawa film.
(E) Exactly three film buffs see the Hitchcock film.

15. Which one of the following could be a complete and accurate list of the film buffs who do NOT see the Hitchcock film?

(A) Ginnie, Marcos
(B) Ginnie Reveka
(C) Ginnie, Ian, Reveka
(D) Ginnie, Marcos, Yow
(E) Ginnie, Viktor, Yow

16. If exactly one film buff sees the Kurosawa film, then which one of the following must be true?

(A) Viktor sees the Hitchcock film.
(B) Ginnie sees the Fellini film.
(C) Marcos sees the Fellini film.
(D) Ian sees the Fellini film.
(E) Reveka sees the Hitchcock film.

17. Which one of the following must be true?

(A) Ginnie sees a different film than Ian does.
(B) Ian sees a different film than Lianna does.
(C) Ian sees a different film than Viktor does.
(D) Ian, Lianna, and Viktor do not all see the same film.
(E) Ginnie, Lianna, and Marcos do not all see the same film.

18. If Viktor sees the same film as Ginnie does, then which one of the following could be true?

(A) Ginnie sees the Fellini film.
(B) Ian sees the Hitchcock film.
(C) Reveka sees the Kurosawa film.
(D) Viktor sees the Hitchcock film.
(E) Yow sees the Fellini film.

19. Each of the following could be complete and accurate list of the film buffs who see the Fellini film EXCEPT:

(A) Ginnie, Ian
(B) Ginnie, Marcos
(C) Ian, Reveka
(D) Marcos, Reveka
(E) Viktor, Yow

GO ON TO THE NEXT PAGE.

Questions 20–24

Six cars are to be arranged in a straight line, and will be numbered 1 through 6, in order, from the front of the line to the back of the line. Each car is exactly one color: two are green, two are orange, and two are purple. The arrangement of cars is restricted as follows:

No car can be the same color as any car next to it in line.
Either car 5 or car 6 must be purple.
Car 1 cannot be orange.
Car 4 cannot be green.

20. The cars in which one of the following pairs CANNOT be the same color as each other?

(A) cars 1 and 4
(B) cars 1 and 5
(C) cars 3 and 5
(D) cars 3 and 6
(E) cars 4 and 6

21. If car 2 is the same color as car 4, then which one of the following statements must be true?

(A) Car 1 is purple.
(B) Car 2 is orange.
(C) Car 3 is green.
(D) Car 5 is purple.
(E) Car 6 is green

22. If car 4 is purple, which one of the following must be true?

(A) Car 1 is orange.
(B) Car 2 is green.
(C) Car 3 is orange.
(D) Car 5 is green.
(E) Car 6 is purple.

23. Which one of the following statements must be false?

(A) Car 2 is green.
(B) Car 4 is orange.
(C) Car 5 is purple.
(D) Car 6 is orange.
(E) Car 6 is green.

24. If one of the two orange cars is replaced by a third green car, and if the arrangement of cars in line must conform to the same restrictions as before, then which one of the following is a complete and accurate list of the cars each of which must be green?

(A) car 1
(B) car 3
(C) car 5
(D) car 1, car 3
(E) car l, car 3, car 5

S T O P

IF YOU FINISH BEFORE TIME IS CALLED, YOU MAY CHECK YOUR WORK ON THIS SECTION ONLY.
DO NOT WORK ON ANY OTHER SECTION IN THE TEST.

SECTION III

Time—35 minutes

25 Questions

Directions: The questions in this section are based on the reasoning contained in brief statements or passages. For some questions, more than one of the choices could conceivably answer the question. However, you are to choose the best answer; that is, the response that most accurately and completely answers the question. You should not make assumptions that are by commonsense standards implausible, superfluous, or incompatible with the passage. After you have chosen the best answer, blacken the corresponding space on your answer sheet.

1. Aristophanes' play *The Clouds*, which was written when the philosopher Socrates was in his mid-forties, portrays Socrates as an atheistic philosopher primarily concerned with issues in natural science. The only other surviving portrayals of Socrates were written after Socrates' death at age 70. They portrayed Socrates as having a religious dimension and a strong focus on ethical issues.

   Which one of the following, if true, would most help to resolve the apparent discrepancy between Aristophanes' portrayal of Socrates and the other surviving portrayals?

   (A) Aristophanes' portrayal of Socrates in *The Clouds* was unflattering, whereas the other portrayals were very flattering.
   (B) Socrates' philosophical views and interests changed sometime after his mid-forties.
   (C) Most of the philosophers who lived before Socrates were primarily concerned with natural science.
   (D) Socrates was a much more controversial figure in the years before his death than he was in his mid-forties.
   (E) Socrates had an influence on many subsequent philosophers who were primarily concerned with natural science.

2. Board member: The J Foundation, a philanthropic organization, gave you this grant on the condition that your resulting work not contain any material detrimental to the J Foundation's reputation. But your resulting work never mentions any of the laudable achievements of our foundation. Hence your work fails to meet the conditions under which the grant was made.

   The reasoning in the board member's argument is vulnerable to criticism on the grounds that the argument

   (A) takes for granted that a work that never mentions any laudable achievements cannot be of high intellectual value
   (B) confuses a condition necessary for the receipt of a grant with a condition sufficient for the receipt of a grant
   (C) presumes, without providing justification, that a work that does not mention a foundation's laudable achievements is harmful to that foundation's reputation
   (D) fails to consider that recipients of a grant usually strive to meet a foundation's conditions
   (E) fails to consider the possibility that the work that was produced with the aid of the grant may have met all conditions other than avoiding detriment to the J Foundation's reputation

3. Psychiatrist: Breaking any habit is difficult, especially when it involves an addictive substance. People who break a habit are more likely to be motivated by immediate concerns than by long-term ones. Therefore, people who succeed in breaking their addiction to smoking cigarettes are more likely to be motivated by the social pressure against smoking—which is an immediate concern—than by health concerns, since ________.

   The conclusion of the psychiatrist's argument is most strongly supported if which one of the following completes the argument?

   (A) a habit that involves an addictive substance is likely to pose a greater health threat than a habit that does not involve any addictive substance
   (B) for most people who successfully quit smoking, smoking does not create an immediate health concern at the time they quit
   (C) some courses of action that exacerbate health concerns can also relieve social pressure
   (D) most people who succeed in quitting smoking succeed only after several attempts
   (E) everyone who succeeds in quitting smoking is motivated either by social pressure or by health concerns

GO ON TO THE NEXT PAGE.

4. Cassie: In order to improve the quality of customer service provided by our real estate agency, we should reduce client loads—the number of clients each agent is expected to serve at one time.

   Melvin: Although smaller client loads are desirable, reducing client loads at our agency is simply not feasible. We already find it very difficult to recruit enough qualified agents; recruiting even more agents, which would be necessary in order to reduce client loads, is out of the question.

   Of the following, which one, if true, is the logically strongest counter that Cassie can make to Melvin's argument?

   (A) Since reducing client loads would improve working conditions for agents, reducing client loads would help recruit additional qualified agents to the real estate agency.
   (B) Many of the real estate agency's current clients have expressed strong support for efforts to reduce client loads.
   (C) Several recently conducted studies of real estate agencies have shown that small client loads are strongly correlated with high customer satisfaction ratings.
   (D) Hiring extra support staff for the real estate agency's main office would have many of the same beneficial effects as reducing client loads.
   (E) Over the last several years, it has become increasingly challenging for the real estate agency to recruit enough qualified agents just to maintain current client loads.

5. The star-nosed mole has a nose that ends in a pair of several-pointed stars, or tentacles that are crucial for hunting, as moles are poor-sighted. These tentacles contain receptors that detect electric fields produced by other animals, enabling the moles to detect and catch suitable prey such as worms and insects.

   Which one of the following is most strongly supported by the information above?

   (A) Both worms and insects produce electric fields.
   (B) The star-nosed mole does not rely at all on its eyesight for survival.
   (C) The star-nosed mole does not rely at all on its sense of smell when hunting.
   (D) Only animals that hunt have noses with tentacles that detect electric fields.
   (E) The star-nosed mole does not produce an electric field.

6. In her recent book a psychologist described several cases that exhibit the following pattern: A child, denied something by its parent, initiates problematic behavior such as screaming; the behavior escalates until finally the exasperated parent acquiesces to the child's demand. At this point the child, having obtained the desired goal, stops the problematic behavior, to the parent's relief. This self-reinforcing pattern of misbehavior and accommodation is repeated with steadily increasing levels of misbehavior by the child.

   The cases described by the psychologist illustrate each of the following generalizations EXCEPT:

   (A) A child can develop problematic behavior patterns as a result of getting what it wants.
   (B) A child and parent can mutually influence each other's behavior.
   (C) Parents, by their choices, can inadvertently increase their child's level of misbehavior.
   (D) A child can unintentionally influence a parent's behavior in ways contrary to the child's intended goals.
   (E) A child can get what it wants by doing what its parent doesn't want it to do.

7. Scientist: In our study, chemical R did not cause cancer in laboratory rats. But we cannot conclude from this that chemical R is safe for humans. After all, many substances known to be carcinogenic to humans cause no cancer in rats; this is probably because some carcinogens cause cancer only via long-term exposure and rats are short lived.

   Which one of the following most precisely describes the role played in the scientist's argument by the statement that chemical R did not cause cancer in laboratory rats?

   (A) It is cited as evidence against the conclusion that chemical R is safe for humans.
   (B) It is advanced to support the contention that test results obtained from laboratory rats cannot be extrapolated to humans.
   (C) It illustrates the claim that rats are too short lived to be suitable as test subjects for the carcinogenic properties of substances to which humans are chronically exposed.
   (D) It is used as evidence to support the hypothesis that chemical R causes cancer in humans via long-term exposure.
   (E) It is cited as being insufficient to support the conclusion that chemical R is safe for humans.

8. Department store manager: There is absolutely no reason to offer our customers free gift wrapping again this holiday season. If most customers take the offer, it will be expensive and time-consuming for us. On the other hand, if only a few customers want it, there is no advantage in offering it.

Which one of the following is an assumption required by the department store manager's argument?

(A) Gift wrapping would cost the store more during this holiday season than in previous holiday seasons.
(B) Anything that slows down shoppers during the holiday season costs the store money.
(C) It would be to the store's advantage to charge customers for gift wrapping services.
(D) It would be expensive to inform customers about the free gift wrapping service.
(E) Either few customers would want free gift wrapping or most customers would want it.

9. Among people who have a history of chronic trouble falling asleep, some rely only on sleeping pills to help them fall asleep, and others practice behavior modification techniques and do not take sleeping pills. Those who rely only on behavior modification fall asleep more quickly than do those who rely only on sleeping pills, so behavior modification is more effective than are sleeping pills in helping people to fall asleep.

Which one of the following, if true, most weakens the argument?

(A) People who do not take sleeping pills spend at least as many total hours asleep each night as do the people who take sleeping pills.
(B) Most people who have trouble falling asleep and who use behavior modification techniques fall asleep more slowly than do most people who have no trouble falling asleep.
(C) Many people who use only behavior modification techniques to help them fall asleep have never used sleeping pills.
(D) The people who are the most likely to take sleeping pills rather than practice behavior modification techniques are those who have previously had the most trouble falling asleep.
(E) The people who are the most likely to practice behavior modification techniques rather than take sleeping pills are those who prefer not to use drugs if other treatments are available.

10. Lawyer: This witness acknowledges being present at the restaurant and watching when my client, a famous television personality, was assaulted. Yet the witness claims to recognize the assailant, but not my famous client. Therefore, the witness's testimony should be excluded.

The lawyer's conclusion follows logically if which one of the following is assumed?

(A) If a witness claims to recognize both parties involved in an assault, then the witness's testimony should be included.
(B) There are other witnesses who can identify the lawyer's client as present during the assault.
(C) It is impossible to determine whether the witness actually recognized the assailant.
(D) The testimony of a witness to an assault should be included only if the witness claims to recognize both parties involved in the assault.
(E) It is unlikely that anyone would fail to recognize the lawyer's client.

11. Biologist: Many paleontologists have suggested that the difficulty of adapting to ice ages was responsible for the evolution of the human brain. But this suggestion must be rejected, for most other animal species adapted to ice ages with no evolutionary changes to their brains.

The biologist's argument is most vulnerable to criticism on which one of the following grounds?

(A) It fails to address adequately the possibility that even if a condition is sufficient to produce an effect in a species, it may not be necessary to produce that effect in that species.
(B) It fails to address adequately the possibility that a condition can produce a change in a species even if it does not produce that change in other species.
(C) It overlooks the possibility that a condition that is needed to produce a change in one species is not needed to produce a similar change in other species.
(D) It presumes without warrant that human beings were presented with greater difficulties during ice ages than were individuals of most other species.
(E) It takes for granted that, if a condition coincided with the emergence of a certain phenomenon, that condition must have been causally responsible for the phenomenon.

GO ON TO THE NEXT PAGE.

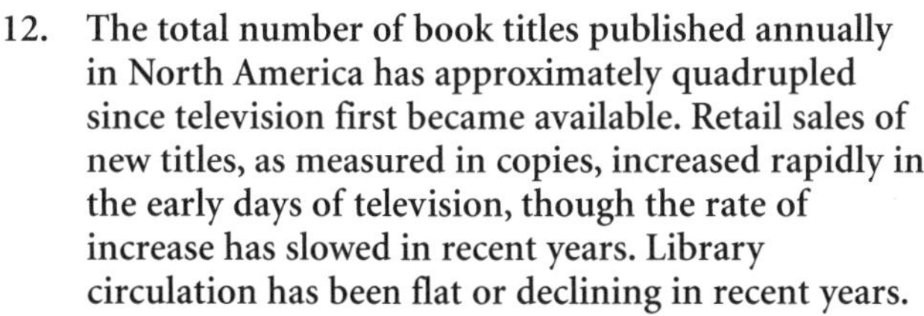

12. The total number of book titles published annually in North America has approximately quadrupled since television first became available. Retail sales of new titles, as measured in copies, increased rapidly in the early days of television, though the rate of increase has slowed in recent years. Library circulation has been flat or declining in recent years.

Which one of the following is most strongly supported by the information above?

(A) Television has, over the years, brought about a reduction in the amount of per capita reading in North America.
(B) The introduction of television usually brings about a decrease in library use.
(C) Book publishers in North America now sell fewer copies per title than they sold in the early days of television.
(D) The availability of television does not always cause a decline in the annual number of book titles published or in the number of books sold.
(E) The introduction of television expanded the market for books in North America.

13. Botanist: It has long been believed that people with children or pets should keep poinsettia plants out of their homes. Although this belief has been encouraged by child-rearing books, which commonly list poinsettias as poisonous and therefore dangerous, it is mistaken. Our research has shown, conclusively, that poinsettias pose no risk to children or pets.

Which one of the following most accurately expresses the conclusion drawn in the botanist's argument?

(A) Child-rearing books should encourage people with children to put poinsettias in their homes.
(B) Poinsettias are not dangerously poisonous.
(C) According to many child-rearing books, poinsettias are dangerous.
(D) The belief that households with children or pets should not have poinsettias is mistaken.
(E) Poinsettias pose no risk to children or pets.

14. Archaeologist: An ancient stone building at our excavation site was composed of three kinds of stone—quartz, granite, and limestone. Of these, only limestone occurs naturally in the area. Most of the buildings at the site from the same time period had limestone as their only stone component, and most were human dwellings. Therefore, the building we are studying probably was not a dwelling.

Which one of the following, if true, would most strengthen the archaeologist's reasoning?

(A) Most of the buildings that were used as dwellings at the site were made, at least in part, of limestone.
(B) Most of the buildings at the site that were not dwellings were made, at least in part, from types of stone that do not occur naturally in the area.
(C) Most of the buildings that were built from stones not naturally occurring in the area were not built with both quartz and granite.
(D) Most of the buildings at the site were used as dwellings.
(E) No quartz has been discovered on the site other than that found in the building being studied.

GO ON TO THE NEXT PAGE.

15. Theodore will be able to file his tax return on time only in the event that he has an accountant prepare his tax return and the accountant does not ask Theodore for any additional documentation of his business expenses. If he does have an accountant prepare his return, the accountant will necessarily ask Theodore to provide this additional documentation. Therefore, Theodore will not be able to file on time.

The pattern of reasoning in which one of the following arguments most closely parallels the pattern of reasoning in the argument above?

(A) Given the demands of Timothy's job, his next free evening will occur next Friday. Since he spent a lot of money on his last evening out, he will probably decide to spend his next free evening at home. Therefore, Timothy will probably be at home next Friday evening.
(B) Tovah cannot attend the concert next week if she is away on business. If she misses that concert, she will not have another opportunity to attend a concert this month. Since she will be away on business, Tovah will not be able to attend a concert this month.
(C) Mark's children will not be content this weekend unless he lets them play video games some of the time. Mark will let them play video games, but only at times when he has no other activities planned. Therefore, unless Mark and his children take a break from planned activities, Mark's children will not be content this weekend.
(D) If Teresa is not seated in first class on her airline flight, she will be seated in business class. Therefore, since she cannot be seated in first class on that flight, she will necessarily be seated in business class.
(E) Susannah will have a relaxing vacation only if her children behave especially well and she does not start to suspect that they are planning some mischief. Since she will certainly start to suspect that they are planning some mischief if they behave especially well, Susannah's vacation cannot possibly be relaxing.

16. When a threat to life is common, as are automobile and industrial accidents, only unusual instances tend to be prominently reported by the news media. Instances of rare threats, such as product tampering, however, are seen as news by reporters and are universally reported in featured stories. People in general tend to estimate the risk of various threats by how frequently those threats come to their attention.

If the statements above are true, which one of the following is most strongly supported on the basis of them?

(A) Whether governmental action will be taken to lessen a common risk depends primarily on the prominence given to the risk by the news media.
(B) People tend to magnify the risk of a threat if the threat seems particularly dreadful or if those who would be affected have no control over it.
(C) Those who get their information primarily from the news media tend to overestimate the risk of uncommon threats relative to the risk of common threats.
(D) Reporters tend not to seek out information about long-range future threats but to concentrate their attention on the immediate past and future.
(E) The resources that are spent on avoiding product tampering are greater than the resources that are spent on avoiding threats that stem from the weather.

GO ON TO THE NEXT PAGE.

17. Real estate agent: Upon selling a home, the sellers are legally entitled to remove any items that are not permanent fixtures. Legally, large appliances like dishwashers are not permanent fixtures. However, since many prospective buyers of the home are likely to assume that large appliances in the home would be included with its purchase, sellers who will be keeping the appliances are morally obliged either to remove them before showing the home or to indicate in some other way that the appliances are not included.

Which one of the following principles, if valid, most helps to justify the real estate agent's argumentation?

(A) If a home's sellers will be keeping any belongings that prospective buyers of the home might assume would be included with the purchase of the home, the sellers are morally obliged to indicate clearly that those belongings are not included.
(B) A home's sellers are morally obliged to ensure that prospective buyers of the home do not assume that any large appliances are permanent fixtures in the home.
(C) A home's sellers are morally obliged to include with the sale of the home at least some of the appliances that are not permanent fixtures but were in the home when it was shown to prospective buyers.
(D) A home's sellers are morally obliged not to deliberately mislead any prospective buyers of their home about which belongings are included with the sale of the home and which are not.
(E) If a home's sellers have indicated in some way that a large appliance is included with the home's purchase, then they are morally obliged not to remove that appliance after showing the home.

18. Many parents rigorously organize their children's activities during playtime, thinking that doing so will enhance their children's cognitive development. But this belief is incorrect. To thoroughly structure a child's playtime and expect this to produce a creative and resourceful child would be like expecting a good novel to be produced by someone who was told exactly what the plot and characters must be.

The argument is most vulnerable to criticism on which one of the following grounds?

(A) It takes for granted that if something is conducive to a certain goal it cannot also be conducive to some other goal.
(B) It overlooks the possibility that many children enjoy rigorously organized playtime.
(C) It takes a necessary condition for something's enhancing a child's creativity and resourcefulness to be a sufficient condition for its doing so.
(D) It fails to consider the possibility that being able to write a good novel requires something more than creativity and resourcefulness.
(E) It fails to consider the possibility that something could enhance a child's overall cognitive development without enhancing the child's creativity and resourcefulness.

19. Bureaucrat: The primary, constant goal of an ideal bureaucracy is to define and classify all possible problems and set out regulations regarding each eventuality. Also, an ideal bureaucracy provides an appeal procedure for any complaint. If a complaint reveals an unanticipated problem, the regulations are expanded to cover the new issue, and for this reason an ideal bureaucracy will have an ever-expanding system of regulations.

Which one of the following is an assumption the bureaucrat's argument requires?

(A) An ideal bureaucracy will provide an appeal procedure for complaints even after it has defined and classified all possible problems and set out regulations regarding each eventuality.
(B) For each problem that an ideal bureaucracy has defined and classified, the bureaucracy has received at least one complaint revealing that problem.
(C) An ideal bureaucracy will never be permanently without complaints about problems that are not covered by that bureaucracy's regulations.
(D) An ideal bureaucracy can reach its primary goal if, but only if, its system of regulations is always expanding to cover problems that had not been anticipated.
(E) Any complaint that an ideal bureaucracy receives will reveal an unanticipated problem that the bureaucracy is capable of defining and classifying.

20. Scientists studying a common type of bacteria have discovered that most bacteria of that type are in hibernation at any given time. Some microbiologists have concluded from this that bacteria in general are usually in hibernation. This conclusion would be reasonable if all types of bacteria were rather similar. But, in fact, since bacteria are extremely diverse, it is unlikely that most types of bacteria hibernate regularly.

Which one of the following most accurately expresses the overall conclusion of the argument?

(A) Bacteria of most types are usually in hibernation.
(B) It is probably not true that most types of bacteria hibernate regularly.
(C) If bacteria are extremely diverse, it is unlikely that most types of bacteria hibernate regularly.
(D) The conclusion that bacteria in general are usually in hibernation would be reasonable if all types of bacteria were rather similar.
(E) It is likely that only one type of bacteria hibernates regularly.

21. Any student who is not required to hand in written homework based on the reading assignments in a course will not complete all of the reading assignments. Even highly motivated students will neglect their reading assignments if they are not required to hand in written homework. Therefore, if the students in a course are given several reading assignments and no written assignments, no student in that course will receive a high grade for the course.

The conclusion of the argument follows logically if which one of the following is assumed?

(A) No student who completes anything less than all of the reading assignments for a course will earn a high grade for that course.
(B) Any student who completes all of the reading and written assignments for a course will earn a high grade in that course.
(C) All highly motivated students who complete all of the reading assignments for a course will receive high grades for that course.
(D) If highly motivated students are required to hand in written homework on their reading assignments, then they will complete all of their reading assignments.
(E) Some highly motivated students will earn high grades in a course if they are required to hand in written homework on their reading assignments.

22. In a study, one group of volunteers was fed a high-protein, low-carbohydrate diet; another group was fed a low-protein, high-carbohydrate diet. Both diets contained the same number of calories, and each volunteer's diet prior to the experiment had contained moderate levels of proteins and carbohydrates. After ten days, those on the low-carbohydrate diet had lost more weight than those on the high-carbohydrate diet. Thus, the most effective way to lose body fat is to eat much protein and shun carbohydrates.

Which one of the following, if true, most weakens the argument above?

(A) A low-protein, high-carbohydrate diet causes the human body to retain water, the added weight of which largely compensates for the weight of any body fat lost, whereas a high-protein, low-carbohydrate diet does not.
(B) Many people who consume large quantities of protein nevertheless gain significant amounts of body fat.
(C) A high-protein, low-carbohydrate diet will often enable the human body to convert some body fat into muscle, without causing any significant overall weight loss.
(D) In the experiment, the volunteers on the high-carbohydrate diet engaged in regular exercise of a kind known to produce weight loss, and those on the low-carbohydrate diet did not.
(E) Many of the volunteers who had been on the low-carbohydrate diet eventually regained much of the weight they had lost on the diet after returning to their normal diets.

GO ON TO THE NEXT PAGE.

23. Essayist: Computers have the capacity to represent and to perform logical transformations on pieces of information. Since exactly the same applies to the human mind, the human mind is a type of computer.

The flawed pattern of reasoning in which one of the following most closely resembles the flawed pattern of reasoning in the essayist's argument?

(A) Often individual animals sacrifice their lives when the survival of their offspring or close relatives is threatened. It is probable, therefore, that there is a biological basis for the fact that human beings are similarly often willing to sacrifice their own well-being for the good of their community.
(B) In the plastic arts, such as sculpture or painting, no work can depend for its effectiveness upon a verbal narrative that explains it. Since the same can be said of poetry, we cannot consider this characteristic as a reasonable criterion for distinguishing the plastic arts from other arts.
(C) In any organism, the proper functioning of each component depends upon the proper functioning of every other component. Thus, communities belong to the category of organisms, since communities are invariably characterized by this same interdependence of components.
(D) Some vitamins require the presence in adequate amounts of some mineral in order to be fully beneficial to the body. Thus, since selenium is needed to make vitamin E fully active, anyone with a selenium deficiency will have a greater risk of contracting those diseases from which vitamin E provides some measure of protection.
(E) Friendship often involves obligations whose fulfillment can be painful or burdensome. The same can be said of various forms of cooperation that cannot strictly be called friendship. Thus cooperation, like friendship, can require that priority be given to goals other than mere self-interest.

24. It is popularly believed that a poem has whatever meaning is assigned to it by the reader. But objective evaluation of poetry is possible only if this popular belief is false; for the aesthetic value of a poem cannot be discussed unless it is possible for at least two readers to agree on the correct interpretation of the poem.

Which one of the following is an assumption required by the argument?

(A) Only if they find the same meaning in a poem can two people each judge that it has aesthetic value.
(B) If two readers agree about the meaning of a given poem, that ensures that an objective evaluation of the poem can be made.
(C) Discussion of a poem is possible only if it is false that a poem has whatever meaning is assigned to it by the reader.
(D) A given poem can be objectively evaluated only if the poem's aesthetic value can be discussed.
(E) Aesthetic evaluation of literature is best accomplished through discussion by more than two readers.

25. Dean: The mathematics department at our university has said that it should be given sole responsibility for teaching the course Statistics for the Social Sciences. But this course has no more mathematics in it than high school algebra does. The fact that a course has mathematics in it does not mean that it needs to be taught by a mathematics professor, any more than a course approaching its subject from a historical perspective must be taught by a history professor. Such demands by the mathematics department are therefore unjustified.

The dean's argument is most vulnerable to criticism on the grounds that it

(A) presumes, without providing justification, that expertise in a subject does not enable one to teach that subject well
(B) purports to refute a view by showing that one possible reason for that view is insufficient
(C) presumes, without providing justification, that most students are as knowledgeable about mathematics as they are about history
(D) fails to establish that mathematics professors are not capable of teaching Statistics for the Social Sciences effectively
(E) presumes, without providing justification, that any policies that apply to history courses must be justified with respect to mathematics courses

S T O P

IF YOU FINISH BEFORE TIME IS CALLED, YOU MAY CHECK YOUR WORK ON THIS SECTION ONLY.
DO NOT WORK ON ANY OTHER SECTION IN THE TEST.

SECTION IV

Time—35 minutes

23 Questions

Directions: Each group of questions in this section is based on a set of conditions. In answering some of the questions, it may be useful to draw a rough diagram. Choose the response that most accurately and completely answers each question and blacken the corresponding space on your answer sheet.

Questions 1–6

There are exactly six law students—Gambini, Little, Mitchum, Richardson, Saito, and Veracruz—in a trial advocacy class. The class is divided into three trial teams—team 1, team 2, and team 3—of exactly two students each. Each student is on exactly one of the teams. Each student prepares exactly one of either the opening argument or the final argument for his or her team. The teams must be formed according to the following specifications:

Mitchum is on the same team as either Gambini or Veracruz.
Little prepares an opening argument.
Either Gambini or Richardson, but not both, prepares a final argument.

1. Which one of the following could be the composition of each team and the argument each student prepares?

(A) team 1: Little, opening; Gambini, final
team 2: Veracruz, opening; Mitchum, final
team 3: Saito, opening; Richardson, final
(B) team 1: Mitchum, opening; Gambini, final
team 2: Veracruz, opening; Little, final
team 3: Richardson, opening; Saito, final
(C) team 1: Richardson, opening; Gambini, final
team 2: Mitchum, opening; Saito, final
team 3: Little, opening; Veracruz, final
(D) team 1: Gambini, opening; Mitchum, final
team 2: Little, opening; Richardson, final
team 3: Veracruz, opening; Saito, final
(E) team 1: Gambini, opening; Mitchum, final
team 2: Richardson, opening; Saito, final
team 3: Little, opening; Veracruz, final

2. If Gambini is on the same team as Mitchum, and if Gambini prepares the final argument for that team, then which one of the following could be true?

(A) Little is on the same team as Veracruz, who prepares the opening argument for the team.
(B) Richardson is on the same team as Saito, who prepares the opening argument for the team.
(C) Richardson is on the same team as Saito, who prepares the final argument for the team.
(D) Saito is on the same team as Veracruz, who prepares the opening argument for the team.
(E) Saito is on the same team as Veracruz, who prepares the final argument for the team.

3. Which one of the following could be true?

(A) Gambini, who prepares a final argument, is on the same team as Richardson.
(B) Gambini, who prepares a final argument, is on the same team as Veracruz.
(C) Gambini, who prepares an opening argument, is on the same team as Little.
(D) Little, who prepares an opening argument, is on the same team as Mitchum.
(E) Mitchum, who prepares an opening argument, is on the same team as Saito.

4. If Richardson is on the same team as Veracruz, then for exactly how many of the students can it be determined which of the arguments he or she prepares?

(A) one
(B) two
(C) three
(D) four
(E) five

5. If Little is on the same team as Richardson, then which one of the following must be true?

(A) Saito is on the same team as Veracruz.
(B) Gambini is on the same team as Mitchum.
(C) Mitchum prepares a final argument.
(D) Veracruz prepares a final argument.
(E) Gambini prepares an opening argument.

6. If Saito prepares an opening argument, then which one of the following pairs of students could be on the same team as each other?

(A) Gambini and Little
(B) Gambini and Saito
(C) Little and Veracruz
(D) Mitchum and Veracruz
(E) Richardson and Veracruz

GO ON TO THE NEXT PAGE.

Questions 7–12

While on vacation, Sukanya receives several e-mail messages from work, each message from one of three associates: Hilary, Jerome, and Lula. Sukanya receives at least one and no more than two messages from each of them. Sukanya receives each message on the day it is sent. No more than one message is sent each day. The messages are received in a manner consistent with the following:

The first message is not from Lula.
Both the first and last messages are from the same person.
Exactly once Sukanya receives a message from Jerome on the day after receiving one from Hilary.
Of the first three messages, exactly one is from Jerome.

7. Which one of the following could be an accurate list of the e-mail messages Sukanya receives, identified by the person each message is from and listed in the order she receives them?

(A) Lula, Hilary, Jerome, Hilary, Jerome, Lula
(B) Jerome, Lula, Hilary, Lula, Jerome
(C) Jerome, Lula, Hilary, Jerome, Hilary
(D) Jerome, Lula, Hilary, Hilary, Jerome
(E) Hilary, Lula, Lula, Jerome, Jerome, Hilary

8. What is the maximum possible number of e-mail messages Sukanya receives after Jerome's first message but before Hilary's first message?

(A) zero
(B) one
(C) two
(D) three
(E) four

9. If Sukanya receives exactly four e-mail messages, then which one of the following must be true?

(A) Exactly one of the messages is from Lula.
(B) Exactly two of the messages are from Jerome.
(C) The second message is from Lula.
(D) The third message is from Hilary.
(E) The fourth message is from Jerome.

10. Which one of the following e-mail messages CANNOT be from Lula?

(A) the second message
(B) the third message
(C) the fourth message
(D) the fifth message (if there is a fifth one)
(E) the sixth message (if there is a sixth one)

11. If Sukanya receives six e-mail messages, the fifth of which is from Lula, which one of the following must be true?

(A) The first message is from Jerome.
(B) The second message is from Lula.
(C) The third message is from Hilary.
(D) The fourth message is from Jerome.
(E) The sixth message is from Lula.

12. If Sukanya receives two e-mail messages from Lula, what is the maximum possible number of e-mail messages Sukanya receives after Lula's first message but before Lula's last message?

(A) zero
(B) one
(C) two
(D) three
(E) four

GO ON TO THE NEXT PAGE.

Questions 13–18

Mercotek carried out a study to compare the productivity of its night shift with that of its day shift. Every week the company's six crews—F, G, H, R, S, and T—were ranked from first (most productive) to sixth (least productive). There were no ties. For any given week, either G and T were the two night-shift crews or else S and H were—the four other crews were the day-shift crews for that week. The following relationships held for every week of the study:

F is more productive than G.
R is more productive than S.
R is more productive than T.
S is more productive than H.
G is more productive than T.

13. Which one of the following could be an accurate ranking of all the crews, in order from first to sixth, for a given week of the study?

(A) F, G, T, R, S, H
(B) F, R, G, T, H, S
(C) G, R, T, S, H, F
(D) R, F, G, S, H, T
(E) R, S, H, T, F, G

14. If F is ranked third for a given week of the study, then which one of the following could also be true of that week?

(A) G ranks second.
(B) H ranks fourth.
(C) R ranks second.
(D) S ranks fourth.
(E) T ranks fourth.

15. Which one of the following CANNOT be the crew ranked fifth for any given week of the study?

(A) G
(B) H
(C) R
(D) S
(E) T

16. For any given week of the study, the ranking of all the crews is completely determined if which one of the following is true?

(A) F ranks second that week.
(B) G ranks fifth that week.
(C) H ranks third that week.
(D) R ranks third that week.
(E) S ranks third that week.

17. If the night-shift crews rank fifth and sixth for a given week of the study, then which one of the following could also be true of that week?

(A) G ranks fourth.
(B) H ranks fifth.
(C) R ranks third.
(D) S ranks fourth.
(E) T ranks fifth.

18. Which one of the following is a complete and accurate list of the crews that CANNOT be ranked third for any given week of the study?

(A) G, H, S
(B) R, T
(C) F, T
(D) G, T
(E) T

GO ON TO THE NEXT PAGE.

Questions 19–23

A shuttle van stops exactly four times—once at Fundy, once at Los Altos, once at Mineola, and once at Simcoe—not necessarily in that order. The van starts with exactly four passengers on board—Greg, Jasmine, Rosa, and Vijay—each of whom gets off at a different stop. The following conditions hold:

Los Altos is the first or second stop.
Rosa is still on board when the van reaches Mineola.
Jasmine is on board longer than Vijay.
If Jasmine is still on board when the van reaches Fundy, then Greg is still on board when the van reaches Simcoe; otherwise, Greg is not still on board when the van reaches Simcoe.

19. Which one of the following could be a complete and accurate matching of stops, listed in the order in which the van stops at them, to the passengers who get off at them?

(A) Los Altos: Greg
Mineola: Vijay
Fundy: Jasmine
Simcoe: Rosa
(B) Simcoe: Vijay
Mineola: Greg
Fundy: Rosa
Los Altos: Jasmine
(C) Los Altos: Jasmine
Mineola: Vijay
Fundy: Greg
Simcoe: Rosa
(D) Los Altos: Rosa
Mineola: Vijay
Fundy: Jasmine
Simcoe: Greg
(E) Los Altos: Vijay
Fundy: Jasmine
Mineola: Rosa
Simcoe: Greg

20. If Mineola is the first stop, which one of the following is a complete and accurate list of the passengers who could possibly get off there?

(A) Rosa
(B) Greg, Rosa
(C) Greg, Vijay
(D) Greg, Rosa, Vijay
(E) Jasmine, Rosa, Vijay

21. If Fundy is the first stop, then which one of the following could accurately list the passengers in order from first to last off?

(A) Greg, Vijay, Jasmine, Rosa
(B) Rosa, Vijay, Greg, Jasmine
(C) Vijay, Greg, Rosa, Jasmine
(D) Vijay, Jasmine, Greg, Rosa
(E) Vijay, Rosa, Jasmine, Greg

22. Which one of the following must be true if Greg is still on board both when the van reaches Los Altos and when it reaches Simcoe, not necessarily in that order, assuming he is the second one off the van?

(A) Vijay is on board when the van reaches Simcoe.
(B) Vijay is on board when the van reaches Los Altos.
(C) Rosa is on board when the van reaches Simcoe.
(D) Rosa is on board when the van reaches Fundy.
(E) Jasmine is on board when the van reaches Mineola.

23. If Greg is not on board when the van reaches Simcoe, then which one of the following must be false?

(A) Greg is on board when the van reaches Fundy.
(B) Jasmine is on board when the van reaches Mineola.
(C) Rosa is on board when the van reaches Fundy.
(D) Vijay is on board when the van reaches Fundy.
(E) Vijay is on board when the van reaches Mineola.

S T O P

IF YOU FINISH BEFORE TIME IS CALLED, YOU MAY CHECK YOUR WORK ON THIS SECTION ONLY.
DO NOT WORK ON ANY OTHER SECTION IN THE TEST.

Acknowledgment is made to the following sources from which material has been adapted for use in this test booklet:

Peter M. Garber, *Famous Bubbles: The Fundamentals of Early Manias*. ©2000 by MIT Press.

John Sandlos, "Purple Loosestrife and the 'Bounding' of Nature in North American Wetlands." ©1997 by Electronic Journal of Sociology.

Linda Ching Sledge, "Oral Tradition in Kingston's *China Men*." ©1990 by The Modern Language Association of America.

Daniel Q. Thompson, Ronald L. Stuckey, and Edith B. Thompson, "Spread, Impact, and Control of Purple Loosestrife (*Lythrum salicaria*) in North American Wetlands." ©1987 by US Fish and Wildlife Service.

LSAT WRITING SAMPLE TOPIC

Directions: The scenario presented below describes two choices, either one of which can be supported on the basis of the information given. Your essay should consider both choices and argue for one over the other, based on the two specified criteria and the facts provided. There is no "right" or "wrong" choice: a reasonable argument can be made for either.

Aña Rodriguez is a shy five-year-old girl. The Rodriguez family must send Aña to either Mercer Preschool or Butte Preschool. The Rodriguezes are equally satisfied with the quality of the teachers and the facilities at both schools. Using the facts below, write an essay in which you argue for one preschool over the other based on the following two criteria:

- The preschool must provide a stimulating social environment for Aña.
- The preschool must be conveniently located.

Aña is an only child who lives on a block with no other children her age. Two children Aña occasionally plays with at the local playground would be in her class at Mercer. The class size at Mercer is eight children. Mercer occupies its students' time, for the most part, with activities for the entire class. There is little unstructured time. Mercer is within easy walking distance of the Rodriguez home. Parking near Mercer is nearly impossible. After the infrequent winter snowstorms, snow is typically left to melt rather than shoveled. Walking can be difficult at such times.

Aña's best friend will be attending Butte. Aña knows none of the other children who would be in her class. The class size at Butte is 12 children. Most of the students' time is not formally structured. The children are free to participate in a number of optional activities with or without their classmates. The few structured activities all involve small groups of two or three children. Butte is a 10-minute drive, or 20-minute bus ride, from the Rodriguez house. Parking is always available since Butte has its own lot. Aña's younger cousin Pablo, who lives on her block, will be attending a different class at Butte.

Scratch Paper

Do not write your essay in this space.

Directions:

1. Use the Answer Key on the next page to check your answers.

2. Use the Scoring Worksheet below to compute your raw score.

3. Use the Score Conversion Chart to convert your raw score into the 120–180 scale.

Scoring Worksheet

1. Enter the number of questions you answered correctly in each section

	Number Correct
SECTION I..........	______
SECTION II.........	______
SECTION III........	______
SECTION IV.........	______

2. Enter the sum here: ______ **This is your Raw Score.**

Conversion Chart

For Converting Raw Score to the 120–180 LSAT Scaled Score
LSAT PrepTest 55

REPORTED SCORE	LOWEST RAW SCORE	HIGHEST RAW SCORE
180	99	100
179	98	98
178	97	97
177	96	96
176	—*	—*
175	95	95
174	94	94
173	—*	—*
172	93	93
171	92	92
170	91	91
169	90	90
168	89	89
167	87	88
166	86	86
165	85	85
164	83	84
163	82	82
162	81	81
161	79	80
160	77	78
159	76	76
158	74	75
157	72	73
156	70	71
155	69	69
154	67	68
153	65	66
152	63	64
151	61	62
150	59	60
149	58	58
148	56	57
147	54	55
146	52	53
145	50	51
144	48	49
143	47	47
142	45	46
141	43	44
140	41	42
139	40	40
138	38	39
137	36	37
136	35	35
135	33	34
134	32	32
133	30	31
132	29	29
131	27	28
130	26	26
129	25	25
128	24	24
127	22	23
126	21	21
125	20	20
124	19	19
123	18	18
122	17	17
121	16	16
120	0	15

*There is no raw score that will produce this scaled score for this PrepTest.

SECTION I

1.	B	8.	D	15.	D	22.	E
2.	A	9.	D	16.	B	23.	B
3.	C	10.	B	17.	D	24.	D
4.	A	11.	E	18.	E	25.	C
5.	B	12.	C	19.	C		
6.	A	13.	D	20.	A		
7.	A	14.	E	21.	B		

SECTION II

1.	D	8.	E	15.	D	22.	D
2.	A	9.	B	16.	C	23.	D
3.	A	10.	E	17.	B	24.	B
4.	B	11.	A	18.	C	25.	B
5.	E	12.	C	19.	D	26.	C
6.	E	13.	A	20.	B	27.	D
7.	A	14.	A	21.	A		

SECTION III

1.	B	8.	E	15.	E	22.	A
2.	C	9.	D	16.	C	23.	C
3.	B	10.	D	17.	A	24.	D
4.	A	11.	B	18.	E	25.	B
5.	A	12.	D	19.	C		
6.	D	13.	D	20.	B		
7.	E	14.	B	21.	A		

SECTION IV

1.	D	8.	C	15.	C	22.	C
2.	C	9.	A	16.	C	23.	D
3.	A	10.	E	17.	C		
4.	B	11.	D	18.	E		
5.	E	12.	B	19.	E		
6.	C	13.	D	20.	D		
7.	D	14.	B	21.	D		

Experimental Section Answer Key
June 1999, PrepTest 27, Section 2

1.	E	8.	E	15.	C	22.	E
2.	E	9.	C	16.	A	23.	A
3.	C	10.	D	17.	E	24.	D
4.	C	11.	A	18.	B		
5.	D	12.	C	19.	E		
6.	B	13.	D	20.	A		
7.	B	14.	A	21.	B		

PrepTest 56
December 2008

Time—35 minutes

26 Questions

Directions: The questions in this section are based on the reasoning contained in brief statements or passages. For some questions, more than one of the choices could conceivably answer the question. However, you are to choose the best answer; that is, the response that most accurately and completely answers the question. You should not make assumptions that are by commonsense standards implausible, superfluous, or incompatible with the passage. After you have chosen the best answer, blacken the corresponding space on your answer sheet.

1. Powell: Private waste-removal companies spend 60 percent of what public waste-removal companies spend per customer, yet give their customers at least as good service. Private waste-removal companies, therefore, work more efficiently.

   Freeman: Your conclusion is unwarranted. Different customers have different waste-removal needs. Since private companies, unlike their public counterparts, can select which customers to serve, they choose to exclude the potential customers whom they judge to be the most costly to serve.

   The issue in dispute between Powell and Freeman is the

   (A) accuracy of the figure of 60 percent with regard to the difference in service costs between private and public waste-removal companies
   (B) reason private waste-removal companies are able to offer service comparable to that offered by public ones while spending less money per customer
   (C) ability of private versus public waste-removal companies to select which customers to serve
   (D) likelihood of the local authorities' turning public waste-removal companies into private ones so that the companies can operate with lower service costs than they now incur
   (E) relationship between the needs of a waste-removal customer and the amount of money it takes to serve that customer

2. Although 90 percent of the population believes itself to be well informed about health care, only 20 percent knows enough about DNA to understand a news story about DNA. So apparently at least 80 percent of the population does not know enough about medical concepts to make well-informed personal medical choices or to make good public policy decisions about health care.

   The argument's reasoning is questionable because the argument fails to demonstrate that

   (A) those people who can understand news stories about DNA are able to make well-informed personal medical choices
   (B) more than 20 percent of the population needs to be well informed about health care for good public policy decisions about health care to be made
   (C) one's being able to make well-informed personal medical choices ensures that one makes good public policy decisions about health care
   (D) an understanding of DNA is essential to making well-informed personal medical choices or to making good public policy decisions about health care
   (E) since 90 percent of the population believes itself to be well informed about health care, at least 70 percent of the population is mistaken in that belief

GO ON TO THE NEXT PAGE.

Questions 3–4

In Yasukawa's month-long study of blackbirds, the percentage of smaller birds that survived the duration of the study exceeded the percentage of larger birds that survived. However, Yasukawa's conclusion that size is a determinant of a blackbird's chances of survival over a month-long period is probably mistaken, since smaller blackbirds are generally younger than larger ones.

3. The statements above, if true, support which one of the following inferences?

   (A) Among the blackbirds that survived the month-long study, there was no relation between size and age.
   (B) Larger blackbirds of a given age are actually more likely to survive over a one-month period than are smaller blackbirds of the same age.
   (C) Among blackbirds of the same size, a difference in age probably does not indicate a difference in chances of survival over a one-month period.
   (D) Among blackbirds of the same age, a difference in size may not indicate a difference in chances of survival over a month-long period.
   (E) With a larger sample of blackbirds, the percentage of smaller birds that survive a one-month period would be the same as the percentage of larger birds that survive.

4. Which one of the following, if true, indicates that the criticism of Yasukawa's research is based on a misunderstanding of it?

   (A) Yasukawa compared the survival chances of two different species of blackbirds, a larger and a small species, rather than of different sizes of birds within one species.
   (B) Yasukawa examined blackbirds in their natural habitat rather than in captivity.
   (C) Yasukawa did not compare the survival chances of blackbirds with those of other kinds of birds.
   (D) Yasukawa noted that the larger blackbirds had more success in fights than did the smaller blackbirds.
   (E) Yasukawa noted that the larger blackbirds tended to have more firmly established social hierarchies than did the smaller blackbirds.

5. During the 1980's Japanese collectors were very active in the market for European art, especially as purchasers of nineteenth-century Impressionist paintings. This striking pattern surely reflects a specific preference on the part of many Japanese collectors for certain aesthetic attributes they found in nineteenth-century Impressionist paintings.

   Which one of the following, if true, most strongly supports the explanation above?

   (A) Impressionist paintings first became popular among art collectors in Europe at the beginning of the twentieth century.
   (B) During the 1980s, the Japanese economy underwent a sustained expansion that was unprecedented in the country's recent history.
   (C) Several nineteenth-century Impressionist painters adopted certain techniques and visual effects found in Japanese prints that are highly esteemed in Japan.
   (D) During the 1960s and 1970s, the prices of nineteenth-century Impressionist paintings often exceeded the prices of paintings by older European masters.
   (E) During the 1980s, collectors from Japan and around the world purchased many paintings and prints by well-known twentieth-century Japanese artists.

GO ON TO THE NEXT PAGE.

6. Frankie: If jelly makers were given incentives to make a certain percentage of their jellies from cloudberries, income for cloudberry gatherers would increase.

Anna: That plan would fail. Cacao, like cloudberries, was once harvested from wild plants. When chocolate became popular in Europe, the cacao gathers could not supply enough to meet the increased demand, and farmers began to grow large quantities of it at low cost. Now all cacao used in commercial chocolate production is grown on farms. Likewise, if the demand for cloudberries increases, domesticated berries grown on farms will completely supplant berries gathered in the wild.

Anna's argument proceeds by

(A) giving a reason why a proposed course of action would be beneficial to all those affected by it
(B) reinterpreting evidence presented in support of a proposal as a reason to reject the proposal
(C) projecting the result of following a proposal in a given situation by comparing that situation with a past situation
(D) proposing a general theory as a way of explaining a specific market situation
(E) contending that the uses for one product are similar to the uses for another product

7. Because of the recent recession in Country A, most magazines published there have experienced decreases in advertising revenue, so much so that the survival of the most widely read magazines is in grave doubt. At the same time, however, more people in Country A are reading more magazines than ever before, and the number of financially successful magazines in Country A is greater than ever.

Which one the following, if true, most helps to resolve the apparent discrepancy in the information above?

(A) Most magazines reduce the amount they charge for advertisements during a recession.
(B) The audience for a successful television show far exceeds the readership of even the most widely read magazine.
(C) Advertising is the main source of revenue only for the most widely read magazines; other magazines rely on circulation for their revenue.
(D) Because of the recession, people in Country A have cut back on magazine subscriptions and are reading borrowed magazines.
(E) More of the new general interest magazines that were launched this year in Country A have survived than survived in previous years.

8. The gray squirrel, introduced into local woodlands ten years ago, threatens the indigenous population of an endangered owl species, because the squirrels' habitual stripping of tree bark destroys the trees in which the owls nest. Some local officials have advocated setting out poison for the gray squirrels. The officials argue that this measure, while eliminating the squirrels, would pose no threat to the owl population, since the poison would be placed in containers accessible only to squirrels and other rodents.

Which one of the following, if true, most calls into question the officials' argument?

(A) One of the species whose members are likely to eat the poison is the red squirrel, a species on which owls do not prey.
(B) The owls whose nesting sites are currently being destroyed by the gray squirrels feed primarily on rodents.
(C) No indigenous population of any other bird species apart from the endangered owls is threatened by the gray squirrels.
(D) The owls that are threatened build their nests in the tops of trees, but the gray squirrels strip away bark from the trunks.
(E) The officials' plan entails adding the poison to food sources that are usually eaten by rodents but not by other animals.

GO ON TO THE NEXT PAGE.

Questions 9–10

Sales manager: Last year the total number of meals sold in our company's restaurants was much higher than it was the year before. Obviously consumers find our meals desirable.

Accountant: If you look at individual restaurants, however, you find that the number of meals sold actually decreased substantially at every one of our restaurants that was in operation both last year and the year before. The desirability of our meals to consumers has clearly decreased, given that this group of restaurants—the only ones for which we have sales figures that permit a comparison between last year and the year before—demonstrates a trend toward fewer sales.

9. If the sales figures cited by the accountant and the sales manager are both accurate, which one of the following must be true?

(A) The company opened at least one new restaurant in the last two years.
(B) The company's meals are less competitive than they once were.
(C) The quality of the company's meals has not improved over the past two years.
(D) The prices of the company's meals have changed over the past two years.
(E) The market share captured by the company's restaurants fell last year.

10. Which one of the following, if true, most seriously calls into question the accountant's argument?

(A) The company's restaurants last year dropped from their menus most of the new dishes that had been introduced the year before.
(B) Prior to last year there was an overall downward trend in the company's sales.
(C) Those of the company's restaurants that did increase their sales last year did not offer large discounts on prices to attract customers.
(D) Sales of the company's most expensive meal contributed little to the overall two-year sales increase.
(E) Most of the company's restaurants that were in operation throughout both last year and the year before are located in areas where residents experienced a severe overall decline in income last year.

11. A local chemical plant produces pesticides that can cause sterility in small mammals such as otters. Soon after the plant began operating, the incidence of sterility among the otters that swim in a nearby river increased dramatically. Therefore, pesticides are definitely contaminating the river.

Which one of the following arguments contains a flaw in reasoning that is similar to one in the argument above?

(A) The bacteria that cause tetanus live in the digestive tract of horses. Tetanus is a highly infectious disease. Consequently it must be that horses contract tetanus more frequently than do most other animals.
(B) A diet low in calcium can cause a drop in egg production in poultry. When chickens on a local farm were let out in the spring to forage for food, their egg production dropped noticeably. So the food found and eaten by the chickens is undeniably low in calcium.
(C) Animals that are undernourished are very susceptible to infection. Animals in the largest metropolitan zoos are not undernourished, so they surely must not be very susceptible to disease.
(D) Apes are defined by having, among other characteristics, opposable thumbs and no external tail. Recently, fossil remains of a previously unknown animal were found. Because this animal had opposable thumbs, it must have been an ape.
(E) The only animal that could have produced a track similar to this one is a bear. But there are no bears in this area of the country, so this animal track is a fake.

GO ON TO THE NEXT PAGE.

12. Clothes made from natural fibers such as cotton, unlike clothes made from artificial fibers such as polyester often shrink when washed at high temperatures. The reason for this shrinkage is that natural fibers are tightly curled in their original state. Since the manufacturer of cloth requires straight fibers, natural fibers are artificially straightened prior to being made into cloth. High temperatures cause all fibers in cloth to return to their original states.

Which one of the following is most strongly supported by the information above?

(A) Washing clothes made from natural fibers at low temperatures causes the fibers to straighten slightly.
(B) High temperatures have no effect on the straightness of fibers in clothes made from a blend of natural and artificial fibers.
(C) Clothes made from natural fibers stretch more easily than do clothes made from artificial fibers.
(D) If natural fibers that have been straightened and used for cloth are curled up again by high temperatures, they cannot be straightened again.
(E) Artificial fibers are straight in their original state.

13. Problems caused by the leaching of pollutants from dumps and landfills are worst in countries with an annual per capita economic output of $4,000 to $5,000, and less severe for considerably poorer and considerably richer countries. This is so because pollution problems increase during the early stages of a country's industrial development but then diminish as increasing industrial development generates adequate resources to tackle such problems. Therefore, problems caused by such leaching in Country X, where the annual per capita economic output is now $5,000, should begin to diminish in the next few years.

Which one of the following is an assumption on which the argument depends?

(A) Within the next few years, Country X will impose a system of fines for illegal waste disposal by its industrial companies.
(B) Countries surrounding Country X will reduce the amount of pollution that their factories release into the air and water.
(C) Industrial development in Country X will increase in the next few years.
(D) Country X will begin the process of industrialization in the next few years.
(E) No other country with a similar amount of industrial development has pollution problems that are as severe as those in Country X.

14. Critic: Many popular psychological theories are poor theories in that they are inelegant and do not help to dispel the mystery that surrounds our psyche. However, this is not really important. The theories produce the right results: therapeutically, they tend to have greater success than their more scientific rivals.

The statement about the relative therapeutic success of many popular psychological theories plays which one of the following roles in the critic's argument?

(A) It is used to disprove evidence against these theories.
(B) It is used to override some considerations against these theories.
(C) It is used to suggest that popular psychological theories are actually better scientific explanations than are their rivals.
(D) It is used to illustrate what the critic takes to be the most important aspect of scientific theories.
(E) It is used to suggest that the popular theories may not be as devoid of explanatory power as one may be led to believe.

15. Tony: Few anarchists have ever performed violent actions. These few are vastly outnumbered by the violent adherents of other political ideologies. Therefore, the special association in the public mind between anarchism and political violence is unwarranted.

Keisha: Anarchists have always been few in number, whereas other ideologies have often spawned mass movements. Therefore, the proportion of anarchists who are violent is possibly greater than the proportion of adherents of other ideologies who are violent.

Keisha responds to Tony's argument in which one of the following ways?

(A) She shows that Tony's conclusion is questionable because Tony bases it on a comparison that inappropriately involves absolute numbers rather than proportions.
(B) She attempts to undermine Tony's conclusion by introducing plausible evidence that is incompatible with the evidence Tony offers in support of that conclusion.
(C) She questions the accuracy of the claims on which Tony bases his conclusion.
(D) She presents evidence that the two groups Tony has compared have no significant qualities in common.
(E) She indicates that Tony has adopted questionable criteria for including certain people in the groups he is comparing.

GO ON TO THE NEXT PAGE.

16. Recent research shows that sound change (pronunciation shift) in a language is not gradual. New sounds often emerge suddenly. This confounds the classical account of sound change, whose central tenet is gradualness. Since this classical account must be discarded, sound-change theory in general must also be.

    Which one of the following, if assumed, does most to justify the argument's conclusion?

    (A) The data on which the classical account of sound-change theory was based are now known to be inaccurate.
    (B) The emergence of new sounds appears to be random.
    (C) The meeting of linguistically disparate cultures can affect the sound of their languages in unpredictable ways.
    (D) All theories of sound change rely heavily on the classical theory.
    (E) For most languages, historical records of their earlier stages are scarce or nonexistent.

17. The stable functioning of a society depends upon the relatively long-term stability of the goals of its citizens. This is clear from the fact that unless the majority of individuals have a predictable and enduring set of aspirations, it will be impossible for a legislature to craft laws that will augment the satisfaction of the citizenry, and it should be obvious that a society is stable only if its laws tend to increase the happiness of its citizens.

    The claim that a society is stable only if its laws tend to increase the happiness of its citizens plays which one of the following roles in the argument?

    (A) It is the conclusion of the argument.
    (B) It helps to support the conclusion of the argument.
    (C) It is a claim that must be refuted if the conclusion is to be established.
    (D) It is a consequence of the argument.
    (E) It is used to illustrate the general principle that the argument presupposes.

18. Astronauts who experience weightlessness frequently get motion sickness. The astronauts see their own motion relative to passing objects, but while the astronauts are weightless their inner ears indicate that their bodies are not moving. The astronauts' experience is best explained by the hypothesis that conflicting information received by the brain about the body's motion causes motion sickness.

    Which one of the following, if true, provides the strongest additional support for the hypotheses above?

    (A) During rough voyages ship passengers in cabins providing a view of the water are less likely to get motion sickness than are passengers in cabins providing no view.
    (B) Many people who are experienced airplane passengers occasionally get motion sickness.
    (C) Some automobile passengers whose inner ears indicate that they are moving and who have a clear view of the objects they are passing get motion sickness.
    (D) People who have aisle seats in trains or airplanes are as likely to get motion sickness as are people who have window seats.
    (E) Some astronauts do not get motion sickness even after being in orbit for several days.

19. Pollen and other allergens can cause cells in the nose to release histamine, a chemical that inflames nasal tissue and causes runny nose, congestion, and sneezing. Antihistamines minimize these allergy symptoms by blocking the action of histamine. In addition, antihistamines have other effects, including drowsiness. However, histamine plays no role in the processes by which colds produce their symptoms.

    If the statements above are true, which one of the following must also be true?

    (A) Pollen and other allergens do not cause colds.
    (B) Colds are more difficult to treat than allergies.
    (C) Antihistamines, when taken alone, are ineffective against congestion caused by colds.
    (D) The sleeplessness that sometimes accompanies allergies can be effectively treated with antihistamines.
    (E) Any effect antihistamines may have in reducing cold symptoms does not result from blocking the action of histamine.

20. A poem is any work of art that exploits some of the musical characteristics of language, such as meter, rhythm, euphony, and rhyme. A novel, though it may be a work of art in language, does not usually exploit the musical characteristics of language. A symphony, though it may be a work of art that exploit the musical characteristics of sounds, rarely involves language. A limerick, though it may exploit some musical characteristics of language, is not, strictly speaking, art.

The statements above, if true, most strongly support which one of the following?

(A) If a creation is neither a poem, nor a novel, nor a symphony, then it is not a work of art.
(B) An example of so-called blank verse, which does not rhyme, is not really a poem.
(C) If a novel exploits meter and rhyme while standing as a work of art, then it is both a novel and a poem.
(D) Limericks constitute a nonartistic type of poetry.
(E) If a symphony does not exploit the musical characteristics of sound, then it is not a work of art.

21. In order to pressure the government of Country S to become less repressive, some legislators in Country R want to ban all exports from R to S. Companies in R that manufacture telecommunication equipment such as telephones and fax machines have argued that exports of their products should be exempted from the ban, on the grounds that it is impossible for a country to remain repressive when telecommunication equipment is widely available to the population of that country.

Which one of the following is an assumption on which the argument given by the manufacturers depends?

(A) The government of S has recently increased the amount of telecommunication equipment it allows to be imported into the country.
(B) The telecommunication equipment that would be imported into S if the exemption were to be granted would not be available solely to top government officials in S.
(C) A majority of the members of R's legislature do not favor exempting telecommunication equipment from the ban on exports to Country S.
(D) Of all exports that could be sent to Country S, telecommunication equipment would be the most effective in helping citizens of S oppose that country's repressive government.
(E) Without pressure from Country R, the government of S would be able to continue repressing its citizens indefinitely.

22. Some people believe that saying that an organization is hierarchical says everything there is to say about how that organization operates. All bureaucratically controlled organizations are hierarchical. Yet the Public Works Department, although bureaucratically controlled, operates quite differently than most other bureaucratically controlled organizations operate.

If the statements above are true, which one of the following must also be true on the basis of them?

(A) The Public Works Department operates more like a nonbureaucratically controlled organization than like a bureaucratically controlled organization.
(B) Any organization that is hierarchical is bureaucratically controlled.
(C) From the fact that a given organization is hierarchical nothing can reliably be concluded about how that organization operates.
(D) Not all hierarchical organizations operate in the same way.
(E) Whether or not an organization is bureaucratically controlled has nothing to do with how that organization operates.

23. Research indicates that 90 percent of extreme insomniacs consume large amount of coffee. Since Tom drinks a lot of coffee, it is quite likely that he is an extreme insomniac.

Which one of the following most accurately describes a flaw in the argument's reasoning?

(A) It fails to acknowledge the possibility that Tom is among the 10 percent of people who drink large amounts of coffee who are not extreme insomniacs.
(B) It fails to consider the possible contribution to extreme insomnia of other causes of insomnia besides coffee.
(C) It relies on evidence that does not indicate the frequency of extreme insomnia among people who drink large amounts of coffee.
(D) It draws an inference about one specific individual from evidence that describes only the characteristics of a class of individuals
(E) It presumes without warrant that drinking coffee always causes insomnia.

GO ON TO THE NEXT PAGE.

24. Folklorist: Oral traditions are often preferable to written ones. Exclusive dependence on speech improves the memory; literate populations grow sluggish in recall, running to written sources whenever they need information. Because writing has no limits, it can proliferate to the point where writer and reader both become confused. Since oral traditions are dependent on memory, what is useless and irrelevant is quickly eradicated.

Which one of the following principles, if valid, most helps to justify the folklorist's argumentation?

(A) Accuracy in communication breeds mental self-reliance.
(B) Literate populations need to make efforts to communicate efficiently.
(C) Tradition is of greater value than accumulation of knowledge.
(D) Economy of expression is to be preferred over verbosity.
(E) Ideas that cannot be discussed clearly should not be discussed at all.

25. When interviewing job candidates, personnel managers not only evaluate a candidate's work experience and educational background but also inquire about hobbies. Personnel managers try to justify these inquiries by noting that the enthusiasm someone shows for a hobby may well carry over to enthusiasm for a job. But such enthusiasm may also indicate that the candidate is less concerned with work than with play. Therefore personnel managers should not inquire about a candidate's hobbies.

The argument is flawed because it overlooks each of the following possibilities EXCEPT:

(A) A candidate's involvement in particular hobbies may indicate a capacity to make long-term commitments.
(B) Candidates who have no hobbies may pretend that they have one when asked in an interview.
(C) Inquiries about a hobby may put candidates at ease, eliciting more honest responses about important questions.
(D) Having certain kinds of hobbies may indicate that a candidate has good organizational skills.
(E) Personnel managers may make better choices among candidates if they are not restricted from asking particular types of questions.

26. Researcher: The vast majority of a person's dreams bear no resemblance whatsoever to real events that follow the dreams. Thus, it is unreasonable to believe that one has extrasensory perception solely on the basis of having had several vivid dreams about events that happen after the dreams.

Which one of the following arguments is most similar in its reasoning to the argument above?

(A) It is unreasonable to believe that a new drug cures heart disease when it is tested, albeit successfully, on only a few patients. Most new drugs require testing on large numbers of patients before they are considered effective.
(B) Many people who undergo surgery for ulcers show no long-term improvement. So it is unreasonable to believe that surgery for ulcers is effective, even though ulcer surgery benefits many people as well.
(C) Even though many cancer patients experience remissions without drinking herbal tea, it is unreasonable to believe that not drinking herbal tea causes such remissions. Several factors are known to be relevant to cancer remission.
(D) A number of people who die prematurely take aspirin. But it is unreasonable to conclude that aspirin is dangerous. Most people who take aspirin do not die prematurely.
(E) A significant number of children raised near power lines develop cancer. So it is unreasonable to deny a connection between living near power lines and developing cancer, even though many people living near power lines never develop cancer.

S T O P

IF YOU FINISH BEFORE TIME IS CALLED, YOU MAY CHECK YOUR WORK ON THIS SECTION ONLY.
DO NOT WORK ON ANY OTHER SECTION IN THE TEST.

SECTION I

Time—35 minutes

23 Questions

Directions: Each group of questions in this section is based on a set of conditions. In answering some of the questions, it may be useful to draw a rough diagram. Choose the response that most accurately and completely answers each question and blacken the corresponding space on your answer sheet.

Questions 1–6

Individual hour-long auditions will be scheduled for each of six saxophonists—Fujimura, Gabrieli, Herman, Jackson, King, and Lauder. The auditions will all take place on the same day. Each audition will begin on the hour, with the first beginning at 1 P.M. and the last at 6 P.M. The schedule of auditions must conform to the following conditions:

Jackson auditions earlier than Herman does.
Gabrieli auditions earlier than King does.
Gabrieli auditions either immediately before or immediately after Lauder does.
Exactly one audition separates the auditions of Jackson and Lauder.

1. Which one of the following is an acceptable schedule for the auditions, listed in order from 1 P.M. through 6 P.M?

(A) Fujimura, Gabrieli, King, Jackson, Herman, Lauder
(B) Fujimura, King, Lauder, Gabrieli, Jackson, Herman
(C) Fujimura, Lauder, Gabrieli, King, Jackson, Herman
(D) Herman, Jackson, Gabrieli, Lauder, King, Fujimura
(E) Jackson, Gabrieli, Lauder, Herman, King, Fujimura

2. Which one of the following must be true?

(A) Lauder is scheduled to audition earlier than Herman.
(B) Lauder is scheduled to audition earlier than King.
(C) Jackson's audition is scheduled to begin at either 1 P.M or 5 P.M
(D) Fujimura and Jackson are not scheduled to audition in consecutive hours.
(E) Gabrieli and King are not scheduled to audition in consecutive hours.

3. The earliest King's audition could be scheduled to begin is

(A) 5 P.M.
(B) 4 P.M.
(C) 3 P.M.
(D) 2 P.M.
(E) 1 P.M.

4. The order in which the saxophonists are scheduled to audition is completely determined if which one of the following is true?

(A) Herman's audition is scheduled to begin at 4 P.M.
(B) Jackson's audition is scheduled to begin at 1 P.M.
(C) Jackson's audition is scheduled to begin at 5 P.M.
(D) Lauder's audition is scheduled to begin at 1 P.M.
(E) Lauder's audition is scheduled to begin at 2 P.M.

5. If Fujimura's audition is not scheduled to begin at 1 P.M., which one of the following could be true?

(A) Herman's audition is scheduled to begin at 6 P.M.
(B) Gabrieli's audition is scheduled to begin at 5 P.M.
(C) Herman's audition is scheduled to begin at 3 P.M.
(D) Jackson's audition is scheduled to begin at 2 P.M.
(E) Jackson's audition is scheduled to begin at 5 P.M.

6. Which one of the following must be true?

(A) Gabrieli's audition is scheduled to begin before 5 P.M.
(B) Herman's audition is scheduled to begin after 2 P.M.
(C) Herman's audition is scheduled to begin before 6 P.M.
(D) King's audition is scheduled to begin before 6 P.M.
(E) Lauder's audition is scheduled to begin before 5 P.M.

GO ON TO THE NEXT PAGE.

Questions 7–11

Four people—Grace, Heather, Josh, and Maria—will help each other move exactly three pieces of furniture—a recliner, a sofa, and a table. Each piece of furniture will be moved by exactly two of the people, and each person will help move at least one of the pieces of furniture, subject to the following constraints:

Grace helps move the sofa if, but only if, Heather helps move the recliner.
If Josh helps move the table, then Maria helps move the recliner.
No piece of furniture is moved by Grace and Josh together.

7. Which one of the following could be an accurate matching of each piece of furniture to the two people who help each other move it?

(A) recliner: Grace and Maria; sofa: Heather and Josh; table: Grace and Heather
(B) recliner: Grace and Maria; sofa: Heather and Maria; table: Grace and Josh
(C) recliner: Heather and Josh; sofa: Grace and Heather; table: Josh and Maria
(D) recliner: Heather and Josh; sofa: Heather and Maria; table: Grace and Maria
(E) recliner: Josh and Maria; sofa: Grace and Heather; table: Grace and Maria

8. If Josh and Maria help each other move the recliner, then which one of the following must be true?

(A) Heather helps move the sofa.
(B) Josh helps move the sofa.
(C) Maria helps move the sofa.
(D) Grace helps move the table.
(E) Heather helps move the table.

9. If Heather helps move each of the pieces of furniture, then which one of the following could be true?

(A) Grace helps move the recliner.
(B) Maria helps move the recliner.
(C) Josh helps move the sofa.
(D) Maria helps move the sofa.
(E) Grace helps move the table.

10. Which one of the following could be a pair of people who help each other move both the recliner and the table?

(A) Grace and Josh
(B) Grace and Maria
(C) Heather and Josh
(D) Heather and Maria
(E) Josh and Maria

11. If Josh and Maria help each other move the sofa, then which one of the following could be true?

(A) Heather and Josh help each other move the recliner.
(B) Heather and Maria help each other move the recliner.
(C) Grace and Josh help each other move the table.
(D) Grace and Maria help each other move the table.
(E) Heather and Maria help each other move the table.

GO ON TO THE NEXT PAGE.

Questions 12–16

A town has exactly two public parks—Graystone Park and Landing Park—which are to be planted with North American trees. There are exactly four varieties of trees available—maples, oaks, sycamores, and tamaracks. The planting of the trees must be in accord with the following:

Each of the parks is planted with exactly three of the varieties.
At least one of the parks is planted with both maples and sycamores.
Any park that is planted with oaks will also be planted with tamaracks.
Graystone Park is planted with maples.

12. Which one of the following could be a complete and accurate list of the varieties of trees planted in each of the parks?

(A) Graystone Park: maples, oaks, sycamores
Landing Park: maples, oaks, sycamores
(B) Graystone Park: maples, oaks, tamaracks
Landing Park: maples, oaks, tamaracks
(C) Graystone Park: maples, sycamores, tamaracks
Landing Park: maples, oaks, sycamores
(D) Graystone Park: maples, sycamores, tamaracks
Landing Park: maples, oaks, tamaracks
(E) Graystone Park: oaks, sycamores, tamaracks
Landing Park: maples, sycamores, tamaracks

13. Which one of the following must be true?

(A) Graystone Park is planted with sycamores.
(B) Landing Park is planted with maples.
(C) Landing Park is planted with tamaracks.
(D) The number of the parks planted with maples is equal to the number of the parks planted with sycamores.
(E) The number of the parks planted with maples is greater than the number of the parks planted with sycamores.

14. If both parks are planted with sycamores, which one of the following could be true?

(A) The number of the parks planted with maples is equal to the number of the parks planted with oaks.
(B) The number of the parks planted with maples is greater than the number of the parks planted with sycamores.
(C) The number of the parks planted with oaks is equal to the number of the parks planted with sycamores.
(D) Graystone Park is planted with both maples and oaks.
(E) Landing Park is planted with both maples and oaks.

15. Which one of the following must be false?

(A) Both parks are planted with oaks.
(B) Both parks are planted with sycamores.
(C) Both parks are planted with tamaracks.
(D) Exactly one of the parks is planted with maples.
(E) Exactly one of the parks is planted with sycamores.

16. Which one of the following could be true?

(A) The number of the parks planted with oaks is equal to the number of the parks planted with tamaracks.
(B) The number of the parks planted with oaks is greater than the number of the parks planted with sycamores.
(C) Exactly one of the parks is planted with tamaracks.
(D) Neither park is planted with tamaracks.
(E) Both parks contain exactly the same three varieties of trees as each other.

GO ON TO THE NEXT PAGE.

Questions 17–23

Five executives—Quinn, Rodriguez, Sasada, Taylor, and Vandercar—are being scheduled to make site visits to three of their company's manufacturing plants—Farmington, Homestead, and Morningside. Each site will be visited by at least one of the executives and each executive will visit just one site. Each of the three site visits will take place on a different day. The schedule of site visits must conform to the following requirements:

The Farmington visit must take place before the Homestead visit.
The Farmington visit will include only one of the executives.
The site visit that includes Quinn must take place before any site visit that includes either Rodriguez or Taylor.
The site visit that includes Sasada cannot take place after any site visit that includes Vandercar.

17. Which one of the following could be the executives included in each of the site visits, with the sites listed in the order in which they are visited?

(A) Farmington: Quinn
Homestead: Rodriguez, Sasada
Morningside: Taylor, Vandercar
(B) Farmington: Quinn
Homestead: Rodriguez, Vandercar
Morningside: Sasada, Taylor
(C) Farmington: Rodriguez
Morningside: Quinn, Taylor
Homestead: Sasada, Vandercar
(D) Homestead: Sasada
Farmington: Quinn
Morningside: Rodriguez, Taylor, Vandercar
(E) Morningside: Quinn
Farmington: Rodriguez, Sasada
Homestead: Taylor, Vandercar

18. If the second of the three site visits includes both Rodriguez and Taylor, which one of the following must be true?

(A) The Farmington visit includes Quinn.
(B) The Homestead visit includes Vandercar.
(C) The Morningside visit includes Sasada.
(D) The second of the three site visits includes Sasada.
(E) The second of the three site visits includes exactly three of the executives.

19. If one of the site visits includes both Quinn and Sasada, which one of the following could be true?

(A) The Farmington visit is the first of the three site visits.
(B) The Homestead visit is the second of the three site visits.
(C) One of the site visits includes only Vandercar.
(D) The second of the three site visits includes Sasada.
(E) The second of the three site visits includes exactly two of the executives.

20. The executives who visit Homestead CANNOT be

(A) Quinn and Vandercar only
(B) Rodriguez and Taylor only
(C) Sasada and Taylor only
(D) Quinn, Sasada, and Vandercar
(E) Rodriguez, Sasada, and Taylor

21. If the Morningside visit includes both Quinn and Vandercar, which one of the following could be true?

(A) One of the site visits includes both Rodriguez and Sasada.
(B) The second of the three site visits includes exactly three of the executives.
(C) The last of the three site visits includes exactly three of the executives.
(D) The Homestead visit takes place earlier than the Morningside visit.
(E) The Morningside visit takes place earlier than the Farmington visit.

22. Which one of the following must be true?

(A) The Farmington visit takes place earlier than the Morningside visit.
(B) The site visit that includes Vandercar takes place earlier than the site visit that includes Rodriguez.
(C) One of the first two site visits includes Sasada.
(D) The second of the three site visits includes at least two of the executives.
(E) At least one of the first two site visits includes only one of the executives.

23. If the Farmington visit includes Sasada, which one of the following must be true?

(A) One of the site visits includes exactly three of the executives.
(B) The last of the three site visits includes Rodriguez.
(C) The Homestead visit includes Quinn.
(D) The Morningside visit includes Taylor.
(E) The site visit that includes Vandercar also includes Quinn.

S T O P

IF YOU FINISH BEFORE TIME IS CALLED, YOU MAY CHECK YOUR WORK ON THIS SECTION ONLY.
DO NOT WORK ON ANY OTHER SECTION IN THE TEST.

SECTION II

Time—35 minutes

25 Questions

Directions: The questions in this section are based on the reasoning contained in brief statements or passages. For some questions, more than one of the choices could conceivably answer the question. However, you are to choose the best answer; that is, the response that most accurately and completely answers the question. You should not make assumptions that are by commonsense standards implausible, superfluous, or incompatible with the passage. After you have chosen the best answer, blacken the corresponding space on your answer sheet.

1. This region's swimmers generally swim during the day because they are too afraid of sharks to swim after dark but feel safe swimming during daylight hours. Yet all recent shark attacks on swimmers in the area have occurred during the day, indicating that, contrary to popular opinion, it is not more dangerous to swim here at night than during the day.

   The reasoning in the argument is most vulnerable to criticism on the grounds that it

   (A) overlooks the possibility that some sharks are primarily nocturnal hunters
   (B) bases its conclusion on evidence from an unreliable source
   (C) overlooks the possibility that swimmers might feel anxiety caused by not being able to see one's surroundings in the dark
   (D) presumes, without providing justification, that swimmers cannot be the most knowledgeable about which times of day are safest for swimming
   (E) fails to take into account the possibility that the number of shark attacks at night would increase dramatically if more people swam at night

2. Denise: Crime will be reduced only when punishment is certain and is sufficiently severe to give anyone considering committing a crime reason to decide against doing so.

   Reshmi: No, crime will be most effectively reduced if educational opportunities are made readily available to everyone, so that those who once viewed criminal activity as the only means of securing a comfortable lifestyle will choose a different path.

   Their dialogue provides the most support for the claim that Denise and Reshmi agree that

   (A) people are capable of choosing whether or not to commit crimes
   (B) crime is the most important issue facing modern society
   (C) reducing crime requires fair and consistent responses to criminal behavior
   (D) crimes are committed in response to economic need
   (E) reducing crime requires focusing on assured punishments

3. Acme Corporation offers unskilled workers excellent opportunities for advancement. As evidence, consider the fact that the president of the company, Ms. Garon, worked as an assembly line worker, an entry-level position requiring no special skills, when she first started at Acme.

   Which one of the following statements, if true, most weakens the reasoning above?

   (A) Acme's vice president of operations also worked as an assembly line worker when he first started at Acme.
   (B) Acme regularly hires top graduates of business schools and employs them briefly in each of a succession of entry-level positions before promoting them to management.
   (C) Acme promotes its own employees to senior management positions much more frequently than it hires senior managers from other companies.
   (D) Ms. Garon worked at Acme for more than 20 years before she was promoted to president.
   (E) Acme pays entry-level employees slightly higher wages than most other businesses in the same industry.

GO ON TO THE NEXT PAGE.

4. The song of the yellow warbler signals to other yellow warblers that a particular area has been appropriated by the singer as its own feeding territory. Although the singing deters other yellow warblers from taking over the feeding territory of the singer, other yellow warblers may range for food within a portion of the singer's territory. However, a warbler sings a special song when it molts (sheds its feathers). Other yellow warblers will not enter the smaller core territory of a yellow warbler singing its molting song. Therefore yellow warblers, which can only fly short distances during molting, have no competition for the food supply within the range of their restricted flying.

The argument makes which one of the following assumptions?

(A) The core areas contain just enough food to sustain one yellow warbler while it molts.
(B) Warblers are the only molting birds that lay claim to core areas of feeding territories by singing.
(C) There are no birds other than yellow warblers that compete with yellow warblers for food.
(D) Warblers often share their feeding areas with other kinds of birds, which often do not eat the same insects or seeds as warblers do.
(E) The core areas of each feeding territory are the same size for each molting warbler.

5. Chinh: Television producers should not pay attention to the preferences of the viewing public when making creative decisions. Great painters do not consider what the museum-going public wants to see.

Lana: But television is expressly for the viewing public. So a producer is more like a CEO than like an artist. Just as a company would be foolhardy not to consider consumers' tastes when developing products, the TV producer must consider viewers' preferences.

According to Lana, Chinh's argument is flawed in that it

(A) is circular
(B) relies on a sample of consumers that is unrepresentative of consumers in general
(C) infers from the effect produced by an action that the action is intended to produce that effect
(D) fails to consider the possibility that painters may in fact try to please the museum-going public
(E) offers a faulty analogy

6. Dietitian: High consumption of sodium increases some people's chances of developing heart disease. To maintain cardiac health without lowering sodium consumption, therefore, these people should eat fresh, rather than canned or frozen, fruit and vegetables, since the potassium in plant foods helps to prevent sodium's malign effects.

Which one of the following is an assumption required by the dietitian's argument?

(A) Fresh fruits and vegetables contain more potassium than sodium.
(B) Food processing businesses often add sodium to foods being canned or frozen.
(C) Potassium is the only mineral that helps to prevent sodium's malign effects.
(D) Potassium in fruits and vegetables has few negative side effects.
(E) Fresh fruits and vegetables contain more potassium than do canned or frozen ones.

7. Dana intentionally watered the plant every other day. But since the plant was a succulent, and needed dry soil, the frequent watering killed the plant. Therefore Dana intentionally killed the plant.

Which one of the following arguments exhibits a flawed pattern of reasoning most similar to the flawed pattern of reasoning exhibited in the argument above?

(A) Jack stole $10 from Kelly and bet it on a race. The bet returned $100 to Jack. Therefore Jack really stole $100 from Kelly.
(B) Celeste knows that coffee is grown in the mountains in Peru and that Peru is in South America. Therefore Celeste should know that coffee is grown in South America.
(C) The restaurant owner decided to take an item off her restaurant's menu. This decision disappointed Jerry because that item was his favorite dish. Therefore the restaurant owner decided to disappoint Jerry.
(D) The heavy rain caused the dam to break, and the breaking of the dam caused the fields downstream to be flooded. Therefore the heavy rain caused the flooding of the fields.
(E) The power plant raised the water temperature, and whatever raised the water temperature is responsible for the decrease in fish. Therefore the power plant is responsible for the decrease in fish.

GO ON TO THE NEXT PAGE.

8. This boulder is volcanic in origin and yet the rest of the rock in this area is sedimentary. Since this area was covered by southward-moving glaciers during the last ice age, this boulder was probably deposited here, hundreds of miles from its geological birthplace, by a glacier.

Which one of the following, if true, most seriously undermines the conclusion drawn in the argument above?

(A) Most boulders that have been moved by glaciers have not been moved more than 100 miles.
(B) The closest geological source of volcanic rock is 50 miles south of this boulder.
(C) The closest geological source of volcanic rock is 50 miles north of this boulder.
(D) There are no geological sources of volcanic rock north of this boulder.
(E) No other boulders of volcanic origin exist within 50 miles of this boulder.

9. Rifka: We do not need to stop and ask for directions. We would not need to do that unless, of course, we were lost.

Craig: The fact that we are lost is precisely why we need to stop.

In the exchange above, the function of Craig's comment is to

(A) contradict the conclusion of Rifka's argument without offering any reason to reject any of Rifka's implicit premises
(B) deny one of Rifka's implicit premises and thereby arrive at a different conclusion
(C) imply that Rifka's argument is invalid by accepting the truth of its premises while rejecting its conclusion
(D) provide a counterexample to Rifka's generalization
(E) affirm the truth of the stated premise of Rifka's argument while remaining noncommittal about its conclusion

10. Critic: The idealized world portrayed in romance literature is diametrically opposed to the debased world portrayed in satirical literature. Nevertheless, the major characters in both types of works have moral qualities that reflect the worlds in which they are presented. Comedy and tragedy, meanwhile, require that the moral qualities of major characters change during the course of the action. Therefore, neither tragedy nor comedy can be classified as satirical literature or romance literature.

The critic's conclusion follows logically if which one of the following is assumed?

(A) Some characters in comedies and tragedies are neither debased nor idealized.
(B) The visions of the world portrayed in works of tragedy and works of comedy change during the course of the action.
(C) If a character in a tragedy is idealized at the beginning of the action depicted in the tragedy, he or she must be debased at the end.
(D) In romance literature and satirical literature, characters' moral qualities do not change during the course of the action.
(E) Both comedy and tragedy require that the moral qualities of minor characters change during the course of the action.

11. Lance: If experience teaches us nothing else, it teaches us that every general rule has at least one exception.

Frank: What you conclude is itself a general rule. If we assume that it is true, then there is at least one general rule that has no exceptions. Therefore, you must withdraw your conclusion.

Frank's argument is an attempt to counter Lance's conclusion by

(A) demonstrating that Lance assumes the very thing he sets out to prove
(B) showing that Lance's conclusion involves him in a contradiction
(C) showing that no general rule can have exceptions
(D) establishing that experience teaches us the opposite of what Lance concludes
(E) showing that it has no implications for any real cases

GO ON TO THE NEXT PAGE.

12. Throughout a certain nation, electricity has actually become increasingly available to people in urban areas while energy production has been subsidized to help residents of rural areas gain access to electricity. However, even with the subsidy, many of the most isolated rural populations still have no access to electricity. Thus, the energy subsidy has failed to achieve its intended purpose.

The reasoning in the argument is most vulnerable to criticism on the grounds that the argument

(A) takes for granted that the subsidy's intended purpose could have been achieved if the subsidy had not existed
(B) takes for granted that if a subsidy has any benefit for those whom it was not intended to benefit, then that subsidy has failed to achieve its intended purpose
(C) presumes, without providing justification, that the intended purpose of the subsidy was to benefit not only rural populations in the nation who have no electricity, but other people in the nation as well
(D) overlooks the possibility that even many of the people in the nation who live in urban areas would have difficulty gaining access to electricity without the subsidy
(E) fails to take into account that the subsidy could have helped many of the rural residents in the nation gain access to electricity even if many other rural residents in the nation were not helped in this way

13. Heart attacks are most likely to occur on Mondays. The accepted explanation is that because Monday is the first day of the workweek, people feel more stress on Mondays than on other days. However, research shows that even unemployed retired people are more likely to have heart attacks on Mondays than on other days.

Which one of the following, if true, most helps to explain the increased likelihood that an unemployed retiree will have a heart attack on a Monday?

(A) Because they associate Monday with work, retired people are more likely to begin large projects on Mondays.
(B) Many retired people take up part-time jobs after they retire from their careers.
(C) People seldom change their dietary and other health habits after retirement.
(D) Stress is the major factor influencing the risk of heart attack.
(E) Unemployed retired people are even more likely to have heart attacks than are people who have jobs.

14. Psychologist: We asked 100 entrepreneurs and 100 business managers to answer various questions and rate how confident they were that their responses were correct. While members of each group were overconfident, in general the entrepreneurs were much more so than the business managers. This indicates that people who are especially overconfident are more likely to attempt to start a business in spite of the enormous odds against success than people who are less confident.

Which one of the following, if true, lends the most support to the psychologist's conclusion?

(A) The questions asked of the entrepreneurs and business managers included personal, political, and business questions.
(B) At least some of the entrepreneurs surveyed had accurately determined before attempting to start their businesses what the odds were against their attempts being successful.
(C) Another survey showed that degree of confidence was highly correlated with success in business.
(D) The business managers who were most overconfident were found to have attempted to start businesses in the past.
(E) How confident each person surveyed was that his or her answers to the questions asked were correct corresponded closely to that person's confidence in his or her business acumen.

GO ON TO THE NEXT PAGE.

15. If Agnes's research proposal is approved, the fourth-floor lab must be cleaned out for her use. Immanuel's proposal, on the other hand, requires less space. So if his proposal is approved, he will continue to work in the second-floor lab. Only those proposals the director supports will be approved. So since the director will support both proposals, the fourth-floor lab must be cleaned out.

The argument's reasoning is flawed because the argument

(A) presumes, without providing justification, that the fourth-floor lab is bigger than the second-floor lab
(B) fails to consider the possibility that a proposal will be rejected even with the director's support
(C) presumes, without providing justification, that the director will support both proposals with equal enthusiasm
(D) fails to consider the possibility that Immanuel will want to move to a bigger lab once his proposal is approved
(E) presumes, without providing justification, that no lab other than the fourth-floor lab would be adequate for Agnes's research

16. In order to expand its mailing lists for e-mail advertising, the Outdoor Sports Company has been offering its customers financial incentives if they provide the e-mail addresses of their friends. However, offering such incentives is an unethical business practice, because it encourages people to exploit their personal relationships for profit, which risks damaging the integrity of those relationships.

Which one of the following principles, if valid, most helps to justify the reasoning in the argument?

(A) It is unethical for people to exploit their personal relationships for profit if in doing so they risk damaging the integrity of those relationships.
(B) If it would be unethical to use information that was gathered in a particular way, then it is unethical to gather that information in the first place.
(C) It is an unethical business practice for a company to deliberately damage the integrity of its customers' personal relationships in any way.
(D) It is unethical to encourage people to engage in behavior that could damage the integrity of their personal relationships.
(E) Providing a friend's personal information to a company in exchange for a financial reward will almost certainly damage the integrity of one's personal relationship with that friend.

17. Glen: An emphasis on law's purely procedural side produces a concern with personal rights that leads to the individual's indifference to society's welfare. Law's primary role should be to create virtuous citizens.

Sara: But such a role would encourage government to decide which modes of life are truly virtuous; that would be more dangerous than government's being overprotective of individuals' rights.

The dialogue provides the most support for the claim that Glen and Sara disagree about whether

(A) citizens can be assumed to be capable of making good choices without governmental interference
(B) virtuousness on the part of citizens is more important than the protection of citizens' rights
(C) there is an inherent danger in allowing government to decide what constitutes virtuous behavior among citizens
(D) an emphasis on law's purely procedural side results in government's being overprotective of citizens' rights
(E) the cultivation of virtue among citizens should be the primary role of law

GO ON TO THE NEXT PAGE.

18. Some credit card companies allow cardholders to skip payments for up to six months under certain circumstances, but it is almost never in a cardholder's interest to do so. Finance charges accumulate during the skipped-payment period, and the cost to the cardholder is much greater in the long run.

Which one of the following arguments illustrates a principle most similar to the principle underlying the argument above?

(A) Although insecticides are effective in ridding the environment of insect pests, they often kill beneficial insects at the same time. Since these beneficial insects are so important, we must find other ways to combat insect pests.
(B) Increasing the base salary of new employees is good for a company. Although the company's payroll will increase, it will be easier for the company to recruit new employees.
(C) It is unwise to use highway maintenance funds for construction of new roads. There is some immediate benefit from new roads, but if these funds are not used for maintenance, the total maintenance cost will be greater in the long run.
(D) It is better to invest in a used piece of equipment than to purchase a new one. Although used equipment requires more repairs and is sometimes more costly in the long run, buying a new machine requires a far greater initial outlay of capital.
(E) Sports cars are impractical for most drivers. While there is undoubtedly a certain thrill associated with driving these cars, their small size makes them incapable of transporting any but the smallest amounts of cargo.

19. None of the students taking literature are taking physics, but several of the students taking physics are taking art. In addition, none of the students taking rhetoric are taking physics.

Which one of the following statements follows logically from the statements above?

(A) There are students who are taking art but not literature.
(B) None of the students taking literature are taking art.
(C) There are students who are taking rhetoric but not literature.
(D) None of the students taking rhetoric are taking literature.
(E) There are students who are taking both art and literature.

20. Psychologist: Psychotherapists who attempt to provide psychotherapy on radio or television talk shows are expected to do so in ways that entertain a broad audience. However, satisfying this demand is nearly always incompatible with providing high-quality psychological help. For this reason, psychotherapists should never provide psychotherapy on talk shows.

Which one of the following principles must be assumed in order for the psychologist's conclusion to be properly drawn?

(A) It is never appropriate for psychotherapists to attempt to entertain a broad audience.
(B) The context in which psychological help is presented has a greater impact on its quality than the nature of the advice that is given.
(C) Psychotherapy should never be provided in a context in which there is any chance that the therapy might be of less than high quality.
(D) Most members of radio and television talk show audiences are seeking entertainment rather than high-quality psychological help.
(E) Psychotherapists should never attempt to provide psychological help in a manner that makes it unlikely to be of high quality.

GO ON TO THE NEXT PAGE.

21. Tania: A good art critic is not fair in the ordinary sense; it is only about things that do not interest one that one can give a truly unbiased opinion. Since art is a passion, good criticism of art cannot be separated from emotion.

Monique: Art is not simply a passion. The best art critics passionately engage with the artwork, but render their criticism only after shedding all of their biases and consulting general principles of aesthetics.

The dialogue most strongly supports the claim that Tania and Monique disagree about whether

(A) art is not simply a passion
(B) good art criticism is sometimes unbiased
(C) art critics should not feel emotion toward artworks
(D) fairness generally requires minimizing the influence of bias
(E) the passionate engagement of the art critic with the artwork is the most important aspect of art criticism

22. The writing styles in works of high literary quality are not well suited to the avoidance of misinterpretation. For this reason, the writing in judicial decisions, which are primarily intended as determinations of law, is rarely of high literary quality. However, it is not uncommon to find writing of high literary quality in dissenting opinions, which are sometimes included in written decisions in cases heard by a panel of judges.

Which one of the following, if true, most helps to resolve the apparent discrepancy in the statements above?

(A) It is not uncommon for more than one judge to have an influence on the way a dissenting opinion is written.
(B) Unlike literary works, legal opinions rely heavily on the use of technical terminology.
(C) The law is not to any great extent determined by dissenting opinions.
(D) Judges spend much more time reading judicial decisions than reading works of high literary quality.
(E) Judicial decisions issued by panels of judges are likely to be more widely read than are judicial decisions issued by a single judge who hears a case alone.

23. Ecologist: Without the intervention of conservationists, squirrel monkeys will become extinct. But they will survive if large tracts of second-growth forest habitat are preserved for them. Squirrel monkeys flourish in second-growth forest because of the plentiful supply of their favorite insects and fruit.

Which one of the following can be properly inferred from the ecologist's statements?

(A) No habitat other than second-growth forest contains plentiful supplies of squirrel monkeys' favorite insects and fruit.
(B) At least some of the conservationists who intervene to help the squirrel monkeys survive will do so by preserving second-growth forest habitat for the monkeys.
(C) Without plentiful supplies of their favorite insects and fruit, squirrel monkeys will become extinct.
(D) If conservationists intervene to help squirrel monkeys survive, then the squirrel monkeys will not become extinct.
(E) Without the intervention of conservationists, large tracts of second-growth forest habitat will not be preserved for squirrel monkeys.

GO ON TO THE NEXT PAGE.

24. Over 40,000 lead seals from the early Byzantine Empire remain today. Apart from the rare cases where the seal authenticated a document of special importance, most seals had served their purpose when the document was opened. Lead was not expensive, but it was not free: most lead seals would have been recast once they had served their purpose. Thus the number of early Byzantine documents sealed in such a fashion must have been many times the number of remaining lead seals.

Which one of the following statements, if true, most strengthens the argument?

(A) Most of the lead seals produced during the early Byzantine Empire were affixed to documents that were then opened during that period.
(B) Most of the lead seals produced during the early Byzantine Empire were affixed to documents that have since been destroyed.
(C) The amount of lead available for seals in the early Byzantine Empire was much greater than the amount of lead that remains in the seals today.
(D) During the time of the early Byzantine Empire there were at most 40,000 documents of enough importance to prevent the removing and recycling of the seal.
(E) During the time of the early Byzantine Empire there were fewer than 40,000 seals affixed to documents at any given time.

25. Farmer: In the long run, it is counterproductive for farmers to use insecticides. Because insects' resistance to insecticides increases with insecticide use, farmers have to use greater and greater amounts of costly insecticides to control insect pests.

Which one of the following most accurately describes the role played in the farmer's argument by the proposition that farmers have to use greater and greater amounts of costly insecticides to control insect pests?

(A) It is the argument's main conclusion, but not its only conclusion.
(B) It is a claim for which a causal explanation is provided and which itself is used as direct support for the argument's only conclusion.
(C) It is the argument's only conclusion.
(D) It is a claim that is used as direct support for an intermediary conclusion, which in turn is used as direct support for the argument's main conclusion.
(E) It identifies a phenomenon for which the argument's main conclusion offers a causal explanation.

S T O P

IF YOU FINISH BEFORE TIME IS CALLED, YOU MAY CHECK YOUR WORK ON THIS SECTION ONLY.
DO NOT WORK ON ANY OTHER SECTION IN THE TEST.

SECTION III

Time—35 minutes

25 Questions

Directions: The questions in this section are based on the reasoning contained in brief statements or passages. For some questions, more than one of the choices could conceivably answer the question. However, you are to choose the best answer; that is, the response that most accurately and completely answers the question. You should not make assumptions that are by commonsense standards implausible, superfluous, or incompatible with the passage. After you have chosen the best answer, blacken the corresponding space on your answer sheet.

1. Anna: Did you know that rainbows always occur opposite the sun, appearing high in the sky when the sun is low, and low in the sky when the sun is high? The Roman scholar Pliny the Elder claimed that this was so, in the first century A.D.

   William: His claim cannot be correct. After all, Pliny the Elder wrote that there are tribes of dog-headed people and beings with no heads or necks but with eyes on their shoulders, and said that smearing snails on your forehead cures headaches!

   William's argument against Anna's claims about rainbows is most vulnerable to criticism because it

   (A) inappropriately distorts Anna's conclusion, making it appear more extreme than it really is
   (B) takes for granted that Pliny the Elder was in bad faith when he reported about unheard-of creatures
   (C) illicitly infers that, because Pliny the Elder made some incorrect assertions, Pliny the Elder's assertions about rainbows are also incorrect
   (D) accepts the assertions of an ancient scholar without presenting contemporary verification of that scholar's views
   (E) implies that Pliny the Elder's writings are too outdated to be of any value

2. Shareholder: The company's current operations are time-proven successes. The move into food services may siphon off funds needed by these other operations. Also, the food service industry is volatile, with a higher inherent risk than with, for instance, pharmaceuticals, another area into which the company has considered expanding.

   If the shareholder's statements are true, which one of the following is most strongly supported by them?

   (A) The company's present operations require increased funding.
   (B) Investment into pharmaceuticals would not siphon off money from other operations.
   (C) The company will lose money as it expands into the food service industry.
   (D) Only if the company expands its operations into pharmaceuticals are increased profits possible.
   (E) The company has a greater chance of losing money in food services than in pharmaceuticals.

3. Mariah: Joanna has argued that Adam should not judge the essay contest because several of his classmates have entered the contest. However, the essays are not identified by author to the judge and, moreover, none of Adam's friends are classmates of his. Still, Adam has no experience in critiquing essays. Therefore, I agree with Joanna that Adam should not judge the contest.

   Which one of the following principles, if valid, most helps to justify Mariah's argument?

   (A) A suspicion of bias is insufficient grounds on which to disqualify someone from judging a contest.
   (B) Expertise should be the primary prerequisite for serving as a contest judge.
   (C) The ability of a judge to make objective decisions is more important than that judge's content expertise.
   (D) In selecting a contest judge, fairness concerns should override concern for the appropriate expertise.
   (E) A contest judge, no matter how well qualified, cannot judge properly if the possibility of bias exists.

GO ON TO THE NEXT PAGE.

4. The manufacturers of NoSmoke claim that their product reduces smokers' cravings for cigarettes. However, in a recent study, smokers given the main ingredient in NoSmoke reported no decrease in cravings for cigarettes. Thus, since NoSmoke has only two ingredients, if similar results are found for the second ingredient, we can conclude that NoSmoke does not reduce smokers' cravings.

The argument above is flawed in that it

(A) illicitly presumes that a whole must lack a certain quality if all of its parts lack that quality
(B) confuses a mere correlation with a cause
(C) relies on a sample that is likely to be unrepresentative
(D) overlooks the possibility that NoSmoke helps people to quit smoking in ways other than by reducing smokers' cravings for cigarettes
(E) illicitly presumes that a claim must be false because the people making the claim are biased

5. Gardener: Researchers encourage us to allow certain kinds of weeds to grow among garden vegetables because they can repel caterpillars from the garden. While it is wise to avoid unnecessary use of insecticides, the researchers' advice is premature. For all we know, those kinds of weeds can deplete the soil of nutrients and moisture that garden crops depend on, and might even attract other kinds of damaging pests.

Which one of the following most accurately expresses the main conclusion of the gardener's argument?

(A) To the extent that it is possible to do so, we should eliminate the use of insecticides in gardening.
(B) Allowing certain kinds of weeds to grow in vegetable gardens may contribute to a net increase in unwanted garden pests.
(C) Allowing the right kinds of weeds to grow in vegetable gardens can help toward controlling caterpillars without the use of insecticides.
(D) We should be cautious about the practice of allowing certain kinds of weeds to grow among garden vegetables.
(E) We should be skeptical about the extent to which certain kinds of weeds can reduce the presence of caterpillars in gardens.

6. Executive: We recently ran a set of advertisements in the print version of a travel magazine and on that magazine's website. We were unable to get any direct information about consumer response to the print ads. However, we found that consumer response to the ads on the website was much more limited than is typical for website ads. We concluded that consumer response to the print ads was probably below par as well.

The executive's reasoning does which one of the following?

(A) bases a prediction of the intensity of a phenomenon on information about the intensity of that phenomenon's cause
(B) uses information about the typical frequency of events of a general kind to draw a conclusion about the probability of a particular event of that kind
(C) infers a statistical generalization from claims about a large number of specific instances
(D) uses a case in which direct evidence is available to draw a conclusion about an analogous case in which direct evidence is unavailable
(E) bases a prediction about future events on facts about recent comparable events

7. Conservation officers justified their decision to remove a pack of ten coyotes from a small island by claiming that the coyotes, which preyed on wild cats and plover, were decimating the plover population and would soon wipe it out. After the coyotes were removed, however, the plover population plummeted dramatically, and within two years plover could no longer be found on the island.

Which one of the following would, if true, most help explain the phenomenon described above?

(A) Plover are ground-nesting birds, which makes them easy prey for coyotes.
(B) Wild cat and plover populations tend to fluctuate together.
(C) Coyotes are not susceptible to any of the diseases that commonly infect plover or wild cats.
(D) The wild cat population on the island was once significantly larger than it is currently.
(E) The coyotes preyed mainly on wild cats, and wild cats prey on plover.

GO ON TO THE NEXT PAGE.

8. Economist: During a recession, a company can cut personnel costs either by laying off some employees without reducing the wages of remaining employees or by reducing the wages of all employees without laying off anyone. Both damage morale, but layoffs damage it less, since the aggrieved have, after all, left. Thus, when companies must reduce personnel costs during recessions, they are likely to lay off employees.

Which one of the following, if true, most strengthens the economist's reasoning?

(A) Employee morale is usually the primary concern driving companies' decisions about whether to lay off employees or to reduce their wages.
(B) In general, companies increase wages only when they are unable to find enough qualified employees.
(C) Some companies will be unable to make a profit during recessions no matter how much they reduce personnel costs.
(D) When companies cut personnel costs during recessions by reducing wages, some employees usually resign.
(E) Some companies that have laid off employees during recessions have had difficulty finding enough qualified employees once economic growth resumed.

9. There are far fewer independent bookstores than there were 20 years ago, largely because chain bookstores prospered and multiplied during that time. Thus, chain bookstores' success has been to the detriment of book consumers, for the shortage of independent bookstores has prevented the variety of readily available books from growing as much as it otherwise would have.

Which one of the following is an assumption on which the argument relies?

(A) Book consumers would be better off if there were a greater variety of readily available books than there currently is.
(B) Independent bookstores typically do not sell the kinds of books that are available in chain bookstores.
(C) The average bookstore today is larger than the average bookstore of 20 years ago.
(D) The average bookstore today is smaller than the average bookstore of 20 years ago.
(E) Some book consumers value low prices more highly than wide selection.

10. Concert promoter: Some critics claim that our concert series lacks popular appeal. But our income from the sales of t-shirts and other memorabilia at the concerts is equal to or greater than that for similar sales at comparable series. So those critics are mistaken.

The concert promoter's argument is flawed in that it

(A) attacks the critics on the basis of emotional considerations rather than factual ones
(B) takes for granted that income from sales of memorabilia is the sole indicator of popular appeal
(C) takes for granted that the comparable series possess popular appeal
(D) draws a conclusion about the popularity of a series based on a comparison with other, dissimilar events
(E) fails to adequately distinguish the series as a whole from individual concerts in it

11. The sun emits two types of ultraviolet radiation that damage skin: UV-A, which causes premature wrinkles, and UV-B, which causes sunburn. Until about ten years ago, sunscreens protected against UV-B radiation but not against UV-A radiation.

Which one of the following is best supported by the information above?

(A) Since about ten years ago, the percentage of people who wear sunscreen every time they spend time in the sun has increased.
(B) Most people whose skin is prematurely wrinkled have spent a large amount of time in the sun without wearing sunscreen.
(C) The specific cause of premature skin wrinkling was not known until about ten years ago.
(D) People who wear sunscreen now are less likely to become sunburned than were people who spent the same amount of time in the sun wearing sunscreen ten years ago.
(E) Until about ten years ago, people who wore sunscreen were no less likely to have premature wrinkles than were people who spent the same amount of time in the sun without wearing sunscreen.

GO ON TO THE NEXT PAGE.

12. Advice columnist: Several scientific studies have shown that, when participating in competitive sports, those people who have recently been experiencing major stress in their lives are several times more likely to suffer serious injuries than are other participants in competitive sports. Since risking serious injury is unwise, no sports activity should be used as a method for coping with stress.

Which one of the following principles, if valid, most helps to justify the reasoning in the advice columnist's argument?

(A) If people recently under stress should avoid a subset of activities of a certain type, they should avoid all activities of that type.
(B) A method for coping with stress should be used only if it has been subjected to scientific study.
(C) People who have not been experiencing major stress in their lives should participate in competitive sports.
(D) When people have been under considerable stress, they should engage in competitive activities in order to relieve the stress.
(E) People with a history of sports injuries should not engage in sports activities if they have recently been under stress.

13. Tent caterpillars' routes between their nests and potential food sources are marked with chemical traces called pheromones that the caterpillars leave behind. Moreover, routes from food sources back to the nest are marked more heavily than are merely exploratory routes that have failed to turn up a food source. Thus, tent caterpillars are apparently among the insect species that engage in communal foraging, which consists in the conveying of information concerning the location of food to other members of the colony, nest, or hive.

Which one of the following, if true, adds the most support to the argument?

(A) A hungry tent caterpillar is more likely to follow heavily marked routes than lightly marked routes.
(B) Tent caterpillars can detect the presence but not the concentration of pheromones.
(C) Sometimes individual tent caterpillars will not return to the nest until a food source is located.
(D) The pheromones left by tent caterpillars are different from the pheromones left by other animals.
(E) The pheromones that tent caterpillars leave behind are detectable by certain other species of caterpillars.

14. Many movies starring top actors will do well at the box office because the actors are already well known and have a loyal following. Movies starring unknown actors are therefore unlikely to do well.

The flawed reasoning in the argument above is most similar to that in which one of the following?

(A) Many animals must devote most of their energy to locating food, or they will not get enough food to maintain optimal energy levels. Thus, if immediate survival requires such an animal to devote most of its energy to some other purpose, optimal energy levels generally will not be maintained.
(B) Often the presence of the flower bee balm in a garden will attract bumblebees that pollinate the plants and enable the garden to produce an abundant crop. So, gardens that lack bee balm usually do not produce abundant crops.
(C) A person's ability to keep confidences is a large part of being a friend, since frequently such an ability enables a high degree of openness in communication. Thus, a high degree of openness in communication is an essential feature of friendship.
(D) Visual aids can be very useful in effectively teaching math skills, because they generally allow vivid conceptualization of math principles. If such visual aids were never employed, therefore, teaching math skills might sometimes be more difficult.
(E) An understanding of the rules of perspective is necessary for achieving success as a painter, since it is the understanding of these most basic rules that allows the painter to paint realistically. Thus, painters with an understanding of the rules of perspective will achieve success.

GO ON TO THE NEXT PAGE.

15. As part of a new trend in the writing of history, an emphasis on the details of historical events and motivations has replaced the previous emphasis on overarching historical trends and movements, with the result that the latter are often overlooked. In consequence, the ominous parallels that may exist between historical trends and current trends are also overlooked, which lessens our ability to learn from history.

The statements above, if true, most strongly support which one of the following?

(A) Studying the details of historical events and motivations lessens our ability to learn from history.
(B) Overarching historical trends and movements can be discerned only when details of historical events and motivations are not emphasized.
(C) Those who attend to overall trends and movements in history and not to details are the best able to learn from history.
(D) A change in emphasis in the interpretation of history has lessened our ability to learn from history.
(E) History should be interpreted in a way that gives equal emphasis to overarching historical trends and movements and to the details of historical events and motivations.

16. Therapist: The ability to trust other people is essential to happiness, for without trust there can be no meaningful emotional connection to another human being, and without meaningful emotional connections to others we feel isolated.

Which one of the following, if assumed, allows the conclusion of the therapist's argument to be properly inferred?

(A) No one who is feeling isolated can feel happy.
(B) Anyone who has a meaningful emotional connection to another human being can be happy.
(C) To avoid feeling isolated, it is essential to trust other people.
(D) At least some people who do not feel isolated are happy.
(E) Anyone who is able to trust other people has a meaningful emotional connection to at least one other human being.

17. Of all the Arabic epic poems that have been popular at various times, only *Sirat Bani Hilal* is still publicly performed. Furthermore, while most other epics were only recited, *Sirat Bani Hilal* has usually been sung. The musical character of the performance, therefore, is the main reason for its longevity.

The argument is most vulnerable to criticism on the grounds that it

(A) relies on evidence that is in principle impossible to corroborate
(B) relies on a source of evidence that may be biased
(C) takes for granted that a particular correlation is causal
(D) takes what may be mere popular opinion to be an established fact
(E) takes a sufficient condition to be a necessary condition

18. Fund-raiser: A charitable organization rarely gives its donors the right to vote on its policies. The inability to directly influence how charities spend contributions makes potential donors feel less of an emotional connection to the charity. Thus, most charities could probably increase the amount of money they raise through donations by giving donors the right to vote.

Which one of the following is an assumption that the fund-raiser's argument depends on?

(A) The most effective way for a charity to give potential donors the ability to directly influence what that charity does is by giving donors the right to vote on the charity's policies.
(B) Most charities that have increased the amount of money they raise through donations have done so by making potential donors feel a greater emotional connection to the charity.
(C) Every charity that has given donors the right to vote on its policies has seen a marked increase in the emotional connection donors have to that charity.
(D) Most potential donors to a charity are unwilling to give that charity any money if there is no possible way for them to have any influence on that charity's policies.
(E) The emotional connection potential donors feel to a charity can affect the amount of money that charity raises through donations.

19. Leslie: I'll show you that your quest for the treasure is irrational. Suppose you found a tablet inscribed, "Whoever touches this tablet will lose a hand, yet will possess the world." Would you touch it?

Erich: Certainly not.

Leslie: Just as I expected! It is clear from your answer that your hands are more important to you than possessing the world. But your entire body is necessarily more important to you than your hands. Yet you are ruining your health and harming your body in your quest for a treasure that is much less valuable than the whole world. I rest my case.

Which one of the following most accurately expresses the main conclusion drawn in Leslie's argument?

(A) Erich would not sacrifice one of his hands in order to possess the world.
(B) Erich should not risk his physical well-being regardless of the possible gains that such risks might bring.
(C) Erich is irrationally risking something that is precious to him for something that is of no value.
(D) Erich can be convinced that his quest for the treasure is irrational.
(E) Erich is engaging in irrational behavior by pursuing his quest for the treasure.

20. Newspaper article: People who take vitamin C supplements tend to be healthier than average. This was shown by a study investigating the relationship between high doses of vitamin C and heart disease, which showed that people who regularly consume high doses of vitamin C supplements have a significantly lower than average risk of heart disease.

Which one of the following, if true, would most weaken the argument in the newspaper article?

(A) Vitamin C taken in the form of supplements has a different effect on the body than does vitamin C taken in food.
(B) The reduction in risk of heart disease due to the consumption of vitamin C is no greater than the reduction due to certain other dietary changes.
(C) Taking both vitamin C supplements and vitamin E supplements lowers one's risk of heart disease far more than does taking either one alone.
(D) High doses of vitamin C supplements tend to reduce slightly one's resistance to certain common infectious diseases.
(E) Taking vitamin C supplements has been found to lower one's risk of developing cancer.

GO ON TO THE NEXT PAGE.

21. George: Throughout the 1980s and early 1990s, hardly anyone learned ballroom dancing. Why is it that a large number of people now take ballroom dancing lessons?

    Boris: It's because, beginning in 1995, many people learned the merengue and several related ballroom dances. Because these dances are so popular, other ballroom dances are now catching on.

    Boris's response to George is most vulnerable to criticism because it fails to

    (A) show that the people who learned the merengue are the same people who are now interested in other ballroom dances
    (B) explain why ballroom dancing was so unpopular before 1995
    (C) relate the merengue to the forms of dancing that were more prevalent before 1995
    (D) account for the beginning of the revival of interest in ballroom dancing
    (E) demonstrate that all types of ballroom dancing are currently popular

22. On the basis of relatively minor morphological differences, some scientists suggest that Neanderthals should be considered a species distinct from Cro-Magnons, the forerunners of modern humans. Yet the fact that the tools used by these two groups of hominids living in different environments were of exactly the same type indicates uncanny behavioral similarities, for only if they faced the same daily challenges and met them in the same way would they have used such similar tools. This suggests that they were members of the same species, and that the morphological differences are due merely to their having lived in different environments.

    If the statements above are true, then each of the following could be true EXCEPT:

    (A) Morphological differences between the members of two populations do not guarantee that the two populations do not belong to the same species.
    (B) The daily challenges with which an environment confronts its inhabitants are unique to that environment.
    (C) There are greater morphological differences between Cro-Magnons and modern humans than there are between Cro-Magnons and Neanderthals.
    (D) Use of similar tools is required if members of two distinct groups of tool-making hominids are to be considered members of the same species.
    (E) Through much of their coexistence, Cro-Magnons and Neanderthals were geographically isolated from one another.

23. A summer day is "pleasant" if there are intermittent periods of wind and the temperature stays below 84°F (29°C) all afternoon. A summer day with high humidity levels is "oppressive" either if the temperature stays above 84°F (29°C) all afternoon or if there is no wind.

    Which one of the following summer weather reports most closely conforms to the principles stated above?

    (A) The temperature on Friday stayed below 82°F (28°C) all day, and there was no wind at all. It was a day of low humidity, and it was a pleasant day.
    (B) On Monday, the temperature ranged from 85°F to 90°F (30°C to 32°C) from early morning until night. It was an oppressive day even though the humidity levels were low.
    (C) On Tuesday, the temperature neither rose above nor fell below 84°F (29°C) throughout late morning and all afternoon. It was a pleasant day because there were occasional periods of wind.
    (D) On Wednesday, a refreshing breeze in the early morning became intermittent by late morning, and the day's humidity levels were constantly high. It was an oppressive day, even though the temperature did not rise above 84°F (29°C) all day.
    (E) On Thursday morning, the air was very still, and it remained windless for the whole day. Humidity levels for the day were high, and even though the temperature fell below 84°F (29°C) between early and late afternoon, it was an oppressive day.

GO ON TO THE NEXT PAGE.

24. The local radio station will not win the regional ratings race this year. In the past ten years the station has never finished better than fifth place in the ratings. The station's manager has not responded to its dismal ratings by changing its musical format or any key personnel, while the competition has often sought to respond to changing tastes in music and has aggressively recruited the region's top radio personalities.

The reasoning in which one of the following is most similar to that in the argument above?

(A) Every swan I have seen was white. Therefore all swans are probably white.
(B) A fair coin was fairly flipped six times and was heads every time. The next flip will probably be heads too.
(C) All lions are mammals. Therefore Leo, the local zoo's oldest lion, is a mammal too.
(D) Recently stock prices have always been lower on Mondays. Therefore they will be lower this coming Monday too.
(E) Only trained swimmers are lifeguards, so it follows that the next lifeguard at the local pool will be a trained swimmer.

25. Chef: This mussel recipe's first step is to sprinkle the live mussels with cornmeal. The cornmeal is used to clean them out: they take the cornmeal in and eject the sand that they contain. But I can skip this step, because the mussels available at seafood markets are farm raised and therefore do not contain sand.

Which one of the following is an assumption required by the chef's argument?

(A) Cornmeal is not used to clean out farm-raised mussels before they reach seafood markets.
(B) Mussels contain no contaminants other than sand.
(C) Sprinkling the mussels with cornmeal does not affect their taste.
(D) The chef's mussel recipe was written before farm-raised mussels became available.
(E) The mussels the chef is using for the mussel recipe came from a seafood market.

S T O P

IF YOU FINISH BEFORE TIME IS CALLED, YOU MAY CHECK YOUR WORK ON THIS SECTION ONLY.
DO NOT WORK ON ANY OTHER SECTION IN THE TEST.

SECTION IV

Time—35 minutes

27 Questions

Directions: Each set of questions in this section is based on a single passage or a pair of passages. The questions are to be answered on the basis of what is stated or implied in the passage or pair of passages. For some of the questions, more than one of the choices could conceivably answer the question. However, you are to choose the best answer; that is, the response that most accurately and completely answers the question, and blacken the corresponding space on your answer sheet.

With his first published works in the 1950s, Amos Tutuola became the first Nigerian writer to receive wide international recognition. Written in a mix of standard English, idiomatic Nigerian English, and literal translation of his native language, Yoruba, Tutuola's works were quick to be praised by many literary critics as fresh, inventive approaches to the form of the novel. Others, however, dismissed his works as simple retellings of local tales, full of unwelcome liberties taken with the details of the well-known story lines. However, to estimate properly Tutuola's rightful position in world literature, it is essential to be clear about the genre in which he wrote; literary critics have assumed too facilely that he wrote novels.

No matter how flexible a definition of the novel one uses, establishing a set of criteria that enable Tutuola's works to be described as such applies to his works a body of assumptions the works are not designed to satisfy. Tutuola is not a novelist but a teller of folktales. Many of his critics are right to suggest that Tutuola's subjects are not strikingly original, but it is important to bear in mind that whereas realism and originality are expected of the novel, the teller of folktales is expected to derive subjects and frameworks from the corpus of traditional lore. The most useful approach to Tutuola's works, then, is one that regards him as working within the African oral tradition.

Within this tradition, a folktale is common property, an expression of a people's culture and social circumstances. The teller of folktales knows that the basic story is already known to most listeners and, equally, that the teller's reputation depends on the inventiveness with which the tale is modified and embellished, for what the audience anticipates is not an accurate retelling of the story but effective improvisation and delivery. Thus, within the framework of the basic story, the teller is allowed considerable room to maneuver—in fact, the most brilliant tellers of folktales transform them into unique works.

Tutuola's adherence to this tradition is clear: specific episodes, for example, are often repeated for emphasis, and he embellishes familiar tales with personal interpretations or by transferring them to modern settings. The blend of English with local idiom and Yoruba grammatical constructs, in which adjectives and verbs are often interchangeable, re-creates the folktales in singular ways. And, perhaps most revealingly, in the majority of Tutuola's works, the traditional accents and techniques of the teller of folktales are clearly discernible, for example in the adoption of an omniscient, summarizing voice at the end of his narratives, a device that is generally recognized as being employed to conclude most folktales.

1. Which one of the following most accurately expresses the main point of the passage?

   (A) Amos Tutuola is an internationally acclaimed writer of folktales whose unique writing style blends together aspects of Yoruba, Nigerian English, and standard English.
   (B) Amos Tutuola's literary works should be evaluated not as novels but as unique and inventively crafted retellings of folktales.
   (C) Amos Tutuola is an important author because he is able to incorporate the traditions of an oral art form into his novels.
   (D) Critics are divided as to whether Amos Tutuola's literary works should be regarded as novels or folktales.
   (E) The folktale is a valuable African literary genre that finds singular expression in the works of Amos Tutuola.

2. Tutuola's approach to writing folktales would be most clearly exemplified by a modern-day Irish author who

   (A) applied conventions of the modern novel to the retelling of Irish folktales
   (B) re-created important elements of the Irish literary style within a purely oral art form
   (C) combined characters from English and Irish folktales to tell a story of modern life
   (D) transplanted traditional Irish folktales from their original setting to contemporary Irish life
   (E) utilized an omniscient narrator in telling original stories about contemporary Irish life

3. Which one of the following most accurately characterizes the author's attitude toward Tutuola's position in world literature?

   (A) convinced that Tutuola's works should be viewed within the context of the African oral tradition
   (B) certain that Tutuola's works will generate a renewed interest in the study of oral traditions
   (C) pleased at the reception that Tutuola's works have received from literary critics
   (D) confident that the original integrity of Tutuola's works will be preserved despite numerous translations
   (E) optimistic that Tutuola's works reflect what will become a growing new trend in literature

4 According to the passage, some critics have criticized Tutuola's work on the ground that

   (A) his literary works do not exhibit enough similarities to the African oral tradition from which they are drawn
   (B) his mixture of languages is not entirely effective as a vehicle for either traditional folktales or contemporary novels
   (C) his attempt to fuse elements of traditional storytelling style with the format of the novel is detrimental to his artistic purposes
   (D) his writing borrows substantially from well-known story lines and at the same time alters their details
   (E) his unique works are not actually novels, even though he characterizes them as such

5. The author attributes each of the following to Tutuola EXCEPT:

   (A) repetition of elements in his stories for emphasis
   (B) relocation of traditional stories to modern settings
   (C) attainment of international recognition
   (D) use of an omniscient narrator in his works
   (E) transformation of Yoruba folktales into modern novels

6. The author refers to the "corpus of traditional lore" (lines 26–27) as part of an attempt to

   (A) distinguish expectations that apply to one literary genre from those that apply to another literary genre
   (B) argue that two sharply differing literary genres are both equally valuable
   (C) challenge critics who ascribe little merit to innovative ways of blending two distinct literary genres
   (D) elucidate those characteristics of one literary genre that have direct counterparts in another, largely dissimilar genre
   (E) argue for a new, more precise analysis of two literary genres whose distinguishing characteristics are poorly understood

7. The primary purpose of the passage is to

   (A) illustrate the wide range of Tutuola's body of work
   (B) explain the significance of the literary genre of the folktale and to defend it as a valid art form
   (C) provide an account of Tutuola's body of work in order to help establish appropriate criteria for its evaluation
   (D) distinguish accurately between the genre of the novel and that of the folktale
   (E) summarize the disagreement among critics regarding Tutuola's place in world literature

GO ON TO THE NEXT PAGE.

Mechanisms for recognizing kin are found throughout the plant and animal kingdoms, regardless of an organism's social or mental complexity. Improvements in the general understanding of these mechanisms have turned some biologists' attention to the question of why kin recognition occurs at all. One response to this question is offered by the inclusive fitness theory, which was developed in the 1960s. The theory is based on the realization that an organism transmits its genetic attributes to succeeding generations not solely through its offspring, but more generally through all of its close relatives. Whereas the traditional view of evolution held that natural selection favors the continued genetic representation of individuals within a species that produce the greatest number of offspring, the inclusive fitness theory posits that natural selection similarly favors organisms that help their relatives, because doing so also increases their own total genetic representation. The theory has helped to explain previously mysterious phenomena, including the evolution of social insect species like the honeybee, most of whose members do not produce offspring and exist only to nurture relatives.

Inclusive fitness theory has also been applied usefully to new findings concerning cannibalism within animal species. Based on the theory, cannibals should have evolved to avoid eating their own kin because of the obvious genetic costs of such a practice. Spadefoot toad tadpoles provide an illustration. Biologists have found that all tadpoles of that species begin life as omnivores, feeding mainly on organic debris in their soon-to-be-dry pool in the desert, but that occasionally one tadpole eats another or eats a freshwater shrimp. This event can trigger changes in the tadpole's physiology and dietary preference, causing the tadpole to become larger and exclusively carnivorous, feasting on other animals including members of its own species. Yet the cannibals have a procedure of discrimination whereby they nip at other tadpoles, eating nonsiblings but releasing siblings unharmed. This suggests that the inclusive fitness theory offers at least a partial answer to why kin recognition develops. Interestingly, a cannibal tadpole is less likely to avoid eating kin when it becomes very hungry, apparently putting its own unique genetic makeup ahead of its siblings'.

But there may be other reasons why organisms recognize kin. For example, it has recently been found that tiger salamander larvae, also either omnivorous or cannibalistic, are plagued in nature by a deadly bacterium. Furthermore, it was determined that cannibal larvae are especially likely to be infected by eating diseased species members. The fact that this bacterium is more deadly when it comes from a close relative with a similar immune system suggests that natural selection may favor cannibals that avoid such pathogens by not eating kin. For tiger salamanders then, kin recognition can be explained simply as a means by which an organism preserves its own life, not as a means to aid in relatives' survival.

8. Which one of the following most accurately expresses the main point of the passage?

(A) Some findings support the hypothesis that kin recognition emerged through natural selection because it increased organisms' total genetic representation, but this hypothesis may not explain all instances of kin recognition.
(B) Current research supports the view that the mechanisms enabling the members of a species to recognize close relatives are as various as the purposes served by that ability.
(C) Recent research involving tiger salamanders undermines the hypothesis concerning the purpose of kin recognition that is espoused by traditional evolutionary theorists.
(D) New research involving tiger salamanders indicates that the traditional theory of natural selection is more strongly supported by the evidence than is thought by those who consider only the case of the spadefoot toad tadpole.
(E) While traditional evolutionary theory was unable to account for the phenomenon of kin recognition, this phenomenon is fully explained by the inclusive fitness theory.

9. The passage states which one of the following about some spadefoot toad tadpoles?

(A) They develop the ability to recognize fellow carnivores.
(B) They feed only upon omnivorous tadpoles.
(C) They change in body size when they become carnivores.
(D) Their carnivorousness constitutes an important piece of evidence that calls into question the inclusive fitness theory.
(E) Their carnivorousness would not occur unless it contributed in some way to the evolutionary success of the spadefoot toad species.

10. Based on the passage, the author would be most likely to agree with which one of the following statements about evolutionary explanations of kin recognition?

(A) It is impossible to understand the mechanisms underlying kin recognition until an evolutionary explanation of such recognition has been attained.
(B) Such explanations require no modifications to traditional evolutionary theory.
(C) For any such explanation to be fully adequate it should ignore the differences of social or mental complexity of the organisms whose abilities it is intended to explain.
(D) Kin recognition may have different evolutionary explanations in different species.
(E) No other evolutionary explanation can account for the wide diversity of unusual phenomena with the same success as the inclusive fitness theory.

11. Which one of the following most accurately describes the function of the last sentence of the second paragraph?

(A) to draw attention to behavior that further complicates the set of facts to be explained by any theory of natural selection that accounts for kin recognition
(B) to explain why cannibals in most species eat their kin less often than do cannibal spadefoot toad tadpoles
(C) to describe behavior that lends support to the account of kin recognition presented in the second paragraph
(D) to offer evidence that the behavior of cannibal spadefoot toad tadpoles is unexplainable
(E) to imply that the described behavior is more relevant to the issue at hand than is the immediately preceding material

12. The passage most strongly supports which one of the following statements about the mechanism by which cannibal spadefoot toad tadpoles recognize their kin?

(A) It is not dependent solely on the use of visual cues.
(B) It is neither utilized nor possessed by those tadpoles that do not become cannibalistic.
(C) It does not always allow a tadpole to distinguish its siblings from tadpoles that are not siblings.
(D) It is rendered unnecessary by physiological changes accompanying the dietary shift from omnivorousness to carnivorousness.
(E) It could not have developed in a species in which all members are omnivorous.

13. The passage states which one of the following about the mechanisms that enable organisms to recognize their close genetic relatives?

(A) The mechanisms are most easily explained if we assume that they have a similar purpose in all species regardless of the species' social or mental complexities.
(B) The mechanisms have become more clearly understood, prompting interest in the purpose they serve.
(C) The mechanisms have become the focus of theoretical attention only since the 1960s.
(D) The detailed workings of these mechanisms must be better understood before their purpose can be fully explained.
(E) The mechanisms operate differently in different species even when they serve exactly the same function.

14. The information in the passage most strongly suggests that the fact that most honeybees exist only to nurture relatives

(A) was not known to be true before the 1960s
(B) can be explained only if we assume that these members are in turn nurtured by the relatives they nurture
(C) is what led most biologists to reject the traditional view of evolution
(D) calls into question the view that evolution proceeds by natural selection
(E) is difficult to explain without at least supplementing the traditional view of evolution with further explanatory hypotheses

15. Which one of the following would, if true, most help to undermine the author's evaluation in the last sentence of the passage?

(A) Many tiger salamander larvae infected by the deadly bacterium are not cannibalistic.
(B) The factor that determines which tiger salamander larvae are carnivorous and which are omnivorous is not contained in the genetic makeup of the larvae.
(C) Kin recognition helps tiger salamanders avoid inbreeding that may be life-threatening to their offspring.
(D) Noncannibalistic tiger salamanders tend to produce fewer offspring than cannibalistic tiger salamanders.
(E) Cannibalistic tiger salamanders are immune to certain diseases to which noncannibalistic salamanders are not.

GO ON TO THE NEXT PAGE.

Passage A

There is no universally accepted definition within international law for the term "national minority." It is most commonly applied to (1) groups of persons—not necessarily citizens—under the jurisdiction of one country who have ethnic ties to another "homeland" country, or (2) groups of citizens of a country who have lasting ties to that country and have no such ties to any other country, but are distinguished from the majority of the population by ethnicity, religion, or language. The terms "people" and "nation" are also vaguely defined in international agreements. Documents that refer to a "nation" generally link the term to the concept of "nationalism," which is often associated with ties to land. It also connotes sovereignty, for which reason, perhaps, "people" is often used instead of "nation" for groups subject to a colonial power.

While the lack of definition of the terms "minority," "people," and "nation" presents difficulties to numerous minority groups, this lack is particularly problematic for the Roma (Gypsies). The Roma are not a colonized people, they do not have a homeland, and many do not bear ties to any currently existing country. Some Roma are not even citizens of any country, in part because of their nomadic way of life, which developed in response to centuries of fleeing persecution. Instead, they have ethnic and linguistic ties to other groups of Roma that reside in other countries.

Passage B

Capotorti's definition of a minority includes four empirical criteria—a group's being numerically smaller than the rest of the population of the state; their being nondominant; their having distinctive ethnic, linguistic, or religious characteristics; and their desiring to preserve their own culture—and one legal criterion, that they be citizens of the state in question. This last element can be problematic, given the previous nomadic character of the Roma, that they still cross borders between European states to avoid persecution, and that some states have denied them citizenship, and thus minority status. Because this element essentially grants the state the arbitrary right to decide if the Roma constitute a minority without reference to empirical characteristics, it seems patently unfair that it should be included in the definition.

However, the Roma easily fulfill the four objective elements of Capotorti's definition and should, therefore, be considered a minority in all major European states. Numerically, they are nowhere near a majority, though they number in the hundreds of thousands, even millions, in some states. Their nondominant position is evident—they are not even acknowledged as a minority in some states. The Roma have a number of distinctive linguistic, ethnic, and religious characteristics. For example, most speak Romani, an Indo-European language descended from Sanskrit. Roma groups also have their own distinctive legal and court systems, which are group oriented rather than individual-rights oriented. That they have preserved their language, customs, and identity through centuries of persecution is evidence enough of their desire to preserve their culture.

16. Which one of the following most accurately expresses the main point of passage A?

    (A) Different definitions of certain key terms in international law conflict with one another in their application to the Roma.
    (B) In at least some countries in which they live, the Roma are not generally considered a minority group.
    (C) The lack of agreement regarding the definitions of such terms as "minority," "people," and "nation" is partly due to the unclear application of the terms to groups such as the Roma.
    (D) Any attempt to define such concepts as people, nation, or minority group will probably fail to apply to certain borderline cases such as the Roma.
    (E) The absence of a clear, generally agreed-upon understanding of what constitutes a people, nation, or minority group is a problem, especially in relation to the Roma.

17. The term "problematic" has which one of the following meanings in both passage A (line 19) and passage B (line 35)?

    (A) giving rise to intense debate
    (B) confusing and unclear
    (C) resulting in difficulties
    (D) difficult to solve
    (E) theoretically incoherent

GO ON TO THE NEXT PAGE.

18. Which one of the following claims about the Roma is NOT made in passage A?

(A) Those living in one country have ethnic ties to Roma in other countries.
(B) Some of them practice a nomadic way of life.
(C) They, as a people, have no recognizable homeland.
(D) In some countries, their population exceeds one million.
(E) The lack of a completely satisfactory definition of "minority" is a greater problem for them than for most.

19. The authors' views regarding the status of the Roma can most accurately be described in which one of the following ways?

(A) The author of passage A, but not the author of passage B, disapproves of the latitude that international law allows individual states in determining their relations to nomadic Roma populations.
(B) The author of passage B, but not the author of passage A, considers the problems of the Roma to be a noteworthy example of how international law can be ineffective.
(C) The author of passage B, but not the author of passage A, considers the Roma to be a paradigmatic example of a people who do not constitute a nation.
(D) Both authors would prefer that the political issues involving the Roma be resolved on a case-by-case basis within each individual country rather than through international law.
(E) Both authors consider the problems that the Roma face in relation to international law to be anomalous and special.

20. The relationship between which one of the following pairs of documents is most analogous to the relationship between passage A and passage B?

(A) "The Lack of Clear-Cut Criteria for Classifying Jobs as Technical Causes Problems for Welders" and "A Point-by-Point Argument That Welding Fulfills the Union's Criteria for Classification of Jobs as 'Technical'"
(B) "Why the Current Criteria for Professional Competence in Welding Have Not Been Effectively Applied" and "A Review of the Essential Elements of Any Formal Statement of Professional Standards"
(C) "The Need for a Revised Definition of the Concept of Welding in Relation to Other Technical Jobs" and "An Enumeration and Description of the Essential Job Duties Usually Carried Out by Union Welders"
(D) "The Lack of Competent Welders in Our Company Can Be Attributed to a General Disregard for Professional and Technical Staff Recruitment" and "A Discussion of the Factors That Companies Should Consider in Recruiting Employees"
(E) "The Conceptual Links Between Professionalism and Technical Expertise" and "A Refutation of the Union's Position Regarding Which Types of Jobs Should Be Classified as Neither Professional nor Technical"

21. Which one of the following is a principle that can be most reasonably considered to underlie the reasoning in both of the passages?

(A) A definition that is vaguely formulated cannot serve as the basis for the provisions contained in a document of international law.
(B) A minority group's not being officially recognized as such by the government that has jurisdiction over it can be detrimental to the group's interests.
(C) Provisions in international law that apply only to minority groups should not be considered valid.
(D) Governments should recognize the legal and court systems used by minority populations within their jurisdictions.
(E) A group that often moves back and forth across a boundary between two countries can be legitimately considered citizens of both countries.

During most of the nineteenth century, many French women continued to be educated according to models long established by custom and religious tradition. One recent observer has termed the failure to institute real and lasting educational reform at the end of the eighteenth century a "missed opportunity"—for in spite of the egalitarian and secular aims of the French Revolution in 1789, a truly nondiscriminatory education system for both women and men would not be established in the country until the 1880s. However, legislators had put forth many proposals for educational reform in the years just after the revolution; two in particular attempted to institute educational systems for women that were, to a great extent, egalitarian.

The first of these proposals endeavored to replace the predominantly religious education that women originally received in convents and at home with reformed curricula. More importantly, the proposal insisted that, because education was a common good that should be offered to both sexes, instruction should be available to everyone. By the same token, teachers would be drawn from both sexes. Thus the proposal held it essential that schools for both men and women be established promptly throughout the country and that these schools be public, a tangible sign of the state's interest in all of its citizens. One limitation of this proposal, however, was that girls, unlike boys, were to leave school at age eight in order to be educated at home in the skills necessary for domestic life and for the raising of families. The second proposal took a more comprehensive approach. It advocated equal education for women and men on the grounds that women and men enjoy the same rights, and it was the only proposal of the time that called for coeducational schools, which were presented as a bulwark against the traditional gender roles enforced by religious tradition. In other respects, however, this proposal also continued to define women in terms of their roles in the domestic sphere and as mothers.

That neither proposal was able to envision a system of education that was fully equal for women, and that neither was adopted into law even as such, bespeaks the immensity of the cultural and political obstacles to egalitarian education for women at the time. Nevertheless, the vision of egalitarian educational reform was not entirely lost. Nearly a century later, in the early 1880s, French legislators recalled the earlier proposals in their justification of new laws that founded public secondary schools for women, abolished fees for education, and established compulsory attendance for all students. In order to pass these reforms, the government needed to demonstrate that its new standards were rooted in a long philosophical, political, and pedagogical tradition. Various of the resulting institutions also made claim to revolutionary origin, as doing so allowed them to appropriate the legitimacy conferred by tradition and historical continuity.

22. It can be inferred from the passage that the French legislators who passed new educational laws in the early 1880s were

(A) committed to removing education in the skills necessary for domestic life from the public school curriculum
(B) unaware of the difficulties that the earlier legislators faced when advocating similar legislation
(C) concerned with improving educational equality across economic strata as well as between the sexes
(D) more open to political compromise than were the legislators who introduced the previous proposals for reform
(E) more inclined to give religious authorities a role in education than were the legislators who introduced the previous proposals for reform

23. Which one of the following most accurately describes the organization of the passage?

(A) Education in France during one historical period is described; two proposals that attempted to reform the educational system are presented; inconsistencies within each proposal are identified and lamented.
(B) The movement toward gender equality in France during one historical period is discussed; two proposals for educational reform are presented; the differences between the proposals and the educational system of that era are outlined.
(C) The traditional nature of French education for women is described; proposed breaks with tradition are discussed, followed by a discussion of why eventual change required less of a break with tradition.
(D) The egalitarian aims in France during one historical period are presented; proposals that foreshadowed eventual reform are described; the initial characterization of the aims is modified.
(E) The nature of education for women in France during one historical period is described; proposals for educational reform are presented; the relationship between the proposals and eventual reform is indicated.

GO ON TO THE NEXT PAGE.

24. Suppose that two proposals were put forward by lawmakers concerning housing reform today. Which one of the following pairs of proposals is most closely analogous to the pair of proposals discussed in the second paragraph of the passage?

(A) "Housing should be made available to all" and "Real estate practices should be nondiscriminatory"
(B) "Housing should be made available to all" and "The quality of housing should be improved"
(C) "There should be housing for all who can pay" and "Housing should be of uniform quality"
(D) "The quality of housing should be improved" and "Real estate practices should be nondiscriminatory"
(E) "Low-cost housing should be constructed" and "Housing should be of uniform quality"

25. According to the passage, the second of the two proposals discussed was distinctive because it asserted that

(A) everyone should both learn and teach
(B) males and females should go to the same schools
(C) education should involve lifelong learning
(D) religious schools should be abolished
(E) education for girls should be both public and secular

26. Based on the passage, the fact that the proposed reforms were introduced shortly after the French Revolution most clearly suggests that the proposals

(A) were a reaction to the excesses of the new government
(B) had their roots in a belief in the power of education
(C) had vast popular support within French society
(D) treated education for women as a prerequisite to the implementation of other reforms
(E) were influenced by egalitarian ideals

27. The author would most likely describe the proposals mentioned in the passage with which one of the following statements?

(A) They espoused reforms that were very modest by the standards of the day.
(B) They were fundamentally unethical due to their incomplete view of equality.
(C) They were well-meaning attempts to do as much as was feasible at the time.
(D) They were reasonable, and it is difficult to understand why they failed.
(E) They were not adopted because their aims were not fully comprehensive.

S T O P

IF YOU FINISH BEFORE TIME IS CALLED, YOU MAY CHECK YOUR WORK ON THIS SECTION ONLY.
DO NOT WORK ON ANY OTHER SECTION IN THE TEST.

Acknowledgment is made to the following sources from which material has been adapted for use in this test booklet:

James P. Draper, ed., *Black Literature Criticism.* ©1992 by Gale Research Inc.

Geneviève Fraisse and Michelle Perrot, eds., *A History of Women in the West.* ©1993 by the President and Fellows of Harvard College.

David W. Pfennig and Paul W. Sherman, "Kin Recognition." ©1995 by Scientific American, Inc.

"Why Wages Do Not Fall in Recessions." ©February 26, 2000 by The Economist Newspaper Limited.

LSAT WRITING SAMPLE TOPIC

Directions: The scenario presented below describes two choices, either one of which can be supported on the basis of the information given. Your essay should consider both choices and argue for one over the other, based on the two specified criteria and the facts provided. There is no "right" or "wrong" choice: a reasonable argument can be made for either.

An online business named It's Yours (IY) is a custom designer and seller of jewelry. IY plans to expand its offerings to include a line of customized watches and must decide how to incorporate the new products into the business—either by adding the customizations itself or by having the watch manufacturer do it. Using the facts below, write an essay in which you argue for one option over the other based on the following two criteria:

- IY wants to maintain control over the quality of the products and service it provides.
- IY wants to be adequately prepared for an anticipated increase in sales volume.

One option is for IY to bring the watch customization in house, adding the watches to its work with the other jewelry lines. IY would need to make substantial investments in specialized equipment and training for its design and assembly staff. In producing its personalized jewelry, IY frequently receives novel, unexpected requests and then works one-on-one with customers to design items. Bringing the watch personalization on board would double its in-house production. Keeping up with demand might require IY to decline orders or delay production.

Alternatively, IY could have the watch manufacturer implement the requested personalizations. The watch manufacturer is a large company that currently has excess production capacity. It has an existing customization capacity. Customization is not the core of its business. Based on its experience with the jewelry production, IY believes that the manufacturer will be able to respond to a substantial range of typical customer requests. IY would have to decline any unusual requests that present a design challenge.

Scratch Paper
Do not write your essay in this space.

Directions:

1. Use the Answer Key on the next page to check your answers.

2. Use the Scoring Worksheet below to compute your raw score.

3. Use the Score Conversion Chart to convert your raw score into the 120–180 scale.

Scoring Worksheet

1. Enter the number of questions you answered correctly in each section

	Number Correct
SECTION I	______
SECTION II	______
SECTION III	______
SECTION IV	______

2. Enter the sum here: ______ This is your Raw Score.

Conversion Chart

For Converting Raw Score to the 120–180 LSAT Scaled Score
LSAT PrepTest 56

REPORTED SCORE	LOWEST RAW SCORE	HIGHEST RAW SCORE
180	98	100
179	97	97
178	96	96
177	__*	__*
176	95	95
175	94	94
174	93	93
173	92	92
172	91	91
171	90	90
170	89	89
169	88	88
168	87	87
167	85	86
166	84	84
165	82	83
164	81	81
163	79	80
162	78	78
161	76	77
160	74	75
159	73	73
158	71	72
157	69	70
156	67	68
155	66	66
154	64	65
153	62	63
152	60	61
151	58	59
150	57	57
149	55	56
148	53	54
147	51	52
146	50	50
145	48	49
144	46	47
143	45	45
142	43	44
141	41	42
140	40	40
139	38	39
138	37	37
137	35	36
136	34	34
135	32	33
134	31	31
133	29	30
132	28	28
131	27	27
130	25	26
129	24	24
128	23	23
127	21	22
126	20	20
125	19	19
124	18	18
123	17	17
122	15	16
121	__*	__*
120	0	14

*There is no raw score that will produce this scaled score for this PrepTest.

SECTION I

1.	E	8.	D	15.	A	22.	E
2.	B	9.	B	16.	E	23.	B
3.	C	10.	B	17.	A		
4.	C	11.	E	18.	A		
5.	A	12.	D	19.	C		
6.	E	13.	C	20.	D		
7.	A	14.	A	21.	E		

SECTION II

1.	E	8.	D	15.	B	22.	C
2.	A	9.	B	16.	D	23.	E
3.	B	10.	D	17.	E	24.	A
4.	C	11.	B	18.	C	25.	B
5.	E	12.	E	19.	A		
6.	E	13.	A	20.	E		
7.	C	14.	D	21.	B		

SECTION III

1.	C	8.	A	15.	D	22.	B
2.	E	9.	A	16.	A	23.	E
3.	B	10.	C	17.	C	24.	D
4.	A	11.	E	18.	E	25.	E
5.	D	12.	A	19.	E		
6.	D	13.	A	20.	D		
7.	E	14.	B	21.	D		

SECTION IV

1.	B	8.	A	15.	C	22.	C
2.	D	9.	C	16.	E	23.	E
3.	A	10.	D	17.	C	24.	A
4.	D	11.	A	18.	D	25.	B
5.	E	12.	A	19.	E	26.	E
6.	A	13.	B	20.	A	27.	C
7.	C	14.	E	21.	B		

Experimental Section Answer Key
June 1999, PrepTest 27, Section 1

1.	B	8.	B	15.	A	22.	D
2.	D	9.	A	16.	D	23.	C
3.	D	10.	E	17.	B	24.	D
4.	A	11.	B	18.	A	25.	B
5.	C	12.	E	19.	E	26.	D
6.	C	13.	C	20.	C		
7.	C	14.	B	21.	B		

PrepTest 57
June 2009

SECTION I

Time—35 minutes

23 Questions

Directions:Each group of questions in this section is based on a set of conditions. In answering some of the questions, it may be useful to draw a rough diagram. Choose the response that most accurately and completely answers each question and blacken the corresponding space on your answer sheet.

Questions 1–5

On a particular Saturday, a student will perform six activities—grocery shopping, hedge trimming, jogging, kitchen cleaning, laundry, and motorbike servicing. Each activity will be performed once, one at a time. The order in which the activities are performed is subject to the following conditions:

Grocery shopping has to be immediately after hedge trimming.
Kitchen cleaning has to be earlier than grocery shopping.
Motorbike servicing has to be earlier than laundry.
Motorbike servicing has to be either immediately before or immediately after jogging.

1. Which one of the following could be the order, from first to last, of the student's activities?

(A) jogging, kitchen cleaning, hedge trimming, grocery shopping, motorbike servicing, laundry
(B) jogging, motorbike servicing, laundry, hedge trimming, grocery shopping, kitchen cleaning
(C) kitchen cleaning, hedge trimming, grocery shopping, laundry, motorbike servicing, jogging
(D) kitchen cleaning, jogging, motorbike servicing, laundry, hedge trimming, grocery shopping
(E) motorbike servicing, jogging, laundry, hedge trimming, kitchen cleaning, grocery shopping

2. Which one of the following activities CANNOT be third?

(A) grocery shopping
(B) hedge trimming
(C) jogging
(D) kitchen cleaning
(E) motorbike servicing

3. Which one of the following CANNOT be true?

(A) Hedge trimming is fourth.
(B) Jogging is fourth.
(C) Kitchen cleaning is second.
(D) Laundry is third.
(E) Motorbike servicing is second.

4. Which one of the following activities CANNOT be fifth?

(A) grocery shopping
(B) hedge trimming
(C) jogging
(D) laundry
(E) motorbike servicing

5. Which one of the following, if substituted for the condition that motorbike servicing has to be earlier than laundry, would have the same effect in determining the order of the student's activities?

(A) Laundry has to be one of the last three activities.
(B) Laundry has to be either immediately before or immediately after jogging.
(C) Jogging has to be earlier than laundry.
(D) Laundry has to be earlier than hedge trimming.
(E) Laundry has to be earlier than jogging.

GO ON TO THE NEXT PAGE.

Questions 6–11

Each of exactly three actors—Gombrich, Otto, and Raines—auditions for parts on exactly two of the following days of a particular week: Wednesday, Thursday, Friday, and Saturday. On each of these days at least one of the actors auditions for parts. The order of that week's auditions must meet the following conditions:

The first day on which Otto auditions is some day before the first day on which Raines auditions.
There is at least one day on which both Gombrich and Raines audition.
At least one of the actors auditions on both Thursday and Saturday.

6. Which one of the following could be an accurate matching of the actors to the days on which they audition?

(A) Gombrich: Thursday, Friday
Otto: Wednesday, Saturday
Raines: Friday, Saturday
(B) Gombrich: Thursday, Saturday
Otto: Wednesday, Friday
Raines: Friday, Saturday
(C) Gombrich: Friday, Saturday
Otto: Thursday, Saturday
Raines: Wednesday, Friday
(D) Gombrich: Wednesday, Thursday
Otto: Wednesday, Saturday
Raines: Thursday, Saturday
(E) Gombrich: Wednesday, Friday
Otto: Wednesday, Thursday
Raines: Thursday, Saturday

7. If Otto auditions on both Thursday and Saturday, then Gombrich could audition on both

(A) Wednesday and Thursday
(B) Wednesday and Friday
(C) Thursday and Friday
(D) Thursday and Saturday
(E) Friday and Saturday

8. Which one of the following CANNOT be true of the week's auditions?

(A) Gombrich's last audition is on Thursday.
(B) Gombrich's last audition is on Friday.
(C) Otto's last audition is on Saturday.
(D) Raines's last audition is on Friday.
(E) Raines's last audition is on Thursday.

9. Which one of the following pairs of days CANNOT be the two days on which Otto auditions?

(A) Wednesday and Thursday
(B) Wednesday and Friday
(C) Wednesday and Saturday
(D) Thursday and Friday
(E) Thursday and Saturday

10. Which one of the following could be true?

(A) All three actors audition on Wednesday.
(B) All three actors audition on Friday.
(C) All three actors audition on Saturday.
(D) Otto auditions on Friday and on Saturday.
(E) Raines auditions on Wednesday and on Friday.

11. If Gombrich auditions on both Wednesday and Saturday, then which one of the following could be true?

(A) Otto auditions on both Wednesday and Thursday.
(B) Otto auditions on both Wednesday and Friday.
(C) Otto auditions on both Wednesday and Saturday.
(D) Raines auditions on both Wednesday and Saturday.
(E) Raines auditions on both Thursday and Friday.

GO ON TO THE NEXT PAGE.

Questions 12–17

Each of seven toy dinosaurs—an iguanadon, a lambeosaur, a plateosaur, a stegosaur, a tyrannosaur, an ultrasaur, and a velociraptor—is completely colored either green, mauve, red, or yellow. A display is to consist entirely of exactly five of these toys. The display must meet the following specifications:

Exactly two mauve toys are included.
The stegosaur is red and is included.
The iguanadon is included only if it is green.
The plateosaur is included only if it is yellow.
The velociraptor is included only if the ultrasaur is not.
If both the lambeosaur and the ultrasaur are included, at least one of them is not mauve.

12. Which one of the following could be the toys included in the display?

(A) the lambeosaur, the plateosaur, the stegosaur, the ultrasaur, the velociraptor
(B) the lambeosaur, the plateosaur, the stegosaur, the tyrannosaur, the ultrasaur
(C) the iguanadon, the lambeosaur, the plateosaur, the stegosaur, the ultrasaur
(D) the iguanadon, the lambeosaur, the plateosaur, the tyrannosaur, the velociraptor
(E) the iguanadon, the lambeosaur, the stegosaur, the ultrasaur, the velociraptor

13. If the tyrannosaur is not included in the display, then the display must contain each of the following EXCEPT:

(A) a green iguanadon
(B) a mauve velociraptor
(C) a mauve lambeosaur
(D) a mauve ultrasaur
(E) a yellow plateosaur

14. Which one of the following is a pair of toys that could be included in the display together?

(A) a green lambeosaur and a mauve velociraptor
(B) a green lambeosaur and a yellow tyrannosaur
(C) a green lambeosaur and a yellow ultrasaur
(D) a yellow tyrannosaur and a green ultrasaur
(E) a yellow tyrannosaur and a red velociraptor

15. If the display includes a yellow tyrannosaur, then which one of the following must be true?

(A) The iguanadon is included in the display.
(B) The plateosaur is not included in the display.
(C) The display includes two yellow toy dinosaurs.
(D) The display contains a green lambeosaur.
(E) The display contains a mauve velociraptor.

16. If both the iguanadon and the ultrasaur are included in the display, then the display must contain which one of the following?

(A) a mauve tyrannosaur
(B) a mauve ultrasaur
(C) a yellow lambeosaur
(D) a yellow plateosaur
(E) a yellow ultrasaur

17. If the display includes two green toys, then which one of the following could be true?

(A) There is exactly one yellow toy included in the display.
(B) The tyrannosaur is included in the display and it is green.
(C) Neither the lambeosaur nor the velociraptor is included in the display.
(D) Neither the tyrannosaur nor the velociraptor is included in the display.
(E) Neither the ultrasaur nor the velociraptor is included in the display.

GO ON TO THE NEXT PAGE.

Questions 18–23

A charitable foundation awards grants in exactly four areas—medical services, theater arts, wildlife preservation, and youth services—each grant being in one of these areas. One or more grants are awarded in each of the four quarters of a calendar year. Additionally, over the course of a calendar year, the following must obtain:

Grants are awarded in all four areas.
No more than six grants are awarded.
No grants in the same area are awarded in the same quarter or in consecutive quarters.
Exactly two medical services grants are awarded.
A wildlife preservation grant is awarded in the second quarter.

18. Which one of the following is a possible allocation of grants in a particular calendar year?

(A) first quarter: theater arts
second quarter: wildlife preservation
third quarter: medical services, youth services
fourth quarter: theater arts

(B) first quarter: wildlife preservation
second quarter: medical services
third quarter: theater arts
fourth quarter: medical services, youth services

(C) first quarter: youth services
second quarter: wildlife preservation, medical services
third quarter: theater arts
fourth quarter: medical services, youth services

(D) first quarter: medical services, theater arts
second quarter: theater arts, wildlife preservation
third quarter: youth services
fourth quarter: medical services

(E) first quarter: medical services, theater arts
second quarter: wildlife preservation, youth services
third quarter: theater arts
fourth quarter: medical services, youth services

19. Which one of the following CANNOT be true in a particular calendar year?

(A) In each of the two quarters in which a medical services grant is awarded, no other grant is awarded.
(B) Exactly two theater arts grants are awarded, one in the second quarter and one in the fourth quarter.
(C) Exactly two youth services grants are awarded, one in the first quarter and one in the third quarter.
(D) Two wildlife preservation grants and two youth services grants are awarded.
(E) Three grants are awarded in the fourth quarter.

20. If a wildlife preservation grant and a youth services grant are awarded in the same quarter of a particular calendar year, then any of the following could be true that year EXCEPT:

(A) A medical services grant is awarded in the second quarter.
(B) A theater arts grant is awarded in the first quarter.
(C) A theater arts grant is awarded in the second quarter.
(D) A wildlife preservation grant is awarded in the fourth quarter.
(E) A youth services grant is awarded in the third quarter.

21. If exactly two grants are awarded in just one of the four quarters of a particular calendar year, then which one of the following could be true that year?

(A) Two youth services grants are awarded.
(B) Neither a medical services grant nor a youth services grant is awarded in the first quarter.
(C) A wildlife preservation grant is awarded in the fourth quarter.
(D) Both a youth services grant and a theater arts grant are awarded in the first quarter.
(E) A youth services grant is awarded in the first quarter and a theater arts grant is awarded in the second quarter.

22. Which one of the following CANNOT be true in a particular calendar year?

(A) Three grants are awarded in a quarter, none of which is a medical services grant.
(B) Exactly two grants are awarded in the first quarter and exactly two in the third quarter.
(C) Exactly two grants are awarded in the first quarter and exactly two in the fourth quarter.
(D) Theater arts grants are awarded in the first and fourth quarters, and no other grants are awarded in those two quarters.
(E) Wildlife preservation grants are awarded in the second and fourth quarters, and no other grants are awarded in those two quarters.

23. It is fully determined which grants are awarded for each quarter of a particular calendar year if which one of the following is true that year?

(A) Two theater arts grants are awarded.
(B) Two youth services grants are awarded.
(C) Three grants are awarded in the first quarter.
(D) Three grants are awarded in the second quarter.
(E) Three grants are awarded in the third quarter.

S T O P

IF YOU FINISH BEFORE TIME IS CALLED, YOU MAY CHECK YOUR WORK ON THIS SECTION ONLY.
DO NOT WORK ON ANY OTHER SECTION IN THE TEST.

SECTION II

Time—35 minutes

26 Questions

Directions: The questions in this section are based on the reasoning contained in brief statements or passages. For some questions, more than one of the choices could conceivably answer the question. However, you are to choose the best answer; that is, the response that most accurately and completely answers the question. You should not make assumptions that are by commonsense standards implausible, superfluous, or incompatible with the passage. After you have chosen the best answer, blacken the corresponding space on your answer sheet.

1. Many doctors cater to patients' demands that they be prescribed antibiotics for their colds. However, colds are caused by viruses, and antibiotics have no effect on viruses, and so antibiotics have no effect on colds. Such treatments are also problematic because antibiotics can have dangerous side effects. So doctors should never prescribe antibiotics to treat colds.

   The reasoning above most closely conforms to which one of the following principles?

   (A) A doctor should not prescribe a drug for a condition if it cannot improve that condition and if the drug potentially has adverse side effects.
   (B) A doctor should not prescribe any drug that might have harmful effects on the patient even if the drug might have a positive effect on the patient.
   (C) A doctor should attempt to prescribe every drug that is likely to affect the patient's health positively.
   (D) A doctor should withhold treatment from a patient if the doctor is uncertain whether the treatment will benefit the patient.
   (E) A doctor should never base the decision to prescribe a certain medication for a patient on the patient's claims about the effectiveness of that medication.

2. Long-distance runners use two different kinds of cognitive strategies: "associative" and "dissociative." Associative strategies involve attending closely to physical sensations, while dissociative strategies involve mostly ignoring physical sensations. Associative strategies, unlike dissociative ones, require so much concentration that they result in mental exhaustion lasting more than a day. Since it is important for long-distance runners to enter a race mentally refreshed, ________.

   Which one of the following most logically completes the argument?

   (A) long-distance runners should not rely heavily on associative strategies during training the day before they run in a race
   (B) unless they regularly train using associative strategies, long-distance runners should use dissociative strategies during races
   (C) maximizing the benefits of training for long-distance running involves frequently alternating associative and dissociative strategies
   (D) long-distance runners are about evenly divided between those who use dissociative strategies during races and those who use associative strategies during races
   (E) in long-distance running, dissociative strategies are generally more effective for a day's training run than are associative strategies

GO ON TO THE NEXT PAGE.

3. MetroBank made loans to ten small companies, in amounts ranging from $1,000 to $100,000. These ten loans all had graduated payment plans, i.e., the scheduled monthly loan payment increased slightly each month over the five-year term of the loan. Nonetheless, the average payment received by MetroBank for these ten loans had decreased by the end of the five-year term.

   Which one of the following, if true, most helps to resolve the apparent discrepancy in the statements above?

   (A) The number of small companies receiving new loans from MetroBank increased over the five-year term.
   (B) Several of the ten small companies also borrowed money from other banks.
   (C) Most banks offer a greater number of loans for under $100,000 than for over $100,000.
   (D) Of the ten small companies, the three that had borrowed the largest amounts paid off their loans within three years.
   (E) For some loans made by MetroBank, the monthly payment decreases slightly over the term of the loan.

4. Professor: A guest speaker recently delivered a talk entitled "The Functions of Democratic Governments" to a Political Ideologies class at this university. The talk was carefully researched and theoretical in nature. But two students who disagreed with the theory hurled vicious taunts at the speaker. Several others applauded their attempt to humiliate the speaker. This incident shows that universities these days do not foster fair-minded and tolerant intellectual debate.

   The professor's reasoning is flawed in that it

   (A) draws a conclusion based on the professor's own opinion rather than on that of the majority of the students present at the talk
   (B) is inconsistent in advocating tolerance while showing intolerance of the dissenting students' views
   (C) relies primarily on an emotional appeal
   (D) draws a general conclusion based on too small a sample
   (E) incorrectly focuses on the behavior of the dissenting students rather than relating the reasons for that behavior

5. Studies reveal that most people select the foods they eat primarily on the basis of flavor, and that nutrition is usually a secondary concern at best. This suggests that health experts would have more success in encouraging people to eat wholesome foods if they emphasized how flavorful those foods truly are rather than how nutritious they are.

   Which one of the following, if true, most strengthens the argument above?

   (A) Most people currently believe that wholesome foods are more flavorful, on average, than unwholesome foods are.
   (B) Few people, when given a choice between foods that are flavorful but not nutritious and foods that are nutritious but not flavorful, will choose the foods that are nutritious but not flavorful.
   (C) Health experts' attempts to encourage people to eat wholesome foods by emphasizing how nutritious those foods are have been moderately successful.
   (D) The studies that revealed that people choose the foods they eat primarily on the basis of flavor also revealed that people rated as most flavorful those foods that were least nutritious.
   (E) In a study, subjects who were told that a given food was very flavorful were more willing to try the food and more likely to enjoy it than were subjects who were told that the food was nutritious.

GO ON TO THE NEXT PAGE.

6. Studies show that individuals with a high propensity for taking risks tend to have fewer ethical principles to which they consciously adhere in their business interactions than do most people. On the other hand, individuals with a strong desire to be accepted socially tend to have more such principles than do most people. And, in general, the more ethical principles to which someone consciously adheres, the more ethical is that person's behavior. Therefore, business schools can promote more ethical behavior among future businesspeople by promoting among their students the desire to be accepted socially and discouraging the propensity for taking risks.

   The reasoning in the argument is flawed because the argument

   (A) infers from the fact that something is usually true that it is always true
   (B) takes for granted that promoting ethical behavior is more important than any other goal
   (C) concludes merely from the fact that two things are correlated that one causes the other
   (D) takes for granted that certain actions are morally wrong simply because most people believe that they are morally wrong
   (E) draws a conclusion that simply restates a claim presented in support of that conclusion

7. Essayist: Lessing contended that an art form's medium dictates the kind of representation the art form must employ in order to be legitimate; painting, for example, must represent simultaneous arrays of colored shapes, while literature, consisting of words read in succession, must represent events or actions occurring in sequence. The claim about literature must be rejected, however, if one regards as legitimate the imagists' poems, which consist solely of amalgams of disparate images.

   Which one of the following, if assumed, enables the essayist's conclusion to be properly drawn?

   (A) An amalgam of disparate images cannot represent a sequence of events or actions.
   (B) Poems whose subject matter is not appropriate to their medium are illegitimate.
   (C) Lessing was not aware that the imagists' poetry consists of an amalgam of disparate images.
   (D) All art, even the imagists' poetry, depicts or represents some subject matter.
   (E) All art represents something either as simultaneous or as successive.

8. A psychiatrist argued that there is no such thing as a multiple personality disorder on the grounds that in all her years of clinical practice, she had never encountered one case of this type.

   Which one of the following most closely parallels the questionable reasoning cited above?

   (A) Anton concluded that colds are seldom fatal on the grounds that in all his years of clinical practice, he never had a patient who died of a cold.
   (B) Lyla said that no one in the area has seen a groundhog and so there are probably no groundhogs in the area.
   (C) Sauda argued that because therapy rarely had an effect on her patient's type of disorder, therapy was not warranted.
   (D) Thomas argued that because Natasha has driven her car to work every day since she bought it, she would probably continue to drive her car to work.
   (E) Jerod had never spotted a deer in his area and concluded from this that there are no deer in the area.

9. Even if many more people in the world excluded meat from their diet, world hunger would not thereby be significantly reduced.

   Which one of the following, if true, most calls into question the claim above?

   (A) Hunger often results from natural disasters like typhoons or hurricanes, which sweep away everything in their path.
   (B) Both herds and crops are susceptible to devastating viral and other diseases.
   (C) The amount of land needed to produce enough meat to feed one person for a week can grow enough grain to feed more than ten people for a week.
   (D) Often people go hungry because they live in remote barren areas where there is no efficient distribution for emergency food relief.
   (E) Most historical cases of famine have been due to bad social and economic policies or catastrophes such as massive crop failure.

GO ON TO THE NEXT PAGE.

10. Dairy farmer: On our farm, we have great concern for our cows' environmental conditions. We have recently made improvements that increase their comfort, such as providing them with special sleeping mattresses. These changes are intended to increase blood flow to the udder. This increased blood flow would boost milk output and thus increase profits.

Of the following propositions, which one is best illustrated by the dairy farmer's statements?

(A) Dairy cows cannot have comfortable living conditions unless farmers have some knowledge about the physiology of milk production.
(B) Farming practices introduced for the sake of maximizing profits can improve the living conditions of farm animals.
(C) More than other farm animals, dairy cows respond favorably to improvements in their living environments.
(D) The productivity of dairy farms should be increased only if the quality of the product is not compromised.
(E) The key to maximizing profits on a dairy farm is having a concern for dairy cows' environment.

11. Pat: E-mail fosters anonymity, which removes barriers to self-revelation. This promotes a degree of intimacy with strangers that would otherwise take years of direct personal contact to attain.

Amar: Frankness is not intimacy. Intimacy requires a real social bond, and social bonds cannot be formed without direct personal contact.

The dialogue most strongly supports the claim that Pat and Amar disagree with each other about whether

(A) barriers to self-revelation hinder the initial growth of intimacy
(B) E-mail can increase intimacy between friends
(C) intimacy between those who communicate with each other solely by e-mail is possible
(D) real social bonds always lead to intimacy
(E) the use of e-mail removes barriers to self-revelation

12. Criminologist: The main purpose of most criminal organizations is to generate profits. The ongoing revolutions in biotechnology and information technology promise to generate enormous profits. Therefore, criminal organizations will undoubtedly try to become increasingly involved in these areas.

The conclusion of the criminologist's argument is properly inferred if which one of the following is assumed?

(A) If an organization tries to become increasingly involved in areas that promise to generate enormous profits, then the main purpose of that organization is to generate profits.
(B) At least some criminal organizations are or will at some point become aware that the ongoing revolutions in biotechnology and information technology promise to generate enormous profits.
(C) Criminal organizations are already heavily involved in every activity that promises to generate enormous profits.
(D) Any organization whose main purpose is to generate profits will try to become increasingly involved in any technological revolution that promises to generate enormous profits.
(E) Most criminal organizations are willing to become involved in legal activities if those activities are sufficiently profitable.

13. Administrators of educational institutions are enthusiastic about the educational use of computers because they believe that it will enable schools to teach far more courses with far fewer teachers than traditional methods allow. Many teachers fear computers for the same reason. But this reason is mistaken. Computerized instruction requires more, not less, time of instructors, which indicates that any reduction in the number of teachers would require an accompanying reduction in courses offered.

The statement that the educational use of computers enables schools to teach far more courses with far fewer teachers figures in the argument in which one of the following ways?

(A) It is presented as a possible explanation for an observation that follows it.
(B) It is a statement of the problem the argument sets out to solve.
(C) It is a statement that the argument is designed to refute.
(D) It is a statement offered in support of the argument's main conclusion.
(E) It is the argument's main conclusion.

14. Scientists have shown that older bees, which usually forage outside the hive for food, tend to have larger brains than do younger bees, which usually do not forage but instead remain in the hive to tend to newly hatched bees. Since foraging requires greater cognitive ability than does tending to newly hatched bees, it appears that foraging leads to the increased brain size of older bees.

Which one of the following, if true, most seriously weakens the argument above?

(A) Bees that have foraged for a long time do not have significantly larger brains than do bees that have foraged for a shorter time.
(B) The brains of older bees that stop foraging to take on other responsibilities do not become smaller after they stop foraging.
(C) Those bees that travel a long distance to find food do not have significantly larger brains than do bees that locate food nearer the hive.
(D) In some species of bees, the brains of older bees are only marginally larger than those of younger bees.
(E) The brains of older bees that never learn to forage are the same size as those of their foraging counterparts of the same age.

15. Carla: Professors at public universities should receive paid leaves of absence to allow them to engage in research. Research not only advances human knowledge, but also improves professors' teaching by keeping them abreast of the latest information in their fields.

David: But even if you are right about the beneficial effects of research, why should our limited resources be devoted to supporting professors taking time off from teaching?

David's response to Carla is most vulnerable to criticism on the grounds that it

(A) ignores the part of Carla's remarks that could provide an answer to David's question
(B) takes for granted that the only function of a university professor is teaching
(C) incorrectly takes Carla's remarks as claiming that all funding for professors comes from tax money
(D) takes for granted that providing the opportunity for research is the only function of paid leaves of absence
(E) presumes, without providing justification, that professors do not need vacations

16. Software reviewer: Dictation software allows a computer to produce a written version of sentences that are spoken to it. Although dictation software has been promoted as a labor-saving invention, it fails to live up to its billing. The laborious part of writing is in the thinking and the editing, not in the typing. And proofreading the software's error-filled output generally squanders any time saved in typing.

Which one of the following most accurately describes the role played in the software reviewer's argument by the claim that dictation software fails to live up to its billing?

(A) It is the argument's main conclusion but not its only conclusion.
(B) It is the argument's only conclusion.
(C) It is an intermediate conclusion that is offered as direct support for the argument's main conclusion.
(D) It is a premise offered in support of the argument's conclusion.
(E) It is a premise offered as direct support for an intermediate conclusion of the argument.

GO ON TO THE NEXT PAGE.

17. Poetry journal patron: Everybody who publishes in *The Brick Wall Review* has to agree in advance that if a poem is printed in one of its regular issues, the magazine also has the right to reprint it, without monetary compensation, in its annual anthology. *The Brick Wall Review* makes enough money from sales of its anthologies to cover most operating expenses. So, if your magazine also published an anthology of poems first printed in your magazine, you could depend less on donations. After all, most poems published in your magazine are very similar to those published in *The Brick Wall Review.*

Which one of the following, if true, most weakens the patron's argument?

(A) Neither *The Brick Wall Review* nor the other magazine under discussion depends on donations to cover most operating expenses.
(B) Many of the poets whose work appears in *The Brick Wall Review* have had several poems rejected for publication by the other magazine under discussion.
(C) The only compensation poets receive for publishing in the regular issues of the magazines under discussion are free copies of the issues in which their poems appear.
(D) *The Brick Wall Review* depends on donations to cover most operating expenses not covered by income from anthology sales.
(E) *The Brick Wall Review*'s annual poetry anthology always contains a number of poems by famous poets not published in the regular issues of the magazine.

18. No one with a serious medical problem would rely on the average person to prescribe treatment. Similarly, since a good public servant has the interest of the public at heart, ________.

Which one of the following statements would most reasonably complete the argument?

(A) public servants should not be concerned about the outcomes of public opinion surveys
(B) the average public servant knows more about what is best for society than the average person does
(C) public servants should be more knowledgeable about the public good than they are
(D) public servants should base decisions on something other than the average person's recommendations
(E) one is a good public servant if one is more knowledgeable about the public good than is the average person

19. Team captain: Winning requires the willingness to cooperate, which in turn requires motivation. So you will not win if you are not motivated.

The pattern of reasoning in which one of the following is most similar to that in the argument above?

(A) Being healthy requires exercise. But exercising involves risk of injury. So, paradoxically, anyone who wants to be healthy will not exercise.
(B) Learning requires making some mistakes. And you must learn if you are to improve. So you will not make mistakes without there being a noticeable improvement.
(C) Our political party will retain its status only if it raises more money. But raising more money requires increased campaigning. So our party will not retain its status unless it increases its campaigning.
(D) You can repair your own bicycle only if you are enthusiastic. And if you are enthusiastic, you will also have mechanical aptitude. So if you are not able to repair your own bicycle, you lack mechanical aptitude.
(E) Getting a ticket requires waiting in line. Waiting in line requires patience. So if you do not wait in line, you lack patience.

GO ON TO THE NEXT PAGE.

20. In the past, when there was no highway speed limit, the highway accident rate increased yearly, peaking a decade ago. At that time, the speed limit on highways was set at 90 kilometers per hour (kph) (55 miles per hour). Every year since the introduction of the highway speed limit, the highway accident rate has been at least 15 percent lower than that of its peak rate. Thus, setting the highway speed limit at 90 kph (55 mph) has reduced the highway accident rate by at least 15 percent.

Which one of the following, if true, most seriously weakens the argument?

(A) In the years prior to the introduction of the highway speed limit, many cars could go faster than 90 kph (55 mph).
(B) Ten years ago, at least 95 percent of all automobile accidents in the area occurred on roads with a speed limit of under 80 kph (50 mph).
(C) Although the speed limit on many highways is officially set at 90 kph (55 mph), most people typically drive faster than the speed limit.
(D) Thanks to changes in automobile design in the past ten years, drivers are better able to maintain control of their cars in dangerous situations.
(E) It was not until shortly after the introduction of the highway speed limit that most cars were equipped with features such as seat belts and airbags designed to prevent harm to passengers.

21. Editorial: It is a travesty of justice, social critics say, that we can launch rockets into outer space but cannot solve social problems that have plagued humanity. The assumption underlying this assertion is that there are greater difficulties involved in a space launch than are involved in ending long-standing social problems, which in turn suggests that a government's failure to achieve the latter is simply a case of misplaced priorities. The criticism is misplaced, however, for rocket technology is much simpler than the human psyche, and until we adequately understand the human psyche we cannot solve the great social problems.

The statement that rocket technology is much simpler than the human psyche plays which one of the following roles in the editorial's argument?

(A) It is cited as a possible objection to the argument's conclusion.
(B) According to the argument, it is a fact that has misled some social critics.
(C) It is the argument's conclusion.
(D) It is claimed to be a false assumption on which the reasoning that the argument seeks to undermine rests.
(E) It is used by the argument to attempt to undermine the reasoning behind a viewpoint.

22. Archaeologist: After the last ice age, groups of paleohumans left Siberia and crossed the Bering land bridge, which no longer exists, into North America. Archaeologists have discovered in Siberia a cache of Clovis points—the distinctive stone spear points made by paleohumans. This shows that, contrary to previous belief, the Clovis point was not invented in North America.

Which one of the following, if true, would most strengthen the archaeologist's argument?

(A) The Clovis points found in Siberia are older than any of those that have been found in North America.
(B) The Bering land bridge disappeared before any of the Clovis points found to date were made.
(C) Clovis points were more effective hunting weapons than earlier spear points had been.
(D) Archaeologists have discovered in Siberia artifacts that date from after the time paleohumans left Siberia.
(E) Some paleohuman groups that migrated from Siberia to North America via the Bering land bridge eventually returned to Siberia.

GO ON TO THE NEXT PAGE.

23. Taxi drivers, whose income is based on the fares they receive, usually decide when to finish work each day by setting a daily income target; they stop when they reach that target. This means that they typically work fewer hours on a busy day than on a slow day.

The facts described above provide the strongest evidence against which one of the following?

(A) The number of hours per day that a person is willing to work depends on that person's financial needs.
(B) People work longer when their effective hourly wage is high than when it is low.
(C) Workers will accept a lower hourly wage in exchange for the freedom to set their own schedules.
(D) People are willing to work many hours a day in order to avoid a reduction in their standard of living.
(E) People who are paid based on their production work more efficiently than those who are paid a fixed hourly wage.

24. Sometimes one reads a poem and believes that the poem expresses contradictory ideas, even if it is a great poem. So it is wrong to think that the meaning of a poem is whatever the author intends to communicate to the reader by means of the poem. No one who is writing a great poem intends it to communicate contradictory ideas.

Which one of the following is an assumption on which the argument depends?

(A) Different readers will usually disagree about what the author of a particular poem intends to communicate by means of that poem.
(B) If someone writes a great poem, he or she intends the poem to express one primary idea.
(C) Readers will not agree about the meaning of a poem if they do not agree about what the author of the poem intended the poem to mean.
(D) Anyone reading a great poem can discern every idea that the author intended to express in the poem.
(E) If a reader believes that a poem expresses a particular idea, then that idea is part of the meaning of the poem.

25. The law of the city of Weston regarding contributions to mayoral campaigns is as follows: all contributions to these campaigns in excess of $100 made by nonresidents of Weston who are not former residents of Weston must be registered with the city council. Brimley's mayoral campaign clearly complied with this law since it accepted contributions only from residents and former residents of Weston.

If all the statements above are true, which one of the following statements must be true?

(A) No nonresident of Weston contributed in excess of $100 to Brimley's campaign.
(B) Some contributions to Brimley's campaign in excess of $100 were registered with the city council.
(C) No contributions to Brimley's campaign needed to be registered with the city council.
(D) All contributions to Brimley's campaign that were registered with the city council were in excess of $100.
(E) Brimley's campaign did not register any contributions with the city council.

26. Historian: Flavius, an ancient Roman governor who believed deeply in the virtues of manual labor and moral temperance, actively sought to discourage the arts by removing state financial support for them. Also, Flavius was widely unpopular among his subjects, as we can conclude from the large number of satirical plays that were written about him during his administration.

The historian's argumentation is most vulnerable to criticism on the grounds that it

(A) fails to consider the percentage of plays written during Flavius's administration that were not explicitly about Flavius
(B) treats the satirical plays as a reliable indicator of Flavius's popularity despite potential bias on the part of the playwrights
(C) presumes, without providing evidence, that Flavius was unfavorably disposed toward the arts
(D) takes for granted that Flavius's attempt to discourage the arts was successful
(E) fails to consider whether manual labor and moral temperance were widely regarded as virtues in ancient Rome

S T O P

IF YOU FINISH BEFORE TIME IS CALLED, YOU MAY CHECK YOUR WORK ON THIS SECTION ONLY.
DO NOT WORK ON ANY OTHER SECTION IN THE TEST.

Time—35 minutes

26 Questions

Directions: Each passage in this section is followed by a group of questions to be answered on the basis of what is stated or implied in the passage. For some of the questions, more than one of the choice could conceivably answer the question. However, you are to choose the best answer; that is, the response that most accurately and completely answers the question, and blacken the corresponding space on your answer sheet.

The expansion of mass media has led to an explosion in news coverage of criminal activities to the point where it has become virtually impossible to find citizens who are unaware of the details of crimes committed in their communities. Since it is generally believed that people who know the facts of a case are more likely than those who do not to hold an opinion about the case, and that it is more desirable to empanel jurors who do not need to set aside personal prejudices in order to render a verdict, empaneling impartial juries has proven to be a daunting task in North American courts, particularly in trials involving issues or people of public interest.

Judges rely on several techniques to minimize partiality in the courtroom, including moving trials to new venues and giving specific instructions to juries. While many judges are convinced that these techniques work, many critics have concluded that they are ineffective. Change of venue, the critics argue, cannot shield potential jurors from pretrial publicity in widely reported cases. Nor, they claim, can judges' instructions to juries to ignore information learned outside the courtroom be relied upon; one critic characterizes such instruction as requiring of jurors "mental contortions which are beyond anyone's power to execute."

The remedy for partiality most favored by judges is *voir dire*, the questioning of potential jurors to determine whether they can be impartial. But critics charge that this method, too, is unreliable for a number of reasons. Some potential jurors, they argue, do not speak out during *voir dire* (French for "to speak the truth") because they are afraid to admit their prejudices, while others confess untruthfully to having prejudices as a way of avoiding jury duty. Moreover, some potential jurors underestimate their own knowledge, claiming ignorance of a case when they have read about it in newspapers or discussed it with friends. Finally, the critics argue, judges sometimes phrase questions in ways that indicate a desired response, and potential jurors simply answer accordingly.

These criticisms have been taken seriously enough by some countries that rely on juries, such as Canada and Great Britain, that they have abandoned *voir dire* except in unusual circumstances. But merely eliminating existing judicial remedies like *voir dire* does not really provide a solution to the problem of impartiality. It merely recognizes that the mass media have made total ignorance of criminal cases among jurors a virtual impossibility. But if a jury is to be truly impartial, it must be composed of informed citizens representative of the community's collective experience; today, this experience includes exposure to mass media. Impartiality does not reside in the mind of any one juror, it instead results from a process of deliberation among the many members of a panel of informed, curious, and even opinionated people.

1. Which one of the following most accurately expresses the main point of the passage?
   - (A) Due to the expansion of mass media, traditional methods for ensuring the impartiality of jurors are flawed and must be eliminated so that other methods can be implemented.
   - (B) Criticisms of traditional methods for ensuring the impartiality of jurors have led some countries to abandon these methods entirely.
   - (C) Of the three traditional methods for ensuring the impartiality of jurors, vior dire is the most popular among judges but is also the most flawed.
   - (D) *Voir dire* is ineffective at ensuring impartiality due to the latitude it offers potential jurors to misrepresent their knowledge of the cases they are called to hear.
   - (E) Due to the expansion of mass media, solving the problem of minimizing partiality in the courtroom requires a redefinition of what constitutes an impartial jury.

2. One critic characterizes judges' instructions as requiring "mental contortions" (line 25) most likely because of the belief that jurors cannot be expected to
   - (A) deliberate only on what they learn in a trial and not on what they knew beforehand
   - (B) distinguish between pretrial speculation and the actual facts of a case
   - (C) hear about a case before trial without forming an opinion about it
   - (D) identify accurately the degree of prior knowledge they may possess about a case
   - (E) protect themselves from widely disseminated pretrial publicity.

GO ON TO THE NEXT PAGE.

3. The primary purpose of the third paragraph is to

   (A) propose a new method of ensuring impartiality
   (B) describe criticisms of one traditional method of ensuring impartiality
   (C) argue against several traditional methods of ensuring impartiality
   (D) explain why judges are wary of certain methods of ensuring impartiality
   (E) criticize the views of those who believe judges to be incapable of ensuring impartiality

4. With which one of the following statements would the author be most likely to agree?

   (A) Flaws in *voir dire* procedures make it unlikely that juries capable of rendering impartial decisions can be selected.
   (B) Knowledge of a case before it goes to trail offers individual jurors the best chance of rendering impartial decisions.
   (C) Jurors who bring prior opinions about a case to their deliberations need not decrease the chance of the jury's rendering an impartial decision.
   (D) Only juries consisting of people who bring no prior knowledge of a case to their deliberations are capable of rendering truly impartial decisions.
   (E) People who know the facts of a case are more opinionated about it than those who do not.

5. The passage suggests that a potential benefit of mass-media coverage on court cases is that it will

   (A) determine which facts are appropriate for juries to hear
   (B) improve the ability of jurors to minimize their biases
   (C) strengthen the process by which juries come to decisions
   (D) change the methods judges use to question potential jurors
   (E) increase potential jurors' awareness of their degree of bias

6. Which one of the following principles is most in keeping with the passage's argument?

   (A) Jurors should put aside their personal experiences when deliberating a case and base their decision only on the available information.
   (B) Jurors should rely on their overall experience when deliberating a case even when the case was subject to mass-media exposure before trial.
   (C) Jurors should make every effort when deliberating a case to ignore information about the case that they may have learned from the mass media.
   (D) Jurors should be selected to hear a case based on their degree of exposure to mass-media coverage of the case before trial.
   (E) Jurors should be selected to hear a case based on their capacity to refrain from reading or viewing mass-media coverage of the case while the trial is in progress.

7. Of the following, the author's primary purpose in writing the passage most likely is to

   (A) search for compromise between proponents and critics of *voir dire*
   (B) call attention to the effects of mass media on court proceedings
   (C) encourage judges to find new ways to ensure impartial jurors
   (D) debate critics who find fault with current *voir dire* procedures
   (E) argue for a change in how courts address the problem of impartiality

GO ON TO THE NEXT PAGE.

Personal names are generally regarded by European thinkers in two major ways, both of which deny that names have any significant semantic content. In philosophy and linguistics, John Stuart Mill's formulation that "proper names are meaningless marks set upon...persons to distinguish them from one another" retains currency; in anthropology, Claude Lévi-Strauss's characterization of names as being primarily instruments of social classification has been very influential. Consequently, interpretation of personal names in societies were names have other functions and meanings has been neglected. Among the Hopi of the southwestern United States, names often refer to historical or ritual events in order both to place individuals within society and to confer an identity upon them. Furthermore, the images used to evoke these events suggest that Hopi names can be seen as a type of poetic composition.

Throughout life, Hopis receive several names in a sequence of ritual initiations. Birth, entry into one of the ritual societies during childhood, and puberty are among the name-giving occasions. Names are conferred by an adult member of a clan other than the child's clan, and names refer to that name giver's clan, sometimes combining characteristics of the clan's totem animal with the child's characteristics. Thus, a name might translate to something as simple as "little rabbit," which reflects both the child's size and the representative animal.

More often, though, the name giver has in mind a specific event that is not apparent in a name's literal translation. One Lizard clan member from the village of Oraibi is named Lomayayva, "beautifully ascended." This translation, however, tells nothing about either the event referred to—who or what ascended—or the name giver's clan. The name giver in this case is from Badger clan. Badger clan is responsible for an annual ceremony featuring a procession in which masked representations of spirits climb the mesa on which Oraibi sits. Combining the name giver's clan association with the receiver's home village, "beautifully ascended" refers to the splendid colors and movements of the procession up the mesa. The condensed image this name evokes—a typical feature of Hopi personal names—displays the same quality of Western Apache place names that led one commentator to call them "tiny imagist poems."

Hopi personal names do several things simultaneously. They indicate social relationships—but only indirectly—and they individuate persons. Equally important, though, is their poetic quality; in a sense they can be understood as oral texts that produce aesthetic delight. This view of Hopi names is thus opposed not only to Mill's claim that personal names are without inherent meaning but also to Lévi-Strauss's purely functional characterization. Interpreters must understand Hopi clan structures and linguistic practices in order to discern the beauty and significance of Hopi names.

8. Which one of the following statements most accurately summarizes the passage's main point?

(A) Unlike European names, which are used exclusively for identification or exclusively for social classification, Hopi names perform both these functions simultaneously.
(B) Unlike European names, Hopi names tend to neglect the functions of identification and social classification in favor of a concentration on compression and poetic effects.
(C) Lacking knowledge of the intricacies of Hopi linguistic and tribal structures, European thinkers have so far been unable to discern the deeper significance of Hopi names.
(D) Although some Hopi names may seem difficult to interpret, they all conform to a formula whereby a reference to the name giver's clan is combined with a reference to the person named.
(E) While performing the functions ascribed to names by European thinkers, Hopi names also possess a significant aesthetic quality that these thinkers have not adequately recognized.

9. The author most likely refers to Western Apache place names (line 46) in order to

(A) offer an example of how names can contain references not evident in their literal translations
(B) apply a commentator's characterization of Western Apache place names to Hopi personal names
(C) contrast Western Apache naming practices with Hopi naming practices
(D) demonstrate that other names besides Hopi names may have some semantic content
(E) explain how a specific Hopi name refers subtly to a particular Western Apache site

10. Which one of the following statements describes an example of the function accorded to personal names under Lévi-Strauss's view?

(A) Some parents select their children's names from impersonal sources such as books.
(B) Some parents wait to give a child a name in order to choose one that reflects the child's looks or personality.
(C) Some parents name their children in honor of friends or famous people.
(D) Some family members have no parts of their names in common.
(E) Some family names originated as identifications of their bearers' occupations.

GO ON TO THE NEXT PAGE.

11. The primary function of the second paragraph is to

(A) present reasons why Hopi personal names can be treated as poetic compositions
(B) support the claim that Hopi personal names make reference to events in the recipient's life
(C) argue that the fact that Hopis receive many names throughout life refutes European theories about naming
(D) illustrate ways in which Hopi personal names may have semantic content
(E) demonstrate that the literal translation of Hopi personal names often obscures their true meaning

12. Based on the passage, with which one of the following statements about Mill's view would the author of the passage be most likely to agree?

(A) Its characterization of the function of names is too narrow to be universally applicable.
(B) It would be correct if it recognized the use of names as instruments of social classification.
(C) Its influence single-handedly led scholars to neglect how names are used outside Europe.
(D) It is more accurate than Lévi-Strauss's characterization of the purpose of names.
(E) It is less relevant than Lévi-Strauss's characterization in understanding Hopi naming practices.

13. It can be inferred from the passage that each of the following features of Hopi personal names contributes to their poetic quality EXCEPT:

(A) their ability to be understood as oral texts
(B) their use of condensed imagery to evoke events
(C) their capacity to produce aesthetic delight
(D) their ability to confer identity upon individuals
(E) their ability to subtly convey meaning

14. The author's primary purpose in writing the passage it to

(A) present an anthropological study of Hopi names
(B) propose a new theory about the origin of name
(C) describe several competing theories of names
(D) criticize two influential views of names
(E) explain the cultural origins of names

GO ON TO THE NEXT PAGE.

Homing pigeons can be taken from their lofts and transported hundreds of kilometers in covered cages to unfamiliar sites and yet, when released, be able to choose fairly accurate homeward bearings within a minute and fly home. Aside from reading the minds of the experimenters (a possibility that has not escaped investigation), there are two basic explanations for the remarkable ability of pigeons to "home": the birds might keep track of their outward displacement (the system of many short-range species such as honeybees); or they might have some sense, known as a "map sense," that would permit them to construct an internal image of their environment and then "place" themselves with respect to home on some internalized coordinate system.

The first alternative seems unlikely. One possible model for such an inertial system might involve an internal magnetic compass to measure the directional leg of each journey. Birds transported to the release site wearing magnets or otherwise subjected to an artificial magnetic field, however, are only occasionally affected. Alternately, if pigeons measure their displacement by consciously keeping track of the direction and degree of acceleration and deceleration of the various turns, and timing the individual legs of the journey, simply transporting them in the dark, with constant rotations, or under complete anesthesia ought to impair or eliminate their ability to orient. These treatments, however, have no effect. Unfortunately, no one has yet performed the crucial experiment of transporting pigeons in total darkness, anesthetized, rotating, and with the magnetic field reversed all at the same time.

The other alternative, that pigeons have a "map sense," seems more promising, yet the nature of this sense remains mysterious. Papi has posited that the map sense is olfactory: that birds come to associate odors borne on the wind with the direction in which the wind is blowing, and so slowly build up an olfactory map of their surroundings. When transported to the release site, then, they only have to sniff the air en route and/or at the site to know the direction of home. Papi conducted a series of experiments showing that pigeons whose nostrils have been plugged are poorly oriented at release and home slowly.

One problem with the hypothesis is that Schmidt-Koenig and Phillips failed to detect any ability in pigeons to distinguish natural air (presumably laden with olfactory map information) from pure, filtered air. Papi's experimental results, moreover, admit of simpler, nonolfactory explanations. It seems likely that the behavior of nostril-plugged birds results from the distracting and traumatic nature of the experiment. When nasal tubes are used to bypass the olfactory chamber but allow for comfortable breathing, no disorientation is evident. Likewise, when the olfactory epithelium is sprayed with anesthetic to block smell-detection but not breathing, orientation is normal.

15. Which one of the following best states the main idea of the passage?

(A) The ability of pigeons to locate and return to their homes from distant points is unlike that of any other species.
(B) It is likely that some map sense accounts for the homing ability of pigeons, but the nature of that sense has not been satisfactorily identified.
(C) The majority of experiments on the homing ability of pigeons have been marked by design flaws.
(D) The mechanisms underlying the homing ability of pigeons can best be identified through a combination of laboratory research and field experimentation.
(E) The homing ability of pigeons is most likely based on a system similar to that used by many short-range species.

16. According to the passage, which one of the following is ordinarily true regarding how homing pigeons "home"?

(A) Each time they are released at a specific site they fly home by the same route.
(B) When they are released they take only a short time to orient themselves before selecting their route home.
(C) Each time they are released at a specific site they take a shorter amount of time to orient themselves before flying home.
(D) They travel fairly long distances in seemingly random patterns before finally deciding on a route home.
(E) Upon release they travel briefly in the direction opposite to the one they eventually choose.

GO ON TO THE NEXT PAGE.

17. Which one of the following experiments would best test the "possibility" referred to in line 6?

(A) an experiment in which the handlers who transported, released, and otherwise came into contact with homing pigeons released at an unfamiliar site were unaware of the location of the pigeons' home
(B) an experiment in which the handlers who transported, released, and otherwise came into contact with homing pigeons released at an unfamiliar site were asked not to display any affection toward the pigeons
(C) an experiment in which the handlers who transported, released, and otherwise came into contact with homing pigeons released at an unfamiliar site were asked not to speak to each other throughout the release process
(D) an experiment in which all the homing pigeons released at an unfamiliar site had been raised and fed by individual researchers rather than by teams of handlers
(E) an experiment in which all the homing pigeons released at an unfamiliar site were exposed to a wide variety of unfamiliar sights and sounds

18. Information in the passage supports which one of the following statements regarding the "first alternative" (line 16) for explaining the ability of pigeons to "home"?

(A) It has been conclusively ruled out by the results of numerous experiments.
(B) It seems unlikely because there are no theoretical models that could explain how pigeons track displacement.
(C) It has not, to date, been supported by experimental data, but neither has it been definitively ruled out.
(D) It seems unlikely in theory, but recent experimental results show that it may in fact be correct.
(E) It is not a useful theory because of the difficulty in designing experiments by which it might be tested.

19. The author refers to "the system of many short-range species such as honeybees" (lines 9–11) most probably in order to

(A) emphasize the universality of the ability to home
(B) suggest that a particular explanation of pigeons' homing ability is worthy of consideration
(C) discredit one of the less convincing theories regarding the homing ability of pigeons
(D) criticize the techniques utilized by scientists investigating the nature of pigeons' homing ability
(E) illustrate why a proposed explanation of pigeons' homing ability is correct

20. Which one of the following, if true, would most weaken Papi's theory regarding homing pigeons' homing ability?

(A) Even pigeons that have been raised in several different lofts in a variety of territories can find their way to their current home when released in unfamiliar territory.
(B) Pigeons whose sense of smell has been partially blocked find their way home more slowly than do pigeons whose sense of smell has not been affected.
(C) Even pigeons that have been raised in the same loft frequently take different routes home when released in unfamiliar territory.
(D) Even pigeons that have been transported well beyond the range of the odors detectable in their home territories can find their way home.
(E) Pigeons' sense of smell is no more acute than that of other birds who do not have the ability to "home."

21. Given the information in the passage, it is most likely that Papi and the author of the passage would both agree with which one of the following statements regarding the homing ability of pigeons?

(A) The map sense of pigeons is most probably related to their olfactory sense.
(B) The mechanism regulating the homing ability of pigeons is most probably similar to that utilized by honeybees.
(C) The homing ability of pigeons is most probably based on a map sense.
(D) The experiments conducted by Papi himself have provided the most valuable evidence yet collected regarding the homing ability of pigeons.
(E) The experiments conducted by Schmidt-Koenig and Phillips have not substantially lessened the probability that Papi's own theory is correct.

GO ON TO THE NEXT PAGE.

Freud's essay on the "Uncanny" can be said to have defined, for our century, what literary criticism once called the Sublime. This apprehension of a beyond or of a daemonic—a sense of transcendence—appears in literature or life, according to Freud, when we feel that something uncanny is being represented, or conjured up, or at least intimated. Freud locates the source of the uncanny in our tendency to believe in the "omnipotence of thought," that is, in the power of our own or of others' minds over the natural world. The uncanny is, thus, a return to animistic conceptions of the universe, and is produced by the psychic defense mechanisms Freud called repression.

It would have seemed likely for Freud to find his literary instances of the uncanny, or at least some of them, in fairy tales, since as much as any other fictions they seem to be connected with repressed desires and archaic forms of thought. But Freud specifically excluded fairy tales from the realm of the uncanny. "Who would be so bold," Freud asks, "as to call it an uncanny moment, for instance, when Snow White opens her eyes once more?" Why not? Because, he goes on to say, in those stories everything is possible, so nothing is incredible, and, therefore, no conflicts in the reader's judgment are provoked. Thus Freud, alas, found fairy tales to be unsuited to his own analysis.

However, the psychoanalyst Bruno Bettelheim, with a kind of wise innocence, has subjected fairy tales to very close, generally orthodox, and wholly reductive Freudian interpretations. Bettelheim's book, although written in apparent ignorance of the vast critical traditions of interpreting literary romance, is nevertheless a splendid achievement, brimming with useful ideas and insights into how young children read and understand.

Bruno Bettelheim's major therapeutic concern has been with autistic children, so inevitably his interpretive activity is directed against a child's tendency to withdraw defensively or abnormally. According to Bettelheim, a child's desperate isolation, loneliness, and inarticulate anxieties are addressed directly by fairy tales. By telling the child such stores themselves, parents strengthen the therapeutic effect of fairy tales, for in the telling, parents impart to the child their approval of the stories.

But why should fairy tales, in themselves, be therapeutic? Bettelheim's answer depends on the child's being an interpreter: "The fairy tale is therapeutic because children find their own solutions, through contemplating what the story seems to imply about their inner conflicts at this moment in their lives." Bettelheim proceeds on the basis of two complementary assumptions: that children will interpret a story benignly, for their own good; and that Freudian interpretations will yield an accurate account of children's interpretations. The child, questing for help, and the analyst, attempting to find helpful patterns in the stories, thus read alike, though in different vocabularies.

22. According to the author, Bettelheim believes that fairy tales help troubled children by

(A) creating fantasy worlds into which they can escape
(B) helping them find solutions to their own problems
(C) providing a means of communication with their parents
(D) showing them other problems worse than their own
(E) solving their problems for them

23. According to the passage, Bettelheim believes that parents' telling fairy tales to troubled children strengthens the tales' therapeutic effect because

(A) most troubled children do not read independently
(B) most children believe whatever their parents tell them
(C) the parents' telling the stories imparts to the children the parents' sanction of the tales
(D) the parents can help the children interpret the stories according to the parents' belief
(E) the parents can reassure the children that the tales are imaginary

GO ON TO THE NEXT PAGE.

24. It can be inferred from the passage that Freud believed that in fairy tales, "nothing is incredible" (line 24) because, in his view,

(A) fairy tales can be read and understood even by young children
(B) everything in fairy tales is purely imaginary
(C) fairy tales are so fantastic that in them nothing seems out of the ordinary
(D) it is uncanny how the patterns of fairy tales fit our unconscious expectations and wishes
(E) the reader represses those elements of fairy tales which might conflict with his or her judgment

25. According to the passage, Bettelheim believes that when children interpret a story benignly, they

(A) find in fairy tales answers to their own needs
(B) do not associate fairy tales with the uncanny
(C) do not find underlying meanings in fairy tales
(D) are aware that fairy tales are fictions
(E) are reassured by parental approval

26. Which one of the following best describes the author's attitude toward Bettelheim's work?

(A) approving of Bettelheim's rejection of orthodox and reductive Freudian interpretations of fairy tales
(B) appalled at Bettelheim's ignorance of the critical traditions of interpreting literary romance
(C) unimpressed with Bettelheim's research methods
(D) skeptical of Bettelheim's claim that fairy tales are therapeutic
(E) appreciative of Bettelheim's accomplishments and practical insights.

S T O P

IF YOU FINISH BEFORE TIME IS CALLED, YOU MAY CHECK YOUR WORK ON THIS SECTION ONLY.
DO NOT WORK ON ANY OTHER SECTION IN THE TEST.

SECTION III

Time—35 minutes

25 Questions

Directions: The questions in this section are based on the reasoning contained in brief statements or passages. For some questions, more than one of the choices could conceivably answer the question. However, you are to choose the best answer; that is, the response that most accurately and completely answers the question. You should not make assumptions that are by commonsense standards implausible, superfluous, or incompatible with the passage. After you have chosen the best answer, blacken the corresponding space on your answer sheet.

1. Educators studied the performance of 200 students in a university's history classes. They found that those students who performed the best had either part-time jobs or full-time jobs, had their history classes early in the morning, and had a very limited social life, whereas those students who performed the worst had no jobs, had their history classes early in the morning, and had a very active social life.

   Which one of the following, if true, most helps to explain the educators' findings?

   (A) The students compensated for any study time lost due to their jobs but they did not compensate for any study time lost due to their social lives.
   (B) The students who had full-time jobs typically worked late-night hours at those jobs.
   (C) Better students tend to choose classes that are scheduled to meet early in the morning.
   (D) A larger percentage of those students interested in majoring in history had part-time jobs than had full-time jobs.
   (E) Although having a job tends to provide a release from stress, thus increasing academic performance, having a full-time job, like having an active social life, can distract a student from studying.

2. Politician: Most of those at the meeting were not persuaded by Kuyler's argument, nor should they have been, for Kuyler's argument implied that it would be improper to enter into a contract with the government; and yet—as many people know— Kuyler's company has had numerous lucrative contracts with the government.

   Which one of the following describes a flaw in the politician's argument?

   (A) It concludes that an argument is defective merely on the grounds that the argument has failed to persuade anyone of the truth of its conclusion.
   (B) It relies on testimony that is likely to be biased.
   (C) It rejects an argument merely on the grounds that the arguer has not behaved in a way that is consistent with the argument.
   (D) It rejects a position merely on the grounds that an inadequate argument has been given for it.
   (E) It rejects an argument on the basis of an appeal to popular opinion.

3. Although free international trade allows countries to specialize, which in turn increases productivity, such specialization carries risks. After all, small countries often rely on one or two products for the bulk of their exports. If those products are raw materials, the supply is finite and can be used up. If they are foodstuffs, a natural disaster can wipe out a season's production overnight.

   Which one of the following most accurately expresses the conclusion of the argument as a whole?

   (A) Specialization within international trade comes with risks.
   (B) A natural disaster can destroy a whole season's production overnight, devastating a small country's economy.
   (C) A small country's supply of raw materials can be used up in a short period.
   (D) Some countries rely on a small number of products for the export-based sectors of their economies.
   (E) When international trade is free, countries can specialize in what they export.

GO ON TO THE NEXT PAGE.

4. Two randomly selected groups of 30 adults each were asked to write short stories on a particular topic. One group was told that the best stories would be awarded cash prizes, while the other group was not told of any prizes. Each story was evaluated by a team of judges who were given no indication of the group from which the story came. The stories submitted by those who thought they were competing for prizes were ranked on average significantly lower than the stories from the other group.

   Which one of the following, if true, most helps to explain the difference in average ranking between the two groups' stories?

   (A) The cash prizes were too small to motivate an average adult to make a significant effort to produce stories of high quality.
   (B) People writing to win prizes show a greater than usual tendency to produce stereotypical stories that show little creativity.
   (C) Most adults show little originality in writing stories on a topic suggested by someone else.
   (D) The team of judges was biased in favor of stories that they judged to be more realistic.
   (E) No one explained clearly to either group what standards would be used in judging their stories.

5. Hernandez: I recommend that staff cars be replaced every four years instead of every three years. Three-year-old cars are still in good condition and this would result in big savings.

   Green: I disagree. Some of our salespeople with big territories wear out their cars in three years.

   Hernandez: I meant three-year-old cars subjected to normal use.

   In the conversation, Hernandez responds to Green's objection in which one of the following ways?

   (A) by explicitly qualifying a premise used earlier
   (B) by criticizing salespeople who wear out their cars in three years
   (C) by disputing the accuracy of Green's evidence
   (D) by changing the subject to the size of sales territories
   (E) by indicating that Green used a phrase ambiguously

6. Economist: As should be obvious, raising the minimum wage significantly would make it more expensive for businesses to pay workers for minimum-wage jobs. Therefore, businesses could not afford to continue to employ as many workers for such jobs. So raising the minimum wage significantly will cause an increase in unemployment.

   Which one of the following, if true, most weakens the economist's argument?

   (A) Businesses typically pass the cost of increased wages on to consumers without adversely affecting profits.
   (B) When the difference between minimum wage and a skilled worker's wage is small, a greater percentage of a business's employees will be skilled workers.
   (C) A modest increase in unemployment is acceptable because the current minimum wage is not a livable wage.
   (D) Most workers are earning more than the current minimum wage.
   (E) The unemployment rate has been declining steadily in recent years.

7. Scientists removed all viruses from a seawater sample and then measured the growth rate of the plankton population in the water. They expected the rate to increase dramatically, but the population actually got smaller.

   Which one of the following, if true, most helps to explain the unexpected result described above?

   (A) Viruses in seawater help to keep the plankton population below the maximum level that the resources in the water will support.
   (B) Plankton and viruses in seawater compete for some of the same nutrients.
   (C) Plankton utilize the nutrients released by the death of organisms killed by viruses.
   (D) The absence of viruses can facilitate the flourishing of bacteria that sometimes damage other organisms.
   (E) At any given time, a considerable portion of the plankton in seawater are already infected by viruses.

GO ON TO THE NEXT PAGE.

8. City council member: The Senior Guild has asked for a temporary exception to the ordinance prohibiting automobiles in municipal parks. Their case does appear to deserve the exception. However, if we grant this exception, we will find ourselves granting many other exceptions to this ordinance, some of which will be undeserved. Before long, we will be granting exceptions to all manner of other city ordinances. If we are to prevent anarchy in our city, we must deny the Senior Guild's request.

The city council member's argument is most vulnerable to criticism on the grounds that it

(A) distorts an argument and then attacks this distorted argument
(B) dismisses a claim because of its source rather than because of its content
(C) presumes, without sufficient warrant, that one event will lead to a particular causal sequence of events
(D) contains premises that contradict one another
(E) fails to make a needed distinction between deserved exceptions and undeserved ones

9. Physician: In comparing our country with two other countries of roughly the same population size, I found that even though we face the same dietary, bacterial, and stress-related causes of ulcers as they do, prescriptions for ulcer medicines in all socioeconomic strata are much rarer here than in those two countries. It's clear that we suffer significantly fewer ulcers, per capita, than they do.

Which one of the following, if true, most strengthens the physician's argument?

(A) The two countries that were compared with the physician's country had approximately the same ulcer rates as each other.
(B) The people of the physician's country have a cultural tradition of stoicism that encourages them to ignore physical ailments rather than to seek remedies for them.
(C) Several other countries not covered in the physician's comparisons have more prescriptions for ulcer medication than does the physician's country.
(D) A person in the physician's country who is suffering from ulcers is just as likely to obtain a prescription for the ailment as is a person suffering from ulcers in one of the other two countries.
(E) The physician's country has a much better system for reporting the number of prescriptions of a given type that are obtained each year than is present in either of the other two countries.

10. Columnist: The failure of bicyclists to obey traffic regulations is a causal factor in more than one quarter of the traffic accidents involving bicycles. Since inadequate bicycle safety equipment is also a factor in more than a quarter of such accidents, bicyclists are at least partially responsible for more than half of the traffic accidents involving bicycles.

The columnist's reasoning is flawed in that it

(A) presumes, without providing justification, that motorists are a factor in less than half of the traffic accidents involving bicycles
(B) improperly infers the presence of a causal connection on the basis of a correlation
(C) fails to consider the possibility that more than one factor may contribute to a given accident
(D) fails to provide the source of the figures it cites
(E) fails to consider that the severity of injuries to bicyclists from traffic accidents can vary widely

11. Many vaccines create immunity to viral diseases by introducing a certain portion of the disease-causing virus's outer coating into the body. Exposure to that part of a virus is as effective as exposure to the whole virus in stimulating production of antibodies that will subsequently recognize and kill the whole virus. To create a successful vaccine of this type, doctors must first isolate in the disease-causing virus a portion that stimulates antibody production. Now that a suitable portion of the virus that causes hepatitis E has been isolated, doctors claim they can produce a vaccine that will produce permanent immunity to that disease.

Which one of the following, if true, most strongly counters the doctors' claim?

(A) Most of the people who contract hepatitis E are young adults who were probably exposed to the virus in childhood also.
(B) Some laboratory animals exposed to one strain of the hepatitis virus developed immunity to all strains of the virus.
(C) Researchers developed a successful vaccine for another strain of hepatitis, hepatitis B, after first isolating the virus that causes it.
(D) The virus that causes hepatitis E is very common in some areas, so the number of people exposed to that virus is likely to be quite high in those areas.
(E) Many children who are exposed to viruses that cause childhood diseases such as chicken pox never develop those diseases.

GO ON TO THE NEXT PAGE.

12. Editorial: To qualify as an effective law, as opposed to merely an impressive declaration, a command must be backed up by an effective enforcement mechanism. That is why societies have police. The power of the police to enforce a society's laws makes those laws effective. But there is currently no international police force. Hence, what is called "international law" is not effective law.

Which one of the following is an assumption required by the editorial's argument?

(A) No one obeys a command unless mechanisms exist to compel obedience.
(B) If an international police force were established, then so-called international law would become effective law.
(C) The only difference between international law and the law of an individual society is the former's lack of an effective enforcement mechanism.
(D) The primary purpose of a police force is to enforce the laws of the society.
(E) Only an international police force could effectively enforce international law.

13. Art historian: More than any other genre of representational painting, still-life painting lends itself naturally to art whose goal is the artist's self-expression, rather than merely the reflection of a preexisting external reality. This is because in still-life painting, the artist invariably chooses, modifies, and arranges the objects to be painted. Thus, the artist has considerably more control over the composition and subject of a still-life painting than over those of a landscape painting or portrait, for example.

Which one of the following is most strongly supported by the art historian's statements?

(A) Landscape painting and portraiture are the artistic genres that lend themselves most naturally to the mere reflection of a preexisting external reality.
(B) The only way in which artists control the composition and subject of a painting is by choosing, modifying, and arranging the objects to be represented in that painting.
(C) Nonrepresentational painting does not lend itself as naturally as still-life painting does to the goal of the artist's self-expression.
(D) In genres of representational painting other than still-life painting, the artist does not always choose, modify, and arrange the objects to be painted.
(E) When painting a portrait, artists rarely attempt to express themselves through the choice, modification, or arrangement of the background elements against which the subject of the portrait is painted.

14. Food labeling regulation: Food of a type that does not ordinarily contain fat cannot be labeled "nonfat" unless most people mistakenly believe the food ordinarily contains fat. If most people mistakenly believe that a food ordinarily contains fat, the food may be labeled "nonfat" if the label also states that the food ordinarily contains no fat.

Which one of the following situations violates the food labeling regulation?

(A) Although most people know that bran flakes do not normally contain fat, Lester's Bran Flakes are not labeled "nonfat."
(B) Although most people are aware that lasagna ordinarily contains fat, Lester's Lasagna, which contains no fat, is not labeled "nonfat."
(C) Although most garlic baguettes contain fat, Lester's Garlic Baguettes are labeled "nonfat."
(D) Although most people are aware that applesauce does not ordinarily contain fat, Lester's Applesauce is labeled "nonfat."
(E) Although most people mistakenly believe that salsa ordinarily contains fat, the label on Lester's Zesty Salsa says "This product, like all salsas, is nonfat."

GO ON TO THE NEXT PAGE.

15. Medical ethicist: Assuming there is a reasonable chance for a cure, it is acceptable to offer experimental treatments for a disease to patients who suffer from extreme symptoms of that disease. Such patients are best able to weigh a treatment's risks against the benefits of a cure. Therefore, it is never acceptable to offer experimental treatments to patients who experience no extreme symptoms of the relevant disease.

The flawed reasoning in which one of the following is most similar to the flawed reasoning in the medical ethicist's argument?

(A) Even a geological engineer with a background in economics can lose money investing in mineral extraction. So, those who are less knowledgeable about geology or economics should not expect to make money in every investment in mineral extraction.
(B) One is always in a better position to judge whether an automobile would be worth its cost if one has test-driven that automobile. Therefore, if an automobile proves to be not worth its cost, it is likely that it was not test-driven.
(C) Someone born and raised in a country, who has lived abroad and then returned, is exceptionally qualified to judge the merits of living in that country. That is why someone who has not lived in that country should not form judgments about the merits of living there.
(D) One can never eliminate all of the risks of daily life, and even trying to avoid every risk in life is costly. Therefore, anyone who is reasonable will accept some of the risks of daily life.
(E) Almost any industrial development will have unwelcome environmental side effects. Therefore, it is not worthwhile to weigh the costs of potential environmental side effects since such side effects are unavoidable.

16. Critic: As modern methods of communication and transportation have continued to improve, the pace of life today has become faster than ever before. This speed has created feelings of impermanence and instability, making us feel as if we never have enough time to achieve what we want—or at least what we think we want.

The critic's statements most closely conform to which one of the following assessments?

(A) The fast pace of modern life has made it difficult for people to achieve their goals.
(B) The disadvantages of technological progress often outweigh the advantages.
(C) Changes in people's feelings about life can result from technological changes.
(D) The perception of impermanence in contemporary life makes it more difficult for people to know what they want.
(E) Changes in people's feelings fuel the need for technological advancement.

17. Consumer: If you buy a watch at a department store and use it only in the way it was intended to be used, but the watch stops working the next day, then the department store will refund your money. So by this very reasonable standard, Bingham's Jewelry Store should give me a refund even though they themselves are not a department store, since the watch I bought from them stopped working the very next day.

The consumer's argument relies on the assumption that

(A) one should not sell something unless one expects that it will function in the way it was originally designed to function
(B) a watch bought at a department store and a watch bought at Bingham's Jewelry Store can both be expected to keep working for about the same length of time if each is used only as it was intended to be used
(C) a seller should refund the money that was paid for a product if the product does not perform as the purchaser expected it to perform
(D) the consumer did not use the watch in a way contrary to the way it was intended to be used
(E) the watch that was purchased from Bingham's Jewelry Store was not a new watch

GO ON TO THE NEXT PAGE.

18. A study found that patients referred by their doctors to psychotherapists practicing a new experimental form of therapy made more progress with respect to their problems than those referred to psychotherapists practicing traditional forms of therapy. Therapists practicing the new form of therapy, therefore, are more effective than therapists practicing traditional forms.

Which one of the following most accurately describes a flaw in the argument?

(A) It ignores the possibility that therapists trained in traditional forms of therapy use the same techniques in treating their patients as therapists trained in the new form of therapy do.
(B) It ignores the possibility that the patients referred to therapists practicing the new form of therapy had problems more amenable to treatment than did those referred to therapists practicing traditional forms.
(C) It presumes, without providing justification, that any psychotherapist trained in traditional forms of therapy is untrained in the new form of therapy.
(D) It ignores the possibility that therapists practicing the new form of therapy systematically differ from therapists practicing traditional forms of therapy with regard to some personality attribute relevant to effective treatment.
(E) It presumes, without providing justification, that the personal rapport between therapist and patient has no influence on the effectiveness of the treatment the patient receives.

19. Essayist: One of the drawbacks of extreme personal and political freedom is that free choices are often made for the worst. To expect people to thrive when they are given the freedom to make unwise decisions is frequently unrealistic. Once people see the destructive consequences of extreme freedom, they may prefer to establish totalitarian political regimes that allow virtually no freedom. Thus, one should not support political systems that allow extreme freedom.

Which one of the following principles, if valid, most helps to justify the essayist's reasoning?

(A) One should not support any political system that will inevitably lead to the establishment of a totalitarian political regime.
(B) One should not expect everyone to thrive even in a political system that maximizes people's freedom in the long run.
(C) One should support only those political systems that give people the freedom to make wise choices.
(D) One should not support any political system whose destructive consequences could lead people to prefer totalitarian political regimes.
(E) One should not support any political system that is based on unrealistic expectations about people's behavior under that system.

GO ON TO THE NEXT PAGE.

20. Ethicist: Every moral action is the keeping of an agreement, and keeping an agreement is nothing more than an act of securing mutual benefit. Clearly, however, not all instances of agreement-keeping are moral actions. Therefore, some acts of securing mutual benefit are not moral actions.

The pattern of reasoning in which one of the following arguments is most similar to that in the ethicist's argument?

(A) All calculators are kinds of computers, and all computers are devices for automated reasoning. However, not all devices for automated reasoning are calculators. Therefore, some devices for automated reasoning are not computers.
(B) All exercise is beneficial, and all things that are beneficial promote health. However, not all things that are beneficial are forms of exercise. Therefore, some exercise does not promote health.
(C) All metaphors are comparisons, and not all comparisons are surprising. However, all metaphors are surprising. Therefore, some comparisons are not metaphors.
(D) All architecture is design and all design is art. However, not all design is architecture. Therefore, some art is not design.
(E) All books are texts, and all texts are documents. However, not all texts are books. Therefore, some documents are not books.

21. Sociologist: The more technologically advanced a society is, the more marked its members' resistance to technological innovations. This is not surprising, because the more technologically advanced a society is, the more aware its members are of technology's drawbacks. Specifically, people realize that sophisticated technologies deeply affect the quality of human relations.

The claim that the more technologically advanced a society is, the more aware its members are of technology's drawbacks plays which one of the following roles in the sociologist's argument?

(A) It is a conclusion supported by the claim that people realize that sophisticated technologies deeply affect the quality of human relations.
(B) It is offered as an explanation of why people's resistance to technological innovations is more marked the more technologically advanced the society in which they live is.
(C) It is a premise in support of the claim that the quality of human relations in technologically advanced societies is extremely poor.
(D) It is a generalization based on the claim that the more people resist technological innovations, the more difficult it is for them to adjust to those innovations.
(E) It is an example presented to illustrate the claim that resistance to technological innovations deeply affects the quality of human relations.

GO ON TO THE NEXT PAGE.

22. To win democratic elections that are not fully subsidized by the government, nonwealthy candidates must be supported by wealthy patrons. This makes plausible the belief that these candidates will compromise their views to win that support. But since the wealthy are dispersed among the various political parties in roughly equal proportion to their percentage in the overall population, this belief is false.

The argument is vulnerable to criticism on the grounds that it fails to consider that

(A) the primary function of political parties in democracies whose governments do not subsidize elections might not be to provide a means of negating the influence of wealth on elections
(B) in democracies in which elections are not fully subsidized by the government, positions endorsed by political parties might be much less varied than the positions taken by candidates
(C) in democracies, government-subsidized elections ensure that the views expressed by the people who run for office might not be overly influenced by the opinions of the wealthiest people in those countries
(D) in democracies in which elections are not fully subsidized by the government, it might be no easier for a wealthy person to win an election than it is for a nonwealthy person to win an election
(E) a democracy in which candidates do not compromise their views in order to be elected to office might have other flaws

23. In modern "brushless" car washes, cloth strips called mitters have replaced brushes. Mitters are easier on most cars' finishes than brushes are. This is especially important with the new clear-coat finishes found on many cars today, which are more easily scratched than older finishes are.

Which one of the following is most strongly supported by the statements above, if those statements are true?

(A) When car washes all used brushes rather than mitters, there were more cars on the road with scratched finishes than there are today.
(B) Modern "brushless" car washes were introduced as a direct response to the use of clear-coat finishes on cars.
(C) Modern "brushless" car washes usually do not produce visible scratches on cars with older finishes.
(D) Brushes are more effective than mitters and are preferred for cleaning cars with older finishes.
(E) More cars in use today have clear-coat finishes rather than older finishes.

24. It is widely believed that lancelets—small, primitive sea animals—do not have hearts. Each lancelet has a contracting vessel, but this vessel is considered an artery rather than a heart. However, this vessel is indeed a heart. After all, it strongly resembles the structure of the heart of certain other sea animals. Moreover, the muscular contractions in the lancelet's vessel closely resemble the muscular contractions of other animals' hearts.

The argument's conclusion follows logically if which one of the following is assumed?

(A) Only animals that have contracting vessels have hearts.
(B) Some primitive animals other than lancelets have what is widely held to be a heart.
(C) A vessel whose structure and actions closely resemble those of other animal hearts is a heart.
(D) For a vessel in an animal to be properly considered a heart, that vessel must undergo muscular contractions.
(E) No animal that has a heart lacks an artery.

25. Manager: I recommend that our company reconsider the decision to completely abandon our allegedly difficult-to-use computer software and replace it companywide with a new software package advertised as more flexible and easier to use. Several other companies in our region officially replaced the software we currently use with the new package, and while their employees can all use the new software, unofficially many continue to use their former software as much as possible.

Which one of the following is most strongly supported by the manager's statements?

(A) The current company software is as flexible as the proposed new software package.
(B) The familiarity that employees have with a computer software package is a more important consideration in selecting software than flexibility or initial ease of use.
(C) The employees of the manager's company would find that the new software package lacks some of the capabilities of the present software.
(D) Adopting the new software package would create two classes of employees, those who can use it and those who cannot.
(E) Many of the employees in the manager's company would not prefer the new software package to the software currently in use.

S T O P

IF YOU FINISH BEFORE TIME IS CALLED, YOU MAY CHECK YOUR WORK ON THIS SECTION ONLY.
DO NOT WORK ON ANY OTHER SECTION IN THE TEST.

SECTION IV

Time—35 minutes

27 Questions

Directions: Each set of questions in this section is based on a single passage or a pair of passages. The questions are to be answered on the basis of what is stated or implied in the passage or pair of passages. For some of the questions, more than one of the choices could conceivably answer the question. However, you are to choose the best answer; that is, the response that most accurately and completely answers the question, and blacken the corresponding space on your answer sheet.

The United States government agency responsible for overseeing television and radio broadcasting, the Federal Communications Commission (FCC), had an early history of addressing only the concerns of parties with an economic interest in broadcasting—chiefly broadcasting companies. The rights of viewers and listeners were not recognized by the FCC, which regarded them merely as members of the public. Unless citizens' groups were applying for broadcasting licenses, citizens did not have the standing necessary to voice their views at an FCC hearing. Consequently, the FCC appeared to be exclusively at the service of the broadcasting industry.

A landmark case changed the course of that history. In 1964, a local television station in Jackson, Mississippi was applying for a renewal of its broadcasting license. The United Church of Christ, representing Jackson's African American population, petitioned the FCC for a hearing about the broadcasting policies of that station. The church charged that the station advocated racial segregation to the point of excluding news and programs supporting integration. Arguing that the church lacked the level of economic interest required for a hearing, the FCC rejected the petition, though it attempted to mollify the church by granting only a short-term, probationary renewal to the station. Further, the FCC claimed that since it accepted the church's contentions with regard to misconduct on the part of the broadcasters, no hearing was necessary. However, that decision raised a question: If the contentions concerning the station were accepted, why was its license renewed at all? The real reason for denying the church a hearing was more likely the prospect that citizens' groups representing community preferences would begin to enter the closed worlds of government and industry.

The church appealed the FCC's decision in court, and in 1967 was granted the right to a public hearing on the station's request for a long-term license. The hearing was to little avail: the FCC dismissed much of the public input and granted a full renewal to the station. The church appealed again, and this time the judge took the unprecedented step of revoking the station's license without remand to the FCC, ruling that the church members were performing a public service in voicing the legitimate concerns of the community and, as such, should be accorded the right to challenge the renewal of the station's broadcasting license.

The case established a formidable precedent for opening up to the public the world of broadcasting. Subsequent rulings have supported the right of the public to question the performance of radio and television licensees before the FCC at renewal time every three years. Along with racial issues, a range of other matters—from the quality of children's programming and the portrayal of violence to equal time for opposing political viewpoints—are now discussed at licensing proceedings because of the church's intervention.

1. Which one of the following most accurately expresses the main point of the passage?

(A) Because of the efforts of a church group in challenging an FCC decision, public input is now considered in broadcast licensing proceedings.
(B) Court rulings have forced the FCC to abandon policies that appeared to encourage biased coverage of public issues.
(C) The history of the FCC is important because it explains why government agencies are now forced to respond to public input.
(D) Because it has begun to serve the interests of the public, the FCC is less responsive to the broadcasting industry.
(E) In response to pressure from citizens' groups, the FCC has decided to open its license renewal hearings to the public.

GO ON TO THE NEXT PAGE.

2. The author mentions some additional topics now discussed at FCC hearings (lines 54–59) primarily in order to

   (A) support the author's claim that the case helped to open up to the public the world of broadcasting
   (B) suggest the level of vigilance that citizens' groups must maintain with regard to broadcasters
   (C) provide an explanation of why the public is allowed to question the performance of broadcasters on such a frequent basis
   (D) illustrate other areas of misconduct with which the station discussed in the passage was charged
   (E) demonstrate that the station discussed in the passage was not the only one to fall short of its obligation to the public

3. Which one of the following statements is affirmed by the passage?

   (A) The broadcasting industry's economic goals can be met most easily by minimizing the attention given to the interests of viewers and listeners.
   (B) The FCC was advised by broadcasters to bar groups with no economic interest in broadcasting from hearings concerning the broadcasting industry.
   (C) The court ruled in the case brought by the United Church of Christ that the FCC had the ultimate authority to decide whether to renew a broadcaster's license.
   (D) Before the United Church of Christ won its case, the FCC would not allow citizens' groups to speak as members of the public at FCC hearings.
   (E) The case brought by the United Church of Christ represents the first time a citizens' group was successful in getting its concerns about government agencies addressed to its satisfaction.

4. Based on information presented in the passage, with which one of the following statements would the author be most likely to agree?

   (A) If the United Church of Christ had not pursued its case, the FCC would not have been aware of the television station's broadcasting policies.
   (B) By their very nature, industrial and business interests are opposed to public interests.
   (C) The recourse of a citizens' group to the courts represents an effective means of protecting public interests.
   (D) Governmental regulation cannot safeguard against individual businesses acting contrary to public interests.
   (E) The government cannot be trusted to favor the rights of the public over broadcasters' economic interests.

5. The passage suggests that which one of the following has been established by the case discussed in the third paragraph?

   (A) Broadcasters are legally obligated to hold regular meetings at which the public can voice its concerns about broadcasting policies.
   (B) Broadcasters are now required by the FCC to consult citizens' groups when making programming decisions.
   (C) Except in cases involving clear misconduct by a broadcaster, the FCC need not seek public input in licensing hearings.
   (D) When evaluating the performance of a broadcaster applying for a license renewal, the FCC must obtain information about the preferences of the public.
   (E) In FCC licensing proceedings, parties representing community preferences should be granted standing along with those with an economic interest in broadcasting.

GO ON TO THE NEXT PAGE.

An effort should be made to dispel the misunderstandings that still prevent the much-needed synthesis and mutual supplementation of science and the humanities. This reconciliation should not be too difficult once it is recognized that the separation is primarily the result of a basic misunderstanding of the philosophical foundations of both science and the humanities.

Some humanists still identify science with an absurd mechanistic reductionism. There are many who feel that the scientist is interested in nothing more than "bodies in motion," in the strictly mathematical, physical, and chemical laws that govern the material world. This is the caricature of science drawn by representatives of the humanities who are ignorant of the nature of modern science and also of the scientific outlook in philosophy. For example, it is claimed that science either ignores or explains away the most essential human values. Those who believe this also assert that there are aspects of the human mind, manifest especially in the domains of morality, religion, and the arts, that contain an irreducible spiritual element and for that reason can never be adequately explained by science.

Some scientists, on the other hand, claim that the humanist is interested in nothing more than emotion and sentiment, exhibiting the vagrant fancies of an undisciplined mind. To such men and women the humanities are useless because they serve no immediate and technological function for the practical survival of human society in the material world. Such pragmatists believe that the areas of morality, religion, and the arts should have only a secondary importance in people's lives.

Thus there are misconceptions among humanists and scientists alike that are in need of correction. This correction leads to a much more acceptable position that could be called "scientific humanism," attempting as it does to combine the common elements of both disciplines. Both science and the humanities attempt to describe and explain. It is true that they begin their descriptions and explanations at widely separated points, but the objectives remain the same: a clearer understanding of people and their world. In achieving this understanding, science in fact does not depend exclusively on measurable data, and the humanities in fact profit from attempts at controlled evaluation. Scientific humanism can combine the scientific attitude with an active interest in the whole scale of human values. If uninformed persons insist on viewing science as only materialistic and the humanities as only idealistic, a fruitful collaboration of both fields is unlikely. The combination of science and the humanities is, however, possible, even probable, if we begin by noting their common objectives, rather than seeing only their different means.

6. Which one of the following best describes the main idea of the passage?

(A) Scientists' failure to understand humanists hinders collaborations between the two groups.
(B) The materialism of science and the idealism of the humanities have both been beneficial to modern society.
(C) Technological development will cease if science and the humanities remain at odds with each other.
(D) The current relationship between science and the humanities is less cooperative than their relationship once was.
(E) A synthesis of science and the humanities is possible and much-needed.

7. Which one of the following would the author be most likely to characterize as an example of a misunderstanding of science by a humanist?

(A) Science encourages the view that emotions are inexplicable.
(B) Science arises out of practical needs but serves other needs as well.
(C) Science depends exclusively on measurable data to support its claims.
(D) Science recognizes an irreducible spiritual element that makes the arts inexplicable.
(E) Science encourages the use of description in the study of human values.

8. It can be inferred from the passage that the author would be most likely to agree with which one of the following statements?

(A) Scientific humanism is characterized by the extension of description and explanation from science to the humanities.
(B) A clearer understanding of people is an objective of humanists that scientists have not yet come to share.
(C) Controlled measures of aesthetic experience are of little use in the study of the humanities.
(D) Humanists have profited from using methods generally considered useful primarily to scientists.
(E) Fruitful collaboration between scientists and humanists is unlikely to become more common.

GO ON TO THE NEXT PAGE.

9. According to the author, which one of the following is the primary cause of the existing separation between science and the humanities?

(A) inflammatory claims by scientists regarding the pragmatic value of the work of humanists
(B) misunderstandings of the philosophical foundations of each by the other
(C) the excessive influence of reductionism on both
(D) the predominance of a concern with mechanics in science
(E) the failure of humanists to develop rigorous methods

10. Which one of the following best describes one of the functions of the last paragraph in the passage?

(A) to show that a proposal introduced in the first paragraph is implausible because of information presented in the second and third paragraphs
(B) to show that the views presented in the second and third paragraphs are correct but capable of reconciliation
(C) to present information supporting one of two opposing views presented in the second and third paragraphs
(D) to present an alternative to views presented in the second and third paragraphs
(E) to offer specific examples of the distinct views presented in the second and third paragraphs

11. The passage suggests that the author would recommend that humanists accept which one of the following modifications of their point of view?

(A) a realization that the scientist is less interested in describing "bodies in motion" than in constructing mathematical models of the material world
(B) an acknowledgement that there is a spiritual element in the arts that science does not account for
(C) an acceptance of the application of controlled evaluation to the examination of human values
(D) a less strident insistence on the primary importance of the arts in people's lives
(E) an emphasis on developing ways for showing how the humanities support the practical survival of mankind

12. In using the phrase "vagrant fancies of an undisciplined mind" (lines 27–28), the author suggests that humanists are sometimes considered to be

(A) wildly emotional
(B) excessively impractical
(C) unnecessarily intransigent
(D) justifiably optimistic
(E) logically inconsistent

GO ON TO THE NEXT PAGE.

The following passages are adapted from critical essays on the American writer Willa Cather (1873–1947).

Passage A

When Cather gave examples of high quality in fiction, she invariably cited Russian writers Ivan Turgenev or Leo Tolstoy or both. Indeed, Edmund Wilson noted in 1922 that Cather followed the manner of Turgenev, not depicting her characters' emotions directly but telling us how they behave and letting their "inner blaze of glory shine through the simple recital." Turgenev's method was to select details that described a character's appearance and actions without trying to explain them. A writer, he said, "must be a psychologist—but a secret one; he must know and feel the roots of phenomena, but only present the phenomena themselves." Similarly, he argued that a writer must have complete knowledge of a character so as to avoid overloading the work with unnecessary detail, concentrating instead on what is characteristic and typical.

Here we have an impressionistic aesthetic that anticipates Cather's: what Turgenev referred to as secret knowledge Cather called "the thing not named." In one essay she writes that "whatever is felt upon the page without being specifically named there—that, one might say, is created." For both writers, there is the absolute importance of selection and simplification; for both, art is the fusing of the physical world of setting and actions with the emotional reality of the characters. What synthesizes all the elements of narrative for these writers is the establishment of a prevailing mood.

Passage B

In a famous 1927 letter, Cather writes of her novel *Death Comes for the Archbishop*, "Many [reviewers] assert vehemently that it is not a novel. Myself, I prefer to call it a narrative." Cather's preference anticipated an important reformulation of the criticism of fiction: the body of literary theory, called "narratology," articulated by French literary theorists in the 1960s. This approach broadens and simplifies the fundamental paradigms according to which we view fiction: they ask of narrative only that it be narrative, that it tell a story. Narratologists tend *not* to focus on the characteristics of narrative's dominant modern Western form, the "realistic novel": direct psychological characterization, realistic treatment of time, causal plotting, logical closure. Such a model of criticism, which takes as its object "narrative" rather than the "novel," seems exactly appropriate to Cather's work.

Indeed, her severest critics have always questioned precisely her capabilities as a *novelist*. Morton Zabel argued that "[Cather's] themes...could readily fail to find the structure and substance that might have given them life or redeemed them from the tenuity of a sketch"; Leon Edel called one of her novels "two inconclusive fragments." These critics and others like them treat as failures some of the central features of Cather's impressionistic technique: unusual treatment of narrative time, unexpected focus, ambiguous conclusions, a preference for the bold, simple, and stylized in character as well as in landscape. These "non-novelistic" structures indirectly articulate the essential and conflicting forces of desire at work throughout Cather's fiction.

13. If the author of passage A were to read passage B, he or she would be most likely to agree with which one of the following?

(A) Though Cather preferred to call *Death Comes for the Archbishop* a narrative rather than a novel, she would be unlikely to view most of her other novels in the same way.
(B) The critics who questioned Cather's abilities as a novelist focused mostly on her failed experiments and ignored her more aesthetically successful novels.
(C) A model of criticism that takes narrative rather than the novel as its object is likely to result in flawed interpretations of Cather's work.
(D) Critics who questioned Cather's abilities as a novelist fail to perceive the extent to which Cather actually embraced the conventions of the realistic novel.
(E) Cather's goal of representing the "thing not named" explains her preference for the bold, simple, and stylized in the presentation of character.

14. Passage B indicates which one of the following?

(A) Narratologists point to Cather's works as prime examples of pure narrative.
(B) Cather disliked the work of many of the novelists who preceded her.
(C) Cather regarded at least one of her works as not fitting straightforwardly into the category of the novel.
(D) Cather's unusual treatment of narrative time was influenced by the Russian writers Turgenev and Tolstoy.
(E) Cather's work was regarded as flawed by most contemporary critics.

GO ON TO THE NEXT PAGE.

15. It can be inferred that both authors would be most likely to regard which one of the following as exemplifying Cather's narrative technique?

(A) A meticulous inventory of the elegant furniture and décor in a character's living room is used to indicate that the character is wealthy.
(B) An account of a character's emotional scars is used to explain the negative effects the character has on his family.
(C) A description of a slightly quivering drink in the hand of a character at a dinner party is used to suggest that the character is timid.
(D) A chronological summary of the events that spark a family conflict is used to supply the context for an in-depth narration of that conflict.
(E) A detailed narration of an unprovoked act of violence and the reprisals it triggers is used to portray the theme that violence begets violence.

16. Which one of the following most accurately states the main point of passage B?

(A) Cather's fiction is best approached by focusing purely on narrative, rather than on the formal characteristics of the novel.
(B) Most commentators on Cather's novels have mistakenly treated her distinctive narrative techniques as aesthetic flaws.
(C) Cather intentionally avoided the realistic psychological characterization that is the central feature of the modern Western novel.
(D) Cather's impressionistic narratives served as an important impetus for the development of narratology in the 1960s.
(E) Cather rejected the narrative constraints of the realistic novel and instead concentrated on portraying her characters by sketching their inner lives.

17. It is most likely that the authors of the two passages would both agree with which one of the following statements?

(A) More than her contemporaries, Cather used stream-of-consciousness narration to portray her characters.
(B) Cather's works were not intended as novels, but rather as narratives.
(C) Narratology is the most appropriate critical approach to Cather's work.
(D) Cather's technique of evoking the "thing not named" had a marked influence on later novelists.
(E) Cather used impressionistic narrative techniques to portray the psychology of her characters.

18. Both authors would be likely to agree that which one of the following, though typical of many novels, would NOT be found in Cather's work?

(A) Description of the salient features of the setting, such as a chair in which a character often sits.
(B) A plot that does not follow chronological time, but rather moves frequently between the novel's past and present.
(C) Description of a character's physical appearance, dress, and facial expressions.
(D) Direct representation of dialogue between the novel's characters, using quotation marks to set off characters' words.
(E) A narration of a character's inner thoughts, including an account of the character's anxieties and wishes.

19. A central purpose of each passage is to

(A) describe the primary influences on Cather's work
(B) identify some of the distinctive characteristics of Cather's work
(C) explain the critical reception Cather's work received in her lifetime
(D) compare Cather's novels to the archetypal form of the realistic novel
(E) examine the impact of European literature and literary theory on Cather's work

GO ON TO THE NEXT PAGE.

Fractal geometry is a mathematical theory devoted to the study of complex shapes called fractals. Although an exact definition of fractals has not been established, fractals commonly exhibit the property of self-similarity: the reiteration of irregular details or patterns at progressively smaller scales so that each part, when magnified, looks basically like the object as a whole. The Koch curve is a significant fractal in mathematics and examining it provides some insight into fractal geometry. To generate the Koch curve, one begins with a straight line. The middle third of the line is removed and replaced with two line segments, each as long as the removed piece, which are positioned so as to meet and form the top of a triangle. At this stage, the curve consists of four connected segments of equal length that form a pointed protrusion in the middle. This process is repeated on the four segments so that all the protrusions are on the same side of the curve, and then the process is repeated indefinitely on the segments at each stage of the construction.

Self-similarity is built into the construction process by treating segments at each stage the same way as the original segment was treated. Since the rules for getting from one stage to another are fully explicit and always the same, images of successive stages of the process can be generated by computer. Theoretically, the Koch curve is the result of infinitely many steps in the construction process, but the finest image approximating the Koch curve will be limited by the fact that eventually the segments will get too short to be drawn or displayed. However, using computer graphics to produce images of successive stages of the construction process dramatically illustrates a major attraction of fractal geometry: simple processes can be responsible for incredibly complex patterns.

A worldwide public has become captivated by fractal geometry after viewing astonishing computer-generated images of fractals; enthusiastic practitioners in the field of fractal geometry consider it a new language for describing complex natural and mathematical forms. They anticipate that fractal geometry's significance will rival that of calculus and expect that proficiency in fractal geometry will allow mathematicians to describe the form of a cloud as easily and precisely as an architect can describe a house using the language of traditional geometry. Other mathematicians have reservations about the fractal geometers' preoccupation with computer-generated graphic images and their lack of interest in theory. These mathematicians point out that traditional mathematics consists of proving theorems, and while many theorems about fractals have already been proven using the notions of pre-fractal mathematics, fractal geometers have proven only a handful of theorems that could not have been proven with pre-fractal mathematics. According to these mathematicians, fractal geometry can attain a lasting role in mathematics only if it becomes a precise language supporting a system of theorems and proofs.

20. Which one of the following most accurately expresses the main point of the passage?

(A) Because of its unique forms, fractal geometry is especially adaptable to computer technology and is therefore likely to grow in importance and render pre-fractal mathematics obsolete.
(B) Though its use in the generation of extremely complex forms makes fractal geometry an intriguing new mathematical theory, it is not yet universally regarded as having attained the theoretical rigor of traditional mathematics.
(C) Fractal geometry is significant because of its use of self-similarity, a concept that has enabled geometers to generate extremely detailed computer images of natural forms.
(D) Using the Koch curve as a model, fractal geometers have developed a new mathematical language that is especially useful in technological contexts because it does not rely on theorems.
(E) Though fractal geometry has thus far been of great value for its capacity to define abstract mathematical shapes, it is not expected to be useful for the description of ordinary natural shapes.

21. Which one of the following is closest to the meaning of the phrase "fully explicit" as used in lines 24–25?

(A) illustrated by an example
(B) uncomplicated
(C) expressed unambiguously
(D) in need of lengthy computation
(E) agreed on by all

22. According to the description in the passage, each one of the following illustrates the concept of self-similarity EXCEPT:

(A) Any branch broken off a tree looks like the tree itself.
(B) Each portion of the intricately patterned frost on a window looks like the pattern as a whole.
(C) The pattern of blood vessels in each part of the human body is similar to the pattern of blood vessels in the entire body.
(D) The seeds of several subspecies of maple tree resemble one another in shape despite differences in size.
(E) The florets composing a cauliflower head resemble the entire cauliflower head.

GO ON TO THE NEXT PAGE.

23. The explanation of how a Koch curve is generated (lines 10–20) serves primarily to

(A) show how fractal geometry can be reduced to traditional geometry
(B) give an example of a natural form that can be described by fractal geometry
(C) anticipate the objection that fractal geometry is not a precise language
(D) illustrate the concept of self-similarity
(E) provide an exact definition of fractals

24. Which one of the following does the author present as a characteristic of fractal geometry?

(A) It is potentially much more important than calculus.
(B) Its role in traditional mathematics will expand as computers become faster.
(C) It is the fastest-growing field of mathematics.
(D) It encourages the use of computer programs to prove mathematical theorems.
(E) It enables geometers to generate complex forms using simple processes.

25. Each of the following statements about the Koch curve can be properly deduced from the information given in the passage EXCEPT:

(A) The total number of protrusions in the Koch curve at any stage of the construction depends on the length of the initial line chosen for the construction.
(B) The line segments at each successive stage of the construction of the Koch curve are shorter than the segments at the previous stage.
(C) Theoretically, as the Koch curve is constructed its line segments become infinitely small.
(D) At every stage of constructing the Koch curve, all the line segments composing it are of equal length.
(E) The length of the line segments in the Koch curve at any stage of its construction depends on the length of the initial line chosen for the construction.

26. The enthusiastic practitioners of fractal geometry mentioned in lines 39–40 would be most likely to agree with which one of the following statements?

(A) The Koch curve is the most easily generated, and therefore the most important, of the forms studied by fractal geometers.
(B) Fractal geometry will eventually be able to be used in the same applications for which traditional geometry is now used.
(C) The greatest importance of computer images of fractals is their ability to bring fractal geometry to the attention of a wider public.
(D) Studying self-similarity was impossible before the development of sophisticated computer technologies.
(E) Certain complex natural forms exhibit a type of self-similarity like that exhibited by fractals.

27. The information in the passage best supports which one of the following assertions?

(A) The appeal of a mathematical theory is limited to those individuals who can grasp the theorems and proofs produced in that theory.
(B) Most of the important recent breakthroughs in mathematical theory would not have been possible without the ability of computers to graphically represent complex shapes.
(C) Fractal geometry holds the potential to replace traditional geometry in most of its engineering applications.
(D) A mathematical theory can be developed and find applications even before it establishes a precise definition of its subject matter.
(E) Only a mathematical theory that supports a system of theorems and proofs will gain enthusiastic support among a significant number of mathematicians.

S T O P

IF YOU FINISH BEFORE TIME IS CALLED, YOU MAY CHECK YOUR WORK ON THIS SECTION ONLY. DO NOT WORK ON ANY OTHER SECTION IN THE TEST.

Acknowledgment is made to the following sources from which material has been adapted for use in this test booklet:

Jerome Barron, *Freedom of the Press for Whom? The Right of Access to Mass Media.* ©1973 by Indiana University Press.

Huw Jones, "Fractals Before Mandelbrot: A Selective History." ©1993 by Springer-Verlag New York Inc.

LSAT WRITING SAMPLE TOPIC

Directions: The scenario presented below describes two choices, either one of which can be supported on the basis of the information given. Your essay should consider both choices and argue for one over the other, based on the two specified criteria and the facts provided. There is no "right" or "wrong" choice: a reasonable argument can be made for either.

Linda intends to spend her vacation walking part of a national trail. Over the course of one week, she will walk the trail while her luggage is taken on ahead of her each day. At this point, she must choose between either making all the arrangements herself or hiring a company that organizes walking tours to do this for her. Using the facts below, write an essay in which you argue for one approach over the other, based on the following two criteria:

- Linda wants to minimize the effort she puts into managing the vacation, both prior to and during the walk.
- She wants to have as much control over each day's experience as possible.

If Linda chooses to design her own walk and make the arrangements herself, she will research the trail and the available accommodations to estimate the distance she can comfortably cover each day and determine appropriate nightly stopover points. She will arrange for the luggage transportation and lodging. During her walk, it will be easy for her to add rest days as needed and otherwise change her itinerary from day to day.

If she hires a company that organizes walking tours, the company will plan the length of each day's walk based on its knowledge of the terrain. Linda will designate any planned rest days ahead of time. The walking company typically chooses among a limited set of nightly accommodations that it has selected based on customer feedback, honoring specific requests when possible. She will walk on her own. Complete lodging and route details will be provided to her the evening before her first day out. The company will oversee day-to-day luggage transportation.

Scratch Paper

Do not write your essay in this space.

Directions:

1. Use the Answer Key on the next page to check your answers.

2. Use the Scoring Worksheet below to compute your raw score.

3. Use the Score Conversion Chart to convert your raw score into the 120–180 scale.

Scoring Worksheet

1. Enter the number of questions you answered correctly in each section.

	Number Correct
SECTION I..........	______
SECTION II..........	______
SECTION III.........	______
SECTION IV.........	______

2. Enter the sum here: ______ **This is your Raw Score.**

Conversion Chart

For Converting Raw Score to the 120–180 LSAT Scaled Score
LSAT PrepTest 57

Reported Score	Lowest Raw Score	Highest Raw Score
180	99	101
179	98	98
178	__*	__*
177	97	97
176	96	96
175	95	95
174	94	94
173	93	93
172	92	92
171	91	91
170	90	90
169	89	89
168	87	88
167	86	86
166	84	85
165	83	83
164	81	82
163	80	80
162	78	79
161	76	77
160	75	75
159	73	74
158	71	72
157	69	70
156	68	68
155	66	67
154	64	65
153	62	63
152	61	61
151	59	60
150	57	58
149	55	56
148	54	54
147	52	53
146	50	51
145	49	49
144	47	48
143	45	46
142	44	44
141	42	43
140	41	41
139	39	40
138	37	38
137	36	36
136	34	35
135	33	33
134	32	32
133	30	31
132	29	29
131	27	28
130	26	26
129	25	25
128	23	24
127	22	22
126	21	21
125	20	20
124	18	19
123	17	17
122	15	16
121	__*	__*
120	0	14

*There is no raw score that will produce this scaled score for this PrepTest.

SECTION I

1.	D	8.	E	15.	E	22.	D
2.	B	9.	D	16.	A	23.	E
3.	C	10.	C	17.	B		
4.	D	11.	B	18.	C		
5.	C	12.	B	19.	D		
6.	B	13.	D	20.	E		
7.	B	14.	A	21.	B		

SECTION II

1.	A	8.	E	15.	A	22.	A
2.	A	9.	C	16.	B	23.	B
3.	D	10.	B	17.	E	24.	E
4.	D	11.	C	18.	D	25.	C
5.	E	12.	D	19.	C	26.	B
6.	C	13.	C	20.	D		
7.	A	14.	E	21.	E		

SECTION III

1.	A	8.	C	15.	C	22.	B
2.	C	9.	D	16.	C	23.	C
3.	A	10.	C	17.	D	24.	C
4.	B	11.	A	18.	B	25.	E
5.	A	12.	E	19.	D		
6.	A	13.	D	20.	E		
7.	C	14.	D	21.	B		

SECTION IV

1.	A	8.	D	15.	C	22.	D
2.	A	9.	B	16.	A	23.	D
3.	D	10.	D	17.	E	24.	E
4.	C	11.	C	18.	E	25.	A
5.	E	12.	B	19.	B	26.	E
6.	E	13.	E	20.	B	27.	D
7.	C	14.	C	21.	C		

Experimental Section Answer Key
June 1999, PrepTest 27, Section 3

1.	E	8.	E	15.	B	22.	B
2.	A	9.	B	16.	B	23.	C
3.	B	10.	E	17.	A	24.	C
4.	C	11.	D	18.	C	25.	A
5.	C	12.	A	19.	B	26.	E
6.	B	13.	D	20.	D		
7.	E	14.	D	21.	C		

PrepTest 58
September 2009

SECTION I

Time—35 minutes

26 Questions

Directions: The questions in this section are based on the reasoning contained in brief statements or passages. For some questions, more than one of the choices could conceivably answer the question. However, you are to choose the best answer; that is, the response that most accurately and completely answers the question. You should not make assumptions that are by commonsense standards implausible, superfluous, or incompatible with the passage. After you have chosen the best answer, blacken the corresponding space on your answer sheet.

1. Commentator: Although the present freshwater supply is adequate for today's patterns of water use, the human population will increase substantially over the next few decades, drastically increasing the need for freshwater. Hence, restrictions on water use will be necessary to meet the freshwater needs of humankind in the not-too-distant future.

Which one of the following is an assumption required by the argument?

(A) Humans will adapt to restrictions on the use of water without resorting to wasteful use of other natural resources.
(B) The total supply of freshwater has not diminished in recent years.
(C) The freshwater supply will not increase sufficiently to meet the increased needs of humankind.
(D) No attempt to synthesize water will have an appreciable effect on the quantity of freshwater available.
(E) No water conservation measure previously attempted yielded an increase in the supply of freshwater available for human use.

2. Psychologist: The best way to recall a certain word or name that one is having trouble remembering is to occupy one's mind with other things, since often the more we strive to remember a certain word or name that we can't think of, the less likely it becomes that the word will come to mind.

The principle that underlies the psychologist's argument underlies which one of the following arguments?

(A) Often, the best way to achieve happiness is to pursue other things besides wealth and fame, for there are wealthy and famous people who are not particularly happy, which suggests that true happiness does not consist in wealth and fame.
(B) The best way to succeed in writing a long document is not to think about how much is left to write but only about the current paragraph, since on many occasions thinking about what remains to be done will be so discouraging that the writer will be tempted to abandon the project.
(C) The best way to overcome a serious mistake is to continue on confidently as though all is well. After all, one can overcome a serious mistake by succeeding in new challenges, and dwelling on one's errors usually distracts one's mind from new challenges.
(D) The best way to fall asleep quickly is to engage in some mental diversion like counting sheep, because frequently the more one concentrates on falling asleep the lower the chance of falling asleep quickly.
(E) The best way to cope with sorrow or grief is to turn one's attention to those who are experiencing even greater hardship, for in many circumstances this will make our own troubles seem bearable by comparison.

GO ON TO THE NEXT PAGE.

3. Letter to the editor: The Planning Department budget increased from $100,000 in 2001 to $524,000 for this year. However, this does not justify your conclusion in yesterday's editorial that the department now spends five times as much money as it did in 2001 to perform the same duties.

Which one of the following, if true, most helps to support the claim made in the letter regarding the justification of the editorial's conclusion?

(A) Departments other than the Planning Department have had much larger budget increases since 2001.
(B) Since 2001, the Planning Department has dramatically reduced its spending on overtime pay.
(C) In some years between 2001 and this year, the Planning Department budget did not increase.
(D) The budget figures used in the original editorial were adjusted for inflation.
(E) A restructuring act, passed in 2003, broadened the duties of the Planning Department.

4. At mock trials in which jury instructions were given in technical legal jargon, jury verdicts tended to mirror the judge's own opinions. Jurors had become aware of the judge's nonverbal behavior: facial expressions, body movements, tone of voice. Jurors who viewed the same case but were given instruction in clear, nontechnical language, however, were comparatively more likely to return verdicts at odds with the judge's opinion.

Which one of the following is best illustrated by the example described above?

(A) Technical language tends to be more precise than nontechnical language.
(B) A person's influence is proportional to that person's perceived status.
(C) Nonverbal behavior is not an effective means of communication.
(D) Real trials are better suited for experimentation than are mock trials.
(E) The way in which a judge instructs a jury can influence the jury's verdict.

5. Doctor: While a few alternative medicines have dangerous side effects, some, such as many herbs, have been proven safe to consume. Thus, though there is little firm evidence of medicinal effect, advocates of these herbs as remedies for serious illnesses should always be allowed to prescribe them, since their patients will not be harmed, and might be helped, by the use of these products.

Which one of the following, if true, most seriously weakens the doctor's argument?

(A) Many practitioners and patients neglect more effective conventional medicines in favor of herbal remedies.
(B) Many herbal remedies are marketed with claims of proven effectiveness when in fact their effectiveness is unproven.
(C) Some patients may have allergic reactions to certain medicines that have been tolerated by other patients.
(D) The vast majority of purveyors of alternative medicines are driven as much by the profit motive as by a regard for their patients' health.
(E) Any pain relief or other benefits of many herbs have been proven to derive entirely from patients' belief in the remedy, rather than from its biochemical properties.

6. When a nation is on the brink of financial crisis, its government does not violate free-market principles if, in order to prevent economic collapse, it limits the extent to which foreign investors and lenders can withdraw their money. After all, the right to free speech does not include the right to shout "Fire!" in a crowded theatre, and the harm done as investors and lenders rush madly to get their money out before everyone else does can be just as real as the harm resulting from a stampede in a theatre.

The argument does which one of the following?

(A) tries to show that a set of principles is limited in a specific way by using an analogy to a similar principle that is limited in a similar way
(B) infers a claim by arguing that the truth of that claim would best explain observed facts
(C) presents numerous experimental results as evidence for a general principle
(D) attempts to demonstrate that an explanation of a phenomenon is flawed by showing that it fails to explain a particular instance of that phenomenon
(E) applies an empirical generalization to reach a conclusion about a particular case

7. Although many political candidates object to being made the target of advertising designed to cast them in an adverse light, such advertising actually benefits its targets because most elections have been won by candidates who were the targets of that kind of advertising.

The pattern of flawed reasoning in the argument most closely parallels that in which one of the following?

(A) Although many people dislike physical exercise, they should exercise because it is a good way to improve their overall health.
(B) Although many actors dislike harsh reviews of their work, such reviews actually help their careers because most of the really prestigious acting awards have gone to actors who have had performances of theirs reviewed harshly.
(C) Although many students dislike studying, it must be a good way to achieve academic success because most students who study pass their courses.
(D) Although many film critics dislike horror films, such films are bound to be successful because a large number of people are eager to attend them.
(E) Although many people dislike feeling sleepy as a result of staying up late the previous night, such sleepiness must be acceptable to those who experience it because most people who stay up late enjoy doing so.

8. Working residents of Springfield live, on average, farther from their workplaces than do working residents of Rorchester. Thus, one would expect that the demand for public transportation would be greater in Springfield than in Rorchester. However, Springfield has only half as many bus routes as Rorchester.

Each of the following, if true, contributes to a resolution of the apparent discrepancy described above EXCEPT:

(A) Three-fourths of the Springfield workforce is employed at the same factory outside the city limits.
(B) The average number of cars per household is higher in Springfield than in Rorchester.
(C) Rorchester has fewer railway lines than Springfield.
(D) Buses in Springfield run more frequently and on longer routes than in Rorchester.
(E) Springfield has a larger population than Rorchester does.

9. People who need to reduce their intake of fat and to consume fewer calories often turn to fat substitutes, especially those with zero calories such as N5. But studies indicate that N5 is of no use to such people. Subjects who ate foods prepared with N5 almost invariably reported feeling hungrier afterwards than after eating foods prepared with real fat and consequently they ate more, quickly making up for the calories initially saved by using N5.

The reasoning in the argument is most vulnerable to criticism on the grounds that the argument fails to consider the possibility that

(A) many foods cannot be prepared with N5
(B) N5 has mild but unpleasant side effects
(C) not everyone who eats foods prepared with N5 pays attention to caloric intake
(D) people who know N5 contains zero calories tend to eat more foods prepared with N5 than do people who are unaware that N5 is calorie-free
(E) the total fat intake of people who eat foods prepared with N5 tends to decrease even if their caloric intake does not

10. Music historian: Some critics lament the fact that impoverished postwar recording studios forced early bebop musicians to record extremely short solos, thus leaving a misleading record of their music. But these musicians' beautifully concise playing makes the recordings superb artistic works instead of mere representations of their live solos. Furthermore, the conciseness characteristic of early bebop musicians' recordings fostered a compactness in their subsequent live playing, which the playing of the next generation lacks.

The music historian's statements, if true, most strongly support which one of the following?

(A) Representations of live solos generally are not valuable artistic works.
(B) The difficult postwar recording conditions had some beneficial consequences for bebop.
(C) Short bebop recordings are always superior to longer ones.
(D) The music of the generation immediately following early bebop is of lower overall quality than early bebop.
(E) Musicians will not record extremely short solos unless difficult recording conditions force them to do so.

GO ON TO THE NEXT PAGE.

11. Recent studies indicate a correlation between damage to human chromosome number six and adult schizophrenia. We know, however, that there are people without damage to this chromosome who develop adult schizophrenia and that some people with damage to chromosome number six do not develop adult schizophrenia. So there is no causal connection between damage to human chromosome number six and adult schizophrenia.

Which one of the following most accurately describes a reasoning flaw in the argument above?

(A) The argument ignores the possibility that some but not all types of damage to chromosome number six lead to schizophrenia.
(B) The argument presumes, without providing evidence, that schizophrenia is caused solely by chromosomal damage.
(C) The argument makes a generalization based on an unrepresentative sample population.
(D) The argument mistakes a cause for an effect.
(E) The argument presumes, without providing warrant, that correlation implies causation.

12. City councilperson: Many city residents oppose the city art commission's proposed purchase of an unusual stone edifice, on the grounds that art critics are divided over whether the edifice really qualifies as art. But I argue that the purpose of art is to cause experts to debate ideas, including ideas about what constitutes art itself. Since the edifice has caused experts to debate what constitutes art itself, it does qualify as art.

Which one of the following, if assumed, enables the conclusion of the city councilperson's argument to be properly inferred?

(A) Nothing qualifies as art unless it causes debate among experts.
(B) If an object causes debate among experts, no expert can be certain whether that object qualifies as art.
(C) The purchase of an object that fulfills the purpose of art should not be opposed.
(D) Any object that fulfills the purpose of art qualifies as art.
(E) The city art commission should purchase the edifice if it qualifies as art.

13. It is a given that to be an intriguing person, one must be able to inspire the perpetual curiosity of others. Constantly broadening one's abilities and extending one's intellectual reach will enable one to inspire that curiosity. For such a perpetual expansion of one's mind makes it impossible to be fully comprehended, making one a constant mystery to others.

Which one of the following most accurately expresses the conclusion drawn in the argument above?

(A) To be an intriguing person, one must be able to inspire the perpetual curiosity of others.
(B) If one constantly broadens one's abilities and extends one's intellectual reach, one will be able to inspire the perpetual curiosity of others.
(C) If one's mind becomes impossible to fully comprehend, one will always be a mystery to others.
(D) To inspire the perpetual curiosity of others, one must constantly broaden one's abilities and extend one's intellectual reach.
(E) If one constantly broadens one's abilities and extends one's intellectual reach, one will always have curiosity.

14. Theater managers will not rent a film if they do not believe it will generate enough total revenue—including food-and-beverage concession revenue—to yield a profit. Therefore, since film producers want their films to be shown as widely as possible, they tend to make films that theater managers consider attractive to younger audiences.

Which one of the following is an assumption required by the argument?

(A) Adults consume less of the sort of foods and beverages sold at movie concession stands than do either children or adolescents.
(B) Movies of the kinds that appeal to younger audiences almost never also appeal to older audiences.
(C) Food-and-beverage concession stands in movie theaters are usually more profitable than the movies that are shown.
(D) Theater managers generally believe that a film that is attractive to younger audiences is more likely to be profitable than other films.
(E) Films that have an appeal to older audiences almost never generate a profit for theaters that show them.

GO ON TO THE NEXT PAGE.

15. Almost all advances in genetic research give rise to ethical dilemmas. Government is the exclusive source of funding for most genetic research; those projects not funded by government are funded solely by corporations. One or the other of these sources of funding is necessary for any genetic research.

If all the statements above are true, then which one of the following must be true?

(A) Most advances in genetic research occur in projects funded by government rather than by corporations.
(B) Most genetic research funded by government results in advances that give rise to ethical dilemmas.
(C) At least some advances in genetic research occur in projects funded by corporations.
(D) No ethical dilemmas resulting from advances in genetic research arise without government or corporate funding.
(E) As long as government continues to fund genetic research, that research will give rise to ethical dilemmas.

16. Corporate businesses, like species, must adapt to survive. Businesses that are no longer efficient will become extinct. But sometimes a business cannot adapt without changing its core corporate philosophy. Hence, sometimes a business can survive only by becoming a different corporation.

Which one of the following is an assumption required by the argument?

(A) No business can survive without changing its core corporate philosophy.
(B) As a business becomes less efficient, it invariably surrenders its core corporate philosophy.
(C) Different corporations have different core corporate philosophies.
(D) If a business keeps its core corporate philosophy intact, it will continue to exist.
(E) A business cannot change its core corporate philosophy without becoming a different corporation.

17. A survey taken ten years ago of residents of area L showed that although living conditions were slightly below their country's average, most residents of L reported general satisfaction with their living conditions. However, this year the same survey found that while living conditions are now about the same as the national average, most residents of L report general dissatisfaction with their living conditions.

Which one of the following, if true, would most help to resolve the apparent conflict between the results of the surveys described above?

(A) Residents of area L typically value aspects of living conditions different from the aspects of living conditions that are valued by residents of adjacent areas.
(B) Between the times that the two surveys were conducted, the average living conditions in L's country had substantially declined.
(C) Optimal living conditions were established in the survey by taking into account governmental policies and public demands on three continents.
(D) Living conditions in an area generally improve only if residents perceive their situation as somehow in need of improvement.
(E) Ten years ago the residents of area L were not aware that their living conditions were below the national average.

GO ON TO THE NEXT PAGE.

18. Travel agent: Although most low-fare airlines have had few, if any, accidents, very few such airlines have been in existence long enough for their safety records to be reliably established. Major airlines, on the other hand, usually have long-standing records reliably indicating their degree of safety. Hence, passengers are safer on a major airline than on one of the newer low-fare airlines.

Of the following, which one is the criticism to which the reasoning in the travel agent's argument is most vulnerable?

(A) The argument fails to address adequately the possibility that the average major airline has had a total number of accidents as great as the average low-fare airline has had.
(B) The argument draws a general conclusion about how safe passengers are on different airlines on the basis of safety records that are each from too brief a period to adequately justify such a conclusion.
(C) The argument fails to consider the possibility that long-standing and reliable records documenting an airline's degree of safety may indicate that the airline is unsafe.
(D) The argument takes for granted that airlines that are the safest are also the most reliable in documenting their safety.
(E) The argument fails to address adequately the possibility that even airlines with long-standing, reliable records indicating their degree of safety are still likely to have one or more accidents.

19. Economist: Our economy's weakness is the direct result of consumers' continued reluctance to spend, which in turn is caused by factors such as high-priced goods and services. This reluctance is exacerbated by the fact that the average income is significantly lower than it was five years ago. Thus, even though it is not a perfect solution, if the government were to lower income taxes, the economy would improve.

Which one of the following is an assumption required by the economist's argument?

(A) Increasing consumer spending will cause prices for goods and services to decrease.
(B) If consumer spending increases, the average income will increase.
(C) If income taxes are not lowered, consumers' wages will decline even further.
(D) Consumers will be less reluctant to spend money if income taxes are lowered.
(E) Lowering income taxes will have no effect on government spending.

20. A person with a type B lipid profile is at much greater risk of heart disease than a person with a type A lipid profile. In an experiment, both type A volunteers and type B volunteers were put on a low-fat diet. The cholesterol levels of the type B volunteers soon dropped substantially, although their lipid profiles were unchanged. The type A volunteers, however, showed no benefit from the diet, and 40 percent of them actually shifted to type B profiles.

If the information above is true, which one of the following must also be true?

(A) In the experiment, most of the volunteers had their risk of heart disease reduced at least marginally as a result of having been put on the diet.
(B) People with type B lipid profiles have higher cholesterol levels, on average, than do people with type A lipid profiles.
(C) Apart from adopting the low-fat diet, most of the volunteers did not substantially change any aspect of their lifestyle that would have affected their cholesterol levels or lipid profiles.
(D) The reduction in cholesterol levels in the volunteers is solely responsible for the change in their lipid profiles.
(E) For at least some of the volunteers in the experiment, the risk of heart disease increased after having been put on the low-fat diet.

GO ON TO THE NEXT PAGE.

21. Columnist: Although there is and should be complete freedom of thought and expression, that does not mean that there is nothing wrong with exploiting depraved popular tastes for the sake of financial gain.

Which one of the following judgments conforms most closely to the principle cited by the columnist?

(A) The government should grant artists the right to create whatever works of art they want to create so long as no one considers those works to be depraved.
(B) People who produce depraved movies have the freedom to do so, but that means that they also have the freedom to refrain from doing so.
(C) There should be no laws restricting what books are published, but publishing books that pander to people with depraved tastes is not thereby morally acceptable.
(D) The public has the freedom to purchase whatever recordings are produced, but that does not mean that the government may not limit the production of recordings deemed to be depraved.
(E) One who advocates complete freedom of speech should not criticize others for saying things that he or she believes to exhibit depraved tastes.

22. When a society undergoes slow change, its younger members find great value in the advice of its older members. But when a society undergoes rapid change, young people think that little in the experience of their elders is relevant to them, and so do not value their advice. Thus, we may measure the rate at which a society is changing by measuring the amount of deference its younger members show to their elders.

Which one of the following is an assumption on which the argument depends?

(A) A society's younger members can often accurately discern whether that society is changing rapidly.
(B) How much deference young people show to their elders depends on how much of the elders' experience is practically useful to them.
(C) The deference young people show to their elders varies according to how much the young value their elders' advice.
(D) The faster a society changes, the less relevant the experience of older members of the society is to younger members.
(E) Young people value their elders' advice just insofar as the elders' experience is practically useful to them.

23. Politician: We should impose a tariff on imported fruit to make it cost consumers more than domestic fruit. Otherwise, growers from other countries who can grow better fruit more cheaply will put domestic fruit growers out of business. This will result in farmland's being converted to more lucrative industrial uses and the consequent vanishing of a unique way of life.

The politician's recommendation most closely conforms to which one of the following principles?

(A) A country should put its own economic interest over that of other countries.
(B) The interests of producers should always take precedence over those of consumers.
(C) Social concerns should sometimes take precedence over economic efficiency.
(D) A country should put the interests of its own citizens ahead of those of citizens of other countries.
(E) Government intervention sometimes creates more economic efficiency than free markets.

24. The Kiffer Forest Preserve, in the northernmost part of the Abbimac Valley, is where most of the bears in the valley reside. During the eight years that the main road through the preserve has been closed the preserve's bear population has nearly doubled. Thus, the valley's bear population will increase if the road is kept closed.

Which one of the following, if true, most undermines the argument?

(A) Most of the increase in the preserve's bear population over the past eight years is due to migration.
(B) Only some of the increase in the preserve's bear population over the past eight years is due to migration of bears from other parts of the Abbimac Valley.
(C) Only some of the increase in the preserve's bear population over the past eight years is due to migration of bears from outside the Abbimac Valley.
(D) The bear population in areas of the Abbimac Valley outside the Kiffer Forest Preserve has decreased over the past eight years.
(E) The bear population in the Abbimac Valley has remained about the same over the past eight years.

GO ON TO THE NEXT PAGE.

25. If a wig has any handmade components, it is more expensive than one with none. Similarly, a made-to-measure wig ranges from medium-priced to expensive. Handmade foundations are never found on wigs that do not use human hair. Furthermore, any wig that contains human hair should be dry-cleaned. So all made-to-measure wigs should be dry-cleaned.

The conclusion of the argument follows logically if which one of the following is assumed?

(A) Any wig whose price falls in the medium-priced to expensive range has a handmade foundation.
(B) If a wig's foundation is handmade, then it is more expensive than one whose foundation is not handmade.
(C) A wig that has any handmade components should be dry-cleaned.
(D) If a wig's foundation is handmade, then its price is at least in the medium range.
(E) Any wig that should be dry-cleaned has a foundation that is handmade.

26. Philosopher: Wolves do not tolerate an attack by one wolf on another if the latter wolf demonstrates submission by baring its throat. The same is true of foxes and domesticated dogs. So it would be erroneous to deny that animals have rights on the grounds that only human beings are capable of obeying moral rules.

The philosopher's argument proceeds by attempting to

(A) provide counterexamples to refute a premise on which a particular conclusion is based
(B) establish inductively that all animals possess some form of morality
(C) cast doubt on the principle that being capable of obeying moral rules is a necessary condition for having rights
(D) establish a claim by showing that the denial of that claim entails a logical contradiction
(E) provide evidence suggesting that the concept of morality is often applied too broadly

S T O P

IF YOU FINISH BEFORE TIME IS CALLED, YOU MAY CHECK YOUR WORK ON THIS SECTION ONLY.
DO NOT WORK ON ANY OTHER SECTION IN THE TEST.

SECTION II

Time—35 minutes

27 Questions

Directions: Each set of questions in this section is based on a single passage or a pair of passages. The questions are to be answered on the basis of what is stated or implied in the passage or pair of passages. For some of the questions, more than one of the choices could conceivably answer the question. However, you are to choose the best answer; that is, the response that most accurately and completely answers the question, and blacken the corresponding space on your answer sheet.

Traditional sources of evidence about ancient history are archaeological remains and surviving texts. Those investigating the crafts practiced by women in ancient times, however, often derive little information from these sources, and the archaeological record is particularly unavailing for the study of ancient textile production, as researchers are thwarted by the perishable nature of cloth. What shreds persisted through millennia were, until recently, often discarded by excavators as useless, as were loom weights, which appeared to be nothing more than blobs of clay. Ancient texts, meanwhile, rarely mention the creation of textiles; moreover, those references that do exist use archaic, unrevealing terminology. Yet despite these obstacles, researchers have learned a great deal about ancient textiles and those who made them, and also about how to piece together a whole picture from many disparate sources of evidence.

Technological advances in the analysis of archaeological remains provide much more information than was previously available, especially about minute remains. Successful modern methods include radiocarbon dating, infrared photography for seeing through dirt without removing it, isotope "fingerprinting" for tracing sources of raw materials, and thin-layer chromatography for analyzing dyes. As if in preparation for such advances, the field of archaeology has also undergone an important philosophical revolution in the past century. Once little more than a self-serving quest for artifacts to stock museums and private collections, the field has transformed itself into a scientific pursuit of knowledge about past cultures. As part of this process, archaeologists adopted the fundamental precept of preserving all objects, even those that have no immediately discernible value. Thus in the 1970s two researchers found the oldest known complete garment, a 5,000-year-old linen shirt, among a tumbled heap of dirty linens that had been preserved as part of the well-known Petrie collection decades before anyone began to study the history of textiles.

The history of textiles and of the craftswomen who produced them has also advanced on a different front: recreating the actual production of cloth. Reconstructing and implementing ancient production methods provides a valuable way of generating and checking hypotheses. For example, these techniques made it possible to confirm that the excavated pieces of clay once considered useless in fact functioned as loom weights. Similarly, scholars have until recently been obliged to speculate as to which one of two statues of Athena, one large and one small, was adorned with a dress created by a group of Athenian women for a festival, as described in surviving texts. Because records show that it took nine months to produce the dress, scholars assumed it must have adorned the large statue. But by investigating the methods of production and the size of the looms used, researchers have ascertained that in fact a dress for the small statue would have taken nine months to produce.

1. Which one of the following most accurately expresses the main point of the passage?

(A) Archaeology is an expanding discipline that has transformed itself in response both to scientific advances and to changing cultural demands such as a recently increasing interest in women's history.

(B) A diversity of new approaches to the study of ancient textiles has enabled researchers to infer much about the history of textiles and their creators in the ancient world from the scant evidence that remains.

(C) Despite many obstacles, research into the textile production methods used by women in the ancient world has advanced over the past century to the point that archaeologists can now replicate ancient equipment and production techniques.

(D) Research into the history of textiles has spurred sweeping changes in the field of archaeology, from the application of advanced technology to the revaluation of ancient artifacts that were once deemed useless.

(E) Though researchers have verified certain theories about the history of textiles by using technological developments such as radiocarbon dating, most significant findings in this field have grown out of the reconstruction of ancient production techniques.

GO ON TO THE NEXT PAGE.

2. The author's attitude concerning the history of ancient textile production can most accurately be described as

(A) skeptical regarding the validity of some of the new hypotheses proposed by researchers
(B) doubtful that any additional useful knowledge can be generated given the nature of the evidence available
(C) impatient about the pace of research in light of the resources available
(D) optimistic that recent scholarly advances will attract increasing numbers of researchers
(E) satisfied that considerable progress is being made in this field

3. The passage indicates that the re-creation of ancient techniques was used in which one of the following?

(A) investigating the meanings of certain previously unintelligible technical terms in ancient texts
(B) tracing the sources of raw materials used in the production of certain fabrics
(C) constructing certain public museum displays concerning cloth-making
(D) verifying that a particular 5,000-year-old cloth was indeed a shirt
(E) exploring the issue of which of two statues of Athena was clothed with a particular garment

4. The author intends the term "traditional sources" (line 1) to exclude which one of the following?

(A) ancient clay objects that cannot be identified as pieces of pottery by the researchers who unearth them
(B) historically significant pieces of cloth discovered in the course of an excavation
(C) the oldest known complete garment, which was found among other pieces of cloth in a collection
(D) re-creations of looms from which inferences about ancient weaving techniques can be made
(E) ancient accounts of the adornment of a statue of Athena with a dress made by Athenian women

5. The passage as a whole functions primarily as

(A) a defense of the controversial methods adopted by certain researchers in a particular discipline
(B) a set of recommendations to guide future activities in a particular field of inquiry
(C) an account of how a particular branch of research has successfully coped with certain difficulties
(D) a rejection of some commonly held views about the methodologies of a certain discipline
(E) a summary of the hypotheses advanced by researchers who have used innovative methods of investigation

6. According to the passage, which one of the following was an element in the transformation of archaeology in the past century?

(A) an increased interest in the crafts practiced in the ancient world
(B) some archaeologists' adoption of textile conservation experts' preservation techniques
(C) innovative methods of restoring damaged artifacts
(D) the discovery of the oldest known complete garment
(E) archaeologists' policy of not discarding ancient objects that have no readily identifiable value

7. Which one of the following most accurately describes the function of the first paragraph in relation to the rest of the passage?

(A) A particularly difficult archaeological problem is described in order to underscore the significance of new methods used to resolve that problem, which are described in the following paragraphs.
(B) A previously neglected body of archaeological evidence is described in order to cast doubt on received views regarding ancient cultures developed from conventional sources of evidence, as described in the following paragraphs.
(C) The fruitfulness of new technologically based methods of analysis is described in order to support the subsequent argument that apparently insignificant archaeological remains ought to be preserved for possible future research.
(D) The findings of recent archaeological research are outlined as the foundation for a claim advanced in the following paragraphs that the role of women in ancient cultures has been underestimated by archaeologists.
(E) A recently developed branch of archaeological research is described as evidence for the subsequent argument that other, more established branches of archaeology should take advantage of new technologies in their research.

GO ON TO THE NEXT PAGE.

This passage was adapted from articles published in the 1990s.

The success that Nigerian-born computer scientist Philip Emeagwali (b. 1954) has had in designing computers that solve real-world problems has been fueled by his willingness to reach beyond established paradigms and draw inspiration for his designs from nature. In the 1980s, Emeagwali achieved breakthroughs in the design of parallel computer systems. Whereas single computers work sequentially, making one calculation at a time, computers connected in parallel can process calculations simultaneously. In 1989, Emeagwali pioneered the use of massively parallel computers that used a network of thousands of smaller computers to solve what is considered one of the most computationally difficult problems: predicting the flow of oil through the subterranean geologic formations that make up oil fields. Until that time, supercomputers had been used for oil field calculations, but because these supercomputers worked sequentially, they were too slow and inefficient to accurately predict such extremely complex movements.

To model oil field flow using a computer requires the simulation of the distribution of the oil at tens of thousands of locations throughout the field. At each location, hundreds of simultaneous calculations must be made at regular time intervals relating to such variables as temperature, direction of oil flow, viscosity, and pressure, as well as geologic properties of the basin holding the oil. In order to solve this problem, Emeagwali designed a massively parallel computer by using the Internet to connect to more than 65,000 smaller computers. One of the great difficulties of parallel computing is dividing up the tasks among the separate smaller computers so that they do not interfere with each other, and it was here that Emeagwali turned to natural processes for ideas, noting that tree species that survive today are those that, over the course of hundreds of millions of years, have developed branching patterns that have maximized the amount of sunlight gathered and the quantity of water and sap delivered. Emeagwali demonstrated that, for modeling certain phenomena such as subterranean oil flow, a network design based on the mathematical principle that underlies the branching structures of trees will enable a massively parallel computer to gather and broadcast the largest quantity of messages to its processing points in the shortest time.

In 1996 Emeagwali had another breakthrough when he presented the design for a massively parallel computer that he claims will be powerful enough to predict global weather patterns a century in advance. The computer's design is based on the geometry of bees' honeycombs, which use an extremely efficient three-dimensional spacing. Emeagwali believes that computer scientists in the future will increasingly look to nature for elegant solutions to complex technical problems. This paradigm shift, he asserts, will enable us to better understand the systems evolved by nature and, thereby, to facilitate the evolution of human technology.

8. Which one of the following most accurately expresses the main point of the passage?

(A) Emeagwali's establishment of new computational paradigms has enabled parallel computer systems to solve a wide array of real-world problems that supercomputers cannot solve.

(B) Emeagwali has shown that scientists' allegiance to established paradigms has until now prevented the solution of many real-world computational problems that could otherwise have been solved with little difficulty.

(C) Emeagwali's discovery of the basic mathematical principles underlying natural systems has led to a growing use of parallel computer systems to solve complex real-world computational problems.

(D) Emeagwali has designed parallel computer systems that are modeled on natural systems and that are aimed at solving real-world computational problems that would be difficult to solve with more traditional designs.

(E) The paradigm shift initiated by Emeagwali's computer designs has made it more likely that scientists will in the future look to systems evolved by nature to facilitate the evolution of human technology.

GO ON TO THE NEXT PAGE.

9. According to the passage, which one of the following is true?

(A) Emeagwali's breakthroughs in computer design have begun to make computers that work sequentially obsolete.
(B) Emeagwali's first breakthrough in computer design came in response to a request by an oil company.
(C) Emeagwali was the first to use a massively parallel computer to predict the flow of oil in oil fields.
(D) Emeagwali was the first computer scientist to use nature as a model for human technology.
(E) Emeagwali was the first to apply parallel processing to solving real-world problems.

10. The passage most strongly suggests that Emeagwali holds which one of the following views?

(A) Some natural systems have arrived at efficient solutions to problems that are analogous in significant ways to technical problems faced by computer scientists.
(B) Global weather is likely too complicated to be accurately predictable more than a few decades in advance.
(C) Most computer designs will in the future be inspired by natural systems.
(D) Massively parallel computers will eventually be practical enough to warrant their use even in relatively mundane computing tasks.
(E) The mathematical structure of branching trees is useful primarily for designing computer systems to predict the flow of oil through oil fields.

11. Which one of the following most accurately describes the function of the first two sentences of the second paragraph?

(A) They provide an example of an established paradigm that Emeagwali's work has challenged.
(B) They help explain why supercomputers are unable to accurately predict the movements of oil through underground geologic formations.
(C) They provide examples of a network design based on the mathematical principles underlying the branching structures of trees.
(D) They describe a mathematical model that Emeagwali used in order to understand a natural system.
(E) They provide specific examples of a paradigm shift that will help scientists understand certain systems evolved by nature.

12. Which one of the following, if true, would provide the most support for Emeagwali's prediction mentioned in lines 55–58?

(A) Until recently, computer scientists have had very limited awareness of many of the mathematical principles that have been shown to underlie a wide variety of natural processes.
(B) Some of the variables affecting global weather patterns have yet to be discovered by scientists who study these patterns.
(C) Computer designs for the prediction of natural phenomena tend to be more successful when those phenomena are not affected by human activities.
(D) Some of the mathematical principles underlying Emeagwali's model of oil field flow also underlie his designs for other massively parallel computer systems.
(E) Underlying the designs for many traditional technologies are mathematical principles of which the designers of those technologies were not explicitly aware.

13. It can be inferred from the passage that one of the reasons massively parallel computers had not been used to model oil field flow prior to 1989 is that

(A) supercomputers are sufficiently powerful to handle most computational problems, including most problems arising from oil production
(B) the possibility of using a network of smaller computers to solve computationally difficult problems had not yet been considered
(C) the general public was not yet aware of the existence or vast capabilities of the Internet
(D) oil companies had not yet perceived the need for modeling the flow of oil in subterranean fields
(E) smaller computers can interfere with one another when they are connected together in parallel to solve a computationally difficult problem

GO ON TO THE NEXT PAGE.

Proponents of the tangible-object theory of copyright argue that copyright and similar intellectual-property rights can be explained as logical extensions of the right to own concrete, tangible objects. This view depends on the claim that every copyrightable work can be manifested in some physical form, such as a manuscript or a videotape. It also accepts the premise that ownership of an object confers a number of rights on the owner, who may essentially do whatever he or she pleases with the object to the extent that this does not violate other people's rights. One may, for example, hide or display the object, copy it, or destroy it. One may also transfer ownership of it to another.

In creating a new and original object from materials that one owns, one becomes the owner of that object and thereby acquires all of the rights that ownership entails. But if the owner transfers ownership of the object, the full complement of rights is not necessarily transferred to the new owner; instead, the original owner may retain one or more of these rights. This notion of retained rights is common in many areas of law; for example, the seller of a piece of land may retain certain rights to the land in the form of easements or building restrictions. Applying the notion of retained rights to the domain of intellectual property, theorists argue that copyrighting a work secures official recognition of one's intention to retain certain rights to that work. Among the rights typically retained by the original producer of an object such as a literary manuscript or a musical score would be the right to copy the object for profit and the right to use it as a guide for the production of similar or analogous things—for example, a public performance of a musical score.

According to proponents of the tangible-object theory, its chief advantage is that it justifies intellectual property rights without recourse to the widely accepted but problematic supposition that one can own abstract, intangible things such as ideas. But while this account seems plausible for copyrightable entities that do, in fact, have enduring tangible forms, it cannot accommodate the standard assumption that such evanescent things as live broadcasts of sporting events can be copyrighted. More importantly, it does not acknowledge that in many cases the work of conceiving ideas is more crucial and more valuable than that of putting them into tangible form. Suppose that a poet dictates a new poem to a friend, who writes it down on paper that the friend has supplied. The creator of the tangible object in this case is not the poet but the friend, and there would seem to be no ground for the poet's claiming copyright unless the poet can be said to already own the ideas expressed in the work.

14. Which one of the following most accurately expresses the main point of the passage?

(A) Copyright and other intellectual-property rights can be explained as logical extensions of the right to own concrete objects.
(B) Attempts to explain copyright and similar intellectual-property rights purely in terms of rights to ownership of physical objects are ultimately misguided.
(C) Copyrighting a work amounts to securing official recognition of one's intention to retain certain rights to that work.
(D) Explanations of copyright and other intellectual-property rights in terms of rights to ownership of tangible objects fail to consider the argument that ideas should be allowed to circulate freely.
(E) Under the tangible-object theory of intellectual property, rights of ownership are straightforwardly applicable to both ideas and physical objects.

15. According to the passage, the theory that copyright and other intellectual-property rights can be construed as logical extensions of the right to own concrete, tangible objects depends on the claim that

(A) any work entitled to intellectual-property protection can be expressed in physical form
(B) only the original creator of an intellectual work can hold the copyright for that work
(C) the work of putting ideas into tangible form is more crucial and more valuable than the work of conceiving those ideas
(D) in a few cases, it is necessary to recognize the right to own abstract, intangible things
(E) the owner of an item of intellectual property may legally destroy it

16. The passage most directly answers which one of the following questions?

(A) Do proponents of the tangible-object theory of intellectual property advocate any changes in existing laws relating to copyright?
(B) Do proponents of the tangible-object theory of intellectual property hold that ownership of anything besides real estate can involve retained rights?
(C) Has the tangible-object theory of intellectual property influenced the ways in which copyright cases or other cases involving issues of intellectual property are decided in the courts?
(D) Does existing copyright law provide protection against unauthorized copying of manuscripts and musical scores in cases in which their creators have not officially applied for copyright protection?
(E) Are there standard procedures governing the transfer of intellectual property that are common to most legal systems?

17. Suppose an inventor describes an innovative idea for an invention to an engineer, who volunteers to draft specifications for a prototype and then produces the prototype using the engineer's own materials. Which one of the following statements would apply to this case under the tangible-object theory of intellectual property, as the author describes that theory?

(A) Only the engineer is entitled to claim the invention as intellectual property.
(B) Only the inventor is entitled to claim the invention as intellectual property.
(C) The inventor and the engineer are equally entitled to claim the invention as intellectual property.
(D) The engineer is entitled to claim the invention as intellectual property, but only if the inventor retains the right to all profits generated by the invention.
(E) The inventor is entitled to claim the invention as intellectual property, but only if the engineer retains the right to all profits generated by the invention.

18. Legal theorists supporting the tangible-object theory of intellectual property are most likely to believe which one of the following?

(A) A literary work cannot receive copyright protection unless it exists in an edition produced by an established publisher.
(B) Most legal systems explicitly rely on the tangible-object theory of intellectual property in order to avoid asserting that one can own abstract things.
(C) Copyright protects the right to copy for profit, but not the right to copy for other reasons.
(D) Some works deserving of copyright protection simply cannot be manifested as concrete, tangible objects.
(E) To afford patent protection for inventions, the law need not invoke the notion of inventors' ownership of abstract ideas.

19. The passage provides the most support for inferring which one of the following statements?

(A) In most transactions involving the transfer of non-intellectual property, at least some rights of ownership are retained by the seller.
(B) The notion of retained rights of ownership is currently applied to only those areas of law that do not involve intellectual property.
(C) The idea that ownership of the right to copy an item for profit can be transferred is compatible with a tangible-object theory of intellectual property.
(D) Ownership of intellectual property is sufficiently protected by the provisions that, under many legal systems, apply to ownership of material things such as land.
(E) Protection of computer programs under intellectual-property law is justifiable only if the programs are likely to be used as a guide for the production of similar or analogous programs.

20. It can be inferred that the author of the passage is most likely to believe which one of the following?

(A) Theorists who suggest that the notion of retained rights is applicable to intellectual property do not fully understand what it means to transfer ownership of property.
(B) If a work does not exist in a concrete, tangible form, there is no valid theoretical basis for claiming that it should have copyright protection.
(C) Under existing statutes, creators of original tangible works that have intellectual or artistic significance generally do not have the legal right to own the abstract ideas embodied in those works.
(D) An adequate theoretical justification of copyright would likely presuppose that a work's creator originally owns the ideas embodied in that work.
(E) It is common, but incorrect, to assume that such evanescent things as live broadcasts of sporting events can be copyrighted.

GO ON TO THE NEXT PAGE.

Passage A

In music, a certain complexity of sounds can be expected to have a positive effect on the listener. A single, pure tone is not that interesting to explore; a measure of intricacy is required to excite human curiosity. Sounds that are too complex or disorganized, however, tend to be overwhelming. We prefer some sort of coherence, a principle that connects the various sounds and makes them comprehensible.

In this respect, music is like human language. Single sounds are in most cases not sufficient to convey meaning in speech, whereas when put together in a sequence they form words and sentences. Likewise, if the tones in music are not perceived to be tied together sequentially or rhythmically—for example, in what is commonly called melody—listeners are less likely to feel any emotional connection or to show appreciation.

Certain music can also have a relaxing effect. The fact that such music tends to be continuous and rhythmical suggests a possible explanation for this effect. In a natural environment, danger tends to be accompanied by sudden, unexpected sounds. Thus, a background of constant noise suggests peaceful conditions; discontinuous sounds demand more attention. Even soft discontinuous sounds that we consciously realize do not signal danger can be disturbing—for example, the erratic dripping of a leaky tap. A continuous sound, particularly one that is judged to be safe, relaxes the brain.

Passage B

There are certain elements within music, such as a change of melodic line or rhythm, that create expectations about the future development of the music. The expectation the listener has about the further course of musical events is a key determinant for the experience of "musical emotions." Music creates expectations that, if not immediately satisfied, create tension. Emotion is experienced in relation to the buildup and release of tension. The more elaborate the buildup of tension, the more intense the emotions that will be experienced. When resolution occurs, relaxation follows.

The interruption of the expected musical course, depending on one's personal involvement, causes the search for an explanation. This results from a "mismatch" between one's musical expectation and the actual course of the music. Negative emotions will be the result of an extreme mismatch between expectations and experience. Positive emotions result if the converse happens.

When we listen to music, we take into account factors such as the complexity and novelty of the music. The degree to which the music sounds familiar determines whether the music is experienced as pleasurable or uncomfortable. The pleasure experienced is minimal when the music is entirely new to the listener, increases with increasing familiarity, and decreases again when the music is totally known. Musical preference is based on one's desire to maintain a constant level of certain preferable emotions. As such, a trained listener will have a greater preference for complex melodies than will a naive listener, as the threshold for experiencing emotion is higher.

21. Which one of the following concepts is linked to positive musical experiences in both passages?

(A) continuous sound
(B) tension
(C) language
(D) improvisation
(E) complexity

22. The passages most strongly suggest that both are targeting an audience that is interested in which one of the following?

(A) the theoretical underpinnings of how music is composed
(B) the nature of the conceptual difference between music and discontinuous sound
(C) the impact music can have on human emotional states
(D) the most effective techniques for teaching novices to appreciate complex music
(E) the influence music has had on the development of spoken language

23. Which one of the following describes a preference that is most analogous to the preference mentioned in the first paragraph of passage A?

(A) the preference of some people for falling asleep to white noise, such as the sound of an electric fan
(B) the preference of many moviegoers for movies with plots that are clear and easy to follow
(C) the preference of many diners for restaurants that serve large portions
(D) the preference of many young listeners for fast music over slower music
(E) the preference of most children for sweet foods over bitter foods

GO ON TO THE NEXT PAGE.

24. Which one of the following most accurately expresses the main point of passage B?

(A) The type of musical emotion experienced by a listener is determined by the level to which the listener's expectations are satisfied.
(B) Trained listeners are more able to consciously manipulate their own emotional experiences of complex music than are naive listeners.
(C) If the development of a piece of music is greatly at odds with the listener's musical expectations, then the listener will experience negative emotions.
(D) Listeners can learn to appreciate changes in melodic line and other musical complexities.
(E) Music that is experienced by listeners as relaxing usually produces a buildup and release of tension in those listeners.

25. Which one of the following most undermines the explanation provided in passage A for the relaxing effect that some music has on listeners?

(A) The musical traditions of different cultures vary greatly in terms of the complexity of the rhythms they employ.
(B) The rhythmic structure of a language is determined in part by the pattern of stressed syllables in the words and sentences of the language.
(C) Many people find the steady and rhythmic sound of a rocking chair to be very unnerving.
(D) The sudden interruption of the expected development of a melody tends to interfere with listeners' perception of the melody as coherent.
(E) Some of the most admired contemporary composers write music that is notably simpler than is most of the music written in previous centuries.

26. Which one of the following would be most appropriate as a title for each of the passages?

(A) "The Biological Underpinnings of Musical Emotions"
(B) "The Psychology of Listener Response to Music"
(C) "How Music Differs from Other Art Forms"
(D) "Cultural Patterns in Listeners' Responses to Music"
(E) "How Composers Convey Meaning Through Music"

27. It can be inferred that both authors would be likely to agree with which one of the following statements?

(A) The more complex a piece of music, the more it is likely to be enjoyed by most listeners.
(B) More knowledgeable listeners tend to prefer music that is discontinuous and unpredictable.
(C) The capacity of music to elicit strong emotional responses from listeners is the central determinant of its artistic value.
(D) Music that lacks a predictable course is unlikely to cause a listener to feel relaxed.
(E) Music that changes from soft to loud is perceived as disturbing and unpleasant by most listeners.

S T O P

IF YOU FINISH BEFORE TIME IS CALLED, YOU MAY CHECK YOUR WORK ON THIS SECTION ONLY.
DO NOT WORK ON ANY OTHER SECTION IN THE TEST.

Time—35 minutes

25 Questions

Directions: The questions in this section are based on the reasoning contained in brief statements or passages. For some questions, more than one of the choices could conceivably answer the question. However, you are to choose the best answer; that is, the response that most accurately and completely answers the question. You should not make assumptions that are by commonsense standards implausible, superfluous, or incompatible with the passage. After you have chosen the best answer, blacken the corresponding space on your answer sheet.

1. Politician: Governments should tax any harmful substance that is available to the general public at a level that the tax would discourage continued use of the substance.

Which one of the following is an application of the politician's principle of taxation?

(A) The tax on products containing sugar is raised in an effort to raise revenue to be applied to the health costs resulting from the long-term use of these products.
(B) The tax on certain pain relievers that, even though harmful, are available over the counter is raised, since studies have shown that the demand for these products will not be affected.
(C) The tax on a pesticide that contains an organic compound harmful to human beings is raised to give people an incentive to purchase pesticides not containing the compound.
(D) The tax on domestically produced alcoholic beverages is not raised, since recent studies show that the tax would have a negative impact on the tourist industry.
(E) The tax on products that emit fluorocarbons, substances that have proven to be harmful to the earth's ozone layer, is lowered to stimulate the development of new, less environmentally harmful ways of using these substances.

2. The average cable television company offers its customers 50 channels, but new fiber-optic lines will enable telephone companies to provide 100 to 150 television channels to their customers for the same price as cable companies charge for 50. Therefore, cable companies will be displaced by the new television services offered by telephone companies within a few years.

Which one of the following, if true, most helps to strengthen the argument?

(A) The initial cost per household of installing new fiber-optic television service will exceed the current cost of installing cable television service.
(B) The most popular movies and programs on channels carried by cable companies will also be offered on channels carried by the fiber-optic lines owned by the telephone companies.
(C) Cable television companies will respond to competition from the telephone companies by increasing the number of channels they offer.
(D) Some telephone companies own cable companies in areas other than those in which they provide telephone services.
(E) The new fiber-optic services offered by telephone companies will be subject to more stringent governmental programming regulations than those to which cable companies are now subject.

GO ON TO THE NEXT PAGE.

3. A just government never restricts the right of its citizens to act upon their desires except when their acting upon their desires is a direct threat to the health or property of other of its citizens.

Which one of the following judgments most closely conforms to the principle cited above?

(A) A just government would not ban the sale of sports cars, but it could prohibit unrestricted racing of them on public highways.
(B) An unjust government would abolish many public services if these services did not require compulsory labor.
(C) A just government would provide emergency funds to survivors of unavoidable accidents but not to survivors of avoidable ones.
(D) A just government would not censor writings of Shakespeare, but it could censor magazines and movies that criticize the government.
(E) An unjust government would incarcerate one of its citizens even though it had been several years since that citizen harmed someone.

4. Mayor: Citing the severity of the city's winters, the city road commissioner has suggested paving our roads with rubberized asphalt, since the pressure of passing vehicles would cause the rubber to flex, breaking up ice on roads and so making ice removal easier and less of a strain on the road-maintenance budget. However, rubberized asphalt is more expensive than plain asphalt and the city's budget for building and maintaining roads cannot be increased. Therefore, the commissioner's suggestion is not financially feasible.

Which one of the following is assumed by the mayor's argument?

(A) Using rubberized asphalt to pave roads would not have any advantages besides facilitating the removal of ice on roads.
(B) The severity of winters in the region in which the city is located does not vary significantly from year to year.
(C) It would cost more to add particles of rubber to asphalt than to add particles of rubber to other materials that are used to pave roads.
(D) Savings in the cost of ice removal would not pay for the increased expense of using rubberized asphalt to pave roads.
(E) The techniques the city currently uses for removing ice from city roads are not the least expensive possible, given the type of road surface in place.

5. Ticks attach themselves to host animals to feed. Having fed to capacity, and not before then, the ticks drop off their host. Deer ticks feeding off white-footed mice invariably drop off their hosts between noon and sunset, regardless of time of attachment. White-footed mice are strictly nocturnal animals that spend all daytime hours in their underground nests.

Which one of the following conclusions can be properly drawn from the statements above?

(A) Deer ticks all attach themselves to white-footed mice during the same part of the day, regardless of day of attachment.
(B) Deer ticks sometimes drop off their hosts without having fed at all.
(C) Deer ticks that feed off white-footed mice drop off their hosts in the hosts' nests.
(D) White-footed mice to which deer ticks have attached themselves are not aware of the ticks.
(E) White-footed mice are hosts to stable numbers of deer ticks, regardless of season of the year.

6. Monarch butterflies spend the winter hibernating on trees in certain forests. Local environmental groups have organized tours of the forests in an effort to protect the butterflies' habitat against woodcutters. Unfortunately, the tourists trample most of the small shrubs that are necessary to the survival of any monarch butterflies that fall of the trees. Therefore, the tour groups themselves are endangering the monarch butterfly population.

Which one of the following would it be most useful to know in evaluating the argument?

(A) the amount of forest land suitable for monarch butterfly hibernation that is not currently used by monarch butterflies for hibernation
(B) the amount of wood cut each year by woodcutters in forests used by monarch butterflies for hibernation
(C) the amount of plant life trampled by the tourists that is not necessary to the survival of monarch butterflies
(D) the proportion of the trees cut down by the woodcutters each year that are cut in the forests used by monarch butterflies for hibernation
(E) the proportion of hibernating monarch butterflies that fall of the trees

GO ON TO THE NEXT PAGE.

7. If you know a lot about history, it will be easy for you to impress people who are intellectuals. But unfortunately, you will not know much about history if you have not, for example, read a large number of history books. Therefore, if you are not well versed in history due to a lack of reading, it will not be easy for you to impress people who are intellectuals.

   The argument's reasoning is flawed because the argument overlooks the possibility that

   (A) many intellectuals are not widely read in history
   (B) there are people who learn about history who do not impress intellectuals
   (C) it is more important to impress people who are not intellectuals than people who are intellectuals
   (D) there are other easy ways to impress intellectuals that do not involve knowing history
   (E) people who are not intellectuals can be impressed more easily than people who are intellectuals

8. People always seem to associate high prices of products with high quality. But price is not necessarily an indicator of quality. The best teas are often no more expensive than the lower-quality teas.

   Which one of the following, if true, does most to explain the apparent counterexample described above?

   (A) Packing and advertising triple the price of all teas.
   (B) Most people buy low-quality tea, thus keeping its price up.
   (C) All types of tea are subject to high import tariffs.
   (D) Low-quality teas are generally easier to obtain than high quality teas.
   (E) The price of tea generally does not vary from region to region.

9. The only physical factor preventing a human journey to Mars has been weight. Carrying enough fuel to propel a conventional spacecraft to Mars and back would make even the lightest craft too heavy to be launched from Earth. A device has recently been invented, however, that allows an otherwise conventional spacecraft to refill the craft's fuel tanks with fuel manufactured from the Martian atmosphere for the return trip. Therefore, it is possible for people to go to Mars in a spacecraft that carries this device and then return.

   Which one of the following is an assumption on which the argument depends?

   (A) The amount of fuel needed for a spacecraft to return from Mars is the same as the amount of fuel needed to travel from Earth to Mars.
   (B) The fuel manufactured from the Martian atmosphere would not differ in composition from the fuel used to travel to Mars.
   (C) The device for manufacturing fuel from the Martian atmosphere would not take up any of the spaceship crew's living space.
   (D) A conventional spacecraft equipped with the device would not be appreciably more expensive to construct than current spacecraft typically are.
   (E) The device for manufacturing fuel for the return to Earth weighs less than the tanks of fuel that a conventional spacecraft would otherwise need to carry from Earth for the return trip.

10. Unplugging a peripheral component such as a "mouse" from a personal computer renders all of the software programs that require that component unusable on that computer. On Fred's personal computer, a software program that requires a mouse has become unusable. So it must be that the mouse for Fred's computer became unplugged.

    The argument is most vulnerable to which one of the following criticisms?

    (A) It contains a shift in the meaning of "unusable" from "permanently unusable" to "temporarily unusable."
    (B) It treats an event that can cause a certain result as though that event is necessary to bring about that result.
    (C) It introduces information unrelated to its conclusion as evidence in support of that conclusion.
    (D) It attempts to support its conclusion by citing a generalization that is too broad.
    (E) It overlooks the possibility that some programs do not require a peripheral component such as a mouse.

GO ON TO THE NEXT PAGE.

<u>Questions 11–12</u>

P: Complying with the new safety regulations is useless. Even if the new regulations had been in effect before last year's laboratory fire, they would not have prevented the fire or the injuries resulting from it because they do not address its underlying causes.

Q: But any regulations that can potentially prevent money from being wasted are useful. If obeyed, the new safety regulations will prevent some accidents, and whenever there is an accident here at the laboratory, money is wasted even if no one is injured.

11. A point at issue between P and Q is whether

(A) last year's fire resulted in costly damage to the laboratory
(B) accidents at the laboratory inevitably result in personal injuries
(C) the new safety regulations address the underlying cause of last year's fire
(D) it is useful to comply with the new safety regulations
(E) the new safety regulations are likely to be obeyed in the laboratory

12. Q responds to P's position by

(A) extending the basis for assessing the utility of complying with the new regulations
(B) citing additional evidence that undermines P's assessment of the extent to which the new regulations would have prevented injuries in last year's laboratory fire
(C) giving examples to show that the uselessness of all regulations cannot validly be inferred from the uselessness of one particular set of regulations
(D) showing that P's argument depends on the false assumption that compliance with any regulations that would have prevented last year's fire would be useful
(E) pointing out a crucial distinction, overlooked by P, between potential benefits and actual benefits

13. Historian: The ancient Greeks failed to recognize that, morally, democracy is no improvement over monarchy. It is wrong for an individual to have the power to choose the course of action for a government, so it is no less wrong to grant this power to society, which is just a collection of individuals.

The pattern of flawed reasoning in the argument above is most similar to that in which one of the following?

(A) There is no point in trying to find someone else to solve that problem. If Robin cannot solve it, then none of Robin's friends would be able to solve it.
(B) We should not pick Hank for the relay team. He has not won a race all season, so there is no reason to expect him to help the relay team win.
(C) Laws that contain exemptions for some individuals based on no relevant consideration are fundamentally immoral. If it is wrong for a given person to commit an act, then it is wrong for anyone else in similar circumstances to commit the act.
(D) There is no point in asking the club to purchase tents and make them available for use by club members. No member of the club can afford one of those tents, so the club is unable to afford any either.
(E) Agreeing with all of the other members of society does not guarantee that one is correct about an issue. With many topics it is possible for society to be mistaken and hence every individual in society to be likewise mistaken.

GO ON TO THE NEXT PAGE.

14. In 1712 the government of Country Y appointed a censor to prohibit the publication of any book critical of Country Y's government; all new books legally published in the country after 1712 were approved by a censor. Under the first censor, one half of the book manuscripts submitted to the censor were not approved for publication. Under the next censor, only one quarter of the book manuscripts submitted were not approved, but the number of book manuscripts that were approved was the same under both censors.

It the statements in the passage are true, which one of the following can be properly concluded from them?

(A) More books critical of Country Y's government were published before the appointment of the first censor than after it.
(B) The first censor and the second censor prohibited the publication of the same number of book manuscripts.
(C) More book manuscripts were submitted for approval to the first censor than to the second.
(D) The second censor allowed some book manuscripts to be published that the first censor would have considered critical of Country Y's government.
(E) The number of writers who wrote published manuscripts was greater under the first censor than under the second.

15. It is often said that beauty is subjective. But this judgment has to be false. If one tries to glean the standard of beauty of earlier cultures from the artistic works they considered most beautiful, one cannot but be impressed by its similarity to our own standard. In many fundamental ways, what was considered beautiful in those cultures is still considered beautiful in our own time.

Which one of the following statements, if true, most weakens the argument?

(A) Few contemporary artists have been significantly exposed to the art of earlier cultures.
(B) The arts held a much more important place in earlier cultures than they do in our culture.
(C) Our own standard of beauty was strongly influenced by our exposure to works that were considered beautiful in earlier cultures.
(D) Much of what passes for important artistic work today would not be considered beautiful even by contemporary standards.
(E) In most cultures art is owned by a small social elite.

16. Nutrition education in schools once promoted daily consumption of food from each of the "four food groups": milk, meat, fruit and vegetables, and breads and cereals. This recommendation was, however, dangerous to health.

Each of the following, if true, provides support for the critique above EXCEPT:

(A) The division into four groups gave the impression that an equal amount of each should be consumed, but milk and meat tend to contain fats that promote heart disease and cancer and should be eaten in lesser amounts.
(B) The omission of fish, which contains beneficial oils, from the names of groups in the list gave erroneous impression that it is less healthy as a food than is red meat.
(C) A healthy diet should include the consumption of several different fruits and vegetables daily, but the recommendation was often interpreted as satisfied by the consumption of a single serving of a fruit or vegetable.
(D) The recommendation that some food from the fruit and vegetable group be consumed daily constituted a reminder not to neglect this group, which provides needed vitamins, minerals, and fiber.
(E) Encouraging the daily consumption of some product from each of the four food groups gave the impression that eating in that manner is sufficient for a healthy diet, but eating in that manner is consistent with the overconsumption of sweets and fats.

GO ON TO THE NEXT PAGE.

17. The Green Ensemble, a nonprofit theater group, has always been financially dependent on contributions from corporations and would have been forced to disband this year if any of its corporate sponsors had withdrawn their financial support. But the Green Ensemble has not only been able to continue in operation throughout the year, but has recently announced its schedule for next year.

Which one of the following is a conclusion that can be properly drawn from the information above?

(A) None of the Green Ensemble's corporate sponsors withdrew their financial support of the group this year.
(B) Earlier this year the Green Ensemble found other sources of funding for next year, making the group less dependent on corporations for financial support.
(C) During this year corporate funding for the Green Ensemble has been steadily increasing.
(D) This year corporate funding was the source of more than half of the Green Ensemble's income.
(E) Corporate funding for nonprofit theater groups like the Green Ensemble has recently increased.

18. Book publishers have traditionally published a few books that they thought were of intrinsic merit even though these books were unlikely to make a profit. Nowadays, however, fewer of these books are being published. It seems, therefore, that publishers now, more than ever, are more interested in making money than in publishing books of intrinsic value.

Which one of the following statements, if true, most seriously weakens the argument?

(A) Book publishers have always been very interested in making money.
(B) There has been a notable decline in the quality of books written in recent years.
(C) In the past, often books of intrinsic value would unexpectedly make a sizable profit.
(D) There have always been authors unwilling to be published unless a profit is guaranteed.
(E) In recent years, profits in the book publishing industry have been declining.

19. Most people feel that they are being confused by the information from broadcast news. This could be the effect of the information's being delivered too quickly or of its being poorly organized. Analysis of the information content of a typical broadcast news story shows that news stories are far lower in information density than the maximum information density with which most people can cope at any one time. So the information in typical broadcast news stories is poorly organized.

Which one of the following is an assumption that the argument requires in order for its conclusion to be properly drawn?

(A) It is not the number of broadcast news stories to which a person is exposed that is the source of the feeling of confusion.
(B) Poor organization of information in a news story makes it impossible to understand the information.
(C) Being exposed to more broadcast news stories within a given day would help a person to better understand the news.
(D) Most people can cope with a very high information density.
(E) Some people are being overwhelmed by too much information.

20. Art Historian: Robbins cannot pass judgment on Stuart's art. While Robbins understands the art of Stuart too well to dismiss it, she does not understand it well enough to praise it.

The art historian's argument depends on the assumption that

(A) in order to pass judgment on Stuart's art, Robbins must be able either to dismiss it or to praise it
(B) if art can be understood well, it should be either dismissed or praised
(C) in order to understand Stuart's art, Robbins must be able to pass judgment on it
(D) Stuart's art can be neither praised nor dismissed
(E) if Robbins understands art well, she will praise it

GO ON TO THE NEXT PAGE.

Questions 21–22

Words like "employee," "payee," and "detainee" support the generalization, crudely stated, that words with the ending *-ee* designate the person affected in the specified way by an action performed by someone else. The word "absentee" seems to be a direct counterexample: it ends in *-ee*, yet, if it makes sense here to speak of an action at all—that of absenting oneself, perhaps—the word can refer to the person who actually performs that action. Clearly, however, putting forward the following resolves the impasse: if a word with the ending *-ee* refers to one party in a two-party transaction, it refers to the party at which the other party's action is directed.

21. The argument does which one of the following in dealing with the counterexample it offers?

(A) provides additional support for the original generalization in part by showing that the supposed force of the counterexample derives from a misanalysis of that example
(B) dismisses the counterexample on the grounds that its force, compared to the weight of the supporting evidence, is insignificant
(C) concedes that the proposed counterexample is an exception to the generalization but maintains the generalization on the grounds that all generalizations have exceptions
(D) narrows the scope of the generalization at issue in such a way that the putative counterexample is no longer relevant
(E) shows how replacing the notion of being affected in the specified way by an action with that of having someone's action directed at oneself reveals the counterexample to be spurious

22. The reasoning in the argument could have remained unchanged in force and focus if which one of the following had been advanced as a counterexample in place of the word "absentee"?

(A) honoree
(B) appointee
(C) nominee
(D) transferee
(E) escapee

23. Much of today's literature is inferior: most of our authors are intellectually and emotionally inexperienced, and their works lack both the intricacy and the focus on the significant that characterize good literature. However, Hypatia's latest novel is promising; it shows a maturity, complexity, and grace that far exceeds that of her earlier works.

Which one of the following statements is most strongly supported by the information in the passage?

(A) Much of today's literature focuses less on the significant than Hypatia's latest novel focuses on the significant.
(B) Much of today's literature at least lacks the property of grace.
(C) Hypatia's latest novel is good literature when judged by today's standards.
(D) Hypatia's latest novel is clearly better than the majority of today's literature.
(E) Hypatia's latest novel has at least one property of good literature to a greater degree than her earlier works.

GO ON TO THE NEXT PAGE.

24. Scientists, puzzled about the development of penicillin-resistant bacteria in patients who had not been taking penicillin, believe they have found an explanation. The relevant group of patients have dental fillings made of mercury-containing amalgam, and the bacteria the patients develop are immune to mercury poisoning. Scientists have concluded that the genes causing resistance to penicillin are closely bundled on the chromosomes of bacteria with the gene that produces immunity to mercury poisoning. Exposure to the mercury kills off bacteria that lack the relevant immunity gene, and leaves room for those that possess both the mercury-immunity gene and the penicillin-resistance gene to flourish.

Which one of the following most accurately characterizes the role played in the passage by the unstated assumption that some patients who take penicillin develop bacteria with an immunity to penicillin?

(A) It is a hypothesis that is taken by the scientists to be conclusively proven by the findings described in the passage.
(B) It is a generalization that, if true, rules out the possibility that some people who do not take penicillin develop bacteria resistant to it.
(C) It is a point that, in conjunction with the fact that some patients who do not take penicillin develop penicillin-resistant bacteria, generates the problem that prompted the research described in the passage.
(D) It is the tentative conclusion of previous research that appears to be falsified by the scientists' discovery of the mechanism by which bacteria become resistant to mercury poisoning.
(E) It is a generalization assumed by the scientists to conclusively prove that the explanation of their problem case must involve reference to the genetic makeup of the penicillin-resistant bacteria.

25. All any reporter knows about the accident is what the press agent has said. Therefore, if the press agent told every reporter everything about the accident, then no reporter knows any more about it than any other reporter. If no reporter knows any more about the accident than any other reporter, then no reporter can scoop all of the other reporters. However, the press agent did not tell every reporter everything about the accident. It follows that some reporter can scoop all of the other reporters.

The argument's reasoning is flawed because the argument fails to recognize that which one of the following is consistent with the facts the argument presents?

(A) The press agent did not tell everything about the accident to any reporter.
(B) Even if some reporter knows more about the accident than all of the other reporters, that reporter need not scoop any other reporter.
(C) Some reporter may have been told something about the accident that the reporter tells all of the other reporters.
(D) The press agent may not know any more about the accident than the most knowledgeable reporter.
(E) No reporter knows any more about the accident than any other reporter.

S T O P

IF YOU FINISH BEFORE TIME IS CALLED, YOU MAY CHECK YOUR WORK ON THIS SECTION ONLY.
DO NOT WORK ON ANY OTHER SECTION IN THE TEST.

SECTION III

Time—35 minutes

23 Questions

Directions: Each group of questions in this section is based on a set of conditions. In answering some of the questions, it may be useful to draw a rough diagram. Choose the response that most accurately and completely answers each question and blacken the corresponding space on your answer sheet.

Questions 1–6

Historical records show that over the course of five consecutive years—601, 602, 603, 604, and 605—a certain emperor began construction of six monuments: F, G, H, L, M, and S. A historian is trying to determine the years in which the individual monuments were begun. The following facts have been established:

L was begun in a later year than G, but in an earlier year than F.

H was begun no earlier than 604.

M was begun earlier than 604.

Two of the monuments were begun in 601, and no other monument was begun in the same year as any of the other monuments.

1. Which one of the following could be an accurate matching of monuments to the years in which they were begun?

	601	602	603	604	605
(A)	601: G;	602: L, S;	603: M;	604: H;	605: F
(B)	601: G,M;	602: L;	603: H;	604: S;	605: F
(C)	601: G, M;	602: S;	603: F;	604: L;	605: H
(D)	601: G, S;	602: L;	603: F;	604: M;	605: H
(E)	601: G, S;	602: L;	603: M;	604: H;	605: F

2. What is the latest year in which L could have been begun?

(A) 601
(B) 602
(C) 603
(D) 604
(E) 605

3. The years in which each of the monuments were begun can be completely determined if which one of the following is discovered to be true?

(A) F was begun in 603.
(B) G was begun in 602.
(C) H was begun in 605.
(D) M was begun in 602.
(E) S was begun in 604.

4. Which one of the following must be true?

(A) F was begun in a later year than M.
(B) F was begun in a later year than S.
(C) H was begun in a later year than F.
(D) H was begun in a later year than S.
(E) M was begun in a later year than G.

5. L must be the monument that was begun in 602 if which one of the following is true?

(A) F was begun in 605.
(B) G was begun in 601.
(C) H was begun in 604.
(D) M was begun in 601.
(E) S was begun in 603.

6. If M was begun in a later year than L, then which one of the following could be true?

(A) F was begun in 603.
(B) G was begun in 602.
(C) H was begun in 605.
(D) L was begun in 603.
(E) S was begun in 604.

GO ON TO THE NEXT PAGE.

Questions 7–12

A company organizing on-site day care consults with a group of parents composed exclusively of volunteers from among the seven employees—Felicia, Leah, Masatomo, Rochelle, Salman, Terry, and Veena—who have become parents this year. The composition of the volunteer group must be consistent with the following:

If Rochelle volunteers, then so does Masatomo.
If Masatomo volunteers, then so does Terry.
If Salman does not volunteer, then Veena volunteers.
If Rochelle does not volunteer, then Leah volunteers.
If Terry volunteers, then neither Felicia nor Veena volunteers.

7. Which one of the following could be a complete and accurate list of the volunteers?

(A) Felicia, Salman
(B) Masatomo, Rochelle
(C) Leah, Salman, Terry
(D) Salman, Rochelle, Veena
(E) Leah, Salman, Terry, Veena

8. If Veena volunteers, then which one of the following could be true?

(A) Felicia and Rochelle also volunteer.
(B) Felicia and Salman also volunteer.
(C) Leah and Masatomo also volunteer.
(D) Leah and Terry also volunteer.
(E) Salman and Terry also volunteer.

9. If Terry does not volunteer, then which one of the following CANNOT be true?

(A) Felicia volunteers.
(B) Leah volunteers.
(C) Rochelle volunteers.
(D) Salman volunteers.
(E) Veena volunteers.

10. If Masatomo volunteers, then which one of the following could be true?

(A) Felicia volunteers.
(B) Leah volunteers.
(C) Veena volunteers.
(D) Salman does not volunteer.
(E) Terry does not volunteer.

11. If Felicia volunteers, then which one of the following must be true?

(A) Leah volunteers.
(B) Salman volunteers.
(C) Veena does not volunteer.
(D) Exactly three of the employees volunteer.
(E) Exactly four of the employees volunteer.

12. Which one of the following pairs of employees is such that at least one member of the pair volunteers?

(A) Felicia and Terry
(B) Leah and Masatomo
(C) Leah and Veena
(D) Rochelle and Salman
(E) Salman and Terry

GO ON TO THE NEXT PAGE.

Questions 13–17

Flyhigh Airlines owns exactly two planes: P and Q. Getaway Airlines owns exactly three planes: R, S, T. On Sunday, each plane makes exactly one flight, according to the following conditions:

Only one plane departs at a time.
Each plane makes either a domestic or an international flight, but not both.
Plane P makes an international flight.
Planes Q and R make domestic flights.
All international flights depart before any domestic flight.
Any Getaway domestic flight departs before Flyhigh's domestic flight.

13. Which one of the following could be the order, from first to last, in which the five planes depart?

(A) P, Q, R, S, T
(B) P, Q, T, S, R
(C) P, S, T, Q, R
(D) P, S, T, R, Q
(E) T, S, R, P, Q

14. The plane that departs second could be any one of exactly how many of the planes?

(A) one
(B) two
(C) three
(D) four
(E) five

15. If plane S departs sometime before plane P, then which one of the following must be false?

(A) Plane S departs first.
(B) Plane S departs third.
(C) Plane T departs second.
(D) Plane T departs third.
(E) Plane T departs fourth.

16. Which one of the following must be true?

(A) Plane P departs first.
(B) Plane Q departs last.
(C) Plane R departs second.
(D) Plane S departs first.
(E) Plane T departs fourth.

17. If plane S departs third, then each of the following can be true EXCEPT:

(A) Plane R departs sometime before plane S and sometime before plane T.
(B) Plane S departs sometime before plane Q and sometime before plane T.
(C) Plane S departs sometime before plane R and sometime before plane T.
(D) Plane T departs sometime before plane P and sometime before plane S.
(E) Plane T departs sometime before plane R and sometime before plane S.

GO ON TO THE NEXT PAGE.

Questions 18–23

A student is choosing courses to take during a summer school session. Each summer school student must take at least three courses from among the following seven: history, linguistics, music, physics, statistics, theater, and writing. The summer school schedule restricts the courses a student can take in the following ways:

If history is taken, then neither statistics nor music can be taken.
If music is taken, then neither physics nor theater can be taken.
If writing is taken, then neither physics nor statistics can be taken.

18. The student could take which one of the following groups of courses during the summer school session?

(A) history, linguistics, and statistics
(B) history, music, and physics
(C) history, physics, and theater
(D) linguistics, physics, theater, and writing
(E) music, theater, and writing

19. What is the maximum number of courses the student could take during the summer school session?

(A) seven
(B) six
(C) five
(D) four
(E) three

20. If the student takes neither physics nor writing, then it could be true that the student also takes neither

(A) history nor linguistics
(B) history nor music
(C) history nor statistics
(D) linguistics nor music
(E) statistics nor theater

21. If the student takes music, then which one of the following must the student also take?

(A) writing
(B) theater
(C) statistics
(D) physics
(E) linguistics

22. The student must take one or the other or both of

(A) history or statistics
(B) linguistics or theater
(C) linguistics or writing
(D) music or physics
(E) theater or writing

23. Which one of the following, if substituted for the restriction that if music is taken, then neither physics nor theater can be taken, would have the same effect in determining which courses the student can take?

(A) If music is taken, then either statistics or writing must also be taken.
(B) The only courses that are eligible to be taken together with music are linguistics, statistics, and writing.
(C) The only courses that are eligible to be taken together with physics are history and linguistics.
(D) The only courses that are eligible to be taken together with theater are history, linguistics, and writing.
(E) If both physics and theater are taken, then music cannot be taken.

S T O P

IF YOU FINISH BEFORE TIME IS CALLED, YOU MAY CHECK YOUR WORK ON THIS SECTION ONLY.
DO NOT WORK ON ANY OTHER SECTION IN THE TEST.

SECTION IV

Time—35 minutes

25 Questions

Directions: The questions in this section are based on the reasoning contained in brief statements or passages. For some questions, more than one of the choices could conceivably answer the question. However, you are to choose the best answer; that is, the response that most accurately and completely answers the question. You should not make assumptions that are by commonsense standards implausible, superfluous, or incompatible with the passage. After you have chosen the best answer, blacken the corresponding space on your answer sheet.

1. Automated flight technology can guide an aircraft very reliably, from navigation to landing. Yet this technology, even when functioning correctly, is not a perfect safeguard against human error.

   Which one of the following, if true, most helps to explain the situation described above?

   (A) Automated flight technology does not always function correctly.
   (B) Smaller aircraft do not always have their automated flight technology updated regularly.
   (C) If a plane's automated flight technology malfunctions, crew members have to operate the plane manually.
   (D) Some airplane crashes are due neither to human error nor to malfunction of automated flight technology.
   (E) Automated flight technology invariably executes exactly the commands that humans give it.

2. To keep one's hands warm during the winter, one never needs gloves or mittens. One can always keep one's hands warm simply by putting on an extra layer of clothing, such as a thermal undershirt or a sweater. After all, keeping one's vital organs warm can keep one's hands warm as well.

   Which one of the following, if true, most weakens the argument?

   (A) Maintaining the temperature of your hands is far less important, physiologically, than maintaining the temperature of your torso.
   (B) Several layers of light garments will keep one's vital organs warmer than will one or two heavy garments.
   (C) Wearing an extra layer of clothing will not keep one's hands warm at temperatures low enough to cause frostbite.
   (D) Keeping one's hands warm by putting on an extra layer of clothing is less effective than turning up the heat.
   (E) The physical effort required to put on an extra layer of clothing does not stimulate circulation enough to warm your hands.

3. The reason music with a simple recurring rhythm exerts a strong primordial appeal is that it reminds us of the womb environment. After all, the first sound heard within the womb is the comforting sound of the mother's regular heartbeat. So in taking away from us the warmth and security of the womb, birth also takes away a primal and constant source of comfort. Thus it is extremely natural that in seeking sensations of warmth and security throughout life, people would be strongly drawn toward simple recurring rhythmic sounds.

   Which one of the following most accurately expresses the main conclusion drawn in the reasoning above?

   (A) The explanation of the strong primordial appeal of music with a simple recurring rhythm is that it reminds us of the womb environment.
   (B) The comforting sound of the mother's regular heartbeat is the first sound that is heard inside the womb.
   (C) Birth deprives us of a primal and constant source of comfort when it takes away the warmth and security of the womb.
   (D) People seek sensations of warmth and security throughout life because birth takes away the warmth and security of the womb.
   (E) The comforting sound of the mother's regular heartbeat is a simple recurring rhythmic sound.

GO ON TO THE NEXT PAGE.

4. Linguist: Most people can tell whether a sequence of words in their own dialect is grammatical. Yet few people who can do so are able to specify the relevant grammatical rules.

Which one of the following best illustrates the principle underlying the linguist's statements?

(A) Some people are able to write cogent and accurate narrative descriptions of events. But these people are not necessarily also capable of composing emotionally moving and satisfying poems.
(B) Engineers who apply the principles of physics to design buildings and bridges must know a great deal more than do the physicists who discover these principles.
(C) Some people are able to tell whether any given piece of music is a waltz. But the majority of these people cannot state the defining characteristics of a waltz.
(D) Those travelers who most enjoy their journeys are not always those most capable of vividly describing the details of those journeys to others.
(E) Quite a few people know the rules of chess, but only a small number of them can play chess very well.

5. Company president: For the management consultant position, we shall interview only those applicants who have worked for management consulting firms generally recognized as in the top 1 percent of firms worldwide. When we finally select somebody, then, we can be sure to have selected one of the best management consultants available.

The company president's reasoning is most vulnerable to criticism on the grounds that it

(A) takes for granted that only the best management consultants have worked for the top management consulting firms
(B) generalizes from too small a sample of management consulting firms worldwide
(C) takes for granted that if something is true of each member of a collection, then it is also true of the collection as a whole
(D) presumes, without providing warrant, that persons who have worked for the top companies will accept a job offer
(E) presumes, without providing justification, that highly competent management consultants are highly competent at every task

6. Beginners typically decide each chess move by considering the consequences. Expert players, in contrast, primarily use pattern-recognition techniques. That is, such a player recognizes having been in a similar position before and makes a decision based on information recalled about the consequences of moves chosen on that prior occasion.

Which one of the following is most strongly supported by the information above?

(A) Beginning chess players are better at thinking through the consequences of chess moves than experts are.
(B) A beginning chess player should use pattern-recognition techniques when deciding what move to make.
(C) One's chess skills will improve only if one learns to use pattern-recognition techniques.
(D) In playing chess, an expert player relies crucially on his or her memory.
(E) Any chess player who played other games that require pattern-recognition skills would thereby improve his or her chess skills.

7. Farmer: Because water content is what makes popcorn pop, the kernels must dry at just the right speed to trap the correct amount of water. The best way to achieve this effect is to have the sun dry the corn while the corn is still in the field, but I always dry the ears on a screen in a warm, dry room.

Which one of the following, if true, most helps to resolve the apparent discrepancy between the farmer's theory and practice?

(A) The region in which the farmer grows popcorn experiences a long, cloudy season that begins shortly before the popcorn in fields would begin to dry.
(B) Leaving popcorn to dry on its stalks in the field is the least expensive method of drying it.
(C) Drying popcorn on its stalks in the field is only one of several methods that allow the kernels' water content to reach acceptable levels.
(D) When popcorn does not dry sufficiently, it will still pop, but it will take several minutes to do so, even under optimal popping conditions.
(E) If popcorn is allowed to dry too much, it will not pop.

GO ON TO THE NEXT PAGE.

8. Factory manager: One reason the automobile parts this factory produces are expensive is that our manufacturing equipment is outdated and inefficient. Our products would be more competitively priced if we were to refurbish the factory completely with new, more efficient equipment. Therefore, since to survive in today's market we have to make our products more competitively priced, we must completely refurbish the factory in order to survive.

The reasoning in the factory manager's argument is flawed because this argument

(A) fails to recognize that the price of a particular commodity can change over time
(B) shifts without justification from treating something as one way of achieving a goal to treating it as the only way of achieving that goal
(C) argues that one thing is the cause of another when the evidence given indicates that the second thing may in fact be the cause of the first
(D) recommends a solution to a problem without first considering any possible causes of that problem
(E) fails to make a definite recommendation and instead merely suggests that some possible course of action might be effective

9. Two months ago a major shipment of pythons arrived from Africa, resulting in a great number of inexpensive pythons in pet stores. Anyone interested in buying a python, however, should beware: many pythons hatched in Africa are afflicted with a deadly liver disease. Although a few pythons recently hatched in North America have this disease, a much greater proportion of African-hatched pythons have it. The disease is difficult to detect in its early stages, and all pythons die within six months of contracting the disease.

Which one of the following statements can be properly inferred from the statements above?

(A) Some pythons hatched in North America may appear fine but will die within six months as a result of the liver disease.
(B) Pythons that hatch in Africa are more susceptible to the liver disease than are pythons that hatch in North America.
(C) Any python that has not died by the age of six months does not have the liver disease.
(D) The pythons are inexpensively priced because many of them suffer from the liver disease.
(E) Pythons hatched in neither Africa nor North America are not afflicted with the liver disease.

10. Nutritionists believe that a person's daily requirement for vitamins can readily be met by eating five servings of fruits and vegetables daily. However, most people eat far less than this. Thus, most people need to take vitamin pills.

Which one of the following statements, if true, most seriously weakens the argument?

(A) Even five servings of fruits and vegetables a day is insufficient unless the intake is varied to ensure that different vitamins are consumed.
(B) Certain commonly available fruits and vegetables contain considerably more nutrients than others.
(C) Nutritionists sometimes disagree on how much of a fruit or vegetable constitutes a complete serving.
(D) Many commonly consumed foods that are neither fruits nor vegetables are fortified by manufacturers with the vitamins found in fruits and vegetables.
(E) Fruits and vegetables are also important sources of fiber, in forms not found in vitamin pills.

11. Researcher: This fall I returned to a research site to recover the armadillos I had tagged there the previous spring. Since a large majority of the armadillos I recaptured were found within a few hundred yards of the location of their tagging last spring, I concluded that armadillos do not move rapidly into new territories.

Which one of the following is an assumption required by the researcher's argument?

(A) Of the armadillos living in the area of the tagging site last spring, few were able to avoid being tagged by the researcher.
(B) Most of the armadillos tagged the previous spring were not recaptured during the subsequent fall.
(C) Predators did not kill any of the armadillos that had been tagged the previous spring.
(D) The tags identifying the armadillos cannot be removed by the armadillos, either by accident or deliberately.
(E) A large majority of the recaptured armadillos did not move to a new territory in the intervening summer and then move back to the old territory by the fall.

GO ON TO THE NEXT PAGE.

12. Sahira: To make a living from their art, artists of great potential would have to produce work that would gain widespread popular acclaim, instead of their best work. That is why governments are justified in subsidizing artists.

Rahima: Your argument for subsidizing art depends on claiming that to gain widespread popular acclaim, artists must produce something other than their best work; but this need not be true.

In her argument, Rahima

(A) disputes an implicit assumption of Sahira's
(B) presents independent support for Sahira's argument
(C) accepts Sahira's conclusion, but for reasons different from those given by Sahira
(D) uses Sahira's premises to reach a conclusion different from that reached by Sahira
(E) argues that a standard that she claims Sahira uses is self-contradictory

13. Adult frogs are vulnerable to dehydration because of their highly permeable skins. Unlike large adult frogs, small adult frogs have such a low ratio of body weight to skin surface area that they cannot survive in arid climates. The animals' moisture requirements constitute the most important factor determining where frogs can live in the Yucatán peninsula, which has an arid climate in the north and a wet climate in the south.

The information above most strongly supports which one of the following conclusions about frogs in the Yucatán peninsula?

(A) Large adult frogs cannot coexist with small adult frogs in the wet areas.
(B) Frogs living in wet areas weigh more on average than frogs in the arid areas.
(C) Large adult frogs can live in more of the area than small adult frogs can.
(D) Fewer small adult frogs live in the south than do large adult frogs.
(E) Small adult frogs in the south have less permeable skins than small adult frogs in the north.

14. Editorial: A recent survey shows that 77 percent of people feel that crime is increasing and that 87 percent feel the judicial system should be handing out tougher sentences. Therefore, the government must firmly address the rising crime rate.

The reasoning in the editorial's argument is most vulnerable to criticism on the grounds that the argument

(A) appeals to survey results that are inconsistent because they suggest that more people are concerned about the sentencing of criminals than are concerned about crime itself
(B) presumes, without providing justification, that there is a correlation between criminal offenders being treated leniently and a high crime rate
(C) fails to consider whether other surveys showing different results have been conducted over the years
(D) fails to distinguish between the crime rate's actually rising and people's believing that the crime rate is rising
(E) presumes, without providing justification, that tougher sentences are the most effective means of alleviating the crime problem

15. Proofs relying crucially on computers provide less certainty than do proofs not requiring computers. Human cognition alone cannot verify computer-dependent proofs; such proofs can never provide the degree of certainty that attends our judgments concerning, for instance, simple arithmetical facts, which can be verified by human calculation. Of course, in these cases one often uses electronic calculators, but here the computer is a convenience rather than a supplement to human cognition.

The statements above, if true, most strongly support which one of the following?

(A) Only if a proof's result is arrived at without the help of a computer can one judge with any degree of certainty that the proof is correct.
(B) We can never be completely sure that proofs relying crucially on computers do not contain errors that humans do not detect.
(C) Whenever a computer replaces human calculation in a proof, the degree of certainty provided by the proof is reduced.
(D) If one can corroborate something by human calculation, one can be completely certain of it.
(E) It is impossible to supplement the cognitive abilities of humans by means of artificial devices such as computers.

GO ON TO THE NEXT PAGE.

16. Madden: Industrialists address problems by simplifying them, but in farming that strategy usually leads to oversimplification. For example, industrialists see water retention and drainage as different and opposite functions—that good topsoil both drains and retains water is a fact alien to industrial logic. To facilitate water retention, they use a terrace or a dam; to facilitate drainage, they use drain tile, a ditch, or a subsoiler. More farming problems are created than solved when agriculture is the domain of the industrialist, not of the farmer.

The situation as Madden describes it best illustrates which one of the following propositions?

(A) The handling of water drainage and retention is the most important part of good farming.
(B) The problems of farming should be viewed in all their complexity.
(C) Farmers are better than anyone else at solving farming problems.
(D) Industrial solutions for problems in farming should never be sought.
(E) The approach to problem solving typical of industrialists is fundamentally flawed.

17. Critic: Works of modern literature cannot be tragedies as those of ancient playwrights and storytellers were unless their protagonists are seen as possessing nobility, which endures through the calamities that befall one. In an age that no longer takes seriously the belief that human endeavors are governed by fate, it is therefore impossible for a contemporary work of literature to be a tragedy.

Which one of the following is an assumption required by the critic's argument?

(A) Whether or not a work of literature is a tragedy should not depend on characteristics of its audience.
(B) The belief that human endeavors are governed by fate is false.
(C) Most plays that were once classified as tragedies were misclassified.
(D) Those whose endeavors are not regarded as governed by fate will not be seen as possessing nobility.
(E) If an ignoble character in a work of literature endures through a series of misfortunes, that work of literature is not a tragedy.

18. Despite the efforts of a small minority of graduate students at one university to unionize, the majority of graduate students there remain unaware of the attempt. Most of those who are aware believe that a union would not represent their interests or that, if it did, it would not effectively pursue them. Thus, the graduate students at the university should not unionize, since the majority of them obviously disapprove of the attempt.

The reasoning in the argument is most vulnerable to criticism on the grounds that the argument

(A) tries to establish a conclusion simply on the premise that the conclusion agrees with a long-standing practice
(B) fails to exclude alternative explanations for why some graduate students disapprove of unionizing
(C) presumes that simply because a majority of a population is unaware of something, it must not be a good idea
(D) ignores the possibility that although a union might not effectively pursue graduate student interests, there are other reasons for unionizing
(E) blurs the distinction between active disapproval and mere lack of approval

19. Anyone who believes in democracy has a high regard for the wisdom of the masses. Griley, however, is an elitist who believes that any artwork that is popular is unlikely to be good. Thus, Griley does not believe in democracy.

The conclusion follows logically if which one of the following is assumed?

(A) Anyone who believes that an artwork is unlikely to be good if it is popular is an elitist.
(B) Anyone who believes that if an artwork is popular it is unlikely to be good does not have a high regard for the wisdom of the masses.
(C) If Griley is not an elitist, then he has a high regard for the wisdom of the masses.
(D) Anyone who does not have a high regard for the wisdom of the masses is an elitist who believes that if an artwork is popular it is unlikely to be good.
(E) Unless Griley believes in democracy, Griley does not have a high regard for the wisdom of the masses.

GO ON TO THE NEXT PAGE.

20. A recent study confirmed that salt intake tends to increase blood pressure and found that, as a result, people with high blood pressure who significantly cut their salt intake during the study had lower blood pressure by the end of the study. However, it was also found that some people who had very high salt intake both before and throughout the study maintained very low blood pressure.

Which one of the following, if true, contributes the most to an explanation of the results of the study?

(A) Study participants with high blood pressure who cut their salt intake only slightly during the study did not have significantly lower blood pressure by the end of the study.
(B) Salt intake is only one of several dietary factors associated with high blood pressure.
(C) For most people who have high blood pressure, reducing salt intake is not the most effective dietary change they can make to reduce their blood pressure.
(D) At the beginning of the study, some people who had very low salt intake also had very high blood pressure.
(E) Persons suffering from abnormally low blood pressure have heightened salt cravings, which ensure that their blood pressure does not drop too low.

21. The odds of winning any major lottery jackpot are extremely slight. However, the very few people who do win major jackpots receive a great deal of attention from the media. Thus, since most people come to have at least some awareness of events that receive extensive media coverage, it is likely that many people greatly overestimate the odds of their winning a major jackpot.

Which one of the following is an assumption on which the argument depends?

(A) Most people who overestimate the likelihood of winning a major jackpot do so at least in part because media coverage of other people who have won major jackpots downplays the odds against winning such a jackpot.
(B) Very few people other than those who win major jackpots receive a great deal of attention from the media.
(C) If it were not for media attention, most people who purchase lottery tickets would not overestimate their chances of winning a jackpot.
(D) Becoming aware of individuals who have won a major jackpot leads at least some people to incorrectly estimate their own chances of winning such a jackpot.
(E) At least some people who are heavily influenced by the media do not believe that the odds of their winning a major jackpot are significant.

GO ON TO THE NEXT PAGE.

22. A book tour will be successful if it is well publicized and the author is an established writer. Julia is an established writer, and her book tour was successful. So her book tour must have been well publicized.

Which one of the following exhibits a pattern of flawed reasoning most closely parallel to the pattern of flawed reasoning exhibited by the argument above?

(A) This recipe will turn out only if one follows it exactly and uses high-quality ingredients. Arthur followed the recipe exactly and it turned out. Thus, Arthur must have used high-quality ingredients.
(B) If a computer has the fastest microprocessor and the most memory available, it will meet Aletha's needs this year. This computer met Aletha's needs last year. So it must have had the fastest microprocessor and the most memory available last year.
(C) If cacti are kept in the shade and watered more than twice weekly, they will die. This cactus was kept in the shade, and it is now dead. Therefore, it must have been watered more than twice weekly.
(D) A house will suffer from dry rot and poor drainage only if it is built near a high water table. This house suffers from dry rot and has poor drainage. Thus, it must have been built near a high water table.
(E) If one wears a suit that has double vents and narrow lapels, one will be fashionably dressed. The suit that Joseph wore to dinner last night had double vents and narrow lapels, so Joseph must have been fashionably dressed.

23. Eight large craters run in a long straight line across a geographical region. Although some of the craters contain rocks that have undergone high-pressure shocks characteristic of meteorites slamming into Earth, these shocks could also have been caused by extreme volcanic events. Because of the linearity of the craters, it is very unlikely that some of them were caused by volcanoes and others were caused by meteorites. Thus, since the craters are all different ages, they were probably caused by volcanic events rather than meteorites.

Which one of the following statements, if true, would most strengthen the argument?

(A) A similar but shorter line of craters that are all the same age is known to have been caused by volcanic activity.
(B) No known natural cause would likely account for eight meteorite craters of different ages forming a straight line.
(C) There is no independent evidence of either meteorites or volcanic activity in the region where the craters are located.
(D) There is no independent evidence of a volcanic event strong enough to have created the high-pressure shocks that are characteristic of meteorites slamming into Earth.
(E) No known single meteor shower has created exactly eight impact craters that form a straight line.

GO ON TO THE NEXT PAGE.

24. The genuine creative genius is someone who is dissatisfied with merely habitual assent to widely held beliefs; thus these rare innovators tend to anger the majority. Those who are dissatisfied with merely habitual assent to widely held beliefs tend to seek out controversy, and controversy seekers enjoy demonstrating the falsehood of popular viewpoints.

The conclusion of the argument follows logically if which one of the following is assumed?

(A) People become angry when they are dissatisfied with merely habitual assent to widely held beliefs.
(B) People who enjoy demonstrating the falsehood of popular viewpoints anger the majority.
(C) People tend to get angry with individuals who hold beliefs not held by a majority of people.
(D) People who anger the majority enjoy demonstrating the falsehood of popular viewpoints.
(E) People who anger the majority are dissatisfied with merely habitual assent to widely held beliefs.

25. Claude: When I'm having lunch with job candidates, I watch to see if they salt their food without first tasting it. If they do, I count that against them, because they're making decisions based on inadequate information.

Larissa: That's silly. It's perfectly reasonable for me to wear a sweater whenever I go into a supermarket, because I already know supermarkets are always too cool inside to suit me. And I never open a credit card offer that comes in the mail, because I already know that no matter how low its interest rate may be, it will never be worthwhile for me.

The two analogies that Larissa offers can most reasonably be interpreted as invoking which one of the following principles to criticize Claude's policy?

(A) In matters involving personal preference, performing an action without first ascertaining whether it is appropriate in the specific circumstances should not be taken as good evidence of faulty decision making, because the action may be based on a reasoned policy relating to knowledge of a general fact about the circumstances.
(B) In professional decision-making contexts, those who have the responsibility of judging other people's suitability for a job should not use observations of job-related behavior as a basis for inferring general conclusions about those people's character.
(C) General conclusions regarding a job candidate's suitability for a position should not be based exclusively on observations of the candidate's behavior in situations that are neither directly job related nor likely to be indicative of a pattern of behavior that the candidate engages in.
(D) Individuals whose behavior in specific circumstances does not conform to generally expected norms should not automatically be considered unconcerned with meeting social expectations, because such individuals may be acting in accordance with reasoned policies that they believe should be generally adopted by people in similar circumstances.
(E) Evidence that a particular individual uses bad decision-making strategies in matters of personal taste should not be considered sufficient to warrant a negative assessment of his or her suitability for a job, because any good decision maker can have occasional lapses of rationality with regard to such matters.

S T O P

IF YOU FINISH BEFORE TIME IS CALLED, YOU MAY CHECK YOUR WORK ON THIS SECTION ONLY.
DO NOT WORK ON ANY OTHER SECTION IN THE TEST.

Acknowledgment is made to the following sources from which material has been adapted for use in this test booklet:

Elizabeth Wayland Barber, *Women's Work: The First 20,000 Years: Women, Cloth, and Society in Early Times.* ©1994 by Elizabeth Wayland Barber.

LSAT WRITING SAMPLE TOPIC

Directions: The scenario presented below describes two choices, either one of which can be supported on the basis of the information given. Your essay should consider both choices and argue for one over the other, based on the two specified criteria and the facts provided. There is no "right" or "wrong" choice: a reasonable argument can be made for either.

A local amateur astronomical association is going to build a new observatory that will house a medium-sized telescope near the association's home town of Brenton. The association has narrowed the possible building sites down to two. Using the facts below, write an essay in which you argue for one site over the other based on the following two criteria:

- The site should provide seeing conditions for the use of the telescope that minimize atmospheric haze and sources of light pollution.
- The site should facilitate holding public observing sessions and lectures on astronomy for people from Brenton.

The first site is on top of a 2,000 foot (600 meter) ridge within a small forest park. This height is above some of the atmosphere's haze. To reach the summit, visitors must drive up a gravel road that is narrow and winding. Light pollution from a relatively distant megalopolis seriously affects about a quarter of the night sky. Currently, the land surrounding the park is mostly undeveloped farmland. How much will be developed is unpredictable.

The second site is almost at sea level in the middle of a large forest park. Some of the land near the site is swampy. City lights cause some light pollution across about a quarter of the night sky. The roads from Brenton to the site are all paved and in good condition. The travel time to this site from Brenton is about a third less than that to the first site. Unscheduled visitors are more likely at this site than at the first site. They could disturb the work of the amateur astronomers.

Scratch Paper

Do not write your essay in this space.

Directions:

1. Use the Answer Key on the next page to check your answers.

2. Use the Scoring Worksheet below to compute your raw score.

3. Use the Score Conversion Chart to convert your raw score into the 120–180 scale.

Scoring Worksheet

1. Enter the number of questions you answered correctly in each section.

	Number Correct
SECTION I..........	______
SECTION II..........	______
SECTION III.........	______
SECTION IV.........	______

2. Enter the sum here: ______ **This is your Raw Score.**

Conversion Chart

For Converting Raw Score to the 120–180 LSAT Scaled Score
LSAT PrepTest 58

REPORTED SCORE	LOWEST RAW SCORE	HIGHEST RAW SCORE
180	99	101
179	—*	—*
178	98	98
177	97	97
176	96	96
175	95	95
174	—*	—*
173	94	94
172	93	93
171	91	92
170	90	90
169	89	89
168	88	88
167	86	87
166	85	85
165	84	84
164	82	83
163	80	81
162	79	79
161	77	78
160	75	76
159	74	74
158	72	73
157	70	71
156	69	69
155	67	68
154	65	66
153	63	64
152	61	62
151	60	60
150	58	59
149	56	57
148	54	55
147	53	53
146	51	52
145	49	50
144	47	48
143	46	46
142	44	45
141	42	43
140	41	41
139	39	40
138	38	38
137	36	37
136	34	35
135	33	33
134	31	32
133	30	30
132	29	29
131	27	28
130	26	26
129	25	25
128	23	24
127	22	22
126	21	21
125	20	20
124	18	19
123	17	17
122	16	16
121	15	15
120	0	14

*There is no raw score that will produce this scaled score for this PrepTest.

SECTION I

1.	C	8.	E	15.	D	22.	C
2.	D	9.	E	16.	E	23.	C
3.	E	10.	B	17.	B	24.	E
4.	E	11.	A	18.	C	25.	A
5.	A	12.	D	19.	D	26.	A
6.	A	13.	B	20.	E		
7.	B	14.	D	21.	C		

SECTION II

1.	B	8.	D	15.	A	22.	C
2.	E	9.	C	16.	B	23.	B
3.	E	10.	A	17.	A	24.	A
4.	D	11.	B	18.	E	25.	C
5.	C	12.	A	19.	C	26.	B
6.	E	13.	E	20.	D	27.	D
7.	A	14.	B	21.	E		

SECTION III

1.	E	8.	B	15.	B	22.	B
2.	C	9.	C	16.	B	23.	B
3.	E	10.	B	17.	C		
4.	A	11.	A	18.	C		
5.	E	12.	B	19.	D		
6.	C	13.	D	20.	B		
7.	C	14.	D	21.	E		

SECTION IV

1.	E	8.	B	15.	B	22.	C
2.	C	9.	A	16.	B	23.	B
3.	A	10.	D	17.	D	24.	B
4.	C	11.	E	18.	E	25.	A
5.	A	12.	A	19.	B		
6.	D	13.	C	20.	E		
7.	A	14.	D	21.	D		

Experimental Section Answer Key
June 1999, PrepTest 27, Section 4

1.	C	8.	B	15.	C	22.	E
2.	B	9.	E	16.	D	23.	E
3.	A	10.	B	17.	A	24.	C
4.	D	11.	D	18.	B	25.	E
5.	C	12.	A	19.	A		
6.	E	13.	D	20.	A		
7.	D	14.	C	21.	D		

PrepTest 59
December 2009

SECTION I

Time—35 minutes

23 Questions

Directions: Each group of questions in this section is based on a set of conditions. In answering some of the questions, it may be useful to draw a rough diagram. Choose the response that most accurately and completely answers each question and blacken the corresponding space on your answer sheet.

Questions 1–5

A law firm has seven departments—family law, health law, injury law, labor law, probate, securities, and tax law. The firm is to occupy a building with three floors—the bottom floor, the middle floor, and the top floor. Each floor can accommodate up to four departments, and no department is to be on more than one floor. Assignment of departments to floors is subject to the following constraints:

Probate must be on the same floor as tax law.
Health law must be on the floor immediately above injury law.
Labor law must occupy an entire floor by itself.

1. Which one of the following could be the assignment of departments to floors?

(A) top floor: labor law
middle floor: injury law, probate, tax law
bottom floor: family law, health law, securities
(B) top floor: family law, health law, probate
middle floor: injury law, securities, tax law
bottom floor: labor law
(C) top floor: health law, probate, tax law
middle floor: family law, injury law, securities
bottom floor: labor law
(D) top floor: health law, probate, tax law
middle floor: injury law, securities
bottom floor: family law, labor law
(E) top floor: family law, health law, probate, tax law
middle floor: labor law
bottom floor: injury law, securities

2. If injury law and probate are both assigned to the middle floor, which one of the following could be true?

(A) Family law is assigned to the middle floor.
(B) Health law is assigned to the middle floor.
(C) Labor law is assigned to the top floor.
(D) Securities is assigned to the bottom floor.
(E) Tax law is assigned to the top floor.

3. Which one of the following CANNOT be the assignment for any of the floors?

(A) family law, health law, probate, and tax law
(B) family law, injury law, probate, and tax law
(C) family law, probate, securities, and tax law
(D) health law, probate, securities, and tax law
(E) injury law, probate, securities, and tax law

4. If family law is assigned to the same floor as securities, which one of the following could be true?

(A) Exactly one department is assigned to the middle floor.
(B) Exactly four departments are assigned to the middle floor.
(C) Exactly two departments are assigned to the bottom floor.
(D) Exactly three departments are assigned to the bottom floor.
(E) Exactly four departments are assigned to the bottom floor.

5. If probate is assigned to the middle floor along with exactly two other departments, then which one of the following must be true?

(A) Family law is assigned to the floor immediately above health law.
(B) Family law is assigned to the floor immediately below labor law.
(C) Family law is assigned to the same floor as securities.
(D) Probate is assigned to the same floor as health law.
(E) Probate is assigned to the same floor as injury law.

GO ON TO THE NEXT PAGE.

Questions 6–10

A museum curator is arranging seven photographs—*Fence*, *Gardenias*, *Hibiscus*, *Irises*, *Katydid*, *Lotus*, and *Magnolia*—on a gallery wall in accordance with the photographer's requirements. The photographs are to be hung along the wall in a row, in seven positions sequentially numbered from first to seventh. The photographer's requirements are as follows:

Gardenias must be immediately before *Katydid*.
Hibiscus must be somewhere before *Katydid* but cannot be the first photograph.
Irises and *Lotus* must be next to one another.
Magnolia must be one of the first three photographs.
Fence must be either first or seventh.

6. Which one of the following could be the positions, from first to seventh, in which the photographs are hung?
   (A) *Fence*, *Hibiscus*, *Gardenias*, *Magnolia*, *Katydid*, *Irises*, *Lotus*
   (B) *Hibiscus*, *Magnolia*, *Gardenias*, *Katydid*, *Irises*, *Lotus*, *Fence*
   (C) *Irises*, *Lotus*, *Magnolia*, *Hibiscus*, *Gardenias*, *Katydid*, *Fence*
   (D) *Lotus*, *Magnolia*, *Irises*, *Hibiscus*, *Gardenias*, *Katydid*, *Fence*
   (E) *Magnolia*, *Fence*, *Hibiscus*, *Gardenias*, *Katydid*, *Lotus*, *Irises*

7. If *Irises* is immediately before *Gardenias*, which one of the following could be true?
   (A) *Gardenias* is fourth.
   (B) *Hibiscus* is fourth.
   (C) *Irises* is third.
   (D) *Lotus* is second.
   (E) *Magnolia* is third.

8. Where each photograph is hung is fully determined if which one of the following is true?
   (A) *Gardenias* is fourth.
   (B) *Hibiscus* is second.
   (C) *Irises* is second.
   (D) *Lotus* is first.
   (E) *Magnolia* is third.

9. If *Magnolia* is second, which one of the following CANNOT be true?
   (A) *Hibiscus* is third.
   (B) *Hibiscus* is fourth.
   (C) *Hibiscus* is fifth.
   (D) *Gardenias* is fourth.
   (E) *Gardenias* is sixth.

10. Which one of the following, if substituted for the condition that *Hibiscus* must be hung somewhere before *Katydid* but cannot be the first photograph, would have the same effect in determining the arrangement of the photographs?
   (A) If *Fence* is seventh, *Hibiscus* is second.
   (B) *Gardenias* is somewhere after *Hibiscus*, and either *Fence* or *Magnolia* is first.
   (C) *Hibiscus* must be somewhere between the first and sixth photographs.
   (D) Unless *Hibiscus* is second, it must be somewhere between *Magnolia* and *Gardenias*.
   (E) *Katydid* is somewhere after *Hibiscus*, which must be somewhere after *Fence*.

GO ON TO THE NEXT PAGE.

Questions 11–16

Alicia will take exactly four courses this semester. She must choose from the following seven courses—Geography, Japanese, Macroeconomics, Psychology, Russian, Statistics (which is offered twice, once each on Tuesdays at 9 A.M. and 3 P.M.), and World History. No one is allowed to take any course more than once per semester. Because of university requirements and time conflicts, the following restrictions apply to Alicia's choices:

She must take Japanese if she does not take Russian.
She cannot take Japanese if she takes Macroeconomics.
She cannot take World History if she takes Statistics at 9 A.M.
She must take Statistics at 9 A.M. if she takes Psychology.
She must take either Geography or World History but cannot take both.

11. Which one of the following could be the list of the four courses Alicia takes?

(A) Geography, Japanese, Psychology, Russian
(B) Geography, Macroeconomics, Psychology, Statistics
(C) Geography, Japanese, Macroeconomics, Russian
(D) Geography, Psychology, Russian, Statistics
(E) Macroeconomics, Psychology, Russian, Statistics

12. Which one of the following could be an accurate list of three of the courses Alicia takes?

(A) Geography, Statistics, World History
(B) Japanese, Macroeconomics, Statistics
(C) Japanese, Psychology, World History
(D) Psychology, Russian, World History
(E) Russian, Statistics, World History

13. Which courses Alicia takes is fully determined if she takes Russian and which one of the following?

(A) World History
(B) Statistics
(C) Psychology
(D) Macroeconomics
(E) Japanese

14. Alicia could take Statistics at either of the available times if she takes which one of the following pairs of courses?

(A) Geography and Japanese
(B) Geography and Psychology
(C) Japanese and World History
(D) Psychology and Russian
(E) Russian and World History

15. If Alicia takes Statistics at 3 P.M. and Geography, then which one of the following courses must she also take?

(A) Japanese
(B) Macroeconomics
(C) Psychology
(D) Russian
(E) World History

16. Suppose that Alicia must take Statistics if she takes Psychology, but rather than being restricted to taking Statistics at 9 A.M. she can take it at either 9 A.M. or at 3 P.M. If all the other restrictions remain the same, then which one of the following could be the list of the four courses Alicia takes?

(A) Psychology, Russian, Statistics, World History
(B) Macroeconomics, Psychology, Statistics, World History
(C) Macroeconomics, Psychology, Russian, World History
(D) Geography, Psychology, Russian, World History
(E) Geography, Macroeconomics, Russian, World History

GO ON TO THE NEXT PAGE.

Questions 17–23

An organization will hold its first six annual meetings in exactly six cities—Los Angeles, Montreal, New York, Toronto, Vancouver, and Washington—using each city only once. The following conditions govern the order in which the cities are used:

Los Angeles must be used in some year after the year in which Toronto is used.

Vancouver must be used either immediately before or immediately after Washington.

The meeting in Toronto must be separated from the meeting in Montreal by meetings in exactly two other cities.

The meeting in Vancouver must be separated from the meeting in Los Angeles by meetings in exactly two other cities.

17. Which one of the following lists the cities in an order in which they could be used for the meetings, from the first year through the sixth?

(A) Toronto, Vancouver, Washington, Montreal, Los Angeles, New York
(B) Vancouver, Washington, Montreal, Los Angeles, New York, Toronto
(C) Vancouver, Washington, Toronto, New York, Los Angeles, Montreal
(D) Washington, Montreal, Vancouver, New York, Toronto, Los Angeles
(E) Washington, Vancouver, New York, Toronto, Los Angeles, Montreal

18. Which one of the following must be true?

(A) Toronto is used in the first year.
(B) Montreal is used in the fourth year.
(C) Toronto is used at some time before Montreal is used.
(D) New York is used either immediately before or immediately after Vancouver.
(E) The meeting in New York is separated from the meeting in Washington by meetings in exactly two other cities.

19. There is exactly one possible order in which the cities are used if which one of the following is true?

(A) Los Angeles is used in the fifth year.
(B) Montreal is used in the sixth year.
(C) New York is used in the fifth year.
(D) Vancouver is used in the first year.
(E) Washington is used in the second year.

20. Which one of the following is a complete and accurate list of the years in which Washington could be used?

(A) 1, 3, 5
(B) 2, 3, 4, 5
(C) 2, 3, 4, 6
(D) 1, 2, 4, 6
(E) 1, 2, 3, 4, 5, 6

21. If Montreal is used in the first year, which one of the following CANNOT be true?

(A) Washington is used in the third year.
(B) Vancouver is used in the third year.
(C) Toronto is used in the fourth year.
(D) New York is used in the fifth year.
(E) Los Angeles is used in the third year.

22. Which one of the following could be true?

(A) Los Angeles is used in the first year.
(B) New York is used in the second year.
(C) Montreal is used in the third year.
(D) Vancouver is used in the fourth year.
(E) Toronto is used in the sixth year.

23. Which one of the following must be false?

(A) Los Angeles is used either immediately before or immediately after New York.
(B) Los Angeles is used either immediately before or immediately after Washington.
(C) New York is used either immediately before or immediately after Toronto.
(D) Toronto is used either immediately before or immediately after Vancouver.
(E) Toronto is used either immediately before or immediately after Washington.

S T O P

IF YOU FINISH BEFORE TIME IS CALLED, YOU MAY CHECK YOUR WORK ON THIS SECTION ONLY. DO NOT WORK ON ANY OTHER SECTION IN THE TEST.

SECTION II

Time—35 minutes

26 Questions

Directions: The questions in this section are based on the reasoning contained in brief statements or passages. For some questions, more than one of the choices could conceivably answer the question. However, you are to choose the best answer; that is, the response that most accurately and completely answers the question. You should not make assumptions that are by commonsense standards implausible, superfluous, or incompatible with the passage. After you have chosen the best answer, blacken the corresponding space on your answer sheet.

1. On the Caribbean island of Guadeloupe, a researcher examined 35 patients with atypical Parkinson's disease and compared their eating habits to those of 65 healthy adults. She found that all of the patients with atypical Parkinson's regularly ate the tropical fruits soursop, custard apple, and pomme cannelle, whereas only 10 of the healthy adults regularly ate these fruits. From this, she concluded that eating these fruits causes atypical Parkinson's.

   Which one of the following, if true, most strengthens the researcher's reasoning?

   (A) For many of the atypical Parkinson's patients, their symptoms stopped getting worse, and in some cases actually abated, when they stopped eating soursop, custard apple, and pomme cannelle.
   (B) Of the healthy adults who did not regularly eat soursop, custard apple, and pomme cannelle, most had eaten each of these fruits on at least one occasion.
   (C) In areas other than Guadeloupe, many people who have never eaten soursop, custard apple, and pomme cannelle have contracted atypical Parkinson's.
   (D) The 10 healthy adults who regularly ate soursop, custard apple, and pomme cannelle ate significantly greater quantities of these fruits, on average, than did the 35 atypical Parkinson's patients.
   (E) Soursop, custard apple, and pomme cannelle contain essential vitamins not contained in any other food that is commonly eaten by residents of Guadeloupe.

2. Price: A corporation's primary responsibility is to its shareholders. They are its most important constituency because they take the greatest risks. If the corporation goes bankrupt, they lose their investment.

   Albrecht: Shareholders typically have diversified investment portfolios. For employees, however, the well-being of the corporation for which they have chosen to work represents their very livelihood. The corporation's primary responsibility should be to them.

   On the basis of their statements, Price and Albrecht are committed to disagreeing about whether

   (A) corporations have a responsibility to their shareholders
   (B) corporations are responsible for the welfare of their employees
   (C) means should be provided for a corporation's investors to recoup their losses if the corporation goes bankrupt
   (D) a corporation's shareholders have more at stake than anyone else does in the corporation's success or failure
   (E) the livelihood of some of the shareholders depends on the corporation's success

GO ON TO THE NEXT PAGE.

3. Despite the enormous number of transactions processed daily by banks nowadays, if a customer's bank account is accidentally credited with a large sum of money, it is extremely unlikely that the error will not be detected by the bank's internal audit procedures.

Which one of the following, if true, most strongly supports the claim above?

(A) Banks initially process all transactions using one set of computer programs, but then use a different set of programs to double-check large transactions.
(B) Recent changes in banking standards require that customers present identification both when making deposits into their accounts and when making withdrawals from their accounts.
(C) Banks are required by law to send each customer a monthly statement detailing every transaction of the previous month.
(D) The average ratio of bank auditors to customer accounts has slowly increased over the past 100 years.
(E) The development of sophisticated security software has rendered bank computers nearly impervious to tampering by computer hackers.

4. Scientist: While studying centuries-old Antarctic ice deposits, I found that several years of relatively severe atmospheric pollution in the 1500s coincided with a period of relatively high global temperatures. So it is clear in this case that atmospheric pollution did cause global temperatures to rise.

The reasoning in the scientist's argument is most vulnerable to criticism on the grounds that the argument

(A) presumes, without providing justification, that a rise in global temperatures is harmful
(B) draws a general conclusion based on a sample that is likely to be unrepresentative
(C) inappropriately generalizes from facts about a specific period of time to a universal claim
(D) takes for granted that the method used for gathering data was reliable
(E) infers, merely from a claim that two phenomena are associated, that one phenomenon causes the other

5. Gilbert: This food label is mistaken. It says that these cookies contain only natural ingredients, but they contain alphahydroxy acids that are chemically synthesized by the cookie company at their plant.

Sabina: The label is not mistaken. After all, alphahydroxy acids also are found occurring naturally in sugarcane.

Which one of the following, if true, would most strengthen Sabina's argument?

(A) The cookie company has recently dropped alphahydroxy acids from its cookie ingredients.
(B) Not all chemicals that are part of the manufacturing process are ingredients of the cookies.
(C) The label was printed before the cookie company decided to switch from sugarcane alphahydroxy acids to synthesized ones.
(D) Many other foods advertising all natural ingredients also contain some ingredients that are chemically synthesized.
(E) All substances except those that do not occur naturally in any source are considered natural.

6. Although Jaaks is a respected historian, her negative review of Yancey's new book on the history of coastal fisheries in the region rests on a mistake. Jaaks's review argues that the book inaccurately portrays the lives of fishery workers. However, Yancey used the same research methods in this book as in her other histories, which have been very popular. This book is also very popular in local bookstores.

The reasoning above is flawed in that it

(A) relies on the word of a scholar who is unqualified in the area in question
(B) attacks the person making the claim at issue rather than addressing the claim
(C) takes for granted that the popularity of a book is evidence of its accuracy
(D) bases a general conclusion on a sample that is likely to be unrepresentative
(E) presumes, without providing justification, that the methods used by Yancey are the only methods that would produce accurate results

GO ON TO THE NEXT PAGE.

7. Columnist: It has been noted that attending a live musical performance is a richer experience than is listening to recorded music. Some say that this is merely because we do not see the performers when we listen to recorded music. However, there must be some other reason, for there is relatively little difference between listening to someone read a story over the radio and listening to someone in the same room read a story.

Which one of the following most accurately expresses the role played in the argument by the observation that attending a live musical performance is a richer experience than is listening to recorded music?

(A) It is what the columnist's argument purports to show.
(B) It is the reason given for the claim that the columnist's argument is attempting to undermine.
(C) It is what the columnist's argument purports to explain.
(D) It is what the columnist's argument purports to refute.
(E) It is what the position that the columnist tries to undermine is purported to explain.

8. Though ice cream is an excellent source of calcium, dairy farmers report that during the past ten years there has been a sharp decline in ice cream sales. And during the same period, sales of cheddar cheese have nearly doubled. Therefore, more and more people must be choosing to increase their intake of calcium by eating cheddar cheese rather than ice cream.

The reasoning above is most vulnerable to criticism on the grounds that it

(A) fails to produce statistical evidence supporting the dairy farmers' claims
(B) fails to consider alternative explanations of the decline in sales of ice cream
(C) relies solely on the testimony of individuals who are likely to be biased
(D) presumes, without providing justification, that ice cream is a better source of calcium than is cheddar cheese
(E) presumes, without providing justification, that people who eat cheddar cheese never eat ice cream

9. No member of the Richardson Theater Group is both a performer and an administrator. Since Leon and Marta are both members of the Richardson Theater Group but neither is an administrator, it follows that both are performers.

Which one of the following arguments displays a flawed pattern of reasoning most similar to that in the argument above?

(A) Not all of the employees of the Tedenco Company are salaried employees of that company. Since Mr. López and Ms. Allen are both salaried employees of the Tedenco Company, it follows that they are not the only employees of the Tedenco Company.
(B) No employee of the Tedenco Company is both an accountant and a corporate attorney. Since Ms. Walsh is both an accountant and a corporate attorney, it follows that she is not an employee of the Tedenco Company.
(C) No company can have its headquarters in both Canada and Mexico. Since neither the Dumone Company nor the Tedenco Company has its headquarters in Mexico, it follows that both have their headquarters in Canada.
(D) No corporate attorney represents both the Dumone Company and the Tedenco Company. Since Ms. Tseung is a corporate attorney who represents the Dumone Company, it follows that she does not also represent the Tedenco Company.
(E) No member of the board of directors of the Dumone Company is also a member of the board of directors of the Tedenco Company. Since neither company has fewer than five board members, it follows that both boards together include at least ten members.

10. Chemical fertilizers not only create potential health hazards, they also destroy earthworms, which are highly beneficial to soil. For this reason alone the use of chemical fertilizers should be avoided. The castings earthworms leave behind are much richer than the soil they ingest, thus making a garden rich in earthworms much more fertile than a garden without them.

Which one of the following most accurately expresses the main conclusion of the argument?

(A) Earthworms are highly beneficial to soil.
(B) Chemical fertilizers destroy earthworms.
(C) The castings that earthworms leave behind are much richer than the soil they ingest.
(D) The use of chemical fertilizers should be avoided.
(E) A garden rich in earthworms is much more fertile than a garden that is devoid of earthworms.

GO ON TO THE NEXT PAGE.

11. Medical research has established that the Beta Diet is healthier than a more conventional diet. But on average, people who have followed the Beta Diet for several decades are much more likely to be in poor health than are people whose diet is more conventional.

Which one of the following, if true, most helps to resolve the apparent conflict between the two statements above?

(A) On average, people who have followed the Beta Diet for their entire lives are much more likely to have a variety of healthful habits than are people whose diet is more conventional.
(B) The Beta Diet is used primarily as a treatment for a condition that adversely affects overall health.
(C) People of average health who switch from a conventional diet to the Beta Diet generally find that their health improves substantially as a result.
(D) The Beta Diet provides dramatic health benefits for some people but only minor benefits for others.
(E) Recent research has shown that a diet high in fruits, vegetables, and skim milk is even healthier than the Beta Diet.

12. A theoretical framework facilitates conceptual organization of material and fruitful expansions of research. Many historians argue that historical analysis is therefore done best within a theoretical framework. But the past is too complex for all of its main trends to be captured within a theoretical framework. Therefore, _______.

Which one of the following most logically completes the argument?

(A) there is no benefit ever to be gained in recommending to historians that they place their work within a theoretical framework
(B) theoretical frameworks are less useful in history than they are in any other discipline
(C) even the best historical analysis done within a theoretical framework fails to capture all of history's main trends
(D) the value of theoretical work in extending research has been emphasized by historians who recommend doing historical analysis within a theoretical framework
(E) there is no difference between historical analysis that is placed within a theoretical framework and historical analysis that is not

13. Bethany: Psychologists have discovered a technique for replacing one's nightmares with pleasant dreams, and have successfully taught it to adults suffering from chronic nightmares. Studies have found that nightmare-prone children are especially likely to suffer from nightmares as adults. Thus, psychologists should direct efforts toward identifying nightmare-prone children so that these children can be taught the technique for replacing their nightmares with pleasant dreams.

Which one of the following principles, if valid, most helps to justify drawing the conclusion in Bethany's argument?

(A) Psychologists should make an effort to determine why certain children are especially prone to nightmares while other children are not.
(B) Any psychological technique that can be successfully taught to a child can also be successfully taught to an adult.
(C) Psychologists should do everything they can to minimize the number of adults troubled by chronic nightmares.
(D) Identifying nightmare-prone children is generally more difficult than teaching adults the technique for replacing nightmares with pleasant dreams.
(E) Psychologists should not teach the technique for replacing nightmares with pleasant dreams to children who are unlikely to suffer from nightmares as adults.

14. At one sitting, a typical doughnut eater consumes 4 doughnuts containing a total of 680 calories and 40 grams of fat. The typical bagel eater consumes exactly one bagel, at 500 calories and one or two grams of fat per sitting, though the addition of spreads can raise calorie and fat content to the four-doughnut range. Thus, as far as total calorie content is concerned, there is very little difference between what a typical doughnut eater and a typical bagel eater each consumes at one sitting.

The argument depends on assuming which one of the following?

(A) The calories and fat in bagels have the same health impact on bagel eaters as the calories and fat in doughnuts have on doughnut eaters.
(B) Most bagel eaters are not fully aware of the calorie and fat content of a bagel.
(C) Eating bagels instead of eating doughnuts provides no real health benefit.
(D) The typical doughnut eater does not add to doughnuts any substances that increase the total caloric intake.
(E) Most typical doughnut eaters are not also bagel eaters.

GO ON TO THE NEXT PAGE.

15. Bowers: A few theorists hold the extreme view that society could flourish in a condition of anarchy, the absence of government. Some of these theorists have even produced interesting arguments to support that position. One writer, for example, contends that anarchy is laissez-faire capitalism taken to its logical extreme. But these theorists' views ignore the fundamental principle of social philosophy—that an acceptable social philosophy must promote peace and order. Any social philosophy that countenances chaos, i.e., anarchy, accordingly deserves no further attention.

The reasoning in Bowers's argument is most vulnerable to criticism on the grounds that

(A) the meaning of a key term shifts illicitly during the course of the argument
(B) the argument fails to show that laissez-faire capitalism deserves to be rejected as a social philosophy
(C) the truth or falsity of a view is not determined by the number of people who accept it as true
(D) the argument presumes, without providing justification, that any peaceful society will flourish
(E) it is unreasonable to reject a view merely because it can be described as extreme

16. All poets, aside from those who write only epigrams, have wit. All lyrical composers are poets. Azriel does not write epigrams, though he is a lyrical composer. So Azriel has wit.

The pattern of reasoning in which one of the following is most similar to that in the argument above?

(A) All squeeze toys, except those designed for cats, are safe for infants. All squeeze toys are sold prewrapped. This item is not designed for cats, and it is sold prewrapped. So it must be safe for infants.
(B) Aside from the dogcatcher and the police chief, all of the politicians in town are lawyers. All of the politicians in town have websites. Sal is a politician in town, but is neither the dogcatcher nor the police chief. Since Sal is a politician in town he must have a website.
(C) All visas are assigned by this office, except for those that are issued through diplomatic channels. All visit permits are visas. Thus, the visit permit in Will's passport was assigned through diplomatic channels.
(D) All of this store's winter garments are on sale, except for the designer clothes. None of the shirts in this store are designer clothes. This shirt, therefore, since it is on sale, is a winter garment.
(E) All residential buildings are subject to the original fire code, except for those built last year. All townhouses are residential buildings. Bloom House was not built last year, and it is a townhouse, so it is subject to the original fire code.

17. Teachers should not do anything to cause their students to lose respect for them. And students can sense when someone is trying to hide his or her ignorance. Therefore, a teacher who does not know the answer to a question a student has asked should not pretend to know the answer.

The conclusion is properly drawn if which one of the following is assumed?

(A) A teacher cannot be effective unless he or she retains the respect of students.
(B) Students respect honesty above all else.
(C) Students' respect for a teacher is independent of the amount of knowledge they attribute to that teacher.
(D) Teachers are able to tell when students respect them.
(E) Students lose respect for teachers whenever they sense that the teachers are trying to hide their ignorance.

18. Contrary to Malthus's arguments, human food-producing capacity has increased more rapidly than human population. Yet, agricultural advances often compromise biological diversity. Therefore, Malthus's prediction that insufficient food will doom humanity to war, pestilence, and famine will likely be proven correct in the future, because a lack of biodiversity will eventually erode our capacity to produce food.

The statement that human food-producing capacity has increased more rapidly than human population plays which one of the following roles in the argument?

(A) It is a hypothesis the argument provides reasons for believing to be presently false.
(B) It is a part of the evidence used in the argument to support the conclusion that a well-known view is misguided.
(C) It is an observation that the argument suggests actually supports Malthus's position.
(D) It is a general fact that the argument offers reason to believe will eventually change.
(E) It is a hypothesis that, according to the argument, is accepted on the basis of inadequate evidence.

GO ON TO THE NEXT PAGE.

19. At a gathering at which bankers, athletes, and lawyers are present, all of the bankers are athletes and none of the lawyers are bankers.

If the statements above are true, which one of the following statements must also be true?

(A) All of the athletes are bankers.
(B) Some of the lawyers are not athletes.
(C) Some of the athletes are not lawyers.
(D) All of the bankers are lawyers.
(E) None of the lawyers are athletes.

20. Quality control investigator: Upon testing samples of products from our supplier that were sent by our field inspectors from various manufacturing locations, our laboratory discovered that over 20 percent of the samples were defective. Since our supplier is contractually required to limit the rate of defects among items it manufactures for us to below 5 percent, it has violated its contract with us.

The reasoning in the quality control investigator's argument is flawed in that the argument

(A) bases its conclusion on too small a sample of items tested by the laboratory
(B) presumes, without providing justification, that the field inspectors were just as likely to choose a defective item for testing as they were to choose a nondefective item
(C) overlooks the possibility that a few of the manufacturing sites are responsible for most of the defective items
(D) overlooks the possibility that the field inspectors tend to choose items for testing that they suspect are defective
(E) presumes, without providing justification, that the field inspectors made an equal number of visits to each of the various manufacturing sites of the supplier

21. Essayist: When the first prehistoric migrations of humans from Asia to North America took place, the small bands of new arrivals encountered many species of animals that would be extinct only 2,000 years later. Since it is implausible that hunting by these small bands of humans could have had such an effect, and since disease-causing microorganisms not native to North America were undoubtedly borne by the new arrivals as well as by the animals that followed them, these microorganisms were probably the crucial factor that accounts for the extinctions.

Which one of the following, if true, most weakens the essayist's argument?

(A) Animals weakened by disease are not only less able to avoid hunters but are also less able to avoid their other predators.
(B) Human beings generally have a substantial degree of biological immunity to the diseases carried by other species.
(C) Very few species of North American animals not hunted by the new arrivals from Asia were extinct 2,000 years after the first migrations.
(D) Individual humans and animals can carry a disease-causing microorganism without themselves suffering from the disease.
(E) Some species of North American animals became extinct more than 2,000 years after the arrival in North America of the first prehistoric human migrants from Asia.

22. A recent study confirms that nutritious breakfasts make workers more productive. For one month, workers at Plant A received free nutritious breakfasts every day before work, while workers in Plant B did not. The productivity of Plant A's workers increased, while that of Plant B's workers did not.

Which one of the following, if true, most strengthens the argument?

(A) Few workers in Plant B consumed nutritious breakfasts during the month of the study.
(B) Workers in the study from Plant A and Plant B started work at the same time of day.
(C) During the month before the study, workers at Plant A and Plant B were equally productive.
(D) Workers from Plant A took fewer vacation days per capita during the month than did workers from Plant B.
(E) Workers in Plant B were more productive during the month of the study than were workers from Plant A.

23. This year a flood devastated a small river town. Hollyville, also a river town, responded with an outpouring of aid in which a majority of its residents participated, a proportion that far surpassed that of a few years ago when Hollyville sent aid to victims of a highly publicized earthquake. This year's circumstances were a reversal of last year's, when Hollyville itself was the scene of a deadly tornado and so the recipient rather than the supplier of emergency aid.

The situation described above most closely conforms to which one of the following generalizations?

(A) People are more likely to aid people they know than they are to aid strangers.
(B) Those who have received aid are more likely to be in favor of government relief programs than are those who have not.
(C) The amount of aid that victims of a disaster receive is unrelated to the extent to which the disaster is publicized.
(D) Once a disaster has struck them, people are more likely to aid others in need than they were before the disaster.
(E) People are more likely to aid those who have experienced a hardship similar to one they themselves have experienced than to aid those who have experienced a dissimilar hardship.

24. Market analyst: According to my research, 59 percent of consumers anticipate paying off their credit card balances in full before interest charges start to accrue, intending to use the cards only to avoid carrying cash and writing checks. This research also suggests that in trying to win business from their competitors, credit card companies tend to concentrate on improving the services their customers are the most interested in. Therefore, my research would lead us to expect that _______.

Which one of the following most logically completes the market analyst's argument?

(A) most consumers would be indifferent about which company's credit card they use
(B) credit card companies would not make the interest rates they charge on cards the main selling point
(C) most consumers would prefer paying interest on credit card debts over borrowing money from banks
(D) most consumers would ignore the length of time a credit card company allows to pay the balance due before interest accrues
(E) the most intense competition among credit card companies would be over the number of places that they can get to accept their credit card

GO ON TO THE NEXT PAGE.

25. About 3 billion years ago, the Sun was only 80 percent as luminous as it is currently. Such conditions today would result in the freezing of Earth's oceans, but geological evidence shows that water rather than ice filled the oceans at that time. Heat is trapped within Earth's atmosphere through the presence of carbon dioxide, which, like methane, is a "greenhouse gas." Only if the level of greenhouse gases were higher 3 billion years ago than it is today would Earth have retained enough heat to keep the oceans from freezing. It is likely, therefore, that the level of carbon dioxide in the atmosphere was significantly higher then than it is today.

Which one of the following, if true, weakens the argument?

(A) Sufficient heat to keep the oceans liquid 3 billion years ago could not have been generated through geological processes such as volcanic activity.
(B) Geological studies indicate that there is much less methane in Earth's atmosphere today than there was 3 billion years ago.
(C) Geological evidence indicates that the oceans contained greater amounts of dissolved minerals 3 billion years ago, but not enough to alter their freezing points significantly.
(D) The increase in the Sun's luminosity over the past 3 billion years roughly coincided with an increasing complexity of life forms on Earth.
(E) Because the distance from Earth to the Sun has not changed significantly over the last 3 billion years, the increase in the Sun's luminosity has resulted in more radiation reaching Earth.

26. Commentator: For a free market to function properly, each prospective buyer of an item must be able to contact a large number of independent prospective sellers and compare the prices charged for the item to what the item is worth. Thus, despite advertised prices and written estimates available from many of its individual businesses, the auto repair industry does not constitute a properly functioning free market.

The conclusion of the commentator's argument follows logically if which one of the following is assumed?

(A) People do not usually shop for auto repairs but instead take their autos to their regular repair shop out of habit.
(B) Some persons who are shopping for auto repairs cannot determine what these repairs are worth.
(C) Not all auto repair shops give customers written estimates.
(D) Many auto repair shops charge more for auto repairs than these repairs are worth.
(E) Because it is not regulated, the auto repair industry does not have standardized prices.

S T O P

IF YOU FINISH BEFORE TIME IS CALLED, YOU MAY CHECK YOUR WORK ON THIS SECTION ONLY.
DO NOT WORK ON ANY OTHER SECTION IN THE TEST.

Time—35 minutes

24 Questions

Directions: Each group of questions in this section is based on a set of conditions. In answering some of the questions, it may be useful to draw a rough diagram. Choose the response that most accurately and completely answers each question and blacken the corresponding space on your answer sheet.

Questions 1–7

Eight physics students—four majors: Frank, Gwen, Henry, and Joan; and four nonmajors: Victor, Wanda, Xavier, and Yvette—are being assigned to four laboratory benches, numbered 1 through 4. Each student is assigned to exactly one bench, and exactly two students are assigned to each bench. Assignments of students to benches must conform to the following conditions:

Exactly one major is assigned to each bench.
Frank and Joan are assigned to consecutively numbered benches, with Frank assigned to the lower-numbered bench.
Frank is assigned to the same bench as Victor.
Gwen is not assigned to the same bench as Wanda.

1. Which one of the following could be the assignment of students to benches?

(A) 1: Frank, Victor; 2: Joan, Gwen; 3: Henry, Wanda; 4: Xavier, Yvette
(B) 1: Gwen, Yvette; 2: Frank, Xavier; 3: Joan, Wanda; 4: Henry, Victor
(C) 1: Henry, Wanda; 2: Gwen, Xavier; 3: Frank, Victor; 4: Joan, Yvette
(D) 1: Henry, Xavier; 2: Joan, Wanda; 3: Frank, Victor; 4: Gwen, Yvette
(E) 1: Henry, Yvette; 2: Gwen, Wanda; 3: Frank, Victor, 4: Joan, Xavier

2. If Victor is assigned to bench 2 and Wanda is assigned to bench 4, which one of the following must be true?

(A) Frank is assigned to bench 1.
(B) Gwen is assigned to bench 1.
(C) Henry is assigned to bench 3.
(D) Xavier is assigned to bench 1.
(E) Yvette is assigned to bench 3.

3. If Gwen and Henry are not assigned to consecutively numbered benches, which one of the following must be true?

(A) Victor is assigned to bench 2.
(B) Victor is assigned to bench 3.
(C) Wanda is assigned to bench 1.
(D) Wanda is assigned to bench 3.
(E) Wanda is assigned to bench 4.

4. If Henry and Yvette are both assigned to bench 1, which one of the following could be true?

(A) Gwen is assigned to bench 3.
(B) Joan is assigned to bench 2.
(C) Wanda is assigned to bench 2.
(D) Wanda is assigned to bench 3.
(E) Xavier is assigned to bench 3.

5. If Gwen is assigned to bench 4 and Xavier is assigned to bench 3, then any one of the following could be true EXCEPT:

(A) Gwen is assigned to the same bench as Yvette.
(B) Henry is assigned to the same bench as Wanda.
(C) Henry is assigned to the same bench as Xavier.
(D) Joan is assigned to the same bench as Xavier.
(E) Joan is assigned to the same bench as Yvette.

6. If Wanda is assigned to a lower-numbered bench than is Joan, then Henry must be assigned to a

(A) lower-numbered bench than is Frank
(B) lower-numbered bench than is Gwen
(C) lower-numbered bench than is Xavier
(D) higher-numbered bench than is Victor
(E) higher-numbered bench than is Yvette

7. Which one of the following could be the assignments for bench 2 and bench 4?

(A) 2: Gwen, Xavier
4: Henry, Yvette
(B) 2: Henry, Yvette
4: Joan, Xavier
(C) 2: Joan, Victor
4: Gwen, Xavier
(D) 2: Joan, Wanda
4: Gwen, Xavier
(E) 2: Joan, Xavier
4: Henry, Yvette

GO ON TO THE NEXT PAGE.

Questions 8–12

A messenger will deliver exactly seven packages—L, M, N, O, P, S, and T—one at a time, not necessarily in that order. The seven deliveries must be made according to the following conditions:

P is delivered either first or seventh.
The messenger delivers N at some time after delivering L.
The messenger delivers T at some time after delivering M.
The messenger delivers exactly one package between delivering L and delivering O, whether or not L is delivered before O.
The messenger delivers exactly one package between delivering M and delivering P, whether or not M is delivered before P.

8. Which one of the following is an order in which the messenger could make the deliveries, from first to seventh?

(A) L, N, S, O, M, T, P
(B) M, T, P, S, L, N, O
(C) O, S, L, N, M, T, P
(D) P, N, M, S, O, T, L
(E) P, T, M, S, L, N, O

9. Which one of the following could be true?

(A) N is delivered first.
(B) T is delivered first.
(C) T is delivered second.
(D) M is delivered fourth.
(E) S is delivered seventh.

10. If N is delivered fourth, which one of the following could be true?

(A) L is delivered first.
(B) L is delivered second.
(C) M is delivered third.
(D) O is delivered fifth.
(E) S is delivered first.

11. If T is delivered fourth, the seventh package delivered must be

(A) L
(B) N
(C) O
(D) P
(E) S

12. If the messenger delivers M at some time after delivering O, the fifth package delivered could be any one of the following EXCEPT:

(A) L
(B) M
(C) N
(D) S
(E) T

GO ON TO THE NEXT PAGE.

Questions 13–18

Each of exactly five persons—Nguyen, Olson, Pike, Tyner, and Valdez—participates in exactly one of three activities: going to a movie, going to a soccer game, or going to a restaurant. The following conditions must apply.

Nguyen and Olson do not participate in the same activity as each other, nor does either one of them participate in the same activity as Pike.

Exactly two persons go to a soccer game.

Tyner and Pike do not participate in the same activity as each other.

If Nguyen or Valdez goes to a movie, they both go to a movie.

13. Which one of the following could be an accurate list of the activities participated in by Nguyen, Olson, Pike, Tyner, and Valdez, respectively?

(A) movie, soccer game, soccer game, restaurant, movie
(B) movie, restaurant, soccer game, soccer game, movie
(C) soccer game, restaurant, movie, soccer game, movie
(D) soccer game, restaurant, movie, soccer game, restaurant
(E) soccer game, restaurant, movie, soccer game, soccer game

14. If Valdez goes to a soccer game, then each of the following could be true EXCEPT:

(A) Olson goes to a movie.
(B) Nguyen goes to a restaurant.
(C) Nguyen goes to a soccer game.
(D) Tyner goes to a soccer game.
(E) Tyner goes to a movie.

15. Which one of the following is a pair of persons who could go to a movie together?

(A) Nguyen and Tyner
(B) Olson and Tyner
(C) Olson and Valdez
(D) Pike and Olson
(E) Pike and Tyner

16. Each of the following statements must be false EXCEPT:

(A) Only Olson goes to a restaurant.
(B) Only Pike goes to a restaurant.
(C) Only Tyner goes to a restaurant.
(D) Only Valdez goes to a restaurant.
(E) Tyner and Valdez go to a restaurant together.

17. If Nguyen goes to a soccer game, then which one of the following is a complete and accurate list of the persons any one of whom could go to a movie?

(A) Olson
(B) Pike, Valdez
(C) Olson, Tyner
(D) Pike, Tyner, Valdez
(E) Olson, Pike, Tyner

18. If the condition that exactly two persons go to a soccer game is changed to require that exactly three persons go to a soccer game, but all other conditions remain the same, then which one of the following persons must participate in an activity other than going to a soccer game?

(A) Nguyen
(B) Olson
(C) Pike
(D) Tyner
(E) Valdez

GO ON TO THE NEXT PAGE.

Questions 19–24

In each of two years exactly two of four lawmakers—Feld, Gibson, Hsu, and Ivins—and exactly two of three scientists—Vega, Young, and Zapora—will serve as members of a four-person panel. In each year, one of the members will be chairperson. The chairperson in the first year cannot serve on the panel in the second year. The chairperson in the second year must have served on the panel in the first year. Service on the panel must obey the following conditions:

Gibson and Vega do not serve on the panel in the same year as each other.

Hsu and Young do not serve on the panel in the same year as each other.

Each year, either Ivins or Vega, but not both, serves on the panel.

19. Which one of the following could be the list of the people who serve on the panel in the first year?

(A) Feld, Gibson, Vega, Zapora
(B) Feld, Hsu, Vega, Zapora
(C) Feld, Ivins, Vega, Zapora
(D) Gibson, Hsu, Ivins, Zapora
(E) Hsu, Ivins, Young, Zapora

20. If Vega is the chairperson in the first year, which one of the following is a pair of people who must serve on the panel in the second year?

(A) Gibson and Young
(B) Gibson and Zapora
(C) Hsu and Ivins
(D) Ivins and Young
(E) Vega and Young

21. If Hsu is the chairperson in the first year, which one of the following could be the chairperson in the second year?

(A) Feld
(B) Gibson
(C) Hsu
(D) Ivins
(E) Young

22. IF Feld serves on the panel in a given year, any one of the following could serve on the panel that year EXCEPT:

(A) Gibson
(B) Hsu
(C) Ivins
(D) Vega
(E) Young

23. If Ivins is the chairperson in the first year, which one of the following could be the chairperson in the second year?

(A) Feld
(B) Gibson
(C) Hsu
(D) Vega
(E) Young

24. Which one of the following must be true?

(A) Feld is on the panel in the second year.
(B) Hsu is on the panel in the first year.
(C) Ivins is on the panel in both years.
(D) Young is on the panel in both years.
(E) Zapora is on the panel in the second year.

S T O P

IF YOU FINISH BEFORE TIME IS CALLED, YOU MAY CHECK YOUR WORK ON THIS SECTION ONLY.
DO NOT WORK ON ANY OTHER SECTION IN THE TEST.

SECTION III

Time—35 minutes

25 Questions

Directions: The questions in this section are based on the reasoning contained in brief statements or passages. For some questions, more than one of the choices could conceivably answer the question. However, you are to choose the best answer; that is, the response that most accurately and completely answers the question. You should not make assumptions that are by commonsense standards implausible, superfluous, or incompatible with the passage. After you have chosen the best answer, blacken the corresponding space on your answer sheet

1. New technologies that promise to extend life and decrease pain involve innovations that require extensive scientific research. Therefore, investment in such technologies is very risky, because innovations requiring extensive scientific research also require large amounts of capital but are unlikely to provide any financial return. Nonetheless, some people are willing to invest in these new technologies.

   Which one of the following, if true, most helps to explain why some people are willing to invest in new technologies that promise to extend life and decrease pain?

   (A) When investments in new technologies that promise to extend life and decrease pain do provide financial return, they generally return many times the original investment, which is much more than the return on safer investments.
   (B) A large variety of new technologies that promise to extend life and decrease pain have been developed in the last decade.
   (C) The development of certain new technologies other than those that promise to extend life and decrease pain is also very risky, because these technologies require large amounts of capital but are unlikely to provide any financial return.
   (D) Some investments that initially seem likely to provide reasonably large financial return ultimately provide no financial return.
   (E) The scientific research necessary to develop new technologies that promise to extend life and decrease pain sometimes leads to no greater understanding of the natural world.

2. A university psychology department received a large donation from a textbook company after agreeing to use one of the company's books for a large introductory course. The department chair admitted that the department would not have received the donation if it used another company's textbook, but insisted that the book was chosen solely for academic reasons. As proof, she noted that the department's textbook committee had given that textbook its highest rating.

   Which one of the following, if true, most weakens the case for the department chair's position?

   (A) The members of the textbook committee were favorably influenced toward the textbook by the prospect of their department receiving a large donation.
   (B) The department has a long-standing policy of using only textbooks that receive the committee's highest rating.
   (C) In the previous year, a different textbook from the same company was used in the introductory course.
   (D) The department chair is one of the members of the textbook committee.
   (E) The textbook company does not routinely make donations to academic departments that use its books.

GO ON TO THE NEXT PAGE.

3. Hemoglobin, a substance in human blood, transports oxygen from the lungs to the rest of the body. With each oxygen molecule it picks up, a hemoglobin molecule becomes more effective at picking up additional oxygen molecules until its maximum capacity of four oxygen molecules is reached. Grabbing an oxygen molecule changes the shape of the hemoglobin molecule, each time causing it literally to open itself to receive more oxygen.

   Which one of the following is most strongly supported by the information above?

   (A) A hemoglobin molecule that has picked up three oxygen molecules will probably acquire a fourth oxygen molecule.
   (B) The only factor determining how effective a hemoglobin molecule is at picking up oxygen molecules is how open the shape of that hemoglobin molecule is.
   (C) A hemoglobin molecule that has picked up three oxygen molecules will be more effective at picking up another oxygen molecule than will a hemoglobin molecule that has picked up only one oxygen molecule.
   (D) A hemoglobin molecule that has picked up four oxygen molecules will have the same shape as a hemoglobin molecule that has not picked up any oxygen molecules.
   (E) Each hemoglobin molecule in human blood picks up between one and four oxygen molecules in or near the lungs and transports them to some other part of the body.

4. On a short trip a driver is more likely to have an accident if there is a passenger in the car, presumably because passengers distract drivers. However, on a long trip a driver is more likely to have an accident if the driver is alone.

   Which one of the following, if true, most helps to explain the facts described above?

   (A) People are much more likely to drive alone on short trips than on long trips.
   (B) Good drivers tend to take more long trips than bad drivers.
   (C) The longer a car trip is, the more likely a passenger is to help the driver maintain alertness.
   (D) On a long trip the likelihood of an accident does not increase with each additional passenger.
   (E) Most drivers take far more short trips than long trips.

5. Challenger: The mayor claims she has vindicated those who supported her in the last election by fulfilling her promise to increase employment opportunities in our city, citing the 8 percent increase in the number of jobs in the city since she took office. But during her administration, the national government relocated an office to our city, bringing along nearly the entire staff from the outside. The 8 percent increase merely represents the jobs held by these newcomers.

   Mayor: Clearly my opponent does not dispute the employment statistics. The unemployed voters in this city want jobs. The 8 percent increase in the number of jobs during my term exceeds that of any of my predecessors.

   As a response to the challenger, the mayor's answer is flawed in that it

   (A) takes for granted that those who supported the mayor in the last election believed job availability to be a significant city issue
   (B) does not consider whether the number of unemployed persons within the city represents more than 8 percent of the eligible voters
   (C) fails to address the challenger's objection that the 8 percent increase did not result in an increase in job availability for those who lived in the city at the time of the last election
   (D) ignores the challenger's contention that the influx of newcomers during the mayor's administration has increased the size of the voting public and altered its priorities
   (E) explicitly attributes to the challenger beliefs that the challenger has neither asserted nor implied

GO ON TO THE NEXT PAGE.

6. A recent magazine editorial criticizes psychologists for not attempting to establish the order in which different areas of the brain are activated during a cognitive task such as imagining the face of a friend. However, the editorial is unfair because there is currently no technology that can detect the order of activation of brain areas.

Which one of the following most closely conforms to the principle to which the reasoning in the passage conforms?

(A) Construction companies have been unfairly criticized for using fewer layers of heating insulation in new houses than the number of layers used in previous years. Recent technology has made insulation more efficient, so fewer layers are required.
(B) Utility companies have been unfairly criticized for not using nuclear fusion to meet the nation's electricity needs. There is no way to harness fusion that could produce enough electricity to supply even one small town.
(C) The food industry has been unfairly criticized for attempting to preserve food longer by treating it with radiation. If food remained edible for longer, the cost of food would decrease substantially.
(D) The school system has been unfairly criticized for not making familiarity with computer technology a requirement. Computer studies could not be added to the curriculum without sacrificing some other subject.
(E) CEOs of large companies have been unfairly criticized for not always using their knowledge of economic theory to run their companies. Economic theory is sometimes irrelevant to making wise corporate decisions.

7. Although most people know what their bad habits are and want to rid themselves of them, a majority of these people find it very difficult to do so. This is because cessation of habitual behavior is immediately and vividly painful, while whatever benefit is to be gained by the absence of the habit is perceived only dimly because it is remote.

The information above most strongly supports the statement that the people who are most successful at ending their bad habits are those who

(A) can vividly imagine remote but attainable benefit
(B) can vividly imagine their present pain being felt in the future
(C) have succeeded in the past at modifying their behavior
(D) are relatively unaware of their own behavioral characteristics
(E) can vividly remember the pain caused them in the past by their bad habits

8. The more modern archaeologists learn about Mayan civilization, the better they understand its intellectual achievements. Not only were numerous scientific observations and predictions made by Mayan astronomers, but the people in general seem to have had a strong grasp of sophisticated mathematical concepts. We know this from the fact that the writings of the Mayan religious scribes exhibit a high degree of mathematical competence.

The argument's reasoning is most vulnerable to criticism on the grounds that the argument

(A) fails to provide an adequate definition of the term "intellectual achievement"
(B) bases a generalization on a sample that is likely to be unrepresentative
(C) overlooks the impressive achievements of other past civilizations
(D) relies on two different senses of the term "scientific"
(E) takes a mere correlation to be evidence of a causal relationship

9. Manager: There is no good reason to suppose that promoting creativity is a proper goal of an employee training program. Many jobs require little or no creativity and, in those positions, using creativity is more likely to be disruptive than innovative. Furthermore, even if creativity were in demand, there is no evidence that it can be taught.

Which one of the following most accurately expresses the main conclusion drawn in the manager's argument?

(A) Using creativity in jobs that require little or no creativity can be disruptive.
(B) Employee training programs are not able to teach employees creativity.
(C) Many jobs require little or no creativity.
(D) There is no good reason to suppose that employee training programs should promote creativity.
(E) Creativity is in demand, but there is no evidence that it can be taught.

GO ON TO THE NEXT PAGE.

10. Producer: It has been argued that, while the government should not censor television shows, the public should boycott the advertisers of shows that promote violence and erode our country's values. But this would be censorship nonetheless, for if the public boycotted the advertisers, then they would cancel their advertisements, causing some shows to go off the air; the result would be a restriction of the shows that the public can watch.

The producer's conclusion is properly inferred if which one of the following is assumed?

(A) If there is neither government censorship nor boycotting of advertisers, there will be no restriction of the television shows that the public can watch.
(B) Public boycotts could force some shows off the air even though the shows neither promote violence nor erode values.
(C) For any television show that promotes violence and erodes values, there will be an audience.
(D) There is widespread public agreement about which television shows promote violence and erode values.
(E) Any action that leads to a restriction of what the public can view is censorship.

11. Predictions that printed books will soon be replaced by books in electronic formats such as CD-ROM are exaggerated. While research libraries may find an electronic format more convenient for scholars and scientists, bookstores and public libraries will stock books in the format desired by the general public, which will be something other than an electronic format.

Which one of the following, if true, most strengthens the argument?

(A) Scholars and scientists find an electronic format for books the most convenient one for quick searching and cross-referencing.
(B) Publishers will continue to print books in the format stocked by bookstores and public libraries.
(C) Scholars and scientists do not usually conduct their research in public libraries.
(D) At some bookstores and libraries, the popularity of books on tape and of videos is beginning to rival that of printed books.
(E) Some members of the general public prefer to purchase books in an electronic format rather than borrow them from the library.

12. To cut costs, a high school modified its air-conditioning system to increase its efficiency. The modified system, however, caused the humidity in the school air to decrease by 18 percent. Twenty-four hours after the decrease in air humidity, a 25 percent increase in the number of visits to the school nurse was reported. This shows that a decrease in humidity can make people ill.

The argument depends on assuming which one of the following?

(A) At least some of the visits to the school nurse after the system was modified were due to illness.
(B) Most of the students at the high school suffered from the decrease in air humidity.
(C) It takes 24 hours after a person is infected with a virus for that person to exhibit symptoms.
(D) A decrease of 18 percent in air humidity causes an increase of 25 percent in one's probability of becoming ill.
(E) Modifying the air-conditioning system proved to be an ineffective way to cut costs.

13. A recent study of 10,000 people who were involved in automobile accidents found that a low percentage of those driving large automobiles at the time of their accidents were injured, but a high percentage of those who were driving small automobiles at the time of their accidents were injured. Thus, one is less likely to be injured in an automobile accident if one drives a large car rather than a small car.

Which one of the following, if true, most seriously weakens the argument?

(A) Most of the accidents analyzed in the study occurred in areas with very high speed limits.
(B) Most people who own small cars also drive large cars on occasion.
(C) Half of the study participants drove medium-sized cars at the time of their accidents.
(D) A large automobile is far more likely to be involved in an accident than is a small automobile.
(E) Only a small percentage of those people involved in an automobile accident are injured as a result.

GO ON TO THE NEXT PAGE.

14. Economist: A country's trade deficit may indicate weakness in its economy, but it does not in itself weaken that economy. So restricting imports to reduce a trade deficit would be like sticking a thermometer into a glass of cold water in the hope of bringing down a patient's feverish temperature.

The economist's argument employs which one of the following techniques?

(A) claiming that a crucial assumption entails a falsehood
(B) demonstrating that an analogy explicitly used to establish a certain conclusion is faulty
(C) appealing to an analogy in order to indicate the futility of a course of action
(D) calling into question the authority on the basis of which a claim is made
(E) showing that a recommended course of action would have disastrous consequences

15. There are circumstances in which it is not immoral to make certain threats, and there are circumstances in which it is not immoral to ask for money or some other favor. Therefore, there are circumstances in which it is not immoral to ask for money or a favor while making a threat.

Which one of the following exhibits a flawed pattern of reasoning most similar to that in the argument above?

(A) There are many business events for which casual dress is appropriate, and there are many social events for which casual dress is appropriate; therefore, if an occasion is neither a business event nor a social event, casual dress is not likely to be appropriate.
(B) It is usually easy to move a piano after you have convinced five people to help you, provided that you do not need to take it up or down stairs. Therefore, it is usually easy to move a piano.
(C) It is healthful to take drug A for a headache, and it is healthful to take drug B for a headache; therefore, it is healthful to take drug A together with drug B for a headache.
(D) Heavy trucks are generally operated in a safe manner, but the ability to drive a truck safely can be impaired by certain prescription drugs. Therefore, heavy trucks cannot be operated safely while the driver is under the effect of a prescription drug.
(E) The mountain roads are treacherous after it rains, and the mountain streams are full after a rain. So, if the roads in the mountains are treacherous, and the mountain streams are full, it surely has rained recently.

16. A common genetic mutation that lowers levels of the enzyme cathepsin C severely reduces a person's ability to ward off periodontitis, or gum disease. The enzyme triggers immunological reactions that destroy diseased cells and eliminate infections in the mouth. But researchers are developing ways to restore the enzyme to normal levels. Once that happens, we will be able to eliminate periodontitis.

Which one of the following is an assumption on which the argument depends?

(A) Restoring cathepsin C to normal levels is the only way to eliminate periodontitis.
(B) Genetic mutation is the only cause of lowered levels of cathepsin C.
(C) Researchers will soon succeed in finding means of restoring cathepsin C to normal levels.
(D) Persons who do not have the genetic mutation that lowers levels of cathepsin C do not get gum disease.
(E) A person whose cathepsin C level has been restored to normal will not suffer from periodontitis.

17. A recent study of major motion pictures revealed that the vast majority of their plots were simply variations on plots that had been used many times before. Despite this fact, many people enjoy seeing several new movies each year.

Each of the following, if true, would contribute to an explanation of the apparent discrepancy in the information above EXCEPT:

(A) Movies based on standard plots are more likely to be financially successful than are ones based on original plots.
(B) If the details of their stories are sufficiently different, two movies with the same basic plot will be perceived by moviegoers as having different plots.
(C) Because of the large number of movies produced each year, the odds of a person seeing two movies with the same general plot structure in a five-year period are fairly low.
(D) A certain aesthetic pleasure is derived from seeing several movies that develop the same plot in slightly different ways.
(E) Although most modern movie plots have been used before, most of those previous uses occurred during the 1940s and 1950s.

GO ON TO THE NEXT PAGE.

18. Those who claim that governments should not continue to devote resources to space exploration are wrong. Although most people's lives are relatively unaffected by the direct consequences of space exploration, many modern technologies that have a tremendous impact on daily life—e.g., fiber optics, computers, and lasers—are unexpected consequences of it. Society might have missed the benefits of these technologies if governments had not devoted resources to space exploration.

Which one of the following most accurately expresses the principle underlying the argument above?

(A) Governments should not be prevented from allocating resources to projects whose intended consequences do not directly benefit most people.
(B) One can never underestimate the beneficial consequences of government support of ambitious technological undertakings.
(C) The less practical the goal of a government-supported project, the more unexpected the consequences of that project.
(D) Governments should continue to support those projects that have, in the past, produced unintended benefits.
(E) In attempting to advance the welfare of society, governments should continue to dedicate resources to ambitious technological undertakings.

19. If understanding a word always involves knowing its dictionary definition, then understanding a word requires understanding the words that occur in that definition. But clearly there are people—for example, all babies—who do not know the dictionary definitions of some of the words they utter.

Which one of the following statements follows logically from the statements above?

(A) Some babies utter individual words that they do not understand.
(B) Any number of people can understand some words without knowing their dictionary definitions.
(C) If some words can be understood without knowing their dictionary definitions, then babies understand some words.
(D) If it is possible to understand a word without knowing its dictionary definition, then it is possible to understand a word without having to understand any other word.
(E) If some babies understand all the words they utter, then understanding a word does not always involve knowing its dictionary definition.

20. The peppered moth avoids predators by blending into its background, typically the bark of trees. In the late nineteenth century, those peppered moths with the lightest pigmentation had the greatest contrast with their backgrounds, and therefore were the most likely to be seen and eaten by predators. It follows, then, that the darkest peppered moths were the least likely to be seen and eaten.

Which one of the following most accurately describes a flaw in the reasoning of the argument?

(A) The argument overlooks the possibility that light peppered moths had more predators than dark peppered moths.
(B) The argument takes for granted that peppered moths are able to control the degree to which they blend into their backgrounds.
(C) The argument presumes, without providing justification, that all peppered moths with the same coloring had the same likelihood of being seen and eaten by a predator.
(D) The argument overlooks the possibility that there were peppered moths of intermediate color that contrasted less with their backgrounds than the darkest peppered moths did.
(E) The argument presumes, without providing justification, that the only defense mechanism available to peppered moths was to blend into their backgrounds.

GO ON TO THE NEXT PAGE.

21. Historian: The standard "QWERTY" configuration of the keys on typewriters and computer keyboards was originally designed to be awkward and limit typing speed. This was because early typewriters would jam frequently if adjacent keys were struck in quick succession. Experiments have shown that keyboard configurations more efficient than QWERTY can double typing speed while tremendously reducing typing effort. However, the expense and inconvenience of switching to a new keyboard configuration prevent any configuration other than QWERTY from attaining widespread use.

Which one of the following is most strongly supported by the historian's statements?

(A) Most people who have tried typing with non-QWERTY keyboards have typed significantly more quickly using those keyboards than they usually have done using QWERTY keyboards.
(B) Early QWERTY typewriters were less likely to jam than were at least some more recent typewriters if adjacent keys were struck in quick succession.
(C) If the designers of early typewriters had foreseen the possibility that technology would make it possible for adjacent keyboard keys to be struck in rapid succession without jamming, then they would not have proposed the QWERTY configuration.
(D) The benefit to society that would result from switching to a keyboard configuration other than QWERTY is significantly greater than the overall cost of such a switch.
(E) If the keyboard had been designed for computers, then it would not have been designed to limit typing speed.

22. Since anyone who makes an agreement has an obligation to fulfill the terms of that agreement, it follows that anyone who is obligated to perform an action has agreed to perform that action. Hence, saying that one has a legal obligation to perform a given action is the same as saying that one is required to fulfill one's agreement to perform that action.

Which one of the following statements most accurately characterizes the argument's reasoning flaws?

(A) The argument fails to make a crucial distinction between an action one is legally obligated to perform and an action with good consequences, and it takes for granted that everything true of legal obligations is true of obligations generally.
(B) The argument takes for granted that there are obligations other than those resulting from agreements made, and it fails to consider the possibility that actions that uphold agreements made are sometimes performed for reasons other than to uphold those agreements.
(C) The argument contains a premise that is logically equivalent to its conclusion, and it takes for granted that there are only certain actions that one should agree to perform.
(D) The argument treats a condition that is sufficient to make something an obligation as also a requirement for something to be an obligation, and it takes for granted that any obligation to perform an action is a legal obligation.
(E) The argument rests on an ambiguous use of the term "action," and it fails to consider the possibility that people are sometimes unwilling to perform actions that they have agreed to perform.

23. To predict that a device will be invented, one must develop a conception of the device that includes some details at least about how it will function and the consequences of its use. But clearly, then, the notion of predicting an invention is self-contradictory, for inventing means developing a detailed conception, and one cannot predict what has already taken place.

Which one of the following most accurately describes the technique of reasoning employed by the argument?

(A) constructing a counterexample to a general hypothesis about the future
(B) appealing to definitions to infer the impossibility of a kind of occurrence
(C) countering a hypothesis by indicating the falsehood of the implications of that hypothesis
(D) pointing out how a problem is widely thought to be scientific yet is really conceptual
(E) attempting to show that predicting any event implies that it has in fact already taken place

GO ON TO THE NEXT PAGE.

24. Eighteenth-century European aesthetics was reasonably successful in providing an understanding of all art, including early abstract art, until the 1960s, when artists self-consciously rebelled against earlier notions of art. Since the work of these rebellious artists is quite beautiful but outside the bounds of the aesthetic theory then current, there can be no complete theory of aesthetics.

The reasoning above is most vulnerable to criticism in that it

(A) takes for granted that it is more important for a complete aesthetic theory to account for the beauty of traditional art than for it to account for the beauty of self-consciously rebellious art
(B) presumes, without providing justification, that artists' rebellion in the 1960s against earlier notions of art was not guided by their knowledge of eighteenth-century European aesthetic theory
(C) presumes, without providing justification, that an aesthetic theory developed in one part of the world cannot be applied in another
(D) presumes, without providing justification, that art from the 1960s is the only art that cannot be adequately addressed by eighteenth-century European aesthetics
(E) presumes, without providing justification, that eighteenth-century European aesthetics is as encompassing as an aesthetic theory can be

25. Science writer: All scientists have beliefs and values that might slant their interpretations of the data from which they draw their conclusions. However, serious scientific papers are carefully reviewed by many other scientists before publication. These reviewers are likely to notice and object to biases that they do not share. Thus, any slanted interpretations of scientific data will generally have been removed before publication.

Which one of the following is an assumption required by the science writer's argument?

(A) The scientists reviewing serious scientific papers for publication do not always have biases likely to slant their interpretations of the data in those papers.
(B) In general, biases that slant interpretations of data in serious scientific papers being reviewed for publication are not shared among all scientists.
(C) Biases that are present in published scientific papers and shared by most scientists, including those who review the papers, are unlikely to impair the scientific value of those papers.
(D) The interpretation of data is the only part of a serious scientific paper that is sometimes slanted by the beliefs and values of scientists.
(E) Slanted interpretations of data in a scientific paper can be removed only through careful review by scientists who do not share the biases of the author or authors of the paper.

S T O P

IF YOU FINISH BEFORE TIME IS CALLED, YOU MAY CHECK YOUR WORK ON THIS SECTION ONLY.
DO NOT WORK ON ANY OTHER SECTION IN THE TEST.

SECTION IV

Time—35 minutes

25 Questions

Directions: Each set of questions in this section is based on a single passage or a pair of passages. The questions are to be answered on the basis of what is stated or implied in the passage or pair of passages. For some of the questions, more than one of the choices could conceivably answer the question. However, you are to choose the best answer; that is, the response that most accurately and completely answers the question, and blacken the corresponding space on your answer sheet.

Passage A

Recent studies have shown that sophisticated computer models of the oceans and atmosphere are capable of simulating large-scale climate trends with remarkable accuracy. But these models make use of large numbers of variables, many of which have wide ranges of possible values. Because even small differences in those values can have a significant impact on what the simulations predict, it is important to determine the impact when values differ even slightly.

Since the interactions between the many variables in climate simulations are highly complex, there is no alternative to a "brute force" exploration of all possible combinations of their values if predictions are to be reliable. This method requires very large numbers of calculations and simulation runs. For example, exhaustive examination of five values for each of only nine variables would require 2 million calculation-intensive simulation runs. Currently available individual computers are completely inadequate for such a task.

However, the continuing increase in computing capacity of the average desktop computer means that climate simulations can now be run on privately owned desktop machines connected to one another via the Internet. The calculations are divided among the individual desktop computers, which work simultaneously on their share of the overall problem. Some public resource computing projects of this kind have already been successful, although only when they captured the public's interest sufficiently to secure widespread participation.

Passage B

Researchers are now learning that many problems in nature, human society, science, and engineering are naturally "parallel"; that is, that they can be effectively solved by using methods that work simultaneously in parallel. These problems share the common characteristic of involving a large number of similar elements such as molecules, animals, even people, whose individual actions are governed by simple rules but, taken collectively, function as a highly complex system.

An example is the method used by ants to forage for food. As Lewis Thomas observed, a solitary ant is little more than a few neurons strung together by fibers. Its behavior follows a few simple rules. But when one sees a dense mass of thousands of ants, crowded together around their anthill retrieving food or repelling an intruder, a more complex picture emerges; it is as if the whole is thinking, planning, calculating. It is an intelligence, a kind of live computer, with crawling bits for wits.

We are now living through a great paradigm shift in the field of computing, a shift from sequential computing (performing one calculation at a time) to massive parallel computing, which employs thousands of computers working simultaneously to solve one computation-intensive problem. Since many computation-intensive problems are inherently parallel, it only makes sense to use a computing model that exploits that parallelism. A computing model that resembles the inherently parallel problem it is trying to solve will perform best. The old paradigm, in contrast, is subject to the speed limits imposed by purely sequential computing.

1. Which one of the following most accurately expresses the main point of passage B?

(A) Many difficult problems in computing are naturally parallel.
(B) Sequential computing is no longer useful because of the speed limits it imposes.
(C) There is currently a paradigm shift occurring in the field of computing toward parallel computing.
(D) Complex biological and social systems are the next frontier in the field of computer simulation.
(E) Inherently parallel computing problems are best solved by means of computers modeled on the human mind.

2. The large-scale climate trends discussed in passage A are most analogous to which one of the following elements in passage B?

(A) the thousands of computers working simultaneously to solve a calculation-intensive problem
(B) the simple rules that shape the behavior of a single ant
(C) the highly complex behavior of a dense mass of thousands of ants
(D) the paradigm shift from sequential to parallel computing
(E) the speed limits imposed by computing purely sequentially

GO ON TO THE NEXT PAGE.

3. It can be inferred that the authors of the two passages would be most likely to agree on which one of the following statements concerning computing systems?
   (A) Massive, parallel computing systems are able to solve complex computation-intensive problems without having to resort to "brute force."
   (B) Computer models are not capable of simulating the behavior of very large biological populations such as insect colonies.
   (C) Parallel computing systems that link privately owned desktop computers via the Internet are not feasible because they rely too heavily on public participation.
   (D) Currently available computers are not well-suited to running simulations, even if the simulated problems are relatively simple.
   (E) Parallel computing systems employing multiple computers are the best means for simulating large-scale climate trends.

4. The author of passage A mentions public participation (lines 30–32) primarily in order to
   (A) encourage public engagement in the sort of computing model discussed in the passage
   (B) identify a factor affecting the feasibility of the computing model advocated in the passage
   (C) indicate that government support of large-scale computing efforts is needed
   (D) demonstrate that adequate support for the type of approach described in the passage already exists
   (E) suggest that a computing model like that proposed in the passage is infeasible because of forces beyond the designers' control

5. Passage B relates to passage A in which one of the following ways?
   (A) The argument in passage B has little bearing on the issues discussed in passage A.
   (B) The explanation offered in passage B shows why the plan proposed in passage A is unlikely to be implemented.
   (C) The ideas advanced in passage B provide a rationale for the solution proposed in passage A.
   (D) The example given in passage B illustrates the need for the "brute force" exploration mentioned in passage A.
   (E) The discussion in passage B conflicts with the assumptions about individual computers made in passage A.

6. The passages share which one of the following as their primary purpose?
   (A) to show that the traditional paradigm in computing is ineffective for many common computing tasks
   (B) to argue that a new approach to computing is an effective way to solve a difficult type of problem
   (C) to convince skeptics of the usefulness of desktop computers for calculation-intensive problems
   (D) to demonstrate that a new computing paradigm has supplanted the traditional paradigm for most large-scale computing problems
   (E) to describe complex and as yet unsolved problems that have recently arisen in computing

7. In calling a population of ants "an intelligence, a kind of live computer" (lines 51–52) the author of passage B most likely means that
   (A) the behavior of the colony of ants functions as a complex, organized whole
   (B) the paradigm shift taking place in computing was inspired by observations of living systems
   (C) computers are agglomerations of elements that can be viewed as being alive in a metaphorical sense
   (D) computer simulations can simulate the behavior of large biological populations with great accuracy
   (E) the simple rules that govern the behavior of individual ants have been adapted for use in computer simulations

8. The author of passage B would be most likely to agree with which one of the following statements regarding the computing system proposed in the last paragraph of passage A?
   (A) It would be a kind of live computer.
   (B) It would be completely inadequate for simulating large-scale climate trends.
   (C) It would impose strict limitations on the number of variables that could be used in any simulation it runs.
   (D) It would be likely to secure widespread public participation.
   (E) It would solve calculation-intensive problems faster than a traditional sequential computer would.

GO ON TO THE NEXT PAGE.

A proficiency in understanding, applying, and even formulating statutes—the actual texts of laws enacted by legislative bodies—is a vital aspect of the practice of law, but statutory law is often given too little attention by law schools. Much of legal education, with its focus on judicial decisions and analysis of cases, can give a law student the impression that the practice of law consists mainly in analyzing past cases to determine their relevance to a client's situation and arriving at a speculative interpretation of the law relevant to the client's legal problem.

Lawyers discover fairly soon, however, that much of their practice does not depend on the kind of painstaking analysis of cases that is performed in law school. For example, a lawyer representing the owner of a business can often find an explicit answer as to what the client should do about a certain tax-related issue by consulting the relevant statutes. In such a case the facts are clear and the statutes' relation to them transparent, so that the client's question can be answered by direct reference to the wording of the statutes. But statutes' meanings and their applicability to relevant situations are not always so obvious, and that is one reason that the ability to interpret them accurately is an essential skill for law students to learn.

Another skill that teaching statutory law would improve is synthesis. Law professors work hard at developing their students' ability to analyze individual cases, but in so doing they favor the ability to apply the law in particular cases over the ability to understand the interrelations among laws. In contrast, the study of all the statutes of a legal system in a certain small area of the law would enable the student to see how these laws form a coherent whole. Students would then be able to apply this ability to synthesize in other areas of statutory law that they encounter in their study or practice. This is especially important because most students intend to specialize in a chosen area, or areas, of the law.

One possible argument against including training in statutory law as a standard part of law school curricula is that many statutes vary from region to region within a nation, so that the mastery of a set of statutes would usually not be generally applicable. There is some truth to this objection; law schools that currently provide some training in statutes generally intend it as a preparation for practice in their particular region, but for schools that are nationally oriented, this could seem to be an inappropriate investment of time and resources. But while the knowledge of a particular region's statutory law is not generally transferable to other regions, the skills acquired in mastering a particular set of statutes are, making the study of statutory law an important undertaking even for law schools with a national orientation.

9. Which one of the following most accurately expresses the main point of the passage?

(A) In spite of the reservations that nationally oriented law schools can be expected to have, law schools can serve the overall needs of law students better by implementing a standard national curriculum in statutory law.
(B) Since the skills promoted by the study of statutory law are ultimately more important than those promoted by case analysis, the relative emphasis that law schools place on these two areas should be reversed.
(C) Although statutes typically vary from region to region, law schools should provide training in statutory law in order to develop students' ability to synthesize legal information and interpret individual statutes.
(D) In the theoretical world of law school training, as opposed to the actual practice of law, a proficiency in case law is often one of the most important assets that students can have.
(E) Law schools generally are deficient in their attention to statutory law training and therefore fail to impart the skills necessary for the analysis of legal information.

10. Which one of the following is cited in the passage as a reason that might be given for not including statutory law training in law school curricula?

(A) Such training would divert resources away from the far more important development of the ability to analyze cases.
(B) Such training is not essentially different from what is already provided in the core areas of law school education.
(C) The goals of such training can better be achieved by other means, most of which are more directly related to the actual practice of law.
(D) Such training would be irrelevant for those students who do not plan to specialize.
(E) The lack of geographic uniformity among statutory laws makes expertise in the statutes of any particular region generally nontransferable.

GO ON TO THE NEXT PAGE.

11. Which one of the following would, if true, most weaken the author's argument as expressed in the passage?

(A) Many law school administrators recommend the inclusion of statutory law training in the curricula of their schools.
(B) Most lawyers easily and quickly develop proficiency in statutory law through their work experiences after law school.
(C) Most lawyers do not practice law in the same geographic area in which they attended law school.
(D) The curricula of many regionally oriented law schools rely primarily on analysis of cases.
(E) Most lawyers who have undergone training in statutory law are thoroughly familiar with only a narrow range of statutes.

12. The author discusses the skill of synthesis in the third paragraph primarily in order to

(A) identify and describe one of the benefits that the author says would result from the change that is advocated in the passage
(B) indicate that law schools currently value certain other skills over this skill and explain why this is so
(C) argue for the greater importance of this skill as compared with certain others that are discussed earlier in the passage
(D) explain why this skill is necessary for the study of statutory law
(E) provide an example of the type of problem typically encountered in the practice of law

13. Which one of the following questions can be most clearly and directly answered by reference to information in the passage?

(A) What are some ways in which synthetic skills are strengthened or encouraged through the analysis of cases and judicial decisions?
(B) In which areas of legal practice is a proficiency in case analysis more valuable than a proficiency in statutory law?
(C) What skills are common to the study of both statutory law and judicial decisions?
(D) What are some objections that have been raised against including the study of statutes in regionally oriented law schools?
(E) What is the primary focus of the curriculum currently offered in most law schools?

14. The information in the passage suggests that the author would most likely agree with which one of the following statements regarding training in statutory law?

(A) While nationally oriented law schools have been deficient in statutory law training, most regionally oriented law schools have been equally deficient in the teaching of case law.
(B) Training in statutory law would help lawyers resolve legal questions for which the answers are not immediately apparent in the relevant statutes.
(C) Lawyers who are trained in statutory law typically also develop a higher level of efficiency in manipulating details of past cases as compared with lawyers who are not trained in this way.
(D) Courses in statutory law are less effective if they focus specifically on the statutes of a particular region or in a particular area of the law.
(E) Lawyers who do not specialize probably have little need for training in statutory law beyond a brief introduction to the subject.

15. Each of the following conforms to the kinds of educational results that the author would expect from the course of action proposed in the passage EXCEPT:

(A) skill in locating references to court decisions on an issue involving a particular statute regarding taxation
(B) an understanding of the ways in which certain underlying purposes are served by an interrelated group of environmental laws
(C) a knowledge of how maritime statutes are formulated
(D) familiarity with the specific wordings of a group of laws applying to businesses in a particular region or locality
(E) an appreciation of the problems of wording involved in drafting antiterrorism laws

GO ON TO THE NEXT PAGE.

The Japanese American sculptor Isamu Noguchi (1904–1988) was an artist who intuitively asked—and responded to—deeply original questions. He might well have become a scientist within a standard scientific discipline, but he instead became an artist who repeatedly veered off at wide angles from the well-known courses followed by conventionally talented artists of both the traditional and modern schools. The story behind one particular sculpture typifies this aspect of his creativeness.

By his early twenties, Noguchi's sculptures showed such exquisite comprehension of human anatomy and deft conceptual realization that he won a Guggenheim Fellowship for travel in Europe. After arriving in Paris in 1927, Noguchi asked the Romanian-born sculptor Constantin Brancusi if he might become his student. When Brancusi said no, that he never took students, Noguchi asked if he needed a stonecutter. Brancusi did. Noguchi cut and polished stone for Brancusi in his studio, frequently also polishing Brancusi's brass and bronze sculptures. Noguchi, with his scientist's mind, pondered the fact that sculptors through the ages had relied exclusively upon negative light—that is, shadows—for their conceptual communication, precisely because no metals, other than the expensive, nonoxidizing gold, could be relied upon to give off positive-light reflections.

Noguchi wanted to create a sculpture that was purely reflective. In 1929, after returning to the United States, he met the architect and philosopher R. Buckminster Fuller, offering to sculpt a portrait of him. When Fuller heard of Noguchi's ideas regarding positive-light sculpture, he suggested using chrome-nickel steel, which Henry Ford, through automotive research and development, had just made commercially available for the first time in history. Here, finally, was a permanently reflective surface, economically available in massive quantities.

In sculpting his portrait of Fuller, Noguchi did not think of it as merely a shiny alternate model of traditional, negative-light sculptures. What he saw was that completely reflective surfaces provided a fundamental invisibility of surface like that of utterly still waters, whose presence can be apprehended only when objects—a ship's mast, a tree, or sky—are reflected in them. Seaplane pilots making offshore landings in dead calm cannot tell where the water is and must glide in, waiting for the unpredictable touchdown. Noguchi conceived a similarly invisible sculpture, hidden in and communicating through the reflections of images surrounding it. Then only the distortion of familiar shapes in the surrounding environment could be seen by the viewer. The viewer's awareness of the "invisible" sculpture's presence and dimensional relationships would be derived only secondarily.

Even after this stunning discovery, Noguchi remained faithful to his inquisitive nature. At the moment when his explorations had won critical recognition of the genius of his original and fundamental conception, Noguchi proceeded to the next phase of his evolution.

16. In saying that "no metals, other than the expensive, nonoxidizing gold, could be relied upon to give off positive-light reflections" (lines 25–27), the author draws a distinction between

(A) a metal that can be made moderately reflective in any sculptural application and metals that can be made highly reflective but only in certain applications
(B) a naturally highly reflective metal that was technically suited for sculpture and other highly reflective metals that were not so suited
(C) metals that can be made highly reflective but lose their reflective properties over time and a metal that does not similarly lose its reflective properties
(D) a highly reflective sculptural material that, because it is a metal, is long lasting and nonmetallic materials that are highly reflective but impermanent
(E) a highly reflective metal that was acceptable to both traditional and modern sculptors and highly reflective metals whose use in sculpture was purely experimental

17. The passage provides information sufficient to answer which one of the following questions?

(A) In what way did Noguchi first begin to acquire experience in the cutting and polishing of stone for use in sculpture?
(B) In the course of his career, did Noguchi ever work in any art form other than sculpture?
(C) What are some materials other than metal that Noguchi used in his sculptures after ending his association with Brancusi?
(D) During Noguchi's lifetime, was there any favorable critical response to his creation of a positive-light sculpture?
(E) Did Noguchi at any time in his career consider creating a transparent or translucent sculpture lighted from within?

GO ON TO THE NEXT PAGE.

18. The passage offers the strongest evidence that the author would agree with which one of the following statements?

(A) Noguchi's work in Paris contributed significantly to the art of sculpture in that it embodied solutions to problems that other sculptors, including Brancusi, had sought unsuccessfully to overcome.
(B) Noguchi's scientific approach to designing sculptures and to selecting materials for sculptures is especially remarkable in that he had no formal scientific training.
(C) Despite the fact that Brancusi was a sculptor and Fuller was not, Fuller played a more pivotal role than did Brancusi in Noguchi's realization of the importance of negative light to the work of previous sculptors.
(D) Noguchi was more interested in addressing fundamental aesthetic questions than in maintaining a consistent artistic style.
(E) Noguchi's work is of special interest for what it reveals not only about the value of scientific thinking in the arts but also about the value of aesthetic approaches to scientific inquiry.

19. In which one of the following is the relation between the two people most analogous to the relation between Ford and Noguchi as indicated by the passage?

(A) A building-materials dealer decides to market a new type of especially durable simulated-wood flooring material after learning that a famous architect has praised the material.
(B) An expert skier begins experimenting with the use of a new type of material in the soles of ski boots after a shoe manufacturer suggests that that material might be appropriate for that use.
(C) A producer of shipping containers begins using a new type of strapping material, which a rock-climbing expert soon finds useful as an especially strong and reliable component of safety ropes for climbing.
(D) A consultant to a book editor suggests the use of a new type of software for typesetting, and after researching the software the editor decides not to adopt it but finds a better alternative as a result of the research.
(E) A friend of a landscaping expert advises the use of a certain material for the creation of retaining walls and, as a result, the landscaper explores the use of several similar materials.

20. The passage most strongly supports which one of the following inferences?

(A) Prior to suggesting the sculptural use of chrome-nickel steel to Noguchi, Fuller himself had made architectural designs that called for the use of this material.
(B) Noguchi believed that the use of industrial materials to create sculptures would make the sculptures more commercially viable.
(C) Noguchi's "invisible" sculpture appears to have no shape or dimensions of its own, but rather those of surrounding objects.
(D) If a positive-light sculpture depicting a person in a realistic manner were coated with a metal subject to oxidation, it would eventually cease to be recognizable as a realistic likeness.
(E) The perception of the shape and dimensions of a negative-light sculpture does not depend on its reflection of objects from the environment around it.

21. Which one of the following inferences about the portrait of Fuller does the passage most strongly support?

(A) The material that Noguchi used in it had been tentatively investigated by other sculptors but not in direct connection with its reflective properties.
(B) It was similar to at least some of the sculptures that Noguchi produced prior to 1927 in that it represented a human form.
(C) Noguchi did not initially think of it as especially innovative or revolutionary and thus was surprised by Fuller's reaction to it.
(D) It was produced as a personal favor to Fuller and thus was not initially intended to be noticed and commented on by art critics.
(E) It was unlike the sculptures that Noguchi had helped Brancusi to produce in that the latter's aesthetic effects did not depend on contrasts of light and shadow.

22. Which one of the following would, if true, most weaken the author's position in the passage?

(A) Between 1927 and 1929, Brancusi experimented with the use of highly reflective material for the creation of positive-light sculptures.
(B) After completing the portrait of Fuller, Noguchi produced only a few positive-light sculptures and in fact changed his style of sculpture repeatedly throughout his career.
(C) When Noguchi arrived in Paris, he was already well aware of the international acclaim that Brancusi's sculptures were receiving at the time.
(D) Many of Noguchi's sculptures were, unlike the portrait of Fuller, entirely abstract.
(E) Despite his inquisitive and scientific approach to the art of sculpture, Noguchi neither thought of himself as a scientist nor had extensive scientific training.

GO ON TO THE NEXT PAGE.

In an experiment, two strangers are given the opportunity to share $100, subject to the following constraints: One person—the "proposer"—is to suggest how to divide the money and can make only one such proposal. The other person—the "responder"— must either accept or reject the offer without qualification. Both parties know that if the offer is accepted, the money will be split as agreed, but if the offer is rejected, neither will receive anything.

This scenario is called the Ultimatum Game. Researchers have conducted it numerous times with a wide variety of volunteers. Many participants in the role of the proposer seem instinctively to feel that they should offer 50 percent to the responder, because such a division is "fair" and therefore likely to be accepted. Two-thirds of proposers offer responders between 40 and 50 percent. Only 4 in 100 offer less than 20 percent. Offering such a small amount is quite risky; most responders reject such offers. This is a puzzle: Why would anyone reject an offer as too small? Responders who reject an offer receive nothing, so if one assumes—as theoretical economics traditionally has—that people make economic decisions primarily out of rational self-interest, one would expect that an individual would accept any offer.

Some theorists explain the insistence on fair divisions in the Ultimatum Game by citing our prehistoric ancestors' need for the support of a strong group. Small groups of hunter-gatherers depended for survival on their members' strengths. It is counterproductive to outcompete rivals within one's group to the point where one can no longer depend on them in contests with other groups. But this hypothesis at best explains why proposers offer large amounts, not why responders reject low offers.

A more compelling explanation is that our emotional apparatus has been shaped by millions of years of living in small groups, where it is hard to keep secrets. Our emotions are therefore not finely tuned to one-time, strictly anonymous interactions. In real life we expect our friends and neighbors to notice our decisions. If people know that someone is content with a small share, they are likely to make that person low offers. But if someone is known to angrily reject low offers, others have an incentive to make that person high offers. Consequently, evolution should have favored angry responses to low offers; if one regularly receives fair offers when food is divided, one is more likely to survive. Because one-shot interactions were rare during human evolution, our emotions do not discriminate between one-shot and repeated interactions. Therefore, we respond emotionally to low offers in the Ultimatum Game because we instinctively feel the need to reject dismal offers in order to keep our self-esteem. This self-esteem helps us to acquire a reputation that is beneficial in future encounters.

23. Which one of the following most accurately summarizes the main idea of the passage?

(A) Contrary to a traditional assumption of theoretical economics, the behavior of participants in the Ultimatum Game demonstrates that people do not make economic decisions out of rational self-interest.
(B) Although the reactions most commonly displayed by participants in the Ultimatum Game appear to conflict with rational self-interest, they probably result from a predisposition that had evolutionary value.
(C) Because our emotional apparatus has been shaped by millions of years of living in small groups in which it is hard to keep secrets, our emotions are not finely tuned to one-shot, anonymous interactions.
(D) People respond emotionally to low offers in the Ultimatum Game because they instinctively feel the need to maintain the strength of the social group to which they belong.
(E) When certain social and evolutionary factors are taken into account, it can be seen that the behavior of participants in the Ultimatum Game is motivated primarily by the need to outcompete rivals.

24. The passage implies that the Ultimatum Game is

(A) one that requires two strangers to develop trust in each other
(B) responsible for overturning a basic assumption of theoretical economics
(C) a situation that elicits unpredictable results
(D) a type of one-shot, anonymous interaction
(E) proof that our emotional apparatus has been shaped by millions of years of living in small groups

25. The author's primary purpose in the passage is to

(A) survey existing interpretations of the puzzling results of an experiment
(B) show how two theories that attempt to explain the puzzling results of an experiment complement each other
(C) argue that the results of an experiment, while puzzling, are valid
(D) offer a plausible explanation for the puzzling results of an experiment
(E) defend an experiment against criticism that methodological flaws caused its puzzling results

GO ON TO THE NEXT PAGE.

26. Which one of the following sentences would most logically conclude the final paragraph of the passage?

(A) Contrary to the assumptions of theoretical economics, human beings do not act primarily out of self-interest.
(B) Unfortunately, one-time, anonymous interactions are becoming increasingly common in contemporary society.
(C) The instinctive urge to acquire a favorable reputation may also help to explain the desire of many proposers in the Ultimatum Game to make “fair” offers.
(D) High self-esteem and a positive reputation offer individuals living in small groups many other benefits as well.
(E) The behavior of participants in the Ultimatum Game sheds light on the question of what constitutes a “fair” division.

27. In the context of the passage, the author would be most likely to consider the explanation in the third paragraph more favorably if it were shown that

(A) our prehistoric ancestors often belonged to large groups of more than a hundred people
(B) in many prehistoric cultures, there were hierarchies within groups that dictated which allocations of goods were to be considered fair and which were not
(C) it is just as difficult to keep secrets in relatively large social groups as it is in small social groups
(D) it is just as counterproductive to a small social group to allow oneself to be outcompeted by one’s rivals within the group as it is to outcompete those rivals
(E) in many social groups, there is a mutual understanding among the group’s members that allocations of goods will be based on individual needs as opposed to equal shares

S T O P

IF YOU FINISH BEFORE TIME IS CALLED, YOU MAY CHECK YOUR WORK ON THIS SECTION ONLY. DO NOT WORK ON ANY OTHER SECTION IN THE TEST.

Acknowledgment is made to the following sources from which material has been adapted for use in this test booklet:

Philip Emeagwali, “The Ways of Counting.” ©1991 by the Regents of the University of Michigan.

R. Buckminster Fuller, Foreword to *Isamu Noguchi: A Sculptor’s World.* ©1968 by Harper & Row, Publishers, Inc.

Judith C. May, “Letters to the Editor.”©1997 by The New York Times.

Karl Sigmund, Ernst Fehr, and Martin A. Nowak, “The Economics of Fair Play.” ©2001 by Scientific American, Inc.

David Stainforth, et al., “Climateprediction.net: Design Principles for Public Resource Modeling Research.” ©November 2002 by IASTED.

Jack Stark, “Teaching Statutory Law.” ©1994 by the Association of American Law Schools.

LSAT WRITING SAMPLE TOPIC

Directions: The scenario presented below describes two choices, either one of which can be supported on the basis of the information given. Your essay should consider both choices and argue for one over the other, based on the two specified criteria and the facts provided. There is no "right" or "wrong" choice: a reasonable argument can be made for either.

A new theater group has received an arts grant to produce an inaugural play. Its members are split over whether to use the money to commission and stage a new play, or to produce an existing play that is likely to attract a larger audience. Using the facts below, write an essay in which you argue for one option over the other based on the following two criteria:

- The theater group wants to serve as an ongoing education and entertainment resource for the people of its city.
- The theater group wants to serve as a creative outlet for the writers and actors residing in its city.

The existing play would be a complex production. It features a large cast and elaborate sets. The play was originally produced six years earlier and was popular enough to justify an extended run. The popularity of a theater group's first production affects the amount of corporate sponsorship that could be expected for future productions, and could determine whether the theater group survives into a full season. The first production by a theater group usually creates the expectation for the public as to what future productions will be like. The play has several challenging major parts that are difficult to cast effectively.

A new play would likely involve a smaller cast with simpler sets. It would give the actors a greater creative role in shaping their characters. It would showcase the work of a local playwright. There are currently no theater groups in the city dedicated to producing locally created material. Productions of original plays are more likely to be restaged in other cities. They result in scripts that could possibly be sold to other theater companies. Plays by local writers have drawn small audiences in the past.

Scratch Paper

Do not write your essay in this space.

Directions:

1. Use the Answer Key on the next page to check your answers.

2. Use the Scoring Worksheet below to compute your raw score.

3. Use the Score Conversion Chart to convert your raw score into the 120–180 scale.

Scoring Worksheet

1. Enter the number of questions you answered correctly in each section.

	Number Correct
SECTION I	______
SECTION II	______
SECTION III	______
SECTION IV	______

2. Enter the sum here: ______ **This is your Raw Score.**

Conversion Chart

For Converting Raw Score to the 120–180 LSAT Scaled Score
LSAT PrepTest 59

Reported Score	Lowest Raw Score	Highest Raw Score
180	98	101
179	97	97
178	96	96
177	95	95
176	94	94
175	93	93
174	92	92
173	91	91
172	90	90
171	89	89
170	87	88
169	86	86
168	85	85
167	83	84
166	82	82
165	81	81
164	79	80
163	78	78
162	76	77
161	74	75
160	73	73
159	71	72
158	70	70
157	68	69
156	66	67
155	65	65
154	63	64
153	61	62
152	60	60
151	58	59
150	57	57
149	55	56
148	53	54
147	52	52
146	50	51
145	49	49
144	47	48
143	45	46
142	44	44
141	42	43
140	41	41
139	39	40
138	38	38
137	36	37
136	35	35
135	33	34
134	32	32
133	30	31
132	29	29
131	28	28
130	26	27
129	25	25
128	24	24
127	23	23
126	21	22
125	20	20
124	19	19
123	17	18
122	15	16
121	__*	__*
120	0	14

*There is no raw score that will produce this scaled score for this PrepTest.

SECTION I

1.	C	8.	D	15.	D	22.	B
2.	A	9.	B	16.	A	23.	B
3.	C	10.	D	17.	A		
4.	D	11.	D	18.	E		
5.	C	12.	E	19.	D		
6.	C	13.	C	20.	E		
7.	E	14.	A	21.	E		

SECTION II

1.	A	8.	B	15.	A	22.	A
2.	D	9.	C	16.	E	23.	D
3.	A	10.	D	17.	E	24.	B
4.	E	11.	B	18.	D	25.	B
5.	E	12.	C	19.	C	26.	B
6.	C	13.	C	20.	D		
7.	E	14.	D	21.	C		

SECTION III

1.	A	8.	B	15.	C	22.	D
2.	A	9.	D	16.	E	23.	B
3.	C	10.	E	17.	A	24.	E
4.	C	11.	B	18.	D	25.	B
5.	C	12.	A	19.	E		
6.	B	13.	D	20.	D		
7.	A	14.	C	21.	E		

SECTION IV

1.	C	8.	E	15.	A	22.	A
2.	C	9.	C	16.	C	23.	B
3.	E	10.	E	17.	D	24.	D
4.	B	11.	B	18.	D	25.	D
5.	C	12.	A	19.	C	26.	C
6.	B	13.	E	20.	E	27.	D
7.	A	14.	B	21.	B		

Experimental Section Answer Key
June 1999, PrepTest 26, Section 1

1.	C	8.	C	15.	B	22.	A
2.	B	9.	E	16.	B	23.	A
3.	A	10.	A	17.	E	24.	E
4.	D	11.	C	18.	C		
5.	E	12.	A	19.	B		
6.	A	13.	D	20.	D		
7.	D	14.	D	21.	A		

PrepTest 60
June 2010

SECTION I

Time—35 minutes

25 Questions

Directions: The questions in this section are based on the reasoning contained in brief statements or passages. For some questions, more than one of the choices could conceivably answer the question. However, you are to choose the best answer; that is, the response that most accurately and completely answers the question. You should not make assumptions that are by commonsense standards implausible, superfluous, or incompatible with the passage. After you have chosen the best answer, blacken the corresponding space on your answer sheet.

1. Jim's teacher asked him to determine whether a sample of a substance contained iron. Jim knew that magnets attract iron, so he placed a magnet near the substance. Jim concluded that the substance did contain iron, because the substance became attached to the magnet.

   Jim's reasoning is questionable in that it fails to consider the possibility that

   (A) iron sometimes fails to be attracted to magnets
   (B) iron is attracted to other objects besides magnets
   (C) the magnet needed to be oriented in a certain way
   (D) magnets attract substances other than iron
   (E) some magnets attract iron more strongly than others

2. All the books in the library have their proper shelf locations recorded in the catalog. The book Horatio wants is missing from its place on the library shelves, and no one in the library is using it. Since it is not checked out to a borrower nor awaiting shelving nor part of a special display, it must have been either misplaced or stolen.

   Which one of the following most accurately describes the method of reasoning used in the argument?

   (A) An observation about one object is used as a basis for a general conclusion regarding the status of similar objects.
   (B) A deficiency in a system is isolated by arguing that the system failed to control one of the objects that it was intended to control.
   (C) A conclusion about a particular object is rebutted by observing that a generalization that applies to most such objects does not apply to the object in question.
   (D) A generalization is rejected by showing that it fails to hold in one particular instance.
   (E) The conclusion is supported by ruling out other possible explanations of an observed fact.

3. The level of sulfur dioxide in the atmosphere is slightly higher than it was ten years ago. This increase is troubling because ten years ago the Interior Ministry imposed new, stricter regulations on emissions from coal-burning power plants. If these regulations had been followed, then the level of sulfur dioxide in the atmosphere would have decreased.

   Which one of the following can be properly inferred from the statements above?

   (A) If current regulations on emissions from coal-burning power plants are not followed from now on, then the level of sulfur dioxide in the atmosphere will continue to increase.
   (B) There have been violations of the regulations on emissions from coal-burning power plants that were imposed ten years ago.
   (C) If the regulations on emissions from coal-burning power plants are made even stronger, the level of sulfur dioxide in the atmosphere still will not decrease.
   (D) Emissions from coal-burning power plants are one of the main sources of air pollution.
   (E) Government regulations will never reduce the level of sulfur dioxide in the atmosphere.

GO ON TO THE NEXT PAGE.

4. Ecologist: Landfills are generally designed to hold ten years' worth of waste. Some people maintain that as the number of active landfills consequently dwindles over the coming decade, there will inevitably be a crisis in landfill availability. However, their prediction obviously relies on the unlikely assumption that no new landfills will open as currently active ones close and is therefore unsound.

The claim that there will be a crisis in landfill availability plays which one of the following roles in the ecologist's argument?

(A) It follows from the claim stated in the argument's first sentence.
(B) It is the main conclusion of the argument.
(C) It establishes the truth of the argument's conclusion.
(D) It is a claim on which the argument as a whole is designed to cast doubt.
(E) It is an intermediate conclusion of the argument.

5. Recent epidemiological studies report that Country X has the lowest incidence of disease P of any country. Nevertheless, residents of Country X who are reported to have contracted disease P are much more likely to die from it than are residents of any other country.

Which one of the following, if true, most helps to resolve the apparent discrepancy described above?

(A) There are several forms of disease P, some of which are more contagious than others.
(B) Most of the fatal cases of disease P found in Country X involve people who do not reside in Country X.
(C) In Country X, diagnosis of disease P seldom occurs except in the most severe cases of the disease.
(D) The number of cases of disease P that occur in any country fluctuates widely from year to year.
(E) Because of its climate, more potentially fatal illnesses occur in Country X than in many other countries.

6. After an oil spill, rehabilitation centers were set up to save sea otters by removing oil from them. The effort was not worthwhile, however, since 357 affected live otters and 900 that had died were counted, but only 222 affected otters, or 18 percent of those counted, were successfully rehabilitated and survived. Further, the percentage of all those affected that were successfully rehabilitated was much lower still, because only a fifth of the otters that died immediately were ever found.

Which one of the following, as potential challenges, most seriously calls into question evidence offered in support of the conclusion above?

(A) Do sea otters of species other than those represented among the otters counted exist in areas that were not affected by the oil spill?
(B) How is it possible to estimate, of the sea otters that died, how many were not found?
(C) Did the process of capturing sea otters unavoidably involve trapping and releasing some otters that were not affected by the spill?
(D) Were other species of wildlife besides sea otters negatively affected by the oil spill?
(E) What was the eventual cost, per otter rehabilitated, of the rehabilitation operation?

7. Psychologist: Research has shown that a weakened immune system increases vulnerability to cancer. So, cancer-patient support groups, though derided by those who believe that disease is a purely biochemical phenomenon, may indeed have genuine therapeutic value, as it is clear that participation in such groups reduces participants' stress levels.

Which one of the following is an assumption required by the psychologist's argument?

(A) Cancer patients can learn to function well under extreme stress.
(B) Disease is not a biochemical phenomenon at all.
(C) Stress can weaken the immune system.
(D) Discussing one's condition eliminates the stress of being in that condition.
(E) Stress is a symptom of a weakened immune system.

GO ON TO THE NEXT PAGE.

8. Adobe is an ideal material for building in desert environments. It conducts heat very slowly. As a result, a house built of adobe retains the warmth of the desert sun during the cool evenings and then remains cool during the heat of the day, thereby helping to maintain a pleasant temperature. In contrast, houses built of other commonly used building materials, which conduct heat more rapidly, grow hot during the day and cold at night.

   Which one of the following most accurately expresses the main conclusion drawn in the argument above?

   (A) Adobe is a suitable substitute for other building materials where the heat-conduction properties of the structure are especially important.
   (B) In the desert, adobe buildings remain cool during the heat of the day but retain the warmth of the sun during the cool evenings.
   (C) Because adobe conducts heat very slowly, adobe houses maintain a pleasant, constant temperature.
   (D) Ideally, a material used for building houses in desert environments should enable those houses to maintain a pleasant, constant temperature.
   (E) Adobe is an especially suitable material to use for building houses in desert environments.

9. In one study of a particular plant species, 70 percent of the plants studied were reported as having patterned stems. In a second study, which covered approximately the same geographical area, only 40 percent of the plants of that species were reported as having patterned stems.

   Which one of the following, if true, most helps to resolve the apparent discrepancy described above?

   (A) The first study was carried out at the time of year when plants of the species are at their most populous.
   (B) The first study, but not the second study, also collected information about patterned stems in other plant species.
   (C) The second study included approximately 15 percent more individual plants than the first study did.
   (D) The first study used a broader definition of "patterned."
   (E) The focus of the second study was patterned stems, while the first study collected information about patterned stems only as a secondary goal.

10. Letter to the editor: Sites are needed for disposal of contaminated dredge spoils from the local harbor. However, the approach you propose would damage commercial fishing operations. One indication of this is that over 20,000 people have signed petitions opposing your approach and favoring instead the use of sand-capped pits in another area.

    Which one of the following most accurately describes a reasoning flaw in the letter's argument?

    (A) The argument distorts the editor's view in a manner that makes that view seem more vulnerable to criticism.
    (B) The argument fails to establish that the alternative approach referred to is a viable one.
    (C) The argument attempts to establish a particular conclusion because doing so is in the letter writer's self-interest rather than because of any genuine concern for the truth of the matter.
    (D) The argument's conclusion is based on the testimony of people who have not been shown to have appropriate expertise.
    (E) The argument takes for granted that no third option is available that will satisfy all the interested parties.

GO ON TO THE NEXT PAGE.

11. Most universities today offer students a more in-depth and cosmopolitan education than ever before. Until recently, for example, most university history courses required only the reading of textbooks that hardly mentioned the history of Africa or Asia after the ancient periods, or the history of the Americas' indigenous cultures. The history courses at most universities no longer display such limitations.

Which one of the following, if true, most strengthens the argument above?

(A) The history courses that university students find most interesting are comprehensive in their coverage of various periods and cultures.
(B) Many students at universities whose history courses require the reading of books covering all periods and world cultures participate in innovative study-abroad programs.
(C) The extent to which the textbooks of university history courses are culturally inclusive is a strong indication of the extent to which students at those universities get an in-depth and cosmopolitan education.
(D) Universities at which the history courses are quite culturally inclusive do not always have courses in other subject areas that show the same inclusiveness.
(E) University students who in their history courses are required only to read textbooks covering the history of a single culture will not get an in-depth and cosmopolitan education from these courses alone.

12. The government has recently adopted a policy of publishing airline statistics, including statistics about each airline's number of near collisions and its fines for safety violations. However, such disclosure actually undermines the government's goal of making the public more informed about airline safety, because airlines will be much less likely to give complete reports if such information will be made available to the public.

The reasoning in the argument is most vulnerable to criticism on the grounds that it

(A) fails to consider that, even if the reports are incomplete, they may nevertheless provide the public with important information about airline safety
(B) presumes, without providing justification, that the public has a right to all information about matters of public safety
(C) presumes, without providing justification, that information about airline safety is impossible to find in the absence of government disclosures
(D) presumes, without providing justification, that airlines, rather than the government, should be held responsible for accurate reporting of safety information
(E) fails to consider whether the publication of airline safety statistics will have an effect on the revenues of airlines

13. Many economists claim that financial rewards provide the strongest incentive for people to choose one job over another. But in many surveys, most people do not name high salary as the most desirable feature of a job. This shows that these economists overestimate the degree to which people are motivated by money in their job choices.

Which one of the following, if true, most weakens the argument?

(A) Even high wages do not enable people to obtain all the goods they desire.
(B) In many surveys, people say that they would prefer a high-wage job to an otherwise identical job with lower wages.
(C) Jobs that pay the same salary often vary considerably in their other financial benefits.
(D) Many people enjoy the challenge of a difficult job, as long as they feel that their efforts are appreciated.
(E) Some people are not aware that jobs with high salaries typically leave very little time for recreation.

14. Editorial: A proposed new law would limit elementary school class sizes to a maximum of 20 students. Most parents support this measure and argue that making classes smaller allows teachers to devote more time to each student, with the result that students become more engaged in the learning process. However, researchers who conducted a recent study conclude from their results that this reasoning is questionable. The researchers studied schools that had undergone recent reductions in class size, and found that despite an increase in the amount of time teachers spent individually with students, the students' average grades were unchanged.

Which one of the following is an assumption required by the researchers' argument?

(A) The only schools appropriate for study are large elementary schools.
(B) Teachers generally devote the same amount of individualized attention to each student in a class.
(C) Reductions in class size would also involve a decrease in the number of teachers.
(D) Degree of student engagement in the learning process correlates well with students' average grades.
(E) Parental support for the proposed law rests solely on expectations of increased student engagement in the learning process.

GO ON TO THE NEXT PAGE.

15. Camille: Manufacturers of water-saving faucets exaggerate the amount of money such faucets can save. Because the faucets handle such a low volume of water, people using them often let the water run longer than they would otherwise.

Rebecca: It is true that showering now takes longer. Nevertheless, I have had lower water bills since I installed a water-saving faucet. Thus, it is not true that the manufacturers' claims are exaggerated.

The reasoning in Rebecca's argument is questionable in that she takes for granted that

(A) the cost of installing her water-saving faucet was less than her overall savings on her water bill
(B) she saved as much on her water bills as the manufacturers' claims suggested she would
(C) the manufacturers' claims about the savings expected from the installation of water-saving faucets are consistent with one another
(D) people who use water-saving faucets are satisfied with the low volume of water handled by such faucets
(E) installing more water-saving faucets in her house would increase her savings

16. Company spokesperson: In lieu of redesigning our plants, our company recently launched an environmental protection campaign to buy and dispose of old cars, which are generally highly pollutive. Our plants account for just 4 percent of the local air pollution, while automobiles that predate 1980 account for 30 percent. Clearly, we will reduce air pollution more by buying old cars than we would by redesigning our plants.

Which one of the following, if true, most seriously weakens the company spokesperson's argument?

(A) Only 1 percent of the automobiles driven in the local area predate 1980.
(B) It would cost the company over $3 million to reduce its plants' toxic emissions, while its car-buying campaign will save the company money by providing it with reusable scrap metal.
(C) Because the company pays only scrap metal prices for used cars, almost none of the cars sold to the company still run.
(D) Automobiles made after 1980 account for over 30 percent of local air pollution.
(E) Since the company launched its car-buying campaign, the number of citizen groups filing complaints about pollution from the company's plants has decreased.

17. Humankind would not have survived, as it clearly has, if our ancestors had not been motivated by the desire to sacrifice themselves when doing so would ensure the survival of their children or other close relatives. But since even this kind of sacrifice is a form of altruism, it follows that our ancestors were at least partially altruistic.

Which one of the following arguments is most similar in its reasoning to the argument above?

(A) Students do not raise their grades if they do not increase the amount of time they spend studying. Increased study time requires good time management. However, some students do raise their grades. So some students manage their time well.
(B) Organisms are capable of manufacturing their own carbohydrate supply if they do not consume other organisms to obtain it. So plants that consume insects must be incapable of photosynthesis, the means by which most plants produce their carbohydrate supplies.
(C) If fragile ecosystems are not protected by government action their endemic species will perish, for endemic species are by definition those that exist nowhere else but in those ecosystems.
(D) The natural resources used by human beings will be depleted if they are not replaced by alternative materials. But since such replacement generally requires more power, the resources used to create that power will become depleted.
(E) Public buildings do not harmonize with their surroundings if they are not well designed. But any well-designed building is expensive to construct. Thus, either public buildings are expensive to construct or else they do not harmonize with their surroundings.

GO ON TO THE NEXT PAGE.

18. Bus driver: Had the garbage truck not been exceeding the speed limit, it would not have collided with the bus I was driving. I, on the other hand, was abiding by all traffic regulations—as the police report confirms. Therefore, although I might have been able to avoid the collision had I reacted more quickly, the bus company should not reprimand me for the accident.

Which one of the following principles, if valid, most helps to justify the reasoning in the bus driver's argument?

(A) If a vehicle whose driver is violating a traffic regulation collides with a vehicle whose driver is not, the driver of the first vehicle is solely responsible for the accident.
(B) A bus company should not reprimand one of its drivers whose bus is involved in a collision if a police report confirms that the collision was completely the fault of the driver of another vehicle.
(C) Whenever a bus driver causes a collision to occur by violating a traffic regulation, the bus company should reprimand that driver.
(D) A company that employs bus drivers should reprimand those drivers only when they become involved in collisions that they reasonably could have been expected to avoid.
(E) When a bus is involved in a collision, the bus driver should not be reprimanded by the bus company if the collision did not result from the bus driver's violating a traffic regulation.

19. Item Removed From Scoring.

20. Historian: Radio drama requires its listeners to think about what they hear, picturing for themselves such dramatic elements as characters' physical appearances and spatial relationships. Hence, while earlier generations, for whom radio drama was the dominant form of popular entertainment, regularly exercised their imaginations, today's generation of television viewers do so less frequently.

Which one of the following is an assumption required by the historian's argument?

(A) People spend as much time watching television today as people spent listening to radio in radio's heyday.
(B) The more familiar a form of popular entertainment becomes, the less likely its consumers are to exercise their imaginations.
(C) Because it inhibits the development of creativity, television is a particularly undesirable form of popular entertainment.
(D) For today's generation of television viewers, nothing fills the gap left by radio as a medium for exercising the imagination.
(E) Television drama does not require its viewers to think about what they see.

GO ON TO THE NEXT PAGE.

21. Each of the candidates in this year's mayoral election is a small-business owner. Most small-business owners are competent managers. Moreover, no competent manager lacks the skills necessary to be a good mayor. So, most of the candidates in this year's mayoral election have the skills necessary to be a good mayor.

The pattern of flawed reasoning in which one of the following is most similar to that in the argument above?

(A) Anyone who has worked in sales at this company has done so for at least a year. Most of this company's management has worked in its sales department. So, since no one who has worked in the sales department for more than a year fails to understand marketing, most of this company's upper management understands marketing.
(B) Everything on the menu at Maddy's Shake Shop is fat-free. Most fat-free foods and drinks are sugar-free. And all sugar-free foods and drinks are low in calories. Hence, most items on the menu at Maddy's are low in calories.
(C) All the books in Ed's apartment are hardcover books. Most hardcover books are more than 100 pages long. Ed has never read a book longer than 100 pages in its entirety in less than 3 hours. So, Ed has never read any of his books in its entirety in less than 3 hours.
(D) Each of the avant-garde films at this year's film festival is less than an hour long. Most films less than an hour long do not become commercially successful. So, since no movie less than an hour long has an intermission, it follows that most of the movies at this year's film festival do not have an intermission.
(E) All of the bicycle helmets sold in this store have some plastic in them. Most of the bicycle helmets sold in this store have some rubber in them. So, since no helmets that have rubber in them do not also have plastic in them, it follows that most of the helmets in this store that have plastic in them have rubber in them.

22. One of the most useful social conventions is money, whose universality across societies is matched only by language. Unlike language, which is rooted in an innate ability, money is an artificial, human invention. Hence, it seems probable that the invention of money occurred independently in more than one society.

The argument's conclusion is properly drawn if which one of the following is assumed?

(A) Some societies have been geographically isolated enough not to have been influenced by any other society.
(B) Language emerged independently in different societies at different times in human history.
(C) Universal features of human society that are not inventions are rooted in innate abilities.
(D) If money were not useful, it would not be so widespread.
(E) No human society that adopted the convention of money has since abandoned it.

23. Libel is defined as damaging the reputation of someone by making false statements. Ironically, strong laws against libel can make it impossible for anyone in the public eye to have a good reputation. For the result of strong libel laws is that, for fear of lawsuits, no one will say anything bad about public figures.

Which one of the following principles, if valid, most helps to justify the reasoning in the argument?

(A) The absence of laws against libel makes it possible for everyone in the public eye to have a good reputation.
(B) Even if laws against libel are extremely strong and rigorously enforced, some public figures will acquire bad reputations.
(C) If one makes statements that one sincerely believes, then those statements should not be considered libelous even if they are in fact false and damaging to the reputation of a public figure.
(D) In countries with strong libel laws, people make negative statements about public figures only when such statements can be proved.
(E) Public figures can have good reputations only if there are other public figures who have bad reputations.

24. Mammals cannot digest cellulose and therefore cannot directly obtain glucose from wood. Mushrooms can, however; and some mushrooms use cellulose to make highly branched polymers, the branches of which are a form of glucose called beta-glucans. Beta-glucan extracts from various types of mushrooms slow, reverse, or prevent the growth of cancerous tumors in mammals, and the antitumor activity of beta-glucans increases as the degree of branching increases. These extracts prevent tumor growth not by killing cancer cells directly but by increasing immune-cell activity.

Which one of the following is most strongly supported by the information above?

(A) Mammals obtain no beneficial health effects from eating cellulose.
(B) If extracts from a type of mushroom slow, reverse, or prevent the growth of cancerous tumors in mammals, then the mushroom is capable of using cellulose to make beta-glucans.
(C) The greater the degree of branching of beta-glucans, the greater the degree of immune-cell activity it triggers in mammals.
(D) Immune-cell activity in mammals does not prevent tumor growth by killing cancer cells.
(E) Any organism capable of obtaining glucose from wood can use cellulose to make beta-glucans.

25. A law is successful primarily because the behavior it prescribes has attained the status of custom. Just as manners are observed not because of sanctions attached to them but because, through repetition, contrary behavior becomes unthinkable, so societal laws are obeyed not because the behavior is ethically required or because penalties await those who act otherwise, but because to act otherwise would be uncustomary.

Which one of the following comparisons is utilized by the argument?

(A) As with manners and other customs, laws vary from society to society.
(B) As with manners, the primary basis for a society to consider when adopting a law is custom.
(C) As with manners, the main factor accounting for compliance with laws is custom.
(D) As with manners, most laws do not prescribe behavior that is ethically required.
(E) As with manners, most laws do not have strict penalties awaiting those who transgress them.

S T O P

IF YOU FINISH BEFORE TIME IS CALLED, YOU MAY CHECK YOUR WORK ON THIS SECTION ONLY.
DO NOT WORK ON ANY OTHER SECTION IN THE TEST.

Time—35 minutes
27 Questions

Directions: Each passage in this section is followed by a group of questions to be answered on the basis of what is stated or implied in the passage. For some of the questions, more than one of the choices could conceivably answer the question. However, you are to choose the best answer; that is, the response that most accurately and completely answers the question, and blacken the corresponding space on your answer sheet.

Opponents of compulsory national service claim that such a program is not in keeping with the liberal principles upon which Western democracies are founded. This reasoning is reminiscent of the argument that a tax on one's income is undemocratic because it violates one's right to property. Such conceptions of the liberal state fail to take into account the intricate character of the social agreement that undergirds our liberties. It is only in the context of a community that the notion of individual rights has any application; individual rights are meant to define the limits of people's actions with respect to other people. Implicit in such a context is the concept of shared sacrifice. Were no taxes paid, there could be no law enforcement, and the enforcement of law is of benefit to everyone in society. Thus, each of us must bear a share of the burden to ensure that the community is protected.

The responsibility to defend one's nation against outside aggression is surely no less than the responsibility to help pay for law enforcement within the nation. Therefore, the state is certainly within its rights to compel citizens to perform national service when it is needed for the benefit of society.

It might be objected that the cases of taxation and national service are not analogous: While taxation must be coerced, the military is quite able to find recruits without resorting to conscription. Furthermore, proponents of national service do not limit its scope to only those duties absolutely necessary to the defense of the nation. Therefore, it may be contended, compulsory national service oversteps the acceptable boundaries of governmental interference in the lives of its citizens.

By responding thus, the opponent of national service has already allowed that it is a right of government to demand service when it is needed. But what is the true scope of the term "need"? If it is granted, say, that present tax policies are legitimate intrusions on the right to property, then it must also be granted that need involves more than just what is necessary for a sound national defense. Even the most conservative of politicians admits that tax money is rightly spent on programs that, while not necessary for the survival of the state, are nevertheless of great benefit to society. Can the opponent of national service truly claim that activities of the military such as quelling civil disorders, rebuilding dams and bridges, or assisting the victims of natural disasters—all extraneous to the defense of society against outside aggression—do not provide a similar benefit to the nation? Upon reflection, opponents of national service must concede that such a broadened conception of what is necessary is in keeping with the ideas of shared sacrifice and community benefit that are essential to the functioning of a liberal democratic state.

1. Which one of the following most accurately describes the author's attitude toward the relationship between citizenship and individual rights in a democracy?

(A) confidence that individual rights are citizens' most important guarantees of personal freedom
(B) satisfaction at how individual rights have protected citizens from unwarranted government intrusion
(C) alarm that so many citizens use individual rights as an excuse to take advantage of one another
(D) concern that individual rights represent citizens' only defense against government interference
(E) dissatisfaction at how some citizens cite individual rights as a way of avoiding certain obligations to their government

GO ON TO THE NEXT PAGE.

2. The author indicates that all politicians agree about the

   (A) legitimacy of funding certain programs that serve the national good
   (B) use of the military to prevent domestic disorders
   (C) similarity of conscription and compulsory taxation
   (D) importance of broadening the definition of necessity
   (E) compatibility of compulsion with democratic principles

3. Which one of the following most accurately characterizes what the author means by the term "social agreement" (line 8)?

   (A) an agreement among members of a community that the scope of their individual liberties is limited somewhat by their obligations to one another
   (B) an agreement among members of a community that they will not act in ways that infringe upon each other's pursuit of individual liberty
   (C) an agreement among members of a community that they will petition the government for redress when government actions limit their rights
   (D) an agreement between citizens and their government detailing which government actions do or do not infringe upon citizens' personal freedoms
   (E) an agreement between citizens and their government stating that the government has the right to suspend individual liberties whenever it sees fit

4. According to the author, national service and taxation are analogous in the sense that both

   (A) do not require that citizens be compelled to help bring them about
   (B) are at odds with the notion of individual rights in a democracy
   (C) require different degrees of sacrifice from different citizens
   (D) allow the government to overstep its boundaries and interfere in the lives of citizens
   (E) serve ends beyond those related to the basic survival of the state

5. Based on the information in the passage, which one of the following would most likely be found objectionable by those who oppose compulsory national service?

   (A) the use of tax revenues to prevent the theft of national secrets by foreign agents
   (B) the use of tax revenues to fund relief efforts for victims of natural disasters in other nations
   (C) the use of tax revenues to support the upkeep of the nation's standing army
   (D) the use of tax revenues to fund programs for the maintenance of domestic dams and bridges
   (E) the use of tax revenues to aid citizens who are victims of natural disasters

GO ON TO THE NEXT PAGE.

James Porter (1905–1970) was the first scholar to identify the African influence on visual art in the Americas, and much of what is known about the cultural legacy that African-American artists inherited from their African forebears has come to us by way of his work. Porter, a painter and art historian, began by studying African-American crafts of the eighteenth and nineteenth centuries. This research revealed that many of the household items created by African-American men and women—walking sticks, jugs, and textiles—displayed characteristics that linked them iconographically to artifacts of West Africa. Porter then went on to establish clearly the range of the cultural territory inherited by later African-American artists.

An example of this aspect of Porter's research occurs in his essay "Robert S. Duncanson, Midwestern Romantic-Realist." The work of Duncanson, a nineteenth-century painter of the Hudson River school, like that of his predecessor in the movement, Joshua Johnston, was commonly thought to have been created by a Euro-American artist. Porter proved definitively that both Duncanson and Johnston were of African ancestry. Porter published this finding and thousands of others in a comprehensive volume tracing the history of African-American art. At the time of its first printing in 1943, only two other books devoted exclusively to the accomplishments of African-American artists existed. Both of these books were written by Alain LeRoy Locke, a professor at the university where Porter also taught. While these earlier studies by Locke are interesting for being the first to survey the field, neither addressed the critical issue of African precursors; Porter's book addressed this issue, painstakingly integrating the history of African-American art into the larger history of art in the Americas without separating it from those qualities that gave it its unique ties to African artisanship. Porter may have been especially attuned to these ties because of his conscious effort to maintain them in his own paintings, many of which combine the style of the genre portrait with evidence of an extensive knowledge of the cultural history of various African peoples.

In his later years, Porter wrote additional chapters for later editions of his book, constantly revising and correcting his findings, some of which had been based of necessity on fragmentary evidence. Among his later achievements were his definitive reckoning of the birth year of the painter Patrick Reason, long a point of scholarly uncertainty, and his identification of an unmarked grave in San Francisco as that of the sculptor Edmonia Lewis. At his death, Porter left extensive notes for an unfinished project aimed at exploring the influence of African art on the art of the Western world generally, a body of research whose riches scholars still have not exhausted.

6. Which one of the following most accurately states the main idea of the passage?

(A) Because the connections between African-American art and other art in the Americas had been established by earlier scholars, Porter's work focused on showing African-American art's connections to African artisanship.
(B) In addition to showing the connections between African-American art and African artisanship, Porter's most important achievement was illustrating the links between African-American art and other art in the Americas.
(C) Despite the fact that his last book remains unfinished, Porter's work was the first to devote its attention exclusively to the accomplishments of African-American artists.
(D) Although showing the connections between African-American art and African artisanship, Porter's work concentrated primarily on placing African-American art in the context of Western art in general.
(E) While not the first body of scholarship to treat the subject of African-American art, Porter's work was the first to show the connections between African-American art and African artisanship.

7. The discussion of Locke's books is intended primarily to

(A) argue that Porter's book depended upon Locke's pioneering scholarship
(B) highlight an important way in which Porter's work differed from previous work in his field
(C) suggest an explanation for why Porter's book was little known outside academic circles
(D) support the claim that Porter was not the first to notice African influences in African-American art
(E) argue that Locke's example was a major influence on Porter's decision to publish his findings.

8. The passage states which one of the following about the 1943 edition of Porter's book on African-American art?

(A) It received little scholarly attention at first.
(B) It was revised and improved upon in later editions.
(C) It took issue with several of Locke's conclusions.
(D) It is considered the definitive versions of Porter's work.
(E) It explored the influence of African art on Western art in general.

GO ON TO THE NEXT PAGE.

9. Given the information in the passage, Porter's identification of the ancestry of Duncanson and Johnston provides conclusive evidence for which one of the following statements?

(A) Some of the characteristics defining the Hudson River school are iconographically linked to West African artisanship.
(B) Some of the works of Duncanson and Johnston are not in the style of the Hudson River school.
(C) Some of the work of Euro-American painters displays similarities to African-American crafts of the eighteenth and nineteenth centuries.
(D) Some of the works of the Hudson River school were done by African-American painters.
(E) Some of the works of Duncanson and Johnston were influenced by West African artifacts.

10. Which one of the following can most reasonably be inferred from the passage about the study that Porter left unfinished at his death?

(A) If completed, it would have contradicted some of the conclusions contained in his earlier book.
(B) If completed, it would have amended some of the conclusions contained in his earlier book.
(C) If completed, it would have brought up to date the comprehensive history of African-American art begun in his earlier book.
(D) If completed, it would have expanded upon the project of his earlier book by broadening the scope of inquiry found in the earlier book.
(E) If completed, it would have supported some of the theories put forth by Porter's contemporaries since the publication of his earlier book.

11. Which one of the following hypothetical observations is most closely analogous to the discoveries Porter made about African-American crafts of the eighteenth and nineteenth centuries?

(A) Contemporary Haitian social customs have a unique character dependent on but different from both their African and French origins.
(B) Popular music in the United States, some of which is based on African musical traditions, often influences music being composed on the African continent.
(C) Many novels written in Canada by Chinese immigrants exhibit narrative themes very similar to those found in Chinese folktales.
(D) Extensive Indian immigration to England has made traditional Indian foods nearly as popular there as the traditional English foods that had been popular there before Indian immigration.
(E) Some Mexican muralists of the early twentieth century consciously imitated the art of native peoples as a response to the Spanish influences that had predominated in Mexican art.

12. The passage most strongly supports which one of the following inferences about Porter's own paintings?

(A) They often contained figures or images derived from the work of African artisans.
(B) They fueled his interest in pursuing a career in art history.
(C) They were used in Porter's book to show the extent of African influence on African-American art.
(D) They were a deliberate attempt to prove his theories about art history.
(E) They were done after all of his academic work had been completed.

13. Based on the passage, which one of the following, if true, would have been most relevant to the project Porter was working on at the time of his death?

(A) African-American crafts of the eighteenth and nineteenth centuries have certain resemblances to European folk crafts of earlier periods.
(B) The paintings of some twentieth-century European artists prefigured certain stylistic developments in North American graphic art.
(C) The designs of many of the quilts made by African-American women in the nineteenth century reflect designs of European trade goods.
(D) After the movement of large numbers of African Americans to cities, the African influences in the work of many African-American painters increased.
(E) Several portraits by certain twentieth-century European painters were modeled after examples of Central African ceremonial masks.

GO ON TO THE NEXT PAGE.

Between June 1987 and May 19888, the bodies of at least 740 bottlenose dolphins out of a total coastal population of 3,000 to 5,000 washed ashore on the Atlantic coast of the United States. Since some of the dead animals never washed ashore, the overall disaster was presumably worse; perhaps 50 percent of the population died. A dolphin die-off of this character and magnitude had never before been observed; furthermore, the dolphins exhibited a startling range of symptoms. The research team that examined the die-off noted the presence of both skin lesions and internal lesions in the liver, lung, pancreas, and heart, which suggested a massive opportunistic bacterial infection of already weakened animals.

Tissues from the stricken dolphins were analyzed for a variety of toxins. Brevetoxin, a toxin produced by the blooming of the alga *Ptychodiscus brevis*, was present in eight out of seventeen dolphins tested. Tests for synthetic pollutants revealed that polychlorinated biphenyls (PCBs) were present in almost all animals tested.

The research team concluded that brevetoxin poisoning was the most likely cause of the illnesses that killed the dolphins. Although *P. brevis* is ordinarily not found along the Atlantic coast, an unusual bloom of this organism—such blooms are called "red tides" because of the reddish color imparted by the blooming algae—did occur in the middle of the affected coastline in October 1987. These researchers believe the toxin accumulated in the tissue of fish and then was ingested by dolphins that preyed on them. The emaciated appearance of many dolphins indicated that they were metabolizing their blubber reserves, thereby reducing their buoyancy and insulation (and adding to overall stress) as well as releasing stores of previously accumulated synthetic pollutants, such as PCBs, which further exacerbated their condition. The combined impact made the dolphins vulnerable to opportunistic bacterial infection, the ultimate cause of death.

For several reasons, however, this explanation is not entirely plausible. First, bottlenose dolphins and *P. brevis* red tides are both common in the Gulf of Mexico, yet no dolphin die-off of a similar magnitude has been noted there. Second, dolphins began dying in June, hundreds of miles north of and some months earlier than the October red tide bloom. Finally, the specific effects of brevetoxin on dolphins are unknown, whereas PCB poisoning is known to impair functioning of the immune system and liver and to cause skin lesions; all of these problems were observed in the diseased animals. An alternative hypothesis, which accounts for these facts, is that a sudden influx of pollutants, perhaps from offshore dumping, triggered a cascade of disorders in animals whose systems were already heavily laden with pollutants. Although brevetoxin may have been a contributing factor, the event that actually precipitated the die-off was a sharp increase in the dolphins' exposure to synthetic pollutants.

14. The passage is primarily concerned with assessing

(A) the effects of a devastating bacterial infection in Atlantic coast bottlenose dolphins
(B) the process by which illnesses in Atlantic coast bottlenose dolphins were correctly diagnosed
(C) the weaknesses in the research methodology used to explore the dolphin die-off
(D) possible alternative explanations for the massive dolphin die-off
(E) relative effects of various marine pollutants on dolphin mortality

15. Which one of the following is mentioned in the passage as evidence for the explanation of the dolphin die-off offered in the final paragraph?

(A) the release of stored brevetoxins from the dolphins' blubber reserves
(B) the date on which offshore dumping was known to have occurred nearby
(C) the presence of dumping sites for PCBs in the area
(D) the synthetic pollutants that were present in the fish eaten by the dolphins
(E) the effects of PCBs on liver function in dolphins

16. Which one of the following is most analogous to the approach taken by the author of the passage with regard to the research described in the third paragraph?

(A) A physics teacher accepts the data from a student's experiment but questions the student's conclusions.
(B) An astronomer provides additional observations to support another astronomer's theory.
(C) A cook revises a traditional recipe by substituting modern ingredients for those used in the original.
(D) A doctor prescribes medication for a patient whose illness was misdiagnosed by another doctor.
(E) A microbiologist sets out to replicate the experiment that yielded a classic theory of cell structure.

GO ON TO THE NEXT PAGE.

17. Which one of the following most accurately describes the organization of the last paragraph?

(A) One explanation is criticized and a different explanation is proposed.
(B) An argument is advanced and then refuted by means of an opposing argument.
(C) Objections against a hypothesis are advanced, the hypothesis is explained more fully, and then the objections are rejected.
(D) New evidence in favor of a theory is described, and then the theory is reaffirmed.
(E) Discrepancies between two explanations are noted, and a third explanation is proposed.

18. It can be inferred from the passage that the author would most probably agree with which one of the following statements about brevetoxin?

(A) It may have been responsible for the dolphins' skin lesions but could not have contributed to the bacterial infection.
(B) It forms more easily when both *P. brevis* and synthetic pollutants are present in the environment simultaneously.
(C) It damages liver function and immune system responses in bottlenose dolphins but may not have triggered this particular dolphin die-off.
(D) It is unlikely to be among the factors that contributed to the dolphin die-off.
(E) It is unlikely to have caused the die-off because it was not present in the dolphins' environment when the die-off began.

19. The explanation for the dolphin die-off given by the research team most strongly supports which one of the following?

(A) The biological mechanism by which brevetoxin affects dolphins is probably different from that by which it affects other marine animals.
(B) When *P. brevis* blooms in an area where it does not usually exist, it is more toxic than it is in its usual habitat.
(C) Opportunistic bacterial infection is usually associated with brevetoxin poisoning in bottlenose dolphins.
(D) The dolphins' emaciated state was probably a symptom of PCB poisoning rather than of brevetoxin poisoning rather than of brevetoxin poisoning.
(E) When a dolphin metabolizes its blubber, the PCBs released may be more dangerous to the dolphin than they were when stored in the blubber.

20. The author refers to dolphins in the Gulf of Mexico in the last paragraph in order to

(A) refute the assertion that dolphins tend not to inhabit areas where *P. brevis* is common
(B) compare the effects of synthetic pollutants on these dolphins and on Atlantic coast dolphins
(C) cast doubt on the belief that *P. brevis* contributes substantially to dolphin die-offs
(D) illustrate the fact that dolphins in relatively pollution-free waters are healthier than dolphins in polluted waters.
(E) provide evidence for the argument that *P. brevis* was probably responsible for the dolphins' deaths

21. Which one of the following factors is explicitly cited as contributing to the dolphins' deaths in both theories discussed in the passage?

(A) the dolphins diet
(B) the presence of *P. brevis* in the Gulf of Mexico
(C) the wide variety of toxins released by the red tide bloom of October 1987
(D) the presence of synthetic pollutants in the dolphins' bodies
(E) the bacterial infection caused by a generalized failure of the dolphins' immune systems

GO ON TO THE NEXT PAGE.

In England before 1660, a husband controlled his wife's property. In the late seventeenth and eighteenth centuries, with the shift from land-based to commercial wealth, marriage began to incorporate certain features of a contract. Historians have traditionally argued that this trend represented a gain for women, one that reflects changing views about democracy and property following the English Restoration in 1660. Susan Staves contests this view; she argues that whatever gains marriage contracts may briefly have represented for women were undermined by judicial decisions about women's contractual rights.

Shifting through the tangled details of court cases, Staves demonstrates that, despite surface changes, a rhetoric of equality, and occasional decisions supporting women's financial power, definitions of men's and women's property remained inconsistent—generally to women's detriment. For example, dower lands (property inherited by wives after their husbands' deaths) could not be sold, but "curtesy" property (inherited by husbands from their wives) could be sold. Furthermore, comparatively new concepts that developed in conjunction with the marriage contract, such as jointure, pin money, and separate maintenance, were compromised by peculiar rules. For instance, if a woman spent her pin money (money paid by the husband according to the marriage contract for the wife's personal items) on possessions other than clothes she could not sell them; in effect they belonged to her husband. In addition, a wife could sue for pin money only up to a year in arrears-which rendered a suit impractical. Similarly, separate maintenance allowances (stated sums of money for the wife's support if husband and wife agreed to live apart) were complicated by the fact that if a couple tried to agree in a marriage contract on an amount, they were admitting that a supposedly indissoluble bond could be dissolved, an assumption courts could not recognize. Eighteenth-century historians underplayed these inconsistencies, calling them "little contrarieties" that would soon vanish. Staves shows, however, that as judges gained power over decisions on marriage contracts, they tended to fall back on pre-1660 assumptions about property.

Staves' work on women's property has general implications for other studies about women in eighteenth-century England. Staves revises her previous claim that separate maintenance allowances proved the weakening of patriarchy; she now finds that an oversimplification. She also challenges the contention by historians Jeanne and Lawrence Stone that in the late eighteenth century wealthy men married widows less often than before because couples began marrying for love rather than for financial reasons. Staves does not completely undermine their contention, but she does counter their assumption that widows had more money than never-married women. She points out that jointure property (a widow's lifetime use of an amount of money specified in the marriage contract) was often lost on remarriage.

22. Which one of the following best expresses the main idea of the passage?

(A) As notions of property and democracy changed in late seventeenth- and eighteenth-century England, marriage settlements began to incorporate contractual features designed to protect women's property rights.
(B) Traditional historians have incorrectly identified the contractual features that were incorporated into marriage contracts in late seventeenth- and eighteenth-century England.
(C) The incorporation of contractual features into marriage settlements in late seventeenth- and eighteenth-century England did not represent a significant gain for women.
(D) An examination of late seventeenth- and eighteenth-century English court cases indicates that most marriage settlements did not incorporate contractual features designed to protect women's property rights.
(E) Before marriage settlements incorporated contractual features protecting women's property rights, women were unable to gain any financial power in England.

23. Which one of the following best describes the function of the last paragraph in the context of the passage as a whole?

(A) It suggests that Staves' recent work has caused significant revision of theories about the rights of women in eighteenth-century England.
(B) It discusses research that may qualify Staves' work on women's property in eighteenth-century England.
(C) It provides further support for Staves' argument by describing more recent research on women's property in eighteenth-century England.
(D) It asserts that Staves' recent work has provided support for two other hypotheses developed by historians of eighteenth-century England.
(E) It suggests the implications Staves' recent research has for other theories about women in eighteenth-century England.

GO ON TO THE NEXT PAGE.

24. The primary purpose of the passage is to

    (A) compare two explanations for the same phenomenon
    (B) summarize research that refutes an argument
    (C) resolve a long-standing controversy
    (D) suggest that a recent hypothesis should be reevaluated
    (E) provide support for a traditional theory

25. According to the passage, Staves' research has which one of the following effects on the Stones' contention about marriage in late eighteenth-century England?

    (A) Staves' research undermines one of the Stones' assumptions but does not effectively invalidate their contention.
    (B) Staves' research refutes the Stones' contention by providing additional data overlooked by the Stones.
    (C) Staves' research shows that the Stones' contention cannot be correct, and that a number of their assumptions are mistaken.
    (D) Staves' research indicates that the Stones' contention is incorrect because it is based on contradictory data.
    (E) Staves' research qualifies the Stones' contention by indicating that it is based on accurate but incomplete data.

26. According to the passage, Staves indicates that which one of the following was true of judicial decisions on contractual rights?

    (A) Judges frequently misunderstood and misapplied laws regarding married women's property.
    (B) Judges were aware of inconsistencies in laws concerning women's contractual rights but claimed that such inconsistencies would soon vanish.
    (C) Judges' decisions about marriage contracts tended to reflect assumptions about property that had been common before 1660.
    (D) Judges had little influence on the development and application of laws concerning married women's property.
    (E) Judges recognized the patriarchal assumptions underlying laws concerning married women's property and tried to interpret the laws in ways that would protect women.

27. The passage suggests that the historians mentioned in line 5 would be most likely to agree with which one of the following statements?

    (A) The shift from land-based to commercial wealth changed views about property but did not significantly benefit married women until the late eighteenth century.
    (B) Despite initial judicial resistance to women's contractual rights, marriage contracts represented a significant gain for married women.
    (C) Although marriage contracts incorporated a series of surface changes and a rhetoric of equality, they did not ultimately benefit married women.
    (D) Changing views about property and democracy in post-Restoration England had an effect on property laws that was beneficial to women.
    (E) Although contractual rights protecting women's property represented a small gain for married women, most laws continued to be more beneficial for men than for women.

S T O P

IF YOU FINISH BEFORE TIME IS CALLED, YOU MAY CHECK YOUR WORK ON THIS SECTION ONLY.
DO NOT WORK ON ANY OTHER SECTION IN THE TEST.

SECTION II

Time—35 minutes

23 Questions

Directions: Each group of questions in this section is based on a set of conditions. In answering some of the questions, it may be useful to draw a rough diagram. Choose the response that most accurately and completely answers each question and blacken the corresponding space on your answer sheet.

Questions 1–6

A community center will host six arts-and-crafts workshops—Jewelry, Kite-making, Needlepoint, Quilting, Rug-making, and Scrapbooking. The workshops will be given on three consecutive days: Wednesday, Thursday, and Friday. Each workshop will be given once, and exactly two workshops will be given per day, one in the morning and one in the afternoon. The schedule for the workshops is subject to the following constraints:

Jewelry must be given in the morning, on the same day as either Kite-making or Quilting.

Rug-making must be given in the afternoon, on the same day as either Needlepoint or Scrapbooking.

Quilting must be given on an earlier day than both Kite-making and Needlepoint.

1. Which one of the following is an acceptable schedule for the workshops, with each day's workshops listed in the order in which they are to be given?

(A) Wednesday: Jewelry, Kite-making
Thursday: Quilting, Scrapbooking
Friday: Needlepoint, Rug-making

(B) Wednesday: Jewelry, Quilting
Thursday: Kite-making, Needlepoint
Friday: Scrapbooking, Rug-making

(C) Wednesday: Quilting, Needlepoint
Thursday: Scrapbooking, Rug-making
Friday: Jewelry, Kite-making

(D) Wednesday: Quilting, Scrapbooking
Thursday: Jewelry, Kite-making
Friday: Rug-making, Needlepoint

(E) Wednesday: Scrapbooking, Rug-making
Thursday: Quilting, Jewelry
Friday: Kite-making, Needlepoint

2. Which one of the following workshops CANNOT be given on Thursday morning?

(A) Jewelry
(B) Kite-making
(C) Needlepoint
(D) Quilting
(E) Scrapbooking

3. Which one of the following pairs of workshops CANNOT be the ones given on Wednesday morning and Wednesday afternoon, respectively?

(A) Jewelry, Kite-making
(B) Jewelry, Quilting
(C) Quilting, Scrapbooking
(D) Scrapbooking, Quilting
(E) Scrapbooking, Rug-making

4. If Kite-making is given on Friday morning, then which one of the following could be true?

(A) Jewelry is given on Thursday morning.
(B) Needlepoint is given on Thursday afternoon.
(C) Quilting is given on Wednesday morning.
(D) Rug-making is given on Friday afternoon.
(E) Scrapbooking is given on Wednesday afternoon.

5. If Quilting is given in the morning, then which one of the following workshops CANNOT be given on Thursday?

(A) Jewelry
(B) Kite-making
(C) Needlepoint
(D) Rug-making
(E) Scrapbooking

6. How many of the workshops are there that could be the one given on Wednesday morning?

(A) one
(B) two
(C) three
(D) four
(E) five

GO ON TO THE NEXT PAGE.

Questions 7–12

Exactly six actors—Geyer, Henson, Jhalani, Lin, Mitchell, and Paredes—will appear one after another in the opening credits of a television program. Their contracts contain certain restrictions that affect the order in which they can appear. Given these restrictions, the order in which the actors appear, from first to sixth, must conform to the following:

Both Lin and Mitchell appear earlier than Henson.
Both Lin and Paredes appear earlier than Jhalani.
If Mitchell appears earlier than Paredes, then Henson appears earlier than Geyer.
Geyer does not appear last.

7. Which one of the following could be the order, from first to last, in which the actors appear?

(A) Geyer, Lin, Jhalani, Paredes, Mitchell, Henson
(B) Geyer, Mitchell, Paredes, Lin, Henson, Jhalani
(C) Henson, Lin, Paredes, Jhalani, Geyer, Mitchell
(D) Lin, Paredes, Mitchell, Henson, Jhalani, Geyer
(E) Paredes, Mitchell, Lin, Jhalani, Geyer, Henson

8. Which one of the following CANNOT be true?

(A) Henson appears earlier than Geyer.
(B) Henson appears sixth.
(C) Lin appears fifth.
(D) Paredes appears earlier than Mitchell.
(E) Paredes appears second.

9. Exactly how many of the actors are there any one of whom could appear sixth?

(A) 5
(B) 4
(C) 3
(D) 2
(E) 1

10. If Jhalani appears earlier than Mitchell, then which one of the following could be the order in which the other four actors appear, from earliest to latest?

(A) Geyer, Lin, Paredes, Henson
(B) Geyer, Paredes, Henson, Lin
(C) Lin, Henson, Geyer, Paredes
(D) Lin, Paredes, Henson, Geyer
(E) Paredes, Lin, Henson, Geyer

11. If Lin appears immediately before Geyer, then which one of the following must be true?

(A) Geyer appears no later than third.
(B) Henson appears last.
(C) Lin appears no later than third.
(D) Mitchell appears earlier than Geyer.
(E) Paredes appears first.

12. If Mitchell appears first, then which one of the following must be true?

(A) Geyer appears fifth.
(B) Henson appears third.
(C) Jhalani appears sixth.
(D) Lin appears second.
(E) Paredes appears fourth.

GO ON TO THE NEXT PAGE.

Questions 13–17

Over the course of one day, a landscaper will use a truck to haul exactly seven loads—three loads of mulch and four loads of stone. The truck's cargo bed will be cleaned in between carrying any two loads of different materials. To meet the landscaper's needs as efficiently as possible, the following constraints apply:

The cargo bed cannot be cleaned more than three times.
The fifth load must be mulch.

13. Which one of the following is a pair of loads that can both be mulch?

(A) the first and the third
(B) the second and the third
(C) the second and the sixth
(D) the third and the sixth
(E) the fourth and the sixth

14. Which one of the following must be true?

(A) The second load is stone.
(B) The first and second loads are the same material.
(C) The second and third loads are different materials.
(D) At least two loads of mulch are hauled consecutively.
(E) At least three loads of stone are hauled consecutively.

15. If the third load is mulch, which one of the following must be true?

(A) The sixth load is a different material than the seventh load.
(B) The first load is a different material than the second load.
(C) The seventh load is mulch.
(D) The sixth load is mulch.
(E) The first load is stone.

16. If the cargo bed is cleaned exactly twice, which one of the following must be true?

(A) The second load is stone.
(B) The third load is mulch.
(C) The third load is stone.
(D) The sixth load is mulch.
(E) The seventh load is mulch.

17. If no more than two loads of the same material are hauled consecutively, then which one of the following could be true?

(A) The first load is stone.
(B) The fourth load is stone.
(C) The third load is mulch.
(D) The sixth load is mulch.
(E) The seventh load is mulch.

GO ON TO THE NEXT PAGE.

Questions 18–23

A travel magazine has hired six interns—Farber, Gombarick, Hall, Jackson, Kanze, and Lha—to assist in covering three stories—Romania, Spain, and Tuscany. Each intern will be trained either as a photographer's assistant or as a writer's assistant. Each story is assigned a team of two interns—one photographer's assistant and one writer's assistant—in accordance with the following conditions:

Gombarick and Lha will be trained in the same field.
Farber and Kanze will be trained in different fields.
Hall will be trained as a photographer's assistant.
Jackson is assigned to Tuscany.
Kanze is not assigned to Spain.

18. Which one of the following could be an acceptable assignment of photographer's assistants to stories?

(A) Romania: Farber
Spain: Hall
Tuscany: Jackson
(B) Romania: Gombarick
Spain: Hall
Tuscany: Farber
(C) Romania: Gombarick
Spain: Hall
Tuscany: Lha
(D) Romania: Gombarick
Spain: Lha
Tuscany: Kanze
(E) Romania: Hall
Spain: Kanze
Tuscany: Jackson

19. If Farber is assigned to Romania, then which one of the following must be true?

(A) Gombarick is assigned to Spain.
(B) Hall is assigned to Spain.
(C) Kanze is assigned to Tuscany.
(D) Lha is assigned to Spain.
(E) Lha is assigned to Tuscany.

20. If Farber and Hall are assigned to the same story as each other, then which one of the following could be true?

(A) Farber is assigned to Tuscany.
(B) Gombarick is assigned to Romania.
(C) Hall is assigned to Romania.
(D) Kanze is assigned to Tuscany.
(E) Lha is assigned to Spain.

21. If Farber is a writer's assistant, then which one of the following pairs could be the team of interns assigned to Romania?

(A) Farber and Gombarick
(B) Gombarick and Hall
(C) Hall and Kanze
(D) Kanze and Lha
(E) Lha and Hall

22. If Gombarick and Kanze are assigned to the same story as each other, then which one of the following could be true?

(A) Farber is assigned to Romania.
(B) Gombarick is assigned to Spain.
(C) Hall is assigned to Romania.
(D) Kanze is assigned to Tuscany.
(E) Lha is assigned to Spain.

23. Which one of the following interns CANNOT be assigned to Tuscany?

(A) Farber
(B) Gombarick
(C) Hall
(D) Kanze
(E) Lha

S T O P

IF YOU FINISH BEFORE TIME IS CALLED, YOU MAY CHECK YOUR WORK ON THIS SECTION ONLY.
DO NOT WORK ON ANY OTHER SECTION IN THE TEST.

SECTION III

Time—35 minutes

25 Questions

Directions: The questions in this section are based on the reasoning contained in brief statements or passages. For some questions, more than one of the choices could conceivably answer the question. However, you are to choose the best answer; that is, the response that most accurately and completely answers the question. You should not make assumptions that are by commonsense standards implausible, superfluous, or incompatible with the passage. After you have chosen the best answer, blacken the corresponding space on your answer sheet.

1. A research study revealed that, in most cases, once existing highways near urban areas are widened and extended in an attempt to reduce traffic congestion and resulting delays for motorists, these problems actually increase rather than decrease.

   Which one of the following, if true, most helps to explain the discrepancy between the intended results of the highway improvements and the results revealed in the study?

   (A) Widened and extended roads tend to attract many more motorists than used them before their improvement.
   (B) Typically, road widening or extension projects are undertaken only after the population near the road in question has increased and then leveled off, leaving a higher average population level.
   (C) As a general rule, the greater the number of lanes on a given length of highway, the lower the rate of accidents per 100,000 vehicles traveling on it.
   (D) Rural, as compared to urban, traffic usually includes a larger proportion of trucks and vehicles used by farmers.
   (E) Urban traffic generally moves at a slower pace and involves more congestion and delays than rural and suburban traffic.

2. A study found that consumers reaching supermarket checkout lines within 40 minutes after the airing of an advertisement for a given product over the store's audio system were significantly more likely to purchase the product advertised than were consumers who checked out prior to the airing. Apparently, these advertisements are effective.

   Which one of the following, if true, most strengthens the argument?

   (A) During the study, for most of the advertisements more people went through the checkout lines after they were aired than before they were aired.
   (B) A large proportion of the consumers who bought a product shortly after the airing of an advertisement for it reported that they had not gone to the store intending to buy that product.
   (C) Many of the consumers reported that they typically bought at least one of the advertised products every time they shopped at the store.
   (D) Many of the consumers who bought an advertised product and who reached the checkout line within 40 minutes of the advertisement's airing reported that they could not remember hearing the advertisement.
   (E) Many of the consumers who bought an advertised product reported that they buy that product only occasionally.

GO ON TO THE NEXT PAGE.

3. Unless the building permit is obtained by February 1 of this year or some of the other activities necessary for construction of the new library can be completed in less time than originally planned, the new library will not be completed on schedule. It is now clear that the building permit cannot be obtained by February 1, so the new library will not be completed on schedule.

The conclusion drawn follows logically from the premises if which one of the following is assumed?

(A) All of the other activities necessary for construction of the library will take at least as much time as originally planned.
(B) The officials in charge of construction of the new library have admitted that it probably will not be completed on schedule.
(C) The application for a building permit was submitted on January 2 of this year, and processing building permits always takes at least two months.
(D) The application for a building permit was rejected the first time it was submitted, and it had to be resubmitted with a revised building plan.
(E) It is not possible to convince authorities to allow construction of the library to begin before the building permit is obtained.

4. In a study of patients who enrolled at a sleep clinic because of insomnia, those who inhaled the scent of peppermint before going to bed were more likely to have difficulty falling asleep than were patients who inhaled the scent of bitter orange. Since it is known that inhaling bitter orange does not help people fall asleep more easily, this study shows that inhaling the scent of peppermint makes insomnia worse.

Which one of the following, if true, most seriously weakens the argument above?

(A) Several studies have shown that inhaling the scent of peppermint tends to have a relaxing effect on people who do not suffer from insomnia.
(B) The patients who inhaled the scent of bitter orange were, on average, suffering from milder cases of insomnia than were the patients who inhaled the scent of peppermint.
(C) Because the scents of peppermint and bitter orange are each very distinctive, it was not possible to prevent the patients from knowing that they were undergoing some sort of study of the effects of inhaling various scents.
(D) Some of the patients who enrolled in the sleep clinic also had difficulty staying asleep once they fell asleep.
(E) Several studies have revealed that in many cases inhaling certain pleasant scents can dramatically affect the degree to which a patient suffers from insomnia.

5. Dogs learn best when they are trained using both voice commands and hand signals. After all, a recent study shows that dogs who were trained using both voice commands and hand signals were twice as likely to obey as were dogs who were trained using only voice commands.

The claim that dogs learn best when they are trained using both voice commands and hand signals figures in the argument in which one of the following ways?

(A) It is an explicit premise of the argument.
(B) It is an implicit assumption of the argument.
(C) It is a statement of background information offered to help facilitate understanding the issue in the argument.
(D) It is a statement that the argument claims is supported by the study.
(E) It is an intermediate conclusion that is offered as direct support for the argument's main conclusion.

6. Of the many test pilots who have flown the new plane, none has found it difficult to operate. So it is unlikely that the test pilot flying the plane tomorrow will find it difficult to operate.

The reasoning in which one of the following arguments is most similar to the reasoning in the argument above?

(A) All of the many book reviewers who read Rachel Nguyen's new novel thought that it was particularly well written. So it is likely that the average reader will enjoy the book.
(B) Many of the book reviewers who read Wim Jashka's new novel before it was published found it very entertaining. So it is unlikely that most people who buy the book will find it boring.
(C) Neither of the two reviewers who enjoyed Sharlene Lo's new novel hoped that Lo would write a sequel. So it is unlikely that the review of the book in next Sunday's newspaper will express hope that Lo will write a sequel.
(D) Many reviewers have read Kip Landau's new novel, but none of them enjoyed it. So it is unlikely that the reviewer for the local newspaper will enjoy the book when she reads it.
(E) None of the reviewers who have read Gray Ornsby's new novel were offended by it. So it is unlikely that the book will offend anyone in the general public who reads it.

GO ON TO THE NEXT PAGE.

7. Scientist: Any theory that is to be taken seriously must affect our perception of the world. Of course, this is not, in itself, enough for a theory to be taken seriously. To see this, one need only consider astrology.

The point of the scientist's mentioning astrology in the argument is to present

(A) an example of a theory that should not be taken seriously because it does not affect our perception of the world
(B) an example of something that should not be considered a theory
(C) an example of a theory that should not be taken seriously despite its affecting our perception of the world
(D) an example of a theory that affects our perception of the world, and thus should be taken seriously
(E) an example of a theory that should be taken seriously, even though it does not affect our perception of the world

8. Clark: Our local community theater often produces plays by critically acclaimed playwrights. In fact, the production director says that critical acclaim is one of the main factors considered in the selection of plays to perform. So, since my neighbor Michaela's new play will be performed by the theater this season, she must be a critically acclaimed playwright.

The reasoning in Clark's argument is most vulnerable to criticism on the grounds that the argument

(A) takes a condition necessary for a playwright's being critically acclaimed to be a condition sufficient for a playwright's being critically acclaimed
(B) fails to consider that several different effects may be produced by a single cause
(C) treats one main factor considered in the selection of plays to perform as though it were a condition that must be met in order for a play to be selected
(D) uses as evidence a source that there is reason to believe is unreliable
(E) provides no evidence that a playwright's being critically acclaimed is the result rather than the cause of his or her plays being selected for production

9. Legal theorist: Governments should not be allowed to use the personal diaries of an individual who is the subject of a criminal prosecution as evidence against that individual. A diary is a silent conversation with oneself and there is no relevant difference between speaking to oneself, writing one's thoughts down, and keeping one's thoughts to oneself.

Which one of the following principles, if valid, provides the most support for the legal theorist's argument?

(A) Governments should not be allowed to compel corporate officials to surrender interoffice memos to government investigators.
(B) When crime is a serious problem, governments should be given increased power to investigate and prosecute suspected wrongdoers, and some restrictions on admissible evidence should be relaxed.
(C) Governments should not be allowed to use an individual's remarks to prosecute the individual for criminal activity unless the remarks were intended for other people.
(D) Governments should not have the power to confiscate an individual's personal correspondence to use as evidence against the individual in a criminal trial.
(E) Governments should do everything in their power to investigate and prosecute suspected wrongdoers.

10. A ring of gas emitting X-rays flickering 450 times per second has been observed in a stable orbit around a black hole. In light of certain widely accepted physical theories, that rate of flickering can best be explained if the ring of gas has a radius of 49 kilometers. But the gas ring could not maintain an orbit so close to a black hole unless the black hole was spinning.

The statements above, if true, most strongly support which one of the following, assuming that the widely accepted physical theories referred to above are correct?

(A) Black holes that have orbiting rings of gas with radii greater than 49 kilometers are usually stationary.
(B) Only rings of gas that are in stable orbits around black holes emit flickering X-rays.
(C) The black hole that is within the ring of gas observed by the astronomers is spinning.
(D) X-rays emitted by rings of gas orbiting black holes cause those black holes to spin.
(E) A black hole is stationary only if it is orbited by a ring of gas with a radius of more than 49 kilometers.

11. A mass of “black water” containing noxious organic material swept through Laurel Bay last year. Some scientists believe that this event was a naturally occurring but infrequent phenomenon. The black water completely wiped out five species of coral in the bay, including mounds of coral that were more than two centuries old. Therefore, even if this black water phenomenon has struck the bay before, it did not reach last year’s intensity at any time in the past two centuries.

Which one of the following is an assumption required by the argument?

(A) Masses of black water such as that observed last summer come into the bay more frequently than just once every two centuries.
(B) Every species of coral in the bay was seriously harmed by the mass of black water that swept in last year.
(C) The mass of black water that swept through the bay last year did not decimate any plant or animal species that makes use of coral.
(D) The mounds of centuries-old coral that were destroyed were not in especially fragile condition just before the black water swept in last year.
(E) Older specimens of coral in the bay were more vulnerable to damage from the influx of black water than were young specimens.

12. Many nurseries sell fruit trees that they label “miniature.” Not all nurseries, however, use this term in the same way. While some nurseries label any nectarine trees of the Stark Sweet Melody variety as “miniature,” for example, others do not. One thing that is clear is that if a variety of fruit tree is not suitable for growing in a tub or a pot, no tree of that variety can be correctly labeled “miniature.”

Which one of the following can be properly inferred from the information above?

(A) Most nurseries mislabel at least some of their fruit trees.
(B) Some of the nurseries have correctly labeled nectarine trees of the Stark Sweet Melody variety only if the variety is unsuitable for growing in a tub or a pot.
(C) Any nectarine tree of the Stark Sweet Melody variety that a nursery labels “miniature” is labeled incorrectly.
(D) Some nectarine trees that are not labeled “miniature” are labeled incorrectly.
(E) Unless the Stark Sweet Melody variety of nectarine tree is suitable for growing in a tub or a pot, some nurseries mislabel this variety of tree.

13. Psychologist: Identical twins are virtually the same genetically. Moreover, according to some studies, identical twins separated at birth and brought up in vastly different environments show a strong tendency to report similar ethical beliefs, dress in the same way, and have similar careers. Thus, many of our inclinations must be genetic in origin, and not subject to environmental influences.

Which one of the following, if true, would most weaken the psychologist’s argument?

(A) Many people, including identical twins, undergo radical changes in their lifestyles at some point in their lives.
(B) While some studies of identical twins separated at birth reveal a high percentage of similar personality traits, they also show a few differences.
(C) Scientists are far from being able to link any specific genes to specific inclinations.
(D) Identical twins who grow up together tend to develop different beliefs, tastes, and careers in order to differentiate themselves from each other.
(E) Twins who are not identical tend to develop different beliefs, tastes, and careers.

14. Human beings can live happily only in a society where love and friendship are the primary motives for actions. Yet economic needs can be satisfied in the absence of this condition, as, for example, in a merchant society where only economic utility motivates action. It is obvious then that human beings _______.

Which one of the following most logically completes the argument?

(A) can live happily only when economic utility is not a motivator in their society
(B) cannot achieve happiness unless their economic needs have already been satisfied
(C) cannot satisfy economic needs by means of interactions with family members and close friends
(D) can satisfy their basic economic needs without obtaining happiness
(E) cannot really be said to have satisfied their economic needs unless they are happy

GO ON TO THE NEXT PAGE.

15. Technologically, it is already possible to produce nonpolluting cars that burn hydrogen rather than gasoline. But the national system of fuel stations that would be needed to provide the hydrogen fuel for such cars does not yet exist. However, this infrastructure is likely to appear and grow rapidly. A century ago no fuel-distribution infrastructure existed for gasoline-powered vehicles, yet it quickly developed in response to consumer demand.

    Which one of the following most accurately expresses the conclusion drawn in the argument?

    (A) It is already technologically possible to produce nonpolluting cars that burn hydrogen rather than gasoline.
    (B) The fuel-distribution infrastructure for hydrogen-powered cars still needs to be created.
    (C) If a new kind of technology is developed, the infrastructure needed to support that technology is likely to quickly develop in response to consumer demands.
    (D) The fuel-distribution infrastructure for hydrogen-powered cars is likely to appear and grow rapidly.
    (E) Hydrogen-powered vehicles will be similar to gasoline-powered vehicles with regard to the amount of consumer demand for their fuel-distribution infrastructure.

16. Wildlife management experts should not interfere with the natural habitats of creatures in the wild, because manipulating the environment to make it easier for an endangered species to survive in a habitat invariably makes it harder for nonendangered species to survive in that habitat.

    The argument is most vulnerable to criticism on the grounds that it

    (A) fails to consider that wildlife management experts probably know best how to facilitate the survival of an endangered species in a habitat
    (B) fails to recognize that a nonendangered species can easily become an endangered species
    (C) overlooks the possibility that saving an endangered species in a habitat is incompatible with preserving the overall diversity of species in that habitat
    (D) presumes, without providing justification, that the survival of each endangered species is equally important to the health of the environment
    (E) takes for granted that preserving a currently endangered species in a habitat does not have higher priority than preserving species in that habitat that are not endangered

17. Any food that is not sterilized and sealed can contain disease-causing bacteria. Once sterilized and properly sealed, however, it contains no bacteria. There are many different acceptable food-preservation techniques; each involves either sterilizing and sealing food or else at least slowing the growth of disease-causing bacteria. Some of the techniques may also destroy natural food enzymes that cause food to spoil or discolor quickly.

    If the statements above are true, which one of the following must be true?

    (A) All food preserved by an acceptable method is free of disease-causing bacteria.
    (B) Preservation methods that destroy enzymes that cause food to spoil do not sterilize the food.
    (C) Food preserved by a sterilization method is less likely to discolor quickly than food preserved with other methods.
    (D) Any nonsterilized food preserved by an acceptable method can contain disease-causing bacteria.
    (E) If a food contains no bacteria, then it has been preserved by an acceptable method.

GO ON TO THE NEXT PAGE.

18. Activities that pose risks to life are acceptable if and only if each person who bears the risks either gains some net benefit that cannot be had without such risks, or bears the risks voluntarily.

Which one of the following judgments most closely conforms to the principle above?

(A) A door-to-door salesperson declines to replace his older car with a new model with more safety features; this is acceptable because the decision not to replace the car is voluntary.
(B) A smoker subjects people to secondhand smoke at an outdoor public meeting; the resulting risks are acceptable because the danger from secondhand smoke is minimal outdoors, where smoke dissipates quickly.
(C) A motorcyclist rides without a helmet; the risk of fatal injury to the motorcyclist thus incurred is acceptable because the motorcyclist incurs this risk willingly.
(D) Motor vehicles are allowed to emit certain low levels of pollution; the resulting health risks are acceptable because all users of motor vehicles share the resulting benefit of inexpensive, convenient travel.
(E) A nation requires all citizens to spend two years in national service; since such service involves no risk to life, the policy is acceptable.

19. Ecologist: One theory attributes the ability of sea butterflies to avoid predation to their appearance, while another attributes this ability to various chemical compounds they produce. Recently we added each of the compounds to food pellets, one compound per pellet. Predators ate the pellets no matter which one of the compounds was present. Thus the compounds the sea butterflies produce are not responsible for their ability to avoid predation.

The reasoning in the ecologist's argument is flawed in that the argument

(A) presumes, without providing justification, that the two theories are incompatible with each other
(B) draws a conclusion about a cause on the basis of nothing more than a statistical correlation
(C) treats a condition sufficient for sea butterflies' ability to avoid predators as a condition required for this ability
(D) infers, from the claim that no individual member of a set has a certain effect, that the set as a whole does not have that effect
(E) draws a conclusion that merely restates material present in one or more of its premises

20. Principle: One should criticize the works or actions of another person only if the criticism will not seriously harm the person criticized and one does so in the hope or expectation of benefiting someone other than oneself.

Application: Jarrett should not have criticized Ostertag's essay in front of the class, since the defects in it were so obvious that pointing them out benefited no one.

Which one of the following, if true, justifies the above application of the principle?

(A) Jarrett knew that the defects in the essay were so obvious that pointing them out would benefit no one.
(B) Jarrett's criticism of the essay would have been to Ostertag's benefit only if Ostertag had been unaware of the defects in the essay at the time.
(C) Jarrett knew that the criticism might antagonize Ostertag.
(D) Jarrett hoped to gain prestige by criticizing Ostertag.
(E) Jarrett did not expect the criticism to be to Ostertag's benefit.

21. Safety consultant: Judged by the number of injuries per licensed vehicle, minivans are the safest vehicles on the road. However, in carefully designed crash tests, minivans show no greater ability to protect their occupants than other vehicles of similar size do. Thus, the reason minivans have such a good safety record is probably not that they are inherently safer than other vehicles, but rather that they are driven primarily by low-risk drivers.

Which one of the following, if true, most strengthens the safety consultant's argument?

(A) When choosing what kind of vehicle to drive, low-risk drivers often select a kind that they know to perform particularly well in crash tests.
(B) Judged by the number of accidents per licensed vehicle, minivans are no safer than most other kinds of vehicles are.
(C) Minivans tend to carry more passengers at any given time than do most other vehicles.
(D) In general, the larger a vehicle is, the greater its ability to protect its occupants.
(E) Minivans generally have worse braking and emergency handling capabilities than other vehicles of similar size.

GO ON TO THE NEXT PAGE.

22. Consumer advocate: There is no doubt that the government is responsible for the increased cost of gasoline, because the government's policies have significantly increased consumer demand for fuel, and as a result of increasing demand, the price of gasoline has risen steadily.

Which one of the following is an assumption required by the consumer advocate's argument?

(A) The government can bear responsibility for that which it indirectly causes.
(B) The government is responsible for some unforeseen consequences of its policies.
(C) Consumer demand for gasoline cannot increase without causing gasoline prices to increase.
(D) The government has an obligation to ensure that demand for fuel does not increase excessively.
(E) If the government pursues policies that do not increase the demand for fuel, gasoline prices tend to remain stable.

23. A species in which mutations frequently occur will develop new evolutionary adaptations in each generation. Since species survive dramatic environmental changes only if they develop new evolutionary adaptations in each generation, a species in which mutations frequently occur will survive dramatic environmental changes.

The flawed pattern of reasoning in which one of the following is most closely parallel to that in the argument above?

(A) In a stone wall that is properly built, every stone supports another stone. Since a wall's being sturdy depends upon its being properly built, only walls that are composed entirely of stones supporting other stones are sturdy.
(B) A play that is performed before a different audience every time will never get the same reaction from any two audiences. Since no plays are performed before the same audience every time, no play ever gets the same reaction from any two audiences.
(C) A person who is perfectly honest will tell the truth in every situation. Since in order to be a morally upright person one must tell the truth at all times, a perfectly honest person will also be a morally upright person.
(D) An herb garden is productive only if the soil that it is planted in is well drained. Since soil that is well drained is good soil, an herb garden is not productive unless it is planted in good soil.
(E) A diet that is healthful is well balanced. Since a well-balanced diet includes fruits and vegetables, one will not be healthy unless one eats fruits and vegetables.

GO ON TO THE NEXT PAGE.

24. Music critic: How well an underground rock group's recordings sell is no mark of that group's success as an underground group. After all, if a recording sells well, it may be because some of the music on the recording is too trendy to be authentically underground; accordingly, many underground musicians consider it desirable for a recording not to sell well. But weak sales may simply be the result of the group's incompetence.

Which one of the following principles, if valid, most helps to justify the music critic's argument?

(A) If an underground rock group is successful as an underground group, its recordings will sell neither especially well nor especially poorly.
(B) An underground rock group is unsuccessful as an underground group if it is incompetent or if any of its music is too trendy to be authentically underground, or both.
(C) Whether an underground group's recordings meet criteria that many underground musicians consider desirable is not a mark of that group's success.
(D) An underground rock group is successful as an underground group if the group is competent but its recordings nonetheless do not sell well.
(E) For an underground rock group, competence and the creation of authentically underground music are not in themselves marks of success.

25. Graham: The defeat of the world's chess champion by a computer shows that any type of human intellectual activity governed by fixed principles can be mastered by machines and thus that a truly intelligent machine will inevitably be devised.

Adelaide: But you are overlooking the fact that the computer in the case you cite was simply an extension of the people who programmed it. It was their successful distillation of the principles of chess that enabled them to defeat a chess champion using a computer.

The statements above provide the most support for holding that Graham and Adelaide disagree about whether

(A) chess is the best example of a human intellectual activity that is governed by fixed principles
(B) chess is a typical example of the sorts of intellectual activities in which human beings characteristically engage
(C) a computer's defeat of a human chess player is an accomplishment that should be attributed to the computer
(D) intelligence can be demonstrated by the performance of an activity in accord with fixed principles
(E) tools can be designed to aid in any human activity that is governed by fixed principles

S T O P

IF YOU FINISH BEFORE TIME IS CALLED, YOU MAY CHECK YOUR WORK ON THIS SECTION ONLY.
DO NOT WORK ON ANY OTHER SECTION IN THE TEST.

Section IV

Time—35 minutes

27 Questions

Directions: Each set of questions in this section is based on a single passage or a pair of passages. The questions are to be answered on the basis of what is stated or implied in the passage or pair of passages. For some of the questions, more than one of the choices could conceivably answer the question. However, you are to choose the best answer; that is, the response that most accurately and completely answers the question, and blacken the corresponding space on your answer sheet.

Over the past 50 years, expansive, low-density communities have proliferated at the edges of many cities in the United States and Canada, creating a phenomenon known as suburban sprawl. Andres Duany, Elizabeth Plater-Zyberk, and Jeff Speck, a group of prominent town planners belonging to a movement called New Urbanism, contend that suburban sprawl contributes to the decline of civic life and civility. For reasons involving the flow of automobile traffic, they note, zoning laws usually dictate that suburban homes, stores, businesses, and schools be built in separate areas, and this separation robs people of communal space where they can interact and get to know one another. It is as difficult to imagine the concept of community without a town square or local pub, these town planners contend, as it is to imagine the concept of family independent of the home.

Suburban housing subdivisions, Duany and his colleagues add, usually contain homes identical not only in appearance but also in price, resulting in a de facto economic segregation of residential neighborhoods. Children growing up in these neighborhoods, whatever their economic circumstances, are certain to be ill prepared for life in a diverse society. Moreover, because the widely separated suburban homes and businesses are connected only by "collector roads," residents are forced to drive, often in heavy traffic, in order to perform many daily tasks. Time that would in a town center involve social interaction within a physical public realm is now spent inside the automobile, where people cease to be community members and instead become motorists, competing for road space, often acting antisocially. Pedestrians rarely act in this manner toward each other. Duany and his colleagues advocate development based on early-twentieth-century urban neighborhoods that mix housing of different prices and offer residents a "gratifying public realm" that includes narrow, tree-lined streets, parks, corner grocery stores, cafes, small neighborhood schools, all within walking distance. This, they believe, would give people of diverse backgrounds and lifestyles an opportunity to interact and thus develop mutual respect.

Opponents of New Urbanism claim that migration to sprawling suburbs is an expression of people's legitimate desire to secure the enjoyment and personal mobility provided by the automobile and the lifestyle that it makes possible. However, the New Urbanists do not question people's right to their own values; instead, they suggest that we should take a more critical view of these values and of the sprawl-conducive zoning and subdivision policies that reflect them. New Urbanists are fundamentally concerned with the long-term social costs of the now-prevailing attitude that individual mobility, consumption, and wealth should be valued absolutely, regardless of their impact on community life.

1. Which one of the following most accurately expresses the main point of the passage?

(A) In their critique of policies that promote suburban sprawl, the New Urbanists neglect to consider the interests and values of those who prefer suburban lifestyles.
(B) The New Urbanists hold that suburban sprawl inhibits social interaction among people of diverse economic circumstances, and they advocate specific reforms of zoning laws as a solution to this problem.
(C) The New Urbanists argue that most people find that life in small urban neighborhoods is generally more gratifying than life in a suburban environment.
(D) The New Urbanists hold that suburban sprawl has a corrosive effect on community life, and as an alternative they advocate development modeled on small urban neighborhoods.
(E) The New Urbanists analyze suburban sprawl as a phenomenon that results from short-sighted traffic policies and advocate changes to these traffic policies as a means of reducing the negative effects of sprawl.

2. According to the passage, the New Urbanists cite which one of the following as a detrimental result of the need for people to travel extensively every day by automobile?

(A) It imposes an extra financial burden on the residents of sprawling suburbs, thus detracting from the advantages of suburban life.
(B) It detracts from the amount of time that people could otherwise devote to productive employment.
(C) It increases the amount of time people spend in situations in which antisocial behavior occurs.
(D) It produces significant amounts of air pollution and thus tends to harm the quality of people's lives.
(E) It decreases the amount of time that parents spend in enjoyable interactions with their children.

GO ON TO THE NEXT PAGE.

3. The passage most strongly suggests that the New Urbanists would agree with which one of the following statements?

(A) The primary factor affecting a neighborhood's conduciveness to the maintenance of civility is the amount of time required to get from one place to another.
(B) Private citizens in suburbs have little opportunity to influence the long-term effects of zoning policies enacted by public officials.
(C) People who live in suburban neighborhoods usually have little difficulty finding easily accessible jobs that do not require commuting to urban centers.
(D) The spatial configuration of suburban neighborhoods both influences and is influenced by the attitudes of those who live in them.
(E) Although people have a right to their own values, personal values should not affect the ways in which neighborhoods are designed.

4. Which one of the following most accurately describes the author's use of the word "communities" in line 2 and "community" in line 15?

(A) They are intended to be understood in almost identical ways, the only significant difference being that one is plural and the other is singular.
(B) The former is intended to refer to dwellings—and their inhabitants—that happen to be clustered together in particular areas; in the latter, the author means that a group of people have a sense of belonging together.
(C) In the former, the author means that the groups referred to are to be defined in terms of the interests of their members; the latter is intended to refer generically to a group of people who have something else in common.
(D) The former is intended to refer to groups of people whose members have professional or political ties to one another; the latter is intended to refer to a geographical area in which people live in close proximity to one another.
(E) In the former, the author means that there are informal personal ties among members of a group of people; the latter is intended to indicate that a group of people have similar backgrounds and lifestyles.

5. Which one of the following, if true, would most weaken the position that the passage attributes to critics of the New Urbanists?

(A) Most people who spend more time than they would like getting from one daily task to another live in central areas of large cities.
(B) Most people who often drive long distances for shopping and entertainment live in small towns rather than in suburban areas surrounding large cities.
(C) Most people who have easy access to shopping and entertainment do not live in suburban areas.
(D) Most people who choose to live in sprawling suburbs do so because comparable housing in neighborhoods that do not require extensive automobile travel is more expensive.
(E) Most people who vote in municipal elections do not cast their votes on the basis of candidates' positions on zoning policies.

6. The passage most strongly suggests that which one of the following would occur if new housing subdivisions in suburban communities were built in accordance with the recommendations of Duany and his colleagues?

(A) The need for zoning laws to help regulate traffic flow would eventually be eliminated.
(B) There would be a decrease in the percentage of suburban buildings that contain two or more apartments.
(C) The amount of time that residents of suburbs spend traveling to the central business districts of cities for work and shopping would increase.
(D) The need for coordination of zoning policies between large-city governments and governments of nearby suburban communities would be eliminated.
(E) There would be an increase in the per capita number of grocery stores and schools in those suburban communities.

7. The second paragraph most strongly supports the inference that the New Urbanists make which one of the following assumptions?

(A) Most of those who buy houses in sprawling suburbs do not pay drastically less than they can afford.
(B) Zoning regulations often cause economically uniform suburbs to become economically diverse.
(C) City dwellers who do not frequently travel in automobiles often have feelings of hostility toward motorists.
(D) Few residents of suburbs are aware of the potential health benefits of walking, instead of driving, to carry out daily tasks.
(E) People generally prefer to live in houses that look very similar to most of the other houses around them.

GO ON TO THE NEXT PAGE.

Passage A

In ancient Greece, Aristotle documented the ability of foraging honeybees to recruit nestmates to a good food source. He did not speculate on how the communication occurred, but he and naturalists since then have observed that a bee that finds a new food source returns to the nest and "dances" for its nestmates. In the 1940s, von Frisch and colleagues discovered a pattern in the dance. They observed a foraging honeybee's dance, deciphered it, and thereby deduced the location of the food source the bee had discovered. Yet questions still remained regarding the precise mechanism used to transmit that information.

In the 1960s, Wenner and Esch each discovered independently that dancing honeybees emit low-frequency sounds, which we now know to come from wing vibrations. Both researchers reasoned that this might explain the bees' ability to communicate effectively even in completely dark nests. But at that time many scientists mistakenly believed that honeybees lack hearing, so the issue remained unresolved. Wenner subsequently proposed that smell rather than hearing was the key to honeybee communication. He hypothesized that honeybees derive information not from sound, but from odors the forager conveys from the food source.

Yet Gould has shown that foragers can dispatch bees to sites they had not actually visited, something that would not be possible if odor were in fact necessary to bees' communication. Finally, using a honeybee robot to simulate the forager's dance, Kirchner and Michelsen showed that sounds emitted during the forager's dance do indeed play an essential role in conveying information about the food's location.

Passage B

All animals communicate in some sense. Bees dance, ants leave trails, some fish emit high-voltage signals. But some species—bees, birds, and primates, for example—communicate symbolically. In an experiment with vervet monkeys in the wild, Seyfarth, Cheney, and Marler found that prerecorded vervet alarm calls from a loudspeaker elicited the same response as did naturally produced vervet calls alerting the group to the presence of a predator of a particular type. Vervets looked upward upon hearing an eagle alarm call, and they scanned the ground below in response to a snake alarm call. These responses suggest that each alarm call represents, for vervets, a specific type of predator.

Karl von Frisch was first to crack the code of the honeybee's dance, which he described as "language." The dance symbolically represents the distance, direction, and quality of newly discovered food. Adrian Wenner and others believed that bees rely on olfactory cues, as well as the dance, to find a food source, but this has turned out not to be so.

While it is true that bees have a simple nervous system, they do not automatically follow just any information. Biologist James Gould trained foraging bees to find food in a boat placed in the middle of a lake and then allowed them to return to the hive to indicate this new location. He found that hive members ignored the foragers' instructions, presumably because no pollinating flowers grow in such a place.

8. The passages have which one of the following aims in common?

   (A) arguing that certain nonhuman animals possess human-like intelligence
   (B) illustrating the sophistication with which certain primates communicate
   (C) describing certain scientific studies concerned with animal communication
   (D) airing a scientific controversy over the function of the honeybee's dance
   (E) analyzing the conditions a symbolic system must meet in order to be considered a language

9. Which one of the following statements most accurately characterizes a difference between the two passages?

   (A) Passage A is concerned solely with honeybee communication, whereas passage B is concerned with other forms of animal communication as well.
   (B) Passage A discusses evidence adduced by scientists in support of certain claims, whereas passage B merely presents some of those claims without discussing the support that has been adduced for them.
   (C) Passage B is entirely about recent theories of honeybee communication, whereas passage A outlines the historic development of theories of honeybee communication.
   (D) Passage B is concerned with explaining the distinction between symbolic and nonsymbolic communication, whereas passage A, though making use of the distinction, does not explain it.
   (E) Passage B is concerned with gaining insight into human communication by considering certain types of nonhuman communication, whereas passage A is concerned with these types of nonhuman communication in their own right.

GO ON TO THE NEXT PAGE.

10. Which one of the following statements is most strongly supported by Gould's research, as reported in the two passages?

    (A) When a forager honeybee does not communicate olfactory information to its nestmates, they will often disregard the forager's directions and go to sites of their own choosing.
    (B) Forager honeybees instinctively know where pollinating flowers usually grow and will not dispatch their nestmates to any other places.
    (C) Only experienced forager honeybees are able to locate the best food sources.
    (D) A forager's dances can draw other honeybees to sites that the forager has not visited and can fail to draw other honeybees to sites that the forager has visited.
    (E) Forager honeybees can communicate with their nestmates about a newly discovered food source by leaving a trail from the food source to the honeybee nest.

11. It can be inferred from the passages that the author of passage A and the author of passage B would accept which one of the following statements?

    (A) Honeybees will ignore the instructions conveyed in the forager's dance if they are unable to detect odors from the food source.
    (B) Wenner and Esch established that both sound and odor play a vital role in most honeybee communication.
    (C) Most animal species can communicate symbolically in some form or other.
    (D) The work of Von Frisch was instrumental in answering fundamental questions about how honeybees communicate.
    (E) Inexperienced forager honeybees that dance to communicate with other bees in their nest learn the intricacies of the dance from more experienced foragers.

12. Which one of the following most accurately describes a relationship between the two passages?

    (A) Passage A discusses and rejects a position that is put forth in passage B.
    (B) Passage A gives several examples of a phenomenon for which passage B gives only one example.
    (C) Passage A is concerned in its entirety with a phenomenon that passage B discusses in support of a more general thesis.
    (D) Passage A proposes a scientific explanation for a phenomenon that passage B argues cannot be plausibly explained.
    (E) Passage A provides a historical account of the origins of a phenomenon that is the primary concern of passage B.

GO ON TO THE NEXT PAGE.

Most scholars of Mexican American history mark César Chávez's unionizing efforts among Mexican and Mexican American farm laborers in California as the beginning of Chicano political activism in the 1960s. By 1965, Chávez's United Farm Workers Union gained international recognition by initiating a worldwide boycott of grapes in an effort to get growers in California to sign union contracts. The year 1965 also marks the birth of contemporary Chicano theater, for that is the year Luis Valdez approached Chávez about using theater to organize farm workers. Valdez and the members of the resulting Teatro Campesino are generally credited by scholars as having initiated the Chicano theater movement, a movement that would reach its apex in the 1970s.

In the fall of 1965, Valdez gathered a group of striking farm workers and asked them to talk about their working conditions. A former farm worker himself, Valdez was no stranger to the players in the daily drama that was fieldwork. He asked people to illustrate what happened on the picket lines, and the less timid in the audience delighted in acting out their ridicule of the strikebreakers. Using the farm workers' basic improvisations, Valdez guided the group toward the creation of what he termed "*actos*," skits or sketches whose roots scholars have traced to various sources that had influenced Valdez as a student and as a member of the San Francisco Mime Troupe. Expanding beyond the initial setting of flatbed-truck stages at the fields' edges, the *acto* became the quintessential form of Chicano theater in the 1960s. According to Valdez, the *acto* should suggest a solution to the problems exposed in the brief comic statement, and, as with any good political theater, it should satirize the opposition and inspire the audience to social action. Because *actos* were based on participants' personal experiences, they had palpable immediacy.

In her book *El Teatro Campesino*, Yolanda Broyles-González rightly criticizes theater historians for having tended to credit Valdez individually with inventing *actos* as a genre, as if the striking farm workers' improvisational talent had depended entirely on his vision and expertise for the form it took. She traces especially the *actos*' connections to a similar genre of informal, often satirical shows known as *carpas* that were performed in tents to mainly working-class audiences. *Carpas* had flourished earlier in the twentieth century in the border area of Mexico and the United States. Many participants in the formation of the Teatro no doubt had substantial cultural links to this tradition and likely adapted it to their improvisations. The early development of the Teatro Campesino was, in fact, a collective accomplishment; still, Valdez's artistic contribution was a crucial one, for the resulting *actos* were neither *carpas* nor theater in the European tradition of Valdez's academic training, but a distinctive genre with connections to both.

13. Which one of the following most accurately expresses the main point of the passage?

(A) Some theater historians have begun to challenge the once widely accepted view that in creating the Teatro Campesino, Luis Valdez was largely uninfluenced by earlier historical forms.

(B) In crediting Luis Valdez with founding the Chicano theater movement, theater historians have neglected the role of César Chávez in its early development.

(C) Although the creation of the early material of the Teatro Campesino was a collective accomplishment, Luis Valdez's efforts and expertise were essential factors in determining the form it took.

(D) The success of the early Teatro Campesino depended on the special insights and talents of the amateur performers who were recruited by Luis Valdez to participate in creating *actos*.

(E) Although, as Yolanda Broyles-González has pointed out, the Teatro Campesino was a collective endeavor, Luis Valdez's political and academic connections helped bring it recognition.

14. The author uses the word "immediacy" (line 39) most likely in order to express

(A) how little physical distance there was between the performers in the late 1960s *actos* and their audiences

(B) the sense of intimacy created by the performers' technique of addressing many of their lines directly to the audience

(C) the ease with which the Teatro Campesino members were able to develop *actos* based on their own experiences

(D) how closely the director and performers of the Teatro Campesino worked together to build a repertoire of *actos*

(E) how vividly the *actos* conveyed the performers' experiences to their audiences

GO ON TO THE NEXT PAGE.

15. The second sentence of the passage functions primarily in which one of the following ways?
    (A) It helps explain both a motivation of those who developed the first *actos* and an important aspect of their subject matter.
    (B) It introduces a major obstacle that Valdez had to overcome in gaining public acceptance of the work of the Teatro Campesino.
    (C) It anticipates and counters a possible objection to the author's view that the *actos* developed by Teatro Campesino were effective as political theater.
    (D) It provides an example of the type of topic on which scholars of Mexican American history have typically focused to the exclusion of theater history.
    (E) It helps explain why theater historians, in their discussions of Valdez, have often treated him as though he were individually responsible for inventing *actos* as a genre.

16. The passage indicates that the early *actos* of the Teatro Campesino and the *carpas* were similar in that
    (A) both had roots in theater in the European tradition
    (B) both were studied by the San Francisco Mime Troupe
    (C) both were initially performed on farms
    (D) both often involved satire
    (E) both were part of union organizing drives

17. It can be inferred from the passage that Valdez most likely held which one of the following views?
    (A) As a theatrical model, the *carpas* of the early twentieth century were ill-suited to the type of theater that he and the Teatro Campesino were trying to create.
    (B) César Chávez should have done more to support the efforts of the Teatro Campesino to use theater to organize striking farm workers.
    (C) Avant-garde theater in the European tradition is largely irrelevant to the theatrical expression of the concerns of a mainly working-class audience.
    (D) Actors do not require formal training in order to achieve effective and artistically successful theatrical performances.
    (E) The aesthetic aspects of a theatrical work should be evaluated independently of its political ramifications.

18. Based on the passage, it can be concluded that the author and Broyles-González hold essentially the same attitude toward
    (A) the influences that shaped *carpas* as a dramatic genre
    (B) the motives of theater historians in exaggerating the originality of Valdez
    (C) the significance of *carpas* for the development of the genre of the *acto*
    (D) the extent of Valdez's acquaintance with *carpas* as a dramatic form
    (E) the role of the European tradition in shaping Valdez's contribution to the development of *actos*

19. The information in the passage most strongly supports which one of the following statements regarding the Teatro Campesino?
    (A) Its efforts to organize farm workers eventually won the acceptance of a few farm owners in California.
    (B) It included among its members a number of individuals who, like Valdez, had previously belonged to the San Francisco Mime Troupe.
    (C) It did not play a major role in the earliest efforts of the United Farm Workers Union to achieve international recognition.
    (D) Although its first performances were entirely in Spanish, it eventually gave some performances partially in English, for the benefit of non-Spanish-speaking audiences.
    (E) Its work drew praise not only from critics in the United States but from critics in Mexico as well.

20. The passage most strongly supports which one of the following?
    (A) The *carpas* tradition has been widely discussed and analyzed by both U.S. and Mexican theater historians concerned with theatrical performance styles and methods.
    (B) Comedy was a prominent feature of Chicano theater in the 1960s.
    (C) In directing the *actos* of the Teatro Campesino, Valdez went to great lengths to simulate or recreate certain aspects of what audiences had experienced in the *carpas*.
    (D) Many of the earliest *actos* were based on scripts composed by Valdez, which the farm-worker actors modified to suit their own diverse aesthetic and pragmatic interests.
    (E) By the early 1970s, Valdez was using *actos* as the basis for other theatrical endeavors and was no longer directly associated with the Teatro Campesino.

GO ON TO THE NEXT PAGE.

In October 1999, the Law Reform Commission of Western Australia (LRCWA) issued its report, "Review of the Civil and Criminal Justice System." Buried within its 400 pages are several important recommendations for introducing contingency fees for lawyers' services into the state of Western Australia. Contingency-fee agreements call for payment only if the lawyer is successful in the case. Because of the lawyer's risk of financial loss, such charges generally exceed regular fees.

Although there are various types of contingency-fee arrangements, the LRCWA has recommended that only one type be introduced: "uplift" fee arrangements, which in the case of a successful outcome require the client to pay the lawyer's normal fee plus an agreed-upon additional percentage of that fee. This restriction is intended to prevent lawyers from gaining disproportionately from awards of damages and thus to ensure that just compensation to plaintiffs is not eroded. A further measure toward this end is found in the recommendation that contingency-fee agreements should be permitted only in cases where two conditions are satisfied: first, the contingency-fee arrangement must be used only as a last resort when all means of avoiding such an arrangement have been exhausted; and second, the lawyer must be satisfied that the client is financially unable to pay the fee in the event that sufficient damages are not awarded.

Unfortunately, under this recommendation, lawyers wishing to enter into an uplift fee arrangement would be forced to investigate not only the legal issues affecting any proposed litigation, but also the financial circumstances of the potential client and the probable cost of the litigation. This process would likely be onerous for a number of reasons, not least of which is the fact that the final cost of litigation depends in large part on factors that may change as the case unfolds, such as strategies adopted by the opposing side.

In addition to being burdensome for lawyers, the proposal to make contingency-fee agreements available only to the least well-off clients would be unfair to other clients. This restriction would unjustly limit freedom of contract and would, in effect, make certain types of litigation inaccessible to middle-income people or even wealthy people who might not be able to liquidate assets to pay the costs of a trial. More importantly, the primary reasons for entering into contingency-fee agreements hold for all clients. First, they provide financing for the costs of pursuing a legal action. Second, they shift the risk of not recovering those costs, and of not obtaining a damages award that will pay their lawyer's fees, from the client to the lawyer. Finally, given the convergence of the lawyer's interest and the client's interest under a contingency-fee arrangement, it is reasonable to assume that such arrangements increase lawyers' diligence and commitment to their cases.

21. As described in the passage, the uplift fee agreements that the LRCWA's report recommends are most closely analogous to which one of the following arrangements?

(A) People who join together to share the costs of purchasing lottery tickets on a regular basis agree to share any eventual proceeds from a lottery drawing in proportion to the amounts they contributed to tickets purchased for that drawing.

(B) A consulting firm reviews a company's operations. The consulting firm will receive payment only if it can substantially reduce the company's operating expenses, in which case it will be paid double its usual fee.

(C) The returns that accrue from the assumption of a large financial risk by members of a business partnership formed to develop and market a new invention are divided among them in proportion to the amount of financial risk each assumed.

(D) The cost of an insurance policy is determined by reference to the likelihood and magnitude of an eventual loss covered by the insurance policy and the administrative and marketing costs involved in marketing and servicing the insurance policy.

(E) A person purchasing a property receives a loan for the purchase from the seller. In order to reduce risk, the seller requires the buyer to pay for an insurance policy that will pay off the loan if the buyer is unable to do so.

22. The passage states which one of the following?

(A) Contingency-fee agreements serve the purpose of transferring the risk of pursuing a legal action from the client to the lawyer.

(B) Contingency-fee agreements of the kind the LRCWA's report recommends would normally not result in lawyers being paid larger fees than they deserve.

(C) At least some of the recommendations in the LRCWA's report are likely to be incorporated into the legal system in the state of Western Australia.

(D) Allowing contingency-fee agreements of the sort recommended in the LRCWA's report would not affect lawyers' diligence and commitment to their cases.

(E) Usually contingency-fee agreements involve an agreement that the fee the lawyer receives will be an agreed-upon percentage of the client's damages.

GO ON TO THE NEXT PAGE.

23. The author's main purpose in the passage is to

(A) defend a proposed reform against criticism
(B) identify the current shortcomings of a legal system and suggest how these should be remedied
(C) support the view that a recommended change would actually worsen the situation it was intended to improve
(D) show that a legal system would not be significantly changed if certain proposed reforms were enacted
(E) explain a suggested reform and critically evaluate it

24. Which one of the following is given by the passage as a reason for the difficulty a lawyer would have in determining whether—according to the LRCWA's recommendations—a prospective client was qualified to enter into an uplift agreement?

(A) The length of time that a trial may last is difficult to predict in advance.
(B) Not all prospective clients would wish to reveal detailed information about their financial circumstances.
(C) Some factors that may affect the cost of litigation can change after the litigation begins.
(D) Uplift agreements should only be used as a last resort.
(E) Investigating whether a client is qualified to enter into an uplift agreement would take time away from investigating the legal issues of the case.

25. The phrase "gaining disproportionately from awards of damages" (lines 18–19) is most likely intended by the author to mean

(A) receiving a payment that is of greater monetary value than the legal services rendered by the lawyer
(B) receiving a higher portion of the total amount awarded in damages than is reasonable compensation for the professional services rendered and the amount of risk assumed
(C) receiving a higher proportion of the damages awarded to the client than the client considers fair
(D) receiving a payment that is higher than the lawyer would have received had the client's case been unsuccessful
(E) receiving a higher proportion of the damages awarded to the client than the judge or the jury that awarded the damages intended the lawyer to receive

26. According to the passage, the LRCWA's report recommended that contingency-fee agreements

(A) be used only when it is reasonable to think that such arrangements will increase lawyers' diligence and commitment to their cases
(B) be used only in cases in which clients are unlikely to be awarded enormous damages
(C) be used if the lawyer is not certain that the client seeking to file a lawsuit could pay the lawyer's regular fee if the suit were to be unsuccessful
(D) not be used in cases in which another type of arrangement is practicable
(E) not be used except in cases where the lawyer is reasonably sure that the client will win damages sufficiently large to cover the lawyer's fees

27. Which one of the following, if true, most seriously undermines the author's criticism of the LRCWA's recommendations concerning contingency-fee agreements?

(A) The proportion of lawsuits filed by the least well-off litigants tends to be higher in areas where uplift fee arrangements have been widely used than in areas in which uplift agreements have not been used.
(B) Before the LRCWA's recommendations, lawyers in Western Australia generally made a careful evaluation of prospective clients' financial circumstances before accepting cases that might involve complex or protracted litigation.
(C) There is strong opposition in Western Australia to any legal reform perceived as favoring lawyers, so it is highly unlikely that the LRCWA's recommendations concerning contingency-fee agreements will be implemented.
(D) The total fees charged by lawyers who successfully litigate cases under uplift fee arrangements are, on average, only marginally higher than the total fees charged by lawyers who litigate cases without contingency agreements.
(E) In most jurisdictions in which contingency-fee agreements are allowed, those of the uplift variety are used much less often than are other types of contingency-fee agreements.

S T O P

IF YOU FINISH BEFORE TIME IS CALLED, YOU MAY CHECK YOUR WORK ON THIS SECTION ONLY. DO NOT WORK ON ANY OTHER SECTION IN THE TEST.

Acknowledgment is made to the following sources from which material has been adapted for use in this test booklet:

Jorge Huerta, "When Sleeping Giants Awaken: Chicano Theatre in the 1960s." ©2002 by The American Society for Theatre Research, Inc.

Jeff Minerd, "Impacts of Sprawl." ©2000 by World Future Society.

GiGi Visscher, "Contingency Fees in Western Australia." ©2000 by eLaw Journal: Murdoch University Electronic Journal of Law. http://www.murdoch.edu.au/elaw/issues/v7n1/visscher71.html.

LSAT Writing Sample Topic

Directions: The scenario presented below describes two choices, either one of which can be supported on the basis of the information given. Your essay should consider both choices and argue for one over the other, based on the two specified criteria and the facts provided. There is no "right" or "wrong" choice: a reasonable argument can be made for either.

In a total solar eclipse, the moon completely covers the sun and casts a rolling shadow along a track on the Earth's surface a few hundred kilometers wide. The eclipse lasts for a few minutes at any location within this track. The Ortegas are planning a trip to observe an upcoming eclipse during their family vacation. They have narrowed the possibilities down to two countries. Using the facts below, write an essay in which you argue in favor of one country over the other based on the following two criteria:

- The Ortegas want to minimize the chance that cloudiness will obscure the eclipse for them.
- The Ortegas want the trip to be worthwhile even if the eclipse is obscured by clouds.

For the first country, climatic data indicate that the probability of cloudiness in the area of the eclipse track is about 75 percent. The family would fly to the capital, which is a cultural center of almost unparalleled richness. Some members of the family have visited the capital before. On some days, they would drive their rental car to other cultural locations in the country. Having a rental car allows some adjustment of eclipse-viewing location according to weather forecasts.

The second country is about twice as far from the family's home as the first country, with correspondingly greater travel expense and inconvenience. No family member has been in the country before. Climatic data indicate that the probability of cloudiness in the area of the eclipse track in the country is about 25 percent. Because the country has some political instability, the family would travel on an eclipse tour organized by a respected company. Visits to several cultural sites are included.

Scratch Paper

Do not write your essay in this space.

Directions:

1. Use the Answer Key on the next page to check your answers.
2. Use the Scoring Worksheet below to compute your raw score.
3. Use the Score Conversion Chart to convert your raw score into the 120–180 scale.

Scoring Worksheet

1. Enter the number of questions you answered correctly in each section

	Number Correct
SECTION I.	______
SECTION II	______
SECTION III	______
SECTION IV	______

2. Enter the sum here: _______
This is your Raw Score.

Conversion Chart

For Converting Raw Score to the 120–180 LSAT Scaled Score
LSAT PrepTest 60

Reported Score	Raw Score Lowest	Raw Score Highest
180	97	99
179	96	96
178	—*	—*
177	95	95
176	94	94
175	93	93
174	92	92
173	91	91
172	90	90
171	89	89
170	87	88
169	86	86
168	85	85
167	83	84
166	82	82
165	80	81
164	79	79
163	77	78
162	75	76
161	74	74
160	72	73
159	70	71
158	68	69
157	67	67
156	65	66
155	63	64
154	62	62
153	60	61
152	58	59
151	56	57
150	55	55
149	53	54
148	51	52
147	50	50
146	48	49
145	47	47
144	45	46
143	43	44
142	42	42
141	40	41
140	39	39
139	37	38
138	36	36
137	35	35
136	33	34
135	32	32
134	31	31
133	29	30
132	28	28
131	27	27
130	26	26
129	25	25
128	24	24
127	23	23
126	22	22
125	21	21
124	20	20
123	19	19
122	18	18
121	17	17
120	0	16

*There is no raw score that will produce this scaled score for this test.

SECTION I

1.	D	8.	E	15.	B	22.	A
2.	E	9.	D	16.	C	23.	E
3.	B	10.	D	17.	A	24.	C
4.	D	11.	C	18.	E	25.	C
5.	C	12.	A	19.	*		
6.	B	13.	C	20.	D		
7.	C	14.	D	21.	B		

SECTION II

1.	B	8.	C	15.	E	22.	E
2.	D	9.	D	16.	A	23.	C
3.	A	10.	A	17.	B		
4.	A	11.	C	18.	A		
5.	E	12.	C	19.	B		
6.	C	13.	E	20.	B		
7.	E	14.	D	21.	D		

SECTION III

1.	A	8.	C	15.	D	22.	A
2.	B	9.	C	16.	E	23.	C
3.	A	10.	C	17.	D	24.	B
4.	B	11.	D	18.	C	25.	C
5.	D	12.	E	19.	D		
6.	D	13.	D	20.	A		
7.	C	14.	D	21.	E		

SECTION IV

1.	D	8.	C	15.	A	22.	A
2.	C	9.	A	16.	D	23.	E
3.	D	10.	D	17.	D	24.	C
4.	B	11.	D	18.	C	25.	B
5.	D	12.	C	19.	C	26.	D
6.	E	13.	C	20.	B	27.	B
7.	A	14.	E	21.	B		

*Item removed from scoring.

Experimental Section Answer Key
June 1999, PrepTest 26, Section 4

1.	E	8.	B	15.	E	22.	C
2.	A	9.	D	16.	A	23.	E
3.	A	10.	D	17.	A	24.	B
4.	E	11.	C	18.	E	25.	A
5.	B	12.	A	19.	E	26.	C
6.	E	13.	E	20.	C	27.	D
7.	B	14.	D	21.	D		

PrepTest 61
October 2010

Section I

Time—35 minutes

27 Questions

Directions: Each set of questions in this section is based on a single passage or a pair of passages. The questions are to be answered on the basis of what is stated or implied in the passage or pair of passages. For some of the questions, more than one of the choices could conceivably answer the question. However, you are to choose the best answer; that is, the response that most accurately and completely answers the question, and blacken the corresponding space on your answer sheet.

The Universal Declaration of Human Rights (UDHR), approved by the United Nations General Assembly in 1948, was the first international treaty to expressly affirm universal respect for human rights. Prior to 1948 no truly international standard of humanitarian beliefs existed. Although Article 1 of the 1945 UN Charter had been written with the express purpose of obligating the UN to "encourage respect for human rights and for fundamental freedoms for all without distinction as to race, sex, language, or religion," there were members of delegations from various small countries and representatives of several nongovernmental organizations who felt that the language of Article 1 was not strong enough, and that the Charter as a whole did not go far enough in its efforts to guarantee basic human rights. This group lobbied vigorously to strengthen the Charter's human rights provisions and proposed that member states be required "to take separate and joint action and to co-operate with the organization for the promotion of human rights." This would have implied an obligation for member states to act on human rights issues. Ultimately, this proposal and others like it were not adopted; instead, the UDHR was commissioned and drafted.

The original mandate for producing the document was given to the UN Commission on Human Rights in February 1946. Between that time and the General Assembly's final approval of the document, the UDHR passed through an elaborate eight-stage drafting process in which it made its way through almost every level of the UN hierarchy. The articles were debated at each stage, and all 30 articles were argued passionately by delegates representing diverse ideologies, traditions, and cultures. The document as it was finally approved set forth the essential principles of freedom and equality for everyone—regardless of sex, race, color, language, religion, political or other opinion, national or social origin, property, birth or other status. It also asserted a number of fundamental human rights, including among others the right to work, the right to rest and leisure, and the right to education.

While the UDHR is in many ways a progressive document, it also has weaknesses, the most regrettable of which is its nonbinding legal status. For all its strong language and high ideals, the UDHR remains a resolution of a purely programmatic nature. Nevertheless, the document has led, even if belatedly, to the creation of legally binding human rights conventions, and it clearly deserves recognition as an international standard-setting piece of work, as a set of aspirations to which UN member states are intended to strive, and as a call to arms in the name of humanity, justice, and freedom.

1. By referring to the Universal Declaration of Human Rights as "purely programmatic" (line 49) in nature, the author most likely intends to emphasize

(A) the likelihood that the document will inspire innovative government programs designed to safeguard human rights
(B) the ability of the document's drafters to translate abstract ideals into concrete standards
(C) the compromises that went into producing a version of the document that would garner the approval of all relevant parties
(D) the fact that the guidelines established by the document are ultimately unenforceable
(E) the frustration experienced by the document's drafters at stubborn resistance from within the UN hierarchy

2. The author most probably quotes directly from both the UN Charter (lines 8–11) and the proposal mentioned in lines 20–22 for which one of the following reasons?

(A) to contrast the different definitions of human rights in the two documents
(B) to compare the strength of the human rights language in the two documents
(C) to identify a bureaucratic vocabulary that is common to the two documents
(D) to highlight what the author believes to be the most important point in each document
(E) to call attention to a significant difference in the prose styles of the two documents

3. The author's stance toward the Universal Declaration of Human Rights can best be described as

(A) unbridled enthusiasm
(B) qualified approval
(C) absolute neutrality
(D) reluctant rejection
(E) strong hostility

GO ON TO THE NEXT PAGE.

4. According to the passage, each of the following is true of the Universal Declaration of Human Rights EXCEPT:

(A) It asserts a right to rest and leisure.
(B) It was drafted after the UN Charter was drafted.
(C) The UN Commission on Human Rights was charged with producing it.
(D) It has had no practical consequences.
(E) It was the first international treaty to explicitly affirm universal respect for human rights.

5. The author would be most likely to agree with which one of the following statements?

(A) The human rights language contained in Article 1 of the UN Charter is so ambiguous as to be almost wholly ineffectual.
(B) The weaknesses of the Universal Declaration of Human Rights generally outweigh the strengths of the document.
(C) It was relatively easy for the drafters of the Universal Declaration of Human Rights to reach a consensus concerning the contents of the document.
(D) The drafters of the Universal Declaration of Human Rights omitted important rights that should be included in a truly comprehensive list of basic human rights.
(E) The Universal Declaration of Human Rights would be truer to the intentions of its staunchest proponents if UN member countries were required by law to abide by its provisions.

6. Suppose that a group of independent journalists has uncovered evidence of human rights abuses being perpetrated by a security agency of a UN member state upon a group of political dissidents. Which one of the following approaches to the situation would most likely be advocated by present-day delegates who share the views of the delegates and representatives mentioned in lines 11–14?

(A) The UN General Assembly authenticates the evidence and then insists upon prompt remedial action on the part of the government of the member state.
(B) The UN General Assembly stipulates that any proposed response must be unanimously accepted by member states before it can be implemented.
(C) The UN issues a report critical of the actions of the member state in question and calls for a censure vote in the General Assembly.
(D) The situation is regarded by the UN as an internal matter that is best left to the discretion of the government of the member state.
(E) The situation is investigated further by nongovernmental humanitarian organizations that promise to disclose their findings to the public via the international media.

GO ON TO THE NEXT PAGE.

It is commonly assumed that even if some forgeries have aesthetic merit, no forgery has as much as an original by the imitated artist would. Yet even the most prominent art specialists can be duped by a talented artist turned forger into mistaking an almost perfect forgery for an original. For instance, artist Han van Meegeren's *The Disciples at Emmaus* (1937)—painted under the forged signature of the acclaimed Dutch master Jan Vermeer (1632–1675)—attracted lavish praise from experts as one of Vermeer's finest works. The painting hung in a Rotterdam museum until 1945, when, to the great embarrassment of the critics, van Meegeren revealed its origin. Astonishingly, there was at least one highly reputed critic who persisted in believing it to be a Vermeer even after van Meegeren's confession.

Given the experts' initial enthusiasm, some philosophers argue that van Meegeren's painting must have possessed aesthetic characteristics that, in a Vermeer original, would have justified the critics' plaudits. Van Meegeren's *Emmaus* thus raises difficult questions regarding the status of superbly executed forgeries. Is a forgery inherently inferior as art? How are we justified, if indeed we are, in revising downwards our critical assessment of a work unmasked as a forgery? Philosopher of art Alfred Lessing proposes convincing answers to these questions.

A forged work is indeed inferior as art, Lessing argues, but not because of a shortfall in aesthetic qualities strictly defined, that is to say, in the qualities perceptible on the picture's surface. For example, in its composition, its technique, and its brilliant use of color, van Meegeren's work is flawless, even beautiful. Lessing argues instead that the deficiency lies in what might be called the painting's intangible qualities. All art, explains Lessing, involves technique, but not all art involves origination of a new vision, and originality of vision is one of the fundamental qualities by which artistic, as opposed to purely aesthetic, accomplishment is measured. Thus Vermeer is acclaimed for having inaugurated, in the seventeenth century, a new way of seeing, and for pioneering techniques for embodying this new way of seeing through distinctive treatment of light, color, and form.

Even if we grant that van Meegeren, with his undoubted mastery of Vermeer's innovative techniques, produced an aesthetically superior painting, he did so about three centuries after Vermeer developed the techniques in question. Whereas Vermeer's origination of these techniques in the seventeenth century represents a truly impressive and historic achievement, van Meegeren's production of *The Disciples at Emmaus* in the twentieth century presents nothing new or creative to the history of art. Van Meegeren's forgery therefore, for all its aesthetic merits, lacks the historical significance that makes Vermeer's work artistically great.

7. Which one of the following most accurately expresses the main point of the passage?

   (A) *The Disciples at Emmaus*, van Meegeren's forgery of a Vermeer, was a failure in both aesthetic and artistic terms.
   (B) The aesthetic value of a work of art is less dependent on the work's visible characteristics than on certain intangible characteristics.
   (C) Forged artworks are artistically inferior to originals because artistic value depends in large part on originality of vision.
   (D) The most skilled forgers can deceive even highly qualified art experts into accepting their work as original.
   (E) Art critics tend to be unreliable judges of the aesthetic and artistic quality of works of art.

8. The passage provides the strongest support for inferring that Lessing holds which one of the following views?

   (A) The judgments of critics who pronounced *The Disciples at Emmaus* to be aesthetically superb were not invalidated by the revelation that the painting is a forgery.
   (B) The financial value of a work of art depends more on its purely aesthetic qualities than on its originality.
   (C) Museum curators would be better off not taking art critics' opinions into account when attempting to determine whether a work of art is authentic.
   (D) Because it is such a skilled imitation of Vermeer, *The Disciples at Emmaus* is as artistically successful as are original paintings by artists who are less significant than Vermeer.
   (E) Works of art that have little or no aesthetic value can still be said to be great achievements in artistic terms.

9. In the first paragraph, the author refers to a highly reputed critic's persistence in believing van Meegeren's forgery to be a genuine Vermeer primarily in order to

   (A) argue that many art critics are inflexible in their judgments
   (B) indicate that the critics who initially praised *The Disciples at Emmaus* were not as knowledgeable as they appeared
   (C) suggest that the painting may yet turn out to be a genuine Vermeer
   (D) emphasize that the concept of forgery itself is internally incoherent
   (E) illustrate the difficulties that skillfully executed forgeries can pose for art critics

10. The reaction described in which one of the following scenarios is most analogous to the reaction of the art critics mentioned in line 13?

(A) lovers of a musical group contemptuously reject a tribute album recorded by various other musicians as a second-rate imitation
(B) art historians extol the work of a little-known painter as innovative until it is discovered that the painter lived much more recently than was originally thought
(C) diners at a famous restaurant effusively praise the food as delicious until they learn that the master chef is away for the night
(D) literary critics enthusiastically applaud a new novel until its author reveals that its central symbols are intended to represent political views that the critics dislike
(E) movie fans evaluate a particular movie more favorably than they otherwise might have because their favorite actor plays the lead role

11. The passage provides the strongest support for inferring that Lessing holds which one of the following views?

(A) It is probable that many paintings currently hanging in important museums are actually forgeries.
(B) The historical circumstances surrounding the creation of a work are important in assessing the artistic value of that work.
(C) The greatness of an innovative artist depends on how much influence he or she has on other artists.
(D) The standards according to which a work is judged to be a forgery tend to vary from one historical period to another.
(E) An artist who makes use of techniques developed by others cannot be said to be innovative.

12. The passage most strongly supports which one of the following statements?

(A) In any historical period, the criteria by which a work is classified as a forgery can be a matter of considerable debate.
(B) An artist who uses techniques that others have developed is most likely a forger.
(C) A successful forger must originate a new artistic vision.
(D) Works of art created early in the career of a great artist are more likely than those created later to embody historic innovations.
(E) A painting can be a forgery even if it is not a copy of a particular original work of art.

13. Which one of the following, if true, would most strengthen Lessing's contention that a painting can display aesthetic excellence without possessing an equally high degree of artistic value?

(A) Many of the most accomplished art forgers have had moderately successful careers as painters of original works.
(B) Reproductions painted by talented young artists whose traditional training consisted in the copying of masterpieces were often seen as beautiful, but never regarded as great art.
(C) While experts can detect most forgeries, they can be duped by a talented forger who knows exactly what characteristics experts expect to find in the work of a particular painter.
(D) Most attempts at art forgery are ultimately unsuccessful because the forger has not mastered the necessary techniques.
(E) The criteria by which aesthetic excellence is judged change significantly from one century to another and from one culture to another.

GO ON TO THE NEXT PAGE.

Passage A

One function of language is to influence others' behavior by changing what they know, believe, or desire. For humans engaged in conversation, the perception of another's mental state is perhaps the most common vocalization stimulus.

While animal vocalizations may have evolved because they can potentially alter listeners' behavior to the signaler's benefit, such communication is—in contrast to human language—inadvertent, because most animals, with the possible exception of chimpanzees, cannot attribute mental states to others. The male *Physalaemus* frog calls because calling causes females to approach and other males to retreat, but there is no evidence that he does so because he attributes knowledge or desire to other frogs, or because he knows his calls will affect their knowledge and that this knowledge will, in turn, affect their behavior. Research also suggests that, in marked contrast to humans, nonhuman primates do not produce vocalizations in response to perception of another's need for information. Macaques, for example, give alarm calls when predators approach and coo calls upon finding food, yet experiments reveal no evidence that individuals were more likely to call about these events when they were aware of them but their offspring were clearly ignorant; similarly, chimpanzees do not appear to adjust their calling to inform ignorant individuals of their own location or that of food. Many animal vocalizations whose production initially seems goal-directed are not as purposeful as they first appear.

Passage B

Many scientists distinguish animal communication systems from human language on the grounds that the former are rigid responses to stimuli, whereas human language is spontaneous and creative.

In this connection, it is commonly stated that no animal can use its communication system to lie. Obviously, a lie requires intention to deceive: to judge whether a particular instance of animal communication is truly prevarication requires knowledge of the animal's intentions. Language philosopher H. P. Grice explains that for an individual to mean something by uttering *x*, the individual must intend, in expressing *x*, to induce an audience to believe something and must also intend the utterance to be recognized as so intended. But conscious intention is a category of mental experience widely believed to be uniquely human. Philosopher Jacques Maritain's discussion of the honeybee's elaborate "waggle-dance" exemplifies this view. Although bees returning to the hive communicate to other bees the distance and direction of food sources, such communication is, Maritain asserts, merely a conditioned reflex: animals may use communicative signs but lack conscious intention regarding their use.

But these arguments are circular: conscious intention is ruled out a priori and then its absence taken as evidence that animal communication is fundamentally different from human language. In fact, the narrowing of the perceived gap between animal communication and human language revealed by recent research with chimpanzees and other animals calls into question not only the assumption that the difference between animal and human communication is qualitative rather than merely quantitative, but also the accompanying assumption that animals respond mechanically to stimuli, whereas humans speak with conscious understanding and intent.

14. Both passages are primarily concerned with addressing which one of the following questions?

(A) Are animals capable of deliberately prevaricating in order to achieve specific goals?
(B) Are the communications of animals characterized by conscious intention?
(C) What kinds of stimuli are most likely to elicit animal vocalizations?
(D) Are the communication systems of nonhuman primates qualitatively different from those of all other animals?
(E) Is there a scientific consensus about the differences between animal communication systems and human language?

15. In discussing the philosopher Maritain, the author of passage B seeks primarily to

(A) describe an interpretation of animal communication that the author believes rests on a logical error
(B) suggest by illustration that there is conscious intention underlying the communicative signs employed by certain animals
(C) present an argument in support of the view that animal communication systems are spontaneous and creative
(D) furnish specific evidence against the theory that most animal communication is merely a conditioned reflex
(E) point to a noted authority on animal communication whose views the author regards with respect

GO ON TO THE NEXT PAGE.

16. The author of passage B would be most likely to agree with which one of the following statements regarding researchers who subscribe to the position articulated in passage A?

(A) They fail to recognize that humans often communicate without any clear idea of their listeners' mental states.
(B) Most of them lack the credentials needed to assess the relevant experimental evidence correctly.
(C) They ignore well-known evidence that animals do in fact practice deception.
(D) They make assumptions about matters that should be determined empirically.
(E) They falsely believe that all communication systems can be explained in terms of their evolutionary benefits.

17. Which one of the following assertions from passage A provides support for the view attributed to Maritain in passage B (lines 50–52)?

(A) One function of language is to influence the behavior of others by changing what they think.
(B) Animal vocalizations may have evolved because they have the potential to alter listeners' behavior to the signaler's benefit.
(C) It is possible that chimpanzees may have the capacity to attribute mental states to others.
(D) There is no evidence that the male *Physalaemus* frog calls because he knows that his calls will affect the knowledge of other frogs.
(E) Macaques give alarm calls when predators approach and coo calls upon finding food.

18. The authors would be most likely to disagree over

(A) the extent to which communication among humans involves the ability to perceive the mental states of others
(B) the importance of determining to what extent animal communication systems differ from human language
(C) whether human language and animal communication differ from one another qualitatively or merely in a matter of degree
(D) whether chimpanzees' vocalizations suggest that they may possess the capacity to attribute mental states to others
(E) whether animals' vocalizations evolved to alter the behavior of other animals in a way that benefits the signaler

19. Passage B differs from passage A in that passage B is more

(A) optimistic regarding the ability of science to answer certain fundamental questions
(B) disapproving of the approach taken by others writing on the same general topic
(C) open-minded in its willingness to accept the validity of apparently conflicting positions
(D) supportive of ongoing research related to the question at hand
(E) circumspect in its refusal to commit itself to any positions with respect to still-unsettled research questions

GO ON TO THE NEXT PAGE.

In contrast to the mainstream of U.S. historiography during the late nineteenth and early twentieth centuries, African American historians of the period, such as George Washington Williams and W. E. B. DuBois, adopted a transnational perspective. This was true for several reasons, not the least of which was the necessity of doing so if certain aspects of the history of African Americans in the United States were to be treated honestly.

First, there was the problem of citizenship. Even after the adoption in 1868 of the Fourteenth Amendment to the U.S. Constitution, which defined citizenship, the question of citizenship for African Americans had not been genuinely resolved. Because of this, emigrationist sentiment was a central issue in black political discourse, and both issues were critical topics for investigation. The implications for historical scholarship and national identity were enormous. While some black leaders insisted on their right to U.S. citizenship, others called on black people to emigrate and find a homeland of their own. Most African Americans were certainly not willing to relinquish their claims to the benefits of U.S. citizenship, but many had reached a point of profound pessimism and had begun to question their allegiance to the United States.

Mainstream U.S. historiography was firmly rooted in a nationalist approach during this period; the glorification of the nation and a focus on the nation-state as a historical force were dominant.The expanding spheres of influence of Europe and the United States prompted the creation of new genealogies of nations, new myths about the inevitability of nations, their "temperaments," their destinies. African American intellectuals who confronted the nationalist approach to historiography were troubled by its implications. Some argued that imperialism was a natural outgrowth of nationalism and its view that a state's strength is measured by the extension of its political power over colonial territory; the scramble for colonial empires was a distinct aspect of nationalism in the latter part of the nineteenth century.

Yet, for all their distrust of U.S. nationalism, most early black historians were themselves engaged in a sort of nation building. Deliberately or not, they contributed to the formation of a collective identity, reconstructing a glorious African past for the purposes of overturning degrading representations of blackness and establishing a firm cultural basis for a shared identity. Thus, one might argue that black historians' internationalism was a manifestation of a kind of nationalism that posits a diasporic community, which, while lacking a sovereign territory or official language, possesses a single culture, however mythical, with singular historical roots. Many members of this diaspora saw themselves as an oppressed "nation" without a homeland, or they imagined Africa as home. Hence, these historians understood their task to be the writing of the history of a people scattered by force and circumstance, a history that began in Africa.

20. Which one of the following most accurately expresses the main idea of the passage?

(A) Historians are now recognizing that the major challenge faced by African Americans in the late nineteenth and early twentieth centuries was the struggle for citizenship.
(B) Early African American historians who practiced a transnational approach to history were primarily interested in advancing an emigrationist project.
(C) U.S. historiography in the late nineteenth and early twentieth centuries was characterized by a conflict between African American historians who viewed history from a transnational perspective and mainstream historians who took a nationalist perspective.
(D) The transnational perspective of early African American historians countered mainstream nationalist historiography, but it was arguably nationalist itself to the extent that it posited a culturally unified diasporic community.
(E) Mainstream U.S. historians in the late nineteenth and early twentieth centuries could no longer justify their nationalist approach to history once they were confronted with the transnational perspective taken by African American historians.

21. Which one of the following phrases most accurately conveys the sense of the word "reconstructing" as it is used in line 47?

(A) correcting a misconception about
(B) determining the sequence of events in
(C) investigating the implications of
(D) rewarding the promoters of
(E) shaping a conception of

22. Which one of the following is most strongly supported by the passage?

(A) Emigrationist sentiment would not have been as strong among African Americans in the late nineteenth century had the promise of U.S. citizenship been fully realized for African Americans at that time.
(B) Scholars writing the history of diasporic communities generally do not discuss the forces that initially caused the scattering of the members of those communities.
(C) Most historians of the late nineteenth and early twentieth centuries endeavored to make the histories of the nations about which they wrote seem more glorious than they actually were.
(D) To be properly considered nationalist, a historical work must ignore the ways in which one nation's foreign policy decisions affected other nations.
(E) A considerable number of early African American historians embraced nationalism and the inevitability of the dominance of the nation-state.

GO ON TO THE NEXT PAGE.

23. As it is described in the passage, the transnational approach employed by African American historians working in the late nineteenth and early twentieth centuries would be best exemplified by a historical study that

(A) investigated the extent to which European and U.S. nationalist mythologies contradicted one another
(B) defined the national characters of the United States and several European nations by focusing on their treatment of minority populations rather than on their territorial ambitions
(C) recounted the attempts by the United States to gain control over new territories during the late nineteenth and early twentieth centuries
(D) considered the impact of emigrationist sentiment among African Americans on U.S. foreign policy in Africa during the late nineteenth century
(E) examined the extent to which African American culture at the turn of the century incorporated traditions that were common to a number of African cultures

24. The passage provides information sufficient to answer which one of the following questions?

(A) Which African nations did early African American historians research in writing their histories of the African diaspora?
(B) What were some of the African languages spoken by the ancestors of the members of the African diasporic community who were living in the United States in the late nineteenth century?
(C) Over which territories abroad did the United States attempt to extend its political power in the latter part of the nineteenth century?
(D) Are there textual ambiguities in the Fourteenth Amendment that spurred the conflict over U.S. citizenship for African Americans?
(E) In what ways did African American leaders respond to the question of citizenship for African Americans in the latter part of the nineteenth century?

25. The author of the passage would be most likely to agree with which one of the following statements?

(A) Members of a particular diasporic community have a common country of origin.
(B) Territorial sovereignty is not a prerequisite for the project of nation building.
(C) Early African American historians who rejected nationalist historiography declined to engage in historical myth-making of any kind.
(D) The most prominent African American historians in the late nineteenth and early twentieth centuries advocated emigration for African Americans.
(E) Historians who employed a nationalist approach focused on entirely different events from those studied and written about by early African American historians.

26. The main purpose of the second paragraph of the passage is to

(A) explain why early African American historians felt compelled to approach historiography in the way that they did
(B) show that governmental actions such as constitutional amendments do not always have the desired effect
(C) support the contention that African American intellectuals in the late nineteenth century were critical of U.S. imperialism
(D) establish that some African American political leaders in the late nineteenth century advocated emigration as an alternative to fighting for the benefits of U.S. citizenship
(E) argue that the definition of citizenship contained in the Fourteenth Amendment to the U.S. Constitution is too limited

27. As it is presented in the passage, the approach to history taken by mainstream U.S. historians of the late nineteenth and early twentieth centuries is most similar to the approach exemplified in which one of the following?

(A) An elected official writes a memo suggesting that because a particular course of action has been successful in the past, the government should continue to pursue that course of action.
(B) A biographer of a famous novelist argues that the precocity apparent in certain of the novelist's early achievements confirms that her success was attributable to innate talent.
(C) A doctor maintains that because a certain medication was developed expressly for the treatment of an illness, it is the best treatment for that illness.
(D) A newspaper runs a series of articles in order to inform the public about the environmentally hazardous practices of a large corporation.
(E) A scientist gets the same result from an experiment several times and therefore concludes that its chemical reactions always proceed in the observed fashion.

S T O P

IF YOU FINISH BEFORE TIME IS CALLED, YOU MAY CHECK YOUR WORK ON THIS SECTION ONLY. DO NOT WORK ON ANY OTHER SECTION IN THE TEST.

SECTION II
Time—35 minutes
25 Questions

Directions: The questions in this section are based on the reasoning contained in brief statements or passages. For some questions, more than one of the choices could conceivably answer the question. However, you are to choose the best answer; that is, the response that most accurately and completely answers the question. You should not make assumptions that are by commonsense standards implausible, superfluous, or incompatible with the passage. After you have chosen the best answer, blacken the corresponding space on your answer sheet.

1. Mary to Jamal: You acknowledge that as the legitimate owner of this business I have the legal right to sell it whenever I wish. But also you claim that because loyal employees will suffer if I sell it, I therefore have no right to do so. Obviously, your statements taken together are absurd.

Mary's reasoning is most vulnerable to the criticism that she

(A) overlooks the possibility that when Jamal claims that she has no right to sell the business, he simply means she has no right to do so at this time
(B) overlooks the possibility that her employees also have rights related to the sale of the business
(C) provides no evidence for the claim that she does have a right to sell the business
(D) overlooks the possibility that Jamal is referring to two different kinds of right
(E) attacks Jamal's character rather than his argument

2. Since there is no survival value in an animal's having an organ that is able to function when all its other organs have broken down to such a degree that the animal dies, it is a result of the efficiency of natural selection that no organ is likely to evolve in such a way that it greatly outlasts the body's other organs.

Of the following, which one illustrates a principle that is most similar to the principle illustrated by the passage?

(A) A store in a lower-income neighborhood finds that it is unable to sell its higher-priced goods and so stocks them only when ordered by a customer.
(B) The body of an animal with a deficient organ is often able to compensate for that deficiency when other organs perform the task the deficient one normally performs.
(C) One car model produced by an automobile manufacturer has a life expectancy that is so much longer than its other models that its great popularity requires the manufacturer to stop producing some of the other models.
(D) Athletes occasionally overdevelop some parts of their bodies to such a great extent that other parts of their bodies are more prone to injury as a result.
(E) Automotive engineers find that it is not cost-effective to manufacture a given automobile part of such high quality that it outlasts all other parts of the automobile, as doing so would not raise the overall quality of the automobile.

GO ON TO THE NEXT PAGE.

3. Commentator: If a political administration is both economically successful and successful at protecting individual liberties, then it is an overall success. Even an administration that fails to care for the environment may succeed overall if it protects individual liberties. So far, the present administration has not cared for the environment but has successfully protected individual liberties.

If all of the statements above are true, then which one of the following must be true?

(A) The present administration is economically successful.
(B) The present administration is not an overall success.
(C) If the present administration is economically successful, then it is an overall success.
(D) If the present administration had been economically successful, it would have cared for the environment.
(E) If the present administration succeeds at environmental protection, then it will be an overall success.

4. The legislature is considering a proposed bill that would prohibit fishing in Eagle Bay. Despite widespread concern over the economic effect this ban would have on the local fishing industry, the bill should be enacted. The bay has one of the highest water pollution levels in the nation, and a recent study of the bay's fish found that 80 percent of them contained toxin levels that exceed governmental safety standards. Continuing to permit fishing in Eagle Bay could thus have grave effects on public health.

The argument proceeds by presenting evidence that

(A) the toxic contamination of fish in Eagle Bay has had grave economic effects on the local fishing industry
(B) the moral principle that an action must be judged on the basis of its foreseeable effects is usually correct
(C) the opponents of the ban have failed to weigh properly its foreseeable negative effects against its positive ones
(D) failure to enact the ban would carry with it unacceptable risks for the public welfare
(E) the ban would reduce the level of toxins in the fish in Eagle Bay

5. Vandenburg: This art museum is not adhering to its purpose. Its founders intended it to devote as much attention to contemporary art as to the art of earlier periods, but its collection of contemporary art is far smaller than its other collections.

Simpson: The relatively small size of the museum's contemporary art collection is appropriate. It's an art museum, not an ethnographic museum designed to collect every style of every period. Its contemporary art collection is small because its curators believe that there is little high-quality contemporary art.

Which one of the following principles, if valid, most helps to justify the reasoning in Simpson's response to Vandenburg?

(A) An art museum should collect only works that its curators consider to be of high artistic quality.
(B) An art museum should not collect any works that violate the purpose defined by the museum's founders.
(C) An art museum's purpose need not be to collect every style of every period.
(D) An ethnographic museum's purpose should be defined according to its curators' beliefs.
(E) The intentions of an art museum's curators should not determine what is collected by that museum.

6. Over the last five years, every new major alternative-energy initiative that initially was promised government funding has since seen that funding severely curtailed. In no such case has the government come even close to providing the level of funds initially earmarked for these projects. Since large corporations have made it a point to discourage alternative-energy projects, it is likely that the corporations' actions influenced the government's funding decisions.

Which one of the following, if true, most strengthens the reasoning above?

(A) For the past two decades, most alternative-energy initiatives have received little or no government funding.
(B) The funding initially earmarked for a government project is always subject to change, given the mechanisms by which the political process operates.
(C) The only research projects whose government funding has been severely curtailed are those that large corporations have made it a point to discourage.
(D) Some projects encouraged by large corporations have seen their funding severely curtailed over the last five years.
(E) All large corporations have made it a point to discourage some forms of research.

GO ON TO THE NEXT PAGE.

7. Talbert: Chess is beneficial for school-age children. It is enjoyable, encourages foresight and logical thinking, and discourages carelessness, inattention, and impulsiveness. In short, it promotes mental maturity.

Sklar: My objection to teaching chess to children is that it diverts mental activity from something with societal value, such as science, into something that has no societal value.

Talbert's and Sklar's statements provide the strongest support for holding that they disagree with each other over whether

(A) chess promotes mental maturity
(B) many activities promote mental maturity just as well as chess does
(C) chess is socially valuable and science is not
(D) children should be taught to play chess
(E) children who neither play chess nor study science are mentally immature

8. Marcia: Not all vegetarian diets lead to nutritional deficiencies. Research shows that vegetarians can obtain a full complement of proteins and minerals from nonanimal foods.

Theodora: You are wrong in claiming that vegetarianism cannot lead to nutritional deficiencies. If most people became vegetarians, some of those losing jobs due to the collapse of many meat-based industries would fall into poverty and hence be unable to afford a nutritionally adequate diet.

Theodora's reply to Marcia's argument is most vulnerable to criticism on the grounds that her reply

(A) is directed toward disproving a claim that Marcia did not make
(B) ignores the results of the research cited by Marcia
(C) takes for granted that no meat-based industries will collapse unless most people become vegetarians
(D) uses the word "diet" in a nontechnical sense whereas Marcia's argument uses this term in a medical sense
(E) takes for granted that people losing jobs in meat-based industries would become vegetarians

9. Musicologist: Classification of a musical instrument depends on the mechanical action through which it produces music. So the piano is properly called a percussion instrument, not a stringed instrument. Even though the vibration of the piano's strings is what makes its sound, the strings are caused to vibrate by the impact of hammers.

Which one of the following most accurately expresses the main conclusion of the musicologist's argument?

(A) Musical instruments should be classified according to the mechanical actions through which they produce sound.
(B) Musical instruments should not be classified based on the way musicians interact with them.
(C) Some people classify the piano as a stringed instrument because of the way the piano produces sound.
(D) The piano should be classified as a stringed instrument rather than as a percussion instrument.
(E) It is correct to classify the piano as a percussion instrument rather than as a stringed instrument.

10. In a vast ocean region, phosphorus levels have doubled in the past few decades due to agricultural runoff pouring out of a large river nearby. The phosphorus stimulates the growth of plankton near the ocean surface. Decaying plankton fall to the ocean floor, where bacteria devour them, consuming oxygen in the process. Due to the resulting oxygen depletion, few fish can survive in this region.

Which one of the following can be properly inferred from the information above?

(A) The agricultural runoff pouring out of the river contributes to the growth of plankton near the ocean surface.
(B) Before phosphorus levels doubled in the ocean region, most fish were able to survive in that region.
(C) If agricultural runoff ceased pouring out of the river, there would be no bacteria on the ocean floor devouring decaying plankton.
(D) The quantity of agricultural runoff pouring out of the river has doubled in the past few decades.
(E) The amount of oxygen in a body of water is in general inversely proportional to the level of phosphorus in that body of water.

11. Psychologists observing a shopping mall parking lot found that, on average, drivers spent 39 seconds leaving a parking space when another car was quietly waiting to enter it, 51 seconds if the driver of the waiting car honked impatiently, but only 32 seconds leaving a space when no one was waiting. This suggests that drivers feel possessive of their parking spaces even when leaving them, and that this possessiveness increases in reaction to indications that another driver wants the space.

Which one of the following, if true, most weakens the reasoning?

(A) The more pressure most drivers feel because others are waiting for them to perform maneuvers with their cars, the less quickly they are able to perform them.
(B) The amount of time drivers spend entering a parking space is not noticeably affected by whether other drivers are waiting for them to do so, nor by whether those other drivers are honking impatiently.
(C) It is considerably more difficult and time-consuming for a driver to maneuver a car out of a parking space if another car waiting to enter that space is nearby.
(D) Parking spaces in shopping mall parking lots are unrepresentative of parking spaces in general with respect to the likelihood that other cars will be waiting to enter them.
(E) Almost any driver leaving a parking space will feel angry at another driver who honks impatiently, and this anger will influence the amount of time spent leaving the space.

12. Shark teeth are among the most common vertebrate fossils; yet fossilized shark skeletons are much less common—indeed, comparatively rare among fossilized vertebrate skeletons.

Which one of the following, if true, most helps to resolve the apparent paradox described above?

(A) Unlike the bony skeletons of other vertebrates, shark skeletons are composed of cartilage, and teeth and bone are much more likely to fossilize than cartilage is.
(B) The rare fossilized skeletons of sharks that are found are often found in areas other than those in which fossils of shark teeth are plentiful.
(C) Fossils of sharks' teeth are quite difficult to distinguish from fossils of other kinds of teeth.
(D) Some species of sharks alive today grow and lose many sets of teeth during their lifetimes.
(E) The physical and chemical processes involved in the fossilization of sharks' teeth are as common as those involved in the fossilization of shark skeletons.

13. Critic: Photographers, by deciding which subjects to depict and how to depict them, express their own worldviews in their photographs, however realistically those photographs may represent reality. Thus, photographs are interpretations of reality.

The argument's conclusion is properly drawn if which one of the following is assumed?

(A) Even representing a subject realistically can involve interpreting that subject.
(B) To express a worldview is to interpret reality.
(C) All visual art expresses the artist's worldview.
(D) Any interpretation of reality involves the expression of a worldview.
(E) Nonrealistic photographs, like realistic photographs, express the worldviews of the photographers who take them.

14. Geologists recently discovered marks that closely resemble worm tracks in a piece of sandstone. These marks were made more than half a billion years earlier than the earliest known traces of multicellular animal life. Therefore, the marks are probably the traces of geological processes rather than of worms.

Which one of the following, if true, most weakens the argument?

(A) It is sometimes difficult to estimate the precise age of a piece of sandstone.
(B) Geological processes left a substantial variety of marks in sandstone more than half a billion years before the earliest known multicellular animal life existed.
(C) There were some early life forms other than worms that are known to have left marks that are hard to distinguish from those found in the piece of sandstone.
(D) At the place where the sandstone was found, the only geological processes that are likely to mark sandstone in ways that resemble worm tracks could not have occurred at the time the marks were made.
(E) Most scientists knowledgeable about early animal life believe that worms are likely to have been among the earliest forms of multicellular animal life on Earth, but evidence of their earliest existence is scarce because they are composed solely of soft tissue.

GO ON TO THE NEXT PAGE.

15. Often a type of organ or body structure is the only physically feasible means of accomplishing a given task, so it should be unsurprising if, like eyes or wings, that type of organ or body structure evolves at different times in a number of completely unrelated species. After all, whatever the difference of heritage and habitat, as organisms animals have fundamentally similar needs and so _______.

Which one of the following most logically completes the last sentence of the passage?

(A) will often live in the same environment as other species quite different from themselves
(B) will in many instances evolve similar adaptations enabling them to satisfy these needs
(C) will develop adaptations allowing them to satisfy these needs
(D) will resemble other species having different biological needs
(E) will all develop eyes or wings as adaptations

16. Engineer: Thermophotovoltaic generators are devices that convert heat into electricity. The process of manufacturing steel produces huge amounts of heat that currently go to waste. So if steel-manufacturing plants could feed the heat they produce into thermophotovoltaic generators, they would greatly reduce their electric bills, thereby saving money.

Which one of the following is an assumption on which the engineer's argument depends?

(A) There is no other means of utilizing the heat produced by the steel-manufacturing process that would be more cost effective than installing thermophotovoltaic generators.
(B) Using current technology, it would be possible for steel-manufacturing plants to feed the heat they produce into thermophotovoltaic generators in such a way that those generators could convert at least some of that heat into electricity.
(C) The amount steel-manufacturing plants would save on their electric bills by feeding heat into thermophotovoltaic generators would be sufficient to cover the cost of purchasing and installing those generators.
(D) At least some steel-manufacturing plants rely on electricity as their primary source of energy in the steel-manufacturing process.
(E) There are at least some steel-manufacturing plants that could greatly reduce their electricity bills only if they used some method of converting wasted heat or other energy from the steel-manufacturing process into electricity.

17. Herbalist: While standard antibiotics typically have just one active ingredient, herbal antibacterial remedies typically contain several. Thus, such herbal remedies are more likely to retain their effectiveness against new, resistant strains of bacteria than are standard antibiotics. For a strain of bacteria, the difficulty of developing resistance to an herbal antibacterial remedy is like a cook's difficulty in trying to prepare a single meal that will please all of several dozen guests, a task far more difficult than preparing one meal that will please a single guest.

In the analogy drawn in the argument above, which one of the following corresponds to a standard antibiotic?

(A) a single guest
(B) several dozen guests
(C) the pleasure experienced by a single guest
(D) a cook
(E) the ingredients available to a cook

18. To find out how barn owls learn how to determine the direction from which sounds originate, scientists put distorting lenses over the eyes of young barn owls before the owls first opened their eyes. The owls with these lenses behaved as if objects making sounds were farther to the right than they actually were. Once the owls matured, the lenses were removed, yet the owls continued to act as if they misjudged the location of the source of sounds. The scientists consequently hypothesized that once a barn owl has developed an auditory scheme for estimating the point from which sounds originate, it ceases to use vision to locate sounds.

The scientists' reasoning is vulnerable to which one of the following criticisms?

(A) It fails to consider whether the owls' vision was permanently impaired by their having worn the lenses while immature.
(B) It assumes that the sense of sight is equally good in all owls.
(C) It attributes human reasoning processes to a nonhuman organism.
(D) It neglects to consider how similar distorting lenses might affect the behavior of other bird species.
(E) It uses as evidence experimental results that were irrelevant to the conclusion.

GO ON TO THE NEXT PAGE.

19. As often now as in the past, newspaper journalists use direct or indirect quotation to report unsupported or false claims made by newsmakers. However, journalists are becoming less likely to openly challenge the veracity of such claims within their articles.

Each of the following, if true, helps to explain the trend in journalism described above EXCEPT:

(A) Newspaper publishers have found that many readers will cancel a subscription simply because a view they take for granted has been disputed by the publication.
(B) The areas of knowledge on which journalists report are growing in specialization and diversity, while journalists themselves are not becoming more broadly knowledgeable.
(C) Persons supporting controversial views more and more frequently choose to speak only to reporters who seem sympathetic to their views.
(D) A basic principle of journalism holds that debate over controversial issues draws the attention of the public.
(E) Journalists who challenge the veracity of claims are often criticized for failing their professional obligation to be objective.

20. When people show signs of having a heart attack an electrocardiograph (EKG) is often used to diagnose their condition. In a study, a computer program for EKG diagnosis of heart attacks was pitted against a very experienced, highly skilled cardiologist. The program correctly diagnosed a significantly higher proportion of the cases that were later confirmed to be heart attacks than did the cardiologist. Interpreting EKG data, therefore, should be left to computer programs.

Which one of the following, if true, most weakens the argument?

(A) Experts agreed that the cardiologist made few obvious mistakes in reading and interpreting the EKG data.
(B) The practice of medicine is as much an art as a science, and computer programs are not easily adapted to making subjective judgments.
(C) The cardiologist correctly diagnosed a significantly higher proportion of the cases in which no heart attack occurred than did the computer program.
(D) In a considerable percentage of cases, EKG data alone are insufficient to enable either computer programs or cardiologists to make accurate diagnoses.
(E) The cardiologist in the study was unrepresentative of cardiologists in general with respect to skill and experience.

21. A government study indicates that raising speed limits to reflect the actual average speeds of traffic on level, straight stretches of high-speed roadways reduces the accident rate. Since the actual average speed for level, straight stretches of high-speed roadways tends to be 120 kilometers per hour (75 miles per hour), that should be set as a uniform national speed limit for level, straight stretches of all such roadways.

Which one of the following principles, if valid, most helps to justify the reasoning above?

(A) Uniform national speed limits should apply only to high-speed roadways.
(B) Traffic laws applying to high-speed roadways should apply uniformly across the nation.
(C) A uniform national speed limit for high-speed roadways should be set only if all such roadways have roughly equal average speeds of traffic.
(D) Long-standing laws that are widely violated are probably not good laws.
(E) Any measure that reduces the rate of traffic accidents should be implemented.

GO ON TO THE NEXT PAGE.

22. Psychiatrist: In treating first-year students at this university, I have noticed that those reporting the highest levels of spending on recreation score at about the same level on standard screening instruments for anxiety and depression as those reporting the lowest levels of spending on recreation. This suggests that the first-year students with high levels of spending on recreation could reduce that spending without increasing their anxiety or depression.

Each of the following, if true, strengthens the psychiatrist's argument EXCEPT:

(A) At other universities, first-year students reporting the highest levels of spending on recreation also show the same degree of anxiety and depression as do those reporting the lowest levels of such spending.
(B) Screening of first-year students at the university who report moderate levels of spending on recreation reveals that those students are less anxious and depressed than both those with the highest and those with the lowest levels of spending on recreation.
(C) Among adults between the ages of 40 and 60, increased levels of spending on recreation are strongly correlated with decreased levels of anxiety and depression.
(D) The screening instruments used by the psychiatrist are extremely accurate in revealing levels of anxiety and depression among university students.
(E) Several of the psychiatrist's patients who are first-year students at the university have reduced their spending on recreation from very high levels to very low levels without increasing their anxiety or depression.

23. Every brick house on River Street has a front yard. Most of the houses on River Street that have front yards also have two stories. So most of the brick houses on River Street have two stories.

Which one of the following is most appropriate as an analogy demonstrating that the reasoning in the argument above is flawed?

(A) By that line of reasoning, we could conclude that most politicians have run for office, since all legislators are politicians and most legislators have run for office.
(B) By that line of reasoning, we could conclude that most public servants are legislators, since most legislators have run for office and most politicians who have run for office are public servants.
(C) By that line of reasoning, we could conclude that not every public servant has run for office, since every legislator is a public servant but some public servants are not legislators.
(D) By that line of reasoning, we could conclude that most legislators have never run for office, since most public servants have never run for office and all legislators are public servants.
(E) By that line of reasoning, we could conclude that most legislators are not public servants, since most public servants have not run for office and most legislators have run for office.

GO ON TO THE NEXT PAGE.

24. Historian: It is unlikely that someone would see history as the working out of moral themes unless he or she held clear and unambiguous moral beliefs. However, one's inclination to morally judge human behavior decreases as one's knowledge of history increases. Consequently, the more history a person knows, the less likely that person is to view history as the working out of moral themes.

The conclusion of the argument is properly drawn if which one of the following is assumed?

(A) Historical events that fail to elicit moral disapproval are generally not considered to exemplify a moral theme.
(B) The less inclined one is to morally judge human behavior, the less likely it is that one holds clear and unambiguous moral beliefs.
(C) Only those who do not understand human history attribute moral significance to historical events.
(D) The more clear and unambiguous one's moral beliefs, the more likely one is to view history as the working out of moral themes.
(E) People tend to be less objective regarding a subject about which they possess extensive knowledge than regarding a subject about which they do not possess extensive knowledge.

25. A recent poll revealed that most students at our university prefer that the university, which is searching for a new president, hire someone who has extensive experience as a university president. However, in the very same poll, the person most students chose from among a list of leading candidates as the one they would most like to see hired was someone who has never served as a university president.

Which one of the following, if true, most helps to account for the apparent discrepancy in the students' preferences?

(A) Because several of the candidates listed in the poll had extensive experience as university presidents, not all of the candidates could be differentiated on this basis alone.
(B) Most of the candidates listed in the poll had extensive experience as university presidents.
(C) Students taking the poll had fewer candidates to choose from than were currently being considered for the position.
(D) Most of the students taking the poll did not know whether any of the leading candidates listed in the poll had ever served as a university president.
(E) Often a person can be well suited to a position even though they have relatively little experience in such a position.

S T O P

IF YOU FINISH BEFORE TIME IS CALLED, YOU MAY CHECK YOUR WORK ON THIS SECTION ONLY.
DO NOT WORK ON ANY OTHER SECTION IN THE TEST.

SECTION III

Time—35 minutes

23 Questions

Directions: Each group of questions in this section is based on a set of conditions. In answering some of the questions, it may be useful to draw a rough diagram. Choose the response that most accurately and completely answers each question and blacken the corresponding space on your answer sheet.

Questions 1–5

Exactly six workers—Faith, Gus, Hannah, Juan, Kenneth, and Lisa—will travel to a business convention in two cars—car 1 and car 2. Each car must carry at least two of the workers, one of whom will be assigned to drive. For the entire trip, the workers will comply with an assignment that also meets the following constraints:

Either Faith or Gus must drive the car in which Hannah travels.

Either Faith or Kenneth must drive the car in which Juan travels.

Gus must travel in the same car as Lisa.

1. Which one of the following is a possible assignment of the workers to the cars?

(A) car 1: Faith (driver), Hannah, and Juan
car 2: Gus (driver), Kenneth, and Lisa

(B) car 1: Faith (driver), Hannah, and Kenneth
car 2: Lisa (driver), Gus, and Juan

(C) car 1: Faith (driver), Juan, Kenneth, and Lisa
car 2: Gus (driver) and Hannah

(D) car 1: Faith (driver) and Juan
car 2: Kenneth (driver), Gus, Hannah, and Lisa

(E) car 1: Gus (driver), Hannah, and Lisa
car 2: Juan (driver), Faith, and Kenneth

2. The two workers who drive the cars CANNOT be

(A) Faith and Gus
(B) Faith and Kenneth
(C) Faith and Lisa
(D) Gus and Kenneth
(E) Kenneth and Lisa

3. If Lisa drives one of the cars, then which one of the following could be true?

(A) Faith travels in the same car as Kenneth.
(B) Faith travels in the same car as Lisa.
(C) Gus travels in the same car as Hannah.
(D) Gus travels in the same car as Juan.
(E) Hannah travels in the same car as Lisa.

4. If Faith travels with two other workers in car 1, and if Faith is not the driver, then the person in car 1 other than Faith and the driver must be

(A) Gus
(B) Hannah
(C) Juan
(D) Kenneth
(E) Lisa

5. Which one of the following CANNOT be true?

(A) Gus is the only person other than the driver in one of the cars.
(B) Hannah is the only person other than the driver in one of the cars.
(C) Juan is the only person other than the driver in one of the cars.
(D) Kenneth is the only person other than the driver in one of the cars.
(E) Lisa is the only person other than the driver in one of the cars.

GO ON TO THE NEXT PAGE.

Questions 6–11

An archaeologist has six ancient artifacts—a figurine, a headdress, a jar, a necklace, a plaque, and a tureen—no two of which are the same age. She will order them from first (oldest) to sixth (most recent). The following has already been determined:

The figurine is older than both the jar and the headdress.
The necklace and the jar are both older than the tureen.
Either the plaque is older than both the headdress and the necklace, or both the headdress and the necklace are older than the plaque.

6. Which one of the following could be the artifacts in the order of their age, from first to sixth?

(A) figurine, headdress, jar, necklace, plaque, tureen
(B) figurine, jar, plaque, headdress, tureen, necklace
(C) figurine, necklace, plaque, headdress, jar, tureen
(D) necklace, jar, figurine, headdress, plaque, tureen
(E) plaque, tureen, figurine, necklace, jar, headdress

7. Exactly how many of the artifacts are there any one of which could be first?

(A) one
(B) two
(C) three
(D) four
(E) five

8. Which one of the following artifacts CANNOT be fourth?

(A) figurine
(B) headdress
(C) jar
(D) necklace
(E) plaque

9. If the figurine is third, which one of the following must be second?

(A) headdress
(B) jar
(C) necklace
(D) plaque
(E) tureen

10. If the plaque is first, then exactly how many artifacts are there any one of which could be second?

(A) one
(B) two
(C) three
(D) four
(E) five

11. Which one of the following, if substituted for the information that the necklace and the jar are both older than the tureen, would have the same effect in determining the order of the artifacts?

(A) The tureen is older than the headdress but not as old as the figurine.
(B) The figurine and the necklace are both older than the tureen.
(C) The necklace is older than the tureen if and only if the jar is.
(D) All of the artifacts except the headdress and the plaque must be older than the tureen.
(E) The plaque is older than the necklace if and only if the plaque is older than the tureen.

GO ON TO THE NEXT PAGE.

Questions 12–17

The coach of a women's track team must determine which four of five runners—Quinn, Ramirez, Smith, Terrell, and Uzoma—will run in the four races of an upcoming track meet. Each of the four runners chosen will run in exactly one of the four races—the first, second, third, or fourth. The coach's selection is bound by the following constraints:

If Quinn runs in the track meet, then Terrell runs in the race immediately after the race in which Quinn runs.

Smith does not run in either the second race or the fourth race.

If Uzoma does not run in the track meet, then Ramirez runs in the second race.

If Ramirez runs in the second race, then Uzoma does not run in the track meet.

12. Which one of the following could be the order in which the runners run, from first to fourth?

(A) Uzoma, Ramirez, Quinn, Terrell
(B) Terrell, Smith, Ramirez, Uzoma
(C) Smith, Ramirez, Terrell, Quinn
(D) Ramirez, Uzoma, Smith, Terrell
(E) Quinn, Terrell, Smith, Ramirez

13. Which one of the following runners must the coach select to run in the track meet?

(A) Quinn
(B) Ramirez
(C) Smith
(D) Terrell
(E) Uzoma

14. The question of which runners will be chosen to run in the track meet and in what races they will run can be completely resolved if which one of the following is true?

(A) Ramirez runs in the first race.
(B) Ramirez runs in the second race.
(C) Ramirez runs in the third race.
(D) Ramirez runs in the fourth race.
(E) Ramirez does not run in the track meet.

15. Which one of the following CANNOT be true?

(A) Ramirez runs in the race immediately before the race in which Smith runs.
(B) Smith runs in the race immediately before the race in which Quinn runs.
(C) Smith runs in the race immediately before the race in which Terrell runs.
(D) Terrell runs in the race immediately before the race in which Ramirez runs.
(E) Uzoma runs in the race immediately before the race in which Terrell runs.

16. If Uzoma runs in the first race, then which one of the following must be true?

(A) Quinn does not run in the track meet.
(B) Smith does not run in the track meet.
(C) Quinn runs in the second race.
(D) Terrell runs in the second race.
(E) Ramirez runs in the fourth race.

17. If both Quinn and Smith run in the track meet, then how many of the runners are there any one of whom could be the one who runs in the first race?

(A) one
(B) two
(C) three
(D) four
(E) five

GO ON TO THE NEXT PAGE.

Questions 18–23

From the 1st through the 7th of next month, seven nurses—Farnham, Griseldi, Heany, Juarez, Khan, Lightfoot, and Moreau—will each conduct one information session at a community center. Each nurse's session will fall on a different day. The nurses' schedule is governed by the following constraints:

At least two of the other nurses' sessions must fall in between Heany's session and Moreau's session.
Griseldi's session must be on the day before Khan's.
Juarez's session must be on a later day than Moreau's.
Farnham's session must be on an earlier day than Khan's but on a later day than Lightfoot's.
Lightfoot cannot conduct the session on the 2nd.

18. Which one of the following could be the order of the nurses' sessions, from first to last?

(A) Farnham, Griseldi, Khan, Moreau, Juarez, Lightfoot, Heany
(B) Heany, Lightfoot, Farnham, Moreau, Juarez, Griseldi, Khan
(C) Juarez, Heany, Lightfoot, Farnham, Moreau, Griseldi, Khan
(D) Lightfoot, Moreau, Farnham, Juarez, Griseldi, Khan, Heany
(E) Moreau, Lightfoot, Heany, Juarez, Farnham, Griseldi, Khan

19. Juarez's session CANNOT be on which one of the following days?

(A) the 2nd
(B) the 3rd
(C) the 5th
(D) the 6th
(E) the 7th

20. If Juarez's session is on the 3rd, then which one of the following could be true?

(A) Moreau's session is on the 1st.
(B) Khan's session is on the 5th.
(C) Heany's session is on the 6th.
(D) Griseldi's session is on the 5th.
(E) Farnham's session is on the 2nd.

21. If Khan's session is on an earlier day than Moreau's, which one of the following could conduct the session on the 3rd?

(A) Griseldi
(B) Heany
(C) Juarez
(D) Lightfoot
(E) Moreau

22. If Griseldi's session is on the 5th, then which one of the following must be true?

(A) Farnham's session is on the 3rd.
(B) Heany's session is on the 7th.
(C) Juarez's session is on the 4th.
(D) Lightfoot's session is on the 1st.
(E) Moreau's session is on the 2nd.

23. Lightfoot's session could be on which one of the following days?

(A) the 3rd
(B) the 4th
(C) the 5th
(D) the 6th
(E) the 7th

S T O P

IF YOU FINISH BEFORE TIME IS CALLED, YOU MAY CHECK YOUR WORK ON THIS SECTION ONLY. DO NOT WORK ON ANY OTHER SECTION IN THE TEST.

Time—35 minutes

25 Questions

Directions: The questions in this section are based on the reasoning contained in brief statements or passages. For some questions, more than one of the choices could conceivably answer the question. However, you are to choose the best answer; that is, the response that most accurately and completely answers the question. You should not make assumptions that are by commonsense standards implausible, superfluous, or incompatible with the passage. After you have chosen the best answer blacken the corresponding space on your answer sheet.

1. Insurance that was to become effective at 9 A.M. on a certain date was taken out on the life of a flight attendant. He died on that date at 10 A.M. local time, which was two hours before 9 A.M. in the time zone where the policy had been purchased. The insurance company contended that the policy had not become effective; a representative of the flight attendant's beneficiary, his mother, countered by arguing that the policy amount should be paid because the attendant had been his mother's sole support, and she was ill.

The representative's argument is flawed as a counter to the insurance company's contention because

(A) the conclusion is no more than a paraphrase of the evidence offered in support of it
(B) it appeals to the emotion of pity rather than addressing the issue raised
(C) it makes an unwarranted distinction between family obligations and business obligations
(D) it substitutes an attack on a person for the giving of reasons
(E) a cause and its effect are mistaken for each other

2. Once a child's imagination becomes developed, a host of imaginary creatures may torment the child. But this newly developed cognitive capacity may also be used to render these creatures harmless. For instance, a child's new toy may be imagined as an ally, powerful enough to ward off any imaginary threats.

The type of situation described above most closely conforms to which one of the following propositions?

(A) Some newly developed capacities only give rise to problems.
(B) Sometimes the cause of a problem may also provide its solution.
(C) Children are not able to distinguish between real and imaginary threats.
(D) The most effective way for children to address their fears is to acknowledge them.
(E) Most problems associated with child-rearing can be solved with a little imagination.

3. Trisha: Today's family is declining in its ability to carry out its functions of child-rearing and providing stability for adult life. There must be a return to the traditional values of commitment and responsibility.

Jerod: We ought to leave what is good enough alone. Contemporary families may be less stable than traditionally, but most people do not find that to be bad. Contemporary criticisms of the family are overblown and destructive.

Trisha and Jerod disagree over whether the institution of the family is

(A) adequate as it is
(B) changing over time
(C) valued by most people
(D) not going to survive
(E) no longer traditional

4. Politician P: My opponent claims that the government is obligated to raise taxes to increase funding for schools and health care. Because raising taxes to increase funding for schools and health care would make taxpayers upset over their loss of buying power, my opponent is simply mistaken.

Politician P's reasoning is questionable because it involves

(A) presupposing that a claim is mistaken on the grounds that the person defending it advocates other unpopular views
(B) assuming that a claim is false on the grounds that the person defending it is of questionable character
(C) concluding that a view is false on the grounds that its implementation would lead to unhappiness
(D) appealing to wholly irrelevant issues to deflect attention away from the real issue
(E) insisting that an obligation exists without offering any evidence that it exists

GO ON TO THE NEXT PAGE.

5. In defending the Hyperion School of Journalism from charges that its program is of little or no value to its students, the dean of the school pointed to its recent success in placing students: 65 percent of its graduates went on to internships or jobs in print or broadcast journalism.

   Which one of the following, if true, most seriously undermines the defense offered by the dean?

   (A) More than half of the school's students came from jobs in journalism to improve their skills.
   (B) Some newspaper editors do not regard journalism schools as a necessary part of the training of a journalist.
   (C) The number of cities with more than one major newspaper has declined sharply over the last 25 years.
   (D) The program offered by the Hyperion School of Journalism is similar in quality and content to those offered by its peer institutions.
   (E) The proportion of applicants to the Hyperion School of Journalism that are admitted is lower than it was ten years ago.

6. The largest volcano on Mars rises 27 kilometers above the surrounding plain and covers an area roughly the size of Romania. Even if the Earth's gravity were as low as the gravity of Mars is, no volcano of such size could exist on Earth, for the Earth's crust, although of essentially the same composition as that of Mars, is too thin to support even a small fraction of that mass and would buckle under it, causing the mountain to sink.

   If the statements above are true, which one of the following must also be true on the basis of them?

   (A) The surface of Mars is less subject to forces of erosion than is the surface of the Earth.
   (B) The highest volcanoes on Mars occur where its crust is thickest.
   (C) On average, volcanoes on Mars are higher than those on Earth.
   (D) The crust of Mars, at least at certain points on the planet, is thicker than the crust of the Earth.
   (E) At least some of the Earth's volcanoes would be larger than they actually are if the Earth's crust were thicker than it is.

7. Speakers of the Caronian language constitute a minority of the population in several large countries. An international body has recommended that the regions where Caronian-speakers live be granted autonomy as an independent nation in which Caronian-speakers would form a majority. But Caronian-speakers live in several, widely scattered areas that cannot be united within a single continuous boundary while at the same time allowing Caronian-speakers to be the majority population. Hence, the recommendation cannot be satisfied.

   The argument relies on which one of the following assumptions?

   (A) A nation once existed in which Caronian-speakers formed the majority of the population.
   (B) Caronian-speakers tend to perceive themselves as constituting a single community.
   (C) The recommendation would not be satisfied by the creation of a nation formed of disconnected regions.
   (D) The new Caronian nation will not include as citizens anyone who does not speak Caronian.
   (E) In most nations several different languages are spoken.

8. Sociologist: The welfare state cannot be successfully implemented because it rests on the assumption that human beings are unselfish—a seemingly false assumption. The welfare state is feasible only if wage earners are prepared to have their hard-earned funds used to help others in greater need, and that requires an unselfish attitude. But people innately seek their own well-being, especially when the interest of others threaten it.

   Which one of the following most accurately expresses the main conclusion of the sociologist's argument?

   (A) The welfare state will not work.
   (B) The welfare state unfairly asks those who work hard to help those in greater need.
   (C) The assumption that human beings are unselfish is false.
   (D) The interests of the less fortunate impinge on the interests of others.
   (E) The welfare state relies on the generosity of wage earners.

GO ON TO THE NEXT PAGE.

9. Early pencil leads were made of solid graphite mined in Cumberland, in Britain. Modern methods of manufacturing pencil leads from powdered graphite are the result of research sponsored by the government of France in the 1790s, when France was at war with Britain and thus had no access to Cumberland graphite.

   The information above most strongly supports which one of the following?

   (A) The world's only deposit of graphite suitable for manufacture of pencils is in Cumberland, in Britain.
   (B) In the 1790s, France's government did not know of any accessible source of solid graphite appropriate to meet France's need for pencils.
   (C) One of the causes of war between France and Britain in the 1790s was the British government's attempt to limit the amount of Cumberland graphite being exported to France.
   (D) Government-sponsored research frequently gives rise to inventions that are of great benefit to society.
   (E) Even today, all pencil leads contain Cumberland graphite.

Questions 10–11

Commercial passenger airplanes can be equipped with a collision-avoidance radar system that provides pilots with information about the proximity of other airplanes. Because the system warns pilots to take evasive action when it indicates a possible collision, passengers are safer on airplanes equipped with the system than on comparable airplanes not so equipped, even though the system frequently warns pilots to evade phantom airplanes.

10. Which one of the following is an assumption on which the argument depends?

    (A) Passengers feel no safer on airplanes equipped with the radar system than on comparable airplanes not so equipped.
    (B) Warnings given by a collision-avoidance system about phantom airplanes are not caused by distorted radar signals.
    (C) The frequency of invalid warnings will not cause pilots routinely to disregard the system's warnings.
    (D) Commercial passenger airplanes are not the only planes that can be equipped with a collision-avoidance system
    (E) The greatest safety risk for passengers traveling on commercial passenger airplanes is that of a midair collision.

11. Which one of the following, if true, most strengthens the argument?

    (A) Evasive action taken in response to the system's warnings poses no risk to the passengers.
    (B) Commercial passenger airplanes are in greater danger of colliding with other airplanes while on the ground than they are while in flight.
    (C) Commercial passenger airplanes are rarely involved in collisions while in flight.
    (D) A study by ground-based air traffic controllers found that 63 percent of the warnings by the system were invalid.
    (E) The collision-avoidance radar system is run by a computerized device on the plane that scans the sky and calculates the distances between planes.

GO ON TO THE NEXT PAGE.

12. The higher the average fat intake among the residents of a country, the higher the incidence of cancer in that country; the lower the average fat intake, the lower the incidence of cancer. So individuals who want to reduce their risk of cancer should reduce their fat intake.

Which one of the following, if true, most weakens the argument?

(A) The differences in average fat intake between countries are often due to the varying makeup of traditional diets.
(B) The countries with a high average fat intake tend to be among the wealthiest in the world.
(C) Cancer is a prominent cause of death in countries with a low average fat intake.
(D) The countries with high average fat intake are also the countries with the highest levels of environmental pollution.
(E) An individual resident of a country whose population has a high average fat intake may have a diet with a low fat intake.

13. A local television station is considering a plan to create a panel of child psychologists to review programs in advance of their airing and rate the level of violence. A program that portrays a high level of violence would be listed in newspapers with four guns after the title. On the other hand, if a show has little violence, one gun would appear after its listing. The station believes that this remedy would forewarn parents about the level of violence in any given program.

Which one of the following must the television station assume in order to conclude that the plan will meet its stated purpose?

(A) Parents would read and pay attention to the ratings listed in the newspapers.
(B) There would be fewer shows rated with one gun than with four guns.
(C) The rating system described in the passage is the most effective system available.
(D) The local television station has an obligation to forewarn parents of the level of violence in television shows.
(E) Television producers of programs rated as having high levels of violence would make an effort to reduce those levels.

14. The common ancestors of Australian land- and tree-dwelling kangaroos had prehensile (grasping) tails and long opposable thumbs, attributes that are well-adapted to tree-dwelling but offer kangaroos few advantages on land. It is hardly surprising, therefore, that land-dwelling kangaroos eventually lost these attributes; what is puzzling is the fact that all modern tree-dwelling kangaroos now lack them as well.

Which one of the following, if true, most helps explain the puzzling fact cited above?

(A) Modern tree-dwelling kangaroos must back down tree trunks slowly and carefully, but the common ancestors of modern tree-and land-dwelling kangaroos used their opposable thumbs to descend trees quickly headfirst.
(B) Modern tree-dwelling kangaroos are smaller than most modern land-dwelling kangaroos but larger than their common ancestors.
(C) Modern tree-dwelling kangaroos' tails cannot grasp branches, but they are somewhat longer and more flexible than those of modern land-dwelling kangaroos.
(D) Modern tree-dwelling kangaroos are descended from species of land-dwelling kangaroos that had been land-dwellers for many generations before modern tree-dwelling kangaroos started to develop.
(E) Modern tree-dwelling kangaroos have smaller and weaker hind legs than modern land-dwelling kangaroos, and they move more slowly on land than do modern land-dwelling kangaroos.

GO ON TO THE NEXT PAGE.

15. Editorialist: Society is obligated to bestow the privileges of adulthood upon its members once they are mature enough to accept the corresponding responsibilities. But science has established that physiological development is completed in most persons by age seventeen. Since this maturing process has been completed by most seventeen-year-olds, there is no reason not to grant these citizens all of the privileges of adulthood.

The editorialist's argument is most vulnerable to criticism on the ground that it

(A) assumes what it is trying to prove
(B) too hastily reaches a general conclusion on the basis of a few examples
(C) equivocates with respect to a central concept
(D) too readily accepts a claim by appeal to inappropriate authority
(E) ignores the fact that some people are mature at age sixteen

16. Every new play that runs for more than three months is either a commercial or a critical success. Last year, all new plays that were critical successes were also commercial successes. Therefore, every new play that ran for more than three months last year was a commercial success.

The pattern of reasoning in which one of the following arguments is most similar to that in the argument above?

(A) Most new restaurants require either good publicity or a good location in order to succeed. But most restaurants with a good location also receive good publicity. Hence, a restaurant that has a good location is guaranteed to succeed.
(B) Every best-selling cookbook published last year is both well written and contains beautiful photographs. The cookbook Cynthia Cleveland published last year is well written and contains beautiful photographs. Therefore, Cleveland's cookbook is a best seller.
(C) All students at the Freeman School of Cooking study either desserts or soups in their second year. This year, all Freeman students studying soups are also studying desserts. Therefore, every second-year student at Freeman is studying desserts this year.
(D) Chefs who become celebrities either open their own restaurants or write books about their craft, but not both. John Endicott is a celebrated chef who opened his own restaurant. Therefore, Endicott does not write books about his craft.
(E) Every catering service in Woodside Township will accept both residential and business catering assignments. Peggy's Fine Foods is a catering service that will not accept business catering assignments. Hence, Peggy's Fine Foods is not in Woodside Township.

17. Commissioner: I have been incorrectly criticized for having made my decision on the power plant issue prematurely. I based my decision on the report prepared by the neighborhood association and, although I have not studied it thoroughly, I am sure that the information it contains is accurate. Moreover, you may recall that when I received input from the neighborhood association on jail relocation, I agreed with its recommendation.

The commissioner's argument is LEAST vulnerable to which one of the following criticisms?

(A) It takes for granted that the association's information is not distorted by bias.
(B) It draws a conclusion about the recommendations of the association from incomplete recollections.
(C) It takes for granted that the association's report is the only direct evidence that needed to be considered.
(D) It hastily concludes that the association's report is accurate, without having studied it in detail.
(E) It takes for granted that agreeing with the association's past recommendation helps to justify agreeing with its current recommendation.

GO ON TO THE NEXT PAGE.

18. Each child in a group of young children read aloud both a short paragraph and a list of randomly ordered words from the paragraph. The more experienced readers among them made fewer pronunciation errors in whichever task they performed second, whether it was the list or the paragraph. The order in which the two tasks were performed, however, had no effect on the performance of beginning readers, who always made fewer pronunciation errors when reading the paragraph than when reading the list.

Which one of the following, if true, most helps to explain why the order in which the tasks were performed was not significant for the beginning readers?

(A) Because several words were used more than once in the paragraph but only once in the list, the list was shorter than the paragraph.
(B) In reading the paragraph, the more experienced readers were better at using context to guess at difficult words than were the beginning readers.
(C) The more experienced readers sounded out difficult words, while the beginning readers relied solely on context to guess at difficult words.
(D) Both tasks used the same words, so that the words the children read in whichever task was performed first would be recognized in the second task.
(E) The beginning readers made more pronunciation errors than the more experienced readers did in reading both the paragraph and the list.

19. Anthropologist: Violence is an extreme form of aggression, and is distinct from the self-expression sufficient for survival under normal conditions. Human beings in certain situations react to unpleasant stimuli with violence—but only because they are conditioned by their culture to react in this manner.

Each of the following can be logically inferred from the anthropologist's statements EXCEPT:

(A) Not all aggression is violent.
(B) The self-expression required for survival is generally nonagressive.
(C) Some behaviors are influenced by the cultures in which human beings live.
(D) In normal circumstances, human beings can survive by responding nonviolently.
(E) Violent behavior is a product of one's cultural environment.

20. Martha's friend, who is very knowledgeable about edible flowers, told Martha that there are no edible daisies, at least not any that are palatable. Martha, however, reasons that since there are daisies that are a kind of chrysanthemum and since there are edible chrysanthemums that are quite palatable, what her friend told her must be incorrect.

Which one of the following has a flawed pattern of reasoning most like that in Martha's reasoning?

(A) Jeanne is a member of the city chorus, and the city chorus is renowned. So Jeanne is an excellent singer.
(B) Rolfe belongs to the library reading group, and all members of that group are avid readers. So Rolfe is an avid reader.
(C) Some of Noriko's sisters are on the debate team, and some members of the debate team are poor students. So at least one of Noriko's sisters must be a poor student.
(D) Most of Leon's friends are good swimmers, and good swimmers are quite strong. So it is likely that at least some of Leon's friends are quite strong.
(E) Many of Teresa's colleagues have written books. Most of the books they have written are on good writing. So some of Teresa's colleagues are good writers.

GO ON TO THE NEXT PAGE.

21. Attorney for Ziegler: My client continued to do consulting work between the time of his arrest for attempted murder and the start of this trial. But I contend that Ziegler was insane at the time that he fired the shot. This is the only reasonable conclusion to draw from the fact that the accusers have submitted no evidence that he was sane at the time he pulled the trigger, only that he was sane some time after he did so.

Which one of the following most accurately describes a flaw in the reasoning of Ziegler's attorney?

(A) It presumes that being a well-educated professional is relevant to being guilty or innocent.
(B) It concludes on the basis of evidence against Ziegler's being sane that there is a lack of evidence for Ziegler's being sane.
(C) It fails to consider that Ziegler might have been insane when he worked as a consultant.
(D) It presumes that whether one is sane is relevant to whether one is morally responsible for one's actions.
(E) It fails to consider the possibility that Ziegler's being sane after the shooting is an indication that he was sane at the time of the shooting.

22. Most students are bored by history courses as they are usually taught, primarily because a large amount of time is spent teaching dates and statistics. The best way to teach history, therefore, is to spend most class time recounting the lives of historical figures and very little on dates and statistics.

Each of the following is an assumption on which the argument depends EXCEPT:

(A) One should avoid boring one's students when teaching a history course.
(B) It is not incompatible with the attainable goals of teaching history to spend very little class time on dates and statistics.
(C) It is possible to recount the lives of historical figures without referring to dates and statistics.
(D) It is compatible with the attainable goals of teaching history to spend most class time recounting the lives of historical figures.
(E) Students are more bored by history courses as they are usually taught than they would be by courses that spend most class time recounting the lives of historical figures.

23. In a certain municipality, a judge overturned a suspect's conviction for possession of an illegal weapon. The suspect had fled upon seeing police and subsequently discarded the illegal weapon after the police gave chase. The judge reasoned as follows: the only cause for the police giving chase was the suspect's flight; by itself, flight from the police does not create a reasonable suspicion of a criminal act; evidence collected during an illegal chase is inadmissible; therefore, the evidence in this case was inadmissible.

Which one of the following principles, if valid, most helps to justify the judge's decision that the evidence was inadmissible?

(A) Flight from the police could create a reasonable suspicion of a criminal act as long as other significant factors are involved.
(B) People can legally flee from the police only when those people are not involved in a criminal act at the time.
(C) Police can legally give chase to a person only when the person's actions have created a reasonable suspicion of a criminal act.
(D) Flight from the police should not itself be considered a criminal act.
(E) In all cases in which a person's actions have created a reasonable suspicion of a criminal act, police can legally give chase to that person.

GO ON TO THE NEXT PAGE.

Questions 24–25

Monica: The sculpture commissioned for our town plaza has been scorned by the public ever since it went up. But since the people in our town do not know very much about contemporary art, the unpopularity of the work says nothing about its artistic merit and thus gives no reason for removing it.

Hector: You may be right about what the sculpture's popularity means about its artistic merit. However, a work of art that was commissioned for a public space ought to benefit the public, and popular opinion is ultimately the only way of determining what the public feels is to its benefit. Thus, if public opinion of this sculpture is what you say, then it certainly ought to be removed.

24. Monica's and Hector's statements commit them to disagreeing about which one of the following principles?

(A) Public opinion of a work of art is an important consideration in determining the work's artistic merit.
(B) Works of art commissioned for public spaces ought at least to have sufficient artistic merit to benefit the public.
(C) The only reason for removing a work of art commissioned for a public space would be that the balance of public opinion is against the work.
(D) The sculpture cannot benefit the public by remaining in the town plaza unless the sculpture has artistic merit.
(E) In determining whether the sculpture should remain in the town plaza, the artistic merit of the sculpture should be a central consideration.

25. The argument Hector makes in responding to Monica depends on the assumption that

(A) no matter what the public's opinion is on an issue affecting the public good, that public opinion ought to be acted on, even though the opinion may not be a knowledgeable one
(B) Monica's assessment of the public's opinion of the sculpture is accurate
(C) if the sculpture had artistic merit, then even a public that was not knowledgeable about modern art would not scorn the sculpture
(D) works of art commissioned for public spaces ought not to be expected to have artistic merit
(E) if the public feels that it does not benefit from the sculpture, this shows that the public does not in fact benefit from the sculpture

S T O P

IF YOU FINISH BEFORE TIME IS CALLED, YOU MAY CHECK YOUR WORK ON THIS SECTION ONLY.
DO NOT WORK ON ANY OTHER SECTION IN THE TEST.

SECTION IV

Time—35 minutes

26 Questions

Directions: The questions in this section are based on the reasoning contained in brief statements or passages. For some questions, more than one of the choices could conceivably answer the question. However, you are to choose the best answer; that is, the response that most accurately and completely answers the question. You should not make assumptions that are by commonsense standards implausible, superfluous, or incompatible with the passage. After you have chosen the best answer, blacken the corresponding space on your answer sheet.

1. Among Trinidadian guppies, males with large spots are more attractive to females than are males with small spots, who consequently are presented with less frequent mating opportunities. Yet guppies with small spots are more likely to avoid detection by predators, so in waters where predators are abundant only guppies with small spots live to maturity.

The situation described above most closely conforms to which one of the following generalizations?

(A) A trait that helps attract mates is sometimes more dangerous to one sex than to another.
(B) Those organisms that are most attractive to the opposite sex have the greatest number of offspring.
(C) Those organisms that survive the longest have the greatest number of offspring.
(D) Whether a trait is harmful to the organisms of a species can depend on which sex possesses it.
(E) A trait that is helpful to procreation can also hinder it in certain environments.

2. Programmer: We computer programmers at Mytheco are demanding raises to make our average salary comparable with that of the technical writers here who receive, on average, 20 percent more in salary and benefits than we do. This pay difference is unfair and intolerable.

Mytheco executive: But many of the technical writers have worked for Mytheco longer than have many of the programmers. Since salary and benefits at Mytheco are directly tied to seniority, the 20 percent pay difference you mention is perfectly acceptable.

Evaluating the adequacy of the Mytheco executive's response requires a clarification of which one of the following?

(A) whether any of the technical writers at Mytheco once worked as programmers at the company
(B) how the average seniority of programmers compares with the average seniority of technical writers
(C) whether the sorts of benefits an employee of Mytheco receives are tied to the salary of that employee
(D) whether the Mytheco executive was at one time a technical writer employed by Mytheco
(E) how the Mytheco executive's salary compares with that of the programmers

3. Cable TV stations have advantages that enable them to attract many more advertisers than broadcast networks attract. For example, cable stations are able to target particular audiences with 24-hour news, sports, or movies, whereas broadcast networks must offer a variety of programming. Cable can also offer lower advertising rates than any broadcast network can, because it is subsidized by viewers through subscriber fees. Additionally, many cable stations have expanded worldwide with multinational programming.

The statements above, if true, provide support for each of the following EXCEPT:

(A) Some broadcast networks can be viewed in several countries.
(B) Broadcast networks do not rely on subscriber fees from viewers.
(C) Low costs are often an important factor for advertisers in selecting a station or network on which to run a TV ad.
(D) Some advertisers prefer to have the opportunity to address a worldwide audience.
(E) The audiences that some advertisers prefer to target watch 24-hour news stations.

4. In polluted industrial English cities during the Industrial Revolution, two plant diseases—black spot, which infects roses, and tar spot, which infects sycamore trees—disappeared. It is likely that air pollution eradicated these diseases.

Which one of the following, if true, most strengthens the reasoning above?

(A) Scientists theorize that some plants can develop a resistance to air pollution.
(B) Certain measures help prevent infection by black spot and tar spot, but once infection occurs, it is very difficult to eliminate.
(C) For many plant species, scientists have not determined the effects of air pollution.
(D) Black spot and tar spot returned when the air in the cities became less polluted.
(E) Black spot and tar spot were the only plant diseases that disappeared in any English cities during the Industrial Revolution.

GO ON TO THE NEXT PAGE.

5. Many scholars are puzzled about who created the seventeenth-century abridgment of Shakespeare's *Hamlet* contained in the First Quarto. Two facts about the work shed light on this question. First, the person who undertook the abridgment clearly did not possess a copy of *Hamlet*. Second, the abridgment contains a very accurate rendering of the speeches of one of the characters, but a slipshod handling of all the other parts.

Which one of the following statements is most supported by the information above?

(A) The abridgment was prepared by Shakespeare.
(B) The abridgment was created to make *Hamlet* easier to produce on stage.
(C) The abridgment was produced by an actor who had played a role in *Hamlet*.
(D) The abridgement was prepared by a spectator of a performance of *Hamlet*.
(E) The abridgment was produced by an actor who was trying to improve the play.

6. Musicologist: Many critics complain of the disproportion between text and music in Handel's *da capo* arias. These texts are generally quite short and often repeated well beyond what is needed for literal understanding. Yet such criticism is refuted by noting that repetition serves a vital function: it frees the audience to focus on the music itself, which can speak to audiences whatever their language.

Which one of the following sentences best expresses the main point of the musicologist's reasoning?

(A) Handel's *da capo* arias contain a disproportionate amount of music.
(B) Handel's *da capo* arias are superior to most in their accessibility to diverse audiences.
(C) At least one frequent criticism of Handel's *da capo* arias is undeserved.
(D) At least some of Handel's *da capo* arias contain unnecessary repetitions.
(E) Most criticism of Handel's *da capo* arias is unwarranted.

7. Baxe Interiors, one of the largest interior design companies in existence, currently has a near monopoly in the corporate market. Several small design companies have won prestigious awards for their corporate work, while Baxe has won none. Nonetheless, the corporate managers who solicit design proposals will only contract with companies they believe are unlikely to go bankrupt, and they believe that only very large companies are unlikely to go bankrupt.

The statements above, if true, most strongly support which one of the following?

(A) There are other very large design companies besides Baxe, but they produce designs that are inferior to Baxe's.
(B) Baxe does not have a near monopoly in the market of any category of interior design other than corporate interiors.
(C) For the most part, designs that are produced by small companies are superior to the designs produced by Baxe.
(D) At least some of the corporate managers who solicit design proposals are unaware that there are designs that are much better than those produced by Baxe.
(E) The existence of interior designs that are superior to those produced by Baxe does not currently threaten its near monopoly in the corporate market.

GO ON TO THE NEXT PAGE.

8. The giant Chicxulub crater in Mexico provides indisputable evidence that a huge asteroid, about six miles across, struck Earth around the time many of the last dinosaur species were becoming extinct. But this catastrophe was probably not responsible for most of these extinctions. Any major asteroid strike kills many organisms in or near the region of the impact, but there is little evidence that such a strike could have a worldwide effect. Indeed, some craters even larger than the Chicxulub crater were made during times in Earth's history when there were no known extinctions.

Which one of the following, if true, would most weaken the argument?

(A) The vast majority of dinosaur species are known to have gone extinct well before the time of the asteroid impact that produced the Chicxulub crater.
(B) The size of a crater caused by an asteroid striking Earth generally depends on both the size of that asteroid and the force of its impact.
(C) Fossils have been discovered of a number of dinosaurs that clearly died as a result of the asteroid impact that produced the Chicxulub crater.
(D) There is no evidence that any other asteroid of equal size struck Earth at the same time as the asteroid that produced the Chicxulub crater.
(E) During the period immediately before the asteroid that produced the Chicxulub crater struck, most of the world's dinosaurs lived in or near the region of the asteroid's impending impact.

9. In a sample containing 1,000 peanuts from lot A and 1,000 peanuts from lot B, 50 of the peanuts from lot A were found to be infected with *Aspergillus*. Two hundred of the peanuts from lot B were found to be infected with *Aspergillus*. Therefore, infection with *Aspergillus* is more widespread in lot B than in lot A.

The reasoning in which one of the following is most similar to the reasoning in the argument above?

(A) Every one of these varied machine parts is of uniformly high quality. Therefore, the machine that we assemble from them will be of equally high quality.
(B) If a plant is carelessly treated, it is likely to develop blight. If a plant develops blight, it is likely to die. Therefore, if a plant is carelessly treated, it is likely to die.
(C) In the past 1,000 experiments, whenever an experimental fungicide was applied to coffee plants infected with coffee rust, the infection disappeared. The coffee rust never disappeared before the fungicide was applied. Therefore, in these experiments, application of the fungicide caused the disappearance of coffee rust.
(D) Three thousand registered voters—1,500 members of the Liberal party and 1,500 members of the Conservative party—were asked which mayoral candidate they favored. Four hundred of the Liberals and 300 of the Conservatives favored Pollack. Therefore, Pollack has more support among Liberals than among Conservatives.
(E) All of my livestock are registered with the regional authority. None of the livestock registered with the regional authority are free-range livestock. Therefore, none of my livestock are free-range livestock.

GO ON TO THE NEXT PAGE.

10. Economist: If the belief were to become widespread that losing one's job is not a sign of personal shortcomings but instead an effect of impersonal social forces (which is surely correct), there would be growth in the societal demand for more government control of the economy to protect individuals from these forces, just as the government now protects them from military invasion. Such extensive government control of the economy would lead to an economic disaster, however.

The economist's statements, if true, most strongly support which one of the following?

(A) Increased knowledge of the causes of job loss could lead to economic disaster.
(B) An individual's belief in his or her own abilities is the only reliable protection against impersonal social forces.
(C) Governments should never interfere with economic forces.
(D) Societal demand for government control of the economy is growing.
(E) In general, people should feel no more responsible for economic disasters than for military invasions.

11. A development company has proposed building an airport near the city of Dalton. If the majority of Dalton's residents favor the proposal, the airport will be built. However, it is unlikely that a majority of Dalton's residents would favor the proposal, for most of them believe that the airport would create noise problems. Thus, it is unlikely that the airport will be built.

The reasoning in the argument is flawed in that the argument

(A) treats a sufficient condition for the airport's being built as a necessary condition
(B) concludes that something must be true, because most people believe it to be true
(C) concludes, on the basis that a certain event is unlikely to occur, that the event will not occur
(D) fails to consider whether people living near Dalton would favor building the airport
(E) overlooks the possibility that a new airport could benefit the local economy

12. After the rush-hour speed limit on the British M25 motorway was lowered from 70 miles per hour (115 kilometers per hour) to 50 miles per hour (80 kilometers per hour), rush-hour travel times decreased by approximately 15 percent.

Which one of the following, if true, most helps to explain the decrease in travel times described above?

(A) After the decrease in the rush-hour speed limit, the average speed on the M25 was significantly lower during rush hours than at other times of the day.
(B) Travel times during periods other than rush hours were essentially unchanged after the rush-hour speed limit was lowered.
(C) Before the rush-hour speed limit was lowered, rush-hour accidents that caused lengthy delays were common, and most of these accidents were caused by high-speed driving.
(D) Enforcement of speed limits on the M25 was quite rigorous both before and after the rush-hour speed limit was lowered.
(E) The number of people who drive on the M25 during rush hours did not increase after the rush-hour speed limit was lowered.

13. An art critic, by ridiculing an artwork, can undermine the pleasure one takes in it; conversely, by lavishing praise upon an artwork, an art critic can render the experience of viewing the artwork more pleasurable. So an artwork's artistic merit can depend not only on the person who creates it but also on those who critically evaluate it.

The conclusion can be properly drawn if which one of the following is assumed?

(A) The merit of an artistic work is determined by the amount of pleasure it elicits.
(B) Most people lack the confidence necessary for making their own evaluations of art.
(C) Art critics understand what gives an artwork artistic merit better than artists do.
(D) Most people seek out critical reviews of particular artworks before viewing those works.
(E) The pleasure people take in something is typically influenced by what they think others feel about it.

GO ON TO THE NEXT PAGE.

14. The number of automobile thefts has declined steadily during the past five years, and it is more likely now than it was five years ago that someone who steals a car will be convicted of the crime.

Which one of the following, if true, most helps to explain the facts cited above?

(A) Although there are fewer car thieves now than there were five years ago, the proportion of thieves who tend to abandon cars before their owners notice that they have been stolen has also decreased.
(B) Car alarms are more common than they were five years ago, but their propensity to be triggered in the absence of any criminal activity has resulted in people generally ignoring them when they are triggered.
(C) An upsurge in home burglaries over the last five years has required police departments to divert limited resources to investigation of these cases.
(D) Because of the increasingly lucrative market for stolen automobile parts, many stolen cars are quickly disassembled and the parts are sold to various buyers across the country.
(E) There are more adolescent car thieves now than there were five years ago, and the sentences given to young criminals tend to be far more lenient than those given to adult criminals.

15. Legislator: My staff conducted a poll in which my constituents were asked whether they favor high taxes. More than 97 percent answered "no." Clearly, then, my constituents would support the bill I recently introduced, which reduces the corporate income tax.

The reasoning in the legislator's argument is most vulnerable to criticism on the grounds that the argument

(A) fails to establish that the opinions of the legislator's constituents are representative of the opinions of the country's population as a whole
(B) fails to consider whether the legislator's constituents consider the current corporate income tax a high tax
(C) confuses an absence of evidence that the legislator's constituents oppose a bill with the existence of evidence that the legislator's constituents support that bill
(D) draws a conclusion that merely restates a claim presented in support of that conclusion
(E) treats a result that proves that the public supports a bill as a result that is merely consistent with public support for that bill

16. Many nursing homes have prohibitions against having pets, and these should be lifted. The presence of an animal companion can yield health benefits by reducing a person's stress. A pet can also make one's time at a home more rewarding, which will be important to more people as the average life span of our population increases.

Which one of the following most accurately expresses the conclusion drawn in the argument above?

(A) As the average life span increases, it will be important to more people that life in nursing homes be rewarding.
(B) Residents of nursing homes should enjoy the same rewarding aspects of life as anyone else.
(C) The policy that many nursing homes have should be changed so that residents are allowed to have pets.
(D) Having a pet can reduce one's stress and thereby make one a healthier person.
(E) The benefits older people derive from having pets need to be recognized, especially as the average life span increases.

17. Near many cities, contamination of lakes and rivers from pollutants in rainwater runoff exceeds that from industrial discharge. As the runoff washes over buildings and pavements, it picks up oil and other pollutants. Thus, water itself is among the biggest water polluters.

The statement that contamination of lakes and rivers from pollutants in rainwater runoff exceeds that from industrial discharge plays which one of the following roles in the argument?

(A) It is a conclusion for which the claim that water itself should be considered a polluter is offered as support.
(B) It is cited as evidence that pollution from rainwater runoff is a more serious problem than pollution from industrial discharge.
(C) It is a generalization based on the observation that rainwater runoff picks up oil and other pollutants as it washes over buildings and pavements.
(D) It is a premise offered in support of the conclusion that water itself is among the biggest water polluters.
(E) It is stated to provide an example of a typical kind of city pollution.

GO ON TO THE NEXT PAGE.

18. Wong: Although all countries are better off as democracies, a transitional autocratic stage is sometimes required before a country can become democratic.

Tate: The freedom and autonomy that democracy provides are of genuine value, but the simple material needs of people are more important. Some countries can better meet these needs as autocracies than as democracies.

Wong's and Tate's statements provide the most support for the claim that they disagree over the truth of which one of the following?

(A) There are some countries that are better off as autocracies than as democracies.
(B) Nothing is more important to a country than the freedom and autonomy of the individuals who live in that country.
(C) In some cases, a country cannot become a democracy.
(D) The freedom and autonomy that democracy provides are of genuine value.
(E) All democracies succeed in meeting the simple material needs of people.

19. Principle: When none of the fully qualified candidates for a new position at Arvue Corporation currently works for that company, it should hire the candidate who would be most productive in that position.

Application: Arvue should not hire Krall for the new position, because Delacruz is a candidate and is fully qualified.

Which one of the following, if true, justifies the above application of the principle?

(A) All of the candidates are fully qualified for the new position, but none already works for Arvue.
(B) Of all the candidates who do not already work for Arvue, Delacruz would be the most productive in the new position.
(C) Krall works for Arvue, but Delacruz is the candidate who would be most productive in the new position.
(D) Several candidates currently work for Arvue, but Krall and Delacruz do not.
(E) None of the candidates already works for Arvue, and Delacruz is the candidate who would be most productive in the new position.

20. Many important types of medicine have been developed from substances discovered in plants that grow only in tropical rain forests. There are thousands of plant species in these rain forests that have not yet been studied by scientists, and it is very likely that many such plants also contain substances of medicinal value. Thus, if the tropical rain forests are not preserved, important types of medicine will never be developed.

Which one of the following is an assumption required by the argument?

(A) There are substances of medicinal value contained in tropical rain forest plants not yet studied by scientists that differ from those substances already discovered in tropical rain forest plants.
(B) Most of the tropical rain forest plants that contain substances of medicinal value can also be found growing in other types of environment.
(C) The majority of plant species that are unique to tropical rain forests and that have been studied by scientists have been discovered to contain substances of medicinal value.
(D) Any substance of medicinal value contained in plant species indigenous to tropical rain forests will eventually be discovered if those species are studied by scientists.
(E) The tropical rain forests should be preserved to make it possible for important medicines to be developed from plant species that have not yet been studied by scientists.

GO ON TO THE NEXT PAGE.

21. In modern deep-diving marine mammals, such as whales, the outer shell of the bones is porous. This has the effect of making the bones light enough so that it is easy for the animals to swim back to the surface after a deep dive. The outer shell of the bones was also porous in the ichthyosaur, an extinct prehistoric marine reptile. We can conclude from this that ichthyosaurs were deep divers.

Which one of the following, if true, most weakens the argument?

(A) Some deep-diving marine species must surface after dives but do not have bones with porous outer shells.
(B) In most modern marine reptile species, the outer shell of the bones is not porous.
(C) In most modern and prehistoric marine reptile species that are not deep divers, the outer shell of the bones is porous.
(D) In addition to the porous outer shells of their bones, whales have at least some characteristics suited to deep diving for which there is no clear evidence whether these were shared by ichthyosaurs.
(E) There is evidence that the bones of ichthyosaurs would have been light enough to allow surfacing even if the outer shells were not porous.

22. Librarian: Some argue that the preservation grant we received should be used to restore our original copy of our town's charter, since if the charter is not restored, it will soon deteriorate beyond repair. But this document, although sentimentally important, has no scholarly value. Copies are readily available. Since we are a research library and not a museum, the money would be better spent preserving documents that have significant scholarly value.

The claim that the town's charter, if not restored, will soon deteriorate beyond repair plays which one of the following roles in the librarian's argument?

(A) It is a claim that the librarian's argument attempts to show to be false.
(B) It is the conclusion of the argument that the librarian's argument rejects.
(C) It is a premise in an argument whose conclusion is rejected by the librarian's argument.
(D) It is a premise used to support the librarian's main conclusion.
(E) It is a claim whose truth is required by the librarian's argument.

23. Columnist: Although much has been learned, we are still largely ignorant of the intricate interrelationships among species of living organisms. We should, therefore, try to preserve the maximum number of species if we have an interest in preserving any, since allowing species toward which we are indifferent to perish might undermine the viability of other species.

Which one of the following principles, if valid, most helps to justify the columnist's argument?

(A) It is strongly in our interest to preserve certain plant and animal species.
(B) We should not take any action until all relevant scientific facts have been established and taken into account.
(C) We should not allow the number of species to diminish any further than is necessary for the flourishing of present and future human populations.
(D) We should not allow a change to occur unless we are assured that that change will not jeopardize anything that is important to us.
(E) We should always undertake the course of action that is likely to have the best consequences in the immediate future.

24. One is likely to feel comfortable approaching a stranger if the stranger is of one's approximate age. Therefore, long-term friends are probably of the same approximate age as each other since most long-term friendships begin because someone felt comfortable approaching a stranger.

The reasoning in the argument is flawed in that it

(A) presumes, without warrant, that one is likely to feel uncomfortable approaching a person only if that person is a stranger
(B) infers that a characteristic is present in a situation from the fact that that characteristic is present in most similar situations
(C) overlooks the possibility that one is less likely to feel comfortable approaching someone who is one's approximate age if that person is a stranger than if that person is not a stranger
(D) presumes, without warrant, that one never approaches a stranger unless one feels comfortable doing so
(E) fails to address whether one is likely to feel comfortable approaching a stranger who is not one's approximate age

GO ON TO THE NEXT PAGE.

25. There can be no individual freedom without the rule of law, for there is no individual freedom without social integrity, and pursuing the good life is not possible without social integrity.

The conclusion drawn above follows logically if which one of the following is assumed?

(A) There can be no rule of law without social integrity.
(B) There can be no social integrity without the rule of law.
(C) One cannot pursue the good life without the rule of law.
(D) Social integrity is possible only if individual freedom prevails.
(E) There can be no rule of law without individual freedom.

26. Economist: Countries with an uneducated population are destined to be weak economically and politically, whereas those with an educated population have governments that display a serious financial commitment to public education. So any nation with a government that has made such a commitment will avoid economic and political weakness.

The pattern of flawed reasoning in which one of the following arguments is most similar to that in the economist's argument?

(A) Animal species with a very narrow diet will have more difficulty surviving if the climate suddenly changes, but a species with a broader diet will not; for changes in the climate can remove the traditional food supply.
(B) People incapable of empathy are not good candidates for public office, but those who do have the capacity for empathy are able to manipulate others easily; hence, people who can manipulate others are good candidates for public office.
(C) People who cannot give orders are those who do not understand the personalities of the people to whom they give orders. Thus, those who can give orders are those who understand the personalities of the people to whom they give orders.
(D) Poets who create poetry of high quality are those who have studied traditional poetry, because poets who have not studied traditional poetry are the poets most likely to create something shockingly inventive, and poetry that is shockingly inventive is rarely fine poetry.
(E) People who dislike exercise are unlikely to lose weight without sharply curtailing their food intake; but since those who dislike activity generally tend to avoid it, people who like to eat but dislike exercise will probably fail to lose weight.

S T O P

IF YOU FINISH BEFORE TIME IS CALLED, YOU MAY CHECK YOUR WORK ON THIS SECTION ONLY. DO NOT WORK ON ANY OTHER SECTION IN THE TEST.

Acknowledgment is made to the following sources from which material has been adapted for use in this test booklet:

Robin D. G. Kelley, "But a Local Phase of a World Problem: Black History's Global Vision, 1883–1950." ©1999 by the Organization of American Historians.

Alfred Lessing, "What Is Wrong With a Forgery?" in *The Forger's Art.* ©1983 by The Regents of the University of California.

David Pitts, "The Noble Endeavor: The Creation of the Universal Declaration of Human Rights." ©2001 by U.S. Department of State, Office of International Information Programs.

Ellen Rosand, "It Bears Repeating." ©1996 by Metropolitan Opera Guild, Inc.

LSAT Writing Sample Topic

Directions: The scenario presented below describes two choices, either one of which can be supported on the basis of the information given. Your essay should consider both choices and argue for one over the other, based on the two specified criteria and the facts provided. There is no "right" or "wrong" choice: a reasonable argument can be made for either.

The attorneys for the plaintiffs in a lawsuit against a major pharmaceutical company are choosing an expert scientific witness to testify that a drug produced by the company was responsible for serious side effects. The attorneys have narrowed their choices down to two people. Using the facts below, write an essay in which you argue for choosing one person over the other based on the following two criteria:

- The attorneys want a witness who will be able to communicate technical information in a clear and effective manner to the jury.
- The attorneys want a witness who is highly knowledgeable in the field of pharmacology.

Dr. Rosa Benally has qualifications similar to those of the defense team's expert witness in that she has a PhD in pharmacology, teaches at a university, and is highly respected for her scientific research. Dr. Benally recently led a series of studies investigating the side effects of the class of drugs that will be under discussion during the trial. She has served effectively as an expert witness in a number of similar trials over the last five years.

Dr. Josephine Rickman is a medical doctor who also has a PhD in pharmacology. She has a busy medical practice. Dr. Rickman sometimes serves as a medical news correspondent on a national news program. She is the author of three best-selling books on medical topics, including one on the pharmaceutical industry. Dr. Rickman prescribed the drug in question to a number of patients who appeared to have experienced side effects like those to be discussed during the trial.

Scratch Paper

Do not write your essay in this space.

Directions:

1. Use the Answer Key on the next page to check your answers.
2. Use the Scoring Worksheet below to compute your raw score.
3. Use the Score Conversion Chart to convert your raw score into the 120–180 scale.

Scoring Worksheet

1. Enter the number of questions you answered correctly in each section

Number Correct

SECTION I. . . . . ______

SECTION II . . . . ______

SECTION III . . . . . . ______

SECTION IV . . . . . . ______

2. Enter the sum here: ______ **This is your Raw Score.**

Conversion Chart

For Converting Raw Score to the 120–180 LSAT Scaled Score
LSAT PrepTest 61

Reported Score	Raw Score Lowest	Raw Score Highest
180	99	101
179	98	98
178	97	97
177	96	96
176	—*	—*
175	95	95
174	94	94
173	93	93
172	92	92
171	91	91
170	89	90
169	88	88
168	87	87
167	85	86
166	84	84
165	82	83
164	81	81
163	79	80
162	78	78
161	76	77
160	74	75
159	73	73
158	71	72
157	69	70
156	67	68
155	66	66
154	64	65
153	62	63
152	60	61
151	58	59
150	57	57
149	55	56
148	53	54
147	52	52
146	50	51
145	48	49
144	47	47
143	45	46
142	43	44
141	42	42
140	40	41
139	39	39
138	37	38
137	36	36
136	34	35
135	33	33
134	31	32
133	30	30
132	29	29
131	27	28
130	26	26
129	25	25
128	24	24
127	22	23
126	21	21
125	20	20
124	19	19
123	18	18
122	16	17
121	—*	—*
120	0	15

*There is no raw score that will produce this scaled score for this test.

SECTION I

1.	D	8.	A	15.	A	22.	A
2.	B	9.	E	16.	D	23.	E
3.	B	10.	C	17.	D	24.	E
4.	D	11.	B	18.	C	25.	B
5.	E	12.	E	19.	B	26.	A
6.	A	13.	B	20.	D	27.	B
7.	C	14.	B	21.	E		

SECTION II

1.	D	8.	A	15.	B	22.	C
2.	E	9.	E	16.	C	23.	D
3.	C	10.	A	17.	A	24.	B
4.	D	11.	A	18.	A	25.	D
5.	A	12.	A	19.	D		
6.	C	13.	B	20.	C		
7.	D	14.	D	21.	E		

SECTION III

1.	A	8.	A	15.	A	22.	B
2.	E	9.	C	16.	E	23.	A
3.	A	10.	B	17.	B		
4.	C	11.	D	18.	D		
5.	D	12.	D	19.	C		
6.	A	13.	D	20.	D		
7.	C	14.	B	21.	B		

SECTION IV

1.	E	8.	E	15.	B	22.	C
2.	B	9.	D	16.	C	23.	D
3.	A	10.	A	17.	D	24.	E
4.	D	11.	A	18.	A	25.	B
5.	C	12.	C	19.	E	26.	B
6.	C	13.	A	20.	A		
7.	E	14.	A	21.	C		

Experimental Section Answer Key
June 1999, PrepTest 26, Section 2

1.	B	8.	A	15.	C	22.	C
2.	B	9.	B	16.	C	23.	C
3.	A	10.	C	17.	B	24.	E
4.	C	11.	A	18.	C	25.	E
5.	A	12.	D	19.	B		
6.	D	13.	A	20.	C		
7.	C	14.	D	21.	E		

PrepTest 62
December 2010

Time—35 minutes

25 Questions

Directions: The questions in this section are based on the reasoning contained in brief statements or passages. For some questions, more than one of the choices could conceivably answer the question. However, you are to choose the best answer; that is, the response that most accurately and completely answers the question. You should not make assumptions that are by commonsense standards implausible, superfluous, or incompatible with the passage. After you have chosen the best answer blacken the corresponding space on your answer sheet.

Questions 1–2

From the tenth century until around the year 1500, there were Norse settlers living in Greenland. During that time, average yearly temperatures fell slightly worldwide, and some people claim that this temperature drop wiped out the Norse settlements by rendering Greenland too cold for human habitation. But this explanation cannot be correct, because Inuit settlers from North America, who were living in Greenland during the time the Norse settlers were there, continued to thrive long after 1500.

1. Which one of the following if true, most helps explain why the Norse settlements in Greenland disappeared while the Inuit settlements survived?
   (A) The drop in average yearly temperature was smaller in Greenland than it was in the world as a whole.
   (B) The Norse settlers' diet, unlike that of the Inuit, was based primarily on livestock and crops that were unable to survive the temperature drop.
   (C) There were settlements in North America during the fifteenth century that were most likely founded by Norse settlers who had come from Greenland.
   (D) The Inuit and the Norse settlements were typically established in coastal areas.
   (E) The Norse community in Norway continued to thrive long after 1500.

2. Which one of the following is a technique of reasoning used in the argument?
   (A) denying the relevance of an analogy
   (B) producing evidence that is inconsistent with the claim being opposed
   (C) presenting an alternative explanation that purports to account for more of the known facts
   (D) citing a general rule that undermines the claim being opposed
   (E) redefining a term in a way that is favorable to the argument's conclusion

3. Even though trading in ivory has been outlawed by international agreement, some piano makers still use ivory, often obtained illegally, to cover piano keys. Recently, experts have devised a synthetic ivory that, unlike earlier ivory substitutes, has found favor with concert pianists throughout the world. But because piano makers have never been major consumers of ivory, the development of the synthetic ivory will therefore probably do little to help curb the killing of elephants, from whose tusks most natural ivory is obtained.

   Which one of the following, if true, most helps to strengthen the argument?
   (A) Most people who play the piano but are not concert pianists can nonetheless easily distinguish between the new synthetic ivory and inferior ivory substitutes.
   (B) The new synthetic ivory can be manufactured to resemble in color and surface texture any of the various types of natural ivory that have commercial uses.
   (C) Other natural products such as bone or tortoise shell have not proven to be acceptable substitutes for natural ivory in piano keys.
   (D) The most common use for natural ivory is in ornamental carvings, which are prized not only for the quality of their workmanship but also for the authenticity of their materials.
   (E) It costs significantly less to produce the new synthetic ivory then it does to produce any of the ivory substitutes that scientists had developed previously.

GO ON TO THE NEXT PAGE.

4. The government has spent heavily to clean groundwater contaminated by toxic chemical spills. Yet not even one spill site has been completely cleaned, and industrial accidents are spilling more toxic chemicals annually than are being cleaned up. More of the government's budget should be redirected to preventing spills. Since prevention is far more effective than cleanup, it makes little sense that the entire annual budget for prevention is less than the amount spent annually on one typical cleanup site.

The proposal about how the government's budget should be redirected plays which one of the following roles in the argument?

(A) It represents an unsupported speculation.
(B) It both supports another claim in the argument and is supported by others.
(C) It is the claim that the argument as a whole is structured to support.
(D) It is a presupposition on which the argument is explicitly based.
(E) It presents an objection to another proposal mentioned in the argument.

5. Consumer: I would like to have the features contained in the latest upgrade to your computer software package, but I am leery of installing the upgrade because a friend has told me he had a problem with it.

Company representative: We have distributed nearly 3,000 copies of the upgrade and we have received fewer than 100 calls saying that it has caused problems. So it is very unlikely that you will experience any problems with the upgrade.

The reasoning in the company representative's argument is most vulnerable to criticism because it fails to consider the possibility that

(A) the company will issue another upgrade that corrects the problems with the current upgrade
(B) some of the problems people have experienced with the upgrade have been quite serious
(C) a significant number of people have experienced problems with the upgrade but have not reported them
(D) the consumer will experience software problems if the upgrade is not installed
(E) some of the reported problems were a result of users failing to follow instructions

6. First legislator: Medical research is predominantly done on groups of patients that include only men. For example, the effects of coffee drinking on health are evaluated only for men, and studies are lacking on hormone treatments for older women. Government-sponsored medical research should be required to include studies of women.

Second legislator: Considerations of male/female balance such as this are inappropriate with respect to research; they have no place in science.

Which one of the following rejoinders, if true, most directly counters the second legislator's objection?

(A) Government-sponsored research is supported by all taxpayers, both male and female.
(B) Serving as a subject for medical research can provide a patient access to new treatments but also can subject the patient to risks.
(C) Government-sponsored medical research is often done in military hospitals or prisons that hold only male residents.
(D) The training of male and female scientists does not differ according to their sex.
(E) Restriction to males of the patient base on which data are collected results in inadequate science.

7. Lack of exercise produces the same or similar bodily effects as aging. In fact, the physical changes that accompany aging can often be slowed down by appropriate exercise. No drug, however, holds any promise for slowing down the changes associated with aging. Therefore, _______.

Which one of the following provides a logical completion to the passage above?

(A) taking drugs has the same effect on aging as does a lack of exercise
(B) people who do not exercise are likely to need drugs to sustain their health
(C) appropriate exercise can prevent the physical changes associated with aging
(D) people who do not exercise when they are young will gain few benefits from beginning to exercise at a later age
(E) if the physical changes of aging are to be slowed, it is more practical to rely on exercise than on drugs

8. Grasses and woody plants are planted on dirt embankments to keep the embankments from eroding. The embankments are mowed to keep the grasses from growing too tall; as a result, clippings pile up. These piles of clippings smother the woody plants, causing their roots, which serve to keep the embankments from eroding, to rot; they also attract rodents that burrow into the dirt and damage the woody plants' roots. Therefore, bringing in predators to eradicate the rodents will prevent erosion of the embankments.

Which one of the following is an error of reasoning in the argument?

(A) Two events that merely co-occur are treated as if one caused the other.
(B) A highly general proposal is based only on an unrepresentative set of facts.
(C) The conclusion is no more than a restatement of one of the pieces of evidence provided to support it.
(D) One possible solution to a problem is claimed to be the only possible solution to that problem.
(E) An action that would eliminate one cause of a problem is treated as if it would solve the entire problem.

9. Scientific and technological discoveries have considerable effects on the development of any society. It follows that predictions of the future condition of societies in which scientific and technological discovery is particularly frequent are particularly untrustworthy.

The argument depends on assuming which one of the following?

(A) Predictions of scientific and technological discoveries or predictions of their effects have harmful consequences in some societies.
(B) The development of a society requires scientific and technological discoveries.
(C) Forecasts of scientific and technological discoveries, or forecasts of their effects, are not entirely reliable.
(D) An advanced scientific and technological society frequently benefits from new discoveries.
(E) It is not as difficult to predict scientific and technological discoveries in a technologically more advanced society as it is in a technologically less advanced society.

10. Tires may be either underinflated, overinflated, or neither. We are pretty safe in assuming that underinflation or overinflation of tires harms their tread. After all, no one has been able to show that these do not harm tire tread.

Which one of the following most accurately describes a flaw in the argument's reasoning?

(A) The argument assumes what it is attempting to demonstrate.
(B) The argument overlooks that what is not in principle susceptible to proof might be false.
(C) The argument fails to specify how it is that underinflation or overinflation harms tire tread.
(D) The argument rejects the possibility that what has not been proven is nevertheless true.
(E) The argument fails to precisely define the terms "underinflation" and "overinflation."

11. Lindsey has been judged to be a bad songwriter simply because her lyrics typically are disjointed and subjective. This judgment is ill founded, however, since the writings of many modern novelists typically are disjointed and subjective and yet these novelists are widely held to be good writers.

Which one of the following is an assumption on which the argument depends?

(A) Disjointed and subjective writing has a comparable effect in modern novels and in songs.
(B) Some readers do not appreciate the subtleties of the disjointed and subjective style adopted by modern novelists.
(C) Song lyrics that are disjointed and subjective have at least as much narrative structure as any other song lyrics do.
(D) A disjointed and subjective style of writing is usually more suitable for novels and song lyrics than it is for any other written works.
(E) The quality of Linsey's songs is better judged by the quality of their lyrics than by the quality of their musical form.

GO ON TO THE NEXT PAGE.

12. The Levant—the area that borders the eastern Mediterranean-was heavily populated in prehistoric times. The southern Levant was abandoned about 6,000 years ago, although the northern Levant, which shared the same climate, remained heavily populated. Recently archaeologists have hypothesized that the sudden depopulation in the southern Levant was due to an economic collapse resulting from deforestation.

If the statements above are true and the archaeologists' hypothesis is correct, which one of the following CANNOT be true?

(A) The sheep and goats herded by the peoples of the southern Levant until 6,000 years ago grazed extensively on the seedlings and saplings of indigenous tree species.
(B) Trees were used in the production of lime plaster, a building material used extensively throughout the southern Levant until 6,000 year ago.
(C) Organic remains from the northern Levant reliably indicate that tree species flourished there without interruption during the period when the southern Levant was being abandoned.
(D) Carbon dating of organic remains from the southern Levant reliably demonstrates that there were no forests present in that area prior to 6,000 years ago.
(E) Since there are few traces of either quarried stone or of mud brick in buildings excavated in the southern Levant, it is likely that the buildings built there prior to 6,000 years ago were made almost entirely of timber.

13. Using rational argument in advertisements does not persuade people to buy the products being advertised. Therefore, advertisers who replace rational argument with nonrational appeals to emotion in advertisements will persuade people to buy the products being advertised.

Which one of the following contains flawed reasoning most similar to the flawed reasoning in the argument above?

(A) People who ask others for favors are refused. Therefore, anyone who has not had the experience of being refused has never asked for a favor.
(B) In the past, people who have tried to solve their problems by discussing them have often failed. Therefore, in the future, people who try to solve their problems by discussing them will often fail.
(C) Using a computer has not improved students' writing skills. Thus, students should to try to improve their writing skills by using a computer.
(D) A person who does to have positive letters of reference cannot get a good job. Therefore, the better the letters of reference a person has, the better the job that person will get.
(E) People never learn to program a computer by reading poorly written directions. Therefore, if people read well-written directions, they will learn to program a computer.

GO ON TO THE NEXT PAGE.

14. A commercial insect trap consists of a small box containing pesticide mixed with glucose, a sweet substance known to attract insect pests. Yet in households where this type of trap has been used regularly for the past several years, recently installed traps are far less effective in eliminating insect pests than were traps of that type installed several years ago. Research scientists have hypothesized that traps in those households decreased in effectiveness because successive generations of the pests developed a resistance to the pesticide in the traps.

Which one of the following, if true, most seriously undermines the hypothesis?

(A) In households where the traps have been used regularly, the proportion of insect pests that have a natural aversion to eating glucose has increased with each successive generation;
(B) Even when only a few individuals out of an entire generation of insects survive the effects of a pesticide, the offspring of those individuals are usually resistant to that pesticide.
(C) After eating glucose mixed with the pesticide, insects that live in households that do not use the trap tend to die in greater numbers than do insects from households where the traps have been used regularly.
(D) After the manufacturer of the traps increased the concentration of the pesticide used in the traps, the traps were no more effective in eliminating household insect pests than were the original traps.
(E) The kind of glucose used to bait the traps is one of several different kinds of glucose that occur naturally.

15. A person's dietary consumption of cholesterol and fat is one of the most important factors determining the level of cholesterol in the person's blood (serum cholesterol). Serum cholesterol levels rise proportionally to increased cholesterol and fat consumption until that consumption reaches a threshold, but once consumption of these substances exceeds that threshold, serum cholesterol levels rise only gradually, even with dramatic increases in consumption. The threshold is one fourth the consumption level of cholesterol and fat in today's average North American diet.

The statements above, if true, most strongly support which one of the following?

(A) The threshold can be lowered by lowering the dietary consumption of cholesterol and fat.
(B) People who consume an average North American diet cannot increase their consumption of cholesterol and fat without dramatically increasing their serum cholesterol levels.
(C) People who consume half as much cholesterol and fat as in the average North American diet will not necessarily have half the average serum cholesterol level.
(D) Serum cholesterol levels cannot be affected by nondietary modifications in behavior, such as exercising more or smoking less.
(E) People who consume less cholesterol and fat than the threshold cannot reduce their serum cholesterol levels.

16. The recently negotiated North American Free Trade Agreement among Canada, Mexico, and the United States is misnamed, because it would not result in truly free trade. Adam Smith, the economist who first articulated the principles of free trade held that any obstacle placed in the way of the free movement of goods, investment, or labor would defeat free trade. So since under the agreement workers would be restricted by national boundaries from seeking the best conditions they could find, the resulting obstruction of the flow of trade would, from a free-trade perspective, be harmful.

The argument proceeds by

(A) ruling out alternatives
(B) using a term in two different senses
(C) citing a nonrepresentative instance
(D) appealing to a relevant authority
(E) responding to a different issue from the one posed

GO ON TO THE NEXT PAGE.

17. Parents who wish to provide a strong foundation for the musical ability of their children should provide them with a good musical education. Since formal instruction is often a part of a good musical education, parents who wish to provide this strong foundation need to ensure that their children receive formal instruction.

The reasoning is most vulnerable to criticism on the grounds that it fails to consider that

(A) parents might not be the only source of a child's musical education
(B) some children might not be interested in receiving a strong foundation for their musical ability
(C) there are many examples of people with formal instruction whose musical ability is poor
(D) formal instruction might not always be a part of a good musical education
(E) some children might become good musicians even if they have not had good musical educations

18. A stingray without parasites is healthier than it would be if it had parasites. Nevertheless, the lack of parasites in stingrays is an indicator that the ecosystem in which the stingrays live is under environmental stress such as pollution.

Which one of the following, if true, most helps to reconcile the discrepancy indicated above?

(A) During part of their life cycles, the parasites of stingrays require as hosts shrimp or oysters, which are environmentally vulnerable organisms.
(B) A stingray is a free-ranging predator that feeds on smaller organisms but has few predators itself.
(C) A parasite drains part of the vitality of its host by drawing nourishment from the host.
(D) An ecosystem can be considered stressed if only a few species of very simple organisms can live there.
(E) Since the life of parasites depends on that of their host, they need to live without killing their host or else not reproduce and infect other individuals before their own host dies.

19. Over the past 20 years, skiing has become a relatively safe sport due to improvements in ski equipment. There has been a 50 percent drop in the number of ski injuries over the last 20 years. Clearly, however, there have not been decreases in the number of injuries in all categories, as statistical data readily show, for although broken legs and ankle injuries have decreased by an astounding 90 percent, knee injuries now represent 16 percent of all ski injuries, up significantly from the 11 percent of 20 years ago.

The reasoning in the argument is flawed because the argument does which one of the following?

(A) It fails to allow for there being ski injuries other than broken legs, ankle injuries, and knee injuries.
(B) It infers disparate effects from the same single cause.
(C) It ignores the possibility that the number of skiers has increased over the past 20 years.
(D) It assumes that an increase in the proportion of knee injuries rules out a decrease in the number of knee injuries.
(E) It proceeds as though there could be a greater decrease in injuries in each category on injury than there is in injuries overall.

GO ON TO THE NEXT PAGE.

20. Only poetry cannot be translated well, and therefore it is poets who preserve languages, for we would not bother to learn a language if we could get everything written in it from translation. So, since we cannot witness the beauty of poetry except in the language in which it is composed, we have motivation to learn the language.

    The information above provides the LEAST support for which one of the following?

    (A) All nonpoetic literature can be translated well.
    (B) One purpose of writing poetry is to preserve the language in which it is written.
    (C) Some translations do not capture all that was expressed in the original language.
    (D) The beauty of poetry is not immediately accessible to people who do not understand the language in which the poetry was written.
    (E) Perfect translation from one language to another is sometimes impossible.

21. The companies that are the prime purchasers of computer software will not buy a software package if the costs of training staff to use it are high, and we know that it is expensive to teach people a software package that demands the memorization of unfamiliar commands. As a result, to be successful, commercial computer software cannot require users to memorize unfamiliar commands.

    The conclusion above follows logically if which one of the following is assumed?

    (A) If most prime purchasers of computer software buy a software product, that product will be successful.
    (B) Commercial computer software that does not require users to memorize unfamiliar commands is no more expensive than software that does.
    (C) Commercial computer software will not be successful unless prime purchasers buy it.
    (D) If the initial cost of computer software is high, but the cost of training users is low, prime purchasers will still buy that software.
    (E) The more difficult it is to learn how to use a piece of software, the more expensive it is to teach a person to use that software.

<u>Questions 22–23</u>

Whenever she considers voting in an election to select one candidate for a position and there is at least one issue important to her, Kay uses the following principle in choosing which course of action to take: it is acceptable for me to vote for a candidate whose opinions differ from mine on at least one issue important to me whenever I disagree with each of the other candidates on even more such issues; it is otherwise unacceptable to vote for that candidate. In the upcoming mayoral election, the three candidates are Legrand, Medina, and Norton. There is only one issue important to Kay, and only Medina shares her opinion on that issue.

22. If the statements in the passage are true, which one of the following must also be true about Kay's course of action in any election to select one candidate for a position?

    (A) If there are no issues important to her, it is unacceptable for her to vote for any candidate in the election.
    (B) If she agrees with each of the candidates on most of the issues important to her, it is unacceptable for her to vote for any candidate in the election.
    (C) If she agrees with a particular candidate on only one issue important to her, it is unacceptable for her to vote for that candidate.
    (D) If she disagrees with each of the candidates on exactly three issues important to her, it is unacceptable for her to vote for any candidate in the election.
    (E) If there are more issues important to her on which she disagrees with a particular candidate than there are such issues on which she agrees with that candidate, it is unacceptable for her to vote for that candidate.

23. According to the principle stated in the passage, in the upcoming mayoral election

    (A) it is acceptable for Kay to vote for either Medina or Legrand, but it is unacceptable for her to vote for Norton
    (B) the only unacceptable courses of action are for Kay to vote for Norton and for her to vote for Legrand
    (C) it is unacceptable for Kay to vote for any of the candidates
    (D) the only unacceptable course of action is for Kay to vote for Medina
    (E) it is acceptable for Kay to vote for any of the candidates

GO ON TO THE NEXT PAGE.

24. Over the last 25 years, the average price paid for a new car has steadily increased in relation to average individual income. This increase indicates that individuals who buy new cars today spend, on average, a larger amount relative to their incomes buying a car than their counterparts did 25 years ago.

Which one of the following, if true, most weakens the argument?

(A) There has been a significant increase over the last 25 years in the proportion of individuals in households with more than one wage earner.
(B) The number of used cars sold annually is the same as it was 25 years ago.
(C) Allowing for inflation, average individual income has significantly declined over the last 25 years.
(D) During the last 25 years, annual new-car sales and the population have both increased, but new-car sales have increased by a greater percentage.
(E) Sales to individuals make up a smaller proportion of all new-car sales than they did 25 years ago.

25. Credit card companies justify charging cardholders additional fees for late payments by asserting the principle that those who expose other individuals, companies, or institutions to financial risk should pay for that risk, and by pointing out that late-paying cardholders present a greater risk of default than other cardholders. Without late fees, the companies argue, they would have to spread the cost of the risk over all cardholders.

The principle invoked by the credit card companies would, if established, be most usefully invoked in which one of the following arguments?

(A) School authorities should use student activity funds to pay for student-caused damages to school property since, even though only a few students cause any significant damage, authorities cannot in most instances determine which students caused the damage.
(B) Insurance companies should demand higher insurance rates of drivers of sports cars than of other drivers, since sports car divers are more likely to cause accidents and thus are more likely to require the companies to pay out money in claims.
(C) Libraries should charge high fines for overdue books, since if they did not do so some people would keep books out indefinitely, risking inconvenience to other library users who might want to use the books.
(D) Cities should impose high fines for littering. The risk of being caught littering is quite low, so the fine for those who are caught must be correspondingly high in order to deter people from littering.
(E) Municipalities should use tax money to pay for the maintenance of municipal roads, since if individuals paid for only those roads they used, some important roads in remote areas would be inadequately maintained.

S T O P

IF YOU FINISH BEFORE TIME IS CALLED, YOU MAY CHECK YOUR WORK ON THIS SECTION ONLY. DO NOT WORK ON ANY OTHER SECTION IN THE TEST.

SECTION I

Time—35 minutes

27 Questions

Directions: Each set of questions in this section is based on a single passage or a pair of passages. The questions are to be answered on the basis of what is stated or implied in the passage or pair of passages. For some of the questions, more than one of the choices could conceivably answer the question. However, you are to choose the best answer; that is, the response that most accurately and completely answers the question, and blacken the corresponding space on your answer sheet.

To study centuries-old earthquakes and the geologic faults that caused them, seismologists usually dig trenches along visible fault lines, looking for sediments that show evidence of having shifted. Using radiocarbon dating, they measure the quantity of the radioactive isotope carbon 14 present in wood or other organic material trapped in the sediments when they shifted. Since carbon 14 occurs naturally in organic materials and decays at a constant rate, the age of organic materials can be reconstructed from the amount of the isotope remaining in them. These data can show the location and frequency of past earthquakes and provide hints about the likelihood and location of future earthquakes.

Geologists William Bull and Mark Brandon have recently developed a new method, called lichenometry, for detecting and dating past earthquakes. Bull and Brandon developed the method based on the fact that large earthquakes generate numerous simultaneous rockfalls in mountain ranges that are sensitive to seismic shaking. Instead of dating fault-line sediments, lichenometry involves measuring the size of lichens growing on the rocks exposed by these rockfalls. Lichens—symbiotic organisms consisting of a fungus and an alga—quickly colonize newly exposed rock surfaces in the wake of rockfalls, and once established they grow radially, flat against the rocks, at a slow but constant rate for as long as 1,000 years if left undisturbed. One species of North American lichen, for example, spreads outward by about 9.5 millimeters each century. Hence, the diameter of the largest lichen on a boulder provides direct evidence of when the boulder was dislodged and repositioned. If many rockfalls over a large geographic area occurred simultaneously, that pattern would imply that there had been a strong earthquake. The location of the earthquake's epicenter can then be determined by mapping these rockfalls, since they decrease in abundance as the distance from the epicenter increases.

Lichenometry has distinct advantages over radiocarbon dating. Radiocarbon dating is accurate only to within plus or minus 40 years, because the amount of the carbon 14 isotope varies naturally in the environment depending on the intensity of the radiation striking Earth's upper atmosphere. Additionally, this intensity has fluctuated greatly during the past 300 years, causing many radiocarbon datings of events during this period to be of little value. Lichenometry, Bull and Brandon claim, can accurately date an earthquake to within ten years. They note, however, that using lichenometry requires careful site selection and accurate calibration of lichen growth rates, adding that the method is best used for earthquakes that occurred within the last 500 years. Sites must be selected to minimize the influence of snow avalanches and other disturbances that would affect normal lichen growth, and conditions like shade and wind that promote faster lichen growth must be factored in.

1. Which one of the following most accurately expresses the main idea of the passage?

(A) Lichenometry is a new method for dating past earthquakes that has advantages over radiocarbon dating.
(B) Despite its limitations, lichenometry has been proven to be more accurate than any other method of discerning the dates of past earthquakes.
(C) Most seismologists today have rejected radiocarbon dating and are embracing lichenometry as the most reliable method for studying past earthquakes.
(D) Two geologists have revolutionized the study of past earthquakes by developing lichenometry, an easily applied method of earthquake detection and dating.
(E) Radiocarbon dating, an unreliable test used in dating past earthquakes, can finally be abandoned now that lichenometry has been developed.

2. The passage provides information that most helps to answer which one of the following questions?

(A) How do scientists measure lichen growth rates under the varying conditions that lichens may encounter?
(B) How do scientists determine the intensity of the radiation striking Earth's upper atmosphere?
(C) What are some of the conditions that encourage lichens to grow at a more rapid rate than usual?
(D) What is the approximate date of the earliest earthquake that lichenometry has been used to identify?
(E) What are some applications of the techniques involved in radiocarbon dating other than their use in studying past earthquakes?

GO ON TO THE NEXT PAGE.

3. What is the author's primary purpose in referring to the rate of growth of a North American lichen species (lines 29–30)?
   (A) to emphasize the rapidity with which lichen colonies can establish themselves on newly exposed rock surfaces
   (B) to offer an example of a lichen species with one of the slowest known rates of growth
   (C) to present additional evidence supporting the claim that environmental conditions can alter lichens' rate of growth
   (D) to explain why lichenometry works best for dating earthquakes that occurred in the last 500 years
   (E) to provide a sense of the sort of timescale on which lichen growth occurs

4. Which one of the following statements is most strongly supported by the passage?
   (A) Lichenometry is less accurate than radiocarbon dating in predicting the likelihood and location of future earthquakes.
   (B) Radiocarbon dating is unlikely to be helpful in dating past earthquakes that have no identifiable fault lines associated with them.
   (C) Radiocarbon dating and lichenometry are currently the only viable methods of detecting and dating past earthquakes.
   (D) Radiocarbon dating is more accurate than lichenometry in dating earthquakes that occurred approximately 400 years ago.
   (E) The usefulness of lichenometry for dating earthquakes is limited to geographic regions where factors that disturb or accelerate lichen growth generally do not occur.

5. The primary purpose of the first paragraph in relation to the rest of the passage is to describe
   (A) a well-known procedure that will then be examined on a step-by-step basis
   (B) an established procedure to which a new procedure will then be compared
   (C) an outdated procedure that will then be shown to be nonetheless useful in some situations
   (D) a traditional procedure that will then be contrasted with other traditional procedures
   (E) a popular procedure that will then be shown to have resulted in erroneous conclusions about a phenomenon

6. It can be inferred that the statements made by Bull and Brandon and reported in lines 50–58 rely on which one of the following assumptions?
   (A) While lichenometry is less accurate when it is used to date earthquakes that occurred more than 500 years ago, it is still more accurate than other methods for dating such earthquakes.
   (B) There is no reliable method for determining the intensity of the radiation now hitting Earth's upper atmosphere.
   (C) Lichens are able to grow only on the types of rocks that are common in mountainous regions.
   (D) The mountain ranges that produce the kinds of rockfalls studied in lichenometry are also subject to more frequent snowfalls and avalanches than other mountain ranges are.
   (E) The extent to which conditions like shade and wind have affected the growth of existing lichen colonies can be determined.

7. The passage indicates that using radiocarbon dating to date past earthquakes may be unreliable due to
   (A) the multiplicity of the types of organic matter that require analysis
   (B) the variable amount of organic materials caught in shifted sediments
   (C) the fact that fault lines related to past earthquakes are not always visible
   (D) the fluctuations in the amount of the carbon 14 isotope in the environment over time
   (E) the possibility that radiation has not always struck the upper atmosphere

8. Given the information in the passage, to which one of the following would lichenometry likely be most applicable?
   (A) identifying the number of times a particular river has flooded in the past 1,000 years
   (B) identifying the age of a fossilized skeleton of a mammal that lived many thousands of years ago
   (C) identifying the age of an ancient beach now underwater approximately 30 kilometers off the present shore
   (D) identifying the rate, in kilometers per century, at which a glacier has been receding up a mountain valley
   (E) identifying local trends in annual rainfall rates in a particular valley over the past five centuries

GO ON TO THE NEXT PAGE.

While courts have long allowed custom-made medical illustrations depicting personal injury to be presented as evidence in legal cases, the issue of whether they have a legitimate place in the courtroom is surrounded by ongoing debate and misinformation. Some opponents of their general use argue that while illustrations are sometimes invaluable in presenting the physical details of a personal injury, in all cases except those involving the most unusual injuries, illustrations from medical textbooks can be adequate. Most injuries, such as fractures and whiplash, they say, are rather generic in nature—certain commonly encountered forces act on particular areas of the body in standard ways—so they can be represented by generic illustrations.

Another line of complaint stems from the belief that custom-made illustrations often misrepresent the facts in order to comply with the partisan interests of litigants. Even some lawyers appear to share a version of this view, believing that such illustrations can be used to bolster a weak case. Illustrators are sometimes approached by lawyers who, unable to find medical experts to support their clients' claims, think that they can replace expert testimony with such deceptive professional illustrations. But this is mistaken. Even if an unscrupulous illustrator could be found, such illustrations would be inadmissible as evidence in the courtroom unless a medical expert were present to testify to their accuracy.

It has also been maintained that custom-made illustrations may subtly distort the issues through the use of emphasis, coloration, and other means, even if they are technically accurate. But professional medical illustrators strive for objective accuracy and avoid devices that have inflammatory potential, sometimes even eschewing the use of color. Unlike illustrations in medical textbooks, which are designed to include the extensive detail required by medical students, custom-made medical illustrations are designed to include only the information that is relevant for those deciding a case. The end user is typically a jury or a judge, for whose benefit the depiction is reduced to the details that are crucial to determining the legally relevant facts. The more complex details often found in textbooks can be deleted so as not to confuse the issue. For example, illustrations of such things as veins and arteries would only get in the way when an illustration is supposed to be used to explain the nature of a bone fracture.

Custom-made medical illustrations, which are based on a plaintiff's X rays, computerized tomography scans, and medical records and reports, are especially valuable in that they provide visual representations of data whose verbal description would be very complex. Expert testimony by medical professionals often relies heavily on the use of technical terminology, which those who are not specially trained in the field find difficult to translate mentally into visual imagery. Since, for most people, adequate understanding of physical data depends on thinking at least partly in visual terms, the clearly presented visual stimulation provided by custom-made illustrations can be quite instructive.

9. Which one of the following is most analogous to the role that, according to the author, custom-made medical illustrations play in personal injury cases?

(A) schematic drawings accompanying an engineer's oral presentation
(B) road maps used by people unfamiliar with an area so that they will not have to get verbal instructions from strangers
(C) children's drawings that psychologists use to detect wishes and anxieties not apparent in the children's behavior
(D) a reproduction of a famous painting in an art history textbook
(E) an artist's preliminary sketches for a painting

10. Based on the passage, which one of the following is the author most likely to believe about illustrations in medical textbooks?

(A) They tend to rely less on the use of color than do custom-made medical illustrations.
(B) They are inadmissible in a courtroom unless a medical expert is present to testify to their accuracy.
(C) They are in many cases drawn by the same individuals who draw custom-made medical illustrations for courtroom use.
(D) They are believed by most lawyers to be less prone than custom-made medical illustrations to misrepresent the nature of a personal injury.
(E) In many cases they are more apt to confuse jurors than are custom-made medical illustrations.

11. The passage states that a role of medical experts in relation to custom-made medical illustrations in the courtroom is to

(A) decide which custom-made medical illustrations should be admissible
(B) temper the impact of the illustrations on judges and jurors who are not medical professionals
(C) make medical illustrations understandable to judges and jurors
(D) provide opinions to attorneys as to which illustrations, if any, would be useful
(E) provide their opinions as to the accuracy of the illustrations

12. According to the passage, one of the ways that medical textbook illustrations differ from custom-made medical illustrations is that

(A) custom-made medical illustrations accurately represent human anatomy, whereas medical textbook illustrations do not
(B) medical textbook illustrations employ color freely, whereas custom-made medical illustrations must avoid color
(C) medical textbook illustrations are objective, while custom-made medical illustrations are subjective
(D) medical textbook illustrations are very detailed, whereas custom-made medical illustrations include only details that are relevant to the case
(E) medical textbook illustrations are readily comprehended by nonmedical audiences, whereas custom-made medical illustrations are not

13. The author's attitude toward the testimony of medical experts in personal injury cases is most accurately described as

(A) appreciation of the difficulty involved in explaining medical data to judges and jurors together with skepticism concerning the effectiveness of such testimony
(B) admiration for the experts' technical knowledge coupled with disdain for the communications skills of medical professionals
(C) acceptance of the accuracy of such testimony accompanied with awareness of the limitations of a presentation that is entirely verbal
(D) respect for the medical profession tempered by apprehension concerning the tendency of medical professionals to try to overwhelm judges and jurors with technical details
(E) respect for expert witnesses combined with intolerance of the use of technical terminology

14. The author's primary purpose in the third paragraph is to

(A) argue for a greater use of custom-made medical illustrations in court cases involving personal injury
(B) reply to a variant of the objection to custom-made medical illustrations raised in the second paragraph
(C) argue against the position that illustrations from medical textbooks are well suited for use in the courtroom
(D) discuss in greater detail why custom-made medical illustrations are controversial
(E) describe the differences between custom-made medical illustrations and illustrations from medical textbooks

GO ON TO THE NEXT PAGE.

Passage A

Because dental caries (decay) is strongly linked to consumption of the sticky, carbohydrate-rich staples of agricultural diets, prehistoric human teeth can provide clues about when a population made the transition from a hunter-gatherer diet to an agricultural one. Caries formation is influenced by several factors, including tooth structure, bacteria in the mouth, and diet. In particular, caries formation is affected by carbohydrates' texture and composition, since carbohydrates more readily stick to teeth.

Many researchers have demonstrated the link between carbohydrate consumption and caries. In North America, Leigh studied caries in archaeologically derived teeth, noting that caries rates differed between indigenous populations that primarily consumed meat (a Sioux sample showed almost no caries) and those heavily dependent on cultivated maize (a Zuni sample had 75 percent carious teeth). Leigh's findings have been frequently confirmed by other researchers, who have shown that, in general, the greater a population's dependence on agriculture is, the higher its rate of caries formation will be.

Under some circumstances, however, nonagricultural populations may exhibit relatively high caries rates. For example, early nonagricultural populations in western North America who consumed large amounts of highly processed stone-ground flour made from gathered acorns show relatively high caries frequencies. And wild plants collected by the Hopi included several species with high cariogenic potential, notably pinyon nuts and wild tubers.

Passage B

Archaeologists recovered human skeletal remains interred over a 2,000-year period in prehistoric Ban Chiang, Thailand. The site's early inhabitants appear to have had a hunter-gatherer-cultivator economy. Evidence indicates that, over time, the population became increasingly dependent on agriculture.

Research suggests that agricultural intensification results in declining human health, including dental health. Studies show that dental caries is uncommon in pre-agricultural populations. Increased caries frequency may result from increased consumption of starchy-sticky foodstuffs or from alterations in tooth wear. The wearing down of tooth crown surfaces reduces caries formation by removing fissures that can trap food particles. A reduction of fiber or grit in a diet may diminish tooth wear, thus increasing caries frequency. However, severe wear that exposes a tooth's pulp cavity may also result in caries.

The diet of Ban Chiang's inhabitants included some cultivated rice and yams from the beginning of the period represented by the recovered remains. These were part of a varied diet that also included wild plant and animal foods. Since both rice and yams are carbohydrates, increased reliance on either or both should theoretically result in increased caries frequency.

Yet comparisons of caries frequency in the Early and Late Ban Chiang Groups indicate that overall caries frequency is slightly greater in the Early Group. Tooth wear patterns do not indicate tooth wear changes between Early and Late Groups that would explain this unexpected finding. It is more likely that, although dependence on agriculture increased, the diet in the Late period remained varied enough that no single food dominated. Furthermore, there may have been a shift from sweeter carbohydrates (yams) toward rice, a less cariogenic carbohydrate.

15. Both passages are primarily concerned with examining which one of the following topics?

(A) evidence of the development of agriculture in the archaeological record
(B) the impact of agriculture on the overall health of human populations
(C) the effects of carbohydrate-rich foods on caries formation in strictly agricultural societies
(D) the archaeological evidence regarding when the first agricultural society arose
(E) the extent to which pre-agricultural populations were able to obtain carbohydrate-rich foods

16. Which one of the following distinguishes the Ban Chiang populations discussed in passage B from the populations discussed in the last paragraph of passage A?

(A) While the Ban Chiang populations consumed several highly cariogenic foods, the populations discussed in the last paragraph of passage A did not.
(B) While the Ban Chiang populations ate cultivated foods, the populations discussed in the last paragraph of passage A did not.
(C) While the Ban Chiang populations consumed a diet consisting primarily of carbohydrates, the populations discussed in the last paragraph of passage A did not.
(D) While the Ban Chiang populations exhibited very high levels of tooth wear, the populations discussed in the last paragraph of passage A did not.
(E) While the Ban Chiang populations ate certain highly processed foods, the populations discussed in the last paragraph of passage A did not.

GO ON TO THE NEXT PAGE.

17. Passage B most strongly supports which one of the following statements about fiber and grit in a diet?

(A) They can either limit or promote caries formation, depending on their prevalence in the diet.
(B) They are typically consumed in greater quantities as a population adopts agriculture.
(C) They have a negative effect on overall health since they have no nutritional value.
(D) They contribute to the formation of fissures in tooth surfaces.
(E) They increase the stickiness of carbohydrate-rich foods.

18. Which one of the following is mentioned in both passages as evidence tending to support the prevailing view regarding the relationship between dental caries and carbohydrate consumption?

(A) the effect of consuming highly processed foods on caries formation
(B) the relatively low incidence of caries among nonagricultural people
(C) the effect of fiber and grit in the diet on caries formation
(D) the effect of the consumption of wild foods on tooth wear
(E) the effect of agricultural intensification on overall human health

19. It is most likely that both authors would agree with which one of the following statements about dental caries?

(A) The incidence of dental caries increases predictably in populations over time.
(B) Dental caries is often difficult to detect in teeth recovered from archaeological sites.
(C) Dental caries tends to be more prevalent in populations with a hunter-gatherer diet than in populations with an agricultural diet.
(D) The frequency of dental caries in a population does not necessarily correspond directly to the population's degree of dependence on agriculture.
(E) The formation of dental caries tends to be more strongly linked to tooth wear than to the consumption of a particular kind of food.

20. Each passage suggests which one of the following about carbohydrate-rich foods?

(A) Varieties that are cultivated have a greater tendency to cause caries than varieties that grow wild.
(B) Those that require substantial processing do not play a role in hunter-gatherer diets.
(C) Some of them naturally have a greater tendency than others to cause caries.
(D) Some of them reduce caries formation because their relatively high fiber content increases tooth wear.
(E) The cariogenic potential of a given variety increases if it is cultivated rather than gathered in the wild.

21. The evidence from Ban Chiang discussed in passage B relates to the generalization reported in the second paragraph of passage A (lines 20–22) in which one of the following ways?

(A) The evidence confirms the generalization.
(B) The evidence tends to support the generalization.
(C) The evidence is irrelevant to the generalization.
(D) The evidence does not conform to the generalization.
(E) The evidence disproves the generalization.

GO ON TO THE NEXT PAGE.

Recent criticism has sought to align Sarah Orne Jewett, a notable writer of regional fiction in the nineteenth-century United States, with the domestic novelists of the previous generation. Her work does resemble the domestic novels of the 1850s in its focus on women, their domestic occupations, and their social interactions, with men relegated to the periphery. But it also differs markedly from these antecedents. The world depicted in the latter revolves around children. Young children play prominent roles in the domestic novels and the work of child rearing—the struggle to instill a mother's values in a child's character—is their chief source of drama. By contrast, children and child rearing are almost entirely absent from the world of Jewett's fiction. Even more strikingly, while the literary world of the earlier domestic novelists is insistently religious, grounded in the structures of Protestant religious belief, to turn from these writers to Jewett is to encounter an almost wholly secular world.

To the extent that these differences do not merely reflect the personal preferences of the authors, we might attribute them to such historical transformations as the migration of the rural young to cities or the increasing secularization of society. But while such factors may help to explain the differences, it can be argued that these differences ultimately reflect different conceptions of the nature and purpose of fiction. The domestic novel of the mid-nineteenth century is based on a conception of fiction as part of a continuum that also included writings devoted to piety and domestic instruction, bound together by a common goal of promoting domestic morality and religious belief. It was not uncommon for the same multipurpose book to be indistinguishably a novel, a child-rearing manual, and a tract on Christian duty. The more didactic aims are absent from Jewett's writing, which rather embodies the late nineteenth-century "high-cultural" conception of fiction as an autonomous sphere with value in and of itself.

This high-cultural aesthetic was one among several conceptions of fiction operative in the United States in the 1850s and 1860s, but it became the dominant one later in the nineteenth century and remained so for most of the twentieth. On this conception, fiction came to be seen as pure art: a work was to be viewed in isolation and valued for the formal arrangement of its elements rather than for its larger social connections or the promotion of extraliterary goods. Thus, unlike the domestic novelists, Jewett intended her works not as a means to an end but as an end in themselves. This fundamental difference should be given more weight in assessing their affinities than any superficial similarity in subject matter.

22. The passage most helps to answer which one of the following questions?

(A) Did any men write domestic novels in the 1850s?
(B) Were any widely read domestic novels written after the 1860s?
(C) How did migration to urban areas affect the development of domestic fiction in the 1850s?
(D) What is an effect that Jewett's conception of literary art had on her fiction?
(E) With what region of the United States were at least some of Jewett's writings concerned?

23. It can be inferred from the passage that the author would be most likely to view the "recent criticism" mentioned in line 1 as

(A) advocating a position that is essentially correct even though some powerful arguments can be made against it
(B) making a true claim about Jewett, but for the wrong reasons
(C) making a claim that is based on some reasonable evidence and is initially plausible but ultimately mistaken
(D) questionable, because it relies on a currently dominant literary aesthetic that takes too narrow a view of the proper goals of fiction
(E) based on speculation for which there is no reasonable support, and therefore worthy of dismissal

24. In saying that domestic fiction was based on a conception of fiction as part of a "continuum" (line 30), the author most likely means which one of the following?

(A) Domestic fiction was part of an ongoing tradition stretching back into the past.
(B) Fiction was not treated as clearly distinct from other categories of writing.
(C) Domestic fiction was often published in serial form.
(D) Fiction is constantly evolving.
(E) Domestic fiction promoted the cohesiveness and hence the continuity of society.

GO ON TO THE NEXT PAGE.

25. Which one of the following most accurately states the primary function of the passage?

(A) It proposes and defends a radical redefinition of several historical categories of literary style.
(B) It proposes an evaluation of a particular style of writing, of which one writer's work is cited as a paradigmatic case.
(C) It argues for a reappraisal of a set of long-held assumptions about the historical connections among a group of writers.
(D) It weighs the merits of two opposing conceptions of the nature of fiction.
(E) It rejects a way of classifying a particular writer's work and defends an alternative view.

26. Which one of the following most accurately represents the structure of the second paragraph?

(A) The author considers and rejects a number of possible explanations for a phenomenon, concluding that any attempt at explanation does violence to the unity of the phenomenon.
(B) The author shows that two explanatory hypotheses are incompatible with each other and gives reasons for preferring one of them.
(C) The author describes several explanatory hypotheses and argues that they are not really distinct from one another.
(D) The author proposes two versions of a classificatory hypothesis, indicates the need for some such hypothesis, and then sets out a counterargument in preparation for rejecting that counterargument in the following paragraph.
(E) The author mentions a number of explanatory hypotheses, gives a mildly favorable comment on them, and then advocates and elaborates another explanation that the author considers to be more fundamental.

27. The differing conceptions of fiction held by Jewett and the domestic novelists can most reasonably be taken as providing an answer to which one of the following questions?

(A) Why was Jewett unwilling to feature children and religious themes as prominently in her works as the domestic novelists featured them in theirs?
(B) Why did both Jewett and the domestic novelists focus primarily on rural as opposed to urban concerns?
(C) Why was Jewett not constrained to feature children and religion as prominently in her works as domestic novelists were?
(D) Why did both Jewett and the domestic novelists focus predominantly on women and their concerns?
(E) Why was Jewett unable to feature children or religion as prominently in her works as the domestic novelists featured them in theirs?

S T O P

IF YOU FINISH BEFORE TIME IS CALLED, YOU MAY CHECK YOUR WORK ON THIS SECTION ONLY.
DO NOT WORK ON ANY OTHER SECTION IN THE TEST.

SECTION II

Time—35 minutes

26 Questions

Directions: The questions in this section are based on the reasoning contained in brief statements or passages. For some questions, more than one of the choices could conceivably answer the question. However, you are to choose the best answer; that is, the response that most accurately and completely answers the question. You should not make assumptions that are by commonsense standards implausible, superfluous, or incompatible with the passage. After you have chosen the best answer, blacken the corresponding space on your answer sheet.

1. In a recent study, a group of young children were taught the word "stairs" while walking up and down a flight of stairs. Later that day, when the children were shown a video of a person climbing a ladder, they all called the ladder stairs.

   Which one of the following principles is best illustrated by the study described above?

   (A) When young children repeatedly hear a word without seeing the object denoted by the word, they sometimes apply the word to objects not denoted by the word.
   (B) Young children best learn words when they are shown how the object denoted by the word is used.
   (C) The earlier in life a child encounters and uses an object, the easier it is for that child to learn how not to misuse the word denoting that object.
   (D) Young children who learn a word by observing how the object denoted by that word is used sometimes apply that word to a different object that is similarly used.
   (E) Young children best learn the names of objects when the objects are present at the time the children learn the words and when no other objects are simultaneously present.

2. Among people who live to the age of 100 or more, a large proportion have led "unhealthy" lives: smoking, consuming alcohol, eating fatty foods, and getting little exercise. Since such behavior often leads to shortened life spans, it is likely that exceptionally long-lived people are genetically disposed to having long lives.

   Which one of the following, if true, most strengthens the argument?

   (A) There is some evidence that consuming a moderate amount of alcohol can counteract the effects of eating fatty foods.
   (B) Some of the exceptionally long-lived people who do not smoke or drink do eat fatty foods and get little exercise.
   (C) Some of the exceptionally long-lived people who exercise regularly and avoid fatty foods do smoke or consume alcohol.
   (D) Some people who do not live to the age of 100 also lead unhealthy lives.
   (E) Nearly all people who live to 100 or more have siblings who are also long-lived.

3. Medications with an unpleasant taste are generally produced only in tablet, capsule, or soft-gel form. The active ingredient in medication M is a waxy substance that cannot tolerate the heat used to manufacture tablets because it has a low melting point. So, since the company developing M does not have soft-gel manufacturing technology and manufactures all its medications itself, M will most likely be produced in capsule form.

   The conclusion is most strongly supported by the reasoning in the argument if which one of the following is assumed?

   (A) Medication M can be produced in liquid form.
   (B) Medication M has an unpleasant taste.
   (C) No medication is produced in both capsule and soft-gel form.
   (D) Most medications with a low melting point are produced in soft-gel form.
   (E) Medications in capsule form taste less unpleasant than those in tablet or soft-gel form.

GO ON TO THE NEXT PAGE.

4. Carol Morris wants to own a majority of the shares of the city's largest newspaper, *The Daily*. The only obstacle to Morris's amassing a majority of these shares is that Azedcorp, which currently owns a majority, has steadfastly refused to sell. Industry analysts nevertheless predict that Morris will soon be the majority owner of *The Daily*.

   Which one of the following, if true, provides the most support for the industry analysts' prediction?

   (A) Azedcorp does not own shares of any newspaper other than *The Daily*.
   (B) Morris has recently offered Azedcorp much more for its shares of *The Daily* than Azedcorp paid for them.
   (C) No one other than Morris has expressed any interest in purchasing a majority of *The Daily*'s shares.
   (D) Morris already owns more shares of *The Daily* than anyone except Azedcorp.
   (E) Azedcorp is financially so weak that bankruptcy will probably soon force the sale of its newspaper holdings.

5. Area resident: Childhood lead poisoning has declined steadily since the 1970s, when leaded gasoline was phased out and lead paint was banned. But recent statistics indicate that 25 percent of this area's homes still contain lead paint that poses significant health hazards. Therefore, if we eliminate the lead paint in those homes, childhood lead poisoning in the area will finally be eradicated.

   The area resident's argument is flawed in that it

   (A) relies on statistical claims that are likely to be unreliable
   (B) relies on an assumption that is tantamount to assuming that the conclusion is true
   (C) fails to consider that there may be other significant sources of lead in the area's environment
   (D) takes for granted that lead paint in homes can be eliminated economically
   (E) takes for granted that children reside in all of the homes in the area that contain lead paint

6. Although some nutritional facts about soft drinks are listed on their labels, exact caffeine content is not. Listing exact caffeine content would make it easier to limit, but not eliminate, one's caffeine intake. If it became easier for people to limit, but not eliminate, their caffeine intake, many people would do so, which would improve their health.

   If all the statements above are true, which one of the following must be true?

   (A) The health of at least some people would improve if exact caffeine content were listed on soft-drink labels.
   (B) Many people will be unable to limit their caffeine intake if exact caffeine content is not listed on soft-drink labels.
   (C) Many people will find it difficult to eliminate their caffeine intake if they have to guess exactly how much caffeine is in their soft drinks.
   (D) People who wish to eliminate, rather than simply limit, their caffeine intake would benefit if exact caffeine content were listed on soft-drink labels.
   (E) The health of at least some people would worsen if everyone knew exactly how much caffeine was in their soft drinks.

7. When the famous art collector Vidmar died, a public auction of her collection, the largest privately owned, was held. "I can't possibly afford any of those works because hers is among the most valuable collections ever assembled by a single person," declared art lover MacNeil.

   The flawed pattern of reasoning in which one of the following is most closely parallel to that in MacNeil's argument?

   (A) Each word in the book is in French. So the whole book is in French.
   (B) The city council voted unanimously to adopt the plan. So councilperson Martinez voted to adopt the plan.
   (C) This paragraph is long. So the sentences that comprise it are long.
   (D) The members of the company are old. So the company itself is old.
   (E) The atoms comprising this molecule are elements. So the molecule itself is an element.

8. A leading critic of space exploration contends that it would be wrong, given current technology, to send a group of explorers to Mars, since the explorers would be unlikely to survive the trip. But that exaggerates the risk. There would be a well-engineered backup system at every stage of the long and complicated journey. A fatal catastrophe is quite unlikely at any given stage if such a backup system is in place.

The reasoning in the argument is flawed in that the argument

(A) infers that something is true of a whole merely from the fact that it is true of each of the parts
(B) infers that something cannot occur merely from the fact that it is unlikely to occur
(C) draws a conclusion about what must be the case based on evidence about what is probably the case
(D) infers that something will work merely because it could work
(E) rejects a view merely on the grounds that an inadequate argument has been made for it

9. A retrospective study is a scientific study that tries to determine the causes of subjects' present characteristics by looking for significant connections between the present characteristics of subjects and what happened to those subjects in the past, before the study began. Because retrospective studies of human subjects must use the subjects' reports about their own pasts, however, such studies cannot reliably determine the causes of human subjects' present characteristics.

Which one of the following, if assumed, enables the argument's conclusion to be properly drawn?

(A) Whether or not a study of human subjects can reliably determine the causes of those subjects' present characteristics may depend at least in part on the extent to which that study uses inaccurate reports about the subjects' pasts.
(B) A retrospective study cannot reliably determine the causes of human subjects' present characteristics unless there exist correlations between the present characteristics of the subjects and what happened to those subjects in the past.
(C) In studies of human subjects that attempt to find connections between subjects' present characteristics and what happened to those subjects in the past, the subjects' reports about their own pasts are highly susceptible to inaccuracy.
(D) If a study of human subjects uses only accurate reports about the subjects' pasts, then that study can reliably determine the causes of those subjects' present characteristics.
(E) Every scientific study in which researchers look for significant connections between the present characteristics of subjects and what happened to those subjects in the past must use the subjects' reports about their own pasts.

GO ON TO THE NEXT PAGE.

10. Gigantic passenger planes currently being developed will have enough space to hold shops and lounges in addition to passenger seating. However, the additional space will more likely be used for more passenger seating. The number of passengers flying the air-traffic system is expected to triple within 20 years, and it will be impossible for airports to accommodate enough normal-sized jet planes to carry that many passengers.

Which one of the following most accurately states the conclusion drawn in the argument?

(A) Gigantic planes currently being developed will have enough space in them to hold shops and lounges as well as passenger seating.
(B) The additional space in the gigantic planes currently being developed is more likely to be filled with passenger seating than with shops and lounges.
(C) The number of passengers flying the air-traffic system is expected to triple within 20 years.
(D) In 20 years, it will be impossible for airports to accommodate enough normal-sized planes to carry the number of passengers that are expected to be flying then.
(E) In 20 years, most airline passengers will be flying in gigantic passenger planes.

11. Scientist: To study the comparative effectiveness of two experimental medications for athlete's foot, a representative sample of people with athlete's foot were randomly assigned to one of two groups. One group received only medication M, and the other received only medication N. The only people whose athlete's foot was cured had been given medication M.

Reporter: This means, then, that if anyone in the study had athlete's foot that was not cured, that person did not receive medication M.

Which one of the following most accurately describes the reporter's error in reasoning?

(A) The reporter concludes from evidence showing only that M can cure athlete's foot that M always cures athlete's foot.
(B) The reporter illicitly draws a conclusion about the population as a whole on the basis of a study conducted only on a sample of the population.
(C) The reporter presumes, without providing justification, that medications M and N are available to people who have athlete's foot but did not participate in the study.
(D) The reporter fails to allow for the possibility that athlete's foot may be cured even if neither of the two medications studied is taken.
(E) The reporter presumes, without providing justification, that there is no sizeable subgroup of people whose athlete's foot will be cured only if they do not take medication M.

12. Paleontologist: Plesiosauromorphs were gigantic, long-necked marine reptiles that ruled the oceans during the age of the dinosaurs. Most experts believe that plesiosauromorphs lurked and quickly ambushed their prey. However, plesiosauromorphs probably hunted by chasing their prey over long distances. Plesiosauromorph fins were quite long and thin, like the wings of birds specialized for long-distance flight.

Which one of the following is an assumption on which the paleontologist's argument depends?

(A) Birds and reptiles share many physical features because they descend from common evolutionary ancestors.
(B) During the age of dinosaurs, plesiosauromorphs were the only marine reptiles that had long, thin fins.
(C) A gigantic marine animal would not be able to find enough food to meet the caloric requirements dictated by its body size if it did not hunt by chasing prey over long distances.
(D) Most marine animals that chase prey over long distances are specialized for long-distance swimming.
(E) The shape of a marine animal's fin affects the way the animal swims in the same way as the shape of a bird's wing affects the way the bird flies.

13. Buying elaborate screensavers—programs that put moving images on a computer monitor to prevent damage—can cost a company far more in employee time than it saves in electricity and monitor protection. Employees cannot resist spending time playing with screensavers that flash interesting graphics across their screens.

Which one of the following most closely conforms to the principle illustrated above?

(A) A school that chooses textbooks based on student preference may not get the most economical package.
(B) An energy-efficient insulation system may cost more up front but will ultimately save money over the life of the house.
(C) The time that it takes to have a pizza delivered may be longer than it takes to cook a complete dinner.
(D) A complicated hotel security system may cost more in customer goodwill than it saves in losses by theft.
(E) An electronic keyboard may be cheaper to buy than a piano but more expensive to repair.

GO ON TO THE NEXT PAGE.

14. Music professor: Because rap musicians can work alone in a recording studio, they need not accommodate supporting musicians' wishes. Further, learning to rap is not as formal a process as learning an instrument. Thus, rap is an extremely individualistic and nontraditional musical form.

Music critic: But rap appeals to tradition by using bits of older songs. Besides, the themes and styles of rap have developed into a tradition. And successful rap musicians do not perform purely idiosyncratically but conform their work to the preferences of the public.

The music critic's response to the music professor's argument

(A) challenges it by offering evidence against one of the stated premises on which its conclusion concerning rap music is based
(B) challenges its conclusion concerning rap music by offering certain additional observations that the music professor does not take into account in his argument
(C) challenges the grounds on which the music professor generalizes from the particular context of rap music to the broader context of musical tradition and individuality
(D) challenges it by offering an alternative explanation of phenomena that the music professor cites as evidence for his thesis about rap music
(E) challenges each of a group of claims about tradition and individuality in music that the music professor gives as evidence in his argument

15. Speaker: Like many contemporary critics, Smith argues that the true meaning of an author's statements can be understood only through insight into the author's social circumstances. But this same line of analysis can be applied to Smith's own words. Thus, if she is right we should be able, at least in part, to discern from Smith's social circumstances the "true meaning" of Smith's statements. This, in turn, suggests that Smith herself is not aware of the true meaning of her own words.

The speaker's main conclusion logically follows if which one of the following is assumed?

(A) Insight into the intended meaning of an author's work is not as important as insight into its true meaning.
(B) Smith lacks insight into her own social circumstances.
(C) There is just one meaning that Smith intends her work to have.
(D) Smith's theory about the relation of social circumstances to the understanding of meaning lacks insight.
(E) The intended meaning of an author's work is not always good evidence of its true meaning.

16. Tissue biopsies taken on patients who have undergone throat surgery show that those who snored frequently were significantly more likely to have serious abnormalities in their throat muscles than those who snored rarely or not at all. This shows that snoring can damage the throat of the snorer.

Which one of the following, if true, most strengthens the argument?

(A) The study relied on the subjects' self-reporting to determine whether or not they snored frequently.
(B) The patients' throat surgery was not undertaken to treat abnormalities in their throat muscles.
(C) All of the test subjects were of similar age and weight and in similar states of health.
(D) People who have undergone throat surgery are no more likely to snore than people who have not undergone throat surgery.
(E) The abnormalities in the throat muscles discovered in the study do not cause snoring.

GO ON TO THE NEXT PAGE.

17. One should never sacrifice one's health in order to acquire money, for without health, happiness is not obtainable.

The conclusion of the argument follows logically if which one of the following is assumed?

(A) Money should be acquired only if its acquisition will not make happiness unobtainable.
(B) In order to be happy one must have either money or health.
(C) Health should be valued only as a precondition for happiness.
(D) Being wealthy is, under certain conditions, conducive to unhappiness.
(E) Health is more conducive to happiness than wealth is.

18. Vanessa: All computer code must be written by a pair of programmers working at a single workstation. This is needed to prevent programmers from writing idiosyncratic code that can be understood only by the original programmer.

Jo: Most programming projects are kept afloat by the best programmers on the team, who are typically at least 100 times more productive than the worst. Since they generally work best when they work alone, the most productive programmers must be allowed to work by themselves.

Each of the following assignments of computer programmers is consistent both with the principle expressed by Vanessa and with the principle expressed by Jo EXCEPT:

(A) Olga and Kensuke are both programmers of roughly average productivity who feel that they are more productive when working alone. They have been assigned to work together at a single workstation.
(B) John is experienced but is not among the most productive programmers on the team. He has been assigned to mentor Tyrone, a new programmer who is not yet very productive. They are to work together at a single workstation.
(C) Although not among the most productive programmers on the team, Chris is more productive than Jennifer. They have been assigned to work together at a single workstation.
(D) Yolanda is the most productive programmer on the team. She has been assigned to work with Mike, who is also very productive. They are to work together at the same workstation.
(E) Kevin and Amy both have a reputation for writing idiosyncratic code; neither is unusually productive. They have been assigned to work together at the same workstation.

19. In West Calverton, most pet stores sell exotic birds, and most of those that sell exotic birds also sell tropical fish. However, any pet store there that sells tropical fish but not exotic birds does sell gerbils; and no independently owned pet stores in West Calverton sell gerbils.

If the statements above are true, which one of the following must be true?

(A) Most pet stores in West Calverton that are not independently owned do not sell exotic birds.
(B) No pet stores in West Calverton that sell tropical fish and exotic birds sell gerbils.
(C) Some pet stores in West Calverton that sell gerbils also sell exotic birds.
(D) No independently owned pet store in West Calverton sells tropical fish but not exotic birds.
(E) Any independently owned pet store in West Calverton that does not sell tropical fish sells exotic birds.

20. Astronomer: Earlier estimates of the distances of certain stars from Earth would mean that these stars are about 1 billion years older than the universe itself, an impossible scenario. My estimates of the distances indicate that these stars are much farther away than previously thought. And the farther away the stars are, the greater their intrinsic brightness must be, given their appearance to us on Earth. So the new estimates of these stars' distances from Earth help resolve the earlier conflict between the ages of these stars and the age of the universe.

Which one of the following, if true, most helps to explain why the astronomer's estimates of the stars' distances from Earth help resolve the earlier conflict between the ages of these stars and the age of the universe?

(A) The stars are the oldest objects yet discovered in the universe.
(B) The younger the universe is, the more bright stars it is likely to have.
(C) The brighter a star is, the younger it is.
(D) How bright celestial objects appear to be depends on how far away from the observer they are.
(E) New telescopes allow astronomers to see a greater number of distant stars.

GO ON TO THE NEXT PAGE.

21. Most large nurseries sell raspberry plants primarily to commercial raspberry growers and sell only plants that are guaranteed to be disease-free. However, the shipment of raspberry plants that Johnson received from Wally's Plants carried a virus that commonly afflicts raspberries.

Which one of the following is most strongly supported by the information above?

(A) If Johnson is a commercial raspberry grower and Wally's Plants is not a large nursery, then the shipment of raspberry plants that Johnson received was probably guaranteed to be disease-free.
(B) Johnson is probably not a commercial raspberry grower if the shipment of raspberry plants that Johnson received from Wally's Plants was not entirely as it was guaranteed to be.
(C) If Johnson is not a commercial raspberry grower, then Wally's Plants is probably not a large nursery.
(D) Wally's Plants is probably not a large, well-run nursery if it sells its raspberry plants primarily to commercial raspberry growers.
(E) If Wally's Plants is a large nursery, then the raspberry plants that Johnson received in the shipment were probably not entirely as they were guaranteed to be.

22. Drug company manager: Our newest product is just not selling. One way to save it would be a new marketing campaign. This would not guarantee success, but it is one chance to save the product, so we should try it.

Which one of the following, if true, most seriously weakens the manager's argument?

(A) The drug company has invested heavily in its newest product, and losses due to this product would be harmful to the company's profits.
(B) Many new products fail whether or not they are supported by marketing campaigns.
(C) The drug company should not undertake a new marketing campaign for its newest product if the campaign has no chance to succeed.
(D) Undertaking a new marketing campaign would endanger the drug company's overall position by necessitating cutbacks in existing marketing campaigns.
(E) Consumer demand for the drug company's other products has been strong in the time since the company's newest product was introduced.

23. Consumer advocate: TMD, a pesticide used on peaches, shows no effects on human health when it is ingested in the amount present in the per capita peach consumption in this country. But while 80 percent of the population eat no peaches, others, including small children, consume much more than the national average, and thus ingest disproportionately large amounts of TMD. So even though the use of TMD on peaches poses minimal risk to most of the population, it has not been shown to be an acceptable practice.

Which one of the following principles, if valid, most helps to justify the consumer advocate's argumentation?

(A) The possibility that more data about a pesticide's health effects might reveal previously unknown risks at low doses warrants caution in assessing that pesticide's overall risks.
(B) The consequences of using a pesticide are unlikely to be acceptable when a majority of the population is likely to ingest it.
(C) Use of a pesticide is acceptable only if it is used for its intended purpose and the pesticide has been shown not to harm any portion of the population.
(D) Society has a special obligation to protect small children from pesticides unless average doses received by the population are low and have not been shown to be harmful to children's health.
(E) Measures taken to protect the population from a harm sometimes turn out to be the cause of a more serious harm to certain segments of the population.

24. Legal commentator: The goal of a recently enacted law that bans smoking in workplaces is to protect employees from secondhand smoke. But the law is written in such a way that it cannot be interpreted as ever prohibiting people from smoking in their own homes.

The statements above, if true, provide a basis for rejecting which one of the following claims?

(A) The law will be interpreted in a way that is inconsistent with the intentions of the legislators who supported it.
(B) Supporters of the law believe that it will have a significant impact on the health of many workers.
(C) The law offers no protection from secondhand smoke for people outside of their workplaces.
(D) Most people believe that smokers have a fundamental right to smoke in their own homes.
(E) The law will protect domestic workers such as housecleaners from secondhand smoke in their workplaces.

25. University president: Our pool of applicants has been shrinking over the past few years. One possible explanation of this unwelcome phenomenon is that we charge too little for tuition and fees. Prospective students and their parents conclude that the quality of education they would receive at this institution is not as high as that offered by institutions with higher tuition. So, if we want to increase the size of our applicant pool, we need to raise our tuition and fees.

The university president's argument requires the assumption that

(A) the proposed explanation for the decline in applications applies in this case
(B) the quality of a university education is dependent on the amount of tuition charged by the university
(C) an increase in tuition and fees at the university would guarantee a larger applicant pool
(D) there is no additional explanation for the university's shrinking applicant pool
(E) the amount charged by the university for tuition has not increased in recent years

26. Editorial: It has been suggested that private, for-profit companies should be hired to supply clean drinking water to areas of the world where it is unavailable now. But water should not be supplied by private companies. After all, clean water is essential for human health, and the purpose of a private company is to produce profit, not to promote health.

Which one of the following principles, if valid, would most help to justify the reasoning in the editorial?

(A) A private company should not be allowed to supply a commodity that is essential to human health unless that commodity is also supplied by a government agency.
(B) If something is essential for human health and private companies are unwilling or unable to supply it, then it should be supplied by a government agency.
(C) Drinking water should never be supplied by an organization that is not able to consistently supply clean, safe water.
(D) The mere fact that something actually promotes human health is not sufficient to show that its purpose is to promote health.
(E) If something is necessary for human health, then it should be provided by an organization whose primary purpose is the promotion of health.

S T O P

IF YOU FINISH BEFORE TIME IS CALLED, YOU MAY CHECK YOUR WORK ON THIS SECTION ONLY.
DO NOT WORK ON ANY OTHER SECTION IN THE TEST.

SECTION III

Time—35 minutes

23 Questions

Directions: Each group of questions in this section is based on a set of conditions. In answering some of the questions, it may be useful to draw a rough diagram. Choose the response that most accurately and completely answers each question and blacken the corresponding space on your answer sheet.

Questions 1–6

A motel operator is scheduling appointments to start up services at a new motel. Appointments for six services—gas, landscaping, power, satellite, telephone, and water—will be scheduled, one appointment per day for the next six days. The schedule for the appointments is subject to the following conditions:

The water appointment must be scheduled for an earlier day than the landscaping appointment.

The power appointment must be scheduled for an earlier day than both the gas and satellite appointments.

The appointments scheduled for the second and third days cannot be for either gas, satellite, or telephone.

The telephone appointment cannot be scheduled for the sixth day.

1. Which one of the following is an acceptable schedule of appointments, listed in order from earliest to latest?
   (A) gas, water, power, telephone, landscaping, satellite
   (B) power, water, landscaping, gas, satellite, telephone
   (C) telephone, power, landscaping, gas, water, satellite
   (D) telephone, water, power, landscaping, gas, satellite
   (E) water, telephone, power, gas, satellite, landscaping

2. If neither the gas nor the satellite nor the telephone appointment is scheduled for the fourth day, which one of the following must be true?
   (A) The gas appointment is scheduled for the fifth day.
   (B) The power appointment is scheduled for the third day.
   (C) The satellite appointment is scheduled for the sixth day.
   (D) The telephone appointment is scheduled for the first day.
   (E) The water appointment is scheduled for the second day.

3. Which one of the following must be true?
   (A) The landscaping appointment is scheduled for an earlier day than the telephone appointment.
   (B) The power appointment is scheduled for an earlier day than the landscaping appointment.
   (C) The telephone appointment is scheduled for an earlier day than the gas appointment.
   (D) The telephone appointment is scheduled for an earlier day than the water appointment.
   (E) The water appointment is scheduled for an earlier day than the gas appointment.

4. Which one of the following CANNOT be the appointments scheduled for the fourth, fifth, and sixth days, listed in that order?
   (A) gas, satellite, landscaping
   (B) landscaping, satellite, gas
   (C) power, satellite, gas
   (D) telephone, satellite, gas
   (E) water, gas, landscaping

5. If neither the gas appointment nor the satellite appointment is scheduled for the sixth day, which one of the following must be true?
   (A) The gas appointment is scheduled for the fifth day.
   (B) The landscaping appointment is scheduled for the sixth day.
   (C) The power appointment is scheduled for the third day.
   (D) The telephone appointment is scheduled for the fourth day.
   (E) The water appointment is scheduled for the second day.

6. Which one of the following, if substituted for the condition that the telephone appointment cannot be scheduled for the sixth day, would have the same effect in determining the order of the appointments?
   (A) The telephone appointment must be scheduled for an earlier day than the gas appointment or the satellite appointment, or both.
   (B) The telephone appointment must be scheduled for the day immediately before either the gas appointment or the satellite appointment.
   (C) The telephone appointment must be scheduled for an earlier day than the landscaping appointment.
   (D) If the telephone appointment is not scheduled for the first day, it must be scheduled for the day immediately before the gas appointment.
   (E) Either the gas appointment or the satellite appointment must be scheduled for the sixth day.

GO ON TO THE NEXT PAGE.

Questions 7–13

An artisan has been hired to create three stained glass windows. The artisan will use exactly five colors of glass: green, orange, purple, rose, and yellow. Each color of glass will be used at least once, and each window will contain at least two different colors of glass. The windows must also conform to the following conditions:

Exactly one of the windows contains both green glass and purple glass.
Exactly two of the windows contain rose glass.
If a window contains yellow glass, then that window contains neither green glass nor orange glass.
If a window does not contain purple glass, then that window contains orange glass.

7. Which one of the following could be the color combinations of the glass in the three windows?

(A) window 1: green, purple, rose, and orange
window 2: rose and yellow
window 3: green and orange
(B) window 1: green, purple, and rose
window 2: green, rose, and orange
window 3: purple and yellow
(C) window 1: green, purple, and rose
window 2: green, purple, and orange
window 3: purple, rose, and yellow
(D) window 1: green, purple, and orange
window 2: rose, orange, and yellow
window 3: purple and rose
(E) window 1: green, purple, and orange
window 2: purple, rose, and yellow
window 3: purple and orange

8. Which one of the following CANNOT be the complete color combination of the glass in one of the windows?

(A) green and orange
(B) green and purple
(C) green and rose
(D) purple and orange
(E) rose and orange

9. If two of the windows are made with exactly two colors of glass each, then the complete color combination of the glass in one of those windows could be

(A) rose and yellow
(B) orange and rose
(C) orange and purple
(D) green and rose
(E) green and orange

10. If the complete color combination of the glass in one of the windows is purple, rose, and orange, then the complete color combination of the glass in one of the other windows could be

(A) green, orange, and rose
(B) green, orange, and purple
(C) orange and rose
(D) orange and purple
(E) green and orange

11. If orange glass is used in more of the windows than green glass, then the complete color combination of the glass in one of the windows could be

(A) orange and purple
(B) green, purple, and rose
(C) green and purple
(D) green and orange
(E) green, orange, and rose

12. Which one of the following could be used in all three windows?

(A) green glass
(B) orange glass
(C) purple glass
(D) rose glass
(E) yellow glass

13. If none of the windows contains both rose glass and orange glass, then the complete color combination of the glass in one of the windows must be

(A) green and purple
(B) green, purple, and orange
(C) green and orange
(D) purple and orange
(E) purple, rose, and yellow

GO ON TO THE NEXT PAGE.

Questions 14–18

A conference on management skills consists of exactly five talks, which are held successively in the following order: Feedback, Goal Sharing, Handling People, Information Overload, and Leadership. Exactly four employees of SoftCorp—Quigley, Rivera, Spivey, and Tran—each attend exactly two of the talks. No talk is attended by more than two of the employees, who attend the talks in accordance with the following conditions:

Quigley attends neither Feedback nor Handling People.
Rivera attends neither Goal Sharing nor Handling People.
Spivey does not attend either of the talks that Tran attends.
Quigley attends the first talk Tran attends.
Spivey attends the first talk Rivera attends.

14. Which one of the following could be a complete and accurate matching of the talks to the SoftCorp employees who attend them?

(A) Feedback: Rivera, Spivey
Goal Sharing: Quigley, Tran
Handling People: None
Information Overload: Quigley, Rivera
Leadership: Spivey, Tran

(B) Feedback: Rivera, Spivey
Goal Sharing: Quigley, Tran
Handling People: Rivera, Tran
Information Overload: Quigley
Leadership: Spivey

(C) Feedback: Rivera, Spivey
Goal Sharing: Quigley, Tran
Handling People: Tran
Information Overload: Quigley, Rivera
Leadership: Spivey

(D) Feedback: Rivera, Spivey
Goal Sharing: Tran
Handling People: Tran
Information Overload: Quigley, Rivera
Leadership: Quigley, Spivey

(E) Feedback: Spivey
Goal Sharing: Quigley, Tran
Handling People: Spivey
Information Overload: Quigley, Rivera
Leadership: Rivera, Tran

15. If none of the SoftCorp employees attends Handling People, then which one of the following must be true?

(A) Rivera attends Feedback.
(B) Rivera attends Leadership.
(C) Spivey attends Information Overload.
(D) Tran attends Goal Sharing.
(E) Tran attends Information Overload.

16. Which one of the following is a complete and accurate list of the talks any one of which Rivera and Spivey could attend together?

(A) Feedback, Information Overload, Leadership
(B) Feedback, Goal Sharing, Information Overload
(C) Information Overload, Leadership
(D) Feedback, Leadership
(E) Feedback, Information Overload

17. If Quigley is the only SoftCorp employee to attend Leadership, then which one of the following could be false?

(A) Rivera attends Feedback.
(B) Rivera attends Information Overload.
(C) Spivey attends Feedback.
(D) Spivey attends Handling People.
(E) Tran attends Goal Sharing.

18. If Rivera is the only SoftCorp employee to attend Information Overload, then which one of the following could be false?

(A) Quigley attends Leadership.
(B) Rivera attends Feedback.
(C) Spivey attends Feedback.
(D) Tran attends Goal Sharing.
(E) Tran attends Handling People.

GO ON TO THE NEXT PAGE.

Questions 19–23

Exactly six witnesses will testify in a trial: Mangione, Ramirez, Sanderson, Tannenbaum, Ujemori, and Wong. The witnesses will testify one by one, and each only once. The order in which the witnesses testify is subject to the following constraints:

Sanderson must testify immediately before either Tannenbaum or Ujemori.

Ujemori must testify earlier than both Ramirez and Wong.

Either Tannenbaum or Wong must testify immediately before Mangione.

19. Which one of the following lists the witnesses in an order in which they could testify?

(A) Ramirez, Sanderson, Tannenbaum, Mangione, Ujemori, Wong
(B) Sanderson, Tannenbaum, Ujemori, Ramirez, Wong, Mangione
(C) Sanderson, Ujemori, Tannenbaum, Wong, Ramirez, Mangione
(D) Tannenbaum, Mangione, Ujemori, Sanderson, Ramirez, Wong
(E) Wong, Ramirez, Sanderson, Tannenbaum, Mangione, Ujemori

20. If Tannenbaum testifies first, then which one of the following could be true?

(A) Ramirez testifies second.
(B) Wong testifies third.
(C) Sanderson testifies fourth.
(D) Ujemori testifies fifth.
(E) Mangione testifies sixth.

21. If Sanderson testifies fifth, then Ujemori must testify

(A) first
(B) second
(C) third
(D) fourth
(E) sixth

22. Which one of the following pairs of witnesses CANNOT testify third and fourth, respectively?

(A) Mangione, Tannenbaum
(B) Ramirez, Sanderson
(C) Sanderson, Ujemori
(D) Tannenbaum, Ramirez
(E) Ujemori, Wong

23. Which one of the following pairs of witnesses CANNOT testify first and second, respectively?

(A) Sanderson, Ujemori
(B) Tannenbaum, Mangione
(C) Tannenbaum, Sanderson
(D) Ujemori, Tannenbaum
(E) Ujemori, Wong

S T O P

IF YOU FINISH BEFORE TIME IS CALLED, YOU MAY CHECK YOUR WORK ON THIS SECTION ONLY. DO NOT WORK ON ANY OTHER SECTION IN THE TEST.

SECTION IV

Time—35 minutes

26 Questions

Directions: The questions in this section are based on the reasoning contained in brief statements or passages. For some questions, more than one of the choices could conceivably answer the question. However, you are to choose the best answer; that is, the response that most accurately and completely answers the question. You should not make assumptions that are by commonsense standards implausible, superfluous, or incompatible with the passage. After you have chosen the best answer, blacken the corresponding space on your answer sheet.

1. Marine biologist: Scientists have long wondered why the fish that live around coral reefs exhibit such brilliant colors. One suggestion is that coral reefs are colorful and, therefore, that colorful fish are camouflaged by them. Many animal species, after all, use camouflage to avoid predators. However, as regards the populations around reefs, this suggestion is mistaken. A reef stripped of its fish is quite monochromatic. Most corals, it turns out, are relatively dull browns and greens.

Which one of the following most accurately expresses the main conclusion drawn in the marine biologist's argument?

(A) One hypothesis about why fish living near coral reefs exhibit such bright colors is that the fish are camouflaged by their bright colors.
(B) The fact that many species use camouflage to avoid predators is one reason to believe that brightly colored fish living near reefs do too.
(C) The suggestion that the fish living around coral reefs exhibit bright colors because they are camouflaged by the reefs is mistaken.
(D) A reef stripped of its fish is relatively monochromatic.
(E) It turns out that the corals in a coral reef are mostly dull hues of brown and green.

2. To discover what percentage of teenagers believe in telekinesis—the psychic ability to move objects without physically touching them—a recent survey asked a representative sample of teenagers whether they agreed with the following statement: "A person's thoughts can influence the movement of physical objects." But because this statement is particularly ambiguous and is amenable to a naturalistic, uncontroversial interpretation, the survey's responses are also ambiguous.

The reasoning above conforms most closely to which one of the following general propositions?

(A) Uncontroversial statements are useless in surveys.
(B) Every statement is amenable to several interpretations.
(C) Responses to surveys are always unambiguous if the survey's questions are well phrased.
(D) Responses people give to poorly phrased questions are likely to be ambiguous.
(E) Statements about psychic phenomena can always be given naturalistic interpretations.

GO ON TO THE NEXT PAGE.

3. A recent study of perfect pitch—the ability to identify the pitch of an isolated musical note—found that a high percentage of people who have perfect pitch are related to someone else who has it. Among those without perfect pitch, the percentage was much lower. This shows that having perfect pitch is a consequence of genetic factors.

Which one of the following, if true, most strengthens the argument?

(A) People who have relatives with perfect pitch generally receive no more musical training than do others.
(B) All of the researchers conducting the study had perfect pitch.
(C) People with perfect pitch are more likely than others to choose music as a career.
(D) People with perfect pitch are more likely than others to make sure that their children receive musical training.
(E) People who have some training in music are more likely to have perfect pitch than those with no such training.

4. Paleontologists recently excavated two corresponding sets of dinosaur tracks, one left by a large grazing dinosaur and the other by a smaller predatory dinosaur. The two sets of tracks make abrupt turns repeatedly in tandem, suggesting that the predator was following the grazing dinosaur and had matched its stride. Modern predatory mammals, such as lions, usually match the stride of prey they are chasing immediately before they strike those prey. This suggests that the predatory dinosaur was chasing the grazing dinosaur and attacked immediately afterwards.

Which one of the following most accurately describes the role played in the argument by the statement that the predatory dinosaur was following the grazing dinosaur and had matched its stride?

(A) It helps establish the scientific importance of the argument's overall conclusion, but is not offered as evidence for that conclusion.
(B) It is a hypothesis that is rejected in favor of the hypothesis stated in the argument's overall conclusion.
(C) It provides the basis for an analogy used in support of the argument's overall conclusion.
(D) It is presented to counteract a possible objection to the argument's overall conclusion.
(E) It is the overall conclusion of the argument.

5. Researchers announced recently that over the past 25 years the incidence of skin cancer caused by exposure to harmful rays from the sun has continued to grow in spite of the increasingly widespread use of sunscreens. This shows that using sunscreen is unlikely to reduce a person's risk of developing such skin cancer.

Which one of the following, if true, most weakens the argument?

(A) Most people who purchase a sunscreen product will not purchase the most expensive brand available.
(B) Skin cancer generally develops among the very old as a result of sunburns experienced when very young.
(C) The development of sunscreens by pharmaceutical companies was based upon research conducted by dermatologists.
(D) People who know that they are especially susceptible to skin cancer are generally disinclined to spend a large amount of time in the sun.
(E) Those who use sunscreens most regularly are people who believe themselves to be most susceptible to skin cancer.

6. University administrator: Any proposal for a new department will not be funded if there are fewer than 50 people per year available for hire in that field and the proposed department would duplicate more than 25 percent of the material covered in one of our existing departments. The proposed Area Studies Department will duplicate more than 25 percent of the material covered in our existing Anthropology Department. However, we will fund the new department.

Which one of the following statements follows logically from the university administrator's statements?

(A) The field of Area Studies has at least 50 people per year available for hire.
(B) The proposed Area Studies Department would not duplicate more than 25 percent of the material covered in any existing department other than Anthropology.
(C) If the proposed Area Studies Department did not duplicate more than 25 percent of the material covered in Anthropology, then the new department would not be funded.
(D) The Anthropology Department duplicates more than 25 percent of the material covered in the proposed Area Studies Department.
(E) The field of Area Studies has fewer than 50 people per year available for hire.

7. Researcher: Over the course of three decades, we kept records of the average beak size of two populations of the same species of bird, one wild population, the other captive. During this period, the average beak size of the captive birds did not change, while the average beak size of the wild birds decreased significantly.

Which one of the following, if true, most helps to explain the researcher's findings?

(A) The small-beaked wild birds were easier to capture and measure than the large-beaked wild birds.
(B) The large-beaked wild birds were easier to capture and measure than the small-beaked wild birds.
(C) Changes in the wild birds' food supply during the study period favored the survival of small-beaked birds over large-beaked birds.
(D) The average body size of the captive birds remained the same over the study period.
(E) The researcher measured the beaks of some of the wild birds on more than one occasion.

8. Storytelling appears to be a universal aspect of both past and present cultures. Comparative study of traditional narratives from widely separated epochs and diverse cultures reveals common themes such as creation, tribal origin, mystical beings and quasi-historical figures, and common story types such as fables and tales in which animals assume human personalities.

The evidence cited above from the study of traditional narratives most supports which one of the following statements?

(A) Storytellers routinely borrow themes from other cultures.
(B) Storytellers have long understood that the narrative is a universal aspect of human culture.
(C) Certain human concerns and interests arise in all of the world's cultures.
(D) Storytelling was no less important in ancient cultures than it is in modern cultures.
(E) The best way to understand a culture is to understand what motivates its storytellers.

9. If a mother's first child is born before its due date, it is likely that her second child will be also. Jackie's second child was not born before its due date, so it is likely that Jackie's first child was not born before its due date either.

The questionable reasoning in the argument above is most similar in its reasoning to which one of the following?

(A) Artisans who finish their projects before the craft fair will probably go to the craft fair. Ben will not finish his project before the fair. So he probably will not go to the craft fair.
(B) All responsible pet owners are likely to be good with children. So anyone who is good with children is probably a responsible pet owner.
(C) If a movie is a box-office hit, it is likely that its sequel will be also. *Hawkman II*, the sequel to *Hawkman I*, was not a box-office hit, so *Hawkman I* was probably not a box-office hit.
(D) If a business is likely to fail, people will not invest in it. Pallid Starr is likely to fail, therefore no one is likely to invest in it.
(E) Tai will go sailing only if the weather is nice. The weather will be nice, thus Tai will probably go sailing.

10. Science journalist: Europa, a moon of Jupiter, is covered with ice. Data recently transmitted by a spacecraft strongly suggest that there are oceans of liquid water deep under the ice. Life as we know it could evolve only in the presence of liquid water. Hence, it is likely that at least primitive life has evolved on Europa.

The science journalist's argument is most vulnerable to criticism on the grounds that it

(A) takes for granted that if a condition would be necessary for the evolution of life as we know it, then such life could not have evolved anywhere that this condition does not hold
(B) fails to address adequately the possibility that there are conditions necessary for the evolution of life in addition to the presence of liquid water
(C) takes for granted that life is likely to be present on Europa if, but only if, life evolved on Europa
(D) overlooks the possibility that there could be unfamiliar forms of life that have evolved without the presence of liquid water
(E) takes for granted that no conditions on Europa other than the supposed presence of liquid water could have accounted for the data transmitted by the spacecraft

GO ON TO THE NEXT PAGE.

11. A bacterial species will inevitably develop greater resistance within a few years to any antibiotics used against it, unless those antibiotics eliminate that species completely. However, no single antibiotic now on the market is powerful enough to eliminate bacterial species X completely.

Which one of the following is most strongly supported by the statements above?

(A) It is unlikely that any antibiotic can be developed that will completely eliminate bacterial species X.
(B) If any antibiotic now on the market is used against bacterial species X, that species will develop greater resistance to it within a few years.
(C) The only way of completely eliminating bacterial species X is by a combination of two or more antibiotics now on the market.
(D) Bacterial species X will inevitably become more virulent in the course of time.
(E) Bacterial species X is more resistant to at least some antibiotics that have been used against it than it was before those antibiotics were used against it.

12. Political scientist: It is not uncommon for a politician to criticize his or her political opponents by claiming that their exposition of their ideas is muddled and incomprehensible. Such criticism, however, is never sincere. Political agendas promoted in a manner that cannot be understood by large numbers of people will not be realized for, as every politician knows, political mobilization requires commonality of purpose.

Which one of the following is the most accurate rendering of the political scientist's main conclusion?

(A) People who promote political agendas in an incomprehensible manner should be regarded as insincere.
(B) Sincere critics of the proponents of a political agenda should not focus their criticisms on the manner in which that agenda is promoted.
(C) The ineffectiveness of a confusingly promoted political agenda is a reason for refraining from, rather than engaging in, criticism of those who are promoting it.
(D) A politician criticizing his or her political opponents for presenting their political agendas in an incomprehensible manner is being insincere.
(E) To mobilize large numbers of people in support of a political agenda, that political agenda must be presented in such a way that it cannot be misunderstood.

13. Many symptoms of mental illnesses are affected by organic factors such as a deficiency in a compound in the brain. What is surprising, however, is the tremendous variation among different countries in the incidence of these symptoms in people with mental illnesses. This variation establishes that the organic factors that affect symptoms of mental illnesses are not distributed evenly around the globe.

The reasoning above is most vulnerable to criticism on the grounds that it

(A) does not say how many different mental illnesses are being discussed
(B) neglects the possibility that nutritional factors that contribute to deficiencies in compounds in the brain vary from culture to culture
(C) fails to consider the possibility that cultural factors significantly affect how mental illnesses manifest themselves in symptoms
(D) presumes, without providing justification, that any change in brain chemistry manifests itself as a change in mental condition
(E) presumes, without providing justification, that mental phenomena are only manifestations of physical phenomena

14. Politician: It has been proposed that the national parks in our country be managed by private companies rather than the government. A similar privatization of the telecommunications industry has benefited consumers by allowing competition among a variety of telephone companies to improve service and force down prices. Therefore, the privatization of the national parks would probably benefit park visitors as well.

Which one of the following, if true, most weakens the politician's argument?

(A) It would not be politically expedient to privatize the national parks even if doing so would, in the long run, improve service and reduce the fees charged to visitors.
(B) The privatization of the telecommunications industry has been problematic in that it has led to significantly increased unemployment and economic instability in that industry.
(C) The vast majority of people visiting the national parks are unaware of proposals to privatize the management of those parks.
(D) Privatizing the national parks would benefit a much smaller number of consumers to a much smaller extent than did the privatization of the telecommunications industry.
(E) The privatization of the national parks would produce much less competition between different companies than did the privatization of the telecommunications industry.

GO ON TO THE NEXT PAGE.

15. Jewel collectors, fearing that their eyes will be deceived by a counterfeit, will not buy a diamond unless the dealer guarantees that it is genuine. But why should a counterfeit give any less aesthetic pleasure when the naked eye cannot distinguish it from a real diamond? Both jewels should be deemed of equal value.

Which one of the following principles, if valid, most helps to justify the reasoning in the argument above?

(A) Jewel collectors should collect only those jewels that provide the most aesthetic pleasure.
(B) The value of a jewel should depend at least partly on market demand.
(C) It should not be assumed that everyone who likes diamonds receives the same degree of aesthetic pleasure from them.
(D) The value of a jewel should derive solely from the aesthetic pleasure it provides.
(E) Jewel collectors should not buy counterfeit jewels unless they are unable to distinguish counterfeit jewels from real ones.

16. All etching tools are either pin-tipped or bladed. While some bladed etching tools are used for engraving, some are not. On the other hand, all pin-tipped etching tools are used for engraving. Thus, there are more etching tools that are used for engraving than there are etching tools that are not used for engraving.

The conclusion of the argument follows logically if which one of the following is assumed?

(A) All tools used for engraving are etching tools as well.
(B) There are as many pin-tipped etching tools as there are bladed etching tools.
(C) No etching tool is both pin-tipped and bladed.
(D) The majority of bladed etching tools are not used for engraving.
(E) All etching tools that are not used for engraving are bladed.

17. A 24-year study of 1,500 adults showed that those subjects with a high intake of foods rich in beta-carotene were much less likely to die from cancer or heart disease than were those with a low intake of such foods. On the other hand, taking beta-carotene supplements for 12 years had no positive or negative effect on the health of subjects in a separate study of 20,000 adults.

Each of the following, if true, would help to resolve the apparent discrepancy between the results of the two studies EXCEPT:

(A) The human body processes the beta-carotene present in foods much more efficiently than it does beta-carotene supplements.
(B) Beta-carotene must be taken for longer than 12 years to have any cancer-preventive effects.
(C) Foods rich in beta-carotene also tend to contain other nutrients that assist in the human body's absorption of beta-carotene.
(D) In the 12-year study, half of the subjects were given beta-carotene supplements and half were given a placebo.
(E) In the 24-year study, the percentage of the subjects who had a high intake of beta-carotene-rich foods who smoked cigarettes was much smaller than the percentage of the subjects with a low intake of beta-carotene-rich foods who smoked.

GO ON TO THE NEXT PAGE.

18. If there are sentient beings on planets outside our solar system, we will not be able to determine this anytime in the near future unless some of these beings are at least as intelligent as humans. We will not be able to send spacecraft to planets outside our solar system anytime in the near future, and any sentient being on another planet capable of communicating with us anytime in the near future would have to be at least as intelligent as we are.

The argument's conclusion can be properly inferred if which one of the following is assumed?

(A) There are no sentient beings on planets in our solar system other than those on Earth.
(B) Any beings that are at least as intelligent as humans would want to communicate with sentient beings outside their own solar systems.
(C) If there is a sentient being on another planet that is as intelligent as humans are, we will not be able to send spacecraft to the being's planet anytime in the near future.
(D) If a sentient being on another planet cannot communicate with us, then the only way to detect its existence is by sending a spacecraft to its planet.
(E) Any sentient beings on planets outside our solar system that are at least as intelligent as humans would be capable of communicating with us.

19. Doctor: Medical researchers recently examined a large group of individuals who said that they had never experienced serious back pain. Half of the members of the group turned out to have bulging or slipped disks in their spines, conditions often blamed for serious back pain. Since these individuals with bulging or slipped disks evidently felt no pain from them, these conditions could not lead to serious back pain in people who do experience such pain.

The reasoning in the doctor's argument is most vulnerable to the criticism that it fails to consider which one of the following possibilities?

(A) A factor that need not be present in order for a certain effect to arise may nonetheless be sufficient to produce that effect.
(B) A factor that is not in itself sufficient to produce a certain effect may nonetheless be partly responsible for that effect in some instances.
(C) An effect that occurs in the absence of a particular phenomenon might not occur when that phenomenon is present.
(D) A characteristic found in half of a given sample of the population might not occur in half of the entire population.
(E) A factor that does not bring about a certain effect may nonetheless be more likely to be present when the effect occurs than when the effect does not occur.

20. Many workers who handled substance T in factories became seriously ill years later. We now know T caused at least some of their illnesses. Earlier ignorance of this connection does not absolve T's manufacturer of all responsibility. For had it investigated the safety of T before allowing workers to be exposed to it, many of their illnesses would have been prevented.

Which one of the following principles most helps to justify the conclusion above?

(A) Employees who are harmed by substances they handle on the job should be compensated for medical costs they incur as a result.
(B) Manufacturers should be held responsible only for the preventable consequences of their actions.
(C) Manufacturers have an obligation to inform workers of health risks of which they are aware.
(D) Whether or not an action's consequences were preventable is irrelevant to whether a manufacturer should be held responsible for those consequences.
(E) Manufacturers should be held responsible for the consequences of any of their actions that harm innocent people if those consequences were preventable.

21. It is virtually certain that the government contract for building the new highway will be awarded to either Phoenix Contracting or Cartwright Company. I have just learned that the government has decided not to award the contract to Cartwright Company. It is therefore almost inevitable that Phoenix Contracting will be awarded the contract.

The argument proceeds by

(A) concluding that it is extremely likely that an event will occur by ruling out the only probable alternative
(B) inferring, from a claim that one of two possible events will occur, that the other event will not occur
(C) refuting a claim that a particular event is inevitable by establishing the possibility of an alternative event
(D) predicting a future event on the basis of an established pattern of past events
(E) inferring a claim about the probability of a particular event from a general statistical statement

GO ON TO THE NEXT PAGE.

22. Researchers have found that children in large families—particularly the younger siblings—generally have fewer allergies than children in small families do. They hypothesize that exposure to germs during infancy makes people less likely to develop allergies.

Which one of the following, if true, most supports the researchers' hypothesis?

(A) In countries where the average number of children per family has decreased over the last century, the incidence of allergies has increased.
(B) Children in small families generally eat more kinds of very allergenic foods than children in large families do.
(C) Some allergies are life threatening, while many diseases caused by germs produce only temporary discomfort.
(D) Children whose parents have allergies have an above-average likelihood of developing allergies themselves.
(E) Children from small families who entered day care before age one were less likely to develop allergies than children from small families who entered day care later.

23. Film preservation requires transferring old movies from their original material—unstable, deteriorating nitrate film—to stable acetate film. But this is a time-consuming, expensive process, and there is no way to transfer all currently deteriorating nitrate films to acetate before they disintegrate. So some films from the earliest years of Hollywood will not be preserved.

Which one of the following is an assumption on which the argument depends?

(A) No new technology for transferring old movies from nitrate film to acetate film will ever be developed.
(B) Transferring films from nitrate to acetate is not the least expensive way of preserving them.
(C) Not many films from the earliest years of Hollywood have already been transferred to acetate.
(D) Some films from the earliest years of Hollywood currently exist solely in their original material.
(E) The least popular films from the earliest years of Hollywood are the ones most likely to be lost.

24. In a recent study of arthritis, researchers tried but failed to find any correlation between pain intensity and any of those features of the weather—humidity, temperature swings, barometric pressure—usually cited by arthritis sufferers as the cause of their increased pain. Those arthritis sufferers in the study who were convinced of the existence of such a correlation gave widely varying accounts of the time delay between the occurrence of what they believed to be the relevant feature of the weather and the increased intensity of the pain. Thus, this study _______.

Of the following, which one most logically completes the argument?

(A) indicates that the weather affects some arthritis sufferers more quickly than it does other arthritis sufferers
(B) indicates that arthritis sufferers' beliefs about the causes of the pain they feel may affect their assessment of the intensity of that pain
(C) suggests that arthritis sufferers are imagining the correlation they assert to exist
(D) suggests that some people are more susceptible to weather-induced arthritis pain than are others
(E) suggests that the scientific investigation of possible links between weather and arthritis pain is impossible

GO ON TO THE NEXT PAGE.

25. Cities with healthy economies typically have plenty of job openings. Cities with high-technology businesses also tend to have healthy economies, so those in search of jobs should move to a city with high-technology businesses.

The reasoning in which one of the following is most similar to the reasoning in the argument above?

(A) Older antiques are usually the most valuable. Antique dealers generally authenticate the age of the antiques they sell, so those collectors who want the most valuable antiques should purchase their antiques from antique dealers.
(B) Antique dealers who authenticate the age of the antiques they sell typically have plenty of antiques for sale. Since the most valuable antiques are those that have had their ages authenticated, antique collectors in search of valuable antiques should purchase their antiques from antique dealers.
(C) Antiques that have had their ages authenticated tend to be valuable. Since antique dealers generally carry antiques that have had their ages authenticated, those collectors who want antiques that are valuable should purchase their antiques from antique dealers.
(D) Many antique collectors know that antique dealers can authenticate the age of the antiques they sell. Since antiques that have had their ages authenticated are always the most valuable, most antique collectors who want antiques that are valuable tend to purchase their antiques from antique dealers.
(E) Many antiques increase in value once they have had their ages authenticated by antique dealers. Since antique dealers tend to have plenty of valuable antiques, antique collectors who prefer to purchase the most valuable antiques should purchase antiques from antique dealers.

26. Sociologist: A recent study of 5,000 individuals found, on the basis of a physical exam, that more than 25 percent of people older than 65 were malnourished, though only 12 percent of the people in this age group fell below government poverty standards. In contrast, a greater percentage of the people 65 or younger fell below poverty standards than were found in the study to be malnourished.

Each of the following, if true, helps to explain the findings of the study cited by the sociologist EXCEPT:

(A) Doctors are less likely to correctly diagnose and treat malnutrition in their patients who are over 65 than in their younger patients.
(B) People over 65 are more likely to take medications that increase their need for certain nutrients than are people 65 or younger.
(C) People over 65 are more likely to suffer from loss of appetite due to medication than are people 65 or younger.
(D) People 65 or younger are no more likely to fall below government poverty standards than are people over 65.
(E) People 65 or younger are less likely to have medical conditions that interfere with their digestion than are people over 65.

S T O P

IF YOU FINISH BEFORE TIME IS CALLED, YOU MAY CHECK YOUR WORK ON THIS SECTION ONLY. DO NOT WORK ON ANY OTHER SECTION IN THE TEST.

Acknowledgment is made to the following sources from which material has been adapted for use in this test booklet:

Richard H. Brodhead, *Cultures of Letters: Scenes of Reading and Writing in Nineteenth-Century America.* ©1993 by the University of Chicago.

Jonathan Glater and Alan Finder, "In Tuition Game, Popularity Rises with Price." ©December 12, 2006 by The New York Times.

Josie Glausiusz, "Seismologists Go Green." ©1999 by the Walt Disney Company.

Michael Pietrusewsky and Michele Toomay Douglas, "Intensification of Agriculture at Ban Chiang: Is There Evidence from the Skeletons?" ©2001 by University of Hawaii Press.

Karen Gust Schollmeyer and Christy G. Turner II, "Dental Caries, Prehistoric Diet, and the Pithouse-to-Pueblo Transition in Southwestern Colorado." ©2004 by Society for American Archaeology.

LSAT Writing Sample Topic

Directions: The scenario presented below describes two choices, either one of which can be supported on the basis of the information given. Your essay should consider both choices and argue for one over the other, based on the two specified criteria and the facts provided. There is no "right" or "wrong" choice: a reasonable argument can be made for either.

The Wangs must arrange summer child care for their ten-year-old child. They have found two summer-long programs that are affordable and in which friends of their child would also be participating. Using the facts below, write an essay in which you argue for one program over the other based on the following two considerations:

- The Wangs want their child to enjoy activities that would add variety to the regular school experience.
- Transportation to the program must be easy for the Wangs to accommodate to their work situations.

City Summer is located at a college near Mrs. Wang's job but a considerable distance from Mr. Wang's. It offers early arrival and late pick-up times for parent convenience. Mrs. Wang has somewhat flexible work hours, but must travel overnight occasionally. City Summer offers classes in the visual arts, dance, drama, music, swimming, and gymnastics, as well as gym activities like basketball and volleyball. In addition, there are organized field trips to museums, plays, and historical sites. The program concludes with a presentation of student work from the classes.

Round Lake Camp is located 30 minutes outside the city. Bus transportation is provided to and from several city schools, one of which is next door to Mr. Wang's job. Pick-up and drop-off are at set times in the early morning and late afternoon. Mr. Wang has flexibility in his work starting time but often must work late. The camp has classes in swimming, sailing, archery, nature study, crafts, and outdoor skills. It also has regular free periods when campers can choose among outdoor activities or just explore the woods. At the end of the summer the campers have an overnight camping trip at a nearby state wilderness area.

Scratch Paper

Do not write your essay in this space.

Directions:

1. Use the Answer Key on the next page to check your answers.
2. Use the Scoring Worksheet below to compute your raw score.
3. Use the Score Conversion Chart to convert your raw score into the 120–180 scale.

Scoring Worksheet

1. Enter the number of questions you answered correctly in each section

	Number Correct
SECTION I.	_______
SECTION II	_______
SECTION III	_______
SECTION IV	_______

2. Enter the sum here: _______
This is your Raw Score.

Conversion Chart

For Converting Raw Score to the 120–180 LSAT Scaled Score
LSAT PrepTest 62

Reported Score	Raw Score Lowest	Raw Score Highest
180	99	102
179	98	98
178	97	97
177	96	96
176	95	95
175	94	94
174	93	93
173	91	92
172	90	90
171	89	89
170	88	88
169	86	87
168	85	85
167	83	84
166	82	82
165	80	81
164	79	79
163	77	78
162	75	76
161	74	74
160	72	73
159	70	71
158	69	69
157	67	68
156	65	66
155	63	64
154	62	62
153	60	61
152	58	59
151	57	57
150	55	56
149	53	54
148	52	52
147	50	51
146	48	49
145	47	47
144	45	46
143	43	44
142	42	42
141	40	41
140	39	39
139	37	38
138	36	36
137	35	35
136	33	34
135	32	32
134	30	31
133	29	29
132	28	28
131	27	27
130	25	26
129	24	24
128	23	23
127	22	22
126	21	21
125	20	20
124	18	19
123	17	17
122	16	16
121	15	15
120	0	14

SECTION I

1.	A	8.	D	15.	A	22.	D
2.	C	9.	A	16.	B	23.	C
3.	E	10.	E	17.	A	24.	B
4.	B	11.	E	18.	B	25.	E
5.	B	12.	D	19.	D	26.	E
6.	E	13.	C	20.	C	27.	C
7.	D	14.	B	21.	D		

SECTION II

1.	D	8.	A	15.	B	22.	D
2.	E	9.	C	16.	E	23.	C
3.	B	10.	B	17.	A	24.	E
4.	E	11.	A	18.	D	25.	A
5.	C	12.	E	19.	D	26.	E
6.	A	13.	D	20.	C		
7.	C	14.	B	21.	E		

SECTION III

1.	D	8.	C	15.	A	22.	A
2.	D	9.	B	16.	A	23.	D
3.	E	10.	B	17.	D		
4.	E	11.	A	18.	E		
5.	B	12.	C	19.	B		
6.	A	13.	E	20.	E		
7.	B	14.	C	21.	A		

SECTION IV

1.	C	8.	C	15.	D	22.	E
2.	D	9.	C	16.	B	23.	D
3.	A	10.	B	17.	D	24.	C
4.	C	11.	B	18.	D	25.	C
5.	B	12.	D	19.	B	26.	D
6.	A	13.	C	20.	E		
7.	C	14.	E	21.	A		

Experimental Section Answer Key
June 1999, PrepTest 26, Section 3

1.	B	8.	E	15.	C	22.	D
2.	B	9.	C	16.	D	23.	B
3.	D	10.	D	17.	D	24.	E
4.	C	11.	A	18.	A	25.	B
5.	C	12.	D	19.	D		
6.	E	13.	E	20.	B		
7.	E	14.	A	21.	C		

PrepTest 63
June 2011

SECTION I

Time—35 minutes

25 Questions

Directions: The questions in this section are based on the reasoning contained in brief statements or passages. For some questions, more than one of the choices could conceivably answer the question. However, you are to choose the best answer; that is, the response that most accurately and completely answers the question. You should not make assumptions that are by commonsense standards implausible, superfluous, or incompatible with the passage. After you have chosen the best answer, blacken the corresponding space on your answer sheet.

1. Backyard gardeners who want to increase the yields of their potato plants should try growing stinging nettles alongside the plants, since stinging nettles attract insects that kill a wide array of insect pests that damage potato plants. It is true that stinging nettles also attract aphids, and that many species of aphids are harmful to potato plants, but that fact in no way contradicts this recommendation, because _______.

   Which one of the following most logically completes the argument?

   (A) stinging nettles require little care and thus are easy to cultivate
   (B) some types of aphids are attracted to stinging nettle plants but do not damage them
   (C) the types of aphids that stinging nettles attract do not damage potato plants
   (D) insect pests typically cause less damage to potato plants than other harmful organisms do
   (E) most aphid species that are harmful to potato plants cause greater harm to other edible food plants

2. Jocko, a chimpanzee, was once given a large bunch of bananas by a zookeeper after the more dominant members of the chimpanzee's troop had wandered off. In his excitement, Jocko uttered some loud "food barks." The other chimpanzees returned and took the bananas away. The next day, Jocko was again found alone and was given a single banana. This time, however, he kept silent. The zookeeper concluded that Jocko's silence was a stratagem to keep the other chimpanzees from his food.

   Which one of the following, if true, most seriously calls into question the zookeeper's conclusion?

   (A) Chimpanzees utter food barks only when their favorite foods are available.
   (B) Chimpanzees utter food barks only when they encounter a sizable quantity of food.
   (C) Chimpanzees frequently take food from other chimpanzees merely to assert dominance.
   (D) Even when they are alone, chimpanzees often make noises that appear to be signals to other chimpanzees.
   (E) Bananas are a food for which all of the chimpanzees at the zoo show a decided preference.

3. A recent survey quizzed journalism students about the sorts of stories they themselves wished to read. A significant majority said they wanted to see stories dealing with serious governmental and political issues and had little tolerance for the present popularity of stories covering lifestyle trends and celebrity gossip. This indicates that today's trends in publishing are based on false assumptions about the interests of the public.

   Which one of the following most accurately describes a flaw in the argument's reasoning?

   (A) It takes what is more likely to be the effect of a phenomenon to be its cause.
   (B) It regards the production of an effect as incontrovertible evidence of an intention to produce that effect.
   (C) It relies on the opinions of a group unlikely to be representative of the group at issue in the conclusion.
   (D) It employs language that unfairly represents those who are likely to reject the argument's conclusion.
   (E) It treats a hypothesis as fact even though it is admittedly unsupported.

GO ON TO THE NEXT PAGE.

4. Electric bug zappers, which work by attracting insects to light, are a very effective means of ridding an area of flying insects. Despite this, most pest control experts now advise against their use, recommending instead such remedies as insect-eating birds or insecticide sprays.

Which one of the following, if true, most helps to account for the pest control experts' recommendation?

(A) Insect-eating birds will take up residence in any insect-rich area if they are provided with nesting boxes, food, and water.
(B) Bug zappers are less effective against mosquitoes, which are among the more harmful insects, than they are against other harmful insects.
(C) Bug zappers use more electricity but provide less light than do most standard outdoor light sources.
(D) Bug zappers kill many more beneficial insects and fewer harmful insects than do insect-eating birds and insecticide sprays.
(E) Developers of certain new insecticide sprays claim that their products contain no chemicals that are harmful to humans, birds, or pets.

5. Gardener: The design of Japanese gardens should display harmony with nature. Hence, rocks chosen for placement in such gardens should vary widely in appearance, since rocks found in nature also vary widely in appearance.

The gardener's argument depends on assuming which one of the following?

(A) The selection of rocks for placement in a Japanese garden should reflect every key value embodied in the design of Japanese gardens.
(B) In the selection of rocks for Japanese gardens, imitation of nature helps to achieve harmony with nature.
(C) The only criterion for selecting rocks for placement in a Japanese garden is the expression of harmony with nature.
(D) Expressing harmony with nature and being natural are the same thing.
(E) Each component of a genuine Japanese garden is varied.

6. Small experimental vacuum tubes can operate in heat that makes semiconductor components fail. Any component whose resistance to heat is greater than that of semiconductors would be preferable for use in digital circuits, but only if that component were also comparable to semiconductors in all other significant respects, such as maximum current capacity. However, vacuum tubes' maximum current capacity is presently not comparable to that of semiconductors.

If the statements above are true, which one of the following must also be true?

(A) Vacuum tubes are not now preferable to semiconductors for use in digital circuits.
(B) Once vacuum tubes and semiconductors have comparable maximum current capacity, vacuum tubes will be used in some digital circuits.
(C) The only reason that vacuum tubes are not now used in digital circuits is that vacuum tubes' maximum current capacity is too low.
(D) Semiconductors will always be preferable to vacuum tubes for use in many applications other than digital circuits.
(E) Resistance to heat is the only advantage that vacuum tubes have over semiconductors.

7. The cause of the epidemic that devastated Athens in 430 B.C. can finally be identified. Accounts of the epidemic mention the hiccups experienced by many victims, a symptom of no known disease except that caused by the recently discovered Ebola virus. Moreover, other symptoms of the disease caused by the Ebola virus are mentioned in the accounts of the Athenian epidemic.

Each of the following, if true, weakens the argument EXCEPT:

(A) Victims of the Ebola virus experience many symptoms that do not appear in any of the accounts of the Athenian epidemic.
(B) Not all of those who are victims of the Ebola virus are afflicted with hiccups.
(C) The Ebola virus's host animals did not live in Athens at the time of the Athenian epidemic.
(D) The Ebola virus is much more contagious than the disease that caused the Athenian epidemic was reported to have been.
(E) The epidemics known to have been caused by the Ebola virus are usually shorter-lived than was the Athenian epidemic.

8. Letter to the editor: Your article was unjustified in criticizing environmentalists for claiming that more wolves on Vancouver Island are killed by hunters than are born each year. You stated that this claim was disproven by recent studies that indicate that the total number of wolves on Vancouver Island has remained roughly constant for 20 years. But you failed to account for the fact that, fearing the extinction of this wolf population, environmentalists have been introducing new wolves into the Vancouver Island wolf population for 20 years.

Which one of the following most accurately expresses the conclusion of the argument in the letter to the editor?

(A) Environmentalists have been successfully maintaining the wolf population on Vancouver Island for 20 years.
(B) As many wolves on Vancouver Island are killed by hunters as are born each year.
(C) The population of wolves on Vancouver Island should be maintained by either reducing the number killed by hunters each year or introducing new wolves into the population.
(D) The recent studies indicating that the total number of wolves on Vancouver Island has remained roughly constant for 20 years were flawed.
(E) The stability in the size of the Vancouver Island wolf population does not warrant the article's criticism of the environmentalists' claim.

9. Computer scientist: For several decades, the number of transistors on new computer microchips, and hence the microchips' computing speed, has doubled about every 18 months. However, from the mid-1990s into the next decade, each such doubling in a microchip's computing speed was accompanied by a doubling in the cost of producing that microchip.

Which one of the following can be properly inferred from the computer scientist's statements?

(A) The only effective way to double the computing speed of computer microchips is to increase the number of transistors per microchip.
(B) From the mid-1990s into the next decade, there was little if any increase in the retail cost of computers as a result of the increased number of transistors on microchips.
(C) For the last several decades, computer engineers have focused on increasing the computing speed of computer microchips without making any attempt to control the cost of producing them.
(D) From the mid-1990s into the next decade, a doubling in the cost of fabricating new computer microchips accompanied each doubling in the number of transistors on those microchips.
(E) It is unlikely that engineers will ever be able to increase the computing speed of microchips without also increasing the cost of producing them.

GO ON TO THE NEXT PAGE.

10. Ms. Sandstrom's newspaper column describing a strange natural phenomenon on the Mendels' farm led many people to trespass on and extensively damage their property. Thus, Ms. Sandstrom should pay for this damage if, as the Mendels claim, she could have reasonably expected that the column would lead people to damage the Mendels' farm.

The argument's conclusion can be properly inferred if which one of the following is assumed?

(A) One should pay for any damage that one's action leads other people to cause if one could have reasonably expected that the action would lead other people to cause damage.
(B) One should pay for damage that one's action leads other people to cause only if, prior to the action, one expected that the action would lead other people to cause that damage.
(C) It is unlikely that the people who trespassed on and caused the damage to the Mendels' property would themselves pay for the damage they caused.
(D) Ms. Sandstrom knew that her column could incite trespassing that could result in damage to the Mendels' farm.
(E) The Mendels believe that Ms. Sandstrom is able to form reasonable expectations about the consequences of her actions.

11. Meyer was found by his employer to have committed scientific fraud by falsifying data. The University of Williamstown, from which Meyer held a PhD, validated this finding and subsequently investigated whether he had falsified data in his doctoral thesis, finding no evidence that he had. But the university decided to revoke Meyer's PhD anyway.

Which one of the following university policies most justifies the decision to revoke Meyer's PhD?

(A) Anyone who holds a PhD from the University of Williamstown and is found to have committed academic fraud in the course of pursuing that PhD will have the PhD revoked.
(B) No PhD program at the University of Williamstown will admit any applicant who has been determined to have committed any sort of academic fraud.
(C) Any University of Williamstown student who is found to have submitted falsified data as academic work will be dismissed from the university.
(D) Anyone who holds a PhD from the University of Williamstown and is found to have committed scientific fraud will have the PhD revoked.
(E) The University of Williamstown will not hire anyone who is under investigation for scientific fraud.

12. Aerobics instructor: Compared to many forms of exercise, kickboxing aerobics is highly risky. Overextending when kicking often leads to hip, knee, or lower-back injuries. Such overextension is very likely to occur when beginners try to match the high kicks of more skilled practitioners.

Which one of the following is most strongly supported by the aerobics instructor's statements?

(A) Skilled practitioners of kickboxing aerobics are unlikely to experience injuries from overextending while kicking.
(B) To reduce the risk of injuries, beginners at kickboxing aerobics should avoid trying to match the high kicks of more skilled practitioners.
(C) Beginners at kickboxing aerobics will not experience injuries if they avoid trying to match the high kicks of more skilled practitioners.
(D) Kickboxing aerobics is more risky than forms of aerobic exercise that do not involve high kicks.
(E) Most beginners at kickboxing aerobics experience injuries from trying to match the high kicks of more skilled practitioners.

13. A large company has been convicted of engaging in monopolistic practices. The penalty imposed on the company will probably have little if any effect on its behavior. Still, the trial was worthwhile, since it provided useful information about the company's practices. After all, this information has emboldened the company's direct competitors, alerted potential rivals, and forced the company to restrain its unfair behavior toward customers and competitors.

Which one of the following most accurately expresses the overall conclusion drawn in the argument?

(A) Even if the company had not been convicted of engaging in monopolistic practices, the trial probably would have had some effect on the company's behavior.
(B) The light shed on the company's practices by the trial has emboldened its competitors, alerted potential rivals, and forced the company to restrain its unfair behavior.
(C) The penalty imposed on the company will likely have little or no effect on its behavior.
(D) The company's trial on charges of engaging in monopolistic practices was worthwhile.
(E) The penalty imposed on the company in the trial should have been larger.

GO ON TO THE NEXT PAGE.

14. Waller: If there were really such a thing as extrasensory perception, it would generally be accepted by the public since anyone with extrasensory powers would be able to convince the general public of its existence by clearly demonstrating those powers. Indeed, anyone who was recognized to have such powers would achieve wealth and renown.

Chin: It's impossible to demonstrate anything to the satisfaction of all skeptics. So long as the cultural elite remains closed-minded to the possibility of extrasensory perception, the popular media reports, and thus public opinion, will always be biased in favor of such skeptics.

Waller's and Chin's statements commit them to disagreeing on whether

(A) extrasensory perception is a real phenomenon
(B) extrasensory perception, if it were a real phenomenon, could be demonstrated to the satisfaction of all skeptics
(C) skeptics about extrasensory perception have a weak case
(D) the failure of the general public to believe in extrasensory perception is good evidence against its existence
(E) the general public believes that extrasensory perception is a real phenomenon

15. Counselor: Hagerle sincerely apologized to the physician for lying to her. So Hagerle owes me a sincere apology as well, because Hagerle told the same lie to both of us.

Which one of the following principles, if valid, most helps to justify the counselor's reasoning?

(A) It is good to apologize for having done something wrong to a person if one is capable of doing so sincerely.
(B) If someone tells the same lie to two different people, then neither of those lied to is owed an apology unless both are.
(C) Someone is owed a sincere apology for having been lied to by a person if someone else has already received a sincere apology for the same lie from that same person.
(D) If one is capable of sincerely apologizing to someone for lying to them, then one owes that person such an apology.
(E) A person should not apologize to someone for telling a lie unless he or she can sincerely apologize to all others to whom the lie was told.

16. A survey of address changes filed with post offices and driver's license bureaus over the last ten years has established that households moving out of the city of Weston outnumbered households moving into the city two to one. Therefore, we can expect that next year's census, which counts all residents regardless of age, will show that the population of Weston has declined since the last census ten years ago.

Which one of the following, if true, most helps strengthen the argument?

(A) Within the past decade many people both moved into the city and also moved out of it.
(B) Over the past century any census of Weston showing a population loss was followed ten years later by a census showing a population gain.
(C) Many people moving into Weston failed to notify either the post office or the driver's license bureau that they had moved to the city.
(D) Most adults moving out of Weston were parents who had children living with them, whereas most adults remaining in or moving into the city were older people who lived alone.
(E) Most people moving out of Weston were young adults who were hoping to begin a career elsewhere, whereas most adults remaining in or moving into the city had long-standing jobs in the city.

17. Psychologist: People tend to make certain cognitive errors when they predict how a given event would affect their future happiness. But people should not necessarily try to rid themselves of this tendency. After all, in a visual context, lines that are actually parallel often appear to people as if they converge. If a surgeon offered to restructure your eyes and visual cortex so that parallel lines would no longer ever appear to converge, it would not be reasonable to take the surgeon up on the offer.

The psychologist's argument does which one of the following?

(A) attempts to refute a claim that a particular event is inevitable by establishing the possibility of an alternative event
(B) attempts to undermine a theory by calling into question an assumption on which the theory is based
(C) argues that an action might not be appropriate by suggesting that a corresponding action in an analogous situation is not appropriate
(D) argues that two situations are similar by establishing that the same action would be reasonable in each situation
(E) attempts to establish a generalization and then uses that generalization to argue against a particular action

18. Principle: Even if an art auction house identifies the descriptions in its catalog as opinions, it is guilty of misrepresentation if such a description is a deliberate attempt to mislead bidders.

Application: Although Healy's, an art auction house, states that all descriptions in its catalog are opinions, Healy's was guilty of misrepresentation when its catalog described a vase as dating from the mid-eighteenth century when it was actually a modern reproduction.

Which one of the following, if true, most justifies the above application of the principle?

(A) An authentic work of art from the mid-eighteenth century will usually sell for at least ten times more than a modern reproduction of a similar work from that period.
(B) Although pottery that is similar to the vase is currently extremely popular among art collectors, none of the collectors who are knowledgeable about such pottery were willing to bid on the vase.
(C) The stated policy of Healy's is to describe works in its catalogs only in terms of their readily perceptible qualities and not to include any information about their age.
(D) Some Healy's staff members believe that the auction house's catalog should not contain any descriptions that have not been certified to be true by independent experts.
(E) Without consulting anyone with expertise in authenticating vases, Healy's described the vase as dating from the mid-eighteenth century merely in order to increase its auction price.

19. Anthropologist: It was formerly believed that prehistoric *Homo sapiens* ancestors of contemporary humans interbred with Neanderthals, but DNA testing of a Neanderthal's remains indicates that this is not the case. The DNA of contemporary humans is significantly different from that of the Neanderthal.

Which one of the following is an assumption required by the anthropologist's argument?

(A) At least some Neanderthals lived at the same time and in the same places as prehistoric *Homo sapiens* ancestors of contemporary humans.
(B) DNA testing of remains is significantly less reliable than DNA testing of samples from living species.
(C) The DNA of prehistoric *Homo sapiens* ancestors of contemporary humans was not significantly more similar to that of Neanderthals than is the DNA of contemporary humans.
(D) Neanderthals and prehistoric *Homo sapiens* ancestors of contemporary humans were completely isolated from each other geographically.
(E) Any similarity in the DNA of two species must be the result of interbreeding.

20. Council member: The profits of downtown businesses will increase if more consumers live in the downtown area, and a decrease in the cost of living in the downtown area will guarantee that the number of consumers living there will increase. However, the profits of downtown businesses will not increase unless downtown traffic congestion decreases.

If all the council member's statements are true, which one of the following must be true?

(A) If downtown traffic congestion decreases, the number of consumers living in the downtown area will increase.
(B) If the cost of living in the downtown area decreases, the profits of downtown businesses will increase.
(C) If downtown traffic congestion decreases, the cost of living in the downtown area will increase.
(D) If downtown traffic congestion decreases, the cost of living in the downtown area will decrease.
(E) If the profits of downtown businesses increase, the number of consumers living in the downtown area will increase.

GO ON TO THE NEXT PAGE.

21. On the Discount Phoneline, any domestic long-distance call starting between 9 A.M. and 5 P.M. costs 15 cents a minute, and any other domestic long-distance call costs 10 cents a minute. So any domestic long-distance call on the Discount Phoneline that does not cost 10 cents a minute costs 15 cents a minute.

The pattern of reasoning in which one of the following arguments is most similar to that in the argument above?

(A) If a university class involves extensive lab work, the class will be conducted in a laboratory; otherwise, it will be conducted in a normal classroom. Thus, if a university class does not involve extensive lab work, it will not be conducted in a laboratory.
(B) If a university class involves extensive lab work, the class will be conducted in a laboratory; otherwise, it will be conducted in a normal classroom. Thus, if a university class is not conducted in a normal classroom, it will involve extensive lab work.
(C) If a university class involves extensive lab work, the class will be conducted in a laboratory; otherwise, it will be conducted in a normal classroom. Thus, if a university class is conducted in a normal classroom, it will not be conducted in a laboratory.
(D) If a university class involves extensive lab work, the class will be conducted in a laboratory; otherwise, it will be conducted in a normal classroom. Thus, if a university class involves extensive lab work, it will not be conducted in a normal classroom.
(E) If a university class involves extensive lab work, the class will be conducted in a laboratory; otherwise, it will be conducted in a normal classroom. Thus, if a university class is not conducted in a normal classroom, it will be conducted in a laboratory.

22. One child pushed another child from behind, injuring the second child. The first child clearly understands the difference between right and wrong, so what was done was wrong if it was intended to injure the second child.

Which one of the following principles, if valid, most helps to justify the reasoning in the argument?

(A) An action that is intended to harm another person is wrong only if the person who performed the action understands the difference between right and wrong.
(B) It is wrong for a person who understands the difference between right and wrong to intentionally harm another person.
(C) Any act that is wrong is done with the intention of causing harm.
(D) An act that harms another person is wrong if the person who did it understands the difference between right and wrong and did not think about whether the act would injure the other person.
(E) A person who does not understand the difference between right and wrong does not bear any responsibility for harming another person.

23. Researcher: Each subject in this experiment owns one car, and was asked to estimate what proportion of all automobiles registered in the nation are the same make as the subject's car. The estimate of nearly every subject has been significantly higher than the actual national statistic for the make of that subject's car. I hypothesize that certain makes of car are more common in some regions of the nation than in other regions; obviously, that would lead many people to overestimate how common their make of car is nationally. That is precisely the result found in this experiment, so certain makes of car must indeed be more common in some areas of the nation than in others.

Which one of the following most accurately expresses a reasoning flaw in the researcher's argument?

(A) The argument fails to estimate the likelihood that most subjects in the experiment did not know the actual statistics about how common their make of car is nationwide.
(B) The argument treats a result that supports a hypothesis as a result that proves a hypothesis.
(C) The argument fails to take into account the possibility that the subject pool may come from a wide variety of geographical regions.
(D) The argument attempts to draw its main conclusion from a set of premises that are mutually contradictory.
(E) The argument applies a statistical generalization to a particular case to which it was not intended to apply.

24. In university towns, police issue far more parking citations during the school year than they do during the times when the students are out of town. Therefore, we know that most parking citations in university towns are issued to students.

Which one of the following is most similar in its flawed reasoning to the flawed reasoning in the argument above?

(A) We know that children buy most of the snacks at cinemas, because popcorn sales increase as the proportion of child moviegoers to adult moviegoers increases.
(B) We know that this houseplant gets more of the sunlight from the window, because it is greener than that houseplant.
(C) We know that most people who go to a university are studious because most of those people study while they attend the university.
(D) We know that consumers buy more fruit during the summer than they buy during the winter, because there are far more varieties of fruit available in the summer than in the winter.
(E) We know that most of the snacks parents buy go to other people's children, because when other people's children come to visit, parents give out more snacks than usual.

25. Counselor: Those who believe that criticism should be gentle rather than harsh should consider the following: change requires a motive, and criticism that is unpleasant provides a motive. Since harsh criticism is unpleasant, harsh criticism provides a motive. Therefore, only harsh criticism will cause the person criticized to change.

The reasoning in the counselor's argument is most vulnerable to criticism on the grounds that the argument

(A) infers that something that is sufficient to provide a motive is necessary to provide a motive
(B) fails to address the possibility that in some cases the primary goal of criticism is something other than bringing about change in the person being criticized
(C) takes for granted that everyone who is motivated to change will change
(D) confuses a motive for doing something with a motive for avoiding something
(E) takes the refutation of an argument to be sufficient to show that the argument's conclusion is false

S T O P

IF YOU FINISH BEFORE TIME IS CALLED, YOU MAY CHECK YOUR WORK ON THIS SECTION ONLY.
DO NOT WORK ON ANY OTHER SECTION IN THE TEST.

Time—35 minutes

25 Questions

Directions: The questions in this section are based on the reasoning contained in brief statements or passages. For some questions, more than one of the choices could conceivably answer the question. However, you are to choose the best answer; that is, the response that most accurately and completely answers the question. You should not make assumptions that are by commonsense standards implausible, superfluous, or incompatible with the passage. After you have chosen the best answer, blacken the corresponding space on your answer sheet.

1. Psychiatrist: We are learning that neurochemical imbalances can cause behavior ranging from extreme mental illness to less serious but irritating behavior such as obsessive fantasizing, petulance, or embarrassment. These findings will promote compassion and tolerance when looking at a mental illness, quirk, or mere difference between two persons, since being mentally healthy can now begin to be seen as simply having the same neurochemical balances as most people.

Which one of the following most accurately expresses the conclusion of the psychiatrist's argument?

(A) Understanding the role of the neurochemical in behavior will foster empathy toward others.
(B) Neurochemical imbalances can cause mental illness and other behaviors.
(C) Neurochemical balances and imbalances are the main determinants of mental behavior.
(D) Being mentally healthy is a matter of having the same neurochemical balances as most people.
(E) Advances in neurochemistry enhance our theories of mental illness.

2. No one wants this job as much as Joshua does, but he is not applying for it. It follows that there will not be any applicants, no matter how high the salary that is being offered.

The flawed reasoning in the argument above most closely parallels that in which one of the following?

(A) Beth knows better than anyone else how to spot errors in a computer program, yet even she has not found any in this program so far. So it is clear that the errors must all be in the rest of the program.
(B) If anyone can decipher this inscription, it is Professor Alvarez, but she is so involved with her new research that it will be impossible to interest her in this sort of task. Therefore, all we can do now is hope to find someone else.
(C) Although he has the strongest motive of anyone for buying Anna's plot of land, Manfred is not pursuing the matter. Therefore, regardless of how low a price Anna is prepared to accept, she will be looking for a buyer in vain.
(D) The person initially most interested in obtaining the contract was Mr. Moore, but he of all people suddenly withdrew his bid. This means that, no matter how discouraged the other bidders had been, they will now redouble their efforts.
(E) Three times Paul would have liked to take advantage of a special vacation package for himself and his family, but each time he was indispensable at the factory just then. So the more seniority Paul acquires, the greater are the constraints on his personal life.

GO ON TO THE NEXT PAGE.

3. Many people limit the intake of calories and cholesterol in their diet in order to lose weight and reduce the level of cholesterol in their blood. When a person loses weight, the fat cells in that person's body decrease in size but not in number. As they decrease in size, fat cells spill the cholesterol they contain into the bloodstream. Therefore, a person who goes on a low-calorie, low cholesterol diet _____.

Which one of the following most logically completes the argument?

(A) might at first have an increased level of cholesterol in his or her blood
(B) will not lose weight any faster than will a person whose diet is high in calories
(C) might lose more weight by going on a low calorie, high-cholesterol diet than by going on the low-calorie, low-cholesterol diet
(D) will not decrease the size of his or her fat cells
(E) will both decrease the level of cholesterol in his or her blood and gain weight

Questions 4-5

Advances in photocopying technology allow criminals with no printing expertise to counterfeit paper currency. One standard anticounterfeiting technique, microprinting, prints paper currency with tiny designs that cannot be photocopied distinctly. Although counterfeits of microprinted currency can be detected easily by experts, such counterfeits often circulate widely before being detected. An alternative, though more costly, printing technique would print currency with a special ink. Currency printed with the ink would change color depending on how ordinary light strikes it, whereas photocopied counterfeits of such currency would not. Because this technique would allow anyone to detect photocopied counterfeit currency easily, it should be adopted instead of microprinting, despite the expense.

4. Which one of the following, if true, provides the most support for the recommendation made by the argument?

(A) When an anticounterfeiting technique depends on the detection of counterfeits by experts, the cost of inspection by experts adds significantly to the cost to society of that technique.
(B) For any anticounterfeiting technique to be effective, the existence of anticounterfeiting techniques should be widely broadcast, but the method by which counterfeits are detected should be kept secret.
(C) The process of microprinting paper currency involves fewer steps than does the printing of paper currency with the special ink.
(D) Before photocopying technology existed, most counterfeits of paper currency were accomplished by master engravers.
(E) Many criminals do not have access to the advanced photocopiers that are needed to produce counterfeits of microprinted paper currency that cashiers will accept as real.

5. Which one of the following, if true, most seriously undermines the argument?

(A) The longer the interval between the time a counterfeit bill passes into circulation and the time the counterfeit is detected, the more difficult it is for law enforcement officials to apprehend the counterfeiter.
(B) Sophisticated counterfeiters could produce currency printed with the special ink but cannot duplicate microprinted currency exactly.
(C) Further advances in photocopying technology will dramatically increase the level of detail that photocopies can reproduce.
(D) The largest quantities of counterfeit currency now entering circulation are produced by ordinary criminals who engage in counterfeiting only briefly.
(E) It is very difficult to make accurate estimates of what the costs to society would be if large amounts of counterfeit currency circulated widely.

GO ON TO THE NEXT PAGE.

6. One test to determine whether a person has been infected with tuberculosis consists of injecting the person with proteins extracted from the tuberculosis bacterium. Once a person has been infected by a bacterium, the person's immune system subsequently recognizes certain proteins present in that bacterium and attacks the bacterium. This recognition also takes place in the test and results in a skin irritation at the injection site. Hence the physicians who designed the test reasoned that anyone who reacts in this manner to an injection with the tuberculosis proteins has been infected with tuberculosis.

Which one of the following is an assumption on which the physicians' reasoning depends?

(A) All of the proteins present in disease-causing bacteria can be recognized by the body's immune system.
(B) Localized skin irritations are a characteristic symptom of tuberculosis in most people.
(C) The ability of the proteins present in the tuberculosis bacterium to trigger the skin irritation is exclusive to that bacterium.
(D) Some people who have been injected with proteins extracted from the tuberculosis bacterium will contract tuberculosis as a result of the injection.
(E) The body's immune system cannot recognize infectious bacteria unless there are sufficient quantities of the bacteria to cause overt symptoms of disease.

7. Generations of European-history students have been taught that a political assassination caused the First World War. Without some qualification, however, this teaching is bound to mislead, since the war would not have happened without the treaties and alliances that were already in effect and the military force that was already amassed. These were the deeper causes of the war, whereas the assassination was a cause only in a trivial sense. It was like the individual spark that happens to ignite a conflagration that was, in the prevailing conditions, inevitable.

Which one of the following most accurately restates the main point of the passage?

(A) The assassination did not cause the war, since the assassination was only the last in a chain of events leading up to the war, each of which had equal claim to being called its "cause."
(B) The war was destined to happen, since the course of history up to that point could not have been altered.
(C) Though the statement that the assassination caused the war is true, the term "cause" more fundamentally applies to the conditions that made it possible for that event to start the war.
(D) If the assassination had occurred when it did but less military force had at that time been amassed, then the war's outbreak might have been considerably delayed or the war might not have occurred at all.
(E) Although the conditions prevailing at the time the war started made war inevitable, if the war had not been triggered by the assassination it would not have taken the course with which students of history are familiar.

GO ON TO THE NEXT PAGE.

8. Toddlers are not being malicious when they bite people. For example, a child may want a toy, and feel that the person he or she bites is preventing him or her from having it.

The situation as described above most closely conforms to which one of the following generalizations?

(A) Biting people is sometimes a way for toddlers to try to solve problems.
(B) Toddlers sometimes engage in biting people in order to get attention from adults.
(C) Toddlers mistakenly believe that biting people is viewed as acceptable behavior by adults.
(D) Toddlers do not recognize that by biting people they often thwart their own ends.
(E) Resorting to biting people is in some cases an effective way for toddlers to get what they want.

9. Consumer advocate: Last year's worldwide alarm about a computer "virus"—a surreptitiously introduced computer program that can destroy other programs and data—was a fraud. Companies selling programs to protect computers against such viruses raised worldwide concern about the possibility that a destructive virus would be activated on a certain date. There was more smoke than fire, however, only about a thousand cases of damage were reported around the world. Multitudes of antivirus programs were sold, so the companies' warning was clearly only an effort to stimulate sales.

The reasoning in the consumer advocate's argument is flawed because this argument

(A) restates its conclusion without attempting to offer a reason to accept it
(B) fails to acknowledge that antivirus programs might protect against viruses other than the particular one described
(C) asserts that the occurrence of one event after another shows that the earlier event was the cause of the later one
(D) uses inflammatory language as a substitute for providing any evidence
(E) overlooks the possibility that the protective steps taken did work and, for many computers, prevented the virus from causing damage

10. Insects can see ultraviolet light and are known to identify important food sources and mating sites by sensing the characteristic patterns of ultraviolet light that these things reflect. Insects are also attracted to *Glomosus* spiderwebs, which reflect ultraviolet light. Thus, insects are probably attracted to these webs because of the specific patterns of ultraviolet light that these webs reflect.

Which one of the following, if true, most strongly supports the argument?

(A) When webs of many different species of spider were illuminated with a uniform source of white light containing an ultraviolet component, many of these webs did not reflect the ultraviolet light.
(B) When the silks of spiders that spin silk only for lining burrows and covering eggs were illuminated with white light containing an ultraviolet component, the silks of these spiders reflected ultraviolet light.
(C) When webs of the comparatively recently evolved common garden spider were illuminated with white light containing an ultraviolet component, only certain portions of these webs reflected ultraviolet light.
(D) When *Drosophila* fruit flies were placed before a *Glomosus* web and a synthetic web of similar pattern that also reflected ultraviolet light and both webs were illuminated with white light containing an ultraviolet component, many of the fruit flies flew to the *Glomosus* web.
(E) When *Drosophila* fruit flies were placed before two *Glomosus* webs, one illuminated with white light containing an ultraviolet component and one illuminated with white light without an ultraviolet component, the majority flew to the ultraviolet reflecting web.

GO ON TO THE NEXT PAGE.

11. A Habitat Conservation Plan (HCP) is based on a law that allows developers to use land inhabited by endangered species in exchange for a promise to preserve critical habitat or provide replacement land nearby. Some individuals of endangered species are lost in return for assurances by the owner or developer that habitat for those remaining animals will be protected. Environmentalists are pleased that HCPs allow them to win concessions from developers who would otherwise ignore rarely enforced environmental laws. Satisfied property owners prefer HCPs to more restrictive prohibitions of land use.

    The situation described above most closely conforms to which one of the following principles?

    (A) In order to avoid protracted legal battles environmentalists should compromise with developers.
    (B) Developers should adhere only to those environmental laws that are not overburdensome.
    (C) Laws should not be designed to serve the interests of all the parties concerned since they are often so weak that no one's interest is served well.
    (D) Laws should be fashioned in such a way as to reconcile the interests of developers and environmentalists.
    (E) The most effective means of preserving endangered species is to refrain from alienating property owners.

12. It has long been thought that lizards evolved from a group of amphibians called anthracosaurs, no fossils of which have been found in any rocks older than 300 million years. However, a fossil of a lizard was recently found that is estimated to be 340 million years old. Lizards could not have evolved from creatures that did not exist until after the first lizards. Therefore, lizards could not have evolved from anthracosaurs.

    An assumption made in the argument is that there are no

    (A) unknown anthracosaur fossils older than 340 million years
    (B) unknown lizard fossils older than 340 million years
    (C) known lizard fossils that predate some anthracosaur fossils
    (D) known anthracosaur fossils that predate some lizard fossils
    (E) known lizard fossils whose age is uncertain

<u>Questions 13–14</u>

Numismatist: In medieval Spain, most gold coins were minted from gold mined in West Africa, in the area that is now Senegal. The gold mined in this region was the purest known. Its gold content of 92 percent allowed coins to be minted without refining the gold, and indeed coins minted from this source of gold can be recognized because they have that gold content. The mints could refine gold and produced other kinds of coins that had much purer gold content, but the Senegalese gold was never refined.

13. Which one of the following inferences about gold coins minted in medieval Spain is most strongly supported by the information the numismatist gives?

    (A) Coins minted from Senegalese gold all contained the same weight, as well as the same proportion, of gold.
    (B) The source of some refined gold from which coins were minted was unrefined gold with a gold content of less than 92 percent.
    (C) Two coins could have the same monetary value even though they differed from each other in the percentage of gold they contained.
    (D) No gold coins were minted that had a gold content of less than 92 percent.
    (E) The only unrefined gold from which coins could be minted was Senegalese gold.

14. As a preliminary to negotiating prices, merchants selling goods often specified that payment should be in the coins minted from Senegalese gold. Which one of the following, if true, most helps to explain this preference?

    (A) Because refined gold varied considerably in purity, specifying a price as a number of refined-gold coins did not fix the quantity of gold received in payment.
    (B) During this period most day-to-day trading was conducted using silver coins, though gold coins were used for costly transactions and long-distance commerce.
    (C) The mints were able to determine the purity, and hence the value, of gold coins by measuring their density.
    (D) Since gold coins' monetary value rested on the gold they contained, payments were frequently made using coins minted in several different countries.
    (E) Merchants obtaining gold to resell for use in jewelry could not sell the metal unless it was first refined.

15. Some plants have extremely sensitive biological thermometers. For example, the leaves of rhododendrons curl when the temperature of the air around them is below 0°C (Celsius). Similarly, mature crocus blossoms open in temperatures above 2°C. So someone who simultaneously observed rhododendrons with uncurled leaves, crocuses with mature but unopened blossoms, and a thermometer showing 1°C could determine that the thermometer's reading was accurate to within plus or minus 1°C.

Which one of the following, if true, most seriously undermines the reasoning above?

(A) Neither rhododendrons nor crocuses bloom for more than a few weeks each year, and the blossoms of rhododendrons growing in any area do not appear until at least several weeks after crocuses growing in that area have ceased to bloom.
(B) Many people find it unpleasant to be outdoors for long periods when the temperature is at or about 1°C.
(C) The climate and soil conditions that favor the growth of rhododendrons are also favorable to the growth of crocuses.
(D) Air temperature surrounding rhododendrons, which can grow 12 feet tall, is likely to differ from air temperature surrounding crocuses, which are normally only a few inches high, by more than 2°C, even if the two plants are growing side by side.
(E) Certain types of thermometers that are commonly used to measure outdoor temperatures can be extremely accurate in moderate temperature ranges but much less accurate in warmer or colder temperature ranges.

16. Political scientist: The dissemination of political theories is in principle able to cause change in existing social structures. However, all political theories are formulated in the educationally privileged setting of the university, leading to convoluted language that is alienating to many individuals outside academia who would be important agents of change. It follows that, with respect to political theory, there is a special role for those outside the university context to render it into accessible, clear language.

Which one of the following is an assumption on which the argument depends?

(A) Persons outside academic settings are the most important agents of change to the social structure.
(B) Persons within academic settings who formulate political theories attempt to change existing social structures.
(C) Persons outside academic settings are better left out of the initial formulation of political theories.
(D) Persons outside academic settings stand to gain more from the dissemination of political theories than persons inside.
(E) Persons within academic settings are less willing or less able than persons outside to write in a straightforward way.

17. Nicotine has long been known to cause heart attacks and high blood pressure. Yet a recent study has shown that the incidence of heart attacks and high blood pressure is significantly higher among cigarette smokers who do not chew tobacco than among nonsmokers exposed to an equal amount of nicotine through tobacco chewing.

Which one of the following, if true, helps LEAST to resolve the apparent discrepancy described above?

(A) People who smoke but do not chew tobacco tend to exercise less than those who chew tobacco but do not smoke.
(B) Chemicals other than nicotine present in chewing tobacco but not present in cigarette smoke mitigate the effects that nicotine has on the cardiovascular system.
(C) People who chew tobacco but do not smoke tend to have healthier diets than those who smoke but do not chew tobacco.
(D) Chemicals other than nicotine present in chewing tobacco but not present in cigarette smoke can cause cancer.
(E) Chemicals other than nicotine present in cigarette smoke but not present in chewing tobacco raise blood pressure.

18. President of Central Supply Company: Profits are at an all-time low this fiscal year because of decreased demand for our products. If this situation continues, the company may have to declare bankruptcy. So it is important to prevent any further decrease in profits. Consequently, the only options are to reduce planned expansion or to eliminate some less profitable existing operations.

Which one of the following most accurately describes a flaw, in the company president's reasoning?

(A) It presumes without giving justification that survival of the company has been a good thing.
(B) It does not take into account that there are alternatives to declaring bankruptcy.
(C) It presumes without giving justification that only decreased demand can ever be the cause of decreased profits.
(D) It does not allow for the possibility that profits will decrease only slightly during the next fiscal year.
(E) It does not take into account that there may be other ways to stop the decrease in profits.

19. In all mammalian species, the period of a young mammal's life in which it is most frequently playful coincides with the period of most rapid growth of the neural connections in the mammal's brain that give rise to various complex patterns of movement, posture, and social response. Indeed, the neural connections created by frequent play during this period later become indispensable for the mammal's survival and well-being as an adult.

The statements above, if true, serve LEAST well as evidence for which one of the following?

(A) Young mammals of species that are preyed on by other animals are likely to engage in forms of sudden mock flight, bolting away from locations where no predators are to be found.
(B) The young of nonmammalian species such as fish, reptiles, and birds do not normally engage in playful behavior that serves the function served by play in the development of young mammals.
(C) Adult mammals are more likely to engage in interactive play with their young if they engaged in similar forms of play when they themselves were young.
(D) Mammals that cannot engage in certain common forms of play when young are likely to show certain deficits that limit their subsequent success as adults.
(E) Young mammals of predatory species tend to practice in their play inoffensive versions of motions and actions that are useful in finding and catching prey when these mammals become adults.

20. Physicist: Determinism is the view that every event has a preceding cause sufficient for its occurrence. That is, if determinism is true, then the events that are presently occurring could not have failed to occur given the state of the universe a moment ago. Determinism, however, is false because it is impossible to know the complete state of the universe at any given time since it is impossible to measure accurately both the position and velocity of any given subatomic particle at a particular time.

The physicist's reasoning is most vulnerable to criticism on which one of the following grounds?

(A) That it is impossible to measure accurately both the position and velocity of any given subatomic particle does not imply that it is impossible to know either the position or velocity of all subatomic particles.
(B) That the complete state of the universe at any given time is unknowable does not imply that the states at that time of the individual subatomic particles making it up are unknowable.
(C) That it is impossible to measure accurately both the position and velocity of any given subatomic particle at a particular time does not imply that its position or velocity cannot be accurately measured separately.
(D) That it is impossible to know the complete state of the universe at any given time does not imply that there is no complete state of the universe at that time.
(E) That the position and velocity of any given subatomic particle cannot be jointly measured with accuracy does not imply that this is the case for the position and velocity of all subatomic particles.

21. If this parking policy is unpopular with the faculty, then we should modify it. If it is unpopular among students, we should adopt a new policy. And, it is bound to be unpopular either with the faculty or among students.

If the statements above are true, which one of the following must also be true?

(A) We should attempt to popularize this parking policy among either the faculty or students.
(B) We should modify this parking policy only if this will not reduce its popularity among students.
(C) We should modify this parking policy if modification will not reduce its popularity with the faculty.
(D) If the parking policy is popular among students, then we should adopt a new policy.
(E) If this parking policy is popular with the faculty, then we should adopt a new policy.

GO ON TO THE NEXT PAGE.

22. It is an absurd idea that whatever artistic endeavor the government refuses to support it does not allow, as one can see by rephrasing the statement to read: No one is allowed to create art without a government subsidy.

The pattern of reasoning in which one of the following is most similar to that in the argument above?

(A) The claim that any driver who is not arrested does not break the law is absurd, as one can see by rewording it: Every driver who breaks the law gets arrested.
(B) The claim that any driver who is not arrested does not break the law is absurd, as one can see by rewording it: Every driver who gets arrested has broken the law.
(C) The notion that every scientist who is supported by a government grant will be successful is absurd, as one can see by rewording it: No scientist who is successful is so without a government grant.
(D) The notion that every scientist who is supported by a government grant will be successful is absurd, as one can see by rewording it: No scientist lacking governmental support will be successful.
(E) The notion that every scientist who has been supported by a government grant will be successful is absurd, as one can see by rewording it: No scientist is allowed to do research without a government grant.

23. Politician: Nobody can deny that homelessness is a problem yet there seems to be little agreement on how to solve it. One thing, however is clear: ignoring the problem will not make it go away. Only if the government steps in and provides the homeless with housing will this problem disappear, and this necessitates increased taxation. For this reason, we should raise taxes.

Which one of the following principles, if valid, most supports the politician's argument?

(A) Only if a measure is required to solve a problem should it be adopted.
(B) Only if a measure is sufficient to solve a problem should it be adopted.
(C) If a measure is required to solve a problem, then it should be adopted.
(D) If a measure is sufficient to solve a problem, then it should be adopted.
(E) If a measure is sufficient to solve a problem, any steps necessitated by that measure should be adopted.

24. Trade official: Country X deserves economic retribution for its protectionism. However, it is crucial that we recognize that there are overriding considerations in this case. We should still sell to X the agricultural equipment it ordered; there is high demand in our country for agricultural imports from X.

The argument depends on assuming which one of the following principles?

(A) Agricultural components of international trade are more important than nonagricultural commodities.
(B) The ability to keep popular products available domestically is less important than our being able to enter international markets.
(C) We should never jeopardize the interests of our people to punish a projectionist country.
(D) In most cases, punishing a projectionist country should have priority over the interests of our people.
(E) We should balance the justice of an action with the consequences for our interests of undertaking that action.

25. Jack's aunt gave him her will, asking him to make it public when she died; he promised to do so. After her death, Jack looked at the will; it stipulated that all her money go to her friend George. Jack knew that if he made the will public, George would squander the money, benefiting neither George nor anyone else. Jack also knew that if he did not make the will public, the money would go to his own mother, who would use it to benefit herself and others, harming no one. After reflection, he decided not to make the will public.

Which one of the following principles, if valid, would require Jack to act as he did in the situation described?

(A) Duties to family members take priority over duties to people who are not family members.
(B) Violating a promise is impermissible whenever doing so would become known by others.
(C) One must choose an alternative that benefits some and harms no one over an alternative that harms some and benefits no one.
(D) When faced with alternatives it is obligatory to choose whichever one will benefit the greatest number of people.
(E) A promise becomes nonbinding when the person to whom the promise was made is no longer living.

S T O P

IF YOU FINISH BEFORE TIME IS CALLED, YOU MAY CHECK YOUR WORK ON THIS SECTION ONLY. DO NOT WORK ON ANY OTHER SECTION IN THE TEST.

SECTION II

Time—35 minutes

23 Questions

Directions: Each group of questions in this section is based on a set of conditions. In answering some of the questions, it may be useful to draw a rough diagram. Choose the response that most accurately and completely answers each question and blacken the corresponding space on your answer sheet.

Questions 1–5

Each of seven candidates for the position of judge—Hamadi, Jefferson, Kurtz, Li, McDonnell, Ortiz, and Perkins—will be appointed to an open position on one of two courts—the appellate court or the trial court. There are three open positions on the appellate court and six open positions on the trial court, but not all of them will be filled at this time. The judicial appointments will conform to the following conditions:

Li must be appointed to the appellate court.
Kurtz must be appointed to the trial court.
Hamadi cannot be appointed to the same court as Perkins.

1. Which one of the following is an acceptable set of appointments of candidates to courts?

(A) appellate: Hamadi, Ortiz
trial: Jefferson, Kurtz, Li, McDonnell, Perkins
(B) appellate: Hamadi, Li, Perkins
trial: Jefferson, Kurtz, McDonnell, Ortiz
(C) appellate: Kurtz, Li, Perkins
trial: Hamadi, Jefferson, McDonnell, Ortiz
(D) appellate: Li, McDonnell, Ortiz
trial: Hamadi, Jefferson, Kurtz, Perkins
(E) appellate: Li, Perkins
trial: Hamadi, Jefferson, Kurtz, McDonnell, Ortiz

2. Which one of the following CANNOT be true?

(A) Hamadi and McDonnell are both appointed to the appellate court.
(B) McDonnell and Ortiz are both appointed to the appellate court.
(C) Ortiz and Perkins are both appointed to the appellate court.
(D) Hamadi and Jefferson are both appointed to the trial court.
(E) Ortiz and Perkins are both appointed to the trial court.

3. Which one of the following CANNOT be true?

(A) Jefferson and McDonnell are both appointed to the appellate court.
(B) Jefferson and McDonnell are both appointed to the trial court.
(C) McDonnell and Ortiz are both appointed to the trial court.
(D) McDonnell and Perkins are both appointed to the appellate court.
(E) McDonnell and Perkins are both appointed to the trial court.

4. If Ortiz is appointed to the appellate court, which one of the following must be true?

(A) Hamadi is appointed to the appellate court.
(B) Jefferson is appointed to the appellate court.
(C) Jefferson is appointed to the trial court.
(D) Perkins is appointed to the appellate court.
(E) Perkins is appointed to the trial court.

5. Which one of the following, if substituted for the condition that Hamadi cannot be appointed to the same court as Perkins, would have the same effect on the appointments of the seven candidates?

(A) Hamadi and Perkins cannot both be appointed to the appellate court.
(B) If Hamadi is not appointed to the trial court, then Perkins must be.
(C) If Perkins is appointed to the same court as Jefferson, then Hamadi cannot be.
(D) If Hamadi is appointed to the same court as Li, then Perkins must be appointed to the same court as Kurtz.
(E) No three of Hamadi, Kurtz, Li, and Perkins can be appointed to the same court as each other.

GO ON TO THE NEXT PAGE.

Questions 6–10

Exactly six members of a skydiving team—Larue, Ohba, Pei, Treviño, Weiss, and Zacny—each dive exactly once, one at a time, from a plane, consistent with the following conditions:

Treviño dives from the plane at some time before Weiss does.
Larue dives from the plane either first or last.
Neither Weiss nor Zacny dives from the plane last.
Pei dives from the plane at some time after either Ohba or Larue but not both.

6. Which one of the following could be an accurate list of the members in the order in which they dive from the plane, from first to last?

(A) Larue, Treviño, Ohba, Zacny, Pei, Weiss
(B) Larue, Treviño, Pei, Zacny, Weiss, Ohba
(C) Weiss, Ohba, Treviño, Zacny, Pei, Larue
(D) Treviño, Weiss, Pei, Ohba, Zacny, Larue
(E) Treviño, Weiss, Zacny, Larue, Pei, Ohba

7. Which one of the following must be true?

(A) At least two of the members dive from the plane after Larue.
(B) At least two of the members dive from the plane after Ohba.
(C) At least two of the members dive from the plane after Pei.
(D) At least two of the members dive from the plane after Treviño.
(E) At least two of the members dive from the plane after Weiss.

8. If Larue dives from the plane last, then each of the following could be true EXCEPT:

(A) Treviño dives from the plane fourth.
(B) Weiss dives from the plane fourth.
(C) Ohba dives from the plane fifth.
(D) Pei dives from the plane fifth.
(E) Zacny dives from the plane fifth.

9. If Zacny dives from the plane immediately after Weiss, then which one of the following must be false?

(A) Larue dives from the plane first.
(B) Treviño dives from the plane third.
(C) Zacny dives from the plane third.
(D) Pei dives from the plane fourth.
(E) Zacny dives from the plane fourth.

10. If Treviño dives from the plane immediately after Larue, then each of the following could be true EXCEPT:

(A) Ohba dives from the plane third.
(B) Weiss dives from the plane third.
(C) Zacny dives from the plane third.
(D) Pei dives from the plane fourth.
(E) Weiss dives from the plane fourth.

GO ON TO THE NEXT PAGE.

Questions 11–17

A company's six vehicles—a hatchback, a limousine, a pickup, a roadster, a sedan, and a van—are serviced during a certain week—Monday through Saturday—one vehicle per day. The following conditions must apply:

At least one of the vehicles is serviced later in the week than the hatchback.

The roadster is serviced later in the week than the van and earlier in the week than the hatchback.

Either the pickup and the van are serviced on consecutive days, or the pickup and the sedan are serviced on consecutive days, but not both.

The sedan is serviced earlier in the week than the pickup or earlier in the week than the limousine, but not both.

11. Which one of the following could be the order in which the vehicles are serviced, from Monday through Saturday?

(A) the hatchback, the pickup, the sedan, the limousine, the van, the roadster
(B) the pickup, the sedan, the van, the roadster, the hatchback, the limousine
(C) the pickup, the van, the sedan, the roadster, the limousine, the hatchback
(D) the van, the roadster, the pickup, the hatchback, the sedan, the limousine
(E) the van, the sedan, the pickup, the roadster, the hatchback, the limousine

12. Which one of the following CANNOT be the vehicle serviced on Thursday?

(A) the hatchback
(B) the limousine
(C) the pickup
(D) the sedan
(E) the van

13. If neither the pickup nor the limousine is serviced on Monday, then which one of the following must be true?

(A) The hatchback and the limousine are serviced on consecutive days.
(B) The hatchback and the sedan are serviced on consecutive days.
(C) The van is serviced on Monday.
(D) The limousine is serviced on Saturday.
(E) The pickup is serviced on Saturday.

14. If the limousine is not serviced on Saturday, then each of the following could be true EXCEPT:

(A) The limousine is serviced on Monday.
(B) The roadster is serviced on Tuesday.
(C) The hatchback is serviced on Wednesday.
(D) The roadster is serviced on Wednesday.
(E) The sedan is serviced on Wednesday.

15. If the sedan is serviced earlier in the week than the pickup, then which one of the following could be true?

(A) The limousine is serviced on Wednesday.
(B) The sedan is serviced on Wednesday.
(C) The van is serviced on Wednesday.
(D) The hatchback is serviced on Friday.
(E) The limousine is serviced on Saturday.

16. If the limousine is serviced on Saturday, then which one of the following must be true?

(A) The pickup is serviced earlier in the week than the roadster.
(B) The pickup is serviced earlier in the week than the sedan.
(C) The sedan is serviced earlier in the week than the roadster.
(D) The hatchback and the limousine are serviced on consecutive days.
(E) The roadster and the hatchback are serviced on consecutive days.

17. Which one of the following could be the list of the vehicles serviced on Tuesday, Wednesday, and Friday, listed in that order?

(A) the pickup, the hatchback, the limousine
(B) the pickup, the roadster, the hatchback
(C) the sedan, the limousine, the hatchback
(D) the van, the limousine, the hatchback
(E) the van, the roadster, the limousine

GO ON TO THE NEXT PAGE.

Questions 18–23

A street entertainer has six boxes stacked one on top of the other and numbered consecutively 1 through 6, from the lowest box up to the highest. Each box contains a single ball, and each ball is one of three colors—green, red, or white. Onlookers are to guess the color of each ball in each box, given that the following conditions hold:

There are more red balls than white balls.

There is a box containing a green ball that is lower in the stack than any box that contains a red ball.

There is a white ball in a box that is immediately below a box that contains a green ball.

18. If there are exactly two white balls, then which one of the following boxes could contain a green ball?

(A) box 1
(B) box 3
(C) box 4
(D) box 5
(E) box 6

19. If there are green balls in boxes 5 and 6, then which one of the following could be true?

(A) There are red balls in boxes 1 and 4.
(B) There are red balls in boxes 2 and 4.
(C) There is a white ball in box 1.
(D) There is a white ball in box 2.
(E) There is a white ball in box 3.

20. The ball in which one of the following boxes must be the same color as at least one of the other balls?

(A) box 2
(B) box 3
(C) box 4
(D) box 5
(E) box 6

21. Which one of the following must be true?

(A) There is a green ball in a box that is lower than box 4.
(B) There is a green ball in a box that is higher than box 4.
(C) There is a red ball in a box that is lower than box 4.
(D) There is a red ball in a box that is higher than box 4.
(E) There is a white ball in a box that is lower than box 4.

22. If there are red balls in boxes 2 and 3, then which one of the following could be true?

(A) There is a red ball in box 1.
(B) There is a white ball in box 1.
(C) There is a green ball in box 4.
(D) There is a red ball in box 5.
(E) There is a white ball in box 6.

23. If boxes 2, 3, and 4 all contain balls that are the same color as each other, then which one of the following must be true?

(A) Exactly two of the boxes contain a green ball.
(B) Exactly three of the boxes contain a green ball.
(C) Exactly three of the boxes contain a red ball.
(D) Exactly one of the boxes contains a white ball.
(E) Exactly two of the boxes contain a white ball.

S T O P

IF YOU FINISH BEFORE TIME IS CALLED, YOU MAY CHECK YOUR WORK ON THIS SECTION ONLY.
DO NOT WORK ON ANY OTHER SECTION IN THE TEST.

SECTION III

Time—35 minutes

26 Questions

Directions: The questions in this section are based on the reasoning contained in brief statements or passages. For some questions, more than one of the choices could conceivably answer the question. However, you are to choose the best answer; that is, the response that most accurately and completely answers the question. You should not make assumptions that are by commonsense standards implausible, superfluous, or incompatible with the passage. After you have chosen the best answer, blacken the corresponding space on your answer sheet.

1. Commentator: In last week's wreck involving one of Acme Engines' older locomotives, the engineer lost control of the train when his knee accidentally struck a fuel shut-down switch. Acme claims it is not liable because it never realized that the knee-level switches were a safety hazard. When asked why it relocated knee-level switches in its newer locomotives, Acme said engineers had complained that they were simply inconvenient. However, it is unlikely that Acme would have spent the $500,000 it took to relocate switches in the newer locomotives merely because of inconvenience. Thus, Acme Engines should be held liable for last week's wreck.

The point that Acme Engines spent $500,000 relocating knee-level switches in its newer locomotives is offered in the commentator's argument as

(A) proof that the engineer is not at all responsible for the train wreck
(B) a reason for believing that the wreck would have occurred even if Acme Engines had remodeled their older locomotives
(C) an explanation of why the train wreck occurred
(D) evidence that knee-level switches are not in fact hazardous
(E) an indication that Acme Engines had been aware of the potential dangers of knee-level switches before the wreck occurred

2. Artist: Almost everyone in this country really wants to be an artist even though they may have to work other jobs to pay the rent. After all, just about everyone I know hopes to someday be able to make a living as a painter, musician, or poet even if they currently work as dishwashers or discount store clerks.

The reasoning in the artist's argument is flawed in that the argument

(A) contains a premise that presupposes the truth of the conclusion
(B) presumes that what is true of each person in a country is also true of the country's population as a whole
(C) defends a view solely on the grounds that the view is widely held
(D) bases its conclusion on a sample that is unlikely to accurately represent people in the country as a whole
(E) fails to make a needed distinction between wanting to be an artist and making a living as an artist

3. The qwerty keyboard became the standard keyboard with the invention of the typewriter and remains the standard for typing devices today. If an alternative known as the Dvorak keyboard were today's standard, typists would type significantly faster. Nevertheless, it is not practical to switch to the Dvorak keyboard because the cost to society of switching, in terms of time, money, and frustration, would be greater than the benefits that would be ultimately gained from faster typing.

The example above best illustrates which one of the following propositions?

(A) Often it is not worthwhile to move to a process that improves speed if it comes at the expense of accuracy.
(B) People usually settle on a standard because that standard is more efficient than any alternatives.
(C) People often remain with an entrenched standard rather than move to a more efficient alternative simply because they dislike change.
(D) The emotional cost associated with change is a factor that sometimes outweighs financial considerations.
(E) The fact that a standard is already in wide use can be a crucial factor in making it a more practical choice than an alternative.

GO ON TO THE NEXT PAGE.

4. Sam: Mountain lions, a protected species, are preying on bighorn sheep, another protected species. We must let nature take its course and hope the bighorns survive.

Meli: Nonsense. We must do what we can to ensure the survival of the bighorn, even if that means limiting the mountain lion population.

Which one of the following is a point of disagreement between Meli and Sam?

(A) Humans should not intervene to protect bighorn sheep from mountain lions.
(B) The preservation of a species as a whole is more important than the loss of a few individuals.
(C) The preservation of a predatory species is easier to ensure than the preservation of the species preyed upon.
(D) Any measures to limit the mountain lion population would likely push the species to extinction.
(E) If the population of mountain lions is not limited, the bighorn sheep species will not survive.

5. Parent: Pushing very young children into rigorous study in an effort to make our nation more competitive does more harm than good. Curricula for these young students must address their special developmental needs, and while rigorous work in secondary school makes sense, the same approach in the early years of primary school produces only short-term gains and may cause young children to burn out on schoolwork. Using very young students as pawns in the race to make the nation economically competitive is unfair and may ultimately work against us.

Which one of the following can be inferred from the parent's statements?

(A) For our nation to be competitive, our secondary school curriculum must include more rigorous study than it now does.
(B) The developmental needs of secondary school students are not now being addressed in our high schools.
(C) Our country can be competitive only if the developmental needs of all our students can be met.
(D) A curriculum of rigorous study does not adequately address the developmental needs of primary school students.
(E) Unless our nation encourages more rigorous study in the early years of primary school, we cannot be economically competitive.

6. A transit company's bus drivers are evaluated by supervisors riding with each driver. Drivers complain that this affects their performance, but because the supervisor's presence affects every driver's performance, those drivers performing best with a supervisor aboard will likely also be the best drivers under normal conditions.

Which one of the following is an assumption on which the argument depends?

(A) There is no effective way of evaluating the bus drivers' performance without having supervisors ride with them.
(B) The supervisors are excellent judges of a bus driver's performance.
(C) For most bus drivers, the presence of a supervisor makes their performance slightly worse than it otherwise would be.
(D) The bus drivers are each affected in roughly the same way and to the same extent by the presence of the supervisor.
(E) The bus drivers themselves are able to deliver accurate assessments of their driving performance.

7. Economic growth accelerates business demand for the development of new technologies. Businesses supplying these new technologies are relatively few, while those wishing to buy them are many. Yet an acceleration of technological change can cause suppliers as well as buyers of new technologies to fail.

Which one of the following is most strongly supported by the information above?

(A) Businesses supplying new technologies are more likely to prosper in times of accelerated technological change than other businesses.
(B) Businesses that supply new technologies may not always benefit from economic growth.
(C) The development of new technologies may accelerate economic growth in general.
(D) Businesses that adopt new technologies are most likely to prosper in a period of general economic growth.
(E) Economic growth increases business failures.

GO ON TO THE NEXT PAGE.

8. Energy analyst: During this record-breaking heat wave, air conditioner use has overloaded the region's electrical power grid, resulting in frequent power blackouts throughout the region. For this reason, residents have been asked to cut back voluntarily on air conditioner use in their homes. But even if this request is heeded, blackouts will probably occur unless the heat wave abates.

   Which one of the following, if true, most helps to resolve the apparent discrepancy in the information above?

   (A) Air-conditioning is not the only significant drain on the electrical system in the area.
   (B) Most air-conditioning in the region is used to cool businesses and factories.
   (C) Most air-conditioning systems could be made more energy efficient by implementing simple design modifications.
   (D) Residents of the region are not likely to reduce their air conditioner use voluntarily during particularly hot weather.
   (E) The heat wave is expected to abate in the near future.

9. Long-term and short-term relaxation training are two common forms of treatment for individuals experiencing problematic levels of anxiety. Yet studies show that on average, regardless of which form of treatment one receives, symptoms of anxiety decrease to a normal level within the short-term-training time period. Thus, for most people the generally more expensive long-term training is unwarranted.

   Which one of the following, if true, most weakens the argument?

   (A) A decrease in symptoms of anxiety often occurs even with no treatment or intervention by a mental health professional.
   (B) Short-term relaxation training conducted by a more experienced practitioner can be more expensive than long-term training conducted by a less experienced practitioner.
   (C) Recipients of long-term training are much less likely than recipients of short-term training to have recurrences of problematic levels of anxiety.
   (D) The fact that an individual thinks that a treatment will reduce his or her anxiety tends, in and of itself, to reduce the individual's anxiety.
   (E) Short-term relaxation training involves the teaching of a wider variety of anxiety-combating relaxation techniques than does long-term training.

10. Editorial: Many critics of consumerism insist that advertising persuades people that they need certain consumer goods when they merely desire them. However, this accusation rests on a fuzzy distinction, that between wants and needs. In life, it is often impossible to determine whether something is merely desirable or whether it is essential to one's happiness.

    Which one of the following most accurately expresses the conclusion drawn in the editorial's argument?

    (A) The claim that advertising persuades people that they need things that they merely want rests on a fuzzy distinction.
    (B) Many critics of consumerism insist that advertising attempts to blur people's ability to distinguish between wants and needs.
    (C) There is nothing wrong with advertising that tries to persuade people that they need certain consumer goods.
    (D) Many critics of consumerism fail to realize that certain things are essential to human happiness.
    (E) Critics of consumerism often use fuzzy distinctions to support their claims.

11. People who browse the web for medical information often cannot discriminate between scientifically valid information and quackery. Much of the quackery is particularly appealing to readers with no medical background because it is usually written more clearly than scientific papers. Thus, people who rely on the web when attempting to diagnose their medical conditions are likely to do themselves more harm than good.

    Which one of the following is an assumption the argument requires?

    (A) People who browse the web for medical information typically do so in an attempt to diagnose their medical conditions.
    (B) People who attempt to diagnose their medical conditions are likely to do themselves more harm than good unless they rely exclusively on scientifically valid information.
    (C) People who have sufficient medical knowledge to discriminate between scientifically valid information and quackery will do themselves no harm if they rely on the web when attempting to diagnose their medical conditions.
    (D) Many people who browse the web assume that information is not scientifically valid unless it is clearly written.
    (E) People attempting to diagnose their medical conditions will do themselves more harm than good only if they rely on quackery instead of scientifically valid information.

12. When adults toss balls to very young children they generally try to toss them as slowly as possible to compensate for the children's developing coordination. But recent studies show that despite their developing coordination, children actually have an easier time catching balls that are thrown at a faster speed.

Which one of the following, if true, most helps to explain why very young children find it easier to catch balls that are thrown at a faster speed?

(A) Balls thrown at a faster speed, unlike balls thrown at a slower speed, trigger regions in the brain that control the tracking of objects for self-defense.
(B) Balls that are tossed more slowly tend to have a higher arc that makes it less likely that the ball will be obscured by the body of the adult tossing it.
(C) Adults generally find it easier to catch balls that are thrown slowly than balls that are thrown at a faster speed.
(D) Children are able to toss balls back to the adults with more accuracy when they throw fast than when they throw the ball back more slowly.
(E) There is a limit to how fast the balls can be tossed to the children before the children start to have more difficulty in catching them.

13. Like a genetic profile, a functional magnetic-resonance image (fMRI) of the brain can contain information that a patient wishes to keep private. An fMRI of a brain also contains enough information about a patient's skull to create a recognizable image of that patient's face. A genetic profile can be linked to a patient only by referring to labels or records.

The statements above, if true, most strongly support which one of the following?

(A) It is not important that medical providers apply labels to fMRIs of patients' brains.
(B) An fMRI has the potential to compromise patient privacy in circumstances in which a genetic profile would not.
(C) In most cases patients cannot be reasonably sure that the information in a genetic profile will be kept private.
(D) Most of the information contained in an fMRI of a person's brain is also contained in that person's genetic profile.
(E) Patients are more concerned about threats to privacy posed by fMRIs than they are about those posed by genetic profiles.

14. Council member: I recommend that the abandoned shoe factory be used as a municipal emergency shelter. Some council members assert that the courthouse would be a better shelter site, but they have provided no evidence of this. Thus, the shoe factory would be a better shelter site.

A questionable technique used in the council member's argument is that of

(A) asserting that a lack of evidence against a view is proof that the view is correct
(B) accepting a claim simply because advocates of an opposing claim have not adequately defended their view
(C) attacking the proponents of the courthouse rather than addressing their argument
(D) attempting to persuade its audience by appealing to their fear
(E) attacking an argument that is not held by any actual council member

15. It was misleading for James to tell the Core Curriculum Committee that the chair of the Anthropology Department had endorsed his proposal. The chair of the Anthropology Department had told James that his proposal had her endorsement, but only if the draft proposal she saw included all the recommendations James would ultimately make to the Core Curriculum Committee.

The argument relies on which one of the following assumptions?

(A) If the chair of the Anthropology Department did not endorse James's proposed recommendations, the Core Curriculum Committee would be unlikely to implement them.
(B) The chair of the Anthropology Department would have been opposed to any recommendations James proposed to the Core Curriculum Committee other than those she had seen.
(C) James thought that the Core Curriculum Committee would implement the proposed recommendations only if they believed that the recommendations had been endorsed by the chair of the Anthropology Department.
(D) James thought that the chair of the Anthropology Department would have endorsed all of the recommendations that he proposed to the Core Curriculum Committee.
(E) The draft proposal that the chair of the Anthropology Department had seen did not include all of the recommendations in James's proposal to the Core Curriculum Committee.

GO ON TO THE NEXT PAGE.

16. Travaillier Corporation has recently hired employees with experience in the bus tour industry, and its executives have also been negotiating with charter bus companies that subcontract with bus tour companies. But Travaillier has traditionally focused on serving consumers who travel primarily by air, and marketing surveys show that Travaillier's traditional consumers have not changed their vacation preferences. Therefore, Travaillier must be attempting to enlarge its consumer base by attracting new customers.

Which one of the following, if true, would most weaken the argument?

(A) In the past, Travaillier has found it very difficult to change its customers' vacation preferences.
(B) Several travel companies other than Travaillier have recently tried and failed to expand into the bus tour business.
(C) At least one of Travaillier's new employees not only has experience in the bus tour industry but has also designed air travel vacation packages.
(D) Some of Travaillier's competitors have increased profits by concentrating their attention on their customers who spend the most on vacations.
(E) The industry consultants employed by Travaillier typically recommend that companies expand by introducing their current customers to new products and services.

17. Educator: Traditional classroom education is ineffective because education in such an environment is not truly a social process and only social processes can develop students' insights. In the traditional classroom, the teacher acts from outside the group and interaction between teachers and students is rigid and artificial.

The educator's conclusion follows logically if which one of the following is assumed?

(A) Development of insight takes place only if genuine education also occurs.
(B) Classroom education is effective if the interaction between teachers and students is neither rigid nor artificial.
(C) All social processes involve interaction that is neither rigid nor artificial.
(D) Education is not effective unless it leads to the development of insight.
(E) The teacher does not act from outside the group in a nontraditional classroom.

18. The probability of avoiding heart disease is increased if one avoids fat in one's diet. Furthermore, one is less likely to eat fat if one avoids eating dairy foods. Thus the probability of maintaining good health is increased by avoiding dairy foods.

The reasoning in the argument is most vulnerable to criticism on which one of the following grounds?

(A) The argument ignores the possibility that, even though a practice may have potentially negative consequences, its elimination may also have negative consequences.
(B) The argument fails to consider the possibility that there are more ways than one of decreasing the risk of a certain type of occurrence.
(C) The argument presumes, without providing justification, that factors that carry increased risks of negative consequences ought to be eliminated.
(D) The argument fails to show that the evidence appealed to is relevant to the conclusion asserted.
(E) The argument fails to consider that what is probable will not necessarily occur.

19. Professor: One cannot frame an accurate conception of one's physical environment on the basis of a single momentary perception, since each such glimpse occurs from only one particular perspective. Similarly, any history book gives only a distorted view of the past, since it reflects the biases and prejudices of its author.

The professor's argument proceeds by

(A) attempting to show that one piece of reasoning is incorrect by comparing it with another, presumably flawed, piece of reasoning
(B) developing a case for one particular conclusion by arguing that if that conclusion were false, absurd consequences would follow
(C) making a case for the conclusion of one argument by showing that argument's resemblance to another, presumably cogent, argument
(D) arguing that because something has a certain group of characteristics, it must also have another, closely related, characteristic
(E) arguing that a type of human cognition is unreliable in one instance because it has been shown to be unreliable under similar circumstances

GO ON TO THE NEXT PAGE.

20. To date, most of the proposals that have been endorsed by the Citizens League have been passed by the city council. Thus, any future proposal that is endorsed by the Citizens League will probably be passed as well.

The pattern of reasoning in which one of the following arguments is most similar to that in the argument above?

(A) Most of the Vasani grants that have been awarded in previous years have gone to academic biologists. Thus, if most of the Vasani grants awarded next year are awarded to academics, most of these will probably be biologists.

(B) Most of the individual trees growing on the coastal islands in this area are deciduous. Therefore, most of the tree species on these islands are probably deciduous varieties.

(C) Most of the editors who have worked for the local newspaper have not been sympathetic to local farmers. Thus, if the newspaper hires someone who is sympathetic to local farmers, they will probably not be hired as an editor.

(D) Most of the entries that were received after the deadline for last year's photography contest were rejected by the judges' committee. Thus, the people whose entries were received after the deadline last year will probably send them in well before the deadline this year.

(E) Most of the stone artifacts that have been found at the archaeological site have been domestic tools. Thus, if the next artifact found at the site is made of stone, it will probably be a domestic tool.

21. Chemist: The molecules of a certain weed-killer are always present in two forms, one the mirror image of the other. One form of the molecule kills weeds, while the other has no effect on them. As a result, the effectiveness of the weed-killer in a given situation is heavily influenced by which of the two forms is more concentrated in the soil, which in turn varies widely because local soil conditions will usually favor the breakdown of one form or the other. Thus, much of the data on the effects of this weed-killer are probably misleading.

Which one of the following, if true, most strengthens the chemist's argument?

(A) In general, if the molecules of a weed-killer are always present in two forms, then it is likely that weeds are killed by one of those two forms but unaffected by the other.

(B) Almost all of the data on the effects of the weed-killer are drawn from laboratory studies in which both forms of the weed-killer's molecules are equally concentrated in the soil and equally likely to break down in that soil.

(C) Of the two forms of the weed-killer's molecules, the one that kills weeds is found in most local soil conditions to be the more concentrated form.

(D) The data on the effects of the weed-killer are drawn from studies of the weed-killer under a variety of soil conditions similar to those in which the weed-killer is normally applied.

(E) Data on the weed-killer's effects that rely solely on the examination of the effects of only one of the two forms of the weed-killer's molecules will almost certainly be misleading.

GO ON TO THE NEXT PAGE.

22. Principle: A police officer is eligible for a Mayor's Commendation if the officer has an exemplary record, but not otherwise; an officer eligible for the award who did something this year that exceeded what could be reasonably expected of a police officer should receive the award if the act saved someone's life.

Conclusion: Officer Franklin should receive a Mayor's Commendation but Officer Penn should not.

From which one of the following sets of facts can the conclusion be properly drawn using the principle?

(A) In saving a child from drowning this year, Franklin and Penn both risked their lives beyond what could be reasonably expected of a police officer. Franklin has an exemplary record but Penn does not.
(B) Both Franklin and Penn have exemplary records, and each officer saved a child from drowning earlier this year. However, in doing so, Franklin went beyond what could be reasonably expected of a police officer; Penn did not.
(C) Neither Franklin nor Penn has an exemplary record. But, in saving the life of an accident victim, Franklin went beyond what could be reasonably expected of a police officer. In the only case in which Penn saved someone's life this year, Penn was merely doing what could be reasonably expected of an officer under the circumstances.
(D) At least once this year, Franklin has saved a person's life in such a way as to exceed what could be reasonably expected of a police officer. Penn has not saved anyone's life this year.
(E) Both Franklin and Penn have exemplary records. On several occasions this year Franklin has saved people's lives, and on many occasions this year Franklin has exceeded what could be reasonably expected of a police officer. On no occasions this year has Penn saved a person's life or exceeded what could be reasonably expected of an officer.

23. Essayist: It is much less difficult to live an enjoyable life if one is able to make lifestyle choices that accord with one's personal beliefs and then see those choices accepted by others. It is possible for people to find this kind of acceptance by choosing friends and associates who share many of their personal beliefs. Thus, no one should be denied the freedom to choose the people with whom he or she will associate.

Which one of the following principles, if valid, most helps to justify the essayist's argument?

(A) No one should be denied the freedom to make lifestyle choices that accord with his or her personal beliefs.
(B) One should associate with at least some people who share many of one's personal beliefs.
(C) If having a given freedom could make it less difficult for someone to live an enjoyable life, then no one should be denied that freedom.
(D) No one whose enjoyment of life depends, at least in part, on friends and associates who share many of the same personal beliefs should be deliberately prevented from having such friends and associates.
(E) One may choose for oneself the people with whom one will associate, if doing so could make it easier to live an enjoyable life.

24. Physician: The rise in blood pressure that commonly accompanies aging often results from a calcium deficiency. This deficiency is frequently caused by a deficiency in the active form of vitamin D needed in order for the body to absorb calcium. Since the calcium in one glass of milk per day can easily make up for any underlying calcium deficiency, some older people can lower their blood pressure by drinking milk.

The physician's conclusion is properly drawn if which one of the following is assumed?

(A) There is in milk, in a form that older people can generally utilize, enough of the active form of vitamin D and any other substances needed in order for the body to absorb the calcium in that milk.
(B) Milk does not contain any substance that is likely to cause increased blood pressure in older people.
(C) Older people's drinking one glass of milk per day does not contribute to a deficiency in the active form of vitamin D needed in order for the body to absorb the calcium in that milk.
(D) People who consume high quantities of calcium together with the active form of vitamin D and any other substances needed in order for the body to absorb calcium have normal blood pressure.
(E) Anyone who has a deficiency in the active form of vitamin D also has a calcium deficiency.

GO ON TO THE NEXT PAGE.

25. Political philosopher: A just system of taxation would require each person's contribution to correspond directly to the amount the society as a whole contributes to serve that person's interests. For purposes of taxation, wealth is the most objective way to determine how well the society has served the interest of any individual. Therefore, each person should be taxed solely in proportion to her or his income.

The flawed reasoning in the political philosopher's argument is most similar to that in which one of the following?

(A) Cars should be taxed in proportion to the danger that they pose. The most reliable measure of this danger is the speed at which a car can travel. Therefore, cars should be taxed only in proportion to their ability to accelerate quickly.
(B) People should be granted autonomy in proportion to their maturity. A certain psychological test was designed to provide an objective measure of maturity. Therefore, those scoring above high school level on the test should be granted complete autonomy.
(C) Everyone should pay taxes solely in proportion to the benefits they receive from government. Many government programs provide subsidies for large corporations. Therefore, a just tax would require corporations to pay a greater share of their income in taxes than individual citizens pay.
(D) Individuals who confer large material benefits upon society should receive high incomes. Those with high incomes should pay correspondingly high taxes. Therefore, we as a society should place high taxes on activities that confer large benefits upon society.
(E) Justice requires that health care be given in proportion to each individual's need. Therefore, we need to ensure that the most seriously ill hospital patients are given the highest priority for receiving care.

26. A recent poll showed that almost half of the city's residents believe that Mayor Walker is guilty of ethics violations. Surprisingly, however, 52 percent of those surveyed judged Walker's performance as mayor to be good or excellent, which is no lower than it was before anyone accused him of ethics violations.

Which one of the following, if true, most helps to explain the surprising fact stated above?

(A) Almost all of the people who believe that Walker is guilty of ethics violations had thought, even before he was accused of those violations, that his performance as mayor was poor.
(B) In the time since Walker was accused of ethics violations, there has been an increase in the percentage of city residents who judge the performance of Walker's political opponents to be good or excellent.
(C) About a fifth of those polled did not know that Walker had been accused of ethics violations.
(D) Walker is currently up for reelection, and anticorruption groups in the city have expressed support for Walker's opponent.
(E) Walker has defended himself against the accusations by arguing that the alleged ethics violations were the result of honest mistakes by his staff members.

S T O P

IF YOU FINISH BEFORE TIME IS CALLED, YOU MAY CHECK YOUR WORK ON THIS SECTION ONLY.
DO NOT WORK ON ANY OTHER SECTION IN THE TEST.

SECTION IV

Time—35 minutes

27 Questions

Directions: Each set of questions in this section is based on a single passage or a pair of passages. The questions are to be answered on the basis of what is stated or implied in the passage or pair of passages. For some of the questions, more than one of the choices could conceivably answer the question. However, you are to choose the best answer; that is, the response that most accurately and completely answers the question, and blacken the corresponding space on your answer sheet.

In Alaska, tradition is a powerful legal concept, appearing in a wide variety of legal contexts relating to natural-resource and public-lands activities. Both state and federal laws in the United States assign privileges and exemptions to individuals engaged in "traditional" activities using otherwise off-limits land and resources. But in spite of its prevalence in statutory law, the term "tradition" is rarely defined. Instead, there seems to be a presumption that its meaning is obvious. Failure to define "tradition" clearly in written law has given rise to problematic and inconsistent legal results.

One of the most prevalent ideas associated with the term "tradition" in the law is that tradition is based on long-standing practice, where "long-standing" refers not only to the passage of time but also to the continuity and regularity of a practice. But two recent court cases involving indigenous use of sea otter pelts illustrate the problems that can arise in the application of this sense of "traditional."

The hunting of sea otters was initially prohibited by the Fur Seal Treaty of 1910. The Marine Mammal Protection Act (MMPA) of 1972 continued the prohibition, but it also included an Alaska Native exemption, which allowed takings of protected animals for use in creating authentic native articles by means of "traditional native handicrafts." The U.S. Fish and Wildlife Service (FWS) subsequently issued regulations defining authentic native articles as those "commonly produced" before 1972, when the MMPA took effect. Not covered by the exemption, according to the FWS, were items produced from sea otter pelts, because Alaska Natives had not produced such handicrafts "within living memory."

In 1986, FWS agents seized articles of clothing made from sea otter pelts from Marina Katelnikoff, an Aleut. She sued, but the district court upheld the FWS regulations. Then in 1991 Katelnikoff joined a similar suit brought by Boyd Dickinson, a Tlingit from whom articles of clothing made from sea otter pelts had also been seized. After hearing testimony establishing that Alaska Natives had made many uses of sea otters before the occupation of the territory by Russia in the late 1700s, the court reconsidered what constituted a traditional item under the statute. The court now held that the FWS's regulations were based on a "strained interpretation" of the word "traditional," and that the reference to "living memory" imposed an excessively restrictive time frame. The court stated, "The fact that Alaskan natives were prevented, by circumstances beyond their control, from exercising a tradition for a given period of time does not mean that it has been lost forever or that it has become any less a 'tradition.' It defies common sense to define 'traditional' in such a way that only those traditions that were exercised during a comparatively short period in history could qualify as 'traditional.'"

1. Which one of the following most accurately expresses the main point of the passage?

(A) Two cases involving the use of sea otter pelts by Alaska Natives illustrate the difficulties surrounding the application of the legal concept of tradition in Alaska.

(B) Two court decisions have challenged the notion that for an activity to be considered "traditional," it must be shown to be a long-standing activity that has been regularly and continually practiced.

(C) Two court cases involving the use of sea otter pelts by Alaska Natives exemplify the wave of lawsuits that are now occurring in response to changes in natural-resource and public-lands regulations.

(D) Definitions of certain legal terms long taken for granted are being reviewed in light of new evidence that has come from historical sources relating to Alaska Native culture.

(E) Alaskan state laws and U.S. federal laws are being challenged by Alaska Natives because the laws are not sufficiently sensitive to indigenous peoples' concerns.

GO ON TO THE NEXT PAGE.

2. The court in the 1991 case referred to the FWS's interpretation of the term "traditional" as "strained" (line 46) because, in the court's view, the interpretation

(A) ignored the ways in which Alaska Natives have historically understood the term "traditional"
(B) was not consonant with any dictionary definition of "traditional"
(C) was inconsistent with what the term "traditional" is normally understood to mean
(D) led the FWS to use the word "traditional" to describe a practice that should not have been described as such
(E) failed to specify which handicrafts qualified to be designated as "traditional"

3. According to the passage, the court's decision in the 1991 case was based on which one of the following?

(A) a narrow interpretation of the term "long-standing"
(B) a common-sense interpretation of the phrase "within living memory"
(C) strict adherence to the intent of FWS regulations
(D) a new interpretation of the Fur Seal Treaty of 1910
(E) testimony establishing certain historical facts

4. The passage most strongly suggests that the court in the 1986 case believed that "traditional" should be defined in a way that

(A) reflects a compromise between the competing concerns surrounding the issue at hand
(B) emphasizes the continuity and regularity of practices to which the term is applied
(C) reflects the term's usage in everyday discourse
(D) encourages the term's application to recently developed, as well as age-old, activities
(E) reflects the concerns of the people engaging in what they consider to be traditional activities

5. Which one of the following is most strongly suggested by the passage?

(A) Between 1910 and 1972, Alaska Natives were prohibited from hunting sea otters.
(B) Traditional items made from sea otter pelts were specifically mentioned in the Alaska Native exemption of the MMPA.
(C) In the late 1700s, Russian hunters pressured the Russian government to bar Alaska Natives from hunting sea otters.
(D) By 1972, the sea otter population in Alaska had returned to the levels at which it had been prior to the late 1700s.
(E) Prior to the late 1700s, sea otters were the marine animal most often hunted by Alaska Natives.

6. The author's reference to the Fur Seal Treaty (line 22) primarily serves to

(A) establish the earliest point in time at which fur seals were considered to be on the brink of extinction
(B) indicate that several animals in addition to sea otters were covered by various regulatory exemptions issued over the years
(C) demonstrate that there is a well-known legal precedent for prohibiting the hunting of protected animals
(D) suggest that the sea otter population was imperiled by Russian seal hunters and not by Alaska Natives
(E) help explain the evolution of Alaska Natives' legal rights with respect to handicrafts defined as "traditional"

7. The ruling in the 1991 case would be most relevant as a precedent for deciding in a future case that which one of the following is a "traditional" Alaska Native handicraft?

(A) A handicraft no longer practiced but shown by archaeological evidence to have been common among indigenous peoples several millennia ago
(B) A handicraft that commonly involves taking the pelts of more than one species that has been designated as endangered
(C) A handicraft that was once common but was discontinued when herd animals necessary for its practice abandoned their local habitat due to industrial development
(D) A handicraft about which only a very few indigenous craftspeople were historically in possession of any knowledge
(E) A handicraft about which young Alaska Natives know little because, while it was once common, few elder Alaska Natives still practice it

GO ON TO THE NEXT PAGE.

The literary development of Kate Chopin, author of *The Awakening* (1899), took her through several phases of nineteenth-century women's fiction. Born in 1850, Chopin grew up with the sentimental novels that formed the bulk of the fiction of the mid–nineteenth century. In these works, authors employed elevated, romantic language to portray female characters whose sole concern was to establish their social positions through courtship and marriage. Later, when she started writing her own fiction, Chopin took as her models the works of a group of women writers known as the local colorists.

After 1865, what had traditionally been regarded as "women's culture" began to dissolve as women entered higher education, the professions, and the political world in greater numbers. The local colorists, who published stories about regional life in the 1870s and 1880s, were attracted to the new worlds opening up to women, and felt free to move within these worlds as artists. Like anthropologists, the local colorists observed culture and character with almost scientific detachment. However, as "women's culture" continued to disappear, the local colorists began to mourn its demise by investing its images with mythic significance. In their stories, the garden became a paradisal sanctuary; the house became an emblem of female nurturing; and the artifacts of domesticity became virtual totemic objects.

Unlike the local colorists, Chopin devoted herself to telling stories of loneliness, isolation, and frustration. But she used the conventions of the local colorists to solve a specific narrative problem: how to deal with extreme psychological states without resorting to the excesses of the sentimental novels she read as a youth. By reporting narrative events as if they were part of a region's "local color," Chopin could tell rather shocking or even melodramatic tales in an uninflected manner.

Chopin did not share the local colorists' growing nostalgia for the past, however, and by the 1890s she was looking beyond them to the more ambitious models offered by a movement known as the New Women. In the form as well as the content of their work, the New Women writers pursued freedom and innovation. They modified the form of the sentimental novel to make room for interludes of fantasy and parable, especially episodes in which women dream of an entirely different world than the one they inhabit. Instead of the crisply plotted short stories that had been the primary genre of the local colorists, the New Women writers experimented with impressionistic methods in an effort to explore hitherto unrecorded aspects of female consciousness. In *The Awakening*, Chopin embraced this impressionistic approach more fully to produce 39 numbered sections of uneven length unified less by their style or content than by their sustained focus on faithfully rendering the workings of the protagonist's mind.

8. Which one of the following statements most accurately summarizes the content of the passage?

   (A) Although Chopin drew a great deal of the material for *The Awakening* from the concerns of the New Women, she adapted them, using the techniques of the local colorists, to recapture the atmosphere of the novels she had read in her youth.

   (B) Avoiding the sentimental excesses of novels she read in her youth, and influenced first by the conventions of the local colorists and then by the innovative methods of the New Women, Chopin developed the literary style she used in *The Awakening*.

   (C) With its stylistic shifts, variety of content, and attention to the internal psychology of its characters, Chopin's *The Awakening* was unlike any work of fiction written during the nineteenth century.

   (D) In *The Awakening*, Chopin rebelled against the stylistic restraint of the local colorists, choosing instead to tell her story in elevated, romantic language that would more accurately convey her protagonist's loneliness and frustration.

   (E) Because she felt a kinship with the subject matter but not the stylistic conventions of the local colorists, Chopin turned to the New Women as models for the style she was struggling to develop in *The Awakening*.

9. With which one of the following statements about the local colorists would Chopin have been most likely to agree?

   (A) Their idealization of settings and objects formerly associated with "women's culture" was misguided.

   (B) Their tendency to observe character dispassionately caused their fiction to have little emotional impact.

   (C) Their chief contribution to literature lay in their status as inspiration for the New Women.

   (D) Their focus on regional life prevented them from addressing the new realms opening up to women.

   (E) Their conventions prevented them from portraying extreme psychological states with scientific detachment.

GO ON TO THE NEXT PAGE.

10. According to the passage, which one of the following conventions did Chopin adopt from other nineteenth-century women writers?

(A) elevated, romantic language
(B) mythic images of "women's culture"
(C) detached narrative stance
(D) strong plot lines
(E) lonely, isolated protagonists

11. As it is used by the author in line 14 of the passage, "women's culture" most probably refers to a culture that was expressed primarily through women's

(A) domestic experiences
(B) regional customs
(C) artistic productions
(D) educational achievements
(E) political activities

12. The author of the passage describes the sentimental novels of the mid–nineteenth century in lines 3–9 primarily in order to

(A) argue that Chopin's style represents an attempt to mimic these novels
(B) explain why Chopin later rejected the work of the local colorists
(C) establish the background against which Chopin's fiction developed
(D) illustrate the excesses to which Chopin believed nostalgic tendencies would lead
(E) prove that women's literature was already flourishing by the time Chopin began to write

13. The passage suggests that one of the differences between *The Awakening* and the work of the New Women was that *The Awakening*

(A) attempted to explore aspects of female consciousness
(B) described the dream world of female characters
(C) employed impressionism more consistently throughout
(D) relied more on fantasy to suggest psychological states
(E) displayed greater unity of style and content

14. The primary purpose of the passage is to

(A) educate readers of *The Awakening* about aspects of Chopin's life that are reflected in the novel
(B) discuss the relationship between Chopin's artistic development and changes in nineteenth-century women's fiction
(C) trace the evolution of nineteenth-century women's fiction using Chopin as a typical example
(D) counter a claim that Chopin's fiction was influenced by external social circumstances
(E) weigh the value of Chopin's novels and stories against those of other writers of her time

15. The work of the New Women, as it is characterized in the passage, gives the most support for which one of the following generalizations?

(A) Works of fiction written in a passionate, engaged style are more apt to effect changes in social customs than are works written in a scientific, detached style.
(B) Even writers who advocate social change can end up regretting the change once it has occurred.
(C) Changes in social customs inevitably lead to changes in literary techniques as writers attempt to make sense of the new social realities.
(D) Innovations in fictional technique grow out of writers' attempts to describe aspects of reality that have been neglected in previous works.
(E) Writers can most accurately depict extreme psychological states by using an uninflected manner.

GO ON TO THE NEXT PAGE.

Until the 1950s, most scientists believed that the geology of the ocean floor had remained essentially unchanged for many millions of years. But this idea became insupportable as new discoveries were made. First, scientists noticed that the ocean floor exhibited odd magnetic variations. Though unexpected, this was not entirely surprising, because it was known that basalt—the volcanic rock making up much of the ocean floor—contains magnetite, a strongly magnetic mineral that was already known to locally distort compass readings on land. This distortion is due to the fact that although some basalt has so-called "normal" polarity—that is, the magnetite in it has the same polarity as the earth's present magnetic field—other basalt has reversed polarity, an alignment opposite that of the present field. This occurs because in magma (molten rock), grains of magnetite—behaving like little compass needles—align themselves with the earth's magnetic field, which has reversed at various times throughout history. When magma cools to form solid basalt, the alignment of the magnetite grains is "locked in," recording the earth's polarity at the time of cooling.

As more of the ocean floor was mapped, the magnetic variations revealed recognizable patterns, particularly in the area around the other great oceanic discovery of the 1950s: the global mid-ocean ridge, an immense submarine mountain range that winds its way around the earth much like the seams of a baseball. Alternating stripes of rock with differing polarities are laid out in rows on either side of the mid-ocean ridge: one stripe with normal polarity and the next with reversed polarity. Scientists theorized that mid-ocean ridges mark structurally weak zones where the ocean floor is being pulled apart along the ridge crest. New magma from deep within the earth rises easily through these weak zones and eventually erupts along the crest of the ridges to create new oceanic crust. Over millions of years, this process, called ocean floor spreading, built the mid-ocean ridge.

This theory was supported by several lines of evidence. First, at or near the ridge crest, the rocks are very young, and they become progressively older away from the crest. Further, the youngest rocks all have normal polarity. Finally, because geophysicists had already determined the ages of continental volcanic rocks and, by measuring the magnetic orientation of these same rocks, had assigned ages to the earth's recent magnetic reversals, they were able to compare these known ages of magnetic reversals with the ocean floor's magnetic striping pattern, enabling scientists to show that, if we assume that the ocean floor moved away from the spreading center at a rate of several centimeters per year, there is a remarkable correlation between the ages of the earth's magnetic reversals and the striping pattern.

16. Which one of the following most accurately expresses the main idea of the passage?

(A) In the 1950s, scientists refined their theories concerning the process by which the ocean floor was formed many millions of years ago.
(B) The discovery of basalt's magnetic properties in the 1950s led scientists to formulate a new theory to account for the magnetic striping on the ocean floor.
(C) In the 1950s, two significant discoveries led to the transformation of scientific views about the geology of the oceans.
(D) Local distortions to compass readings are caused, scientists have discovered, by magma that rises through weak zones in the ocean floor to create new oceanic crust.
(E) The discovery of the ocean floor's magnetic variations convinced scientists of the need to map the entire ocean floor, which in turn led to the discovery of the global mid-ocean ridge.

17. The author characterizes the correlation mentioned in the last sentence of the passage as "remarkable" in order to suggest that the correlation

(A) indicates that ocean floor spreading occurs at an extremely slow rate
(B) explains the existence of the global mid-ocean ridge
(C) demonstrates that the earth's magnetic field is considerably stronger than previously believed
(D) provides strong confirmation of the ocean floor spreading theory
(E) reveals that the earth's magnetic reversals have occurred at very regular intervals

18. According to the passage, which one of the following is true of magnetite grains?

(A) In the youngest basalt, they are aligned with the earth's current polarity.
(B) In magma, most but not all of them align themselves with the earth's magnetic field.
(C) They are not found in other types of rock besides basalt.
(D) They are about the size of typical grains of sand.
(E) They are too small to be visible to the naked eye.

GO ON TO THE NEXT PAGE.

19. If the time intervals between the earth's magnetic field reversals fluctuate greatly, then, based on the passage, which one of the following is most likely to be true?

(A) Compass readings are most likely to be distorted near the peaks of the mid-ocean ridge.
(B) It is this fluctuation that causes the ridge to wind around the earth like the seams on a baseball.
(C) Some of the magnetic stripes of basalt on the ocean floor are much wider than others.
(D) Continental rock is a more reliable indicator of the earth's magnetic field reversals than is oceanic rock.
(E) Within any given magnetic stripe on the ocean floor, the age of the basalt does not vary.

20. Which one of the following would, if true, most help to support the ocean floor spreading theory?

(A) There are types of rock other than basalt that are known to distort compass readings.
(B) The ages of the earth's magnetic reversals have been verified by means other than examining magnetite grains in rock.
(C) Pieces of basalt similar to the type found on the mid-ocean ridge have been found on the continents.
(D) Along its length, the peak of the mid-ocean ridge varies greatly in height above the ocean floor.
(E) Basalt is the only type of volcanic rock found in portions of the ocean floor nearest to the continents.

21. Which one of the following is most strongly supported by the passage?

(A) Submarine basalt found near the continents is likely to be some of the oldest rock on the ocean floor.
(B) The older a sample of basalt is, the more times it has reversed its polarity.
(C) Compass readings are more likely to become distorted at sea than on land.
(D) The magnetic fields surrounding magnetite grains gradually weaken over millions of years on the ocean floor.
(E) Any rock that exhibits present-day magnetic polarity was formed after the latest reversal of the earth's magnetic field.

GO ON TO THE NEXT PAGE.

Passage A

Central to the historian's profession and scholarship has been the ideal of objectivity. The assumptions upon which this ideal rests include a commitment to the reality of the past, a sharp separation between fact and value, and above all, a distinction between history and fiction.

According to this ideal, historical facts are prior to and independent of interpretation: the value of an interpretation should be judged by how well it accounts for the facts; if an interpretation is contradicted by facts, it should be abandoned. The fact that successive generations of historians have ascribed different meanings to past events does not mean, as relativist historians claim, that the events themselves lack fixed or absolute meanings.

Objective historians see their role as that of a neutral judge, one who must never become an advocate or, worse, propagandist. Their conclusions should display the judicial qualities of balance and evenhandedness. As with the judiciary, these qualities require insulation from political considerations, and avoidance of partisanship or bias. Thus objective historians must purge themselves of external loyalties; their primary allegiance is to objective historical truth and to colleagues who share a commitment to its discovery.

Passage B

The very possibility of historical scholarship as an enterprise distinct from propaganda requires of its practitioners that self-discipline that enables them to do such things as abandon wishful thinking, assimilate bad news, and discard pleasing interpretations that fail elementary tests of evidence and logic.

Yet objectivity, for the historian, should not be confused with neutrality. Objectivity is perfectly compatible with strong political commitment. The objective thinker does not value detachment as an end in itself but only as an indispensable means of achieving deeper understanding. In historical scholarship, the ideal of objectivity is most compellingly embodied in the *powerful argument*—one that reveals by its every twist and turn its respectful appreciation of the alternative arguments it rejects. Such a text attains power precisely because its author has managed to suspend momentarily his or her own perceptions so as to anticipate and take into account objections and alternative constructions—not those of straw men, but those that truly issue from the rival's position, understood as sensitively and stated as eloquently as the rival could desire. To mount a telling attack on a position, one must first inhabit it. Those so habituated to their customary intellectual abode that they cannot even explore others can never be persuasive to anyone but fellow habitués.

Such arguments are often more faithful to the complexity of historical interpretation—more faithful even to the irreducible plurality of human perspectives—than texts that abjure position-taking altogether. The powerful argument is the highest fruit of the kind of thinking I would call objective, and in it neutrality plays no part. Authentic objectivity bears no resemblance to the television newscaster's mechanical gesture of allocating the same number of seconds to both sides of a question, editorially splitting the difference between them, irrespective of their perceived merits.

22. Both passages are concerned with answering which one of the following questions?

(A) What are the most serious flaws found in recent historical scholarship?
(B) What must historians do in order to avoid bias in their scholarship?
(C) How did the ideal of objectivity first develop?
(D) Is the scholarship produced by relativist historians sound?
(E) Why do the prevailing interpretations of past events change from one era to the next?

23. Both passages identify which one of the following as a requirement for historical research?

(A) the historian's willingness to borrow methods of analysis from other disciplines when evaluating evidence
(B) the historian's willingness to employ methodologies favored by proponents of competing views when evaluating evidence
(C) the historian's willingness to relinquish favored interpretations in light of the discovery of facts inconsistent with them
(D) the historian's willingness to answer in detail all possible objections that might be made against his or her interpretation
(E) the historian's willingness to accord respectful consideration to rival interpretations

GO ON TO THE NEXT PAGE.

24. The author of passage B and the kind of objective historian described in passage A would be most likely to disagree over whether
    (A) detachment aids the historian in achieving an objective view of past events
    (B) an objective historical account can include a strong political commitment
    (C) historians today are less objective than they were previously
    (D) propaganda is an essential tool of historical scholarship
    (E) historians of different eras have arrived at differing interpretations of the same historical events

25. Which one of the following most accurately describes an attitude toward objectivity present in each passage?
    (A) Objectivity is a goal that few historians can claim to achieve.
    (B) Objectivity is essential to the practice of historical scholarship.
    (C) Objectivity cannot be achieved unless historians set aside political allegiances.
    (D) Historians are not good judges of their own objectivity.
    (E) Historians who value objectivity are becoming less common.

26. Both passages mention propaganda primarily in order to
    (A) refute a claim made by proponents of a rival approach to historical scholarship
    (B) suggest that scholars in fields other than history tend to be more biased than historians
    (C) point to a type of scholarship that has recently been discredited
    (D) identify one extreme to which historians may tend
    (E) draw contrasts with other kinds of persuasive writing

27. The argument described in passage A and the argument made by the author of passage B are both advanced by
    (A) citing historical scholarship that fails to achieve objectivity
    (B) showing how certain recent developments in historical scholarship have undermined the credibility of the profession
    (C) summarizing opposing arguments in order to point out their flaws
    (D) suggesting that historians should adopt standards used by professionals in certain other fields
    (E) identifying what are seen as obstacles to achieving objectivity

S T O P

IF YOU FINISH BEFORE TIME IS CALLED, YOU MAY CHECK YOUR WORK ON THIS SECTION ONLY.
DO NOT WORK ON ANY OTHER SECTION IN THE TEST.

Acknowledgment is made to the following sources from which material has been adapted for use in this test booklet:

W. Jacquelyne Kious and Robert I. Tilling, *This Dynamic Earth: The Story of Plate Tectonics*. ©1996 by the United States Geological Survey.

"Open Your Mind." ©2002 by The Economist Newspaper Limited.

Elaine Showalter, *Sister's Choice: Tradition and Change in American Women's Writing*. ©1991 by Elaine Showalter.

Jennifer L. Tomsen, "'Traditional' Resource Uses and Activities: Articulating Values and Examining Conflicts in Alaska." ©2002 by Alaska Law Review.

LSAT Writing Sample Topic

Directions: The scenario presented below describes two choices, either one of which can be supported on the basis of the information given. Your essay should consider both choices and argue for one over the other, based on the two specified criteria and the facts provided. There is no "right" or "wrong" choice: a reasonable argument can be made for either.

The biggest newspaper in a large market is deciding whether to continue to write all of its local stories in-house or to contract out much of this work off-site to local freelancers. The largest section of the newspaper is devoted to local coverage. Using the facts below, write an essay in which you argue for one choice over the other based on the following two criteria:

- The newspaper wants to maximize the quality of its local coverage.
- The newspaper wants to minimize the costs of producing local stories.

Writing all local stories in-house requires maintaining an extensive staff for this purpose. This involves expenditures for salaries, benefits, and overhead. Staff must also be reimbursed for employee business expenses associated with gathering stories. The day-to-day management of personnel frictions in a sizable staff can be challenging. Training and communicating with in-house staff is direct. This allows for the effective adoption and maintenance of strict standards. Different approaches and innovation tend to be discouraged.

Contracting out much of the responsibility for local coverage would tend to encourage different approaches and innovation. It would free up some staff time for potentially more rewarding work such as conducting in-depth investigations of local concerns. The only compensation for the freelancers contracted for local coverage would be a fixed amount for each accepted story, depending on its length after editing by in-house staff. There would be a high turnover of these freelancers. Their loyalty to the company would be relatively low. Hiring replacements would require staff time. Training and communicating with freelancers would be relatively difficult. This includes efforts to inculcate and enforce strict standards.

Scratch Paper
Do not write your essay in this space.

Directions:

1. Use the Answer Key on the next page to check your answers.

2. Use the Scoring Worksheet below to compute your raw score.

3. Use the Score Conversion Chart to convert your raw score into the 120–180 scale.

Scoring Worksheet

1. Enter the number of questions you answered correctly in each section.

	Number Correct
SECTION I.	_______
SECTION II	_______
SECTION III	_______
SECTION IV	_______

2. Enter the sum here: _______

This is your Raw Score.

Conversion Chart

For Converting Raw Score to the 120–180 LSAT Scaled Score
LSAT PrepTest 63

Reported Score	Raw Score Lowest	Raw Score Highest
180	100	101
179	99	99
178	98	98
177	97	97
176	—*	—*
175	96	96
174	95	95
173	94	94
172	93	93
171	92	92
170	90	91
169	89	89
168	88	88
167	86	87
166	85	85
165	83	84
164	82	82
163	80	81
162	78	79
161	77	77
160	75	76
159	73	74
158	71	72
157	69	70
156	67	68
155	66	66
154	64	65
153	62	63
152	60	61
151	58	59
150	56	57
149	54	55
148	53	53
147	51	52
146	49	50
145	47	48
144	46	46
143	44	45
142	42	43
141	41	41
140	39	40
139	38	38
138	36	37
137	35	35
136	33	34
135	32	32
134	30	31
133	29	29
132	28	28
131	27	27
130	25	26
129	24	24
128	23	23
127	22	22
126	21	21
125	20	20
124	19	19
123	18	18
122	—*	—*
121	17	17
120	0	16

*There is no raw score that will produce this scaled score for this test.

SECTION I

1.	C	8.	E	15.	C	22.	B
2.	B	9.	D	16.	D	23.	B
3.	C	10.	A	17.	C	24.	E
4.	D	11.	D	18.	E	25.	A
5.	B	12.	B	19.	C		
6.	A	13.	D	20.	B		
7.	B	14.	D	21.	E		

SECTION II

1.	E	8.	C	15.	A	22.	C
2.	B	9.	D	16.	B	23.	D
3.	A	10.	A	17.	B		
4.	C	11.	B	18.	B		
5.	E	12.	E	19.	C		
6.	B	13.	C	20.	E		
7.	D	14.	E	21.	A		

SECTION III

1.	E	8.	B	15.	E	22.	A
2.	D	9.	C	16.	E	23.	C
3.	E	10.	A	17.	D	24.	A
4.	A	11.	B	18.	A	25.	A
5.	D	12.	A	19.	C	26.	A
6.	D	13.	B	20.	E		
7.	B	14.	B	21.	B		

SECTION IV

1.	A	8.	B	15.	D	22.	B
2.	C	9.	A	16.	C	23.	C
3.	E	10.	C	17.	D	24.	B
4.	B	11.	A	18.	A	25.	B
5.	A	12.	C	19.	C	26.	D
6.	E	13.	C	20.	B	27.	E
7.	C	14.	B	21.	A		

Experimental Section Answer Key
June 1999, PrepTest 25, Section 2

1.	A	8.	A	15.	D	22.	A
2.	C	9.	E	16.	E	23.	C
3.	A	10.	E	17.	D	24.	E
4.	A	11.	D	18.	E	25.	D
5.	B	12.	A	19.	B		
6.	C	13.	B	20.	D		
7.	C	14.	A	21.	E		

PrepTest 64
October 2011

SECTION I

Time—35 minutes

25 Questions

Directions: The questions in this section are based on the reasoning contained in brief statements or passages. For some questions, more than one of the choices could conceivably answer the question. However, you are to choose the best answer; that is, the response that most accurately and completely answers the question. You should not make assumptions that are by commonsense standards implausible, superfluous, or incompatible with the passage. After you have chosen the best answer, blacken the corresponding space on your answer sheet.

1. Sometimes it is advisable for a medical patient to seek a second opinion. But this process can be awkward for both the patient and the physicians, since the patient often worries that the first physician will be alienated. In addition, for the first physician there is the issue of pride: a second opinion tacitly highlights a physician's fallibility. And the second physician is in the position of evaluating not only a patient's health, but also, inevitably and uncomfortably, a colleague's work.

   Which one of the following most accurately states the conclusion of the argument as a whole?

   (A) Because of the awkwardness involved, it is best for patients not to seek second opinions unless it is absolutely necessary.
   (B) In cases in which second opinions are necessary, the first physician often feels that his or her professional judgment is called into question.
   (C) The process of obtaining a second medical opinion can be awkward for those involved.
   (D) Physicians who are called upon to offer second opinions are always uncomfortable about evaluating the work of colleagues.
   (E) In many cases in which medical patients seek second opinions, they are concerned about offending the first physician.

2. There are 70 to 100 Florida panthers alive today. This represents a very large increase over their numbers in the 1970s, but their population must reach at least 250 if it is to be self-sustaining. Their current habitat is not large enough to support any more of these animals, however.

   If the statements above are true, which one of the following must also be true?

   (A) Some part of the panthers' current habitat is only of marginal quality.
   (B) If the population of Florida panthers ever exceeds 250, it will be self-sustaining.
   (C) Unless Florida panthers acquire a larger habitat, their population will not be self-sustaining.
   (D) The population of Florida panthers will never increase much beyond its current level.
   (E) Today, Florida panthers occupy a larger habitat than they did in the 1970s.

3. Political scientist: Efforts to create a more egalitarian society are often wrongly criticized on the grounds that total equality would necessarily force everyone into a common mold. Equality is presumed by such critics to require unacceptably bland uniformity. But this is not so. By promoting complementary human interests, a society can achieve a greater and more prosperous equality while enhancing rather than minimizing diversity.

   The political scientist's argument proceeds by

   (A) undermining a view by showing that its general acceptance would lead to undesirable consequences
   (B) rebutting an objection by attacking the assumption on which it is said to be based
   (C) attacking a view by claiming that those who propose it are motivated only by self-interest
   (D) claiming that whatever is true of a group must be true of each of the members of the group
   (E) undermining an apparent counterexample to a universal claim

GO ON TO THE NEXT PAGE.

4. Physician: In an experiment, 50 patients with chronic back pain were divided into two groups. Small magnets were applied to the backs of one group; the other group received no treatment. Most of the patients in the first group, but very few in the second group, reported a significant reduction in pain. This shows that magnetic fields are probably effective at relieving some back pain.

Which one of the following, if true, constitutes the logically strongest counter to the physician's argument?

(A) A patient's merely knowing that a treatment has been applied can lead to improvement in his or her condition.
(B) Most physicians believe that medication relieves chronic back pain more effectively than magnets do.
(C) No other experiments have been done showing that magnetic fields reduce pain in any area other than the back.
(D) Some of the scientists who helped design the experiment believed even before the experiment that magnetic fields relieve back pain, but they were not directly involved in conducting the experiment.
(E) There was wide variation in the specific causes of the chronic back pain suffered by the patients in the experiment.

5. Kennel club members who frequently discipline their dogs report a higher incidence of misbehavior than do members who rarely or never discipline their dogs. We can conclude from this that discipline does not improve dogs' behavior; on the contrary, it encourages misbehavior.

The argument is flawed in that it fails to consider the possibility that

(A) dogs' misbehavior is the cause of, rather than the result of, frequent discipline
(B) dogs learn from past experience how their owners are likely to react to misbehavior
(C) discipline does not cause misbehavior on the part of animals other than dogs
(D) kennel club members tend to be more skilled at raising dogs than are other dog owners
(E) kennel club members are more likely to use discipline than are other dog owners

6. The number of tornadoes recorded annually in North America has more than tripled since 1953. Yet meteorologists insist that the climatic factors affecting the creation of tornadoes are unchanged.

Which one of the following, if true, most helps to resolve the apparent discrepancy described above?

(A) The factors affecting the creation of tornadoes were not well known to meteorologists before 1953.
(B) The intensity of the average tornado is greater now than it was in 1953.
(C) The number of tornadoes recorded annually has increased only slightly in the last five years.
(D) The amount of property damage done by tornadoes has grown substantially since 1953.
(E) Many more citizens are helping authorities detect tornadoes now than in 1953.

7. Recently, a report commissioned by a confectioners trade association noted that chocolate, formerly considered a health scourge, is an effective antioxidant and so has health benefits. Another earlier claim was that oily foods clog arteries, leading to heart disease, yet reports now state that olive oil has a positive influence on the circulatory system. From these examples, it is clear that if you wait long enough, almost any food will be reported to be healthful.

The reasoning in the argument is flawed in that the argument

(A) relies on the truth of a claim by a source that is likely to be biased
(B) applies a general rule to specific cases to which it does not pertain
(C) bases an overly broad generalization on just a few instances
(D) takes for granted that all results of nutritional research are eventually reported
(E) fails to consider that there are many foods that are reported to be unhealthful

GO ON TO THE NEXT PAGE.

8. According to the "bottom-up" theory of how ecosystems are structured, the availability of edible plants is what primarily determines an ecosystem's characteristics since it determines how many herbivores the ecosystem can support, which in turn determines how many predators it can support. This theory also holds that a reduction in the number of predators will have little impact on the rest of the ecosystem.

Which one of the following, if true, would provide evidence against the bottom-up theory?

(A) In an effort to build up the population of a rare species of monkey on Vahique Island, monkeys were bred in zoos and released into the wild. However, the effort failed because the trees on which the monkeys fed were also nearly extinct.
(B) After hunting virtually eliminated predators on Rigu Island, the population of many herbivore species increased more than tenfold, causing the density of plants to be dramatically reduced.
(C) After many of the trees on Jaevix Island were cleared, the island's leaf-cutter ants, which require a forested ecosystem, experienced a substantial decrease in population, as did the island's anteaters.
(D) After a new species of fern was introduced to Lisdok Island, native ferns were almost eliminated. However, this did not affect the population of the herbivores that had eaten the native ferns, since they also thrived on a diet of the new fern.
(E) Plants that are a dietary staple of wild pigs on Sedif Island have flourished over the last three decades, and the population of the pigs has not changed much in spite of extensive hunting.

9. If a child is to develop healthy bones, the child's diet must include sufficient calcium. It therefore follows that the diets of children who do not develop healthy bones do not include sufficient calcium.

Flawed reasoning in which one of the following most closely parallels the flawed reasoning in the argument above?

(A) If bread is to have a firm crust, it must be baked at the right temperature. It therefore follows that bread that is not baked at the right temperature will not have a firm crust.
(B) A cake must contain the right amount of flour in order to taste good. It therefore follows that cakes that do not taste good do not contain the right amount of flour.
(C) The Bake-a-Thon, which is open to contestants of all ages, has never been won by a person under the age of 30. It therefore follows that the winner of this year's Bake-a-Thon will not be under the age of 30.
(D) Both yeast and baking powder can cause sweet rolls to rise. It therefore follows that yeast can always be substituted for baking powder in a recipe for sweet rolls.
(E) In recipe contests, there are always more contestants in the pie category than there are in the cake category. It therefore follows that contestants generally have a better chance of winning in the cake category than in the pie category.

10. History provides many examples of technological innovations being strongly resisted by people whose working conditions without those innovations were miserable. This shows that social inertia is a more powerful determinant of human behavior than is the desire for comfort or safety.

Which one of the following, if true, most seriously undermines the reasoning in the argument?

(A) People correctly believe that technological innovations often cause job loss.
(B) People are often reluctant to take on new challenges.
(C) Some examples of technological innovation have been embraced by workers.
(D) People tend to adapt easily to gradually implemented technological innovations.
(E) People correctly believe that technological innovations almost always increase workers' productivity.

GO ON TO THE NEXT PAGE.

11. In considering the fact that many people believe that promotions are often given to undeserving employees because the employees successfully flatter their supervisors, a psychologist argued that although many people who flatter their supervisors are subsequently promoted, flattery generally is not the reason for their success, because almost all flattery is so blatant that it is obvious even to those toward whom it is directed.

Which one of the following, if assumed, enables the psychologist's conclusion to be properly drawn?

(A) People in positions of responsibility expect to be flattered.
(B) Official guidelines for granting promotion tend to focus on merit.
(C) Flattery that is not noticed by the person being flattered is ineffective.
(D) Many people interpret insincere flattery as sincere admiration.
(E) Supervisors are almost never influenced by flattery when they notice it.

12. The government is being urged to prevent organizations devoted to certain views on human nutrition from advocating a diet that includes large portions of uncooked meat, because eating uncooked meat can be very dangerous. However, this purported fact does not justify the government's silencing the groups, for surely the government would not be justified in silencing a purely political group merely on the grounds that the policies the group advocates could be harmful to some members of society. The same should be true for silencing groups with certain views on human nutrition.

Which one of the following principles most helps to justify the reasoning in the argument?

(A) The government should not silence any group for advocating a position that a significant proportion of society believes to be beneficial.
(B) The government ought to do whatever is in the best interest of society.
(C) One ought to advocate a position only if one believes that it is true or would be beneficial.
(D) The government ought not to silence an opinion merely on the grounds that it could be harmful to disseminate the opinion.
(E) One ought to urge the government to do only those things the government is justified in doing.

13. Medical researcher: Scientists compared a large group of joggers who habitually stretch before jogging to an equal number of joggers who do not stretch before jogging. Both groups of joggers incurred roughly the same number of injuries. This indicates that stretching before jogging does not help to prevent injuries.

Which one of the following, if true, would most weaken the medical researcher's argument?

(A) For both groups of joggers compared by the scientists, the rate of jogging injuries during the study was lower than the overall rate of jogging injuries.
(B) Among the joggers in the groups compared by the scientists, many of those previously injured while jogging experienced difficulty in their efforts to perform stretches.
(C) Most jogging injuries result from falls, collisions, and other mishaps on which the flexibility resulting from stretching would have little if any effect.
(D) The more prone a jogger is to jogging injuries, the more likely he or she is to develop the habit of performing stretches before jogging.
(E) Studies have found that, for certain forms of exercise, stretching beforehand can reduce the severity of injuries resulting from that exercise.

GO ON TO THE NEXT PAGE.

14. Superconductor development will enable energy to be transported farther with less energy lost in transit. This will probably improve industrial productivity, for a similar improvement resulted when oil and natural gas replaced coal as the primary fossil fuels used in North America. Shipping costs, a function of the distance fossil fuels are shipped and the losses of material in transit, decreased for factory owners at that time.

The claim that superconductor development will probably improve industrial productivity plays which one of the following roles in the argument?

(A) It is a conclusion for which the claim that shipping costs for fossil fuels are partly a function of the losses of material in transit is offered as partial support.
(B) It is a generalization for which the claim that superconductor development will enable energy to be transported farther with less energy lost in transit is offered as an illustration.
(C) It is an assumption supporting the conclusion that superconductor development will enable energy to be transported farther with less energy lost in transit.
(D) It is a premise offered to support the claim that oil and natural gas have replaced coal as the primary fossil fuels used in North America.
(E) It is cited as evidence that shipping costs are a function of the distances fossil fuels are shipped and the losses of material in transit.

15. The French novelist Colette (1873–1954) has been widely praised for the vividness of her language. But many critics complain that her novels are indifferent to important moral questions. This charge is unfair. Each of her novels is a poetic condensation of a major emotional crisis in the life of an ordinary person of her time. Such emotional crises almost invariably raise important moral questions.

Which one of the following is an assumption on which the argument depends?

(A) Critics who suggest that Colette's novels are indifferent to great moral questions of her time greatly underestimate her literary achievements.
(B) A novel that poetically condenses a major emotional crisis does not have to be indifferent to the important moral questions raised by that crisis.
(C) To deserve the level of praise that Colette has received, a novelist's work must concern itself with important moral questions.
(D) The vividness of Colette's language was not itself the result of poetic condensation.
(E) Colette's purpose in poetically condensing emotional crises in the lives of characters in her novels was to explore some of the important moral questions of her time.

16. The view that every person is concerned exclusively with her or his own self-interest implies that government by consent is impossible. Thus, social theorists who believe that people are concerned only with their self-interest evidently believe that aspiring to democracy is futile, since democracy is not possible in the absence of government by consent.

The reasoning in the argument is flawed in that the argument

(A) infers merely from the fact of someone's holding a belief that he or she believes an implication of that belief
(B) infers that because something is true of a group of people, it is true of each individual member of the group
(C) infers that because something is true of each individual person belonging to a group, it is true of the group as a whole
(D) attempts to discredit a theory by discrediting those who espouse that theory
(E) fails to consider that, even if an argument's conclusion is false, some of the assumptions used to justify that conclusion may nonetheless be true

17. Archaeologist: The mosaics that were removed from Zeugma, the ancient city now flooded by the runoff from Turkey's Birecik Dam, should have been left there. We had all the information about them that we needed to draw archaeological conclusions, and future archaeologists studying the site, who may not have access to our records, might be misled by their absence.

Which one of the following, if assumed, most helps to justify the reasoning in the archaeologist's argument?

(A) The only considerations that bear upon the question of whether the mosaics should have been removed are archaeological.
(B) Archaeologists studying a site can tell whether or not that site had been flooded at some time.
(C) The materials used in the construction of a mosaic are readily apparent when the mosaic is examined in its original location.
(D) Archaeological sites from which artifacts have been removed rarely mislead archaeologists who later study the site.
(E) The removal of artifacts from archaeological sites rarely has any environmental impact.

GO ON TO THE NEXT PAGE.

18. Traffic engineers have increased the capacity of the Krakkenbak Bridge to handle rush-hour traffic flow. The resultant increase in rush-hour traffic flow would not have occurred had the city not invested in computer modeling technology last year at the request of the city's mayor, and the city's financial predicament would not have been resolved if the traffic flow across the bridge during rush hour had not been increased.

Which one of the following can be properly inferred from the information above?

(A) The city's financial predicament would not have been resolved had the city chosen a competing computer modeling software package.
(B) The city's financial predicament would not have been resolved had the city not invested in computer modeling technology.
(C) On an average day, more traffic crosses the Krakkenbak Bridge this year as compared to last year.
(D) Traffic flow across the Krakkenbak Bridge during rush hour would not have increased had the city's mayor not made investing in computer modeling technology the highest budgetary priority last year.
(E) The city's mayor was a proponent of investing in computer modeling technology because of the city's need to increase traffic flow across the Krakkenbak Bridge during rush hour.

19. Court analyst: Courts should not allow the use of DNA tests in criminal cases. There exists considerable controversy among scientific experts about how reliable these tests are. Unless there is widespread agreement in the scientific community about how reliable a certain test is, it is unreasonable for the courts to allow evidence based on that test.

The court analyst's reasoning is flawed because it fails to take into account that

(A) courts have the authority to admit or exclude any evidence irrespective of what experts have to say about its reliability
(B) the standard against which evidence in a criminal case is measured should not be absolute certainty
(C) experts may agree that the tests are highly reliable while disagreeing about exactly how reliable they are
(D) data should not be admitted as evidence in a court of law without scientific witnesses having agreed about how reliable they are
(E) there are also controversies about reliability of evidence in noncriminal cases

20. Members of the VideoKing Frequent Viewers club can now receive a special discount coupon. Members of the club who have rented more than ten videos in the past month can receive the discount coupon only at the VideoKing location from which the member last rented a movie. Members of the Frequent Viewers club who have not rented more than ten videos in the past month can receive the coupon only at the Main Street location. Pat, who has not rented more than ten videos in the past month, can receive the special discount coupon at the Walnut Lane location of VideoKing.

If all of the statements above are true, which one of the following must be true?

(A) The only people who can receive the special discount coupon at the Main Street location are Frequent Viewers club members who have not rented more than ten videos.
(B) Some members of the Frequent Viewers club have not rented more than ten videos.
(C) Some members of the Frequent Viewers club can receive the special discount coupon at more than one location of VideoKing.
(D) Some people who are not members of the Frequent Viewers club can receive the special discount coupon.
(E) If Pat rents a movie from the Main Street location, then she will not receive the special discount coupon.

GO ON TO THE NEXT PAGE.

21. Game show winners choosing between two equally desirable prizes will choose either the one that is more expensive or the one with which they are more familiar. Today's winner, Ed, is choosing between two equally desirable and equally unfamiliar prizes, A and B. He will thus choose A, which is more expensive.

The reasoning in which one of the following is most similar to the reasoning above?

(A) With a book contract, an academic writer receives either an advance or a guarantee of royalties. Professor al-Sofi received an advance for a book contract, so al-Sofi did not receive a guarantee of royalties.
(B) When entering this amusement park, children always choose to take their first ride on either the Rocket or the Mouse. Janine insisted on the Rocket for her first ride. Thus, Janine would not have been standing near the Mouse during her first half hour in the amusement park.
(C) The elliptical orbit of an asteroid is only slightly eccentric unless it is affected by the gravitational pull of a planet. Asteroid Y is affected by Jupiter's gravitational pull and asteroid X is not. Thus, the orbit of asteroid Y is the more eccentric of the two.
(D) New students in this program must choose either a physics class or an art class. Miyoko has no desire to take a class in either of those fields, so Miyoko will probably not enter this program.
(E) To avoid predators, rabbits will either double back on their pursuers or flee for nearby cover. The rabbit being pursued by a fox in this wildlife film is in a field that offers no opportunity for nearby cover, so it will try to double back on the fox.

22. Microbiologist: Because heavy metals are normally concentrated in sewage sludge during the sewage treatment process, the bacteria that survive in the sludge have evolved the unusual ability to resist heavy-metal poisoning. The same bacteria also show a strong resistance to antibiotics. This suggests that the bacteria's exposure to the heavy metals in the sewage sludge has somehow promoted their resistance to antibiotics.

Which one of the following, if true, most strengthens the microbiologist's argument?

(A) Most bacteria that are not resistant to antibiotics are not resistant to heavy-metal poisoning either.
(B) Bacteria that live in sewage sludge that is free of heavy metals, but is in other respects similar to normal sewage, are generally resistant to neither heavy-metal poisoning nor antibiotics.
(C) Antibiotic resistance of bacteria that survive in sewage sludge in which heavy metals are concentrated contributes to their resistance to heavy-metal poisoning.
(D) Sewage sludge that contains high concentrations of heavy metals almost always contains significant concentrations of antibiotics.
(E) Many kinds of bacteria that do not live in sewage sludge are resistant to both heavy-metal poisoning and antibiotics.

23. Ethicist: Marital vows often contain the promise to love "until death do us part." If "love" here refers to a feeling, then this promise makes no sense, for feelings are not within one's control, and a promise to do something not within one's control makes no sense. Thus, no one—including those making marital vows—should take "love" in this context to be referring to feelings.

The ethicist's conclusion follows logically if which one of the following is assumed?

(A) None of our feelings are within our control.
(B) People should not make promises to do something that is not within their control.
(C) "Love" can legitimately be taken to refer to something other than feelings.
(D) Promises should not be interpreted in such a way that they make no sense.
(E) Promises that cannot be kept do not make any sense.

GO ON TO THE NEXT PAGE.

24. Principle: If a food product contains ingredients whose presence most consumers of that product would be upset to discover in it, then the food should be labeled as containing those ingredients.

Application: Crackly Crisps need not be labeled as containing genetically engineered ingredients, since most consumers of Crackly Crisps would not care if they discovered that fact.

The application of the principle is most vulnerable to criticism on the grounds that it

(A) fails to address the possibility that consumers of a specific food may not be representative of consumers of food in general
(B) fails to address the possibility that the genetically engineered ingredients in Crackly Crisps may have been proven safe for human consumption
(C) implicitly makes use of a value judgment that is incompatible with the principle being applied
(D) takes for granted that if most consumers of a product would buy it even if they knew several of the ingredients in it, then they would buy the product even if they knew all the ingredients in it
(E) confuses a claim that under certain conditions a certain action should be taken with a claim that the action need not be taken in the absence of those conditions

25. Editorial: The town would not need to spend as much as it does on removing trash if all town residents sorted their household garbage. However, while telling residents that they must sort their garbage would get some of them to do so, many would resent the order and refuse to comply. The current voluntary system, then, is to be preferred, because it costs about as much as a nonvoluntary system would and it does not engender nearly as much resentment.

The contention that the town would not have to spend as much as it does on removing trash if all town residents sorted their garbage plays which one of the following roles in the editorial's argument?

(A) It is a claim that the editorial is trying to show is false.
(B) It is a fact granted by the editorial that lends some support to an alternative to the practice that the editorial defends as preferable.
(C) It is an example of a difficulty facing the claim that the editorial is attempting to refute.
(D) It is a premise that the editorial's argument relies on in reaching its conclusion.
(E) It is the conclusion that the editorial's argument purports to establish.

S T O P

IF YOU FINISH BEFORE TIME IS CALLED, YOU MAY CHECK YOUR WORK ON THIS SECTION ONLY.
DO NOT WORK ON ANY OTHER SECTION IN THE TEST.

SECTION II

Time—35 minutes

23 Questions

Directions: Each group of questions in this section is based on a set of conditions. In answering some of the questions, it may be useful to draw a rough diagram. Choose the response that most accurately and completely answers each question and blacken the corresponding space on your answer sheet.

Questions 1–6

An administrator must assign parking spaces to six new employees: Robertson, Souza, Togowa, Vaughn, Xu, and Young. Each of the six employees must be assigned one of the following parking spaces: #1, #2, #3, #4, #5, or #6. No two employees can be assigned the same parking space. The following rules govern the assignment of parking spaces:

Young must be assigned a higher-numbered parking space than Togowa.

Xu must be assigned a higher-numbered parking space than Souza.

Robertson must be assigned a higher-numbered parking space than Young.

Robertson must be assigned parking space #1, #2, #3, or #4.

1. Which one of the following could be the assignment of parking spaces to the new employees?

(A) #1: Young; #2: Souza; #3: Vaughn; #4: Robertson; #5: Togowa; #6: Xu
(B) #1: Vaughn; #2: Togowa; #3: Young; #4: Souza; #5: Robertson; #6: Xu
(C) #1: Togowa; #2: Young; #3: Xu; #4: Robertson; #5: Souza; #6: Vaughn
(D) #1: Togowa; #2: Robertson; #3: Young; #4: Souza; #5: Vaughn; #6: Xu
(E) #1: Souza; #2: Togowa; #3: Young; #4: Robertson; #5: Xu; #6: Vaughn

2. If Togowa is assigned a higher-numbered parking space than Souza, then which one of the following could be true?

(A) Young is assigned parking space #2.
(B) Vaughn is assigned parking space #5.
(C) Togowa is assigned parking space #3.
(D) Souza is assigned parking space #2.
(E) Robertson is assigned parking space #3.

3. The assignment of parking spaces to each of the new employees is fully and uniquely determined if which one of the following is true?

(A) Souza is assigned parking space #1.
(B) Young is assigned parking space #2.
(C) Vaughn is assigned parking space #3.
(D) Robertson is assigned parking space #4.
(E) Xu is assigned parking space #5.

4. For how many of the six new employees is the assignment of a parking space limited to one of only two possible spaces?

(A) none
(B) two
(C) three
(D) four
(E) five

5. If Young is assigned a higher-numbered parking space than Souza, then which one of the following could be true?

(A) Togowa is assigned parking space #1.
(B) Young is assigned parking space #2.
(C) Robertson is assigned parking space #3.
(D) Souza is assigned parking space #3.
(E) Vaughn is assigned parking space #4.

6. If Robertson is assigned parking space #3, then which one of the following must be true?

(A) Souza is assigned parking space #4.
(B) Togowa is assigned parking space #2.
(C) Vaughn is assigned parking space #5.
(D) Xu is assigned parking space #6.
(E) Young is assigned parking space #2.

Questions 7–12

A government needs to assign new ambassadors to Venezuela, Yemen, and Zambia. The candidates for these ambassadorships are Jaramillo, Kayne, Landon, Novetzke, and Ong. One ambassador will be assigned to each country, and no ambassador will be assigned to more than one country. The assignment of the ambassadors must meet the following constraints:

Either Kayne or Novetzke, but not both, is assigned to one of the ambassadorships.
If Jaramillo is assigned to one of the ambassadorships, then so is Kayne.
If Ong is assigned as ambassador to Venezuela, Kayne is not assigned as ambassador to Yemen.
If Landon is assigned to an ambassadorship, it is to Zambia.

7. Which one of the following could be the assignment of the ambassadors?

(A) Venezuela: Jaramillo
Yemen: Ong
Zambia: Novetzke
(B) Venezuela: Kayne
Yemen: Jaramillo
Zambia: Landon
(C) Venezuela: Landon
Yemen: Novetzke
Zambia: Ong
(D) Venezuela: Novetzke
Yemen: Jaramillo
Zambia: Kayne
(E) Venezuela: Ong
Yemen: Kayne
Zambia: Landon

8. The pair of candidates who are not assigned to ambassadorships could be

(A) Jaramillo and Novetzke
(B) Jaramillo and Ong
(C) Kayne and Landon
(D) Kayne and Novetzke
(E) Landon and Ong

9. If Ong is assigned as ambassador to Venezuela, then the other two ambassadors assigned could be

(A) Jaramillo and Landon
(B) Jaramillo and Novetzke
(C) Kayne and Landon
(D) Kayne and Novetzke
(E) Landon and Novetzke

10. If Kayne is assigned as ambassador to Yemen, which one of the following must be true?

(A) Jaramillo is assigned as ambassador to Venezuela.
(B) Landon is assigned as ambassador to Zambia.
(C) Ong is assigned as ambassador to Zambia.
(D) Jaramillo is not assigned to an ambassadorship.
(E) Ong is not assigned to an ambassadorship.

11. Which one of the following CANNOT be true?

(A) Jaramillo is assigned as ambassador to Zambia.
(B) Kayne is assigned as ambassador to Zambia.
(C) Novetzke is assigned as ambassador to Zambia.
(D) Landon is not assigned to an ambassadorship.
(E) Ong is not assigned to an ambassadorship.

12. Which one of the following, if substituted for the constraint that if Jaramillo is assigned to one of the ambassadorships, then so is Kayne, would have the same effect in determining the assignment of the ambassadors?

(A) If Kayne is assigned to an ambassadorship, then so is Jaramillo.
(B) If Landon and Ong are both assigned to ambassadorships, then so is Novetzke.
(C) If Ong is not assigned to an ambassadorship, then Kayne is assigned to an ambassadorship.
(D) Jaramillo and Novetzke are not both assigned to ambassadorships.
(E) Novetzke and Ong are not both assigned to ambassadorships.

GO ON TO THE NEXT PAGE.

Questions 13–18

On the first day of a two-day study for a cycling magazine, four riders—Reynaldo, Seamus, Theresa, and Yuki—will each test one of four bicycles—F, G, H, and J. Each rider will then test a different one of the bicycles on the second day. Each rider tests only one bicycle per day, and all four bicycles are tested each day. The assignment of riders to bicycles is subject to the following conditions:

Reynaldo cannot test F.
Yuki cannot test J.
Theresa must be one of the testers for H.
The bicycle that Yuki tests on the first day must be tested by Seamus on the second day.

13. Which one of the following is a possible assignment of riders to bicycles, with the riders for each bicycle listed in the order in which they test the bicycle?

(A) F: Seamus, Reynaldo; G: Yuki, Seamus; H: Theresa, Yuki; J: Reynaldo, Theresa
(B) F: Seamus, Yuki; G: Reynaldo, Theresa; H: Yuki, Seamus; J: Theresa, Reynaldo
(C) F: Yuki, Seamus; G: Seamus, Reynaldo; H: Theresa, Yuki; J: Reynaldo, Theresa
(D) F: Yuki, Seamus; G: Theresa, Reynaldo; H: Reynaldo, Theresa; J: Seamus, Yuki
(E) F: Yuki, Theresa; G: Seamus, Yuki; H: Theresa, Reynaldo; J: Reynaldo, Seamus

14. If Theresa tests G on the second day, then which one of the following must be true?

(A) Reynaldo tests H on the first day.
(B) Reynaldo tests J on the first day.
(C) Theresa tests H on the second day.
(D) Theresa tests J on the first day.
(E) Yuki tests H on the second day.

15. Any of the following could be true EXCEPT:

(A) Reynaldo tests J on the first day.
(B) Reynaldo tests J on the second day.
(C) Seamus tests H on the first day.
(D) Yuki tests H on the first day.
(E) Yuki tests H on the second day.

16. Which one of the following CANNOT be true?

(A) Reynaldo tests G on the second day.
(B) Seamus tests F on the first day.
(C) Theresa tests F on the second day.
(D) Reynaldo tests H on the first day.
(E) Yuki tests F on the second day.

17. If Theresa tests J on the first day, then which one of the following could be true?

(A) Reynaldo tests G on the second day.
(B) Seamus tests H on the first day.
(C) Yuki tests H on the second day.
(D) Seamus is one of the testers for J.
(E) Theresa is one of the testers for G.

18. Which one of the following CANNOT be true?

(A) Both Reynaldo and Seamus test J.
(B) Both Reynaldo and Theresa test J.
(C) Both Reynaldo and Yuki test G.
(D) Both Seamus and Theresa test G.
(E) Both Theresa and Yuki test F.

GO ON TO THE NEXT PAGE.

Questions 19–23

Exactly eight books—F, G, H, I, K, L, M, O—are placed on a bookcase with exactly three shelves—the top shelf, the middle shelf, and the bottom shelf. At least two books are placed on each shelf. The following conditions must apply:

More of the books are placed on the bottom shelf than the top shelf.
I is placed on the middle shelf.
K is placed on a higher shelf than F.
O is placed on a higher shelf than L.
F is placed on the same shelf as M.

19. Which one of the following could be a complete and accurate list of the books placed on the bottom shelf?

(A) F, M
(B) F, H, M
(C) G, H, K
(D) F, G, M, O
(E) G, H, L, M

20. It is fully determined which of the shelves each of the books is placed on if which one of the following is true?

(A) I and M are placed on the same shelf as each other.
(B) K and G are placed on the same shelf as each other.
(C) L and F are placed on the same shelf as each other.
(D) M and H are placed on the same shelf as each other.
(E) H and O are placed on the same shelf as each other.

21. Which one of the following must be true?

(A) O is placed on a shelf higher than the shelf M is placed on.
(B) K is placed on a shelf higher than the shelf G is placed on.
(C) I is placed on a shelf higher than the shelf F is placed on.
(D) G is placed on a shelf higher than the shelf O is placed on.
(E) F is placed on a shelf higher than the shelf L is placed on.

22. If G is placed on the top shelf, then which one of the following could be a complete and accurate list of the books placed on the middle shelf?

(A) H, I
(B) I, L
(C) H, I, L
(D) I, K, L
(E) F, I, M

23. If L is placed on a shelf higher than the shelf H is placed on, then which one of the following must be true?

(A) F and G are placed on the same shelf as each other.
(B) G and H are placed on the same shelf as each other.
(C) H and M are placed on the same shelf as each other.
(D) I and G are placed on the same shelf as each other.
(E) K and O are placed on the same shelf as each other.

S T O P

IF YOU FINISH BEFORE TIME IS CALLED, YOU MAY CHECK YOUR WORK ON THIS SECTION ONLY. DO NOT WORK ON ANY OTHER SECTION IN THE TEST.

Time—35 minutes

26 Questions

Directions: Each passage in this section is followed by a group of questions to be answered on the basis of what is stated or implied in the passage. For some of the questions, more than one of the choices could conceivably answer the question. However, you are to choose the best answer; that is, the response that most accurately and completely answers the question, and blacken the corresponding space on your answer sheet.

Most office workers assume that the messages they send to each other via electronic mail are as private as a telephone call or a face-to-face meeting. That assumption is wrong. Although it is illegal in many areas for an employer to eavesdrop on private conversations or telephone calls—even if they take place on a company-owned telephone—there are no clear rules governing electronic mail. In fact, the question of how private electronic mail transmissions should be has emerged as one of the more complicated legal issues of the electronic age.

People's opinions about the degree of privacy that electronic mail should have vary depending on whose electronic mail system is being used and who is reading the messages. Does a government office, for example, have the right to destroy electronic messages created in the course of running the government, thereby denying public access to such documents? Some hold that government offices should issue guidelines that allow their staff to delete such electronic records, and defend this practice by claiming that the messages thus deleted already exist in paper versions whose destruction is forbidden. Opponents of such practices argue that the paper versions often omit such information as who received the messages and when they received them, information commonly carried on electronic mail systems. Government officials, opponents maintain, are civil servants; the public should thus have the right to review any documents created during the conducting of government business.

Questions about electronic mail privacy have also arisen in the private sector. Recently, two employees of an automotive company were discovered to have been communicating disparaging information about their supervisor via electronic mail. The supervisor, who had been monitoring the communication, threatened to fire the employees. When the employees filed a grievance complaining that their privacy had been violated, they were let go. Later, their court case for unlawful termination was dismissed; the company's lawyers successfully argued that because the company owned the computer system, its supervisors had the right to read anything created on it.

In some areas, laws prohibit outside interception of electronic mail by a third party without proper authorization such as a search warrant. However, these laws to not cover "inside" interception such as occurred at the automotive company. In the past, courts have ruled that interoffice communications may be considered private only if employees have a "reasonable expectation" of privacy when they send the messages. The fact is that no absolute guarantee of privacy exists in any computer system. The only solution may be for users to scramble their own messages with encryption codes; unfortunately, such complex codes are likely to undermine the principal virtue of electronic mail: its convenience.

1. Which one of the following statements most accurately summarizes the main point of the passage?

(A) Until the legal questions surrounding the privacy of electronic mail in both the public and private sectors have been resolved, office workers will need to scramble their electronic mail messages with encryption codes.

(B) The legal questions surrounding the privacy of electronic mail in the workplace can best be resolved by treating such communications as if they were as private as telephone conversations or face-to-face meetings.

(C) Any attempt to resolve the legal questions surrounding the privacy of electronic mail in the workplace must take into account the essential difference between public-sector and private-sector business.

(D) At present, in both the public and private sectors, there seem to be no clear general answers to the legal questions surrounding the privacy of electronic mail in the workplace.

(E) The legal questions surrounding the privacy of electronic mail in the workplace can best be resolved by allowing supervisors in public-sector but not private-sector offices to monitor their employees' communications.

GO ON TO THE NEXT PAGE.

2. According to the passage, which one of the following best expresses the reason some people use to oppose the deletion of electronic mail records at government offices?

   (A) Such deletion reveals the extent of government's unhealthy obsession with secrecy.
   (B) Such deletion runs counter to the notion of government's accountability to its constituency.
   (C) Such deletion clearly violates the legal requirement that government offices keep duplicate copies of all their transactions.
   (D) Such deletion violates the government's own guidelines against destruction of electronic records.
   (E) Such deletion harms relations between government employees and their supervisors.

3. Which one of the following most accurately states the organization of the passage?

   (A) A problem is introduced, followed by specific examples illustrating the problem; a possible solution is suggested, followed by an acknowledgment of its shortcomings.
   (B) A problem is introduced, followed by explications of two possible solutions to the problem; the first solution is preferred to the second, and reasons are given for why it is the better alternative.
   (C) A problem is introduced, followed by analysis of the historical circumstances that helped bring the problem about; a possible solution is offered and rejected as being only a partial remedy.
   (D) A problem is introduced, followed by enumeration of various questions that need to be answered before a solution can be found; one possible solution is proposed and argued for.
   (E) A problem is introduced, followed by descriptions of two contrasting approaches to thinking about the problem; the second approach is preferred to the first, and reasons are given for why it is more likely to yield a successful solution.

4. Based on the passage, the author's attitude toward interception of electronic mail can most accurately be described as

   (A) outright disapproval of the practice
   (B) support for employers who engage in it
   (C) support for employees who lose their jobs because of it
   (D) intellectual interest in its legal issues
   (E) cynicism about the motives behind the practice

5. It can be inferred from the passage that the author would most likely hold which one of the following opinions about an encryption system that could encode and decode electronic mail messages with a single keystroke?

   (A) It would be an unreasonable burden on a company's ability to monitor electronic mail created by its employees.
   (B) It would significantly reduce the difficulty of attempting to safeguard the privacy of electronic mail.
   (C) It would create substantial legal complications for companies trying to prevent employees from revealing trade secrets to competitors.
   (D) It would guarantee only a minimal level of employee privacy, and so would not be worth the cost involved in installing such a system.
   (E) It would require a change in the legal definition of "reasonable expectation of privacy" as it applies to employer-employee relations.

6. Given the information in the passage, which one of the following hypothetical events is LEAST likely to occur?

   (A) A court rules that a government office's practice of deleting its electronic mail is not in the public's best interests.
   (B) A private-sector employer is found liable for wiretapping an office telephone conversation in which two employees exchanged disparaging information about their supervisor.
   (C) A court upholds the right of a government office to destroy both paper and electronic versions of its in-house documents.
   (D) A court upholds a private-sector employer's right to monitor messages sent between employees over the company's in-house electronic mail system.
   (E) A court rules in favor of a private-sector employee whose supervisor stated that in-house electronic mail would not be monitored but later fired the employee for communicating disparaging information via electronic mail.

7. The author's primary purpose in writing the passage is to

   (A) demonstrate that the individual right to privacy has been eroded by advances in computer technology
   (B) compare the legal status of electronic mail in the public and private sectors
   (C) draw an extended analogy between the privacy of electronic mail and the privacy of telephone conversations or face-to-face meetings
   (D) illustrate the complexities of the privacy issues surrounding electronic mail in the workplace
   (E) explain why the courts have not been able to rule definitively on the issue of the privacy of electronic mail

While a new surge of critical interest in the ancient Greek poems conventionally ascribed to Homer has taken place in the last twenty years or so, it was nonspecialists rather than professional scholars who studied the poetic aspects of the *Iliad* and the *Odyssey* between, roughly, 1935 and 1970. During these years, while such nonacademic intellectuals as Simone Weil and Erich Auerbach were trying to define the qualities that made these epic accounts of the Trojan War and its aftermath great poetry, the questions that occupied the specialists were directed elsewhere: "Did the Trojan War really happen?" "Does the bard preserve Indo-European folk memories?" "How did the poems get written down?" Something was driving scholars away from the actual works to peripheral issues. Scholars produced books about archaeology, and gift-exchange in ancient societies, about the development of oral poetry, about virtually anything except the *Iliad* and the *Odyssey* themselves as unique reflections or distillations of life itself—as, in short, great poetry. The observations of the English poet Alexander Pope seemed as applicable in 1970 as they had been when he wrote them in 1715: according to Pope, the remarks of critics "are rather Philosophical, Historical, Geographical . . . or rather anything than Critical and Poetical."

Ironically, the modern manifestation of this "nonpoetical" emphasis can be traced to the profoundly influential work of Milman Parry, who attempted to demonstrate in detail how the Homeric poems, believed to have been recorded nearly three thousand years ago, were the products of a long and highly developed tradition of oral poetry about the Trojan War. Parry proposed that this tradition built up its diction and its content by a process of constant accumulation and refinement over many generations of storytellers. But after Parry's death in 1935, his legacy was taken up by scholars who, unlike Parry, forsook intensive analysis of the poetry itself and focused instead on only one element of Parry's work: the creative limitations and possibilities of oral composition, concentrating on fixed elements and inflexibilities, focusing on the things that oral poetry allegedly can and cannot do. The dryness of this kind of study drove many of the more inventive scholars away from the poems into the rapidly developing field of Homer's archaeological and historical background.

Appropriately, Milman Parry's son Adam was among those scholars responsible for a renewed interest in Homer's poetry as literary art. Building on his father's work, the younger Parry argued that the Homeric poems exist both within and against a tradition. The *Iliad* and the *Odyssey* were, Adam Parry thought, the beneficiaries of an inherited store of diction, scenes, and concepts, and at the same time highly individual works that surpassed these conventions. Adam Parry helped prepare the ground for the recent Homeric revival by affirming his father's belief in a strong inherited tradition, but also by emphasizing Homer's unique contributions within that tradition.

8. Which one of the following best states the main idea of the passage?
   - (A) The Homeric poems are most fruitfully studied as records of the time and place in which they were written.
   - (B) The Homeric poems are the products of a highly developed and complicated tradition of oral poetry.
   - (C) The Homeric poems are currently enjoying a resurgence of critical interest after an age of scholarship largely devoted to the poems' nonpoetic elements.
   - (D) The Homeric poems are currently enjoying a resurgence of scholarly interest after an age during which most studies were authored by nonacademic writers.
   - (E) Before Milman Parry published his pioneering work in the early twentieth century, it was difficult to assign a date or an author to the Homeric poems.

9. According to the passage, the work of Simone Weil and Erich Auerbach on Homer was primarily concerned with which one of the following?
   - (A) considerations of why criticism of Homer had moved to peripheral issues
   - (B) analyses of the poetry itself in terms of its literary qualities
   - (C) studies in the history and nature of oral poetry
   - (D) analyses of the already ancient epic tradition inherited by Homer
   - (E) critiques of the highly technical analyses of academic critics

GO ON TO THE NEXT PAGE.

10. The passage suggests which one of the following about scholarship on Homer that has appeared since 1970?

 (A) It has dealt extensively with the Homeric poems as literary art.
 (B) It is more incisive than the work of the Parrys.
 (C) It has rejected as irrelevant the scholarship produced by specialists between 1935 and 1970.
 (D) It has ignored the work of Simone Weil and Erich Auerbach.
 (E) It has attempted to confirm that the *Iliad* and the *Odyssey* were written by Homer.

11. The author of the passage most probably quotes Alexander Pope (lines 24–26) in order to

 (A) indicate that the Homeric poems have generally received poor treatment at the hands of English critics
 (B) prove that poets as well as critics have emphasized elements peripheral to the poems
 (C) illustrate that the nonpoetical emphasis also existed in an earlier century
 (D) emphasize the problems inherent in rendering classical Greek poetry into modern English
 (E) argue that poets and literary critics have seldom agreed about the interpretation of poetry

12. According to the passage, which one of the following is true of Milman Parry's immediate successors in the field of Homeric studies?

 (A) They reconciled Homer's poetry with archaeological and historical concerns.
 (B) They acknowledged the tradition of oral poetry, but focused on the uniqueness of Homer's poetry within the tradition.
 (C) They occupied themselves with the question of what qualities made for great poetry.
 (D) They emphasized the boundaries of oral poetry.
 (E) They called for a revival of Homer's popularity.

13. Which one of the following best describes the organization of the passage?

 (A) A situation is identified and its origins are examined.
 (B) A series of hypotheses is reviewed and one is advocated.
 (C) The works of two influential scholars are summarized.
 (D) Several issues contributing to a current debate are summarized.
 (E) Three possible solutions to a long-standing problem are posed.

GO ON TO THE NEXT PAGE.

Even in the midst of its resurgence as a vital tradition, many sociologists have viewed the current form of the powwow, a ceremonial gathering of native Americans, as a sign that tribal culture is in decline. Focusing on the dances and rituals that have recently come to be shared by most tribes, they suggest that an intertribal movement is now in ascension and claim the inevitable outcome of this tendency is the eventual dissolution of tribes and the complete assimilation of native Americans into Euroamerican society. Proponents of this "Pan-Indian" theory point to the greater frequency of travel and communication between reservations, the greater urbanization of native Americans, and, most recently, their increasing politicization in response to common grievances as the chief causes of the shift toward intertribalism.

Indeed, the rapid diffusion of dance styles, outfits, and songs from one reservation to another offers compelling evidence that intertribalism has been increasing. However, these sociologists have failed to note the concurrent revitalization of many traditions unique to individual tribes. Among the Lakota, for instance, the Sun Dance was revived, after a forty-year hiatus, during the 1950's. Similarly, the Black Legging Society of the Kiowa and the Hethuska Society of the Ponca—both traditional groups within their respective tribes—have gained new popularity. Obviously, a more complex societal shift is taking place than the theory of Pan-Indianism can account for.

An examination of the theory's underpinnings may be critical at this point, especially given that native Americans themselves chafe most against the Pan-Indian classification. Like other assimilationist theories with which it is associated, the Pan-Indian view is predicated upon an a priori assumption about the nature of cultural contact: that upon contact minority societies immediately begin to succumb in every respect—biologically, linguistically, and culturally—to the majority society. However, there is no evidence that this is happening to native American groups.

Yet the fact remains that intertribal activities are a major facet of native American culture today. Certain dances at powwows, for instance, are announced as intertribal, other as traditional. Likewise, speeches given at the beginnings of powwows are often delivered in English, while the prayer that follows is usually spoken in a native language. Cultural borrowing is, of course, old news. What is important to note is the conscious distinction native Americans make between tribal and intertribal tendencies.

Tribalism, although greatly altered by modern history, remains a potent force among native Americans: It forms a basis for tribal identity, and aligns music and dance with other social and cultural activities important to individual tribes. Intertribal activities, on the other hand, reinforce native American identity along a broader front, where this identity is directly threatened by outside influences.

14. Which one of the following best summarizes the main idea of the passage?

(A) Despite the fact that sociologists have only recently begun to understand its importance, intertribalism has always been an influential factor in native American culture.
(B) Native Americans are currently struggling with an identity crisis caused primarily by the two competing forces of tribalism and intertribalism.
(C) The recent growth of intertribalism is unlikely to eliminate tribalism because the two forces do not oppose one another but instead reinforce distinct elements of native American identity.
(D) The tendency toward intertribalism, although prevalent within native American culture, has had a minimal effect on the way native Americans interact with the broader community around them.
(E) Despite the recent revival of many native American tribal traditions, the recent trend toward intertribalism is likely to erode cultural differences among the various native American tribes.

15. The author most likely states that "cultural borrowing is, of course, old news" (lines 47–48) primarily to

(A) acknowledge that in itself the existence of intertribal tendencies at powwows is unsurprising
(B) suggest that native Americans' use of English in powwows should be accepted as unavoidable
(C) argue that the deliberate distinction of intertribal and traditional dances is not a recent development
(D) suggest that the recent increase in intertribal activity is the result of native Americans
(E) indicate that the powwow itself could have originated by combining practices drawn from both native and non-native American cultures

16. The author of the passage would most likely agree with which one of the following assertions?

(A) Though some believe the current form of the powwow signals the decline of tribal culture, the powwow contains elements that indicate the continuing strength of tribalism.
(B) The logical outcome of the recent increase in intertribal activity is the eventual disappearance of tribal culture.
(C) Native Americans who participate in both tribal and intertribal activities usually base their identities on intertribal rather than tribal affiliations.
(D) The conclusions of some sociologists about the health of native American cultures show that these sociologists are in fact biased against such cultures.
(E) Until it is balanced by revitalization of tribal customs, intertribalism will continue to weaken the native American sense of identity.

GO ON TO THE NEXT PAGE.

17. The primary function of the third paragraph is to

(A) search for evidence to corroborate the basic assumption of the theory of Pan-Indianism
(B) demonstrate the incorrectness of the theory of Pan-Indianism by pointing out that native American groups themselves disagree with the theory
(C) explain the origin of the theory of Pan-Indianism by showing how it evolved from other assimilationist theories
(D) examine several assimilationist theories in order to demonstrate that they rest on a common assumption
(E) criticize the theory of Pan-Indianism by pointing out that it rests upon an assumption for which there is no supporting evidence

18. Which one of the following most accurately describes the author's attitude toward the theory of Pan-Indianism?

(A) critical of its tendency to attribute political motives to cultural practices
(B) discomfort at its negative characterization of cultural borrowing by native Americans
(C) hopeful about its chances for preserving tribal culture
(D) offended by its claim that assimilation is a desirable consequence of cultural contact
(E) skeptical that it is a complete explanation of recent changes in native American society

19. With which one of the following statements would the author of the passage be most likely to agree?

(A) The resurgence of the powwow is a sign that native American customs are beginning to have an important influence on Euroamerican society.
(B) Although native Americans draw conscious distinctions between tribal and intertribal activities, there is no difference in how the two types of activity actually function within the context of native American society.
(C) Without intertribal activities, it would be more difficult for native Americans to maintain the cultural differences between native American and Euroamerican society.
(D) The powwow was recently revived, after an extended hiatus, in order to strengthen native Americans' sense of ethnic identity.
(E) The degree of urbanization, intertribal communication, and politicization among native Americans has been exaggerated by proponents of the theory of Pan-Indianism.

20. Which one of the following situations most clearly illustrates the phenomenon of intertribalism, as that phenomenon is described in the passage?

(A) a native American tribe in which a number of powerful societies attempt to prevent the revival of a traditional dance
(B) a native American tribe whose members attempt to learn the native languages of several other tribes
(C) a native American tribe whose members attempt to form a political organization in order to redress several grievances important to that tribe
(D) a native American tribe in which a significant percentage of the members have forsaken their tribal identity and become assimilated into Euroamerican society
(E) a native American tribe whose members often travel to other parts of the reservation in order to visit friends and relatives

21. In the passage, the author is primarily concerned with doing which one of the following?

(A) identifying an assumption common to various assimilationist theories and then criticizing these theories by showing this assumption to be false
(B) arguing that the recent revival of a number of tribal practices shows sociologists are mistaken in believing intertribalism to be a potent force among native American societies
(C) questioning the belief that native American societies will eventually be assimilated into Euroamerican society by arguing that intertribalism helps strengthen native American identity
(D) showing how the recent resurgence of tribal activities is a deliberate attempt to counteract the growing influence of intertribalism
(E) proposing an explanation of why the ascension of intertribalism could result in the eventual dissolution of tribes and complete assimilation of native American into Euroamerican society

GO ON TO THE NEXT PAGE.

Scientists typically advocate the analytic method of studying complex systems: systems are divided into component parts that are investigated separately. But nineteenth-century critics of this method claimed that when a system's parts are isolated its complexity tends to be lost. To address the perceived weaknesses of the analytic method these critics put forward a concept called organicism, which posited that the whole determines the nature of its parts and that the parts of a whole are interdependent.

Organicism depended upon the theory of internal relations, which states that relations between entities are possible only within some whole that embraces them, and that entities are altered by the relationships into which they enter. If an entity stands in a relationship with another entity, it has some property as a consequence. Without this relationship, and hence without the property, the entity would be different—and so would be another entity. Thus, the property is one of the entity's defining characteristics. Each of an entity's relationships likewise determines a defining characteristic of the entity.

One problem with the theory of internal relations is that not all properties of an entity are defining characteristics: numerous properties are accompanying characteristics—even if they are always present, their presence does not influence the entity's identity. Thus, even if it is admitted that every relationship into which an entity enters determines some characteristic of the entity, it is not necessarily true that such characteristics will define the entity; it is possible for the entity to enter into a relationship yet remain essentially unchanged.

The ultimate difficulty with the theory of internal relations is that it renders the acquisition of knowledge impossible. To truly know an entity, we must know all of its relationships; but because the entity is related to everything in each whole of which it is a part, these wholes must be known completely before the entity can be known. This seems to be a prerequisite impossible to satisfy.

Organicists' criticism of the analytic method arose from their failure to fully comprehend the method. In rejecting the analytic method, organicists overlooked the fact that before the proponents of the method analyzed the component parts of a system, they first determined both the laws applicable to the whole system and the initial conditions of the system; proponents of the method thus did not study parts of a system in full isolation from the system as a whole. Since organicists failed to recognize this, they never advanced any argument to show that laws and initial conditions of complex systems cannot be discovered. Hence, organicists offered no valid reason for rejecting the analytic method or for adopting organicism as a replacement for it.

22. Which one of the following most completely and accurately summarizes the argument of the passage?

(A) By calling into question the possibility that complex systems can be studied in their entirety, organicists offered an alternative to the analytic method favored by nineteenth-century scientists.
(B) Organicists did not offer a useful method of studying complex systems because they did not acknowledge that there are relationships into which an entity may enter that do not alter the entity's identity.
(C) Organicism is flawed because it relies on a theory that both ignores the fact that not all characteristics of entities are defining and ultimately makes the acquisition of knowledge impossible.
(D) Organicism does not offer a valid challenge to the analytic method both because it relies on faulty theory and because it is based on a misrepresentation of the analytic method.
(E) In criticizing the analytic method, organicists neglected to disprove that scientists who employ the method are able to discover the laws and initial conditions of the systems they study.

23. According to the passage, organicists' chief objection to the analytic method was that the method

(A) oversimplified systems by isolating their components
(B) assumed that a system can be divided into component parts
(C) ignored the laws applicable to the system as a whole
(D) claimed that the parts of a system are more important than the system as a whole
(E) denied the claim that entities enter into relationships

GO ON TO THE NEXT PAGE.

24. The passage offers information to help answer each of the following questions EXCEPT:

(A) Why does the theory of internal relations appear to make the acquisition of knowledge impossible?
(B) Why did the organicists propose replacing the analytic method?
(C) What is the difference between a defining characteristic and an accompanying characteristic?
(D) What did organicists claim are the effects of an entity's entering into a relationship with another entity?
(E) What are some of the advantages of separating out the parts of a system for study?

25. The passage most strongly supports the ascription of which one of the following views to scientists who use the analytic method?

(A) A complex system is best understood by studying its component parts in full isolation from the system as a whole.
(B) The parts of a system should be studied with an awareness of the laws and initial conditions that govern the system.
(C) It is not possible to determine the laws governing a system until the system's parts are separated from one another.
(D) Because the parts of a system are interdependent, they cannot be studied separately without destroying the system's complexity.
(E) Studying the parts of a system individually eliminates the need to determine which characteristics of the parts are defining characteristics.

26. Which one of the following is a principle upon which the author bases an argument against the theory of internal relations?

(A) An adequate theory of complex systems must define the entities of which the system is composed.
(B) An acceptable theory cannot have consequences that contradict its basic purpose.
(C) An adequate method of study of complex systems should reveal the actual complexity of the systems it studies.
(D) An acceptable theory must describe the laws and initial conditions of a complex system.
(E) An acceptable method of studying complex systems should not study parts of the system in isolation from the system as a whole.

S T O P

IF YOU FINISH BEFORE TIME IS CALLED, YOU MAY CHECK YOUR WORK ON THIS SECTION ONLY.
DO NOT WORK ON ANY OTHER SECTION IN THE TEST.

SECTION III

Time—35 minutes

26 Questions

Directions: The questions in this section are based on the reasoning contained in brief statements or passages. For some questions, more than one of the choices could conceivably answer the question. However, you are to choose the best answer; that is, the response that most accurately and completely answers the question. You should not make assumptions that are by commonsense standards implausible, superfluous, or incompatible with the passage. After you have chosen the best answer, blacken the corresponding space on your answer sheet.

1. "Hot spot" is a term that ecologists use to describe those habitats with the greatest concentrations of species found only in one place—so-called "endemic" species. Many of these hot spots are vulnerable to habitat loss due to commercial development. Furthermore, loss of endemic species accounts for most modern-day extinctions. Thus, given that only a limited number of environmental battles can be waged, it would be reasonable for organizations dedicated to preserving species to _______.

   Which one of the following most logically completes the argument?

   (A) try to help only those species who are threatened with extinction because of habitat loss
   (B) concentrate their resources on protecting hot spot habitats
   (C) treat all endemic species as equally valuable and equally in need of preservation
   (D) accept that most endemic species will become extinct
   (E) expand the definition of "hot spot" to include vulnerable habitats that are not currently home to many endangered species

2. Principle: If you sell an item that you know to be defective, telling the buyer that the item is sound, you thereby commit fraud.

   Application: Wilton sold a used bicycle to Harris, knowing very little about its condition. Wilton told Harris that the bicycle was in good working condition, but Harris soon learned that the brakes were defective. Wilton was therefore guilty of fraud.

   The application of the principle is most vulnerable to criticism on the grounds that

   (A) the application fails to establish whether Wilton was given the opportunity to repair the brakes
   (B) the application fails to indicate how much money Wilton received for the bicycle
   (C) the application uses the word "defective" in a sense that is crucially different from how it is used in the statement of the principle
   (D) Harris might not have believed Wilton's statement about the bicycle's condition
   (E) asserting something without justification is not the same as asserting something one knows to be false

3. Engine noise from boats travelling through killer whales' habitats ranges in frequency from 100 hertz to 3,000 hertz, an acoustical range that overlaps that in which the whales communicate through screams and squeals. Though killer whales do not seem to behave differently around running boat engines, engine noise from boats can be loud enough to damage their hearing over time. Therefore, _______.

   Which one of the following most logically completes the argument?

   (A) younger killer whales are better able to tolerate engine noise from boats than older whales are
   (B) killer whales are less likely to attempt to communicate with one another when boat engines are operating nearby
   (C) noise from boat engines may impair killer whales' ability to communicate
   (D) killer whales are most likely to prefer areas where boat traffic is present, but light
   (E) killer whales would probably be more successful in finding food if boats did not travel through their habitats

GO ON TO THE NEXT PAGE.

4. Journalist: A manufacturers' trade group that has long kept its membership list secret inadvertently sent me a document listing hundreds of manufacturing companies. A representative of the trade group later confirmed that every company listed in the document does indeed belong to the trade group. Because Bruch Industries is not listed on the document, it is evidently not a member of the trade group.

The journalist's reasoning in the argument is flawed in that the journalist

(A) gives no reason to think that Bruch Industries would want to belong to the trade group
(B) does not present any evidence that the document names every member of the trade group
(C) does not explain how it is that the trade group could have inadvertently sent out a secret document
(D) presents no reason why Bruch Industries would not want its membership in the trade group to be known
(E) takes for granted the accuracy of a statement by a representative who had a reason to withhold information

5. Peter: Unlike in the past, most children's stories nowadays don't have clearly immoral characters in them. They should, though. Children need to learn the consequences of being bad.

Yoko: Children's stories still tend to have clearly immoral characters in them, but now these characters tend not to be the sort that frighten children. Surely that's an improvement.

Peter and Yoko disagree over whether today's children's stories

(A) should be less frightening than they are
(B) tend to be less frightening than earlier children's stories were
(C) differ significantly in overall quality from earlier children's stories
(D) tend to have clearly immoral characters in them
(E) should help children learn the consequences of being bad

6. Local resident: An overabundance of algae must be harmful to the smaller fish in this pond. During the fifteen or so years that I have lived here, the few times that I have seen large numbers of dead small fish wash ashore in late summer coincide exactly with the times that I have noticed abnormally large amounts of algae in the water.

The local resident's argument is most vulnerable to criticism on the grounds that it

(A) presumes, without providing justification, that smaller fish are somehow more susceptible to harm as a result of overabundant algae than are larger fish
(B) fails to consider that the effects on smaller fish of overabundant algae may be less severe in larger bodies of water with more diverse ecosystems
(C) ignores the possibility that the same cause might have different effects on fish of different sizes
(D) ignores the possibility that the overabundance of algae and the deaths of smaller fish are independent effects of a common cause
(E) ignores the possibility that below-normal amounts of algae are detrimental to the pond's smaller fish

7. Tanner: The public should demand political debates before any election. Voters are better able to choose the candidate best suited for office if they watch the candidates seriously debate one another.

Saldana: Political debates almost always benefit the candidate who has the better debating skills. Thus, they don't really help voters determine which candidate is most qualified for office.

The dialogue provides the most support for the claim that Tanner and Saldana disagree over which one of the following?

(A) Political candidates with strong debating skills are more likely to win elections than those with weak debating skills.
(B) A voter who watches a political debate will likely be better able, as a result, to determine which candidate is more qualified for office.
(C) Debating skills are of little use to politicians in doing their jobs once they are elected to office.
(D) The candidates with the best debating skills are the ones who are most qualified for the political offices for which they are running.
(E) Political debates tend to have a major effect on which candidate among those participating in a debate will win the election.

GO ON TO THE NEXT PAGE.

8. A recent study shows that those highways that carry the most traffic, and thus tend to be the most congested, have the lowest rate of fatal traffic accidents.

Which one of the following, if true, most helps to explain the phenomenon described above?

(A) Drivers have more accidents when they become distracted.
(B) The highways that have the highest rate of fatal accidents have moderate volumes of traffic.
(C) Most of the motorists on very heavily traveled highways tend to be commuting to or from work.
(D) Most serious accidents occur when vehicles are moving at a high rate of speed.
(E) Heavily traveled highways do not always carry a higher proportion of large trucks.

9. In some jurisdictions, lawmakers have instituted sentencing guidelines that mandate a penalty for theft that is identical to the one they have mandated for bribery. Hence, lawmakers in those jurisdictions evidently consider the harm resulting from theft to be equal to the harm resulting from bribery.

Which one of the following, if true, would most strengthen the argument?

(A) In general, lawmakers mandate penalties for crimes that are proportional to the harm they believe to result from those crimes.
(B) In most cases, lawmakers assess the level of harm resulting from an act in determining whether to make that act illegal.
(C) Often, in response to the unusually great harm resulting from a particular instance of a crime, lawmakers will mandate an increased penalty for that crime.
(D) In most cases, a victim of theft is harmed no more than a victim of bribery is harmed.
(E) If lawmakers mandate penalties for crimes that are proportional to the harm resulting from those crimes, crime in those lawmakers' jurisdictions will be effectively deterred.

10. People often admonish us to learn the lessons of history, but, even if it were easy to discover what the past was really like, it is nearly impossible to discover its lessons. We are supposed, for example, to learn the lessons of World War I. But what are they? And were we ever to discover what they are, it is not clear that we could ever apply them, for we shall never again have a situation just like World War I.

That we should learn the lessons of history figures in the argument in which one of the following ways?

(A) It sets out a problem the argument as a whole is designed to resolve.
(B) It is compatible with accepting the argument's conclusion and with denying it.
(C) It is a position that the argument simply takes for granted is false.
(D) It expresses the position the argument as a whole is directed toward discrediting.
(E) It is an assumption that is required in order to establish the argument's conclusion.

11. Sigerson argues that the city should adopt ethical guidelines that preclude its politicians from accepting campaign contributions from companies that do business with the city. Sigerson's proposal is dishonest, however, because he has taken contributions from such companies throughout his career in city politics.

The reasoning in the argument is most vulnerable to criticism on the grounds that the argument

(A) confuses a sufficient condition for adopting ethical guidelines for politicians with a necessary condition for adopting such guidelines
(B) rejects a proposal on the grounds that an inadequate argument has been given for it
(C) fails to adequately address the possibility that other city politicians would resist Sigerson's proposal
(D) rejects a proposal on the grounds that the person offering it is unfamiliar with the issues it raises
(E) overlooks the fact that Sigerson's proposal would apply only to the future conduct of city politicians

GO ON TO THE NEXT PAGE.

12. Some gardening books published by Garden Path Press recommend tilling the soil and adding compost before starting a new garden on a site, but they do not explain the difference between hot and cold composting. Since any gardening book that recommends adding compost is flawed if it does not explain at least the basics of composting, some books published by Garden Path are flawed.

The argument requires the assumption that

(A) some gardening books that recommend tilling the soil and adding compost before starting a new garden are not flawed
(B) gardeners should not add compost to the soil unless they have a thorough understanding of composting
(C) an explanation of the basics of composting must include an explanation of the difference between hot and cold composting
(D) everyone who understands the difference between hot and cold composting understands at least the basics of composting
(E) no gardening book that includes an explanation of at least the basics of composting is flawed

13. Astronomers have found new evidence that the number of galaxies in the universe is not 10 billion, as previously believed, but 50 billion. This discovery will have an important effect on theories about how galaxies are formed. But even though astronomers now believe 40 billion more galaxies exist, many astronomers' estimates of the universe's total mass remain virtually unchanged.

Which one of the following, if true, does most to explain why the estimates remain virtually unchanged?

(A) The mass of galaxies is thought to make up only a tiny percentage of the universe's total mass.
(B) The overwhelming majority of galaxies are so far from Earth that their mass can be only roughly estimated.
(C) The number of galaxies that astronomers believe exist tends to grow as the instruments used to detect galaxies become more sophisticated.
(D) Theories about how galaxies are formed are rarely affected by estimates of the universe's total mass.
(E) There is no consensus among astronomers on the proper procedures for estimating the universe's total mass.

14. Newspaper subscriber: Arnot's editorial argues that by making certain fundamental changes in government we would virtually eliminate our most vexing social ills. But clearly this conclusion is false. After all, the argument Arnot makes for this claim depends on the dubious assumption that government can be trusted to act in the interest of the public.

Which one of the following most accurately expresses a flaw in the argument's reasoning?

(A) it repudiates a claim merely on the grounds that an inadequate argument has been given for it
(B) it treats a change that is required for virtual elimination of society's most vexing social ills as a change that will guarantee the virtual elimination of those ills
(C) it fails to consider that, even if an argument's conclusion is false, some of the assumptions used to justify that conclusion may nonetheless be true
(D) it distorts the opponent's argument and then attacks this distorted argument
(E) it uses the key term "government" in one sense in a premise and in another sense in the conclusion

15. Columnist: Shortsighted motorists learn the hard way about the wisdom of preventive auto maintenance; such maintenance almost always pays off in the long run. Our usually shortsighted city council should be praised for using similar wisdom when they hired a long-term economic development adviser. In hiring this adviser, the council made an investment that is likely to have a big payoff in several years. Other cities in this region that have devoted resources to economic development planning have earned large returns on such an investment.

Which one of the following, if true, most weakens the columnist's argument?

(A) Even some cars that receive regular preventive maintenance break down, requiring costly repairs.
(B) The columnist's city has a much smaller population and economy than the other cities did when they began devoting resources to economic development planning.
(C) Most motorists who fail to perform preventive maintenance on their cars do so for nonfinancial reasons.
(D) Qualified economic development advisers generally demand higher salaries than many city councils are willing to spend.
(E) Cities that have earned large returns due to hiring economic development advisers did not earn any returns at all in the advisers' first few years of employment.

16. Editorial: Cell-phone usage on buses and trains is annoying to other passengers. This suggests that recent proposals to allow use of cell phones on airplanes are ill-advised. Cell-phone use would be far more upsetting on airplanes than it is on buses and trains. Airline passengers are usually packed in tightly. And if airline passengers are offended by the cell-phone excesses of their seatmates, they often cannot move to another seat.

Which one of the following most accurately describes the role played in the editorial's argument by the statement that cell-phone use would be far more upsetting on airplanes than it is on buses and trains?

(A) It is the main conclusion of the argument.
(B) It is a claim that the argument tries to rebut.
(C) It is a premise that indirectly supports the main conclusion of the argument by supporting a premise for that conclusion.
(D) It is a conclusion for which support is provided and that itself is used in turn to directly support the argument's main conclusion.
(E) It provides background information that plays no role in the reasoning in the argument.

17. Science writer: The deterioration of cognitive faculties associated with Alzheimer's disease is evidently caused by the activities of microglia—the brain's own immune cells. For one thing, this deterioration can be slowed by some anti-inflammatory drugs, such as acetylsalicylic acid. Furthermore, patients with Alzheimer's are unable to eliminate the protein BA from the brain, where it accumulates and forms deposits. The microglia attack these protein deposits by releasing poisons that destroy surrounding healthy brain cells, thereby impairing the brain's cognitive functions.

Which one of the following, if true, most helps to support the science writer's argument?

(A) The inability of Alzheimer's patients to eliminate the protein BA from the brain is due to a deficiency in the brain's immune system.
(B) Acetylsalicylic acid reduces the production of immune cells in the brain.
(C) The activity of microglia results in a decrease in the buildup of protein deposits in the brain.
(D) The protein BA directly interferes with the cognitive functions of the brain.
(E) Immune reactions by microglia occur in certain diseases of the brain other than Alzheimer's.

18. Lawyer: One is justified in accessing information in computer files without securing authorization from the computer's owner only if the computer is typically used in the operation of a business. If, in addition, there exist reasonable grounds for believing that such a computer contains data usable as evidence in a legal proceeding against the computer's owner, then accessing the data in those computer files without the owner's authorization is justified.

The principles stated by the lawyer most strongly support which one of the following judgments?

(A) Rey gave his friend Sunok a key to the store where he worked and asked her to use the store owners' computer to look up their friend Jim's phone number, which Rey kept on the computer. Because Sunok had Rey's permission, her action was justified.
(B) Police department investigators accessed the electronic accounting files of the central computer owned by a consulting firm that was on trial for fraudulent business practices without seeking permission from the firm's owners. Contrary to the investigators' reasonable beliefs, however, the files ultimately provided no evidence of wrongdoing. Nevertheless, the investigators' action was justified.
(C) A police officer accessed, without Natalie's permission, files on the computer that Natalie owned and used exclusively in the operation of her small business. Since the police officer's search of the files on Natalie's computer produced no evidence usable in any legal proceeding against Natalie, the police officer's action was clearly not justified.
(D) Customs officials examined all of the files stored on a laptop computer confiscated from an importer whom they suspected of smuggling. Because there were reasonable grounds for believing that the computer had typically been used in the operation of the importer's legitimate business, the customs officials' action was justified.
(E) Against the company owner's wishes, a police officer accessed some of the files on one of the company's computers. Although the computer was typically used in the operation of the company's business, the particular files accessed by the police officer were personal letters written by one of the company's employees. Thus, the police officer's unauthorized use of the computer was not justified.

GO ON TO THE NEXT PAGE.

19. The conventional process for tanning leather uses large amounts of calcium oxide and sodium sulfide. Tanning leather using biological catalysts costs about the same as using these conventional chemicals if the cost of waste disposal is left out of the comparison. However, nearly 20 percent less waste is produced with biological catalysts, and waste disposal is a substantial part of the overall cost of tanning. It is therefore less costly to tan leather if biological catalysts are used instead.

Which one of the following is an assumption required by the argument?

(A) Leather tanned using the conventional process is not lower in quality than is leather tanned using biological catalysts.
(B) The biological catalysts that can be used in the tanning process are less costly by weight than are calcium oxide and sodium sulfide.
(C) New technological innovations have recently made the use of biological catalysts in the tanning process much more cost effective.
(D) Disposal of tanning waste produced with biological catalysts does not cost significantly more than disposal of the same amount of waste produced with the conventional process.
(E) The labor costs associated with tanning leather using biological catalysts are not any greater than the labor costs associated with the conventional tanning process.

20. One should not play a practical joke on someone if it shows contempt for that person or if one believes it might bring significant harm to that person.

The principle stated above, if valid, most helps to justify the reasoning in which one of the following arguments?

(A) I should not have played that practical joke on you yesterday. Even if it was not contemptuous, I should have realized that it would bring significant harm to someone.
(B) I have no reason to think that the practical joke I want to play would harm anyone. So, since the joke would show no contempt for the person the joke is played on, it would not be wrong for me to play it.
(C) Because of the circumstances, it would be wrong for me to play the practical joke I had intended to play on you. Even though it would not show contempt for anyone, it could easily bring you significant harm.
(D) It would have been wrong for me to play the practical joke that I had intended to play on you. Even though I did not have reason to think that it would significantly harm anyone, I did think that it would show contempt for someone.
(E) Someone was harmed as a result of my practical joke. Thus, even though it did not show contempt for the person I played the joke on, I should not have played it.

21. Economics professor: Marty's Pizza and Checkers Pizza are the two major pizza parlors in our town. Marty's sold coupon books including coupons good for one large plain pizza at any local pizza parlor, at Marty's expense. But Checkers refused to accept these coupons, even though they were redeemed by all other local pizza parlors. Accepting them would have cost Checkers nothing and would have satisfied those of its potential customers who had purchased the coupon books. This shows that Checkers's motive in refusing to accept the coupons was simply to hurt Marty's Pizza.

Which one of the following, if assumed, enables the economics professor's conclusion to be properly drawn?

(A) Any company that refuses to accept coupons issued by a competitor when doing so would satisfy some of the company's potential customers is motivated solely by the desire to hurt that competitor.
(B) Any company that wishes to hurt a competitor by refusing to accept coupons issued by that competitor will refuse to accept them even when accepting them would cost nothing and would satisfy its potential customers.
(C) At least one company has refused to accept coupons issued by its major local competitor simply in order to hurt that competitor, even though those coupons were accepted by all other local competitors.
(D) Any company that accepts its major competitor's coupons helps its competitor by doing so, even if it also satisfies its own actual or potential customers.
(E) If accepting coupons issued by a competitor would not enable a company to satisfy its actual or potential customers, then that company's refusal to accept the coupons is motivated by the desire to satisfy customers.

GO ON TO THE NEXT PAGE.

22. Science writer: Scientists' astounding success rate with research problems they have been called upon to solve causes the public to believe falsely that science can solve any problem. In fact, the problems scientists are called upon to solve are typically selected by scientists themselves. When the problems are instead selected by politicians or business leaders, their formulation is nevertheless guided by scientists in such a way as to make scientific solutions feasible. Scientists are almost never asked to solve problems that are not subject to such formulation.

The science writer's statements, if true, most strongly support which one of the following?

(A) If a problem can be formulated in such a way as to make a scientific solution feasible, scientists will usually be called upon to solve that problem.
(B) Any problem a scientist can solve can be formulated in such a way as to make a scientific solution feasible.
(C) Scientists would probably have a lower success rate with research problems if their grounds for selecting such problems were less narrow.
(D) Most of the problems scientists are called upon to solve are problems that politicians and business leaders want solved, but whose formulation the scientists have helped to guide.
(E) The only reason for the astounding success rate of science is that the problems scientists are called upon to solve are usually selected by the scientists themselves.

23. Most auto mechanics have extensive experience. Furthermore, most mechanics with extensive experience understand electronic circuits. Thus, most auto mechanics understand electronic circuits.

The pattern of flawed reasoning in which one of the following arguments is most similar to that in the argument above?

(A) During times of the year when automobile traffic increases, gas prices also increase. Increases in gas prices lead to increases in consumer complaints. Thus, increased automobile traffic causes increased consumer complaints.
(B) The most common species of birds in this region are migratory. Moreover, most migratory birds have left this region by the end of November. Hence, few birds remain in this region during the winter.
(C) It is not surprising that most speeding tickets in this region are issued to drivers of sports cars. After all, most drivers who are not interested in driving fast do not buy sports cars.
(D) Most nature photographers find portrait photography boring. Moreover, most portrait photographers especially enjoy photographing dignitaries. Thus, most nature photographers find photographing dignitaries especially boring.
(E) Most snow-removal companies run lawn-care services during the summer. Also, most companies that run lawn-care services during the summer hire additional workers in the summer. Thus, most snow-removal companies hire additional workers in the summer.

24. If one wants to succeed, then one should act as though one were genuinely confident about one's abilities, even if one actually distrusts one's skills. Success is much more easily obtained by those who genuinely believe themselves capable of succeeding than by those filled with self-doubts.

Which one of the following statements, if true, most strengthens the argument?

(A) Those who convince others that they are capable of succeeding usually have few self-doubts.
(B) Genuine confidence is often a by-product of pretended self-confidence.
(C) Success is usually more a matter of luck or determination than of skill.
(D) Many people who behave in a self-confident manner are genuinely confident about their abilities.
(E) Self-doubt can hamper as well as aid the development of the skills necessary for success.

25. Journalist: The trade union members at AutoFaber Inc. are planning to go on strike. Independent arbitration would avert a strike, but only if both sides agree to accept the arbitrator's recommendations as binding. However, based on past experience, the union is quite unlikely to agree to this, so a strike is likely.

Which one of the following arguments exhibits a pattern of reasoning most similar to that exhibited by the journalist's argument?

(A) The company will downsize unless more stock is issued. Furthermore, if the company downsizes, the shareholders will demand a change. Since no more stock is being issued, we can be sure that the shareholders will demand a change.

(B) Rodriguez will donate her paintings to the museum only if the new wing is named after her. The only other person the new wing could be named after is the museum's founder, Wu. But it was decided yesterday that the gardens, not the new wing, would be named after Wu. So Rodriguez will donate her paintings to the museum.

(C) Reynolds and Khripkova would not make suitable business partners, since they are constantly squabbling, whereas good business partners know how to get along with each other most of the time and, if they quarrel, know how to resolve their differences.

(D) Lopez will run in tomorrow's marathon. Lopez will win the marathon only if his sponsors do a good job of keeping him hydrated. But his sponsors are known to be poor at keeping their athletes hydrated. So it is probable that Lopez will not win the marathon.

(E) The new course in microeconomics is offered either in the fall or in the spring. The new course will be offered in the spring if there is a qualified instructor available. Since the economics department currently lacks a qualified instructor for such courses, however, the course will not be offered in the spring.

26. Acquiring complete detailed information about all the pros and cons of a product one might purchase would clearly be difficult and expensive. It is rational not to acquire such information unless one expects that the benefits of doing so will outweigh the cost and difficulty of doing so. Therefore, consumers who do not bother to acquire such information are thereby behaving rationally.

The conclusion of the argument is properly drawn if which one of the following is assumed?

(A) Rational consumers who do not expect that the benefits outweigh the cost and difficulty of acquiring detailed information about a product they might purchase usually do not bother to acquire such information.

(B) Whenever it is rational not to acquire detailed information about a product, it would be irrational to bother to acquire such information.

(C) The benefits of acquiring detailed information about a product one might purchase usually do not outweigh the cost and difficulty of doing so.

(D) Rational consumers usually expect that the benefits of acquiring detailed information about a product they might purchase would not outweigh the cost and difficulty of doing so.

(E) Consumers who do not bother to acquire complete detailed information about a product they might purchase do not expect that the benefits of acquiring such information will outweigh the cost and difficulty of doing so.

S T O P

IF YOU FINISH BEFORE TIME IS CALLED, YOU MAY CHECK YOUR WORK ON THIS SECTION ONLY.
DO NOT WORK ON ANY OTHER SECTION IN THE TEST.

SECTION IV

Time—35 minutes

27 Questions

Directions: Each set of questions in this section is based on a single passage or a pair of passages. The questions are to be answered on the basis of what is stated or implied in the passage or pair of passages. For some of the questions, more than one of the choices could conceivably answer the question. However, you are to choose the best answer; that is, the response that most accurately and completely answers the question, and blacken the corresponding space on your answer sheet.

Determining the most effective way to deter deliberate crimes, such as fraud, as opposed to impulsive crimes, such as crimes of passion, is a problem currently being debated in the legal community. On one side of the debate are those scholars who believe that deliberate crimes are a product of the influence of societal norms and institutions on individuals. These scholars suggest that changing people's beliefs about crime, increasing the access of the most economically alienated individuals to economic institutions, and rehabilitating those convicted of this type of crime will reduce the crime rate. On the other side are those legal scholars who believe that the decision to commit a deliberate crime is primarily the result of individual choice. They suggest that increasing the fines and penalties associated with criminal activity, along with efficacious law enforcement, is the best deterrence method. However, some recent legal scholarship has changed the nature of this debate by introducing an economic principle that shows that these two positions, far from being antithetical, are surprisingly complementary.

The economic principle that reconciles the two positions is that of utility maximization, which holds that, given a choice of actions, rational individuals will choose the action that maximizes their anticipated overall satisfaction, or expected utility. The expected utility of an action is ascertained by determining the utilities of the possible outcomes of that action, weighing them according to the likelihood of each outcome's coming to pass, and then adding up those weighted utilities. Using this economic framework, an individual's decision to commit a crime can be analyzed as a rational economic choice.

According to the utility maximization principle a person who responds rationally to economic incentives or disincentives will commit a crime if the expected utility from doing so, given the chance of getting caught, exceeds the expected utility from activity that is lawful. Within this framework the two crime-deterrence methods have the same overall effect. For instance, the recommendations on one side of the crime deterrence debate to increase penalties for crimes and strengthen law enforcement result in an increased likelihood of detection and punishment and impose an increased cost to the individual if detected and punished. This lowers the expected utility from criminal activity, thereby making a person less likely to choose to commit a deliberate crime. The recommendations on the other side of the debate, such as increasing the economic opportunities of individuals most alienated from economic institutions, also affect the utility equation. All else being equal, enacting these types of policies will effectively increase the expected utility from lawful activity. This economic analysis demonstrates that the two positions are not fundamentally in conflict, and that the optimal approach to crime deterrence would include elements of both deterrence strategies.

1. Which one of the following most accurately states the main point of the passage?

(A) The principle of utility maximization provides an economic framework that allows legal scholars to analyze an individual's decision to commit a crime as a rational economic choice that maximizes that individual's expected utility.

(B) Legal scholars have found that deliberate criminal acts are motivated by neither external influences nor individual choices alone but that instead both of these factors are important in the decision to commit a crime.

(C) The utility maximization principle can be used to quantify the effects both of methods of deterrence that revolve around individual factors and of those that emphasize the impact of societal norms on the decision to commit a deliberate crime.

(D) Introduction of the utility maximization principle into the current crime deterrence debate indicates that both sides in the debate offer useful recommendations that can work together in deterring deliberate crime.

(E) The utility maximization principle demonstrates that deliberate criminal acts are the result of the rational economic choices of individuals and are not influenced by societal norms or the policies and practices of societal institutions.

GO ON TO THE NEXT PAGE.

2. The author mentions "crimes of passion" in line 3 primarily in order to

(A) give an example of a kind of deliberate crime
(B) provide a contrast that helps to define a deliberate crime
(C) demonstrate that not all crimes can be deterred
(D) help illustrate one side of the current debate in the legal community
(E) mention a crime that is a product of the influence of societal norms

3. The explanation of the utility maximization principle in the passage suggests that which one of the following would be least appropriately described as a rational response to economic incentives and disincentives?

(A) In order to reduce his taxes, a waiter conceals a large part of his tip income from the government because he believes that it is very unlikely that this will be detected and he will be penalized.
(B) A motorist avoids speeding on a certain stretch of road because she knows that it is heavily patrolled and that a speeding ticket will lead to loss of her driver's license.
(C) An industrialist continues to illegally discharge an untreated pollutant into a river because the cost of treatment far exceeds the fine for illegally discharging the pollutant.
(D) A government official in an impoverished country risks prosecution for soliciting bribes because rampant inflation has rendered her government salary inadequate to support her and her family.
(E) A worker physically assaults his former supervisor in a crowded workplace because he has been dismissed from his job and he believes that the dismissal was unwarranted and unfair.

4. Based on the passage, which one of the following scenarios is most similar to some legal scholars' use of the utility maximization principle regarding the crime deterrence debate?

(A) an astronomer's use of a paradox employed by certain ancient cosmologists as a metaphor to help describe a phenomenon recently observed with the aid of new technologies
(B) a drawing instructor's use of a law of optics from physics to demonstrate that two lines that appear to diverge actually run parallel to each other
(C) a botanist's use of a quotation from a legendary Olympic athlete to make a point about the competitive nature of plants in a forest
(D) a judge's use of evidence from anthropology to support a decision in a controversial legal case
(E) a mediator's use of a short quotation from a well-known novel in an attempt to set a tone of collegiality and good conduct at the start of a bargaining session

5. Which one of the following most accurately describes the organization of the passage?

(A) Two sides of a debate are described and a general principle is used to resolve the conflict between them.
(B) Two sides of a debate are described and an economic principle is applied to decide between them.
(C) Two beliefs are described and a principle is introduced to discredit them.
(D) A general principle is described and instantiated by two different ways of solving a problem.
(E) A general principle is described and used to highlight the differences between two sides in a debate.

6. The passage suggests that the author would be likely to agree with each of the following statements EXCEPT:

(A) The rate at which criminals return to criminal activity is likely to fall if laws requiring stronger punishments for repeat offenders are adopted.
(B) The rate at which criminals return to criminal activity is likely to increase if efforts to rehabilitate them are ended.
(C) The rate of deliberate crimes is likely to decrease if the expected utility of lawful activities decreases.
(D) The rate of deliberate crimes is likely to increase if the access of individuals to economic institutions decreases.
(E) The rate of deliberate crimes will tend to vary inversely with the level of law enforcement.

Mexican Americans share with speakers of Spanish throughout the world a rich and varied repertoire of proverbs as well as a vital tradition of proverb use. The term "proverb" refers to a self-contained saying that can be understood independent of a specific verbal context and that has as its main purpose the carrying of a message or piece of wisdom. The great majority of Spanish-language proverbs reached Mexico from peninsular Spain, though they did not all originate there. Many belong, in fact, to the common proverb tradition of Europe and have exact equivalents in English-language proverbial speech.

Each use of a proverb is an individual act whose meaning varies depending on the individual speaker and the particular social context in which the use occurs. Nonetheless, it is important to recognize that proverb use is also shaped by the larger community with which the individual interacts. The fact that proverbs often serve a didactic purpose points us to one important function that proverbs serve in Mexican American communities: the instruction of the young. In fact, this function seems to be much more prominent in Mexican tradition in general than in English-speaking traditions. Adolescents of Mexican descent in the United States consistently report the frequent use of proverbs by their parents as a teaching tool, in areas ranging from the inculcation of table manners to the regulation of peer-group relationships. The latter area is a particularly frequent focus of proverb use within Mexican American communities: one of the most frequently used proverbs, for example, translates roughly as, "Tell me who you run with and I'll tell you who you are." Perhaps this emphasis on peer-group relations derives from a sense that traditional, community-approved norms are threatened by those prevalent in the surrounding society, or from a sense that, in dealing with older children especially, parents need to appeal to traditional wisdom to bolster their authority.

Another dimension of proverb use within Mexican American communities is that proverbs often serve to foster a consciousness of ethnicity, that is, of membership in a particular ethnic group possessing features that distinguish it from other groups within a multiethnic environment. Even those Mexican American proverbs that do not have an explicitly didactic purpose nevertheless serve as a vehicle for the transmission of both the Spanish language and Mexican culture. It is in these sayings that links to folklore and other aspects of Mexican culture are established and maintained. Proverbs thus provide a means of enhancing Mexican American young people's familiarity with their heritage, thereby strengthening their ties to Mexican tradition.

7. Which one of the following most accurately expresses the main point of the passage?
   - (A) The Mexican American tradition of Spanish-language proverb use differs in important ways from the common proverb tradition of Europe.
   - (B) Spanish-language proverbs figure prominently in Mexican American communities, where they are used both to instruct the young and to promote the young's familiarity with their heritage.
   - (C) Most proverbs that are commonly used in Mexican American communities have their origins in either peninsular Spain or the common proverb tradition of Europe.
   - (D) Many people in Mexican American communities use proverbs to teach young people about a wide range of social behaviors and norms.
   - (E) As is illustrated in the Spanish-language tradition, the use of proverbs can serve a wide range of purposes within a community.

8. The author provides a translation of a proverb in lines 32–33 primarily in order to
   - (A) illustrate the relation between proverb use and education about peer-group relationships in Mexican American communities
   - (B) provide an example of the tone of a proverb that is frequently used in Mexican American communities
   - (C) illustrate how a proverb can function as an appeal to traditional wisdom
   - (D) provide an example of how some Spanish-language proverbs can be clearly translated into English
   - (E) illustrate the effectiveness of proverbs as educational tools in Mexican American communities

GO ON TO THE NEXT PAGE.

9. The passage provides information that most helps to answer which one of the following questions?

(A) In what other areas besides Europe did Spanish-language proverbs currently used in Mexican American communities originate?
(B) Are any proverbs that are used frequently in the English-language tradition derived from Mexican American proverbs?
(C) What kinds of messages and pieces of wisdom are most often communicated by proverbs in the English-language tradition?
(D) In what other ethnic groups besides Mexican Americans do proverbs function to maintain ties to the traditions of those groups?
(E) Is the use of proverbs in teaching young people more common in Mexican American communities than in the English-language tradition?

10. The passage most strongly suggests which one of the following about the use of proverbs?

(A) Proverb use is seldom intended to reinforce community-approved norms.
(B) The way in which a proverb is used depends, at least in part, on the community in which it is used.
(C) The most frequent use of proverbs in Mexican American communities is for the purpose of regulating peer-group relationships.
(D) Proverbs are often used to help teach young people languages.
(E) When a proverb is used as an educational tool, it is usually intended to serve more than one purpose.

11. The author of the passage would be most likely to agree with which one of the following statements?

(A) Most Mexican American proverbs have their origin in the common proverb tradition of Europe.
(B) Mexican American parents are more likely to emphasize the value of traditional wisdom than are most other parents in the United States.
(C) There are more Spanish-language proverbs than there are proverbs in the common proverb tradition of Europe.
(D) Proverb use in some communities may reflect parental concern that the young will not embrace traditional norms.
(E) Most proverbs cannot be accurately translated from one language to another.

12. Which one of the following is most strongly implied by the passage?

(A) If a proverb is used to inculcate table manners, then its primary purpose is to maintain ties to an ethnic tradition.
(B) The frequent use of proverbs within any community functions, at least in part, to convey a sense of their ethnicity to children within that community.
(C) The ways in which Mexican Americans use Spanish-language proverbs are typical of the ways in which Spanish speakers throughout the world use those proverbs.
(D) There are some sayings that do not require a verbal context to be understood but whose meaning for each particular use depends on the social context in which that use occurs.
(E) The emphasis within Mexican American communities on teaching children about peer-group relationships distinguishes those communities from other communities within the United States.

GO ON TO THE NEXT PAGE.

Passage A

Evolutionary psychology has taught us to examine human behavior from the standpoint of the theory of evolution—to explain a given type of human behavior by examining how it contributes to the reproductive success of individuals exhibiting the behavior, and thereby to the proliferation of the genetic material responsible for causing that behavior. From an evolutionary standpoint, the problem of altruism is a thorny one: what accounts for the evolution of behavior in which an individual expends energy or other valuable resources promoting the welfare of another individual?

The answer probably lies in the psychological experiences of identification and empathy. Such experiences could have initially arisen in response to cues (like physical resemblance) that indicated the presence of shared genetic material in human ancestors. The psychological states provoked by these cues could have increased the chances of related individuals' receiving assistance, thereby enhancing the survival and replication of genes influencing the capacity for identification and empathy. This would account, for example, for a mother's rushing to help her injured child; genes promoting their own self-propagation may thus operate through instinctive actions that appear unselfish.

Since human ancestors lived in small, kin-based groups, the application of altruistic mechanisms to the entire group would have promoted the propagation of the genes responsible for those mechanisms. Later, these mechanisms may have come to apply to humans who are not kin when communities grew larger. In this way, apparently altruistic mechanisms may have arisen within a genetically "selfish" system.

Passage B

Evolutionary psychology is a kind of conspiracy theory; that is, it explains behavior by imputing an interest (the proliferation of genes) that the agent of the behavior does not openly acknowledge, or indeed, is not even aware of. Thus, what seemed to be your unsurprising interest in your child's well-being turns out to be your genes' conspiracy to propagate themselves.

Such arguments can appear persuasive on the face of it. According to some evolutionary psychologists, an interest in the proliferation of genes explains monogamous families in animals whose offspring mature slowly. Human offspring mature slowly; and, at least in numerical terms, our species favors monogamous families. Evolutionary psychologists take this as evidence that humans form monogamous families because of our interest in propagating our genes. Are they right?

Maybe yes, maybe no; this kind of inference needs to be handled with great care. There are, most often, all sorts of interests that would explain any given behavior. What is needed to make it decisive that a particular interest explains a particular behavior is that the behavior would be reasonable *only* if one had that interest. But such cases are vanishingly rare: an interest in Y might explain doing X, but so too would an interest in doing X. A concern to propagate one's genes would explain promoting the welfare of one's children; but so too would an interest in the welfare of one's children. Not all of one's motives can be instrumental, after all; there must be some things that one cares for just for their own sakes.

13. Which one of the following most accurately states the main point of passage A?

(A) Altruistic behavior is problematic for evolutionary psychology because it tends to diminish the reproductive success of individuals that exhibit it.
(B) New evidence may explain the evolution of altruistic behavior in early humans by showing that genes promote their own self-propagation.
(C) Altruistic behavior originally served evolutionary purposes that it does not serve today because humans no longer live in small, kin-based groups.
(D) Contrary to what critics of evolutionary psychology say, most significant types of human behavior are prompted by genetically selfish motivations.
(E) An evolutionary explanation of altruistic behavior may lie in the psychological states brought about in early humans by cues of kinship or familiarity.

14. The approaches toward evolutionary psychology exhibited by the two authors differ in which one of the following ways?

(A) The author of passage A is more interested in examining the logical implications of evolutionary psychology than the author of passage B is.
(B) The author of passage A is more committed to the principles of evolutionary psychology than the author of passage B is.
(C) The author of passage A is more willing to consider nonevolutionary explanations for human behavior than the author of passage B is.
(D) The author of passage B is more skeptical of evolutionary theory in general than the author of passage A is.
(E) The author of passage B is more critical of the motives of evolutionary psychologists than the author of passage A is.

GO ON TO THE NEXT PAGE.

15. According to passage B, which one of the following is an example of a human characteristic for which evolutionary psychologists propose a questionable explanation?

(A) the early human tendency to live in small communities
(B) the slow maturation of human offspring
(C) forming monogamous families
(D) misinterpreting the interests that motivate human actions
(E) caring for some things for their own sakes

16. According to passage A, certain types of human behavior developed through evolutionary processes because they

(A) helped spread the genes responsible for those same behaviors
(B) prompted individuals to behave unselfishly
(C) improved the physical health of individuals who exhibited the behaviors
(D) made individuals who exhibited the behaviors more adept at finding food
(E) prompted early humans to live in mutually dependent groups

17. How does the purpose of passage B relate to the content of passage A?

(A) The author of passage B seeks to support the main claims made in passage A by presenting additional arguments in support of those claims.
(B) The author of passage B criticizes the type of argument made in passage A by attempting to create an analogous argument with a conclusion that is clearly false.
(C) The author of passage B argues that the type of evidence used in passage A is often derived from inaccurate observation.
(D) The author of passage B maintains that the claims made in passage A are vacuous because no possible evidence could confirm or disconfirm them.
(E) The author of passage B seeks to undermine the type of argument made in passage A by suggesting that it relies on questionable reasoning.

18. Which one of the following assertions from passage A most clearly exemplifies what the author of passage B means in calling evolutionary psychology a "conspiracy theory" (lines 35–36)?

(A) Evolutionary psychologists seek to examine human behavior from the point of view of the theory of evolution.
(B) Altruism presents a difficult problem for evolutionary psychology.
(C) An altruistic individual uses valuable resources to promote the well-being of another individual.
(D) Genes may promote their self-propagation through actions that appear unselfish.
(E) Early humans lived in small, kin-based groups.

19. It can be inferred that the author of passage B would regard which one of the following as a mistaken assumption underlying arguments like that made in passage A?

(A) Most of the physical features characteristic of modern humans developed as the result of evolutionary pressures.
(B) Any action performed by an early human was necessarily orchestrated by that individual's genes to promote the genes' self-propagation.
(C) To explain a type of human behavior in evolutionary terms, it is sufficient to show that the behavior would have improved the reproductive success of early humans.
(D) Evolutionary psychology can be used to explain human behavior but not animal behavior, since animal behavior is driven largely by instinct.
(E) Most early human behaviors that significantly hindered reproductive success were eliminated by evolutionary competition.

GO ON TO THE NEXT PAGE.

During Dostoyevsky's time there were two significant and opposing directions in Russian literary criticism. One position maintained that art stood high above the present and the everyday, while the radical view maintained that art had a right to exist only if it found its sources in concrete reality, and, through the exposure of want and injustice, it contributed to the creation of a new society; literature, in other words, should be useful. Dostoyevsky took a third position. As a realist, he never doubted that reality was literature's crucial source. But his understanding of reality went deeper than the one prevailing among radical critics, since for Dostoyevsky there was no distinction in principle between fantasy and reality, and reality was far more than the merely tangible.

The radical critics' demand that reality be depicted "as it is" was meaningless for Dostoyevsky; reality was necessarily shaped by the person who experienced it: what may not be reality for you may be reality for me. The task of the writer was to explode the boundaries of the so-called real world. Within perceptible "reality" exists another sphere, the fantastic, which is not in any way superfluous to a writer's concerns: "The fantastic must be so intimately bound up with the real that one almost believes in it."

The radical critics' insistence that art must serve a particular political view was for Dostoyevsky the equivalent of assigning to art "a shameful destiny." A literary work must stand or fall on its "artistic merit," he explained. The utilitarian claim that the formal aspects of a work were of secondary importance so long as its goal was good and its purpose clear struck Dostoyevsky as a contradiction in terms. Only fully realized artistic works could fulfill their goals. But what does it mean to say that a work is "artistic"? Dostoyevsky defined it thus: "To say that a novelist is 'artistic' means that he possesses a talent to express his thoughts in characters and images so that when the reader has finished the novel, he has fully understood the author's thoughts. Therefore, artistry is quite simply the ability to write well."

The radical critics' requirement that art must at all costs be "useful" to people and society seemed to Dostoyevsky unsatisfactory. How can we know what will show itself to be useful? Can we say with assurance how useful the *Iliad* has been to humankind? No, Dostoyevsky believed, when it comes to this we encounter breadths that cannot be measured with any precision; sometimes a work of art may appear to deviate from reality and serve no useful purpose because we cannot see clearly what paths it may take to become useful.

20. Which one of the following most accurately expresses the main point of the passage?

(A) By drawing on elements from the two opposing strains of Russian literary criticism, Dostoyevsky developed the theoretical apparatus for a new direction in Russian literature.

(B) In opposition to the views of the two most prominent groups of Russian literary critics, Dostoyevsky believed that literature should keep itself removed from reality.

(C) Dostoyevsky's indictment of the radical Russian critics rested solely on his objection to the radical critics' stipulation that literature be useful to society.

(D) In his critical writings, Dostoyevsky championed the freedom of the artist against the narrow constraints imposed by the radical Russian critics' concern with the depiction of reality.

(E) Dostoyevsky's position on literature differed sharply from that of the radical Russian critics with respect to the nature of reality, the importance of formal aspects in a literary work, and the utility of art.

21. Which one of the following works most clearly exemplifies writing Dostoyevsky would have deemed "artistic"?

(A) a fictionalized account based on interviews with patients that illustrates the brutal facts of illness

(B) a novel in which the author's ideas are given substance through suitable characters and events

(C) a novel in which the author attempted to use allegory to communicate a criticism of feudal society

(D) an autobiographical essay in which the author chronicles the outstanding events in his life

(E) a short story in which the characters debate how to solve various social problems

GO ON TO THE NEXT PAGE.

22. According to the passage, Dostoyevsky disagreed with the radical critics' view of realism in literature because he believed

(A) reality is not independent of the experiences of individuals
(B) realism is unequal to the task of representing political views
(C) art should be elevated above the portrayal of reality
(D) realism does not in fact facilitate the exposure of social inequities or contribute to the creation of a new society
(E) reality is not the crucial source of successful literature

23. In the context of the passage, the description of a work of literature as "useful" mainly refers to its

(A) proficiency at depicting the realm of the fantastic
(B) effectiveness at communicating the author's ideas
(C) ability to help bring about social change
(D) facility for exploding the boundaries of the tangible world
(E) capacity to advance a particular theory of literature

24. Which one of the following most accurately describes the organization of the material presented in the passage?

(A) Three positions are presented and each is elaborated in detail.
(B) Three positions are presented and the third is differentiated from the first two in detail.
(C) Three positions are presented and the third is differentiated from the second in detail.
(D) Three positions are presented and the third is shown to be superior to the first two.
(E) Three positions are presented and the third is shown to be inferior to the second.

25. It can be inferred from the passage that Dostoyevsky would most likely have agreed with which one of the following statements about the view held by some Russian critics that art should stand high above the present and everyday?

(A) It is correct because of its requirement that art have a strong element of the fantastic.
(B) It is correct because it recognizes that reality is more than just an enumeration of the mundane details of life.
(C) It is incorrect because reality must be the foundation of all literature.
(D) It is incorrect because it makes no distinction between reality and fantasy.
(E) It is incorrect because of its insistence that art further some societal end.

26. Given the information in the passage, Dostoyevsky would have been most likely to agree with which one of the following statements about works of literature?

(A) Only works of literature that are well written can serve a particular political view.
(B) Only works of literature that serve a particular political view can be said to be well written.
(C) Works of literature that are not well written always attempt to serve a particular political view.
(D) A work of literature that is well written cannot serve any particular political view.
(E) A work of literature that serves a particular political view cannot be well written.

27. The passage suggests that Dostoyevsky's attitude toward the radical critics' view would be most softened if the radical critics were to

(A) draw a sharper distinction between reality and fantasy when evaluating the content of a literary work
(B) put clarity of purpose ahead of formal aspects when evaluating a literary work
(C) acknowledge the importance of eliminating elements of concrete reality from literary works
(D) recognize the full significance of artistic merit when evaluating literary works
(E) explain more fully their demand that reality be depicted as it is

S T O P

IF YOU FINISH BEFORE TIME IS CALLED, YOU MAY CHECK YOUR WORK ON THIS SECTION ONLY.
DO NOT WORK ON ANY OTHER SECTION IN THE TEST.

Acknowledgment is made to the following sources from which material has been adapted for use in this test booklet:

Jerry Fodor, "The Trouble with Psychological Darwinism." ©1998 by LRB Ltd.

Werner Z. Hirsch, *Law and Economics: An Introductory Analysis.* ©1979 by Academic Press, Inc.

Geir Kjetsaa, *Fyodor Dostoyevsky: A Writer's Life.* tr. Siri Hustvedt and David McDuff. ©1987 by Viking Penguin Inc.

D. J. Kruger, "Evolution and Altruism: Combining Psychological Mediators with Naturally Selected Tendencies." ©2003 by the Human Behavior and Evolution Society.

LSAT Writing Sample Topic

Directions: The scenario presented below describes two choices, either one of which can be supported on the basis of the information given. Your essay should consider both choices and argue for one over the other, based on the two specified criteria and the facts provided. There is no "right" or "wrong" choice: a reasonable argument can be made for either.

ZM Corporation, a major household appliance manufacturer, is in bankruptcy and must decide whether to sell SB, a foreign-based appliance company it owns, or shut it down permanently. Using the facts below, write an essay in which you argue for one option over the other based on the following two criteria:

- ZM wants to emerge from bankruptcy financially sound and do so as quickly as possible.
- ZM wants to focus on developing its own brands and strengthening their sales.

The sale of SB would produce an immediate injection of cash for ZM. Two bidders have a strong interest in SB. The SB brand has a strong reputation for technological innovation. SB has highly dedicated customers in several key markets. SB has lost money in nine of the past ten years. Recently ZM has invested heavily in developing updated products for SB that use some of ZM's most advanced technology. ZM would continue to sell parts and technology to SB for these appliances. An independent SB would compete with some of ZM's brands in certain markets.

Shutting down SB would involve substantial short-term costs and would be a long process. ZM would have to pay off SB's creditors and make settlements with SB's unions, as well as honor warranties and provide parts and service for SB customers. There is some possibility that selling off SB's assets piecemeal after shutdown might, in the long term, bring in more net money than selling SB intact. A shutdown would allow ZM to retain exclusive control of its advanced technology. Some of SB's highly anticipated new products could be rebranded as ZM products.

Scratch Paper

Do not write your essay in this space.

Directions:

1. Use the Answer Key on the next page to check your answers.

2. Use the Scoring Worksheet below to compute your raw score.

3. Use the Score Conversion Chart to convert your raw score into the 120–180 scale.

Scoring Worksheet

1. Enter the number of questions you answered correctly in each section.

	Number Correct
SECTION I.	______
SECTION II	______
SECTION III	______
SECTION IV	______

2. Enter the sum here: _______

This is your Raw Score.

Conversion Chart

For Converting Raw Score to the 120–180 LSAT Scaled Score
LSAT PrepTest 64

Reported Score	Raw Score Lowest	Raw Score Highest
180	99	101
179	98	98
178	97	97
177	96	96
176	95	95
175	94	94
174	93	93
173	91	92
172	90	90
171	89	89
170	88	88
169	86	87
168	85	85
167	84	84
166	82	83
165	81	81
164	79	80
163	78	78
162	76	77
161	74	75
160	73	73
159	71	72
158	69	70
157	68	68
156	66	67
155	64	65
154	63	63
153	61	62
152	59	60
151	58	58
150	56	57
149	54	55
148	53	53
147	51	52
146	50	50
145	48	49
144	46	47
143	45	45
142	43	44
141	42	42
140	40	41
139	39	39
138	37	38
137	36	36
136	34	35
135	33	33
134	32	32
133	30	31
132	29	29
131	28	28
130	26	27
129	25	25
128	24	24
127	23	23
126	21	22
125	20	20
124	19	19
123	18	18
122	17	17
121	16	16
120	0	15

SECTION I

1.	C	8.	B	15.	B	22.	B
2.	C	9.	B	16.	A	23.	D
3.	B	10.	A	17.	A	24.	E
4.	A	11.	E	18.	B	25.	B
5.	A	12.	D	19.	C		
6.	E	13.	D	20.	D		
7.	C	14.	A	21.	E		

SECTION II

1.	E	8.	A	15.	D	22.	D
2.	B	9.	E	16.	C	23.	C
3.	C	10.	A	17.	B		
4.	D	11.	C	18.	D		
5.	A	12.	D	19.	B		
6.	E	13.	C	20.	A		
7.	B	14.	E	21.	A		

SECTION III

1.	B	8.	D	15.	B	22.	C
2.	E	9.	A	16.	D	23.	E
3.	C	10.	D	17.	B	24.	B
4.	B	11.	E	18.	B	25.	D
5.	D	12.	C	19.	D	26.	E
6.	D	13.	A	20.	C		
7.	B	14.	A	21.	A		

SECTION IV

1.	D	8.	A	15.	C	22.	A
2.	B	9.	E	16.	A	23.	C
3.	E	10.	B	17.	E	24.	C
4.	B	11.	D	18.	D	25.	C
5.	A	12.	D	19.	C	26.	A
6.	C	13.	E	20.	E	27.	D
7.	B	14.	B	21.	B		

Experimental Section Answer Key
June 1999, PrepTest 25, Section 1

1.	D	8.	C	15.	A	22.	D
2.	B	9.	B	16.	A	23.	A
3.	A	10.	A	17.	E	24.	E
4.	D	11.	C	18.	E	25.	B
5.	B	12.	D	19.	C	26.	B
6.	C	13.	A	20.	B		
7.	D	14.	C	21.	C		

PrepTest 65
December 2011

Time—35 minutes

26 Questions

Directions: The questions in this section are based on the reasoning contained in brief statements or passages. For some questions, more than one of the choices could conceivably answer the question. However, you are to choose the best answer; that is, the response that most accurately and completely answers the question. You should not make assumptions that are by commonsense standards implausible, superfluous, or incompatible with the passage. After you have chosen the best answer, blacken the corresponding space on your answer sheet.

1. Taxpayer: For the last ten years, Metro City's bridge-maintenance budget of $1 million annually has been a prime example of fiscal irresponsibility. In a well-run bridge program, the city would spend $15 million a year on maintenance, which would prevent severe deterioration, thus limiting capital expenses for needed bridge reconstruction to $10 million. However, as a result of its attempt to economize, the city is now faced with spending $400 million over two years on emergency reconstruction of its bridges.

The main point of the taxpayer's argument is that Metro City

(A) should have budgeted substantially more money for maintenance of its bridges
(B) would have had a well-run bridge program if it had spent more money for reconstruction of its bridges
(C) is spending more than it needs to on maintenance of its bridges
(D) is economizing on its bridge program to save money in case of emergencies
(E) has bridges that are more expensive to maintain than they were to build

2. Twenty professional income-tax advisors were given identical records from which to prepare an income-tax return. The advisors were not aware that they were dealing with fictitious records compiled by a financial magazine. No two of the completed tax returns agreed with each other, and only one was technically correct.

If the information above is correct, which one of the following conclusions can be properly drawn on the basis of it?

(A) Only one out of every twenty income-tax returns prepared by any given professional income-tax advisor will be correct.
(B) The fact that a tax return has been prepared by a professional income-tax advisor provides no guarantee that the tax return has been correctly prepared.
(C) In order to insure that tax returns are correct, it is necessary to hire professional income-tax advisors to prepare them.
(D) All professional income-tax advisors make mistakes on at least some of the tax returns they prepare.
(E) People are more likely to have an incorrectly prepared tax return if they prepare their own tax returns than if they hire a professional income-tax advisor.

GO ON TO THE NEXT PAGE.

3. The manager of a nuclear power plant defended the claim that the plant was safe by revealing its rate of injury for current workers: only 3.2 injuries per 200,000 hours of work, a rate less than half the national average for all industrial plants. The manager claimed that, therefore, by the standard of how many injuries occur, the plant was safer than most other plants where the employees could work.

Which one of the following, if true, most calls into question the manager's claim?

(A) Workers at nuclear power plants are required to receive extra training in safety precautions on their own time and at their own expense.
(B) Workers at nuclear power plants are required to report to the manager any cases of accidental exposure to radiation.
(C) The exposure of the workers to radiation at nuclear power plants was within levels the government considers safe.
(D) Workers at nuclear power plants have filed only a few lawsuits against the management concerning unsafe working conditions.
(E) Medical problems arising from work at a nuclear power plant are unusual in that they are not likely to appear until after an employee has left employment at the plant.

4. Columnist: The country is presently debating legislation that, if passed, would force manufacturers to increase the number of paid vacation days for employees, to pay higher overtime wages, and to pay all day-care expenses for children of each employee. This legislation is being supported by members of groups that have resorted to violent tactics in the past, and by individuals who are facing indictment on tax-evasion charges. We must defeat this legislation and what it stands for.

The columnist's argument is flawed because it

(A) attacks legislation by calling into question the integrity of the originators of the legislation
(B) assails legislation on the basis of the questionable character of supporters of the legislation
(C) attempts to discredit legislation by appealing to public sentiment for those who would be adversely affected
(D) presupposes that legislation is bad legislation whenever it has only a small number of supporters outside the country's national legislative body
(E) rejects legislation on the grounds that its supporters act inconsistently in seeking to place burdens on manufacturers upon whose business success the supporters depend

5. If the ivory trade continues, experts believe, the elephant will soon become extinct in Africa, because poaching is rife in many areas. A total ban on ivory trading would probably prevent the extinction. However, the country of Zimbabwe—which has virtually eliminated poaching within its borders and which relies on income from carefully culling elephant herds that threaten to become too big—objects to such a ban. Zimbabwe holds that the problem lies not with the ivory trade but with the conservation policies of other countries.

Which one of the following principles forms a logical basis for Zimbabwe's objection to a ban?

(A) International measures to correct a problem should not adversely affect countries that are not responsible for the problem.
(B) Freedom of trade is not a right but a consequence of agreements among nations.
(C) Respecting a country's sovereignty is more important than preventing the extinction of a species.
(D) Prohibitions affecting several countries should be enforced by a supranational agency.
(E) Effective conservation cannot be achieved without eliminating poaching.

6. The male sage grouse has air sacs that, when not inflated, lie hidden beneath the grouse's neck feathers. During its spring courtship ritual, the male sage grouse inflates these air sacs and displays them to the female sage grouse. Some scientists hypothesize that this courtship ritual serves as a means for female sage grouse to select healthy mates.

Which one of the following, if true, most strongly supports the scientists' hypothesis?

(A) Some female sage grouse mate with unhealthy male sage grouse.
(B) When diseased male sage grouse were treated with antibiotics, they were not selected by female sage grouse during the courtship ritual.
(C) Some healthy male sage grouse do not inflate their air sacs as part of the courtship ritual.
(D) Male sage grouse are prone to parasitic infections that exhibit symptoms visible on the birds' air sacs.
(E) The sage grouse is commonly afflicted with a strain of malaria that tends to change as the organism that causes it undergoes mutation.

GO ON TO THE NEXT PAGE.

7. Consumers will be hurt by the new lower ceilings on halibut catches. Given the law of supply and demand these restrictions are likely to result in an increase in the price of the fish.

Which one of the following, if assumed, would do most to justify the claim that the price of halibut will increase?

(A) The demand for halibut will not decrease substantially after the new restrictions are imposed.
(B) There is a connection between the supply of halibut and the demand for it.
(C) The lost production of halibut will not be replaced by increased production of other fish.
(D) The demand for other fish will be affected by the new restrictions.
(E) The amount of halibut consumed represents a very small proportion of all fish consumed.

8. Knowledge of an ancient language is essential for reading original ancient documents. Most ancient historical documents, however, have been translated into modern languages, so scholars of ancient history can read them for their research without learning ancient languages. Therefore, aspirants to careers as ancient-history scholars no longer need to take the time to learn ancient languages.

The argument is vulnerable to criticism on which one of the following grounds?

(A) It concludes that something is never necessary on the grounds that it is not always necessary.
(B) A statement of fact is treated as if it were merely a statement of opinion.
(C) The conclusion is no more than a restatement of the evidence provided as support of that conclusion.
(D) The judgment of experts is applied to a matter in which their expertise is irrelevant.
(E) Some of the evidence presented in support of the conclusion is inconsistent with other evidence provided.

Questions 9–10

The Board of Trustees of the Federici Art Museum has decided to sell some works from its collection in order to raise the funds necessary to refurbish its galleries. Although this may seem like a drastic remedy, the curator has long maintained that among the paintings that the late Ms. Federici collected for the museum were several unsuccessful immature works by Renoir and Cézanne that should be sold because they are of inferior quality and so add nothing to the overall quality of the museum's collection. Hence, the board's action will not detract from the quality of the museum's collection.

9. The conclusion drawn depends on which one of the following assumptions?

(A) Art speculators are unable to distinguish an inferior painting by Renoir from a masterpiece by him.
(B) All of the paintings that the board of trustees sells will be among those that the curator recommends selling.
(C) All of the paintings by Renior and Cézanne that are owned by the Federici Art Museum were purchased by Ms. Federici herself.
(D) Only an avid collector of paintings by Cézanne would be willing to pay a high price for early works by this artist.
(E) A great work of art can be truly appreciated only if it is displayed in a carefully designed and well-maintained gallery.

10. Which one of the following, if true, most weakens the argument?

(A) The directors of an art museum can generally raise funds for refurbishing the building in which the museum's collection is housed by means other than selling part of its collection.
(B) The quality of an art collection is determined not just by the quality of its paintings, but by what its collection demonstrates about the development of the artistic talent and ideas of the artists represented.
(C) The immature works by Renoir and Cézanne that were purchased by Ms. Federici were at that time thought by some critics to be unimportant juvenile works.
(D) Those people who speculate in art by purchasing artworks merely to sell them at much higher prices welcome inflation in the art market, but curators of art museums regret the inflation in the art market.
(E) The best work of a great artist demands much higher prices in the art market than the worst work of that same artist.

GO ON TO THE NEXT PAGE.

11. Taken together, some 2,000 stocks recommended on a popular television show over the course of the past 12 years by the show's guests, most of whom are successful consultants for multibillion-dollar stock portfolios, performed less successfully than the market as a whole for this 12-year period. So clearly, no one should ever follow any recommendations by these so-called experts.

    Each of the following, if true, weakens the argument EXCEPT:

    (A) Taken together, the stocks recommended on the television show performed better than the market as a whole for the past year.
    (B) Taken together, the stocks recommended on the television show performed better for the past 12-year period than stock portfolios that were actually selected by any other means.
    (C) Performance of the stocks recommended on the telephone show was measured by stock dividends, whereas the performance of the market as a whole was measured by change in share value.
    (D) Performance of the stocks recommended on the television show was measured independently by a number of analysts, and the results of all the measurements concurred.
    (E) The stock portfolios for which the guests were consultants performed better for the past 12-year period than the market as a whole.

12. The school principal insisted that student failures are caused by bad teaching. In a relatively short time failing grades disappeared from the school. The principal happily recognized this as evidence that the teaching had improved at the school.

    The flawed pattern of reasoning in the above is most similar to that in which one of the following?

    (A) The nutritionist insisted that the weight gain that team members complained of was caused by overeating. In a brief time all the members stopped overeating. The nutritionist was pleased to conclude that they had stopped gaining weight.
    (B) The manager insisted that the workers who filed complaints had too many different tasks. The manager simplified the jobs, and complaints stopped. The manager happily concluded that the working environment has been improved.
    (C) The nutritionist insisted that the weight gain that team members complained of was merely in their imagination. Members were given weight charts for the last three months. The nutritionist was pleased to conclude that the complaints of weight gain had stopped.
    (D) The manager insisted that the workers who filed complaints did not have enough to do. Soon there were no more complaints filed. The manager was pleased to conclude that the workers were now productively filling their time.
    (E) The nutritionist insisted that the weight gain that team members complained of was caused by their thinking of food too often. The nutritionist was happy to conclude that the weight gain had stopped once the team members reported that they had stopped thinking of food so often.

GO ON TO THE NEXT PAGE.

13. Unlike other primroses, self-pollinating primroses do not need to rely on insects for pollination. In many years insect pollinators are scarce, and in those years a typical non-self-pollinating primrose produces fewer seeds than does a typical self-pollinating primrose. In other years, seed production is approximately equal. Thus, self-pollinating primroses have the advantage of higher average seed production. Aside from seed production, these self-pollinating primroses are indistinguishable from non-self-pollinating primroses. Nevertheless, self-pollinating primrose plants remain rare among primroses.

Which one of the following, if true, most helps to resolve the apparent discrepancy in the information above?

(A) Insects that collect pollen from primroses do not discriminate between self-pollinating primroses and non-self-pollinating primroses.
(B) When insect pollinators are scarce, non-self-pollinating primroses produce larger seeds that are more likely to germinate than are seeds from self-pollinating primroses.
(C) Self-pollinating primroses that are located in areas with few insects produce no fewer seeds than do self-pollinating primroses that are located in areas with many insects.
(D) Many primroses are located in areas in which the soil conditions that are optimal for seed germination are not present.
(E) Self-pollinating primroses can be assisted by insects during pollination but do not require the assistance of insects to be pollinated.

14. We have a moral obligation not to destroy books, even if they belong to us. The reason is quite simple: If preserved, books will almost certainly contribute to the intellectual and emotional enrichment of future generations.

Which one of the following most accurately expresses the principle underlying the argument?

(A) It is morally incumbent upon us to devote effort to performing actions that have at least some chance of improving other people's lives.
(B) We are morally obligated to preserve anything that past generations had preserved for our intellectual and emotional enrichment.
(C) The moral commitments we have to future generations supersede the moral commitments we have to the present generation.
(D) We are morally obligated not to destroy anything that will most likely enrich, either intellectually or emotionally, for posterity.
(E) Being morally obligated not to destroy something requires that we be reasonably assured that that thing will lead to the betterment of someone we know.

15. The southern half of a certain region of the earth was covered entirely by water during the Cretaceous period, the last 75 million years of the Mesozoic era, the era when dinosaurs roamed the earth. Dinosaurs lived only on land. Thus, plesiosaurs—swimming reptiles that lived during the Cretaceous period exclusively—were not dinosaurs. No single species of dinosaur lived throughout the entire Mesozoic era.

If the statements in the passage are true, each of the following could be true EXCEPT:

(A) Dinosaurs inhabited the northern half of the region throughout the entire Mesozoic era.
(B) Plesiosaurs did not inhabit the southern half of the region during the Cretaceous period.
(C) Plesiosaurs did not inhabit the southern half of the region before the Cretaceous period.
(D) Dinosaurs did not inhabit the northern half of the region during the Cretaceous period.
(E) Dinosaurs inhabited the southern half of the region throughout the entire Mesozoic era.

16. Essayist: Wisdom and intelligence are desirable qualities. However, being intelligent does not imply that one is wise, nor does being wise imply that one is intelligent. In my own experience, the people I meet have one or the other of these qualities but not both.

If the essayist's statements are true, then each of the following could be true EXCEPT:

(A) Most people are neither intelligent or wise.
(B) Most people are both intelligent and wise.
(C) No one is both wise and intelligent.
(D) No one is either wise or intelligent.
(E) Many people are intelligent and yet lack wisdom.

GO ON TO THE NEXT PAGE.

17. Concerned citizen: The mayor, an outspoken critic of the proposed restoration of city hall, is right when he notes that the building is outdated, but that the restoration would be expensive at a time when the budget is already tight. We cannot afford such a luxury item in this time of financial restraint, he says. However, I respectfully disagree. The building provides the last remaining link to the days of the city's founding, and preserving a sense of municipal history is crucial to maintaining respect for our city government and its authority. So to the question, "Can we really afford to?" I can only respond, "Can we afford not to?"

Which one of the following most accurately characterizes a flaw in the concerned citizen's argument?

(A) The argument is solely an emotional appeal to history.
(B) The argument ambiguously uses the word "afford."
(C) The argument inappropriately appeals to the authority of the mayor.
(D) The argument incorrectly presumes that the restoration would be expensive.
(E) The argument inappropriately relies on the emotional connotations of words such as "outdated" and "luxury."

18. Obviously, we cannot in any real sense mistreat plants. Plants do not have nervous systems, and having a nervous system is necessary to experience pain.

The conclusion above follows logically if which one of the following is assumed?

(A) Any organism that can experience pain can be mistreated.
(B) Only organisms that have nervous systems can experience pain.
(C) Any organism that has nervous system can experience pain.
(D) Only organisms that can experience pain can be mistreated.
(E) Any organism that has nervous system can be mistreated.

19. Inez: In these poor economic times, people want to be sure they are getting good value for their money. I predict people would be more willing to buy antiques at our fair if we first have the object inspected by professional appraisers who would remove any objects of questionable authenticity.

Anika: I disagree with your prediction. Our customers already are antiques experts. Furthermore, hiring professional appraisers would push up our costs considerably, thus forcing us to raise the prices on all our antiques.

Anika's response proceeds by

(A) indicating that a particular plan would have an effect contrary to the anticipated effect
(B) claiming that a particular plan should not be adopted because, while effective, it would have at least one undesirable consequence
(C) arguing that an alternative plan could achieve a desired result more easily than the plan originally proposed
(D) questioning the assumption that authorities are available who have special knowledge of the problem under discussion
(E) offering a counterexample in order to show that a particular general claim is too broadly stated

20. In some ill-considered popularizations of interesting current research, it is argued that higher apes have the capacity for language but have never put it to use—a remarkable biological miracle, given the enormous selectional advantage of even minimal linguistic skills. It is rather like claiming that some animal has wings adequate for flight but has never thought to fly.

Which one of the following is most similar in its reasoning to the argument above?

(A) Arguing that there are some humans who never sleep is rather like discovering a species of lion that does not eat meat.
(B) Arguing that Earth has been visited by aliens from outer space is rather like claiming that early explorers had visited North America but never founded cities.
(C) Arguing that the human brain has telekinetic powers that no humans have ever exercised is rather like arguing that some insect has legs but never uses them to walk.
(D) Claiming that some people raised tobacco but did not smoke it is rather like claiming that a society that knew how to brew alcohol never drank it.
(E) Arguing that not all people with cars will drive them is rather like claiming that humans invented gasoline long before they used it as fuel for transportation.

GO ON TO THE NEXT PAGE.

Questions 21–22

Sarah: Some schools seek to foster a habit of volunteering in their students by requiring them to perform community service. But since a person who has been forced to do something has not really volunteered and since the habit of volunteering cannot be said to have been fostered in a person who has not yet volunteered for anything, there is no way this policy can succeed by itself.

Paul: I disagree. Some students forced to perform community service have enjoyed it so much that they subsequently actually volunteer to do something similar. In such cases, the policy can clearly be said to have fostered a habit of volunteering.

21. Paul responds to Sarah's argument using which one of the following argumentative techniques?

(A) He argues that Sarah is assuming just what she sets out to prove.
(B) He argues that Sarah's conception of what it means to volunteer excludes certain activities that ought to be considered instances of volunteering.
(C) He introduces considerations that call into question one of Sarah's assumptions.
(D) He questions Sarah's motives for advancing an argument against the school policy.
(E) He argues that a policy Sarah fails to consider could accomplish the same aim as the policy that Sarah considers.

22. The main point at issue between Sarah and Paul is whether

(A) there are any circumstances under which an individual forced to perform a task can correctly be said to have genuinely volunteered to perform that task
(B) being forced to perform community service can provide enjoyment to the individual who is forced to perform such service
(C) being forced to perform community service can by itself encourage a genuine habit of volunteering in those students who are forced to perform such service
(D) it is possible for schools to develop policies that foster the habit of volunteering in their students
(E) students who develop a habit of volunteering while in school are inclined to perform community service later in their lives

23. Only computer scientists understand the architecture of personal computers, and only those who understand the architecture of personal computers appreciate the advances in technology made in the last decade. It follows that only those who appreciate these advances are computer scientists.

Which one of the following most accurately describes a flaw in the reasoning in the argument?

(A) The argument contains no stated or implied relationship between computer scientists and those who appreciate the advances in technology in the last decade.
(B) The argument ignores the fact that some computer scientists may not appreciate the advances in technology made in the last decade.
(C) The argument ignores the fact that computer scientists may appreciate other things besides the advances in technology made in the last decade.
(D) The premises of the argument are stated in such a way that they exclude the possibility of drawing any logical conclusion.
(E) The premises of the argument presuppose that everyone understands the architecture of personal computers.

24. Sociologist: Research shows, contrary to popular opinion, that, all other things being equal, most people who have pets are less happy than most people who do not. Therefore, any person who wants to be as happy as possible would do well to consider not having a pet.

Which one of the following, if true, most seriously weakens the sociologist's argument?

(A) Some people who have pets are happier than most people who do not.
(B) Most people who have no pets occasionally wish that they had pets.
(C) Most people who have pets are reasonably happy.
(D) Most people who have pets feel happier because they have pets.
(E) All people who have no pets admit to feeling unhappy sometimes.

GO ON TO THE NEXT PAGE.

25. The dwarf masked owl, a rare migratory bird of prey, normally makes its winter home on the Baja peninsula, where it nests in the spiny cactus. In fact, there are no other suitable nesting sites for the dwarf masked owl on the Baja peninsula. But a blight last spring destroyed all of the spiny cacti on the Baja peninsula. So unless steps are taken to reestablish the spiny cactus population, the dwarf masked owl will not make its home on the Baja peninsula this winter.

The argument depends on assuming which one of the following?

(A) No birds of prey other than the dwarf masked owl nest in the spiny cactus.
(B) If the Baja peninsula contains spiny cacti, then the dwarf masked owl makes its winter home there.
(C) On occasion the dwarf masked owl has been known to make its winter home far from its normal migratory route.
(D) The dwarf masked owl will not make its winter home on the Baja peninsula only if that region contains no spiny cacti.
(E) Suitable nesting sites must be present where the dwarf masked owl makes its winter home.

26. At night, a flock of crows will generally perch close together in a small place—often a piece of wooded land—called a roost. Each morning, the crows leave the roost and fan out in small groups to hunt and scavenge the surrounding area. For most flocks, the crows' hunting extends as far as 100 to 130 kilometers (60 to 80 miles) from the roost. Normally, a flock will continue to occupy the same roost for several consecutive years, and when it abandons a roost site for a new one, the new roost is usually less than eight kilometers (five miles) away:

Of the following claims, which one can most justifiably be rejected on the basis of the statements above?

(A) Crows will abandon their roost site only in response to increases in the population of the flock.
(B) When there is a shortage of food in the area in which a flock of crows normally hunts and scavenges, some members of the flock will begin to hunt and scavenge outside that area.
(C) Most of the hunting and scavenging that crows do occurs more than eight kilometers (five miles) from their roost.
(D) Once a flock of crows has settled on a new roost site, it is extremely difficult to force it to abandon that site for another.
(E) When a flock of crows moves to a new roost site, it generally does so because the area in which it has hunted and scavenged has been depleted of food sources.

S T O P

IF YOU FINISH BEFORE TIME IS CALLED, YOU MAY CHECK YOUR WORK ON THIS SECTION ONLY.
DO NOT WORK ON ANY OTHER SECTION IN THE TEST.

SECTION I

Time—35 minutes

25 Questions

Directions: The questions in this section are based on the reasoning contained in brief statements or passages. For some questions, more than one of the choices could conceivably answer the question. However, you are to choose the best answer; that is, the response that most accurately and completely answers the question. You should not make assumptions that are by commonsense standards implausible, superfluous, or incompatible with the passage. After you have chosen the best answer, blacken the corresponding space on your answer sheet.

1. In a recent study of more than 400 North American men and women whose previous heart attack put them at risk for a second heart attack, about half were told to switch to a "Mediterranean-type diet"—one rich in fish, vegetables, olive oil, and grains—while the other half were advised to eat a more traditional "Western" diet but to limit their fat intake. Those following the Mediterranean diet were significantly less likely than those in the other group to have a second heart attack. But the Mediterranean diet includes a fair amount of fat from fish and olive oil, so the research suggests that a diet may not have to be extremely low in fat in order to protect the heart.

   Which one of the following, if true, most strengthens the argument?

   (A) Research has shown that eliminating almost all fat from one's diet can be effective in decreasing the likelihood of a second heart attack.
   (B) Studies suggest that the kinds of oils in the fat included in the Mediterranean diet may protect the heart against potentially fatal disruptions of heart rhythms and other causes of heart attacks.
   (C) The patients who consumed the Mediterranean diet enjoyed the food and continued to follow the diet after the experiment was concluded.
   (D) Many people who have had heart attacks are advised by their cardiologists to begin an exercise regimen in addition to changing their diet.
   (E) Some cardiologists believe that the protection afforded by the Mediterranean diet might be enhanced by drugs that lower blood-cholesterol levels.

2. Florist: Some people like to have green carnations on St. Patrick's Day. But flowers that are naturally green are extremely rare. Thus, it is very difficult for plant breeders to produce green carnations. Before St. Patrick's Day, then, it is wise for florists to stock up on white carnations, which are fairly inexpensive and quite easy to dye green.

   Which one of the following most accurately expresses the overall conclusion of the florist's argument?

   (A) It is a good idea for florists to stock up on white carnations before St. Patrick's Day.
   (B) Flowers that are naturally green are very rare.
   (C) There are some people who like to have green carnations on St. Patrick's Day.
   (D) White carnations are fairly inexpensive and can easily be dyed green.
   (E) It is very difficult to breed green carnations.

3. Millions of homes are now using low-energy lighting, but millions more have still to make the switch, a fact that the government and the home lighting industry are eager to change. Although low-wattage bulbs cost more per bulb than normal bulbs, their advantages to the homeowner are enormous, and therefore everyone should use low-wattage bulbs.

   Information about which one of the following would be LEAST useful in evaluating the argument?

   (A) the actual cost of burning low-wattage bulbs compared to that of burning normal bulbs
   (B) the profits the home lighting industry expects to make from sales of low-wattage bulbs
   (C) the specific cost of a low-wattage bulb compared with that of a normal bulb
   (D) the opinion of current users of low-wattage bulbs as to their effectiveness
   (E) the average life of a low-wattage bulb compared with that of a normal bulb

GO ON TO THE NEXT PAGE.

4. Swimming pools should be fenced to protect children from drowning, but teaching children to swim is even more important. And there is a principle involved here that applies to childrearing generally. Thus, while we should restrict children's access to the soft drinks and candies advertised on television shows directed towards children, it is even more important to teach them _______.

Which one of the following most logically completes the passage?

(A) that television can be a good source of accurate information about many things
(B) that television advertisements are deceptive and misleading
(C) how to make nutritional choices that are conducive to their well-being
(D) the importance of physical activity to health and well-being
(E) how to creatively entertain themselves without watching television

5. In its coverage of a controversy regarding a proposal to build a new freeway, a television news program showed interviews with several people who would be affected by the proposed freeway. Of the interviews shown, those conducted with people against the new freeway outnumbered those conducted with people for it two to one. The television program is therefore biased against the proposed freeway.

Which one of the following, if true, most seriously weakens the argument?

(A) Most of the people who watched the program were aware of the freeway controversy beforehand.
(B) Most viewers of television news programs do not expect those programs to be completely free of bias.
(C) In the interviews, the people against the new freeway expressed their opinions with more emotion than the people for the freeway did.
(D) Before the program aired, over twice as many people were against building the freeway than were in favor of it.
(E) The business interests of the television station that produced the program would be harmed by the construction of a new freeway.

6. Evan: I am a vegetarian because I believe it is immoral to inflict pain on animals to obtain food. Some vegetarians who share this moral reason nonetheless consume some seafood, on the grounds that it is not known whether certain sea creatures can experience pleasure or pain. But if it is truly wrong to inflict needless suffering, we should extend the benefit of the doubt to sea animals and refrain from eating seafood.

Which one of the following most closely conforms to the principle illustrated by Evan's criticism of vegetarians who eat seafood?

(A) I do not know if I have repaid Farah the money she lent me for a movie ticket. She says that she does not remember whether or not I repaid her. In order to be sure that I have repaid her, I will give her the money now.
(B) It is uncertain whether all owners of the defective vehicles know that their vehicles are being recalled by the manufacturer. Thus, we should expect that some vehicles that have been recalled have not been returned.
(C) I am opposed to using incentives such as reduced taxes to attract businesses to our region. These incentives would attract businesses interested only in short-term profits. Such businesses would make our region's economy less stable, because they have no long-term commitment to the community.
(D) Updating our computer security system could lead to new contracts. The present system has no problems, but we could benefit from emphasizing a state-of-the-art system in new proposals. If we do not get new customers, the new system could be financed through higher fees for current customers.
(E) Isabel Allende lived through the tragic events of her country's recent history; no doubt her novels have been inspired by her memories of those events. Yet Allende's characters are hopeful and full of joy, indicating that Allende's own view of life has not been negatively marked by her experiences.

GO ON TO THE NEXT PAGE.

7. Economist: Government intervention in the free market in pursuit of socially desirable goals can affect supply and demand, thereby distorting prices. The ethics of such intervention is comparable to that of administering medicines. Most medicines have harmful as well as beneficial effects, so the use of a type of medicine is ethically justified only when its nonuse would be significantly more harmful than its use. Similarly, government intervention in the free market is justified only when it _______.

Which one of the following most logically completes the final sentence above?

(A) would likely be approved of by the majority of the affected participants
(B) has been shown to have few if any significantly harmful effects
(C) is believed unlikely to significantly exacerbate any existing problems
(D) would do less damage than would result from the government's not intervening
(E) provides a solution to some otherwise insoluble problem

8. The proportion of fat calories in the diets of people who read the nutrition labels on food products is significantly lower than it is in the diets of people who do not read nutrition labels. This shows that reading these labels promotes healthful dietary behavior.

The reasoning in the argument above is flawed in that the argument

(A) illicitly infers a cause from a correlation
(B) relies on a sample that is unlikely to be representative of the group as a whole
(C) confuses a condition that is necessary for a phenomenon to occur with a condition that is sufficient for that phenomenon to occur
(D) takes for granted that there are only two possible alternative explanations of a phenomenon
(E) draws a conclusion about the intentions of a group of people based solely on data about the consequences of their behavior

9. Some paleontologists have suggested that *Apatosaurus*, a huge dinosaur, was able to gallop. This, however, is unlikely, because galloping would probably have broken *Apatosaurus*'s legs. Experiments with modern bones show how much strain they can withstand before breaking. By taking into account the diameter and density of *Apatosaurus* leg bones, it is possible to calculate that those bones could not have withstood the strains of galloping.

Which one of the following most accurately expresses the conclusion drawn by the argument as a whole?

(A) Galloping would probably have broken the legs of *Apatosaurus*.
(B) It is possible to calculate that *Apatosaurus* leg bones could not have withstood the strain of galloping.
(C) The claim of paleontologists that *Apatosaurus* was able to gallop is likely to be incorrect.
(D) If galloping would have broken the legs of *Apatosaurus*, then *Apatosaurus* was probably unable to gallop.
(E) Modern bones are quite similar in structure and physical properties to the bones of *Apatosaurus*.

10. A new process enables ordinary table salt to be fortified with iron. This advance could help reduce the high incidence of anemia in the world's population due to a deficiency of iron in the diet. Salt is used as a preservative for food and a flavor enhancer all over the globe, and people consume salt in quantities that would provide iron in significant amounts.

Which one of the following most accurately describes the role played in the argument by the statement that people consume salt in quantities that would provide iron in significant amounts?

(A) It is the conclusion of the argument.
(B) It provides support for the conclusion of the argument.
(C) It is a claim that the argument is directed against.
(D) It qualifies the conclusion of the argument.
(E) It illustrates a principle that underlies the argument.

11. Inspector: The only fingerprints on the premises are those of the owner, Mr. Tannisch. Therefore, whoever now has his guest's missing diamonds must have worn gloves.

Which one of the following exhibits a flaw in its reasoning most similar to that in the inspector's reasoning?

(A) The campers at Big Lake Camp, all of whom became ill this afternoon, have eaten food only from the camp cafeteria. Therefore, the cause of the illness must not have been something they ate.
(B) The second prototype did not perform as well in inclement weather as did the first prototype. Hence, the production of the second prototype might have deviated from the design followed for the first.
(C) Each of the swimmers at this meet more often loses than wins. Therefore, it is unlikely that any of them will win.
(D) All of Marjorie's cavities are on the left side of her mouth. Hence, she must chew more on the left side than on the right.
(E) All of these tomato plants are twice as big as they were last year. So if we grow peas, they will probably be twice as big as last year's peas.

12. Populations of a shrimp species at eleven different Indonesian coral reefs show substantial genetic differences from one reef to another. This is surprising because the area's strong ocean currents probably carry baby shrimp between the different reefs, which would allow the populations to interbreed and become genetically indistinguishable.

Which one of the following, if true, most helps to explain the substantial genetic differences among the shrimp populations?

(A) The genetic differences between the shrimp populations are much less significant than those between shrimp and any other marine species.
(B) The individual shrimp within a given population at any given Indonesian coral reef differ from one another genetically, even though there is widespread interbreeding within any such population.
(C) Before breeding, shrimp of the species examined migrate back to the coral reef at which they were hatched.
(D) Most shrimp hatched at a given Indonesian coral reef are no longer present at that coral reef upon becoming old enough to breed.
(E) Ocean currents probably carry many of the baby shrimp hatched at a given Indonesian coral reef out into the open ocean rather than to another coral reef.

GO ON TO THE NEXT PAGE.

13. Researchers have studied the cost-effectiveness of growing halophytes—salt-tolerant plant species—for animal forage. Halophytes require more water than conventional crops, but can be irrigated with seawater, and pumping seawater into farms near sea level is much cheaper than pumping freshwater from deep wells. Thus, seawater agriculture near sea level should be cost-effective in desert regions although its yields are smaller than traditional, freshwater agriculture.

Which one of the following, if true, most strengthens the argument above?

(A) A given volume of halophytes is significantly different in nutritional value for animal forage from the same volume of conventional forage crops.
(B) Some halophytes not only tolerate seawater but require salt in order to thrive.
(C) Large research expenditures are needed to develop the strains of halophytes best suited for agricultural purposes.
(D) Costs other than the costs of irrigation are different for halophytes grown by means of seawater irrigation than for conventional crops.
(E) Pumping water for irrigation is proportionally one of the largest costs involved in growing, harvesting, and distributing any forage crop for animals.

14. Principle: If an insurance policy is written in such a way that a reasonable person seeking insurance would not read it thoroughly before signing it, then the reasonable expectations of the policyholder concerning the policy's coverage should take legal precedence over specific language in the written policy itself.

Application: The insurance company should be required to cover the hail damage to Celia's car, even though specific language in the written policy Celia signed excluded coverage for hail damage.

Which one of the following, if true, most justifies the above application of the principle?

(A) Celia is a reasonable person, and she expected the insurance policy to cover hail damage to her car.
(B) Given the way it was written, a reasonable person would not have read Celia's insurance policy thoroughly before signing it, and Celia reasonably expected the policy to cover hail damage.
(C) The insurance policy that Celia signed was written in such a way that a reasonable person would not read it thoroughly before signing it, but Celia did read the policy thoroughly before signing it.
(D) Celia did not read the insurance policy thoroughly before signing it, and a reasonable person in her position would assume that the policy would cover hail damage.
(E) Celia did not read the written insurance policy thoroughly before signing it, and a reasonable person in her position would not have done so either.

GO ON TO THE NEXT PAGE.

15. Researcher: Every year approximately the same number of people die of iatrogenic "disease"—that is, as a direct result of medical treatments or hospitalization—as die of all other causes combined. Therefore, if medicine could find ways of preventing all iatrogenic disease, the number of deaths per year would decrease by half.

The reasoning in the researcher's argument is flawed because the argument fails to consider that

(A) prevention of noniatrogenic disease will have an effect on the occurrence of iatrogenic disease
(B) some medical treatments can be replaced by less invasive or damaging alternatives
(C) people who do not die of one cause may soon die of another cause
(D) there is no one way to prevent all cases of death from iatrogenic disease
(E) whenever a noniatrogenic disease occurs, there is a risk of iatrogenic disease

16. Activist: Any member of the city council ought either to vote against the proposal or to abstain. But if all the members abstain, the matter will be decided by the city's voters. So at least one member of the city council should vote against the proposal.

The conclusion of the activist's argument follows logically if which one of the following is assumed?

(A) If all the members of the city council abstain in the vote on the proposal, the city's voters will definitely decide in favor of the proposal.
(B) The proposal should not be decided by the city's voters.
(C) No members of the city council will vote in favor of the proposal.
(D) If not every member of the city council abstains in the vote on the proposal, the matter will not be decided by the city's voters.
(E) If one member of the city council ought to vote against the proposal, the other members should abstain in the vote on the proposal.

17. Economist: Some critics of the media have contended that negative news reports on the state of the economy can actually harm the economy because such reports damage people's confidence in it, and this lack of confidence in turn adversely affects people's willingness to spend money. But studies show that spending trends correlate very closely with people's confidence in their own immediate economic situations. Thus these media critics are mistaken.

The economist's argument is flawed in that it fails to consider the possibility that

(A) one's level of confidence in one's own economic situation affects how one perceives reports about the overall state of the economy
(B) news reports about the state of the economy are not always accurate
(C) people who pay no attention to economic reports in the media always judge accurately whether their own economic situation is likely to deteriorate or improve
(D) people who have little confidence in the overall economy generally take a pessimistic view concerning their own immediate economic situations
(E) an economic slowdown usually has a greater impact on the economic situations of individuals if it takes people by surprise than if people are forewarned

GO ON TO THE NEXT PAGE.

18. Zoologist: Every domesticated large mammal species now in existence was domesticated thousands of years ago. Since those days, people undoubtedly tried innumerable times to domesticate each of the wild large mammal species that seemed worth domesticating. Clearly, therefore, most wild large mammal species in existence today either would be difficult to domesticate or would not be worth domesticating.

The zoologist's argument requires the assumption that

(A) in spite of the difficulties encountered, at one time or another people have tried to domesticate each wild large mammal species
(B) it is not much easier today to domesticate wild large mammal species than it was in the past
(C) not all of the large mammal species that were domesticated in the past are still in existence
(D) the easier it is to domesticate a wild large mammal species, the more worthwhile it is to do so
(E) of all the domesticated large mammal species in existence today, the very first to be domesticated were the easiest to domesticate

19. Last winter was mild enough to allow most bird species to forage naturally, which explains why the proportion of birds visiting feeders was much lower than usual. The mild winter also allowed many species to stay in their summer range all winter without migrating south, thereby limiting the usual attrition accompanying migration. Hence, last year's mild winter is responsible for this year's larger-than-usual bird population.

Which one of the following, if true, would most strengthen the reasoning in the argument?

(A) Increases in bird populations sometimes occur following unusual weather patterns.
(B) When birds do not migrate south, the mating behaviors they exhibit differ from those they exhibit when they do migrate.
(C) Birds eating at feeders are more vulnerable to predators than are birds foraging naturally.
(D) Birds that remain in their summer range all winter often exhaust that range's food supply before spring.
(E) Birds sometimes visit feeders even when they are able to find sufficient food for survival by foraging naturally.

20. Journalist: Newspapers generally report on only those scientific studies whose findings sound dramatic. Furthermore, newspaper stories about small observational studies, which are somewhat unreliable, are more frequent than newspaper stories about large randomized trials, which generate stronger scientific evidence. Therefore, a small observational study must be more likely to have dramatic findings than a large randomized trial.

Which one of the following most accurately expresses a flaw in the journalist's reasoning?

(A) It casts doubt on the reliability of a study by questioning the motives of those reporting it.
(B) It fails to consider that even if a study's findings sound dramatic, the scientific evidence for those findings may be strong.
(C) It confuses a claim about scientific studies whose findings sound dramatic with a similar claim about small observational studies.
(D) It overlooks the possibility that small observational studies are far more common than large randomized trials.
(E) It fails to rule out the possibility that a study's having findings that sound dramatic is an effect rather than a cause of the study's being reported on.

21. In several countries, to slow global warming, many farmers are planting trees on their land because of government incentives. These incentives arose from research indicating that vegetation absorbs carbon dioxide that might otherwise trap heat in the atmosphere. A recent study, however, indicates that trees absorb and store carbon dioxide less effectively than native grasses. Therefore, these incentives are helping to hasten global warming.

The argument requires the assumption that

(A) trees not only absorb carbon dioxide but also emit it
(B) most farmers do not plant any trees on their land unless there is an incentive to do so
(C) land that has been deforested seldom later sustains native grasses
(D) some of the trees planted in response to the incentives are planted where native grasses would otherwise be growing
(E) few if any governments have been interested in promoting the growth of native grasses

GO ON TO THE NEXT PAGE.

22. Does the position of a car driver's seat have a significant impact on driving safety? It probably does. Driving position affects both comfort and the ability to see the road clearly. A driver who is uncomfortable eventually becomes fatigued, which makes it difficult to concentrate on the road. Likewise, the better the visibility from the driver's seat, the more aware the driver can be of road conditions and other vehicles.

Which one of the following most accurately describes the role played in the argument by the claim that driving position affects both comfort and the ability to see the road clearly?

(A) It is the conclusion drawn in the argument.
(B) It is a claim that the argument shows to be inconsistent with available evidence.
(C) It is used to provide a causal explanation for an observed phenomenon.
(D) It describes evidence that the argument ultimately refutes.
(E) It is a premise offered in support of the conclusion drawn in the argument.

23. Physician: There were approximately 83,400 trampoline-related injuries last year. This suggests that trampolines are quite dangerous and should therefore be used only under professional supervision.

Trampoline enthusiast: I disagree. In the past ten years sales of home trampolines have increased much more than trampoline-related injuries have: 260 percent in sales compared with 154 percent in injuries. Every exercise activity carries risks, even when carried out under professional supervision.

The dialogue provides the most support for the claim that the physician and the trampoline enthusiast disagree over whether

(A) trampolines cause injuries to a significant number of people using them
(B) home trampolines are the main source of trampoline-related injuries
(C) the rate of trampoline-related injuries, in terms of the number of injuries per trampoline user, is declining
(D) professional supervision of trampoline use tends to reduce the number of trampoline-related injuries
(E) trampoline use is an activity that warrants mandatory professional supervision

24. Editorial: One of our local television stations has been criticized for its recent coverage of the personal problems of a local politician's nephew, but the coverage was in fact good journalism. The information was accurate. Furthermore, the newscast had significantly more viewers than it normally does, because many people are curious about the politician's nephew's problems.

Which one of the following principles, if valid, would most help to justify the reasoning in the editorial?

(A) Journalism deserves to be criticized if it does not provide information that people want.
(B) Any journalism that intentionally misrepresents the facts of a case deserves to be criticized.
(C) Any journalism that provides accurate information on a subject about which there is considerable interest is good journalism.
(D) Good journalism will always provide people with information that they desire or need.
(E) Journalism that neither satisfies the public's curiosity nor provides accurate information can never be considered good journalism.

25. Interior decorator: All coffeehouses and restaurants are public places. Most well-designed public places feature artwork. But if a public place is uncomfortable it is not well designed, and all comfortable public places have spacious interiors.

If all of the interior decorator's statements are true, then which one of the following must be true?

(A) Any restaurant that has a spacious interior is comfortable.
(B) Most public places that feature artwork are well designed.
(C) Most coffeehouses that are well designed feature artwork.
(D) Any well-designed coffeehouse or restaurant has a spacious interior.
(E) Any coffeehouse that has a spacious interior is a well-designed public place.

S T O P

IF YOU FINISH BEFORE TIME IS CALLED, YOU MAY CHECK YOUR WORK ON THIS SECTION ONLY.
DO NOT WORK ON ANY OTHER SECTION IN THE TEST.

SECTION II

Time—35 minutes

23 Questions

Directions: Each group of questions in this section is based on a set of conditions. In answering some of the questions, it may be useful to draw a rough diagram. Choose the response that most accurately and completely answers each question and blacken the corresponding space on your answer sheet.

Questions 1–5

A professor must determine the order in which five of her students—Fernando, Ginny, Hakim, Juanita, and Kevin—will perform in an upcoming piano recital. Each student performs one piece, and no two performances overlap. The following constraints apply:

Ginny must perform earlier than Fernando.
Kevin must perform earlier than Hakim and Juanita.
Hakim must perform either immediately before or immediately after Fernando.

1. Which one of the following could be the order, from first to last, in which the students perform?

(A) Ginny, Fernando, Hakim, Kevin, Juanita
(B) Ginny, Juanita, Kevin, Hakim, Fernando
(C) Ginny, Kevin, Hakim, Juanita, Fernando
(D) Kevin, Ginny, Juanita, Fernando, Hakim
(E) Kevin, Juanita, Fernando, Hakim, Ginny

2. If Juanita performs earlier than Ginny, then which one of the following could be true?

(A) Fernando performs fourth.
(B) Ginny performs second.
(C) Hakim performs third.
(D) Juanita performs third.
(E) Kevin performs second.

3. Which one of the following CANNOT be true?

(A) Fernando performs immediately before Juanita.
(B) Ginny performs immediately before Hakim.
(C) Hakim performs immediately before Ginny.
(D) Juanita performs immediately before Ginny.
(E) Kevin performs immediately before Hakim.

4. The order in which the students perform is fully determined if which one of the following is true?

(A) Fernando performs immediately before Hakim.
(B) Ginny performs immediately before Fernando.
(C) Hakim performs immediately before Juanita.
(D) Juanita performs immediately before Hakim.
(E) Kevin performs immediately before Fernando.

5. How many of the students are there any one of whom could perform fourth?

(A) one
(B) two
(C) three
(D) four
(E) five

GO ON TO THE NEXT PAGE.

Questions 6–11

As part of an open house at a crafts studio, three teachers—Jiang, Kudrow, and Lanning—will give six consecutive presentations on six different subjects. Jiang will present on needlework and origami; Kudrow on pottery, stenciling, and textile making; and Lanning on woodworking. The order of their presentations will meet the following conditions:

Kudrow cannot give two presentations in a row.

The presentation on stenciling must be given earlier than the one on origami.

The presentation on textile making must be given earlier than the one on woodworking.

6. Which one of the following could be the order of the presentations, from first to sixth?

(A) stenciling, origami, needlework, textile making, pottery, woodworking
(B) stenciling, origami, pottery, woodworking, needlework, textile making
(C) stenciling, origami, textile making, woodworking, needlework, pottery
(D) textile making, origami, stenciling, woodworking, needlework, pottery
(E) textile making, stenciling, woodworking, needlework, pottery, origami

7. If textile making is presented fifth, which one of the following could be true?

(A) Needlework is presented sixth.
(B) Pottery is presented fourth.
(C) Stenciling is presented second.
(D) Stenciling is presented third.
(E) Woodworking is presented second.

8. If needlework is presented first, which one of the following could be true?

(A) Origami is presented sixth.
(B) Pottery is presented second.
(C) Stenciling is presented third.
(D) Textile making is presented fifth.
(E) Woodworking is presented third.

9. Jiang CANNOT give both

(A) the first and third presentations
(B) the first and fourth presentations
(C) the first and fifth presentations
(D) the second and third presentations
(E) the second and fourth presentations

10. If needlework is presented sixth, which one of the following must be true?

(A) Origami is presented fourth.
(B) Pottery is presented fifth.
(C) Stenciling is presented third.
(D) Textile making is presented first.
(E) Woodworking is presented fourth.

11. Which one of the following CANNOT be the subject of the second presentation?

(A) needlework
(B) origami
(C) pottery
(D) textile making
(E) woodworking

GO ON TO THE NEXT PAGE.

Questions 12–16

The organizer of a luncheon will select exactly five foods to be served from among exactly eight foods: two desserts—F and G; three main courses—N, O, and P; three side dishes—T, V, and W. Only F, N, and T are hot foods. The following requirements will be satisfied:

At least one dessert, at least one main course, and at least one side dish must be selected.
At least one hot food must be selected.
If either P or W is selected, both must be selected.
If G is selected, O must be selected.
If N is selected, V cannot be selected.

12. Which one of the following is a list of foods that could be the foods selected?

(A) F, N, O, T, V
(B) F, O, P, T, W
(C) G, N, P, T, W
(D) G, O, P, T, V
(E) G, O, P, V, W

13. Which one of the following is a pair of foods of which the organizer of the luncheon must select at least one?

(A) F, T
(B) G, O
(C) N, T
(D) O, P
(E) V, W

14. If O is the only main course selected, then which one of the following CANNOT be selected?

(A) F
(B) G
(C) T
(D) V
(E) W

15. If F is not selected, which one of the following could be true?

(A) P is the only main course selected.
(B) T is the only side dish selected.
(C) Exactly two hot foods are selected.
(D) Exactly three main courses are selected.
(E) Exactly three side dishes are selected.

16. If T and V are the only side dishes selected, then which one of the following is a pair of foods each of which must be selected?

(A) F and G
(B) F and N
(C) F and P
(D) N and O
(E) O and P

GO ON TO THE NEXT PAGE.

Questions 17–23

A television programming director is scheduling a three-hour block of programs beginning at 1 P.M. The programs that are to fill this time block include an hour-long program called *Generations* and four half-hour programs: *Roamin'*, *Sundown*, *Terry*, and *Waterloo*. The programs will be shown one after the other, each program shown exactly once. The schedule must meet the following constraints:

Generations starts on the hour rather than the half hour.
Terry starts on the half hour rather than the hour.
Roamin' is shown earlier than *Sundown*.
If *Waterloo* is shown earlier than *Terry*, it is shown immediately before *Terry*.

17. Which one of the following could be the order in which the programs are shown, from earliest to latest?

(A) *Generations*, *Roamin'*, *Waterloo*, *Terry*, *Sundown*
(B) *Roamin'*, *Sundown*, *Waterloo*, *Terry*, *Generations*
(C) *Roamin'*, *Terry*, *Waterloo*, *Generations*, *Sundown*
(D) *Waterloo*, *Roamin'*, *Sundown*, *Terry*, *Generations*
(E) *Waterloo*, *Terry*, *Sundown*, *Roamin'*, *Generations*

18. If *Waterloo* is the first program, then how many orders are there in which the remaining programs could be shown?

(A) one
(B) two
(C) three
(D) four
(E) five

19. If *Roamin'* is the second program, then each of the following could be true EXCEPT:

(A) *Sundown* is the third program.
(B) *Sundown* is the fourth program.
(C) *Terry* is the fifth program.
(D) *Waterloo* is the third program.
(E) *Waterloo* is the fifth program.

20. If *Sundown* is the third program, then which one of the following must be true?

(A) *Generations* is the first program.
(B) *Roamin'* is the first program.
(C) *Roamin'* is the second program.
(D) *Terry* is the fifth program.
(E) *Waterloo* is the fourth program.

21. If *Generations* is the third program, then which one of the following could be true?

(A) *Roamin'* is the second program.
(B) *Roamin'* is the fifth program.
(C) *Sundown* is the fourth program.
(D) *Terry* is the fourth program.
(E) *Waterloo* is the second program.

22. Which one of the following CANNOT be true?

(A) *Sundown* is shown immediately before *Generations*.
(B) *Waterloo* is shown immediately before *Roamin'*.
(C) *Generations* is shown immediately before *Sundown*.
(D) *Roamin'* is shown immediately before *Terry*.
(E) *Terry* is shown immediately before *Waterloo*.

23. Which one of the following, if substituted for the constraint that *Generations* starts on the hour rather than the half hour, would have the same effect in determining the order in which the programs are shown?

(A) *Generations* is not shown immediately before *Terry*.
(B) *Generations* is either the first program or the fifth.
(C) *Generations* is neither the second program nor the fourth.
(D) If *Generations* is shown third, then *Roamin'* is shown first.
(E) If *Generations* is not shown first, then it is shown later than *Terry*.

S T O P

IF YOU FINISH BEFORE TIME IS CALLED, YOU MAY CHECK YOUR WORK ON THIS SECTION ONLY. DO NOT WORK ON ANY OTHER SECTION IN THE TEST.

SECTION III

Time—35 minutes

27 Questions

Directions: Each set of questions in this section is based on a single passage or a pair of passages. The questions are to be answered on the basis of what is stated or implied in the passage or pair of passages. For some of the questions, more than one of the choices could conceivably answer the question. However, you are to choose the best answer; that is, the response that most accurately and completely answers the question, and blacken the corresponding space on your answer sheet.

In the 1980s there was a proliferation of poetry collections, short stories, and novels published by women of Latin American descent in the United States. By the end of the decade, another genre of U.S. Latina writing, the autobiography, also came into prominence with the publication of three notable autobiographical collections: *Loving in the War Years: Lo Que Nunca Pasó Por Sus Labios*, by Cherríe Moraga; *Getting Home Alive*, by Aurora Levins Morales and Rosario Morales; and *Borderlands/ La Frontera*, by Gloria Anzaldúa.

These collections are innovative at many levels. They confront traditional linguistic boundaries by using a mix of English and Spanish, and they each address the politics of multiple cultural identities by exploring the interrelationships among such factors as ethnicity, gender, and language. This effort manifests itself in the generically mixed structure of these works, which combine essays, sketches, short stories, poems, and journal entries without, for the most part, giving preference to any of these modes of presentation.

In *Borderlands/La Frontera*, Anzaldúa presents her personal history and the history of the Mexican American community to which she belongs by juxtaposing narrative sequences and poetry. Moraga's *Loving in the War Years* is likewise characterized by a mixture of genres, and, as she states in her introduction, the events in her life story are not arranged chronologically, but rather in terms of her political development. According to one literary critic who specializes in the genre of autobiography, this departure from chronological ordering represents an important difference between autobiographies written by women and those traditionally written by men. *Getting Home Alive* departs even further from the conventions typical of autobiography by bringing together the voices of two people, a mother and her daughter, each of whom authors a portion of the text. The narratives and poems of each author are not assigned to separate sections of the text, but rather are woven together, with a piece by one sometimes commenting on a piece by the other. While this ordering may seem fragmentary and confusing, it is in fact a fully intentional and carefully designed experiment with literary structure. In a sense, this mixing of structures parallels the content of these autobiographies: the writers employ multigeneric and multivocal forms to express the complexities inherent in the formation of their identities.

Rather than forcing their personal histories to conform to existing generic parameters, these writers have revolutionized the genre of autobiography, redrawing the boundaries of this literary form to make it more amenable to the expression of their own experiences. In doing so, they have shown a strong determination to speak for themselves in a world that they feel has for too long taken their silence for granted.

1. Which one of the following most accurately expresses the main point of the passage?

(A) Certain Latina writers who formerly wrote mostly poetry and fiction have found through experimentation that the genre of autobiography suits their artistic purposes especially well.
(B) Latina autobiographers writing in the late 1980s set aside some standard conventions of autobiography in an effort to make the genre more suitable for the expression of their personal histories.
(C) There is a great diversity of styles and narrative strategies among recent traditional and nontraditional Latina autobiographers.
(D) Through recent experimentation in autobiography, Latina writers have shown that nonfictional narrative can be effectively combined with other genres in a single literary work.
(E) Recent writings by Latina authors have prompted some literary critics who specialize in autobiography to acknowledge that differences in gender and ethnicity often underlie differences in writing styles.

2. According to the passage, which one of the following was a motivating factor in certain Latina authors' decisions regarding the structure of their autobiographical writings?

(A) the importance of chronological ordering to those authors' artistic goals
(B) those authors' stated intention of avoiding certain nonnarrative genres
(C) those authors' preference to avoid overt political expression
(D) the complexities of identity formation faced by those authors
(E) those authors' judgment that poetry should not be a narrative medium

GO ON TO THE NEXT PAGE.

3. The author's discussion of *Getting Home Alive* serves primarily to

   (A) distinguish one type of experimental autobiography from two other types by Latina writers
   (B) explain how certain Latina autobiographers combine journal entries and poems in their works
   (C) demonstrate that the use of multiple voices is a common feature of Latina autobiography
   (D) show why readers have difficulty understanding certain autobiographies by Latina writers
   (E) illustrate the extent of certain Latina autobiographers' experimentation with form and structure

4. The passage indicates which one of the following about the Latina autobiographies that the author discusses?

   (A) Each contains some material that would ordinarily be regarded as belonging to a genre of literature other than autobiography.
   (B) Each quotes from previously unpublished private journals or other private documents.
   (C) Each contains analysis of the ways in which its content was influenced by its author's cultural background.
   (D) Each contains writings that were produced by more than one author.
   (E) Each includes explanations of the methodologies that its author, or authors, used in writing the autobiography.

5. Based on the passage, the author's attitude regarding *Getting Home Alive*, by Aurora Levins Morales and Rosario Morales, can be most accurately described as

   (A) disappointment in scholars' failure to recognize it as an appropriate sequel to its authors' purely fictional and poetic works
   (B) expectation that readers in general might not readily recognize that there is a clear purpose for its unconventional organization
   (C) surprise that academic commentators have treated it as having significance as a historical document
   (D) confidence that it will be widely recognized by scholars as a work of both history and literary criticism
   (E) insistence that it should be credited with having helped to broaden critics' understanding of what counts as autobiography

6. The author most likely intends to include which one of the following principles among the "existing generic parameters" referred to in line 52?

   (A) The events presented in an autobiography should be arranged sequentially according to when they actually happened.
   (B) When different modes of presentation are combined in one literary work, no one mode should be given preference.
   (C) Autobiographical writing should not have political overtones.
   (D) Sketches and poems collected together in a single work need not be separated by genre within that work.
   (E) Personal experiences can be represented in a compelling way in any literary genre.

7. Which one of the following would, if true, most undermine the author's claim in lines 51–56 about the effect that the Latina autobiographies discussed had on the genre of autobiography?

   (A) Few autobiographical works published after 1985 have been recognized for their effective use of chronologically linear prose as a means of portraying the complexities of membership in multiple cultures.
   (B) Few critically acclaimed books written by Latina authors have been autobiographical collections consisting partly or wholly of essays, poems, short stories, sketches, and journal entries.
   (C) Many autobiographies have been written by authors in the United States since 1985, and some of these present a unified, chronologically linear prose narrative in a single language.
   (D) Several nineteenth-century autobiographies that are generally unknown among contemporary critics of twentieth-century autobiography are characterized by generically mixed structure and multiple authorship.
   (E) Several multigeneric, nonautobiographical collections consisting at least partly of poetry, short stories, or essays by Latina authors have been published since 1985, and many of these have been critically acclaimed for their innovative structures.

GO ON TO THE NEXT PAGE.

While recent decades have seen more information recorded than any other era, the potential for losing this information is now greater than ever. This prospect is of great concern to archivists, who are charged with preserving vital records and documents indefinitely. One archivist notes that while the quantity of material being saved has increased exponentially, the durability of recording media has decreased almost as rapidly. The clay tablets that contain the laws of ancient Mesopotamia, for example, are still displayed in museums around the world, and many medieval manuscripts written on animal parchment still look as though they were copied yesterday, whereas books printed on acidic paper as recently as the 1980s are already unreadable. Black-and-white photographs will last for a couple of centuries, but most color photographs become unstable within 40 years, and videotapes last only about 20 years.

Computer technology would seem to offer archivists an answer, as maps, photographs, films, videotapes, and all forms of printed material may now be transferred to and stored electronically on computer disks or tape, occupying very little space. But as the pace of technological change increases, so too does the speed with which each new generation of technology supplants the last. For example, many documents and images transferred in the 1980s to optical computer disks—then the cutting edge of technology—may not now be retrievable because they depend on computer software and hardware that are no longer available. And recent generations of digital storage tape are considered safe from deterioration for only ten years. Yet, even as some archivists are reluctant to become dependent on ever-changing computer technology, they are also quickly running out of time.

Even if viable storage systems are developed—new computer technologies are emerging that may soon provide archivists with the information storage durability they require—decisions about what to keep and what to discard will have to be made quickly, as materials recorded on conventional media continue to deteriorate. Ideally, these decisions should be informed by an assessment of the value of each document. Printed versions of ancient works by Homer and Virgil, for example, survived intact because their enduring popularity resulted in multiple copies of the works being made at different historical moments. But many great works, including those of Plato, were lost for several centuries and are known today only because random copies turned up in the archives of medieval monasteries or in other scholarly collections. Undoubtedly, many important works have not survived at all. The danger now is not so much that some recent masterpiece will be lost for an extended period of time, but rather that the sheer volume of accumulated records stored on nondurable media will make it virtually impossible for archivists to sort the essential from the dispensable in time to save it.

8. Which one of the following most accurately expresses the main point of the passage?

(A) The increasing volume of information being stored and the decreasing durability of modern storage media are making it more and more difficult for archivists to carry out their charge.

(B) Modern data storage-and-retrieval techniques have enabled archivists to distinguish essential from dispensable information with greater efficiency than ever before.

(C) Many archivists have come to believe that documents and images preserved on conventional storage media are likely to endure longer than those recorded on electronic storage media.

(D) Given the limitations on the capacity of modern storage media, it is increasingly important for archivists to save only those documents that they believe to have genuine value.

(E) Modern electronic media enable us to record and store information so easily that much of what is stored is not considered by archivists to be essential or valuable.

9. The passage provides information sufficient to answer which one of the following questions?

(A) Are there any copies of the works of Homer and Virgil stored on parchment?

(B) Why is information stored on acidic paper more unstable than information stored on digital storage tape?

(C) When were optical storage disks a state-of-the-art storage medium?

(D) Approximately how many of the original clay tablets recording Mesopotamian law are still in existence?

(E) How were the works of Plato originally recorded?

GO ON TO THE NEXT PAGE.

10. The passage most strongly suggests that the author holds which one of the following views?

    (A) Archivists have little choice but to become dependent on computer technology to store information.
    (B) Archivists should wait for truly durable data storage systems to be developed before electronically storing any more vital information.
    (C) The problems concerning media durability facing most archivists would diminish greatly if their information were not stored electronically at all.
    (D) Storing paintings, photographs, and other images presents greater overall problems for archivists than storing text does.
    (E) Generally, the more information one attempts to store in a given amount of space, the less durable the storage of that information will be.

11. Which one of the following describes the author's primary purpose in mentioning the fact that a wide variety of images and documents can now be stored electronically (lines 19–23)?

    (A) to provide evidence to justify the assertion made in the first sentence of the passage
    (B) to identify an ostensible solution to the problem raised in the first paragraph
    (C) to argue a point that is rejected in the last sentence of the passage
    (D) to offer an additional example of the problem stated at the end of the first paragraph
    (E) to suggest that the danger described in the last paragraph has been exaggerated

12. The passage provides the most support for inferring which one of the following statements?

    (A) Information stored electronically is more vulnerable than information stored on paper to unauthorized use or theft.
    (B) Much of the information stored on optical computer disks in the 1980s was subsequently transferred to digital storage tape.
    (C) The high cost of new electronic data storage systems is prohibiting many archivists from transferring their archives to computer disks and tape.
    (D) Media used recently to store information electronically may ultimately be less durable than older, conventional media such as photographs and videotapes.
    (E) The percentage of information considered essential by archivists has increased proportionally as the amount of information stored has increased.

13. The passage most strongly suggests that the author holds which one of the following views?

    (A) Future electronic information storage systems will not provide archivists with capabilities any more viable in the long term than those available today.
    (B) As much information should be stored by archivists as possible, as there is no way to predict which piece of information will someday be considered a great work.
    (C) The general public has been misled by manufacturers as to the long-term storage capabilities of electronic information storage systems.
    (D) Distinguishing what is dispensable from what is essential has only recently become a concern for archivists.
    (E) Value judgments made by today's archivists will influence how future generations view and understand the past.

GO ON TO THE NEXT PAGE.

The following passages are adapted from articles recently published in North American law review journals.

Passage A

In Canadian and United States common law, blackmail is unique among major crimes: no one has yet adequately explained why it ought to be illegal. The heart of the problem—known as the blackmail paradox—is that two acts, each of which is legally permissible separately, become illegal when combined. If I threaten to expose a criminal act or embarrassing private information unless I am paid money, I have committed blackmail. But the right to free speech protects my right to make such a disclosure, and, in many circumstances, I have a legal right to seek money. So why is it illegal to combine them?

The lack of a successful theory of blackmail has damaging consequences: drawing a clear line between legal and illegal acts has proved impossible without one. Consequently, most blackmail statutes broadly prohibit behavior that no one really believes is criminal and rely on the good judgment of prosecutors not to enforce relevant statutes precisely as written.

It is possible, however, to articulate a coherent theory of blackmail. The key to the wrongness of the blackmail transaction is its triangular structure. The blackmailer obtains what he wants by using a supplementary leverage, leverage that depends upon a third party. The blackmail victim pays to avoid being harmed by persons other than the blackmailer. For example, when a blackmailer threatens to turn in a criminal unless paid money, the blackmailer is bargaining with the state's chip. Thus, blackmail is criminal because it involves the misuse of a third party for the blackmailer's own benefit.

Passage B

Classical Roman law had no special category for blackmail; it was not necessary. Roman jurists began their evaluation of specific categories of actions by considering whether the action caused harm, not by considering the legality or illegality of the action itself.

Their assumption—true enough, it seems—was that a victim of blackmail would be harmed if shameful but private information were revealed to the world. And if the shame would cause harm to the person's status or reputation, then prima facie the threatened act of revelation was unlawful. The burden of proof shifted to the possessor of the information: the party who had or threatened to reveal shameful facts had to show positive cause for the privilege of revealing the information.

In short, assertion of the truth of the shameful fact being revealed was not, in itself, sufficient to constitute a legal privilege. Granted, truth was not wholly irrelevant; false disclosures were granted even less protection than true ones. But even if it were true, the revelation of shameful information was protected only if the revelation had been made for a legitimate purpose and dealt with a matter that the public authorities had an interest in having revealed. Just because something shameful happened to be true did not mean it was lawful to reveal it.

14. Which one of the following is the central topic of each passage?

(A) why triangular transactions are illegal
(B) the role of the right to free speech in a given legal system
(C) how blackmail has been handled in a given legal system
(D) the history of blackmail as a legal concept
(E) why no good explanation of the illegality of blackmail exists

15. In using the phrase "the state's chip" (line 30), the author of passage A most clearly means to refer to a government's

(A) legal authority to determine what actions are crimes
(B) legitimate interest in learning about crimes committed in its jurisdiction
(C) legitimate interest in preventing crimes before they occur
(D) exclusive reliance on private citizens as a source of important information
(E) legal ability to compel its citizens to testify in court regarding crimes they have witnessed

16. Which one of the following statements is most strongly supported by information given in the passages?

(A) In Roman law, there was no blackmail paradox because free speech protections comparable to those in Canadian and U.S. common law were not an issue.
(B) Blackmail was more widely practiced in Roman antiquity than it is now because Roman law did not specifically prohibit blackmail.
(C) In general, Canadian and U.S. common law grant more freedoms than classical Roman law granted.
(D) The best justification for the illegality of blackmail in Canadian and U.S. common law is the damage blackmail can cause to the victim's reputation.
(E) Unlike Roman law, Canadian and U.S. common law do not recognize the interest of public authorities in having certain types of information revealed.

GO ON TO THE NEXT PAGE.

17. Which one of the following is a statement that is true of blackmail under Canadian and U.S. common law, according to passage A, but that would not have been true of blackmail in the Roman legal context, according to passage B?

(A) It combines two acts that are each legal separately.
(B) It is a transaction with a triangular structure.
(C) The laws pertaining to it are meant to be enforced precisely as written.
(D) The blackmail victim pays to avoid being harmed by persons other than the blackmailer.
(E) Canadian and U.S. common law have no special category pertaining to blackmail.

18. Based on what can be inferred from the passages, which one of the following acts would have been illegal under Roman law, but would not be illegal under Canadian and U.S. common law?

(A) bribing tax officials in order to avoid paying taxes
(B) revealing to public authorities that a high-ranking military officer has embezzled funds from the military's budget
(C) testifying in court to a defendant's innocence while knowing that the defendant is guilty
(D) informing a government tax agency that one's employers have concealed their true income
(E) revealing to the public that a prominent politician had once had an adulterous affair

19. The relationship between the ways in which Canadian and U.S. common law and classical Roman law treat blackmail, as described in the passages, is most analogous to the relationship between which one of the following pairs?

(A) One country legally requires anyone working as a carpenter to be licensed and insured; another country has no such requirement.
(B) One country makes it illegal to use cell phones on trains; another country makes it illegal to use cell phones on both trains and buses.
(C) One country legally allows many income tax deductions and exemptions; another country legally allows relatively few deductions and exemptions.
(D) One country makes it illegal for felons to own guns; another country has no such ban because it makes gun ownership illegal for everyone but police and the military.
(E) One country makes it illegal to drive motorcycles with racing-grade engines on its roads; another country legally permits such motorcycles but fines riders who commit traffic violations higher amounts than it does other motorists.

GO ON TO THE NEXT PAGE.

As part of an international effort to address environmental problems resulting from agricultural overproduction, hundreds of thousands of acres of surplus farmland throughout Europe will be taken out of production in coming years. Restoring a natural balance of flora to this land will be difficult, however, because the nutrients in soil that has been in constant agricultural use are depleted. Moreover, much of this land has been heavily fertilized, and when such land is left unplanted, problem weeds like thistles often proliferate, preventing many native plants from establishing themselves. While the quickest way to restore heavily fertilized land is to remove and replace the topsoil, this is impractical on a large scale such as that of the European effort. And while it is generally believed that damaged ecological systems will restore themselves very gradually over time, a study underway in the Netherlands is investigating the possibility of artificially accelerating the processes through which nature slowly reestablishes plant diversity on previously farmed land.

In the study, a former cornfield was raked to get rid of cornstalks and weeds, then divided into 20 plots of roughly equal size. Control plots were replanted with corn or sown with nothing at all. The remaining plots were divided into two groups: plots in one group were sown with a mixture of native grasses and herbs; those in the other group received the same mixture of grasses and herbs together with clover and toadflax. After three years, thistles have been forced out of the plots where the broadest variety of species was sown and have also disappeared from mats of grass in the plots sown with fewer seed varieties. On the control plots that were left untouched, thistles have become dominant.

On some of the plots sown with seeds of native plant species, soil from nearby land that had been taken out of production 20 years earlier was scattered to see what effect introducing nematodes, fungi, and other beneficial microorganisms associated with later stages of natural soil development might have on the process of native plant repopulation. The seeds sown on these enriched plots have fared better than seeds sown on the unenriched plots, but still not as well as those growing naturally on the nearby land. Researchers have concluded that this is because fields farmed for many years are overrun with aggressive disease organisms, while, for example, beneficial mycorrhiza—fungi that live symbiotically on plant roots and strengthen them against the effects of disease organisms—are lacking. These preliminary results suggest that restoring natural plant diversity to overfarmed land hinges on restoring a natural balance of microorganisms in the soil. In other words, diversity underground fosters diversity aboveground. Researchers now believe that both kinds of diversity can be restored more quickly to damaged land if beneficial microorganisms are "sown" systematically into the soil along with a wide variety of native plant seeds.

20. Which one of the following most accurately expresses the central idea of the passage?

(A) The rehabilitation of land damaged by agricultural overproduction can be accelerated by means of a two-pronged strategy aimed at restoring biological diversity.
(B) Restoring plant diversity to overused farmland requires many years and considerable effort.
(C) The damaging effects of long-term agricultural overproduction argue for the modification of current agricultural practices.
(D) Soil on farmland damaged by overproduction will gradually replenish and restore itself over time if left untouched.
(E) Agricultural overproduction tends to encourage the proliferation of disease organisms in the soil as well as problem weeds.

21. Which one of the following most accurately describes the organization of the passage?

(A) A study is described, the results of the study are scrutinized, and the results are judged to be inconclusive but promising.
(B) A hypothesis is presented, evidence both supporting and undermining the hypothesis is given, and a modification of the hypothesis is argued for.
(C) A study is evaluated, a plan of action based on the study's findings is suggested, and conclusions are drawn concerning the likely effectiveness of the plan.
(D) A goal is stated, studies are discussed that argue for modifying the goal's objectives, and a methodology is detailed to achieve the revised goal.
(E) A problem is presented, a study addressing the problem is described, and a course of action based on the study's findings is given.

22. The passage offers which one of the following as an explanation for why native plant varieties grew better when sown on land that had been out of production for 20 years than when sown on the plots enriched with soil taken from that land?

(A) Land that has been farmed for many years lacks certain key nutrients.
(B) Land that has been farmed for many years is usually overrun with harmful and aggressive organisms.
(C) Land that has been farmed for many years has usually been subjected to overfertilization.
(D) The soil that was taken from the land that had been out of production was lacking in fungi and other beneficial organisms.
(E) The soil that was taken from the land that had been out of production contained harmful organisms that attack plant roots.

GO ON TO THE NEXT PAGE.

23. Based on the passage, which one of the following is most likely to be true of any soil used to replace topsoil in the process mentioned in the first paragraph?

    (A) Thistles cannot grow in it.
    (B) It does not contain significant amounts of fungi.
    (C) It contains very few seeds of native grasses and herbs.
    (D) It does not contain large amounts of fertilizer.
    (E) It was never used for growing corn or other commercial crops.

24. The author's reference to the belief that "damaged ecological systems will restore themselves very gradually over time" (lines 16–17) primarily serves to

    (A) introduce a long-held belief that the Netherlands study is attempting to discredit
    (B) cite the justification generally used by people favoring intense agricultural production
    (C) suggest that the consequences of agricultural overproduction are not as dire as people generally believe
    (D) present the most common perception of why agricultural overproduction is problematic
    (E) describe the circumstances surrounding and motivating the Netherlands study

25. In which one of the following circumstances would it be LEAST advantageous to use the methods researched in the Netherlands study in order to restore to its natural state a field that has been in constant agricultural use?

    (A) The field's natural nutrients have been depleted through overproduction.
    (B) The field's topsoil can easily be removed and replaced.
    (C) The field has been heavily fertilized for many decades.
    (D) The field has the potential to support commercial grass plants such as rye.
    (E) The field is adjacent to other fields where corn is growing and will continue to be grown.

26. It can be inferred from the passage that if the disease organisms mentioned in line 48 were eliminated in a plot of land that had been in constant agricultural use, which one of the following would be the most likely to occur?

    (A) Populations of symbiotic mycorrhiza that live in the soil would initially decline.
    (B) Unwanted plant species like thistles would be unable to survive.
    (C) The chance of survival of a beneficial native plant would increase.
    (D) The number of all types of beneficial microorganisms would increase in the long term.
    (E) Populations of other types of disease organisms would increase proportionally.

27. Which one of the following is most analogous to the process, described in the last paragraph, by which the spread of thistles can be curtailed?

    (A) A newspaper works to prevent Party A from winning a majority of seats in the legislature by publishing editorials encouraging that party's supporters to switch their allegiance and vote for candidates from a rival party.
    (B) A newspaper works to prevent Party A from winning a majority of seats in the legislature by publishing editorials defending candidates from a rival party against attacks by certain broadcast journalists.
    (C) A newspaper works to prevent Party A from winning a majority of seats in the legislature by publishing editorials intended to discourage supporters of Party A from voting in the upcoming election.
    (D) A newspaper works to prevent Party A from winning a majority of seats in the legislature by publishing editorials attacking certain public figures who support candidates from Party A.
    (E) A newspaper works to prevent Party A from winning a majority of seats in the legislature by publishing editorials intended to create antagonism between two factions within that party.

S T O P

IF YOU FINISH BEFORE TIME IS CALLED, YOU MAY CHECK YOUR WORK ON THIS SECTION ONLY.
DO NOT WORK ON ANY OTHER SECTION IN THE TEST.

SECTION IV

Time—35 minutes

26 Questions

Directions: The questions in this section are based on the reasoning contained in brief statements or passages. For some questions, more than one of the choices could conceivably answer the question. However, you are to choose the best answer; that is, the response that most accurately and completely answers the question. You should not make assumptions that are by commonsense standards implausible, superfluous, or incompatible with the passage. After you have chosen the best answer, blacken the corresponding space on your answer sheet.

1. When a forest is subject to acid rain, the calcium level in the soil declines. Spruce, fir, and sugar maple trees all need calcium to survive. However, sugar maples in forests that receive significant acid rain are much more likely to show signs of decline consistent with calcium deficiency than are spruces or firs in such forests.

Which one of the following, if true, most helps to explain the greater decline among sugar maples?

(A) Soil in which calcium levels are significantly diminished by acid rain is also likely to be damaged in other ways by acid rain.
(B) Sugar maples that do not receive enough calcium deteriorate less rapidly than spruces or firs that do not receive enough calcium.
(C) Spruces and firs, unlike sugar maples, can extract calcium from a mineral compound that is common in soil and is not affected by acid rain.
(D) Sugar maples require more calcium in the spring and summer than they do in the fall and winter.
(E) Unlike spruces or firs, most sugar maples are native to areas that receive a lot of acid rain.

2. Syndicated political columnists often use their newspaper columns to try to persuade readers to vote a certain way. However, their efforts to persuade voters rarely succeed, for by the time such a column appears, nearly all who will vote in the election will have already made a decision about which candidate to vote for.

Which one of the following is an assumption required by the argument?

(A) Syndicated columnists influence the votes of most of their readers who have not yet decided which candidate to vote for.
(B) The attempts of syndicated political columnists to persuade readers to vote a certain way in an election can instead cause them to vote a different way.
(C) People who regularly read columns by syndicated political columnists mainly read those written by columnists with whom they already largely agree.
(D) Regular readers of columns by syndicated political columnists are less likely to be persuaded to vote a certain way by such columns than are people who seldom read such columns.
(E) People rarely can be persuaded to change their minds about which candidate to vote for once they have made a decision.

GO ON TO THE NEXT PAGE.

3. Travel industry consultant: Several airlines are increasing elbow room and leg room in business class, because surveys show that business travelers value additional space more than, say, better meals. But airlines are overconcerned about the comfort of passengers flying on business; they should instead focus on the comfort of leisure travelers, because those travelers purchase 80 percent of all airline tickets.

Which one of the following, if true, most weakens the reasoning in the travel industry consultant's argument?

(A) Business travelers often make travel decisions based on whether they feel a given airline values their business.
(B) Some airlines have indicated that they will undertake alterations in seating space throughout the entire passenger area of their planes in the near future.
(C) Sleeping in comfort during long flights is not the primary concern of leisure travelers.
(D) A far greater proportion of an airline's revenues is derived from business travelers than from leisure travelers.
(E) Most leisure travelers buy airline tickets only when fares are discounted.

4. Gaby: In school, children should be allowed fully to follow their own interests, supported by experienced teachers who offer minimal guidance. This enables them to be most successful in their adult lives.

Logan: I disagree. Schoolchildren should acquire the fundamental knowledge necessary for future success, and they learn such fundamentals only through disciplined, systematic instruction from accredited teachers.

Gaby's and Logan's comments provide most support for the claim that they disagree about

(A) the way in which schoolchildren best acquire fundamental knowledge
(B) the extent to which teachers should direct schoolchildren's education
(C) the importance of having qualified teachers involved in schoolchildren's education
(D) the sort of school environment that most fosters children's creativity
(E) the extent to which schoolchildren are interested in fundamental academic subjects

5. Judge: The case before me involves a plaintiff and three codefendants. The plaintiff has applied to the court for an order permitting her to question each defendant without their codefendants or their codefendants' legal counsel being present. Two of the codefendants, however, share the same legal counsel. The court will not order any codefendant to find new legal counsel. Therefore, the order requested by the plaintiff cannot be granted.

The conclusion of the judge's argument is most strongly supported if which one of the following principles is assumed to hold?

(A) A court cannot issue an order that forces legal counsel to disclose information revealed by a client.
(B) Defendants have the right to have their legal counsel present when being questioned.
(C) People being questioned in legal proceedings may refuse to answer questions that are self-incriminating.
(D) A plaintiff in a legal case should never be granted a right that is denied to a defendant.
(E) A defendant's legal counsel has the right to question the plaintiff.

6. The calm, shallow waters of coastal estuaries are easily polluted by nutrient-rich sewage. When estuary waters become overnutrified as a result, algae proliferate. The abundant algae, in turn, sometimes provide a rich food source for microorganisms that are toxic to fish, thereby killing most of the fish in the estuary.

Which one of the following can be properly inferred from the information above?

(A) Fish in an estuary that has been polluted by sewage are generally more likely to die from pollution than are fish in an estuary that has been polluted in some other way.
(B) In estuary waters that contain abundant algae, microorganisms that are toxic to fish reproduce more quickly than other types of microorganisms.
(C) Nutrients and other components of sewage do not harm fish in coastal estuaries in any way other than through the resulting proliferation of toxic microorganisms.
(D) Algae will not proliferate in coastal estuaries that are not polluted by nutrient-rich sewage.
(E) Overnutrifying estuary waters by sewage can result in the death of most of the fish in the estuary.

GO ON TO THE NEXT PAGE.

7. The ruins of the prehistoric Bolivian city of Tiwanaku feature green andacite stones weighing up to 40 tons. These stones were quarried at Copacabana, which is across a lake and about 90 kilometers away. Archaeologists hypothesize that the stones were brought to Tiwanaku on reed boats. To show this was possible, experimenters transported a 9-ton stone from Copacabana to Tiwanaku using a reed boat built with locally available materials and techniques traditional to the area.

Which one of the following would be most useful to know in order to evaluate the support for the archaeologists' hypothesis?

(A) whether the traditional techniques for building reed boats were in use at the time Tiwanaku was inhabited
(B) whether green andacite stones quarried at the time Tiwanaku was inhabited were used at any sites near Copacabana
(C) whether reed boats are commonly used today on the lake
(D) whether the green andacite stones at Tiwanaku are the largest stones at the site
(E) whether the reed boat built for the experimenters is durable enough to remain usable for several years

8. Union member: Some members of our labor union are calling for an immediate strike. But a strike would cut into our strike fund and would in addition lead to a steep fine, causing us to suffer a major financial loss. Therefore, we must not strike now.

The union member's argument is most vulnerable to criticism on the grounds that it

(A) fails to consider that a strike might cause the union to suffer a financial loss even if no fine were imposed
(B) fails to define adequately what constitutes a major financial loss
(C) fails to consider that the benefits to be gained from a strike might outweigh the costs
(D) takes for granted that the most important factor in the labor union's bargaining position is the union's financial strength
(E) fails to establish that there will be a better opportunity to strike at a later time

9. Birds and mammals can be infected with West Nile virus only through mosquito bites. Mosquitoes, in turn, become infected with the virus when they bite certain infected birds or mammals. The virus was originally detected in northern Africa and spread to North America in the 1990s. Humans sometimes catch West Nile virus, but the virus never becomes abundant enough in human blood to infect a mosquito.

The statements above, if true, most strongly support which one of the following?

(A) West Nile virus will never be a common disease among humans.
(B) West Nile virus is most common in those parts of North America with the highest density of mosquitoes.
(C) Some people who become infected with West Nile virus never show symptoms of illness.
(D) West Nile virus infects more people in northern Africa than it does in North America.
(E) West Nile virus was not carried to North America via an infected person.

10. In trying to reduce the amount of fat in their diet, on average people have decreased their consumption of red meat by one-half in the last two decades. However, on average those who have reduced their consumption of red meat actually consume substantially more fat than those who have not.

Which one of the following, if true, most helps to resolve the apparent discrepancy described above?

(A) Many more people have reduced their consumption of red meat over the last two decades than have not.
(B) Higher prices over the last two decades have done as much to decrease the consumption of red meat as health concerns have.
(C) People who reduce their consumption of red meat tend to consume as much of other foods that are high in fat as do those who have not reduced their consumption of red meat.
(D) People who reduce their consumption of red meat tend to replace it with cheese and baked goods, which are richer in fat than red meat.
(E) Studies have shown that red meat contains slightly less fat than previously thought.

GO ON TO THE NEXT PAGE.

11. Rolanda: The house on Oak Avenue has a larger yard than any other house we've looked at in Prairieview, so that's the best one to rent.

Tom: No, it isn't. Its yard isn't really as big as it looks. Property lines in Prairieview actually start 20 feet from the street. So what looks like part of the yard is really city property.

Rolanda: But that's true of all the other properties we've looked at too!

Rolanda's response to Tom suggests that Tom commits which one of the following reasoning errors?

(A) He fails to take into account the possibility that there are advantages to having a small yard.
(B) He presumes, without providing justification, that property that belongs to the city is available for private use.
(C) He improperly applies a generalization to an instance that it was not intended to cover.
(D) He fails to apply a general rule to all relevant instances.
(E) He presumes, without providing justification, that whatever is true of a part of a thing is also true of the whole.

12. The best jazz singers use their voices much as horn players use their instruments. The great Billie Holiday thought of her singing voice as a horn, reshaping melody and words to increase their impact. Conversely, jazz horn players achieve their distinctive sounds by emulating the spontaneous twists and turns of an impassioned voice. So jazz consists largely of voicelike horns and hornlike voices.

Which one of the following most accurately describes the role played in the argument by the claim that the best jazz singers use their voices much as horn players use their instruments?

(A) It is the argument's main conclusion and is supported by another statement, which is itself supported by a further statement.
(B) It is the argument's only conclusion, and each of the other statements in the argument is used to support it.
(C) It is a statement for which some evidence is provided and which in turn is used to provide support for the argument's main conclusion.
(D) It is a statement for which no evidence is provided but which itself is used to support the argument's only conclusion.
(E) It is a statement used to support a conclusion that in turn is used to support the argument's main conclusion.

13. Educator: Reducing class sizes in our school district would require hiring more teachers. However, there is already a shortage of qualified teachers in the region. Although students receive more individualized instruction when classes are smaller, education suffers when teachers are underqualified. Therefore, reducing class sizes in our district would probably not improve overall student achievement.

Which one of the following is an assumption required by the educator's argument?

(A) Class sizes in the school district should be reduced only if doing so would improve overall student achievement.
(B) At least some qualified teachers in the school district would be able to improve the overall achievement of students in their classes if class sizes were reduced.
(C) Students place a greater value on having qualified teachers than on having smaller classes.
(D) Hiring more teachers would not improve the achievement of any students in the school district if most or all of the teachers hired were underqualified.
(E) Qualified teachers could not be persuaded to relocate in significant numbers to the educator's region to take teaching jobs.

14. Geographer: Because tropical storms require heat and moisture, they form especially over ocean surfaces of at least 26 degrees Celsius (79 degrees Fahrenheit), ocean temperatures that global warming would encourage. For this reason, many early discussions of global warming predicted that it would cause more frequent and intense tropical storms. But recent research shows that this prediction is unlikely to be borne out. Other factors, such as instabilities in wind flow, are likely to counteract global warming's effects on tropical storm development.

Which one of the following most accurately expresses the conclusion drawn in the geographer's argument?

(A) Tropical storms are especially likely to form over warm ocean surfaces.
(B) Contrary to early discussions, global warming is not the only factor affecting the frequency and intensity of tropical storms.
(C) If global warming were reversed, tropical storms would be less frequent and less intense.
(D) Instabilities in wind flow will negate the effect of global warming on the formation of tropical storms.
(E) Global warming probably will not produce more frequent and intense tropical storms.

GO ON TO THE NEXT PAGE.

15. Copyright was originally the grant of a temporary government-supported monopoly on copying a work. Its sole purpose was to encourage the circulation of ideas by giving authors the opportunity to derive a reasonable financial reward from their works. However, copyright sometimes goes beyond its original purpose since sometimes _______.

The conclusion of the argument is most strongly supported if which one of the following completes the passage?

(A) publication of copyrighted works is not the only way to circulate ideas
(B) authors are willing to circulate their works even without any financial reward
(C) authors are unable to find a publisher for their copyrighted work
(D) there is no practical way to enforce copyrights
(E) copyrights hold for many years after an author's death

16. Critic to economist: In yet another of your bumbling forecasts, last year you predicted that this country's economy would soon go into recession if current economic policies were not changed. Instead, economic growth is even stronger this year.

Economist: There was nothing at all bumbling about my warning. Indeed, it convinced the country's leaders to change economic policies, which is what prevented a recession.

The economist responds to the critic by

(A) indicating that the state of affairs on which the economist's prediction was conditioned did not obtain
(B) distinguishing between a prediction that has not yet turned out to be correct and one that has turned out to be incorrect
(C) attempting to show that the critic's statements are mutually inconsistent
(D) offering a particular counterexample to a general claim asserted by the critic
(E) offering evidence against one of the critic's factual premises

17. Watching music videos from the 1970s would give the viewer the impression that the music of the time was dominated by synthesizer pop and punk rock. But this would be a misleading impression. Because music videos were a new art form at the time, they attracted primarily cutting-edge musicians.

Which one of the following arguments is most similar in its reasoning to that of the argument above?

(A) Our view of pre-printing-press literature can never be accurate, because the surviving works of ancient authors are those that were deemed by copyists most likely to be of interest to future readers.
(B) Our memory of 1960s TV shows could hardly be improved, because so many of the television programs of the era are still rerun today.
(C) Future generations' understanding of today's publishing trends will be distorted if they judge by works published in CD-ROM format, since it is primarily publishers interested in computer games that are using CD-ROM.
(D) Our understanding of silent films is incomplete, because few filmmakers of the time realized that the film stock they were using would disintegrate over time.
(E) Our notion of fashion trends will probably be accurate if we rely on TV fashion programs, despite the fact that these programs deliberately select the most outrageous outfits in order to get the viewers' attention.

18. Hospitals, universities, labor unions, and other institutions may well have public purposes and be quite successful at achieving them even though each of their individual staff members does what he or she does only for selfish reasons.

Which one of the following generalizations is most clearly illustrated by the passage?

(A) What is true of some social organizations is not necessarily true of all such organizations.
(B) An organization can have a property that not all of its members possess.
(C) People often claim altruistic motives for actions that are in fact selfish.
(D) Many social institutions have social consequences unintended by those who founded them.
(E) Often an instrument created for one purpose will be found to serve another purpose just as effectively.

GO ON TO THE NEXT PAGE.

19. Consumer advocate: In some countries, certain produce is routinely irradiated with gamma rays in order to extend shelf life. There are, however, good reasons to avoid irradiated foods. First, they are exposed to the radioactive substances that produce the gamma rays. Second, irradiation can reduce the vitamin content of fresh foods, leaving behind harmful chemical residues. Third, irradiation spawns unique radiolytic products that cause serious health problems, including cancer.

Each of the following, if true, weakens the consumer advocate's argument EXCEPT:

(A) Unique radiolytic products have seldom been found in any irradiated food.
(B) Cancer and other serious health problems have many causes that are unrelated to radioactive substances and gamma rays.
(C) A study showed that irradiation leaves the vitamin content of virtually all fruits and vegetables unchanged.
(D) The amount of harmful chemicals found in irradiated foods is less than the amount that occurs naturally in most kinds of foods.
(E) A study showed that the cancer rate is no higher among people who eat irradiated food than among those who do not.

20. When teaching art students about the use of color, teachers should use colored paper rather than paint in their demonstrations. Colored paper is preferable because it readily permits a repeated use of exactly the same color in different compositions, which allows for a precise comparison of that color's impact in varying contexts. With paint, however, it is difficult to mix exactly the same color twice, and the varying textures of the applied paint can interfere with the pure effect of the color itself.

Which one of the following is an assumption required by the argument?

(A) Two pieces of paper of exactly the same color will have the same effect in a given context, even if they are of different textures.
(B) A slight difference in the color of two pieces of paper is more difficult to notice than a similar difference in the color of two samples of paint.
(C) Changing light conditions have less of an effect on the apparent color of a piece of paper than on the apparent color of a sample of paint.
(D) Observing the impacts of colors across varying contexts helps students to learn about the use of color.
(E) It is important that art students understand how the effects of using colored paper in various compositions differ from those of using paint in those compositions.

21. Philosopher: To explain the causes of cultural phenomena, a social scientist needs data about several societies: one cannot be sure, for example, that a given political structure is brought about only by certain ecological or climatic factors unless one knows that there are no similarly structured societies not subject to those factors, and no societies that, though subject to those factors, are not so structured.

The claim that to explain the causes of cultural phenomena, a social scientist needs data about several societies plays which one of the following roles in the philosopher's reasoning?

(A) It describes a problem that the philosopher claims is caused by the social scientist's need for certainty.
(B) It is a premise used to support a general theoretical claim about the nature of cause and effect relationships.
(C) It is a general hypothesis that is illustrated with an example showing that there is a causal relationship between political structures and environmental conditions.
(D) It is a dilemma that, it is argued, is faced by every social scientist because of the difficulty of determining whether a given cultural phenomenon is the cause or the effect of a given factor.
(E) It is a claim that the philosopher attempts to justify by appeal to the requirements for establishing the existence of one kind of causal relationship.

22. Scientist: Physicists claim that their system of careful peer review prevents scientific fraud in physics effectively. But biologists claimed the same thing for their field 20 years ago, and they turned out to be wrong. Since then, biologists have greatly enhanced their discipline's safeguards against scientific fraud, thus preventing further major incidents. It would be conducive to progress in physics if physicists were to do the same thing.

The conclusion of the scientist's argument is most strongly supported if which one of the following is assumed?

(A) Major incidents of scientific fraud in a scientific discipline are deleterious to progress in that discipline.
(B) Very few incidents of even minor scientific fraud have occurred in biology over the last 20 years.
(C) No system of careful peer review is completely effective in preventing scientific fraud in any scientific discipline.
(D) Twenty years ago the system of peer review in biology was less effective in preventing scientific fraud than the system of peer review in physics is today.
(E) Over the years, there have been relatively few, if any, major incidents of scientific fraud in physics.

23. Biologist: Researchers believe that dogs are the descendants of domesticated wolves that were bred to be better companions for humans. It has recently been found that some breeds of dog are much more closely related genetically to wolves than to most other breeds of dog. This shows that some dogs are descended from wolves that were domesticated much more recently than others.

Which one of the following principles underlies the biologist's argument?

(A) If one breed of dog is descended from wolves that were domesticated more recently than were the wolves from which most other breeds of dog are descended, the former breed may be more closely related to wolves than those other breeds are.
(B) If one breed of dog is more closely related to wolves than to another breed of dog, then the former breed of dog has more recent undomesticated wolf ancestors than the latter breed has.
(C) Any breed of dog descended from wolves that were domesticated is more closely related genetically to at least some other breeds of dog than to wolves.
(D) If one breed of dog is more closely related to wolves than another breed of dog is, then the former breed of dog is more closely related to wolves than to the latter breed of dog.
(E) Any two breeds of dog that are more closely related to each other than to wolves are both descended from wolves that were domesticated long ago.

24. Paleomycologists, scientists who study ancient forms of fungi, are invariably acquainted with the scholarly publications of all other paleomycologists. Professor Mansour is acquainted with the scholarly publications of Professor DeAngelis, who is a paleomycologist. Therefore, Professor Mansour must also be a paleomycologist.

The flawed pattern of reasoning in the argument above is most similar to that in which one of the following arguments?

(A) When a flight on Global Airlines is delayed, all connecting Global Airlines flights are also delayed so that the passengers can make their connections. Since Frieda's connecting flight on Global was delayed, her first flight must have also been a delayed Global Airlines flight.
(B) Any time that one of Global Airlines' local ticket agents misses a shift, the other agents on that shift need to work harder than usual. Since none of Global's local ticket agents missed a shift last week, the airline's local ticket agents did not have to work harder than usual last week.
(C) Any time the price of fuel decreases, Global Airlines' expenses decrease and its income is unaffected. The price of fuel decreased several times last year. Therefore, Global Airlines must have made a profit last year.
(D) All employees of Global Airlines can participate in its retirement plan after they have been with the company a year or more. Gavin has been with Global Airlines for three years. We can therefore be sure that he participates in Global's retirement plan.
(E) Whenever a competitor of Global Airlines reduces its fares, Global must follow suit or lose passengers. Global carried more passengers last year than it did the year before. Therefore, Global must have reduced its fares last year to match reductions in its competitors' fares.

GO ON TO THE NEXT PAGE.

25. Lutsina: Because futuristic science fiction does not need to represent current social realities, its writers can envisage radically new social arrangements. Thus it has the potential to be a richer source of social criticism than is conventional fiction.

Priscilla: That futuristic science fiction writers more skillfully envisage radically new technologies than new social arrangements shows how writers' imaginations are constrained by current realities. Because of this limitation, the most effective social criticism results from faithfully presenting the current social realities for critical examination, as happens in conventional fiction.

Lutsina and Priscilla disagree with each other about whether

(A) some science fiction writers have succeeded in envisaging convincing, radically new social arrangements
(B) writers of conventional fiction are more skillful than are writers of futuristic science fiction
(C) futuristic science fiction has more promise as a source of social criticism than does conventional fiction
(D) envisaging radically new technologies rather than radically new social arrangements is a shortcoming of futuristic science fiction
(E) criticism of current social arrangements is not effective when those arrangements are contrasted with radically different ones

26. Because our club recruited the best volleyball players in the city, we will have the best team in the city. Moreover, since the best team in the city will be the team most likely to win the city championship, our club will almost certainly be city champions this year.

The reasoning in the argument is flawed because the argument

(A) presumes, without presenting relevant evidence, that an entity can be distinguished as the best only on the basis of competition
(B) predicts the success of an entity on the basis of features that are not relevant to the quality of that entity
(C) predicts the outcome of a competition merely on the basis of a comparison between the parties in that competition
(D) presumes, without providing warrant, that if an entity is the best among its competitors, then each individual part of that entity must also be the best
(E) concludes that because an event is the most likely of a set of possible events, that event is more likely to occur than not

S T O P

IF YOU FINISH BEFORE TIME IS CALLED, YOU MAY CHECK YOUR WORK ON THIS SECTION ONLY. DO NOT WORK ON ANY OTHER SECTION IN THE TEST.

Acknowledgment is made to the following sources from which material has been adapted for use in this test booklet:

"A Radical Rethink." ©2003 by The Economist Newspaper Limited.

Larry Katzenstein, "Good Food You Can't Get." ©July 1993 by Reader's Digest.

"Revealing Ancient Bolivia." ©2002 by the Archaeological Institute of America.

Marion de Boo, "Dutch Farmland: Back to Nature." ©1999 by the Stanley Foundation.

R. H. Helmholz, "The Roman Law of Blackmail." ©2001 by The University of Chicago Press.

James Lindgren, "Unraveling the Paradox of Blackmail." ©1984 by Columbia Law Review Association, Inc.

Alexander Stille, "Overload." ©1999 by Condé Nast Publications, Inc.

Lourdes Torres, "The Construction of the Self in U.S. Latina Autobiographies." ©1991 by Indiana University Press.

LSAT Writing Sample Topic

Directions: The scenario presented below describes two choices, either one of which can be supported on the basis of the information given. Your essay should consider both choices and argue for one over the other, based on the two specified criteria and the facts provided. There is no "right" or "wrong" choice: a reasonable argument can be made for either.

Two pediatricians are deciding whether to relocate their small practice 10 miles away, to a large medical pavilion downtown, or to keep their present office and also open a second office about 20 miles away across the city. Using the facts below, write an essay in which you argue for one choice over the other based on the following two criteria:

- The doctors want to attract new patients.
- The doctors want to keep their current patients.

The Laurel Medical Pavilion is a new collection of medical office buildings adjacent to the city's major hospital. The pavilion is convenient to public transportation. It offers ample free parking space. Although office space in the pavilion is expensive, it is going fast. The space the pediatricians would lease includes five examination rooms, sufficient office space, and a large waiting area that the doctors would be able to furnish as they like. The pavilion leases space to doctors in a wide variety of fields. It contains facilities for a wide range of laboratory and diagnostic testing.

The space the doctors are considering leasing as a second office is, like their present premises, a 100-year-old Victorian house in a largely residential area full of young families. The house has a large fenced-in yard and off-street parking space for five vehicles. The first floor of the house was recently remodeled to suit the needs of a small medical practice. Like their present premises, it contains three examination rooms, a small waiting area, and ample office space. The second floor has not been converted into suitable working space. The option of doing so is available to the doctors.

Scratch Paper

Do not write your essay in this space.

Directions:

1. Use the Answer Key on the next page to check your answers.
2. Use the Scoring Worksheet below to compute your raw score.
3. Use the Score Conversion Chart to convert your raw score into the 120–180 scale.

Scoring Worksheet

1. Enter the number of questions you answered correctly in each section

	Number Correct
SECTION I.	______
SECTION II	______
SECTION III	______
SECTION IV	______
SECTION V	______

2. Enter the sum here: ______

This is your Raw Score.

Conversion Chart

For Converting Raw Score to the 120–180 LSAT Scaled Score
LSAT PrepTest 65

Reported Score	Raw Score Lowest	Raw Score Highest
180	98	101
179	97	97
178	96	96
177	95	95
176	94	94
175	93	93
174	92	92
173	91	91
172	90	90
171	88	89
170	87	87
169	86	86
168	85	85
167	83	84
166	82	82
165	80	81
164	79	79
163	77	78
162	76	76
161	74	75
160	73	73
159	71	72
158	69	70
157	68	68
156	66	67
155	64	65
154	63	63
153	61	62
152	59	60
151	57	58
150	56	56
149	54	55
148	52	53
147	51	51
146	49	50
145	47	48
144	46	46
143	44	45
142	43	43
141	41	42
140	39	40
139	38	38
138	36	37
137	35	35
136	34	34
135	32	33
134	31	31
133	30	30
132	28	29
131	27	27
130	26	26
129	25	25
128	23	24
127	22	22
126	21	21
125	20	20
124	19	19
123	18	18
122	16	17
121	—*	—*
120	0	15

*There is no raw score that will produce this scaled score for this test.

SECTION I

1.	B	8.	A	15.	C	22.	E
2.	A	9.	C	16.	B	23.	E
3.	B	10.	B	17.	D	24.	C
4.	C	11.	A	18.	B	25.	D
5.	D	12.	C	19.	C		
6.	A	13.	E	20.	D		
7.	D	14.	B	21.	D		

SECTION II

1.	D	8.	E	15.	D	22.	B
2.	A	9.	B	16.	A	23.	C
3.	C	10.	B	17.	B		
4.	E	11.	C	18.	B		
5.	B	12.	B	19.	D		
6.	C	13.	D	20.	E		
7.	D	14.	E	21.	C		

SECTION III

1.	B	8.	A	15.	B	22.	B
2.	D	9.	C	16.	A	23.	D
3.	E	10.	A	17.	A	24.	E
4.	A	11.	B	18.	E	25.	B
5.	B	12.	D	19.	D	26.	C
6.	A	13.	E	20.	A	27.	B
7.	D	14.	C	21.	E		

SECTION IV

1.	C	8.	C	15.	E	22.	A
2.	E	9.	E	16.	A	23.	B
3.	D	10.	D	17.	C	24.	A
4.	B	11.	D	18.	B	25.	C
5.	B	12.	C	19.	B	26.	E
6.	E	13.	E	20.	D		
7.	A	14.	E	21.	E		

Experimental Section Answer Key
June 1999, PrepTest 25, Section 4

1.	A	8.	A	15.	E	22.	C
2.	B	9.	B	16.	D	23.	B
3.	E	10.	B	17.	B	24.	D
4.	B	11.	D	18.	D	25.	E
5.	A	12.	D	19.	A	26.	E
6.	D	14.	B	20.	C		
7.	A	15.	D	21.	C		

INSTRUCTIONS FOR COMPLETING THE BIOGRAPHICAL AREA ARE ON THE BACK COVER OF YOUR TEST BOOKLET.

USE ONLY A NO. 2 OR HB PENCIL TO COMPLETE THIS ANSWER SHEET. DO NOT USE INK.

USE A NO. 2 PENCIL ONLY — Right Mark — Wrong Marks

A

1 LAST NAME | FIRST NAME | MI
(A–Z)

2 SOCIAL SECURITY/ SOCIAL INSURANCE NO.
(0–9)

3 LSAC ACCOUNT NUMBER
L (0–9)

4 DATE OF BIRTH

MONTH: Jan, Feb, Mar, Apr, May, June, July, Aug, Sept, Oct, Nov, Dec | DAY | YEAR

5 RACIAL/ETHNIC DESCRIPTION

- 1 American Indian/ Alaskan Native
- 2 Asian/Pacific Islander
- 3 Black/African Amer.
- 4 Canadian Aboriginal
- 5 Caucasian/White
- 6 Chicano/Mex. Amer.
- 7 Hispanic/Latino
- 8 Puerto Rican
- 9 Other

6 GENDER
- Male
- Female

7 DOMINANT LANGUAGE
- English
- Other

8 ENGLISH FLUENCY
- Yes
- No

9 TEST BOOK SERIAL NO.

10 TEST FORM

11 TEST DATE

MONTH / DAY / YEAR

12 CENTER NUMBER
(0–9)

13 TEST FORM CODE
(0–9)

Law School Admission Test

Mark one and only one answer to each question. Be sure to fill in completely the space for your intended answer choice. If you erase, do so completely. Make no stray marks.

SECTION 1	SECTION 2	SECTION 3	SECTION 4	SECTION 5
1 A B C D E	1 A B C D E	1 A B C D E	1 A B C D E	1 A B C D E
2 A B C D E	2 A B C D E	2 A B C D E	2 A B C D E	2 A B C D E
3 A B C D E	3 A B C D E	3 A B C D E	3 A B C D E	3 A B C D E
4 A B C D E	4 A B C D E	4 A B C D E	4 A B C D E	4 A B C D E
5 A B C D E	5 A B C D E	5 A B C D E	5 A B C D E	5 A B C D E
6 A B C D E	6 A B C D E	6 A B C D E	6 A B C D E	6 A B C D E
7 A B C D E	7 A B C D E	7 A B C D E	7 A B C D E	7 A B C D E
8 A B C D E	8 A B C D E	8 A B C D E	8 A B C D E	8 A B C D E
9 A B C D E	9 A B C D E	9 A B C D E	9 A B C D E	9 A B C D E
10 A B C D E	10 A B C D E	10 A B C D E	10 A B C D E	10 A B C D E
11 A B C D E	11 A B C D E	11 A B C D E	11 A B C D E	11 A B C D E
12 A B C D E	12 A B C D E	12 A B C D E	12 A B C D E	12 A B C D E
13 A B C D E	13 A B C D E	13 A B C D E	13 A B C D E	13 A B C D E
14 A B C D E	14 A B C D E	14 A B C D E	14 A B C D E	14 A B C D E
15 A B C D E	15 A B C D E	15 A B C D E	15 A B C D E	15 A B C D E
16 A B C D E	16 A B C D E	16 A B C D E	16 A B C D E	16 A B C D E
17 A B C D E	17 A B C D E	17 A B C D E	17 A B C D E	17 A B C D E
18 A B C D E	18 A B C D E	18 A B C D E	18 A B C D E	18 A B C D E
19 A B C D E	19 A B C D E	19 A B C D E	19 A B C D E	19 A B C D E
20 A B C D E	20 A B C D E	20 A B C D E	20 A B C D E	20 A B C D E
21 A B C D E	21 A B C D E	21 A B C D E	21 A B C D E	21 A B C D E
22 A B C D E	22 A B C D E	22 A B C D E	22 A B C D E	22 A B C D E
23 A B C D E	23 A B C D E	23 A B C D E	23 A B C D E	23 A B C D E
24 A B C D E	24 A B C D E	24 A B C D E	24 A B C D E	24 A B C D E
25 A B C D E	25 A B C D E	25 A B C D E	25 A B C D E	25 A B C D E
26 A B C D E	26 A B C D E	26 A B C D E	26 A B C D E	26 A B C D E
27 A B C D E	27 A B C D E	27 A B C D E	27 A B C D E	27 A B C D E
28 A B C D E	28 A B C D E	28 A B C D E	28 A B C D E	28 A B C D E
29 A B C D E	29 A B C D E	29 A B C D E	29 A B C D E	29 A B C D E
30 A B C D E	30 A B C D E	30 A B C D E	30 A B C D E	30 A B C D E

14 PLEASE PRINT ALL INFORMATION

LAST NAME FIRST

SOCIAL SECURITY/SOCIAL INSURANCE NO.

DATE OF BIRTH

MAILING ADDRESS

NOTE: If you have a new address, you must write LSAC at Box 2000-C, Newtown, PA 18940 or call (215) 968-1001.

FOR LSAC USE ONLY

LR	LW	LCS

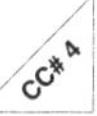

EliteView™ forms by NCS Pearson EM-250133-6:654321 Printed in U.S.A. SIDE 1

INSTRUCTIONS FOR COMPLETING THE BIOGRAPHICAL AREA ARE ON THE BACK COVER OF YOUR TEST BOOKLET.

USE ONLY A NO. 2 OR HB PENCIL TO COMPLETE THIS ANSWER SHEET. DO NOT USE INK.

A

USE A NO. 2 PENCIL ONLY

Right Mark — Wrong Marks

1 LAST NAME | FIRST NAME | MI

2 SOCIAL SECURITY/ SOCIAL INSURANCE NO.

3 LSAC ACCOUNT NUMBER

L

4 DATE OF BIRTH

MONTH | DAY | YEAR

Jan, Feb, Mar, Apr, May, June, July, Aug, Sept, Oct, Nov, Dec

5 RACIAL/ETHNIC DESCRIPTION

- 1 American Indian/ Alaskan Native
- 2 Asian/Pacific Islander
- 3 Black/African Amer.
- 4 Canadian Aboriginal
- 5 Caucasian/White
- 6 Chicano/Mex. Amer.
- 7 Hispanic/Latino
- 8 Puerto Rican
- 9 Other

6 GENDER

- Male
- Female

7 DOMINANT LANGUAGE

- English
- Other

8 ENGLISH FLUENCY

- Yes
- No

9 TEST BOOK SERIAL NO.

10 TEST FORM

11 TEST DATE

MONTH / DAY / YEAR

12 CENTER NUMBER

13 TEST FORM CODE

Law School Admission Test

Mark one and only one answer to each question. Be sure to fill in completely the space for your intended answer choice. If you erase, do so completely. Make no stray marks.

SECTION 1 | SECTION 2 | SECTION 3 | SECTION 4 | SECTION 5

(Questions 1–30, choices A B C D E, in each section)

14 PLEASE PRINT ALL INFORMATION

LAST NAME FIRST

SOCIAL SECURITY/SOCIAL INSURANCE NO.

DATE OF BIRTH

MAILING ADDRESS

NOTE: If you have a new address, you must write LSAC at Box 2000-C, Newtown, PA 18940 or call (215) 968-1001.

FOR LSAC USE ONLY

LR	LW	LCS

B

INSTRUCTIONS FOR COMPLETING THE BIOGRAPHICAL AREA ARE ON THE BACK COVER OF YOUR TEST BOOKLET.

USE ONLY A NO. 2 OR HB PENCIL TO COMPLETE THIS ANSWER SHEET. DO NOT USE INK.

A

USE A NO. 2 PENCIL ONLY — Right Mark — Wrong Marks

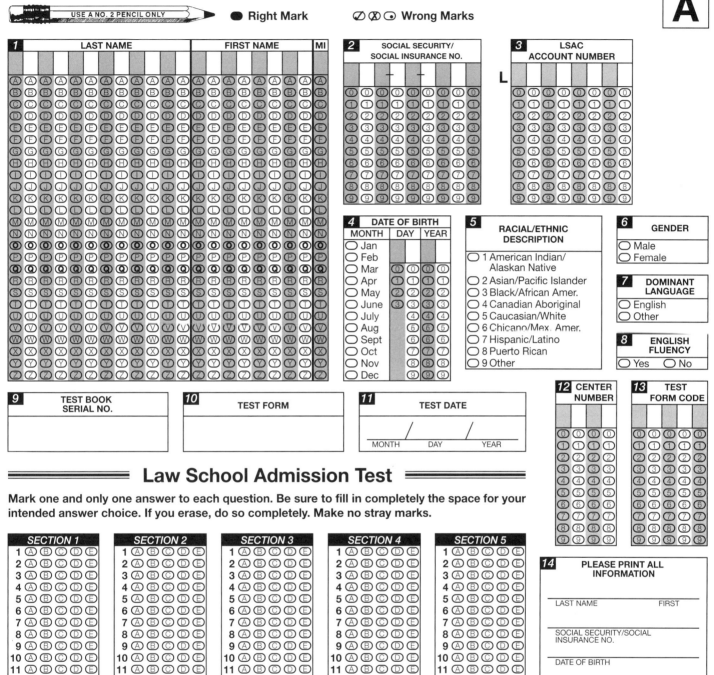

1 LAST NAME | FIRST NAME | MI

A B C D E F G H I J K L M N O P Q R S T U V W X Y Z

2 SOCIAL SECURITY/ SOCIAL INSURANCE NO.

0 1 2 3 4 5 6 7 8 9

3 LSAC ACCOUNT NUMBER

L

0 1 2 3 4 5 6 7 8 9

4 DATE OF BIRTH

MONTH	DAY	YEAR
Jan		
Feb		
Mar	0 0	0 0
Apr	1 1	1 1
May	2 2	2 2
June	3 3	3 3
July	4	4 4
Aug	5	5 5
Sept	6	6 6
Oct	7	7 7
Nov	8	8 8
Dec	9	9 9

5 RACIAL/ETHNIC DESCRIPTION

- 1 American Indian/ Alaskan Native
- 2 Asian/Pacific Islander
- 3 Black/African Amer.
- 4 Canadian Aboriginal
- 5 Caucasian/White
- 6 Chicano/Mex. Amer.
- 7 Hispanic/Latino
- 8 Puerto Rican
- 9 Other

6 GENDER

- Male
- Female

7 DOMINANT LANGUAGE

- English
- Other

8 ENGLISH FLUENCY

- Yes
- No

9 TEST BOOK SERIAL NO.

10 TEST FORM

11 TEST DATE

MONTH / DAY / YEAR

12 CENTER NUMBER

0 1 2 3 4 5 6 7 8 9

13 TEST FORM CODE

0 1 2 3 4 5 6 7 8 9

Law School Admission Test

Mark one and only one answer to each question. Be sure to fill in completely the space for your intended answer choice. If you erase, do so completely. Make no stray marks.

	SECTION 1	SECTION 2	SECTION 3	SECTION 4	SECTION 5
1	A B C D E	A B C D E	A B C D E	A B C D E	A B C D E
2	A B C D E	A B C D E	A B C D E	A B C D E	A B C D E
3	A B C D E	A B C D E	A B C D E	A B C D E	A B C D E
4	A B C D E	A B C D E	A B C D E	A B C D E	A B C D E
5	A B C D E	A B C D E	A B C D E	A B C D E	A B C D E
6	A B C D E	A B C D E	A B C D E	A B C D E	A B C D E
7	A B C D E	A B C D E	A B C D E	A B C D E	A B C D E
8	A B C D E	A B C D E	A B C D E	A B C D E	A B C D E
9	A B C D E	A B C D E	A B C D E	A B C D E	A B C D E
10	A B C D E	A B C D E	A B C D E	A B C D E	A B C D E
11	A B C D E	A B C D E	A B C D E	A B C D E	A B C D E
12	A B C D E	A B C D E	A B C D E	A B C D E	A B C D E
13	A B C D E	A B C D E	A B C D E	A B C D E	A B C D E
14	A B C D E	A B C D E	A B C D E	A B C D E	A B C D E
15	A B C D E	A B C D E	A B C D E	A B C D E	A B C D E
16	A B C D E	A B C D E	A B C D E	A B C D E	A B C D E
17	A B C D E	A B C D E	A B C D E	A B C D E	A B C D E
18	A B C D E	A B C D E	A B C D E	A B C D E	A B C D E
19	A B C D E	A B C D E	A B C D E	A B C D E	A B C D E
20	A B C D E	A B C D E	A B C D E	A B C D E	A B C D E
21	A B C D E	A B C D E	A B C D E	A B C D E	A B C D E
22	A B C D E	A B C D E	A B C D E	A B C D E	A B C D E
23	A B C D E	A B C D E	A B C D E	A B C D E	A B C D E
24	A B C D E	A B C D E	A B C D E	A B C D E	A B C D E
25	A B C D E	A B C D E	A B C D E	A B C D E	A B C D E
26	A B C D E	A B C D E	A B C D E	A B C D E	A B C D E
27	A B C D E	A B C D E	A B C D E	A B C D E	A B C D E
28	A B C D E	A B C D E	A B C D E	A B C D E	A B C D E
29	A B C D E	A B C D E	A B C D E	A B C D E	A B C D E
30	A B C D E	A B C D E	A B C D E	A B C D E	A B C D E

14 PLEASE PRINT ALL INFORMATION

LAST NAME FIRST

SOCIAL SECURITY/SOCIAL INSURANCE NO.

DATE OF BIRTH

MAILING ADDRESS

NOTE: If you have a new address, you must write LSAC at Box 2000-C, Newtown, PA 18940 or call (215) 968-1001.

FOR LSAC USE ONLY

LR	LW	LCS

EliteView™ forms by NCS Pearson EM-250133-6:654321 Printed in U.S.A. **SIDE 1**

INSTRUCTIONS FOR COMPLETING THE BIOGRAPHICAL AREA ARE ON THE BACK COVER OF YOUR TEST BOOKLET.

USE ONLY A NO. 2 OR HB PENCIL TO COMPLETE THIS ANSWER SHEET. DO NOT USE INK.

A

USE A NO. 2 PENCIL ONLY

● Right Mark ⊘ ⊗ ⊙ Wrong Marks

1 LAST NAME | FIRST NAME | MI

2 SOCIAL SECURITY/ SOCIAL INSURANCE NO.

3 LSAC ACCOUNT NUMBER

L

4 DATE OF BIRTH

MONTH | DAY | YEAR

Jan, Feb, Mar, Apr, May, June, July, Aug, Sept, Oct, Nov, Dec

5 RACIAL/ETHNIC DESCRIPTION

- 1 American Indian/ Alaskan Native
- 2 Asian/Pacific Islander
- 3 Black/African Amer.
- 4 Canadian Aboriginal
- 5 Caucasian/White
- 6 Chicano/Mex. Amer.
- 7 Hispanic/Latino
- 8 Puerto Rican
- 9 Other

6 GENDER

- Male
- Female

7 DOMINANT LANGUAGE

- English
- Other

8 ENGLISH FLUENCY

- Yes
- No

9 TEST BOOK SERIAL NO.

10 TEST FORM

11 TEST DATE

MONTH / DAY / YEAR

12 CENTER NUMBER

13 TEST FORM CODE

Law School Admission Test

Mark one and only one answer to each question. Be sure to fill in completely the space for your intended answer choice. If you erase, do so completely. Make no stray marks.

SECTION 1 | SECTION 2 | SECTION 3 | SECTION 4 | SECTION 5

(Questions 1–30 in each section, answer choices A B C D E)

14 PLEASE PRINT ALL INFORMATION

LAST NAME FIRST

SOCIAL SECURITY/SOCIAL INSURANCE NO.

DATE OF BIRTH

MAILING ADDRESS

NOTE: If you have a new address, you must write LSAC at Box 2000-C, Newtown, PA 18940 or call (215) 968-1001.

FOR LSAC USE ONLY

LR	LW	LCS

● Ⓑ

INSTRUCTIONS FOR COMPLETING THE BIOGRAPHICAL AREA ARE ON THE BACK COVER OF YOUR TEST BOOKLET.

USE ONLY A NO. 2 OR HB PENCIL TO COMPLETE THIS ANSWER SHEET. DO NOT USE INK.

A

USE A NO. 2 PENCIL ONLY — ● Right Mark — Wrong Marks

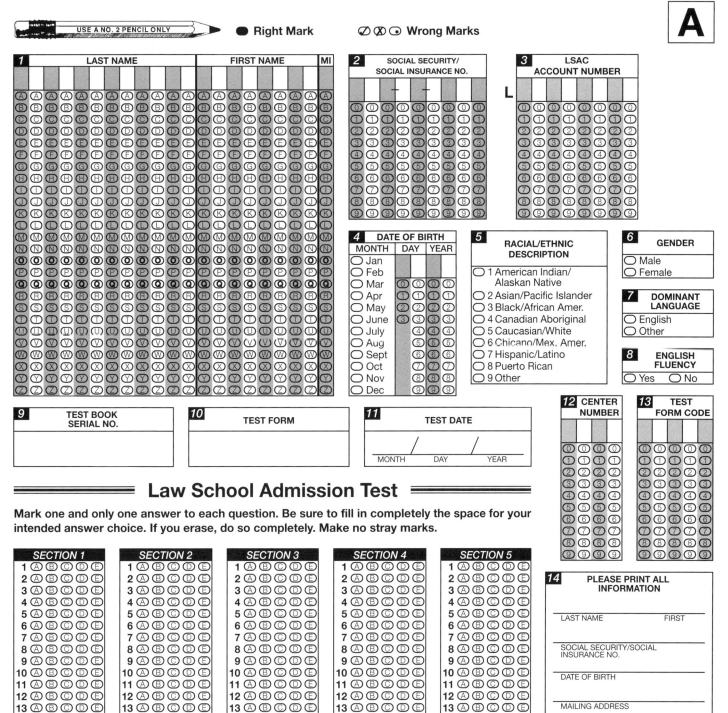

1 LAST NAME | FIRST NAME | MI (bubbles A–Z for each letter)

2 SOCIAL SECURITY/ SOCIAL INSURANCE NO. (bubbles 0–9)

3 LSAC ACCOUNT NUMBER L (bubbles 0–9)

4 DATE OF BIRTH

MONTH	DAY	YEAR
Jan		
Feb		
Mar	0 0	0 0
Apr	1 1	1 1
May	2 2	2 2
June	3 3	3 3
July	4	4 4
Aug	5	5 5
Sept	6	6 6
Oct	7	7 7
Nov	8	8 8
Dec	9	9 9

5 RACIAL/ETHNIC DESCRIPTION

- 1 American Indian/ Alaskan Native
- 2 Asian/Pacific Islander
- 3 Black/African Amer.
- 4 Canadian Aboriginal
- 5 Caucasian/White
- 6 Chicano/Mex. Amer.
- 7 Hispanic/Latino
- 8 Puerto Rican
- 9 Other

6 GENDER

- Male
- Female

7 DOMINANT LANGUAGE

- English
- Other

8 ENGLISH FLUENCY

- Yes
- No

9 TEST BOOK SERIAL NO.

10 TEST FORM

11 TEST DATE

MONTH / DAY / YEAR

12 CENTER NUMBER (bubbles 0–9)

13 TEST FORM CODE (bubbles 0–9)

Law School Admission Test

Mark one and only one answer to each question. Be sure to fill in completely the space for your intended answer choice. If you erase, do so completely. Make no stray marks.

	SECTION 1	SECTION 2	SECTION 3	SECTION 4	SECTION 5
1	A B C D E	A B C D E	A B C D E	A B C D E	A B C D E
2	A B C D E	A B C D E	A B C D E	A B C D E	A B C D E
3	A B C D E	A B C D E	A B C D E	A B C D E	A B C D E
4	A B C D E	A B C D E	A B C D E	A B C D E	A B C D E
5	A B C D E	A B C D E	A B C D E	A B C D E	A B C D E
6	A B C D E	A B C D E	A B C D E	A B C D E	A B C D E
7	A B C D E	A B C D E	A B C D E	A B C D E	A B C D E
8	A B C D E	A B C D E	A B C D E	A B C D E	A B C D E
9	A B C D E	A B C D E	A B C D E	A B C D E	A B C D E
10	A B C D E	A B C D E	A B C D E	A B C D E	A B C D E
11	A B C D E	A B C D E	A B C D E	A B C D E	A B C D E
12	A B C D E	A B C D E	A B C D E	A B C D E	A B C D E
13	A B C D E	A B C D E	A B C D E	A B C D E	A B C D E
14	A B C D E	A B C D E	A B C D E	A B C D E	A B C D E
15	A B C D E	A B C D E	A B C D E	A B C D E	A B C D E
16	A B C D E	A B C D E	A B C D E	A B C D E	A B C D E
17	A B C D E	A B C D E	A B C D E	A B C D E	A B C D E
18	A B C D E	A B C D E	A B C D E	A B C D E	A B C D E
19	A B C D E	A B C D E	A B C D E	A B C D E	A B C D E
20	A B C D E	A B C D E	A B C D E	A B C D E	A B C D E
21	A B C D E	A B C D E	A B C D E	A B C D E	A B C D E
22	A B C D E	A B C D E	A B C D E	A B C D E	A B C D E
23	A B C D E	A B C D E	A B C D E	A B C D E	A B C D E
24	A B C D E	A B C D E	A B C D E	A B C D E	A B C D E
25	A B C D E	A B C D E	A B C D E	A B C D E	A B C D E
26	A B C D E	A B C D E	A B C D E	A B C D E	A B C D E
27	A B C D E	A B C D E	A B C D E	A B C D E	A B C D E
28	A B C D E	A B C D E	A B C D E	A B C D E	A B C D E
29	A B C D E	A B C D E	A B C D E	A B C D E	A B C D E
30	A B C D E	A B C D E	A B C D E	A B C D E	A B C D E

14 PLEASE PRINT ALL INFORMATION

LAST NAME FIRST

SOCIAL SECURITY/SOCIAL INSURANCE NO.

DATE OF BIRTH

MAILING ADDRESS

NOTE: If you have a new address, you must write LSAC at Box 2000-C, Newtown, PA 18940 or call (215) 968-1001.

FOR LSAC USE ONLY

LR	LW	LCS

EliteView™ forms by NCS Pearson EM-250133-6:654321 Printed in U.S.A. SIDE 1

INSTRUCTIONS FOR COMPLETING THE BIOGRAPHICAL AREA ARE ON THE BACK COVER OF YOUR TEST BOOKLET.
USE ONLY A NO. 2 OR HB PENCIL TO COMPLETE THIS ANSWER SHEET. DO NOT USE INK.

A

USE A NO. 2 PENCIL ONLY — Right Mark — Wrong Marks

1 LAST NAME | FIRST NAME | MI

2 SOCIAL SECURITY/ SOCIAL INSURANCE NO.

3 LSAC ACCOUNT NUMBER — L

4 DATE OF BIRTH — MONTH | DAY | YEAR
Jan, Feb, Mar, Apr, May, June, July, Aug, Sept, Oct, Nov, Dec

5 RACIAL/ETHNIC DESCRIPTION
1 American Indian/ Alaskan Native
2 Asian/Pacific Islander
3 Black/African Amer.
4 Canadian Aboriginal
5 Caucasian/White
6 Chicano/Mex. Amer.
7 Hispanic/Latino
8 Puerto Rican
9 Other

6 GENDER
Male
Female

7 DOMINANT LANGUAGE
English
Other

8 ENGLISH FLUENCY
Yes No

9 TEST BOOK SERIAL NO.

10 TEST FORM

11 TEST DATE
MONTH / DAY / YEAR

12 CENTER NUMBER

13 TEST FORM CODE

Law School Admission Test

Mark one and only one answer to each question. Be sure to fill in completely the space for your intended answer choice. If you erase, do so completely. Make no stray marks.

SECTION 1 | SECTION 2 | SECTION 3 | SECTION 4 | SECTION 5 — questions 1–30, answer choices A B C D E

14 PLEASE PRINT ALL INFORMATION

LAST NAME FIRST

SOCIAL SECURITY/SOCIAL INSURANCE NO.

DATE OF BIRTH

MAILING ADDRESS

NOTE: If you have a new address, you must write LSAC at Box 2000-C, Newtown, PA 18940 or call (215) 968-1001.

FOR LSAC USE ONLY

LR	LW	LCS

B

INSTRUCTIONS FOR COMPLETING THE BIOGRAPHICAL AREA ARE ON THE BACK COVER OF YOUR TEST BOOKLET.

USE ONLY A NO. 2 OR HB PENCIL TO COMPLETE THIS ANSWER SHEET. DO NOT USE INK.

A

USE A NO. 2 PENCIL ONLY — Right Mark — Wrong Marks

1 LAST NAME | FIRST NAME | MI

2 SOCIAL SECURITY/ SOCIAL INSURANCE NO.

3 LSAC ACCOUNT NUMBER

L

4 DATE OF BIRTH

MONTH	DAY	YEAR
Jan		
Feb		
Mar	0 0	0 0
Apr	1 1	1 1
May	2 2	2 2
June	3 3	3 3
July	4	4 4
Aug	5	5 5
Sept	6	6 6
Oct	7	7 7
Nov	8	8 8
Dec	9	9 9

5 RACIAL/ETHNIC DESCRIPTION

- 1 American Indian/ Alaskan Native
- 2 Asian/Pacific Islander
- 3 Black/African Amer.
- 4 Canadian Aboriginal
- 5 Caucasian/White
- 6 Chicano/Mex. Amer.
- 7 Hispanic/Latino
- 8 Puerto Rican
- 9 Other

6 GENDER

- Male
- Female

7 DOMINANT LANGUAGE

- English
- Other

8 ENGLISH FLUENCY

- Yes
- No

9 TEST BOOK SERIAL NO.

10 TEST FORM

11 TEST DATE

MONTH / DAY / YEAR

12 CENTER NUMBER

13 TEST FORM CODE

Law School Admission Test

Mark one and only one answer to each question. Be sure to fill in completely the space for your intended answer choice. If you erase, do so completely. Make no stray marks.

SECTION 1 | SECTION 2 | SECTION 3 | SECTION 4 | SECTION 5

1–30 Ⓐ Ⓑ Ⓒ Ⓓ Ⓔ (each section)

14 PLEASE PRINT ALL INFORMATION

LAST NAME FIRST

SOCIAL SECURITY/SOCIAL INSURANCE NO.

DATE OF BIRTH

MAILING ADDRESS

NOTE: If you have a new address, you must write LSAC at Box 2000-C, Newtown, PA 18940 or call (215) 968-1001.

FOR LSAC USE ONLY

LR	LW	LCS

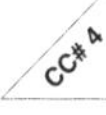

INSTRUCTIONS FOR COMPLETING THE BIOGRAPHICAL AREA ARE ON THE BACK COVER OF YOUR TEST BOOKLET.

USE ONLY A NO. 2 OR HB PENCIL TO COMPLETE THIS ANSWER SHEET. DO NOT USE INK.

A

USE A NO. 2 PENCIL ONLY

● Right Mark   Ⓐ Ⓧ ⊙ Wrong Marks

1 LAST NAME | FIRST NAME | MI

A B C D E F G H I J K L M N O P Q R S T U V W X Y Z

2 SOCIAL SECURITY/ SOCIAL INSURANCE NO.

0 1 2 3 4 5 6 7 8 9

3 LSAC ACCOUNT NUMBER

L

0 1 2 3 4 5 6 7 8 9

4 DATE OF BIRTH

MONTH	DAY	YEAR
Jan		
Feb		
Mar	0 0	0 0
Apr	1 1	1 1
May	2 2	2 2
June	3 3	3 3
July	4	4 4
Aug	5	5 5
Sept	6	6 6
Oct	7	7 7
Nov	8	8 8
Dec	9	9 9

5 RACIAL/ETHNIC DESCRIPTION

- 1 American Indian/ Alaskan Native
- 2 Asian/Pacific Islander
- 3 Black/African Amer.
- 4 Canadian Aboriginal
- 5 Caucasian/White
- 6 Chicano/Mex. Amer.
- 7 Hispanic/Latino
- 8 Puerto Rican
- 9 Other

6 GENDER

- Male
- Female

7 DOMINANT LANGUAGE

- English
- Other

8 ENGLISH FLUENCY

- Yes
- No

9 TEST BOOK SERIAL NO.

10 TEST FORM

11 TEST DATE

MONTH / DAY / YEAR

12 CENTER NUMBER

0 1 2 3 4 5 6 7 8 9

13 TEST FORM CODE

0 1 2 3 4 5 6 7 8 9

Law School Admission Test

Mark one and only one answer to each question. Be sure to fill in completely the space for your intended answer choice. If you erase, do so completely. Make no stray marks.

SECTION 1	SECTION 2	SECTION 3	SECTION 4	SECTION 5
1 A B C D E	1 A B C D E	1 A B C D E	1 A B C D E	1 A B C D E
2 A B C D E	2 A B C D E	2 A B C D E	2 A B C D E	2 A B C D E
3 A B C D E	3 A B C D E	3 A B C D E	3 A B C D E	3 A B C D E
4 A B C D E	4 A B C D E	4 A B C D E	4 A B C D E	4 A B C D E
5 A B C D E	5 A B C D E	5 A B C D E	5 A B C D E	5 A B C D E
6 A B C D E	6 A B C D E	6 A B C D E	6 A B C D E	6 A B C D E
7 A B C D E	7 A B C D E	7 A B C D E	7 A B C D E	7 A B C D E
8 A B C D E	8 A B C D E	8 A B C D E	8 A B C D E	8 A B C D E
9 A B C D E	9 A B C D E	9 A B C D E	9 A B C D E	9 A B C D E
10 A B C D E	10 A B C D E	10 A B C D E	10 A B C D E	10 A B C D E
11 A B C D E	11 A B C D E	11 A B C D E	11 A B C D E	11 A B C D E
12 A B C D E	12 A B C D E	12 A B C D E	12 A B C D E	12 A B C D E
13 A B C D E	13 A B C D E	13 A B C D E	13 A B C D E	13 A B C D E
14 A B C D E	14 A B C D E	14 A B C D E	14 A B C D E	14 A B C D E
15 A B C D E	15 A B C D E	15 A B C D E	15 A B C D E	15 A B C D E
16 A B C D E	16 A B C D E	16 A B C D E	16 A B C D E	16 A B C D E
17 A B C D E	17 A B C D E	17 A B C D E	17 A B C D E	17 A B C D E
18 A B C D E	18 A B C D E	18 A B C D E	18 A B C D E	18 A B C D E
19 A B C D E	19 A B C D E	19 A B C D E	19 A B C D E	19 A B C D E
20 A B C D E	20 A B C D E	20 A B C D E	20 A B C D E	20 A B C D E
21 A B C D E	21 A B C D E	21 A B C D E	21 A B C D E	21 A B C D E
22 A B C D E	22 A B C D E	22 A B C D E	22 A B C D E	22 A B C D E
23 A B C D E	23 A B C D E	23 A B C D E	23 A B C D E	23 A B C D E
24 A B C D E	24 A B C D E	24 A B C D E	24 A B C D E	24 A B C D E
25 A B C D E	25 A B C D E	25 A B C D E	25 A B C D E	25 A B C D E
26 A B C D E	26 A B C D E	26 A B C D E	26 A B C D E	26 A B C D E
27 A B C D E	27 A B C D E	27 A B C D E	27 A B C D E	27 A B C D E
28 A B C D E	28 A B C D E	28 A B C D E	28 A B C D E	28 A B C D E
29 A B C D E	29 A B C D E	29 A B C D E	29 A B C D E	29 A B C D E
30 A B C D E	30 A B C D E	30 A B C D E	30 A B C D E	30 A B C D E

14 PLEASE PRINT ALL INFORMATION

LAST NAME FIRST

SOCIAL SECURITY/SOCIAL INSURANCE NO.

DATE OF BIRTH

MAILING ADDRESS

NOTE: If you have a new address, you must write LSAC at Box 2000-C, Newtown, PA 18940 or call (215) 968-1001.

FOR LSAC USE ONLY

LR	LW	LCS

● B

INSTRUCTIONS FOR COMPLETING THE BIOGRAPHICAL AREA ARE ON THE BACK COVER OF YOUR TEST BOOKLET.

USE ONLY A NO. 2 OR HB PENCIL TO COMPLETE THIS ANSWER SHEET. DO NOT USE INK.

A

USE A NO. 2 PENCIL ONLY — Right Mark — Wrong Marks

1 LAST NAME | FIRST NAME | MI

Ⓐ Ⓑ Ⓒ Ⓓ Ⓔ Ⓕ Ⓖ Ⓗ Ⓘ Ⓙ Ⓚ Ⓛ Ⓜ Ⓝ Ⓞ Ⓟ Ⓠ Ⓡ Ⓢ Ⓣ Ⓤ Ⓥ Ⓦ Ⓧ Ⓨ Ⓩ

2 SOCIAL SECURITY/ SOCIAL INSURANCE NO.

0 1 2 3 4 5 6 7 8 9

3 LSAC ACCOUNT NUMBER

L

0 1 2 3 4 5 6 7 8 9

4 DATE OF BIRTH

MONTH	DAY	YEAR
Jan		
Feb		
Mar	0 0	0 0
Apr	1 1	1 1
May	2 2	2 2
June	3 3	3 3
July	4	4 4
Aug	5	5 5
Sept	6	6 6
Oct	7	7 7
Nov	8	8 8
Dec	9	9 9

5 RACIAL/ETHNIC DESCRIPTION

- 1 American Indian/ Alaskan Native
- 2 Asian/Pacific Islander
- 3 Black/African Amer.
- 4 Canadian Aboriginal
- 5 Caucasian/White
- 6 Chicano/Mex. Amer.
- 7 Hispanic/Latino
- 8 Puerto Rican
- 9 Other

6 GENDER

- Male
- Female

7 DOMINANT LANGUAGE

- English
- Other

8 ENGLISH FLUENCY

- Yes
- No

9 TEST BOOK SERIAL NO.

10 TEST FORM

11 TEST DATE

MONTH / DAY / YEAR

12 CENTER NUMBER

0 1 2 3 4 5 6 7 8 9

13 TEST FORM CODE

0 1 2 3 4 5 6 7 8 9

Law School Admission Test

Mark one and only one answer to each question. Be sure to fill in completely the space for your intended answer choice. If you erase, do so completely. Make no stray marks.

SECTION 1	SECTION 2	SECTION 3	SECTION 4	SECTION 5
1 Ⓐ Ⓑ Ⓒ Ⓓ Ⓔ	1 Ⓐ Ⓑ Ⓒ Ⓓ Ⓔ	1 Ⓐ Ⓑ Ⓒ Ⓓ Ⓔ	1 Ⓐ Ⓑ Ⓒ Ⓓ Ⓔ	1 Ⓐ Ⓑ Ⓒ Ⓓ Ⓔ
2 Ⓐ Ⓑ Ⓒ Ⓓ Ⓔ	2 Ⓐ Ⓑ Ⓒ Ⓓ Ⓔ	2 Ⓐ Ⓑ Ⓒ Ⓓ Ⓔ	2 Ⓐ Ⓑ Ⓒ Ⓓ Ⓔ	2 Ⓐ Ⓑ Ⓒ Ⓓ Ⓔ
3 Ⓐ Ⓑ Ⓒ Ⓓ Ⓔ	3 Ⓐ Ⓑ Ⓒ Ⓓ Ⓔ	3 Ⓐ Ⓑ Ⓒ Ⓓ Ⓔ	3 Ⓐ Ⓑ Ⓒ Ⓓ Ⓔ	3 Ⓐ Ⓑ Ⓒ Ⓓ Ⓔ
4 Ⓐ Ⓑ Ⓒ Ⓓ Ⓔ	4 Ⓐ Ⓑ Ⓒ Ⓓ Ⓔ	4 Ⓐ Ⓑ Ⓒ Ⓓ Ⓔ	4 Ⓐ Ⓑ Ⓒ Ⓓ Ⓔ	4 Ⓐ Ⓑ Ⓒ Ⓓ Ⓔ
5 Ⓐ Ⓑ Ⓒ Ⓓ Ⓔ	5 Ⓐ Ⓑ Ⓒ Ⓓ Ⓔ	5 Ⓐ Ⓑ Ⓒ Ⓓ Ⓔ	5 Ⓐ Ⓑ Ⓒ Ⓓ Ⓔ	5 Ⓐ Ⓑ Ⓒ Ⓓ Ⓔ
6 Ⓐ Ⓑ Ⓒ Ⓓ Ⓔ	6 Ⓐ Ⓑ Ⓒ Ⓓ Ⓔ	6 Ⓐ Ⓑ Ⓒ Ⓓ Ⓔ	6 Ⓐ Ⓑ Ⓒ Ⓓ Ⓔ	6 Ⓐ Ⓑ Ⓒ Ⓓ Ⓔ
7 Ⓐ Ⓑ Ⓒ Ⓓ Ⓔ	7 Ⓐ Ⓑ Ⓒ Ⓓ Ⓔ	7 Ⓐ Ⓑ Ⓒ Ⓓ Ⓔ	7 Ⓐ Ⓑ Ⓒ Ⓓ Ⓔ	7 Ⓐ Ⓑ Ⓒ Ⓓ Ⓔ
8 Ⓐ Ⓑ Ⓒ Ⓓ Ⓔ	8 Ⓐ Ⓑ Ⓒ Ⓓ Ⓔ	8 Ⓐ Ⓑ Ⓒ Ⓓ Ⓔ	8 Ⓐ Ⓑ Ⓒ Ⓓ Ⓔ	8 Ⓐ Ⓑ Ⓒ Ⓓ Ⓔ
9 Ⓐ Ⓑ Ⓒ Ⓓ Ⓔ	9 Ⓐ Ⓑ Ⓒ Ⓓ Ⓔ	9 Ⓐ Ⓑ Ⓒ Ⓓ Ⓔ	9 Ⓐ Ⓑ Ⓒ Ⓓ Ⓔ	9 Ⓐ Ⓑ Ⓒ Ⓓ Ⓔ
10 Ⓐ Ⓑ Ⓒ Ⓓ Ⓔ	10 Ⓐ Ⓑ Ⓒ Ⓓ Ⓔ	10 Ⓐ Ⓑ Ⓒ Ⓓ Ⓔ	10 Ⓐ Ⓑ Ⓒ Ⓓ Ⓔ	10 Ⓐ Ⓑ Ⓒ Ⓓ Ⓔ
11 Ⓐ Ⓑ Ⓒ Ⓓ Ⓔ	11 Ⓐ Ⓑ Ⓒ Ⓓ Ⓔ	11 Ⓐ Ⓑ Ⓒ Ⓓ Ⓔ	11 Ⓐ Ⓑ Ⓒ Ⓓ Ⓔ	11 Ⓐ Ⓑ Ⓒ Ⓓ Ⓔ
12 Ⓐ Ⓑ Ⓒ Ⓓ Ⓔ	12 Ⓐ Ⓑ Ⓒ Ⓓ Ⓔ	12 Ⓐ Ⓑ Ⓒ Ⓓ Ⓔ	12 Ⓐ Ⓑ Ⓒ Ⓓ Ⓔ	12 Ⓐ Ⓑ Ⓒ Ⓓ Ⓔ
13 Ⓐ Ⓑ Ⓒ Ⓓ Ⓔ	13 Ⓐ Ⓑ Ⓒ Ⓓ Ⓔ	13 Ⓐ Ⓑ Ⓒ Ⓓ Ⓔ	13 Ⓐ Ⓑ Ⓒ Ⓓ Ⓔ	13 Ⓐ Ⓑ Ⓒ Ⓓ Ⓔ
14 Ⓐ Ⓑ Ⓒ Ⓓ Ⓔ	14 Ⓐ Ⓑ Ⓒ Ⓓ Ⓔ	14 Ⓐ Ⓑ Ⓒ Ⓓ Ⓔ	14 Ⓐ Ⓑ Ⓒ Ⓓ Ⓔ	14 Ⓐ Ⓑ Ⓒ Ⓓ Ⓔ
15 Ⓐ Ⓑ Ⓒ Ⓓ Ⓔ	15 Ⓐ Ⓑ Ⓒ Ⓓ Ⓔ	15 Ⓐ Ⓑ Ⓒ Ⓓ Ⓔ	15 Ⓐ Ⓑ Ⓒ Ⓓ Ⓔ	15 Ⓐ Ⓑ Ⓒ Ⓓ Ⓔ
16 Ⓐ Ⓑ Ⓒ Ⓓ Ⓔ	16 Ⓐ Ⓑ Ⓒ Ⓓ Ⓔ	16 Ⓐ Ⓑ Ⓒ Ⓓ Ⓔ	16 Ⓐ Ⓑ Ⓒ Ⓓ Ⓔ	16 Ⓐ Ⓑ Ⓒ Ⓓ Ⓔ
17 Ⓐ Ⓑ Ⓒ Ⓓ Ⓔ	17 Ⓐ Ⓑ Ⓒ Ⓓ Ⓔ	17 Ⓐ Ⓑ Ⓒ Ⓓ Ⓔ	17 Ⓐ Ⓑ Ⓒ Ⓓ Ⓔ	17 Ⓐ Ⓑ Ⓒ Ⓓ Ⓔ
18 Ⓐ Ⓑ Ⓒ Ⓓ Ⓔ	18 Ⓐ Ⓑ Ⓒ Ⓓ Ⓔ	18 Ⓐ Ⓑ Ⓒ Ⓓ Ⓔ	18 Ⓐ Ⓑ Ⓒ Ⓓ Ⓔ	18 Ⓐ Ⓑ Ⓒ Ⓓ Ⓔ
19 Ⓐ Ⓑ Ⓒ Ⓓ Ⓔ	19 Ⓐ Ⓑ Ⓒ Ⓓ Ⓔ	19 Ⓐ Ⓑ Ⓒ Ⓓ Ⓔ	19 Ⓐ Ⓑ Ⓒ Ⓓ Ⓔ	19 Ⓐ Ⓑ Ⓒ Ⓓ Ⓔ
20 Ⓐ Ⓑ Ⓒ Ⓓ Ⓔ	20 Ⓐ Ⓑ Ⓒ Ⓓ Ⓔ	20 Ⓐ Ⓑ Ⓒ Ⓓ Ⓔ	20 Ⓐ Ⓑ Ⓒ Ⓓ Ⓔ	20 Ⓐ Ⓑ Ⓒ Ⓓ Ⓔ
21 Ⓐ Ⓑ Ⓒ Ⓓ Ⓔ	21 Ⓐ Ⓑ Ⓒ Ⓓ Ⓔ	21 Ⓐ Ⓑ Ⓒ Ⓓ Ⓔ	21 Ⓐ Ⓑ Ⓒ Ⓓ Ⓔ	21 Ⓐ Ⓑ Ⓒ Ⓓ Ⓔ
22 Ⓐ Ⓑ Ⓒ Ⓓ Ⓔ	22 Ⓐ Ⓑ Ⓒ Ⓓ Ⓔ	22 Ⓐ Ⓑ Ⓒ Ⓓ Ⓔ	22 Ⓐ Ⓑ Ⓒ Ⓓ Ⓔ	22 Ⓐ Ⓑ Ⓒ Ⓓ Ⓔ
23 Ⓐ Ⓑ Ⓒ Ⓓ Ⓔ	23 Ⓐ Ⓑ Ⓒ Ⓓ Ⓔ	23 Ⓐ Ⓑ Ⓒ Ⓓ Ⓔ	23 Ⓐ Ⓑ Ⓒ Ⓓ Ⓔ	23 Ⓐ Ⓑ Ⓒ Ⓓ Ⓔ
24 Ⓐ Ⓑ Ⓒ Ⓓ Ⓔ	24 Ⓐ Ⓑ Ⓒ Ⓓ Ⓔ	24 Ⓐ Ⓑ Ⓒ Ⓓ Ⓔ	24 Ⓐ Ⓑ Ⓒ Ⓓ Ⓔ	24 Ⓐ Ⓑ Ⓒ Ⓓ Ⓔ
25 Ⓐ Ⓑ Ⓒ Ⓓ Ⓔ	25 Ⓐ Ⓑ Ⓒ Ⓓ Ⓔ	25 Ⓐ Ⓑ Ⓒ Ⓓ Ⓔ	25 Ⓐ Ⓑ Ⓒ Ⓓ Ⓔ	25 Ⓐ Ⓑ Ⓒ Ⓓ Ⓔ
26 Ⓐ Ⓑ Ⓒ Ⓓ Ⓔ	26 Ⓐ Ⓑ Ⓒ Ⓓ Ⓔ	26 Ⓐ Ⓑ Ⓒ Ⓓ Ⓔ	26 Ⓐ Ⓑ Ⓒ Ⓓ Ⓔ	26 Ⓐ Ⓑ Ⓒ Ⓓ Ⓔ
27 Ⓐ Ⓑ Ⓒ Ⓓ Ⓔ	27 Ⓐ Ⓑ Ⓒ Ⓓ Ⓔ	27 Ⓐ Ⓑ Ⓒ Ⓓ Ⓔ	27 Ⓐ Ⓑ Ⓒ Ⓓ Ⓔ	27 Ⓐ Ⓑ Ⓒ Ⓓ Ⓔ
28 Ⓐ Ⓑ Ⓒ Ⓓ Ⓔ	28 Ⓐ Ⓑ Ⓒ Ⓓ Ⓔ	28 Ⓐ Ⓑ Ⓒ Ⓓ Ⓔ	28 Ⓐ Ⓑ Ⓒ Ⓓ Ⓔ	28 Ⓐ Ⓑ Ⓒ Ⓓ Ⓔ
29 Ⓐ Ⓑ Ⓒ Ⓓ Ⓔ	29 Ⓐ Ⓑ Ⓒ Ⓓ Ⓔ	29 Ⓐ Ⓑ Ⓒ Ⓓ Ⓔ	29 Ⓐ Ⓑ Ⓒ Ⓓ Ⓔ	29 Ⓐ Ⓑ Ⓒ Ⓓ Ⓔ
30 Ⓐ Ⓑ Ⓒ Ⓓ Ⓔ	30 Ⓐ Ⓑ Ⓒ Ⓓ Ⓔ	30 Ⓐ Ⓑ Ⓒ Ⓓ Ⓔ	30 Ⓐ Ⓑ Ⓒ Ⓓ Ⓔ	30 Ⓐ Ⓑ Ⓒ Ⓓ Ⓔ

14 PLEASE PRINT ALL INFORMATION

LAST NAME FIRST

SOCIAL SECURITY/SOCIAL INSURANCE NO.

DATE OF BIRTH

MAILING ADDRESS

NOTE: If you have a new address, you must write LSAC at Box 2000-C, Newtown, PA 18940 or call (215) 968-1001.

FOR LSAC USE ONLY

LR	LW	LCS

EliteView™ forms by NCS Pearson EM-250133-6:654321 Printed in U.S.A.

SIDE 1

INSTRUCTIONS FOR COMPLETING THE BIOGRAPHICAL AREA ARE ON THE BACK COVER OF YOUR TEST BOOKLET.

USE ONLY A NO. 2 OR HB PENCIL TO COMPLETE THIS ANSWER SHEET. DO NOT USE INK.

A

USE A NO. 2 PENCIL ONLY

● Right Mark ⊘ ⊗ ⊙ Wrong Marks

1 LAST NAME | FIRST NAME | MI

A B C D E F G H I J K L M N O P Q R S T U V W X Y Z

2 SOCIAL SECURITY/ SOCIAL INSURANCE NO.

0 1 2 3 4 5 6 7 8 9

3 LSAC ACCOUNT NUMBER

L

0 1 2 3 4 5 6 7 8 9

4 DATE OF BIRTH

MONTH	DAY	YEAR
Jan		
Feb		
Mar	0 0	0 0
Apr	1 1	1 1
May	2 2	2 2
June	3 3	3 3
July	4	4 4
Aug	5	5 5
Sept	6	6 6
Oct	7	7 7
Nov	8	8 8
Dec	9	9 9

5 RACIAL/ETHNIC DESCRIPTION

- 1 American Indian/ Alaskan Native
- 2 Asian/Pacific Islander
- 3 Black/African Amer.
- 4 Canadian Aboriginal
- 5 Caucasian/White
- 6 Chicano/Mex. Amer.
- 7 Hispanic/Latino
- 8 Puerto Rican
- 9 Other

6 GENDER

- Male
- Female

7 DOMINANT LANGUAGE

- English
- Other

8 ENGLISH FLUENCY

- Yes
- No

9 TEST BOOK SERIAL NO.

10 TEST FORM

11 TEST DATE

MONTH / DAY / YEAR

12 CENTER NUMBER

0 1 2 3 4 5 6 7 8 9

13 TEST FORM CODE

0 1 2 3 4 5 6 7 8 9

Law School Admission Test

Mark one and only one answer to each question. Be sure to fill in completely the space for your intended answer choice. If you erase, do so completely. Make no stray marks.

	SECTION 1	SECTION 2	SECTION 3	SECTION 4	SECTION 5
1	A B C D E	A B C D E	A B C D E	A B C D E	A B C D E
2	A B C D E	A B C D E	A B C D E	A B C D E	A B C D E
3	A B C D E	A B C D E	A B C D E	A B C D E	A B C D E
4	A B C D E	A B C D E	A B C D E	A B C D E	A B C D E
5	A B C D E	A B C D E	A B C D E	A B C D E	A B C D E
6	A B C D E	A B C D E	A B C D E	A B C D E	A B C D E
7	A B C D E	A B C D E	A B C D E	A B C D E	A B C D E
8	A B C D E	A B C D E	A B C D E	A B C D E	A B C D E
9	A B C D E	A B C D E	A B C D E	A B C D E	A B C D E
10	A B C D E	A B C D E	A B C D E	A B C D E	A B C D E
11	A B C D E	A B C D E	A B C D E	A B C D E	A B C D E
12	A B C D E	A B C D E	A B C D E	A B C D E	A B C D E
13	A B C D E	A B C D E	A B C D E	A B C D E	A B C D E
14	A B C D E	A B C D E	A B C D E	A B C D E	A B C D E
15	A B C D E	A B C D E	A B C D E	A B C D E	A B C D E
16	A B C D E	A B C D E	A B C D E	A B C D E	A B C D E
17	A B C D E	A B C D E	A B C D E	A B C D E	A B C D E
18	A B C D E	A B C D E	A B C D E	A B C D E	A B C D E
19	A B C D E	A B C D E	A B C D E	A B C D E	A B C D E
20	A B C D E	A B C D E	A B C D E	A B C D E	A B C D E
21	A B C D E	A B C D E	A B C D E	A B C D E	A B C D E
22	A B C D E	A B C D E	A B C D E	A B C D E	A B C D E
23	A B C D E	A B C D E	A B C D E	A B C D E	A B C D E
24	A B C D E	A B C D E	A B C D E	A B C D E	A B C D E
25	A B C D E	A B C D E	A B C D E	A B C D E	A B C D E
26	A B C D E	A B C D E	A B C D E	A B C D E	A B C D E
27	A B C D E	A B C D E	A B C D E	A B C D E	A B C D E
28	A B C D E	A B C D E	A B C D E	A B C D E	A B C D E
29	A B C D E	A B C D E	A B C D E	A B C D E	A B C D E
30	A B C D E	A B C D E	A B C D E	A B C D E	A B C D E

14 PLEASE PRINT ALL INFORMATION

LAST NAME FIRST

SOCIAL SECURITY/SOCIAL INSURANCE NO.

DATE OF BIRTH

MAILING ADDRESS

NOTE: If you have a new address, you must write LSAC at Box 2000-C, Newtown, PA 18940 or call (215) 968-1001.

FOR LSAC USE ONLY

LR	LW	LCS

INSTRUCTIONS FOR COMPLETING THE BIOGRAPHICAL AREA ARE ON THE BACK COVER OF YOUR TEST BOOKLET.

USE ONLY A NO. 2 OR HB PENCIL TO COMPLETE THIS ANSWER SHEET. DO NOT USE INK.

A

USE A NO. 2 PENCIL ONLY — Right Mark — Wrong Marks

1 LAST NAME | FIRST NAME | MI

A B C D E F G H I J K L M N O P Q R S T U V W X Y Z

2 SOCIAL SECURITY/ SOCIAL INSURANCE NO.

0 1 2 3 4 5 6 7 8 9

3 LSAC ACCOUNT NUMBER

L

0 1 2 3 4 5 6 7 8 9

4 DATE OF BIRTH

MONTH	DAY	YEAR
Jan		
Feb		
Mar	0 0	0 0
Apr	1 1	1 1
May	2 2	2 2
June	3 3	3 3
July	4	4 4
Aug	5	5 5
Sept	6	6 6
Oct	7	7 7
Nov	8	8 8
Dec	9	9 9

5 RACIAL/ETHNIC DESCRIPTION

- 1 American Indian/ Alaskan Native
- 2 Asian/Pacific Islander
- 3 Black/African Amer.
- 4 Canadian Aboriginal
- 5 Caucasian/White
- 6 Chicano/Mex. Amer.
- 7 Hispanic/Latino
- 8 Puerto Rican
- 9 Other

6 GENDER

- Male
- Female

7 DOMINANT LANGUAGE

- English
- Other

8 ENGLISH FLUENCY

- Yes
- No

9 TEST BOOK SERIAL NO.

10 TEST FORM

11 TEST DATE

MONTH / DAY / YEAR

12 CENTER NUMBER

0 1 2 3 4 5 6 7 8 9

13 TEST FORM CODE

0 1 2 3 4 5 6 7 8 9

Law School Admission Test

Mark one and only one answer to each question. Be sure to fill in completely the space for your intended answer choice. If you erase, do so completely. Make no stray marks.

SECTION 1	SECTION 2	SECTION 3	SECTION 4	SECTION 5
1 A B C D E	1 A B C D E	1 A B C D E	1 A B C D E	1 A B C D E
2 A B C D E	2 A B C D E	2 A B C D E	2 A B C D E	2 A B C D E
3 A B C D E	3 A B C D E	3 A B C D E	3 A B C D E	3 A B C D E
4 A B C D E	4 A B C D E	4 A B C D E	4 A B C D E	4 A B C D E
5 A B C D E	5 A B C D E	5 A B C D E	5 A B C D E	5 A B C D E
6 A B C D E	6 A B C D E	6 A B C D E	6 A B C D E	6 A B C D E
7 A B C D E	7 A B C D E	7 A B C D E	7 A B C D E	7 A B C D E
8 A B C D E	8 A B C D E	8 A B C D E	8 A B C D E	8 A B C D E
9 A B C D E	9 A B C D E	9 A B C D E	9 A B C D E	9 A B C D E
10 A B C D E	10 A B C D E	10 A B C D E	10 A B C D E	10 A B C D E
11 A B C D E	11 A B C D E	11 A B C D E	11 A B C D E	11 A B C D E
12 A B C D E	12 A B C D E	12 A B C D E	12 A B C D E	12 A B C D E
13 A B C D E	13 A B C D E	13 A B C D E	13 A B C D E	13 A B C D E
14 A B C D E	14 A B C D E	14 A B C D E	14 A B C D E	14 A B C D E
15 A B C D E	15 A B C D E	15 A B C D E	15 A B C D E	15 A B C D E
16 A B C D E	16 A B C D E	16 A B C D E	16 A B C D E	16 A B C D E
17 A B C D E	17 A B C D E	17 A B C D E	17 A B C D E	17 A B C D E
18 A B C D E	18 A B C D E	18 A B C D E	18 A B C D E	18 A B C D E
19 A B C D E	19 A B C D E	19 A B C D E	19 A B C D E	19 A B C D E
20 A B C D E	20 A B C D E	20 A B C D E	20 A B C D E	20 A B C D E
21 A B C D E	21 A B C D E	21 A B C D E	21 A B C D E	21 A B C D E
22 A B C D E	22 A B C D E	22 A B C D E	22 A B C D E	22 A B C D E
23 A B C D E	23 A B C D E	23 A B C D E	23 A B C D E	23 A B C D E
24 A B C D E	24 A B C D E	24 A B C D E	24 A B C D E	24 A B C D E
25 A B C D E	25 A B C D E	25 A B C D E	25 A B C D E	25 A B C D E
26 A B C D E	26 A B C D E	26 A B C D E	26 A B C D E	26 A B C D E
27 A B C D E	27 A B C D E	27 A B C D E	27 A B C D E	27 A B C D E
28 A B C D E	28 A B C D E	28 A B C D E	28 A B C D E	28 A B C D E
29 A B C D E	29 A B C D E	29 A B C D E	29 A B C D E	29 A B C D E
30 A B C D E	30 A B C D E	30 A B C D E	30 A B C D E	30 A B C D E

14 PLEASE PRINT ALL INFORMATION

LAST NAME FIRST

SOCIAL SECURITY/SOCIAL INSURANCE NO.

DATE OF BIRTH

MAILING ADDRESS

NOTE: If you have a new address, you must write LSAC at Box 2000-C, Newtown, PA 18940 or call (215) 968-1001.

FOR LSAC USE ONLY

LR	LW	LCS

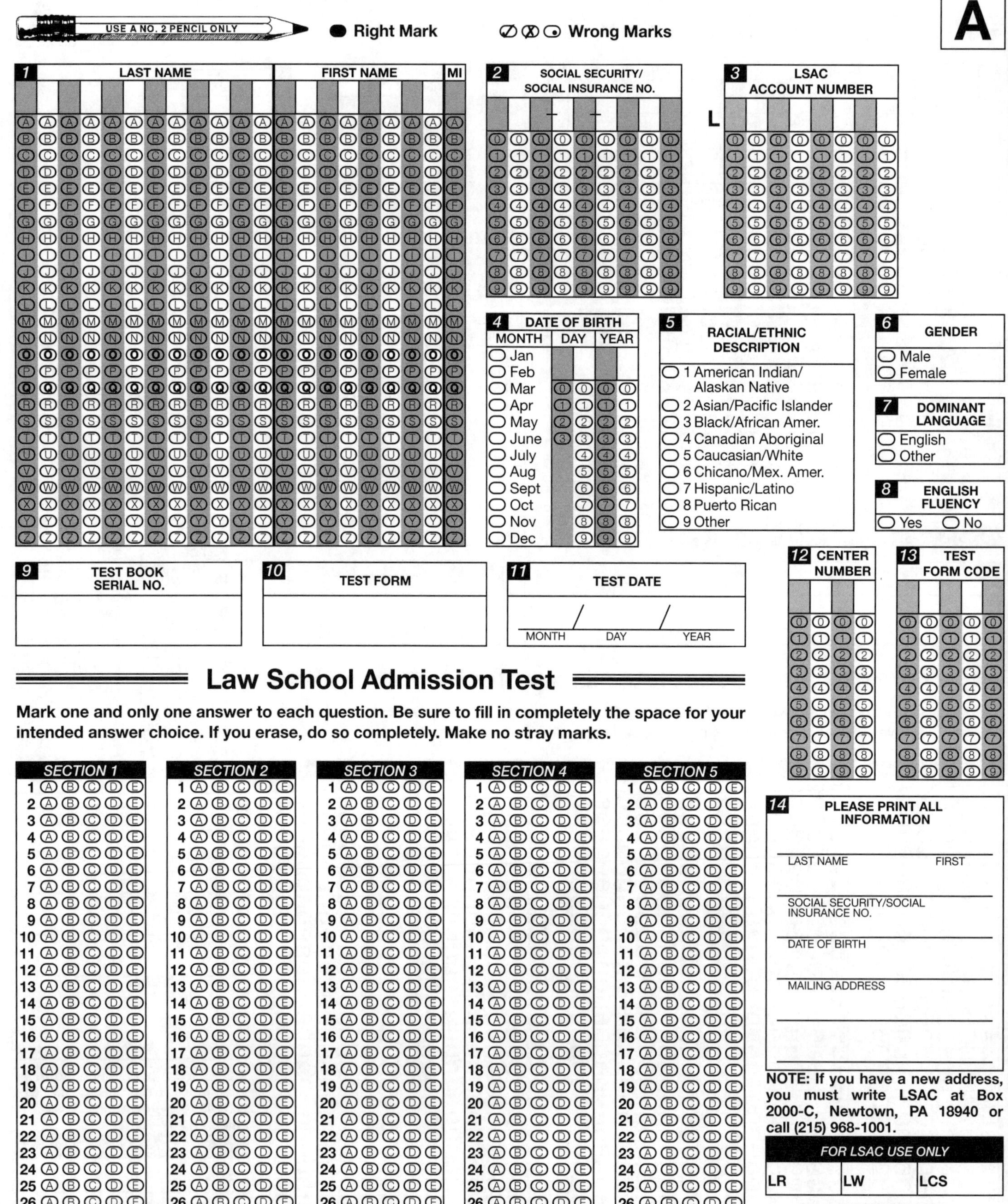

EliteView™ forms by NCS Pearson EM-250133-6:654321 Printed in U.S.A. **SIDE 1**

INSTRUCTIONS FOR COMPLETING THE BIOGRAPHICAL AREA ARE ON THE BACK COVER OF YOUR TEST BOOKLET.

USE ONLY A NO. 2 OR HB PENCIL TO COMPLETE THIS ANSWER SHEET. DO NOT USE INK.

A

USE A NO. 2 PENCIL ONLY

Right Mark **Wrong Marks**

1 LAST NAME | FIRST NAME | MI

2 SOCIAL SECURITY/ SOCIAL INSURANCE NO.

3 LSAC ACCOUNT NUMBER

L

4 DATE OF BIRTH

MONTH | DAY | YEAR

Jan, Feb, Mar, Apr, May, June, July, Aug, Sept, Oct, Nov, Dec

5 RACIAL/ETHNIC DESCRIPTION

1 American Indian/ Alaskan Native
2 Asian/Pacific Islander
3 Black/African Amer.
4 Canadian Aboriginal
5 Caucasian/White
6 Chicano/Mex. Amer.
7 Hispanic/Latino
8 Puerto Rican
9 Other

6 GENDER

Male
Female

7 DOMINANT LANGUAGE

English
Other

8 ENGLISH FLUENCY

Yes No

9 TEST BOOK SERIAL NO.

10 TEST FORM

11 TEST DATE

MONTH / DAY / YEAR

12 CENTER NUMBER

13 TEST FORM CODE

Law School Admission Test

Mark one and only one answer to each question. Be sure to fill in completely the space for your intended answer choice. If you erase, do so completely. Make no stray marks.

SECTION 1 | SECTION 2 | SECTION 3 | SECTION 4 | SECTION 5

1–30 Ⓐ Ⓑ Ⓒ Ⓓ Ⓔ

14 PLEASE PRINT ALL INFORMATION

LAST NAME FIRST

SOCIAL SECURITY/SOCIAL INSURANCE NO.

DATE OF BIRTH

MAILING ADDRESS

NOTE: If you have a new address, you must write LSAC at Box 2000-C, Newtown, PA 18940 or call (215) 968-1001.

FOR LSAC USE ONLY

LR	LW	LCS

● Ⓑ

INSTRUCTIONS FOR COMPLETING THE BIOGRAPHICAL AREA ARE ON THE BACK COVER OF YOUR TEST BOOKLET.

USE ONLY A NO. 2 OR HB PENCIL TO COMPLETE THIS ANSWER SHEET. DO NOT USE INK.

A

USE A NO. 2 PENCIL ONLY

● Right Mark

Wrong Marks

1 LAST NAME | FIRST NAME | MI

A B C D E F G H I J K L M N O P Q R S T U V W X Y Z

2 SOCIAL SECURITY/ SOCIAL INSURANCE NO.

0 1 2 3 4 5 6 7 8 9

3 LSAC ACCOUNT NUMBER

L

0 1 2 3 4 5 6 7 8 9

4 DATE OF BIRTH

MONTH	DAY	YEAR
Jan		
Feb		
Mar	0 0	0 0
Apr	1 1	1 1
May	2 2	2 2
June	3 3	3 3
July	4	4 4
Aug	5	5 5
Sept	6	6 6
Oct	7	7 7
Nov	8	8 8
Dec	9	9 9

5 RACIAL/ETHNIC DESCRIPTION

- 1 American Indian/ Alaskan Native
- 2 Asian/Pacific Islander
- 3 Black/African Amer.
- 4 Canadian Aboriginal
- 5 Caucasian/White
- 6 Chicano/Mex. Amer.
- 7 Hispanic/Latino
- 8 Puerto Rican
- 9 Other

6 GENDER

- Male
- Female

7 DOMINANT LANGUAGE

- English
- Other

8 ENGLISH FLUENCY

- Yes
- No

9 TEST BOOK SERIAL NO.

10 TEST FORM

11 TEST DATE

MONTH / DAY / YEAR

12 CENTER NUMBER

0 1 2 3 4 5 6 7 8 9

13 TEST FORM CODE

0 1 2 3 4 5 6 7 8 9

Law School Admission Test

Mark one and only one answer to each question. Be sure to fill in completely the space for your intended answer choice. If you erase, do so completely. Make no stray marks.

	SECTION 1	SECTION 2	SECTION 3	SECTION 4	SECTION 5
1	A B C D E	A B C D E	A B C D E	A B C D E	A B C D E
2	A B C D E	A B C D E	A B C D E	A B C D E	A B C D E
3	A B C D E	A B C D E	A B C D E	A B C D E	A B C D E
4	A B C D E	A B C D E	A B C D E	A B C D E	A B C D E
5	A B C D E	A B C D E	A B C D E	A B C D E	A B C D E
6	A B C D E	A B C D E	A B C D E	A B C D E	A B C D E
7	A B C D E	A B C D E	A B C D E	A B C D E	A B C D E
8	A B C D E	A B C D E	A B C D E	A B C D E	A B C D E
9	A B C D E	A B C D E	A B C D E	A B C D E	A B C D E
10	A B C D E	A B C D E	A B C D E	A B C D E	A B C D E
11	A B C D E	A B C D E	A B C D E	A B C D E	A B C D E
12	A B C D E	A B C D E	A B C D E	A B C D E	A B C D E
13	A B C D E	A B C D E	A B C D E	A B C D E	A B C D E
14	A B C D E	A B C D E	A B C D E	A B C D E	A B C D E
15	A B C D E	A B C D E	A B C D E	A B C D E	A B C D E
16	A B C D E	A B C D E	A B C D E	A B C D E	A B C D E
17	A B C D E	A B C D E	A B C D E	A B C D E	A B C D E
18	A B C D E	A B C D E	A B C D E	A B C D E	A B C D E
19	A B C D E	A B C D E	A B C D E	A B C D E	A B C D E
20	A B C D E	A B C D E	A B C D E	A B C D E	A B C D E
21	A B C D E	A B C D E	A B C D E	A B C D E	A B C D E
22	A B C D E	A B C D E	A B C D E	A B C D E	A B C D E
23	A B C D E	A B C D E	A B C D E	A B C D E	A B C D E
24	A B C D E	A B C D E	A B C D E	A B C D E	A B C D E
25	A B C D E	A B C D E	A B C D E	A B C D E	A B C D E
26	A B C D E	A B C D E	A B C D E	A B C D E	A B C D E
27	A B C D E	A B C D E	A B C D E	A B C D E	A B C D E
28	A B C D E	A B C D E	A B C D E	A B C D E	A B C D E
29	A B C D E	A B C D E	A B C D E	A B C D E	A B C D E
30	A B C D E	A B C D E	A B C D E	A B C D E	A B C D E

14 PLEASE PRINT ALL INFORMATION

LAST NAME FIRST

SOCIAL SECURITY/SOCIAL INSURANCE NO.

DATE OF BIRTH

MAILING ADDRESS

NOTE: If you have a new address, you must write LSAC at Box 2000-C, Newtown, PA 18940 or call (215) 968-1001.

FOR LSAC USE ONLY

LR	LW	LCS

INSTRUCTIONS FOR COMPLETING THE BIOGRAPHICAL AREA ARE ON THE BACK COVER OF YOUR TEST BOOKLET.

USE ONLY A NO. 2 OR HB PENCIL TO COMPLETE THIS ANSWER SHEET. DO NOT USE INK.

A

USE A NO. 2 PENCIL ONLY

Right Mark **Wrong Marks**

1 LAST NAME | FIRST NAME | MI

2 SOCIAL SECURITY/ SOCIAL INSURANCE NO.

3 LSAC ACCOUNT NUMBER

L

4 DATE OF BIRTH

MONTH	DAY	YEAR
Jan		
Feb		
Mar		
Apr		
May		
June		
July		
Aug		
Sept		
Oct		
Nov		
Dec		

5 RACIAL/ETHNIC DESCRIPTION

1 American Indian/ Alaskan Native
2 Asian/Pacific Islander
3 Black/African Amer.
4 Canadian Aboriginal
5 Caucasian/White
6 Chicano/Mex. Amer.
7 Hispanic/Latino
8 Puerto Rican
9 Other

6 GENDER

Male
Female

7 DOMINANT LANGUAGE

English
Other

8 ENGLISH FLUENCY

Yes No

9 TEST BOOK SERIAL NO.

10 TEST FORM

11 TEST DATE

MONTH / DAY / YEAR

12 CENTER NUMBER

13 TEST FORM CODE

Law School Admission Test

Mark one and only one answer to each question. Be sure to fill in completely the space for your intended answer choice. If you erase, do so completely. Make no stray marks.

SECTION 1 | SECTION 2 | SECTION 3 | SECTION 4 | SECTION 5

1–30 (A) (B) (C) (D) (E)

14 PLEASE PRINT ALL INFORMATION

LAST NAME FIRST

SOCIAL SECURITY/SOCIAL INSURANCE NO.

DATE OF BIRTH

MAILING ADDRESS

NOTE: If you have a new address, you must write LSAC at Box 2000-C, Newtown, PA 18940 or call (215) 968-1001.

FOR LSAC USE ONLY

LR	LW	LCS

(B)

INSTRUCTIONS FOR COMPLETING THE BIOGRAPHICAL AREA ARE ON THE BACK COVER OF YOUR TEST BOOKLET.

USE ONLY A NO. 2 OR HB PENCIL TO COMPLETE THIS ANSWER SHEET. DO NOT USE INK.

A

USE A NO. 2 PENCIL ONLY

Right Mark

Wrong Marks

1 LAST NAME | FIRST NAME | MI

A B C D E F G H I J K L M N O P Q R S T U V W X Y Z

2 SOCIAL SECURITY/ SOCIAL INSURANCE NO.

0 1 2 3 4 5 6 7 8 9

3 LSAC ACCOUNT NUMBER

L

0 1 2 3 4 5 6 7 8 9

4 DATE OF BIRTH

MONTH	DAY	YEAR
Jan		
Feb		
Mar	0 0	0 0
Apr	1 1	1 1
May	2 2	2 2
June	3 3	3 3
July	4	4 4
Aug	5	5 5
Sept	6	6 6
Oct	7	7 7
Nov	8	8 8
Dec	9	9 9

5 RACIAL/ETHNIC DESCRIPTION

- 1 American Indian/ Alaskan Native
- 2 Asian/Pacific Islander
- 3 Black/African Amer.
- 4 Canadian Aboriginal
- 5 Caucasian/White
- 6 Chicano/Mex. Amer
- 7 Hispanic/Latino
- 8 Puerto Rican
- 9 Other

6 GENDER

- Male
- Female

7 DOMINANT LANGUAGE

- English
- Other

8 ENGLISH FLUENCY

- Yes
- No

9 TEST BOOK SERIAL NO.

10 TEST FORM

11 TEST DATE

MONTH / DAY / YEAR

12 CENTER NUMBER

0 1 2 3 4 5 6 7 8 9

13 TEST FORM CODE

0 1 2 3 4 5 6 7 8 9

Law School Admission Test

Mark one and only one answer to each question. Be sure to fill in completely the space for your intended answer choice. If you erase, do so completely. Make no stray marks.

	SECTION 1	SECTION 2	SECTION 3	SECTION 4	SECTION 5
1	A B C D E	A B C D E	A B C D E	A B C D E	A B C D E
2	A B C D E	A B C D E	A B C D E	A B C D E	A B C D E
3	A B C D E	A B C D E	A B C D E	A B C D E	A B C D E
4	A B C D E	A B C D E	A B C D E	A B C D E	A B C D E
5	A B C D E	A B C D E	A B C D E	A B C D E	A B C D E
6	A B C D E	A B C D E	A B C D E	A B C D E	A B C D E
7	A B C D E	A B C D E	A B C D E	A B C D E	A B C D E
8	A B C D E	A B C D E	A B C D E	A B C D E	A B C D E
9	A B C D E	A B C D E	A B C D E	A B C D E	A B C D E
10	A B C D E	A B C D E	A B C D E	A B C D E	A B C D E
11	A B C D E	A B C D E	A B C D E	A B C D E	A B C D E
12	A B C D E	A B C D E	A B C D E	A B C D E	A B C D E
13	A B C D E	A B C D E	A B C D E	A B C D E	A B C D E
14	A B C D E	A B C D E	A B C D E	A B C D E	A B C D E
15	A B C D E	A B C D E	A B C D E	A B C D E	A B C D E
16	A B C D E	A B C D E	A B C D E	A B C D E	A B C D E
17	A B C D E	A B C D E	A B C D E	A B C D E	A B C D E
18	A B C D E	A B C D E	A B C D E	A B C D E	A B C D E
19	A B C D E	A B C D E	A B C D E	A B C D E	A B C D E
20	A B C D E	A B C D E	A B C D E	A B C D E	A B C D E
21	A B C D E	A B C D E	A B C D E	A B C D E	A B C D E
22	A B C D E	A B C D E	A B C D E	A B C D E	A B C D E
23	A B C D E	A B C D E	A B C D E	A B C D E	A B C D E
24	A B C D E	A B C D E	A B C D E	A B C D E	A B C D E
25	A B C D E	A B C D E	A B C D E	A B C D E	A B C D E
26	A B C D E	A B C D E	A B C D E	A B C D E	A B C D E
27	A B C D E	A B C D E	A B C D E	A B C D E	A B C D E
28	A B C D E	A B C D E	A B C D E	A B C D E	A B C D E
29	A B C D E	A B C D E	A B C D E	A B C D E	A B C D E
30	A B C D E	A B C D E	A B C D E	A B C D E	A B C D E

14 PLEASE PRINT ALL INFORMATION

LAST NAME FIRST

SOCIAL SECURITY/SOCIAL INSURANCE NO.

DATE OF BIRTH

MAILING ADDRESS

NOTE: If you have a new address, you must write LSAC at Box 2000-C, Newtown, PA 18940 or call (215) 968-1001.

FOR LSAC USE ONLY

LR	LW	LCS